ENCYCLOPEDIA OF
THE JFK
ASSASSINATION

ENCYCLOPEDIA OF
THE JFK
ASSASSINATION

Michael Benson

Checkmark Books®

An imprint of Facts On File, Inc.

ENCYCLOPEDIA OF THE JFK ASSASSINATION

Checkmark Books
An imprint of Facts On File, Inc.
132 West 31st Street
New York NY 10001

Library of Congress Cataloging-in-Publication Data

Benson, Michael.
Encyclopedia of the JFK assassination / Michael Benson.
    p. cm.
Includes bibliographical references and index.
ISBN 0-8160-4476-7 (hc) — 0-8160-4477-5 (pbk.)
1. Kennedy, John F. (John Fitzgerald), 1917–1963—Assassination—Encyclopedias.
    I. Title
E842.9.B45 2002
973.922—dc21   2001053212

Text design by Erika K. Arroyo
Maps by Jim A. Pearson and Jeremy Eagle
Cover design by Cathy Rincon

Printed in the United States of America

VB FOF 10 9 8 7 6 5 4 3 2

This book is printed on acid-free paper.

CONTENTS

INTRODUCTION

This is an encyclopedia of people, places, and things relevant to the crimes of November 22–24, 1963, in Dallas, Texas. These crimes are the assassination of U.S. president John F. Kennedy, the wounding of Texas governor John B. Connally and bystander James T. Tague, the murder of Dallas police officer J. D. Tippit, and the murder by Jack Ruby of accused assassin Lee Harvey Oswald.

For those readers unfamiliar with these history-changing events, start by reading this introduction, which will give you an overview of those events and their effect on history. Then read the entry for Lee Harvey Oswald (look under "O"), the man arrested and accused of murdering President Kennedy, who was then slain himself while handcuffed to a policeman. Next read the entry for Jack Ruby (under "R") the Dallas nightclub owner who shot Oswald in the basement of the Dallas police station before horrified millions of television spectators.

We know that, somehow, both Oswald and Ruby were involved with these crimes, so after you have finished reading their entries, follow the cross references for those two men. (Cross-references appear both inserted into the text of an entry, if the reference is to a specific point in the entry, and, more commonly, listed at the bottom of each entry.) At this point, choose a favorite "assassination theory" and follow the instructions later in this introduction as to how to research each major theory.

Because that's what almost all of this is—theory. Problems with determining the facts from the fiction regarding the assassination started almost immediately. Official investigation on a local level was shut down early by the federal government, which seemed reluctant to dig too deeply into the matter. So the "official scenario" is the least believed. As I wrote years ago: "The assassination is a murder mystery with the final page torn out, a sleazy slice of grotesque Americana, a dreamlike labyrinth of characters and deeply layered plot. It is a trip down the rabbit hole into a mirrored maze of corrupt power and greed, a story short on heroes. The men we most expected to respond gallantly to a national crisis either scrambled to cover themselves or stuck their heads in the sand."

There is evidence that intelligence agencies—domestic, foreign and private—have purposefully spread false information regarding the assassination, attempts to either obfuscate the truth or use the crime for its political potential or both. Eyewitnesses have lied. This includes people who saw things but deny it, people who falsely claim to have observed suspicious behavior—and people who are covering up their own shady behavior, even though it had nothing to do with the assassination. So never base your assassination theories on one piece of information, no matter how trusted the source. In this case, it would appear, even the good guys are lying. Search the clues for patterns or motifs. A lot of people who knew Oswald were geologists. I wonder if? . . . In 1963, did every city have a "Russian-speaking community" made up of anticommunists like the one in Dallas? How come there are so many pilots? Why were there so many clumsy attempts to make the assassination look like a communist conspiracy? If everyone thought the first report was a firecracker, maybe it was a firecracker. And so on.

For you experts, feel free to read this book any way you please. The entries are long enough so that you can read it front to back without feeling too much like the ball in a pinball machine. Besides, you know your favorite topics. Look them up. Even readers who are experts should keep an eye on the cross references at the bottom (and sometimes inside) of each entry. Even information with which you are familiar may be linked together in unexpected ways.

Below is the overview of that horrible weekend's events, which I call:

THE ORIGINAL NIGHTMARE ON ELM STREET

U.S. president John F. Kennedy—the oldest living son of Irish-American entrepreneur Joseph Kennedy—was killed by rifle fire at approximately 12:30 P.M., on November 22,

1963, as he rode westward in a motorcade. At the time of the shooting the presidential limousine was heading down a slight slope on Elm Street, on the north side of a symmetrically landscaped area called Dealey Plaza at the western edge of the downtown section of Dallas, Texas. Just ahead, from the limo, an underpass could be seen, Dallas's triple underpass. Then loud explosions were heard.

Three weeks earlier, on November 1, assassins' bullets had forced a change in the leadership of South Vietnam, a nation that hundreds and thousands of American soldiers would be fighting to protect only five years later. The leaders of South Vietnam, Diem and Nhu, were assassinated.

Kennedy had come to Dallas to mend political fences in the Texas Democratic Party and to campaign for reelection in 1964. He came at the invitation of the Dallas Citizen's Council, the Dallas Assembly, and the Science Research Center. The Citizen's Council was an organization of powerful Dallas businessmen, which was thought by many to "run Dallas." This was President Kennedy's second visit to Dallas during his presidency. He had come before to say a deathbed goodbye to Speaker of the House Sam Rayburn, who died on November 16, 1961.

At the time of the shooting, President Kennedy's motorcade had just completed a slow journey through downtown Dallas, heading from Love Field airport to the Trade Mart, where the president was scheduled to deliver a luncheon speech. Security during the motorcade was unusually lax—perhaps uniquely so. First Lady Jacqueline Kennedy, was riding beside the president on his left in the limousine's back seat. Only a month before, Jackie, who was grieving over the death of her newborn son, Patrick, had gone for an extended Mediterranean cruise on Aristotle Onassis's yacht, the *Christina*—which was actually a converted destroyer that carried extensive communications equipment. Despite this, the First Lady and the boat had been reported "missing" for several days. (See also KENNEDY, JACQUELINE.)

In Dallas, the gunfire blew off a major portion of President Kennedy's head. Also seriously wounded in the ambush was Governor John Connally of Texas, who was sitting in a jump seat in front of President Kennedy, slightly below Kennedy and about eight inches to his left. Connally's wife, Nellie, sat at the governor's left. Only the politicians were struck by gunfire. (For details on President Kennedy's wounds, see PARKLAND HOSPITAL and AUTOPSY OF JOHN F. KENNEDY.)

The driver and front passenger seats were occupied by veteran agents of the Secret Service, the organization whose duty it was to protect the president and his family from harm. The Secret Service's performance was dismal in Dallas. (See SECRET SERVICE, U.S.)

At the scene of the crime there was much confusion. Policemen ran toward the triple underpass seeking the

The crowds were enthusiastic, and everyone seemed happy as the presidential limousine made its way through downtown Dallas. *(Collector's Archive)*

source of the shots. One policeman, a motorcycle patrolman who had been riding at the back of the motorcade, ran directly into the Texas School Book Depository.

Though there were fewer people watching the motorcade in Dealey Plaza than there had been during the parade's slow journey through downtown Dallas, there were still more than 200 witnesses to the crime. The key statements of many of them will be included in this book. Because there are so many of them, assassination witnesses have been listed separately. It is impossible to include statements from all of the eyewitnesses because so many of them have preferred to remain anonymous. (Some stayed to talk to authorities or members of the press about what they saw. Others simply left the scene, perhaps in shock, perhaps not fully understanding what had happened, and their identities and whereabouts remain unknown to this day.) And there's no doubt that several of the people who today claim to be eyewitnesses to the assassination were in reality nowhere near Dealey Plaza on the fateful day. And, because human nature is what it is, there are many legitimate eyewitnesses whose testimony has grown increasingly dramatic over the years, with new details popping up every now and again to keep listeners happy.

Many witnesses said that the shots came from in front of the president's limousine, from behind a wooden fence atop a grassy slope on the north side of Elm Street, adjacent to the triple underpass—the notorious "grassy knoll." Puffs of smoke were also seen by many eyewitnesses, waffing across Elm Street after the shooting, originating from this location.

DEALEY PLAZA, DALLAS, TEXAS

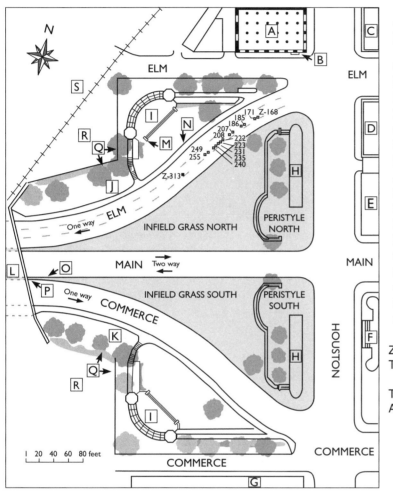

A Texas School Book Depository
B Alleged assassin's lair location
    (sixth-floor window)
C Dal-Tex Building
D Dallas County Records Building
E Dallas County Criminal Courts Building
F Old Court House
G United States Post Office building
H Peristyles and reflecting pools
I Pergolas
J "Grassy knoll" north
K "Grassy knoll" south
L Triple underpass
M Position of Abraham Zapruder
N Stemmons road sign
O Approximate location of curbstone hit
P Position of James T. Tague
Q Stockade fences
R Parking lots
S Rail line

Z-168 to Z-313: Zapruder film frame position
Total distance from frames 168–313:
    137 ft. 0 in.
Total elapsed time: 7 seconds
Assumes Zapruder film is historically
    correct document.

Other witnesses thought the shots came from the buildings to President Kennedy's rear, at the northeast corner of the plaza. Some heard shots coming from both directions.

It should be kept in mind that the assassination of John F. Kennedy took place well after the invention of the silencer, and at least one suspect was reported to have ordered a rifle silencer several weeks before the assassination. (See WEATHERFORD, HARRY.) It is not written in stone that the sounds of Dealey Plaza are any indication whatsoever of the number of shots that were fired. The reports heard may have been nothing more than diversions.

Special attention was drawn to the Texas School Book Depository—the building where Lee Harvey Oswald, the alleged assassin, worked. Oswald was a Marxist—an ex-Marine who had lived for several years in the Soviet Union, who had married a Soviet woman and had returned to the United States where he had gotten into legal trouble while handing out leaflets in New Orleans

supporting Fidel Castro's communist regime in Cuba. (See also OSWALD, LEE HARVEY; OSWALD IN THE MARINES; and TEXAS SCHOOL BOOK DEPOSITORY.)

The School Book Depository was at the northwest corner of Elm and Houston Streets. It was from this building that some eyewitnesses had seen a gun protruding from a sixth-floor window.

A search of the sixth floor produced several shell casings and a rifle. It was initially reported that only two shells had been found. This was later changed to three, leading to speculation that all three shell casings may not have been found simultaneously at the same location.

The rifle, too, had a shifting identification. Called a German Mauser during the early hours of the investigation, the rifle was finally determined to be an Italian Mannlicher-Carcano. A subsequent check of mail-order records revealed that the rifle had seemingly been mail-ordered by Oswald under the pseudonym A. J. Hidell. The weapon was in bad shape, rusty, scope poorly aligned. Weeks later, during FBI tests, federal sharpshooters refused to fire the weapon until it was repaired.

Oswald had fled the building following the shooting and was arrested later in the afternoon in the Texas Theatre in connection with the shooting murder of a police officer.

According to the official scenario, Oswald had walked out the front door of his building and had gotten on a bus. When the bus became stuck in traffic, trapped by the gridlock caused by the presidential motorcade and subsequent assassination, Oswald got off and walked to the Greyhound Bus Station where he took a cab home.

The cleaning lady in his rooming house (see ROBERTS, EARLENE) saw him come into the house hurriedly, go to his room, and exit several minutes later zipping up a jacket. While he was in his room, Roberts said that a Dallas Police car pulled up in front of the house, honked its horn twice, and pulled away. The last she saw of Oswald he was standing outside the house waiting at a bus stop.

However, several eyewitnesses in Dealey Plaza, most notably Deputy Sheriff Roger Craig, saw a man resembling Oswald run from the School Book Depository and get into a light-colored Nash Rambler station wagon with a luggage rack on top.

At Parkland Hospital a pristine bullet (sometimes referred to as "the magic bullet," or as Commission Exhibit 399) was found on a stretcher near the emergency rooms where President Kennedy and Governor Connally were treated. (See MAGIC BULLET.) The bullet ballistically linked the Book Depository rifle with the crime, even though the bullet didn't appear to have struck anything solid.

Officials almost immediately disregarded all eyewitnesses who said that the shots came from anywhere other than the Book Depository, including those who said that the shots came from behind the motorcade, but from buildings other than the Book Depository.

Some thought the shots came from either the Dal-Tex Building or the County Records Building, which are on the east side of Houston Street facing the plaza. Still, dissenters continued to talk, keeping alive the now accepted implausibility of the lone-gunman theory.

One eyewitness, Abraham Zapruder, made an 8mm film of the assassination from his position atop a pergola wall only a few feet east of the picket fence atop the knoll. (See ZAPRUDER FILM, THE.) Zapruder's film was taken from him and developed by authorities. Although frames from the film were published in *Life* magazine, the film was not shown to the American public for more than 10 years.

For years it was assumed that the film was an accurate record of what actually occurred in Dealey Plaza, and, by

using it, investigators could create a timetable of events, thus concluding that a lone gunman using the alleged assassination weapon had time to fire only three shots during the shooting sequence. Unfortunately, evidence of extreme editing in the film has recently been discovered, creating doubt about the film and what it shows.

Still, for authorities during the days following the assassination, three shots were considered the maximum number of shots that could have been fired by one man, and the possibility that more than one man had been firing was never officially considered.

Governor Connally's wounds had been severe. He had an entrance wound in his back, a shattered rib, an exit wound in his chest, a shattered wrist, and a minor wound to his thigh. Explaining all of President Kennedy and Governor Connally's wounds with three shots stretched believability. Since the ricochet of a shot that missed wounded a bystander named James T. Tague—a fact that the FBI never officially recognized—more than one shooter becomes a necessity to provide a reasonable explanation.

Connally recovered from his wounds. Several metal fragments were removed from his body during operations in the hours and days after the shooting, and he carried several fragments inside him for the rest of his life.

The Zapruder film shows President Kennedy's head driven backward and to the left by the fatal shot, fueling suspicions that the fatal shot came from in front of him and to his right.

On the afternoon of the shooting, three vagrants with recent haircuts were apprehended in a railroad car behind the grassy knoll. (See THREE TRAMPS.) The men were escorted across Dealey Plaza by police and, in the process, were repeatedly photographed. Who these three "tramps" were and what connection, if any, they had to the assassination remains a matter of controversy.

President Kennedy and Governor Connally were rushed to Parkland Hospital where the president was pronounced dead at 1:00 P.M. At Parkland, emergency personnel, well experienced in the treatment of gunshot wounds, were unanimous in their opinion that the president had been shot at least once from the front—in the throat, at approximately the location of the knot of his necktie. Others felt his head wound had been caused by a bullet to the right temple, which had struck almost tangentially from the front. This bullet had then blown out the right rear of the president's head, explaining why a motorcycle policeman to the rear of President Kennedy's limousine had been splattered with blood and brain matter by the shot. All at Parkland agreed that there was a large wound in the right rear of JFK's head. (See PARKLAND HOSPITAL.)

The throat wound was slit with a scalpel so that a tracheotomy could be performed. This procedure ended up causing much confusion later. Since the emergency doctors never turned President Kennedy over, an alleged entrance wound in the president's back wasn't seen until the autopsy.

Yet, that night, when President Kennedy's body was autopsied at Bethesda Naval Medical Center in Bethesda, Maryland, by medical examiners unfamiliar with gunshot wounds, well after Oswald's arrest and the assumption of his position in the sixth-floor window, it was determined that the president had been shot exclusively from the rear. (See AUTOPSY OF JOHN F. KENNEDY.)

The autopsy report, which was insufficient in a myriad of ways, said that the president was shot once in the back (the throat wound, therefore, was one of exit) and once in the back of the head. For several days afterward, the fact that there was an autopsy was not made public, and the chief surgeon admitted destroying his original notes.

All photos and X rays of the autopsy agree with the autopsists. (The authenticity of those photographs and X rays, however, has been questioned. Photographic experts have called the images composites.) Is this a case of mass hallucination in Dallas or a massive cover-up in Washington? A third theory, less likely, is that everyone is telling the truth but that JFK's body was altered, his wounds somehow changed in appearance, somewhere between the two hospitals.

One man using a Mannlicher-Carcano rifle could only have fired three shots during the shooting sequence as it appeared in the Zapruder film. Since one bullet, apparently one that had struck President Kennedy in the head, had fragmented and had been found inside the limousine after the shooting, and the bullet that missed has never been found, the "magic bullet" found on the stretcher at Parkland Hospital had to account for all of the nonfatal wounds suffered by President Kennedy and Governor Connally.

President Kennedy's back wound and throat wound, as well as all of Governor Connally's wounds, had to be caused by a bullet that hardly looked as if it had been fired.

The best argument available—out of many—against the lone-nut theory is that Governor Connally held inside his body for the remainder of his life more metal than could possibly be missing from the bullet that had to have caused all of his wounds for the lone-nut theory to remain plausible. Yet, the Warren Commission, a panel of powerful and unimpeachable men commissioned by President Lyndon B. Johnson, sold the magic-bullet myth. Why? Did they do it because they believed it to be true, to cover up a coup d'état, or because they felt the lie was in the best interests of the country? To all but the most paranoid and sordidly cynical, the latter explanation is the more appealing.

It would appear that an effort was made to make the assassination look as if it were the result of a communist conspiracy, specifically of Cuban origin—an anti-détente conspiracy that would lead to an invasion of Cuba. (See OSWALD IN MEXICO.)

To counteract that result, it has been theorized, the Warren Commission and other lone-nut supporters have put forth the lone-nut myth under the belief that, with this lie, they have kept the world from the brink of World War III. (See PHASE-ONE COVER-UP; PHASE-TWO COVER-UP.)

There is evidence that the Dallas police and District Attorney's Office were going to treat the crime as an international conspiracy. (See ALEXANDER, WILLIAM.) The investigation into the assassination by the local authorities was stopped within hours of the shooting at the direct orders of Lyndon Johnson. The FBI took over the investigation and limited their curiosity to information that would support Oswald's lone guilt.

Forty-six minutes or less after the assassination, Dallas Police officer J. D. Tippit was murdered with a handgun near the corner of Tenth Street and Patton Avenue in the Oak Cliff section of Dallas. (See TIPPIT, J. D.; TIPPIT, MURDER OF.)

This crime effectively cleared the initial crime scene of most of its investigation. Many of the Dallas policemen who had reported to Dealey Plaza now abruptly left that location to go to Oak Cliff to investigate the shooting of the policeman.

Many conspiracy theorists have questioned why Dallas police immediately assumed that the Tippit shooting had had something to do with JFK's assassination. This ignores the fact that Tippit was the first Dallas police officer to be killed in the line of duty in 12 years, the last having been Officer Johnny Sides in 1951. Since the crime had been committed only 45 minutes after the biggest crime ever to be committed in Dallas, the presumption that there was a connection seems justified.

Once again, eyewitnesses disagreed strongly on what happened. Still, most said that one man shot Tippit and that the man fleeing the scene was Oswald. Others saw two assailants, either both fleeing in opposite directions on foot or one fleeing on foot and one fleeing in a car.

There was only one witness, Mrs. Helen Markham, a frightened and perhaps slightly pixilated woman, who saw the shooting and later identified the shooter as Oswald. All other identifications were by those who first saw the assailant after the shooting.

One of those witnesses, Warren Reynolds, refused to identify Oswald as the murderer, but he was subsequently ambushed and shot in the head. After miraculously recovering, Reynolds decided that, yes, it was Oswald he had seen fleeing the scene.

DALLAS DOWNTOWN AND CENTRAL OAK CLIFF AREAS

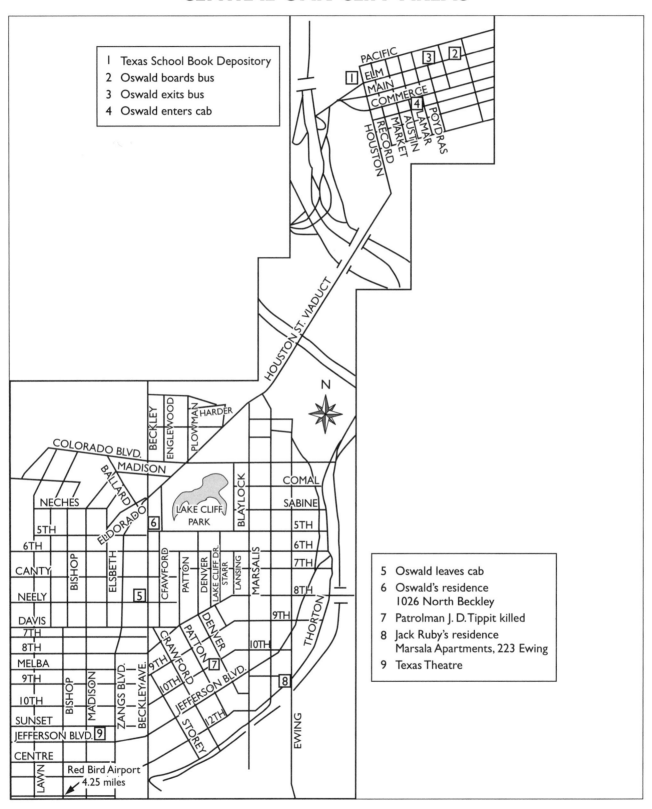

1 Texas School Book Depository
2 Oswald boards bus
3 Oswald exits bus
4 Oswald enters cab

5 Oswald leaves cab
6 Oswald's residence
  1026 North Beckley
7 Patrolman J. D. Tippit killed
8 Jack Ruby's residence
  Marsala Apartments, 223 Ewing
9 Texas Theatre

Red Bird Airport
4.25 miles

Reynolds says that, after he was shot, he received a phone call from General Edwin Walker, a right-wing Dallasite. This was the same General Walker who was supposedly an earlier target for an Oswald shooting attempt. Reynolds, at first, did not link the attempt on his life with the Tippit killing. He thought it had been a mere burglary attempt. General Walker made sure that Reynolds understood that the Tippit shooting and his own shooting must have been connected. One woman who saw Tippit shot, Acquila Clemons, whose version of the crime disagreed with the official scenario, claims that she was threatened by police and told that she should keep her mouth shut. Less than an hour after the murder of Tippit, Oswald was arrested inside an Oak Cliff movie house called the Texas Theatre. Police had been alerted that a suspicious man had entered the theater without buying a ticket. Oswald was reportedly arrested while in possession of the gun that had killed Tippit and fake identification that linked him to the Book Depository rifle.

Dallas police, the FBI, and the Secret Service interrogated Oswald for almost two days in the Dallas Police station without allowing him a lawyer. As far as we know, no stenographic or tape recordings were kept of Oswald's interrogations. The only verifiable quotes from Oswald after his arrest are statements he screamed to the press while being moved from one place to another within the station.

Oswald was later painted as a political fanatic who killed the president so that he would be considered a "great man." The accused assassin, however, couldn't have acted less like a self-aggrandizing zealot after his arrest. He "emphatically denied the charges." He called himself a "patsy."

He seemed more like his Marine nickname "Ozzie Rabbit," who had cinched his guilty appearance by fleeing the crime scene. (His middle name "Harvey," was also a famous rabbit.) During her Warren Commission testimony, Marina Oswald, Lee's Russian wife, in a strange moment perhaps attributable to her interpreter, calls her husband "my frightened rabbit."

In order for someone to be a patsy, others must set him up. If anyone at any time asked Oswald who those others might be, the question was never recorded. Nor was the answer.

There is evidence that Oswald's self-described role in the assassination plot as a patsy was an accurate one. The accused assassin had a public persona created through a number of seemingly staged incidents in his life, which made him perfectly suited to a frame-up. (See OSWALD, LEE HARVEY.)

Oswald's private persona, however—with his connections to organized crime, the Central Intelligence Agency (CIA), the Federal Bureau of Investigation (FBI), the Soviet foreign-intelligence service known as the KGB, anti-Castro exiles etc.—was so complex that it virtually assured that the crime would never be adequately investigated. Whether guilty or frightened of being made into a scapegoat, the agencies, which might otherwise be expected to investigate the crime thoroughly, instead covered up their own involvement with the accused and checked off on the lone-gunman scenario they had been spoon fed.

As mentioned, international tensions in 1963 also contributed to the inevitability that no conspiracy would be unveiled. This was a time when the world hovered on the edge of nuclear holocaust, and the evil specter of conspiracy was frightening even to those whose own reputations and well-being were not protected by the cover-up.

On Sunday morning, November 24, 1963, a Dallas strip-club owner with ties to organized crime named Jack Ruby shot Oswald to death in the basement of the Dallas police station while Oswald was being transferred from the city jail to the county facility.

Ruby, a Jew from Chicago, claimed to have spontaneously shot Oswald. Ruby was the owner of the Carousel Club, which was near the Dallas police headquarters where he shot Oswald.

Ruby's organized crime ties dated back to his childhood in Chicago working for Al Capone. After coming from Chicago to Dallas in late 1947, it has been alleged that Ruby became a liaison between Chicago mobsters who wanted to control vice in Dallas and officials in Dallas who needed to be bribed in order for that plan to work.

Ruby was also a police-phile, friendly with many members of the Dallas police force. Policemen were allowed to drink in the Carousel Club for free and Ruby had been known to fix police officers up with women who worked in the club.

The relationship between the Dallas police and Ruby caused that department much embarrassment as they tried to explain how Ruby had walked right through supposedly stringent security to kill Oswald.

Ruby's bio includes some of the same sort of intrigue as Oswald's. Ruby was alleged by several witnesses to be involved with anti-Castro Cubans and American soldiers of fortune in smuggling weapons into Cuba.

Within days of President Kennedy's death, Lyndon Baines Johnson, the new president, appointed an "investigatory" commission. It became known as the Warren Commission, as it was chaired by Earl Warren, who was at the time the Chief Justice of the Supreme Court.

The Warren Commission was not investigatory, however. The real reason for the commission was to put an official government stamp of approval on the lone gunman/no conspiracy theory that had already been put forth by the FBI.

In fact, the commission was handicapped by the fact that members had little investigatory power of their own and were limited to information and conclusions already put forth by the FBI and the CIA—both of which had reasons to be less than truthful with the commission.

The FBI, for example, was busy suppressing rumors that Oswald had been a paid informant for that organization. The CIA, whose possible direct involvement with Oswald was better obfuscated, was concerned that CIA plans to assassinate communist Cuban leader Fidel Castro would be revealed if the commission were given all the facts.

The Warren Commission was also reluctant to publish some of the information the FBI did provide them, such as details of a visit to the Russian and Cuban embassies in Mexico City during late September and early October of 1963 by Oswald or someone claiming to be Oswald. During that visit the man calling himself Oswald met with a Soviet who may have been in charge of a KGB assassination program. (See KOSTIKOV, VALERI; OSWALD IN MEXICO.)

When the *Warren Report* was published, along with 26 volumes of accompanying testimony and exhibits, it became clear to those who read the whole thing that the report's conclusions were predetermined and not based on its own accumulated evidence.

Books pointing out the evidence of conspiracy in the murder of the president were published within months of the assassination. A man writing under the name Thomas G. Buchanan wrote *Who Killed Kennedy?*, which appeared in 1964. The book theorized that a right-wing conspiracy had killed JFK, funded by Texas oil money.

That same year Joachim Joesten wrote *Oswald: Assassin or Fall Guy?* Attorney Mark Lane, who had been retained by Marguerite Oswald, the alleged assassin's mother, to defend the memory of her son, wrote the best-selling book *Rush to Judgment* in 1966. The book strongly argued that Oswald had been framed.

In 1967, New Orleans district attorney Jim Garrison began investigating the assassination. Garrison considered this to be within his jurisdiction based on the fact that Oswald had spent the summer of 1963 in New Orleans in the company of men who, according to reports received by Garrison, were plotting to kill President Kennedy. (See GARRISON INVESTIGATION.)

Garrison focused his early investigation upon a bizarre hairless, middle-aged man named David Ferrie. Ferrie was a CIA pilot, a private investigator for Carlos Marcello of the New Orleans mob, a soldier of fortune, and a homosexual pedophile who had taught Oswald as a teenager when both were involved in the Civil Air Patrol.

Ferrie died under suspicious circumstances (officially suicide). His death came only hours before Garrison was going to arrest him, so the New Orleans district attorney

instead arrested New Orleans import-export millionaire Clay Shaw, who had also been seen before the assassination by witnesses—using the name "Clay" or "Clem Bertrand"—in the company of Oswald and Ferrie, discussing President Kennedy's assassination.

From the onset of his investigation, Garrison faced a seemingly organized media campaign to stop him. Garrison's requests for help from other government agencies and elected officials brought only refusals. Several of Garrison's key witnesses died before they could testify. Shaw—who was later revealed to be a CIA informant and a board member of an organization linked to assassination attempts on French president Charles de Gaulle—was acquitted. (See PERMINDEX.)

In 1976, the people of the United States saw the Zapruder film for the first time and learned that earlier reports from Dan Rather of CBS News and *Life* magazine, stating that President Kennedy's head snapped forward at the time of the fatal head shot, appeared to be false. As the film depicted the events, the opposite was true: President Kennedy was rocketed backward by the fatal shot.

The public outcry caused by public showing led directly to the formation of the House Select Committee on Assassinations. The House Committee reopened the case, as well as that of the 1968 assassination of Dr. Martin Luther King Jr. in Memphis, Tennessee.

The committee had to deal with internal squabbles, as well as its own share of dying witnesses, and concluded that a number of organized crime figures (Carlos Marcello, Santos Trafficante, Jimmy Hoffa, and Sam Giancana) had the motive, means, and opportunity to order President Kennedy's assassination.

The committee, however, uncovered no evidence directly linking these men with the crime.

Using acoustic evidence seemingly recorded at the assassination scene, the committee concluded that there had been a fourth shot and that it had come from the direction of the grassy knoll. But since the autopsy showed no signs of a shot hitting President Kennedy from the front, the committee determined that the knoll shot had missed.

All wounds, they concluded, had been caused by Oswald firing from the Book Depository. Having run out of time and money, the House Select Committee disbanded—recommending that the Justice Department continue the investigation. The Justice Department did not take up the recommendation. Instead, it issued a statement discrediting the committee's acoustic evidence and reverted the official conclusion back to that of the Warren Commission—one gunman, three bullets, no conspiracy. Hundreds of assassination theories and variations of theories have been put forth by experts, involving both those who pulled the triggers in Dealey Plaza and those who ordered and financed the assassination, but there are four basic primary suspects:

- Organized crime (See GIANCANA, MOMO SALVATORE (SAM); MARCELLO, CARLOS; TRAFFICANTE, SANTOS.)
- the CIA (See ANGLETON, JAMES JESUS; CENTRAL INTELLIGENCE AGENCY; COLBY, WILLIAM; DEMOHRENSCHILDT, GEORGE; DULLES, ALLEN; HELMS, RICHARD; HUNT, E. HOWARD; MK/ULTRA.)
- the military-industrial complex (See ARMY INTELLIGENCE; OSWALD IN THE MARINES; PAINE, RUTH AND MICHAEL R.; WILLOUGHBY, CHARLES.)
- an international web of Fascists (See PERMINDEX; TORBITT DOCUMENT; WHITE RUSSIANS.)

Many theories involve a combination of these groups. Mobsters, some of whom had rigged voting booths to get Kennedy elected, now hated JFK because his brother, Attorney General Robert Kennedy, was waging war against organized crime.

For details on an involved theory that has Greek shipping magnate Aristotle Onassis as the mastermind behind President Kennedy's death see the GEMSTONE FILE.

There were CIA agents and their assets who wanted President Kennedy dead because they considered him too easy on communism. These men felt betrayed by what they perceived as his failure to give them adequate air support during the Bay of Pigs invasion of Cuba, which had been carried out by a group of CIA agents and their Cuban-exile soldiers.

The feeling of betrayal ran both ways, as Kennedy felt that the CIA, a Cold War creation, was not adequately accountable for its actions. JFK had threatened to dissolve the intelligence agency.

Organized crime, which wanted Castro out of Cuba so it could reclaim its casinos in Havana, the CIA, and anti-Castro Cubans had been working hand-in-hand in attempts to assassinate Castro. It is feasible that these same groups got together to change U.S. leadership.

The military-industrial complex, a combination of the military and its massive defense contractors, hated President Kennedy because, so the story goes, he was resisting their attempts to start a long munitions-consumptive war in Vietnam—a war that would become, after President Kennedy's death, highly profitable for a select few.

There is a theory that the best way to solve a murder is to isolate those who gained from the victim's death. *Qui bono* is the legal term for this process. Keep this in mind when reading the entries for Lyndon Johnson and Richard Nixon, the two men who followed Kennedy as the leader of the Free World.

Lyndon Johnson, who gained the most because of the assassination, not only became the new president but also avoided a career-ending financial scandal. (See JOHNSON, LYNDON BAINES.) President Kennedy had already told his secretary that Johnson was not going to be his running mate on the 1964 presidential ticket.

J. Edgar Hoover, who loathed the Kennedys, was approaching the age of mandatory retirement, a rule that President Kennedy was unlikely to waive. With Hoover's long-time friend and neighbor Lyndon Johnson in the White House, Hoover's career was extended.

Oil billionaire H. L. Hunt, who spent millions every year on anticommunist propaganda, maintained his own intelligence network, which worked both within and without the intelligence agencies sponsored by the U.S. government. The oilmen of Texas wanted John Kennedy out of the White House and their friend Lyndon Johnson in because Kennedy had threatened to eliminate a tax loophole called the oil-depletion allowance, which was saving them millions of dollars a year.

Here then, in this book, is a comprehensive assemblage of JFK assassination facts and theories.

ACKNOWLEDGMENTS

Research Consultants: Mitch Highfill, David Henry Jacobs, and Richard Erickson.

And also: Sawnie Aldredge, Rita Benson, Tekla and Matthew Benson, Wanda Boudreaux, James Chambers, Regina Sampogna, Michele Cohen, The Collector's Archives, Anne Darrigan, Richard and Jenny Doherty, Jake Elwell, Michael Gingold, Gary Goldstein, Mr. and Mrs. Anthony Grasso, Lisa M. Grasso, David Hutchison, Norman Jacobs, The JFK Assassination Information Center, Arlene Jones, Kimberly Lyons, Paul McCaffrey, Raymond and Cindy Merrow, Jim A. Pearson, George Napolitano, the New York Public Library, Greig O'Brien, Katharine Repole, Frank Rosner, José Soto, Bert Randolph Sugar, Anthony Timpone, Ruthcarol and Colin Touhey, Nathan Versace, and Andrew Winiarczyk at the Last Hurrah Bookshop.

ENTRIES A–Z

Abundant Life Temple

Large church, standing tall above the Oak Cliff section of Dallas, located at the corner of Tenth and Crawford streets, slightly more than a block west of the scene of Officer J. D. Tippit's murder, in the direction of the Texas Theatre.

According to Dallas police sergeant Gerald Hill, one unnamed eyewitness saw a man who was fleeing the scene of the Tippit murder disappear into the church's back entrance.

The alley that ran behind the church was the same alley that ran behind the Texas Theatre. Directly across that alley from the church was the parking lot where a jacket, allegedly shed by the assailant, was found.

Before the Dallas police, in pursuit of Tippit's killer, could search the church, they were called away to a false alarm at the nearby Jefferson Branch of the Dallas Public Library.

After the report that the assailant had run into the Temple, the building was briefly visited by Hill and Assistant District Attorney William Alexander. Two ladies answered the door, Alexander and Hill said. According to Hill, they asked the ladies if they had seen anyone, and the ladies said no.

It was Hill who had called into the Dallas police dispatcher, saying, "A witness said he saw him last at the Abundant Life Temple at Tenth, about the 400 block. We're fixing to go in and shake it down."

Hill later said that Tenth Street, at the time of the assassination, had more churches on it than any other street in the United States. This claim has not been confirmed.

The Abundant Life Temple was affiliated with the American Council of Christian Churches, the acting director of which in 1963 was oil billionaire H. L. Hunt.

(See also ALEXANDER, WILLIAM; HILL, GERALD; TORBITT DOCUMENT.)

Acoustic Evidence

Assassination researcher Gary Mack suggested to the House Select Committee on Assassinations that Dallas Police transmissions from Dealey Plaza recorded at the time of the assassination might reveal the sounds of the shots. While Department Channel 1 was used for communications during the motorcade, Channel 2 recorded more than five minutes of the sounds around a solitary vehicle when the microphone button on that vehicle became stuck in the open position.

According to Gary Mack, a copy of the original tape was made by Dallas police sergeant Gerald Hill, who gave the copy to author Judy Bonner. Bonner, in turn, gave a copy to assassination archivist Mary Ferrell, who made copies for researchers Penn Jones Jr. and J. Gary Shaw.

In May 1978, the House Select Committee contracted the firm of Bolt, Beranek and Newman to analyze the Dallas police dictabelt recordings. Dr. James Barger found six "impulse sequences" on the Channel 2 recording that he said *could* have been caused by gunshots. It is important to note that there are no *audible* gunshots on the tapes. Belief in the scientific findings was always oddly reminiscent of the belief in flea circuses—the experts had to tell you that the fleas were actually there. Professor Mark Weiss and his research associate Ernest Ashkenasy of Queens College in New York City were asked to review Dr. Barger's findings. They verified the six sounds. So, on August 20, 1978, 36 microphones were set up around Dealey Plaza while guns were fired at various locations where it was thought assassins might have fired. Four-hundred and thirty-two shots were recorded. Weiss and Ashkenasy concluded that, though unable to verify that the impulses on the police recordings were actually caused by gunfire, they found that four of those impulses were *probably* caused by gunfire. It was determined using "sound fingerprints" that three of the shots had come from the sixth floor of the Texas School Book Depository and a fourth shot had come from behind the wooden fence on top of the grassy knoll. Weiss and Ashkenasy said that they had matched "sound fingerprints" from the police recordings to the test recordings and were "95 percent certain" that impulse number three came from the grassy knoll. At last, it was believed, a conspiracy had been scientifically proven.

But there was a problem. In order to create the "sound fingerprints" the acoustics experts had to determine the location of the open microphone that had recorded on Channel 2. They determined that the microphone had belonged to motorcycle officer H. B. McLain, who had ridden in the motorcade well back from the presidential limousine. McLain strongly protested that his microphone had not been stuck open and there was evidence to support his denial.

Among the sounds on the tape that could actually be heard were the increasing and diminishing sound of a siren, apparently passing by—and a sound that resembled that of a carillon bell. There was no crowd noise on the tape. There were indications that the open mike had been stationary and some distance from Dealey Plaza.

Then, in 1979, an Ohio researcher named Stephan N. Barber noticed "cross talk" on Channel 2—that is, the open mike on Channel 2 was close enough to a police radio to record what was happening on Channel 1. The cross talk proved that the "impulses" that had produced the "sound fingerprints" were not recorded until more than a minute after the assassination. To the embarrassment of the acoustics experts who had been so sure, the acoustic evidence was proven invalid.

In 1963, James C. Bowles was the communications supervisor in the dispatch office (Radio Division) for the Dallas police. He was the first to transcribe the police radio tape made at the time of the assassination. His was the transcription used by the Warren Commission. Bowles retired from the Dallas Police Department in 1981 and became sheriff of Dallas County in 1984. On the recordings one can hear the Morse code signal for "V" (victory). Bowles told Harrison Edward Livingstone that this was merely a coincidence. "It's just a heterodyning," he said. Bowles is a vocal opponent of the acoustic evidence. "This is nonsense, utter nonsense," Bowles says. He said that, in his opinion, the open mike that reportedly recorded the assassination was at the Dallas Trade Mart and could not have recorded the shots.

After the House Select Committee reported that the acoustic evidence was proof of a fourth shot, the National Academy of Sciences reviewed the evidence itself and said that not only did the tape not constitute evidence of a fourth shot but there were no shots on the tape at all, just static.

(See also HILL, GERALD.)

Adams, Victoria Elizabeth

Adams witnessed the assassination from the fourth floor of the Texas School Book Depository. She watched the motorcade with coworkers Sandra Styles, Elsie Dorman, and Dorothy Ann Garner. Adams told the FBI that the shots came from below and to the right from her perspective—in other words from the direction of the grassy knoll. After the shooting, she saw a man who resembled Jack Ruby—whom she later saw on television but did not know—questioning people at the corner of Houston and Elm. She said that, at the time, she thought the man was a policeman.

Air Force One

The presidential plane known as Air Force One was a VC-137C, tail number 26000, that arrived for the first time at Andrews Air Force Base on October 12, 1962, joining the MAC Special Missions Wing. In May 1963 the plane flew from Washington, D.C., to Moscow in what was then called the Soviet Union in eight hours and 39 minutes. The trip broke 14 U.S. Air Force transport records. The plane could fly as high as 43,000 feet and had a cruising speed of 575 miles per hour. Its range was 4,600 nautical miles and it carried a crew of 23. It was last used as Air Force One in the early 1980s and currently resides in the Air Force Museum. It transported President and Mrs. Kennedy from Fort Worth to Dallas, Texas, on the morning of the assassination. It was the site of President Johnson's swearing in as president and it transported President Kennedy's body from Love Field in Dallas to Andrews Air Force Base on the late afternoon/early evening of the assassination. Judge Sarah Hughes swore in Lyndon Johnson as the 36th president of the United States aboard Air Force One at Love Field, Dallas, at 2:38 P.M., November 22, 1963. The jet, when flying from Dallas to Washington, D.C., took a zigzag route in case the United States was under attack.

Alemán, José Braulio, Jr.

A wealthy Cuban exile and FBI informant who had a meeting with Florida mobster Santos Trafficante in September 1962 at the Scott Byron Hotel in Miami Beach. According to Alemán, Trafficante was angry about the way the

Kennedys were treating Jimmy Hoffa. He said, "[President Kennedy] doesn't know that this kind of encounter is very delicate. Mark my words, this man Kennedy is in trouble, and he will get what is coming to him."

Testifying before the House Select Committee on Assassinations on March 12, 1977, Alemán quoted Trafficante as saying, "He's not going to be reelected, he's going to be hit."

Alemán's luck went downhill after he testified before the congressional committee. By July 1983, Alemán was broke and hiding in Miami. Then, for no apparent reason, Alemán became crazed and murdered his aunt. He wounded three others. Police were called. A shoot-out ensued. During the gunfight, Alemán allegedly put his gun to his head and committed suicide.

Alexander, William

Alexander, who had served in the infantry in Italy during World War II before joining the Dallas District Attorney's Office, was the Dallas assistant district attorney (ADA) who talked briefly with Jack Ruby on November 23, the day before Ruby murdered Oswald. Alexander claimed the meeting was to discuss bad checks Ruby had received.

Alexander was the ADA who most vigorously presented the case against Oswald to the public immediately following the assassination. According to Harrison Edward Livingstone and Robert Groden in their book *High Treason,* "It has been suggested that Alexander was in the car that stopped in front of Oswald's house around 30 minutes after the assassination."

Alexander says that he did go to Oak Cliff during the late morning of November 22, 1963, to pick up a few items at a hardware store, and that he was on his way back to downtown Dallas, coming across the Houston Street viaduct when he heard sirens and knew something had happened in the Dealey Plaza area. He was outside the Texas School Book Depository when the radio report came in that a police officer had been shot in Oak Cliff. Alexander went from Dealey Plaza to the scene of the Tippit murder in a police car driven by Sergeant Calvin Bud Owens of the Dallas police. Also in the car was Sergeant Gerald Hill. Alexander says that when they arrived at the corner of Tenth Street and Patton Avenue the ambulance carrying Tippit's body was just pulling away. When a call came in that the suspect had been seen entering the Jefferson Branch Library on Jefferson Boulevard, most of the police officers on the scene went there in pursuit, but Alexander, along with Sergeant Gerald Hill, went to the nearby Abundant Life Temple, at the corner of Tenth and Crawford, to see if the suspect was there.

Alexander was present at the arrest of Oswald. After the arrest, Alexander said, seemingly oblivious to the international crisis he might cause, "Yes, he's a goddamned communist."

Alexander was involved in the initial search of Oswald's room on Beckley Avenue, as well as the first official interview with Mrs. Earlene Roberts, the cleaning lady at the rooming house.

Again, according to *High Treason,* "[Alexander] was waiting with a group of policemen in the alley behind the theater. It is believed that someone intended to murder Oswald there, but was foiled when Oswald didn't run out of the theater."

According to Penn Jones Jr., a local publisher, who was among the first to publish items that questioned the official version of the assassination: "Three policemen and . . . Alexander were waiting for him at the back door. Had Oswald run out that door, his execution would have been quick and painless, and the lone gunman theory would have been intact completely."

At 6:30 P.M. on the day of the assassination, Alexander—along with Captain Will Fritz, ADA Jim Allen, and Secret Service agent Forrest Sorrels—left the Dallas police station and went across the street to the Majestic Cafe to "think clearly about the case." Alexander, in a 1985 interview with researcher Dale K. Myers, said, "The question was, did we have enough to file charges against Oswald? As far as the Tippit murder, the answer was yes. We figured this would be enough to hold Oswald without bond, and would give us more time to gather evidence in the president's death, which we didn't have much on."

By November 23, Alexander publicly said he was ready to prosecute Oswald "as part of an international communist conspiracy."

Alexander later prosecuted Ruby for Oswald's murder. During the New Orleans trial of Clay Shaw for conspiracy to assassinate the president, Alexander helped witness Sergio Arcacha Smith successfully resist extradition.

Alexander had a permanent pass to Ruby's Carousel Club. The card, bearing Alexander's signature, was found among Ruby's belongings following Ruby's arrest. Warren Commission Exhibit 1322 describes all of the cards found and lists the names on them. Alexander's name is there. However, a microfilm of the actual cards shows all of them except Alexander's.

During Ruby's time in the Dallas jail following his arrest, he repeatedly stated that his life was in danger in Dallas and that he could not talk to officials freely as long as he was in that city. Ruby asked that he be removed from Dallas to be given a polygraph examination. The Warren Commission agreed to allow Ruby to take the lie detector test, but insisted that he remain in Dallas. When the test was given, Alexander was in the room. The test was administered in the presence of Alexander—the same man who would later tell the Warren Commission that there was no evidence of Ruby's involvement with organized crime.

Alexander participated vigorously in Ruby's prosecution. According to attorney/author Elmer Gertz, a member of the defense team who successfully appealed Ruby's death sentence: "There were 80 people in the [Dallas District Attorney's] office in 1963 . . . and it would be hard to find a more dedicated, and indelicate, lieutenant than . . . 'Bill' Alexander. . . . The gun which he carried was a symbol to him of the strength of the law. . . . For years Ruby had regarded Alexander as his friend; Alexander did not deny it, but friendship did not deter him in the least from his grim task. He was determined to 'fry' his friend, and to that end he would devote his shrewd, resourceful, and remorseless mind. . . . Whether or not Alexander mourned the assassination of the president, he could not resist a typical crack when a St. Patrick's Day parade was held in 1964 on the street of the president's death, 'Don't you think we're pushing our luck a little having another parade for an Irishman around here?' Using humor in the same vein, Alexander described his political philosophy as being 'just to the left of Little Orphan Annie and just to the right of the John Birchers.'"

Penn Jones Jr. wrote: "[Alexander] is alleged to have threatened to kill a man in the Court House by jamming a pistol to the man's head and saying, 'You son of a bitch, I will kill you right here.' . . . In view of the close relationship attested to by both Ruby and Alexander, and in view of a visit to Alexander's office by Ruby on the day before the assassination, we feel it is necessary to ask Alexander if he was the 'officer Alexander' making the [according to Earlene Roberts' Warren Commission testimony] periodic visits to the [Oswald's] rooming house." (See ROBERTS, EARLENE.)

The Warren Commission called a psychiatrist named Dr. William Robert Beavers to testify that Ruby was mentally unstable. Beavers illustrated Ruby's instability by quoting Ruby's comment, before he was given a polygraph test, that he would rather have Bill Alexander in the room than his defense attorney, Joe Tonahill.

A man charged with a capital crime who preferred an ADA's presence to his own defense lawyer, Beavers argued, is not aware of the situation. After Beavers's statements to the Warren Commission, Alexander was allowed by commission counsel Arlen Specter to ask Beavers a few questions.

Immediately, Bill's ego got into the thick of his query: "Did it appear to you that Ruby [during his polygraph examination] was looking to me for aid in framing some of the questions because of my peculiar knowledge of the case, in that I was in on it from the moment of the assassination of the president?"

Beavers replied, "I noticed that he did look to you in terms of getting some sort of support or information or possibly framing questions."

Today Alexander has a private law practice in Dallas.

Allen, William Gaston

A witness to the assassination and news photographer for the *Dallas Times Herald,* born April 19, 1936, in Little Rock, Arkansas. Allen took more than 90 photographs in Dealey Plaza after the assassination. Allen, with Joe Smith of the *Fort Worth Star* and Jack Beers of the *Dallas Morning News,* was one of three photographers to take photos of the three "tramps" as they were led by police out of Dealey Plaza, presumably to be questioned.

Ten minutes after the shooting, Allen photographed Deputy Sheriff Buddy Walthers and an unidentified man wearing a plastic ear piece. The men were standing on the south side of Elm Street in Dealey Plaza. The photos show the unknown man picking something up out of the grass and putting it in his pocket. (See figures, pp. 277–79.)

Allman, Pierce

Radio reporter who, according to Sylvia Meagher, was the man to whom Oswald gave directions to a telephone as Oswald exited the Texas School Book Depository minutes after the assassination. Oswald recalled meeting a "Secret Service man" at the doorway of the building who asked him the whereabouts of a public telephone. It has been speculated that NBC reporter Robert MacNeil may have been the man who encountered Oswald, but best guess is that it was Allman.

(See also MACNEIL, ROBERT.)

Alpha 66

The best funded, best publicized, most organized, and most dangerous of the anti-Castro groups working in the United States at the time of the assassination. Alpha 66, which received funding and other help from the CIA, was founded by Antonio Veciana, the man who later claimed to have seen Lee Harvey Oswald in Dallas in the company of a CIA man code-named Maurice Bishop. (According to Veciana, it was Bishop who had first suggested forming Alpha 66, and it was Bishop who had developed plans to assassinate Castro in October 1961.)

The name came because Alpha symbolized the beginning of the end for Castro, while the number 66 represented the same number of fellow accountants that Veciana recruited when he started his anti-Castro activities.

Even during and after the Cuban missile crisis, and long after President Kennedy ordered a halt to such missions, Alpha 66 continued to kill Soviet troops inside Cuba, as well as attack international ships on their way to Cuba to make deliveries. Of all the anti-Castro groups, Alpha 66 seemed most interested in provoking a war between the United States and the Soviet Union.

Alpha 66 also received a major boost from *Life* magazine, which would routinely send along a reporter on Alpha 66 missions so that their successes could receive maximum publicity.

Alpha 66 apparently had a favorite meeting spot in Dallas. On November 23, 1963, Deputy Sheriff Buddy Walthers wrote a memo to Sheriff Bill Decker stating that an informant had told him that Cubans had used the house at 3128 Harlendale Street in Dallas for meetings on weekends and that "Oswald had been to this house before."

A March 1976 article in the *Saturday Evening Post* called "Dallas: The Cuban Connection," written by assassination researchers Paul Hoch and George O'Toole, states that Veciana used to travel from city to city visiting Alpha 66 headquarters, and that the one in Dallas was located at "3126 Hollandale" (sic).

According to reporter Robert Sam Anson, the leader of the Alpha 66 meetings in Dallas—and who is identified in Warren Commission Document 23.4 as the Oswald look-alike seen at the meetings—was Manuel Rodríguez. It is more likely that the Oswald look-alike was John Thomas Masen, a known Oswald look-alike who was also known to be selling arms and ammunition to Alpha 66.

Manuel Rodríguez Orcarberro was investigated by the Protective Research Division of the Secret Service following the assassination because of the anti-JFK remarks he had made after the Bay of Pigs defeat. According to George Evica, whose source is an unnamed FBI informant, Rodríguez was president of SNFE/Alpha 66/MRP. Evica writes, "Rodriguez worked for the Coca-Cola bottling Company in Cuba until 1958 when he joined Castro. Rodriguez may have been involved in clandestine anti-Castro activity while seemingly cooperating with the revolutionary leader. After Castro come to power, Rodriguez returned to Coca-Cola, probably plotting against the Cuban premier, but soon took refuge in the Brazilian embassy in Havana, escaping to the United States in November 1960. Rodriguez obtained a job as a dishwasher in a Miami Beach hotel, staying there until September 1963. . . . In September 1963 . . . Rodriguez registered as an alien in Dallas, Texas, and headed the Alpha 66 anti-Castro operation which met at 3126 Harlendale Avenue [sic]." A home belonging to Jorge Salazar, this address is alleged to have been "the headquarters for the assassination teams in the JFK assassination plot," according to former CIA agent Robert Morrow. Morrow testified to the House Select Committee on Assassinations that Rodríguez "was known to have worked closely with [Mario] Kohly's Free Cuba Committee, [Guy] Banister's Citizens for a Free Cuba Committee, and Loran Hall's funder, the Committee to Free Cuba, etc."

(See also CHERAMIE, ROSE; D.R.E.; MASEN, JOHN THOMAS.)

Altgens, James Williams (Ike)

Born on April 28, 1919, Altgens was a life-long resident of Dallas who, in 1938, became an Associated Press photographer. Altgens took one of the most famous photos of the assassination sequence.

Altgens had gone to Dealey Plaza to photograph the president with his 35mm Nikkorex-F single lens reflex camera mounted with a 105mm telephoto lens and loaded with Kodak Tri-X pan film. He was standing on the south side of Elm Street, between the Texas School Book Depository and the grassy knoll. By counting the lines in the center of Elm Street to the corner in his photo, it is possible to determine that the first shot hit Kennedy while the view of his limo was still obscured by a tree from the "sniper's nest" window.

Altgens told researcher Larry A. Sneed, "My original intent was to make my picture from the triple underpass, and I would have done that. That was the first place that I went. But the police chased me off because they said it was private property. It belonged to the railroad so unless I was a railroad employee, I would not be allowed to stay up there even though I had credentials. At that time there was no one up there other than the police, one on either side of the underpass. . . . So, I . . . came through the School Book Depository parking lot area and came on through Dealey Plaza and down to the corner of Houston and Main Street. . . . While I was at the corner of Houston and Main, there was a young man [Jerry Belknap] who suffered what appeared to be an epileptic seizure. . . . The policeman [Dallas police sergeant D. V. Harkness] near where I was standing, who was on a three-wheel motorcycle, said, 'We'd better call an ambulance.' . . . As they picked him up and as the ambulance was leaving, you could then see the red lights of the president's caravan. . . . After I made my picture at Main and Houston, I ran down to get ahead of the caravan again to make additional pictures. I happened to look up at the triple underpass, noticed that it was loaded with people."

Altgens told researcher David Lifton on November 1, 1965, that he remembered, just before the motorcade arrived, that a number of people appeared behind the wall on the knoll "to the right of the stairs as you face the knoll." There were police among them.

Altgens told Sneed, "I took a diagonal run right across Dealey Plaza. . . . I was able then to make the picture that turned out to be [of] the first shot that Kennedy received."

To the Warren Commission Altgens testified: "I made one picture at the time I heard a noise that sounded like a firecracker . . . the sound was not of such a volume that it would indicate to me it was a high-velocity rifle. . . . It sounded like it was coming up from behind the car."

Altgen's comment that he saw people to the right of the stairs on the north side of Elm is physically impossible because of the layout of Dealey Plaza. Because those stairs curve right after disappearing from his view, what appeared to him to be on the right of the stairs was actually to the left of the stairs and behind them.

The famous photo also shows that the Secret Service agents assigned to protect Vice President Lyndon Johnson may have reacted faster than President Kennedy's guards. While the presidential Secret Service agents had merely turned to look back at the Texas School Book Depository, Vice President Johnson's protectors already had their car door open. A review of photos taken throughout the motorcade reveals that this door was kept ajar during other moments in the parade, however—so perhaps it was standard procedure.

In Altgens's photo that shows the Depository, there is a man standing on the front steps of the building who greatly resembles Lee Harvey Oswald. Evidence shows that the man was probably Oswald look-alike Billy Lovelady, a fellow employee of the building. Sarah Stanton, a Book Depository clerk who stood on the building's front steps, is among those who verify that Billy Lovelady also watched from that position. Other photographs taken during the assassination help to corroborate that Lovelady, who died on January 14, 1979, at the age of 41 of a heart attack in Colorado, was the man in the doorway.

Altgens told Warren Commission counsel that, because of the direction of flying brain matter, he thought the bullet had exited the left side of President Kennedy's head.

This photo, taken by Associated Press photographer James Altgens, captures the exact moment that President John F. Kennedy was shot. The president appears to slump in the car, as his wife, Jacqueline, holds his arm in an effort to aid him. Governor John Connally of Texas, who was in the front seat, was also shot. *(AP/Wide World Photos)*

President John F. Kennedy is slumped down in the backseat of the car after being fatally wounded, while his wife leans over him and a Secret Service Agent stands on the bumper. This photo was taken by James Altgens a moment after the shooting. (AP/Wide World Photos)

Altgens told Sneed, "The tissue, perhaps bone, a lot of fragments, all came my way. It came in my direction because I was standing right by the curb area on the south side of Elm Street which means that it came right across Jackie Kennedy, perhaps fifteen feet from the limousine, some of this, of course, falling in the car, some out of the car. But the majority of the mass that was coming from his head came directly like a straight shot out my way on to the left in a straight line. When he fell over into her lap, the blood was on the left side of his face. There was no blood on the right-hand side which suggested to me that the wound was more to the left than it was to the right."

Following the shooting, Altgens ran toward the grassy knoll like many other witnesses. He said he was following several law enforcement officials who were running in that direction with their guns drawn.

Altgens worked for the Associated Press until the latter part of 1979 when he went to work for the Ford Motor Company in their Display and Exhibits Department in Detroit. On December 12, 1995, Altgens and his wife Clara were both found dead in their home in Dallas, apparently victims of carbon monoxide poisoning.

(See also EPILEPTIC SEIZURE; OSWALD LOOK-ALIKES.)

Alvarado, Gilberto Ugarte   See OSWALD IN MEXICO; PHASE-ONE COVERUP.

Alyea, Tom

WFAA-TV cameraman who entered the Texas School Book Depository immediately after the assassination, before the Dallas police sealed off the building. Alyea told researcher

Gary Mack in 1985 that federal agents on the scene were "bent on getting me out of the place," but local cops allowed him to stay.

When he had trouble filming the shells on the sixth floor because of the boxes that surrounded them, Captain Will Fritz picked them up and held them in his hand so that they could be photographed, then threw them back down. This occurred before the crime scene search unit had arrived. This means that, according to Alyea, the official photographs do not show the shells as they were found, but as they were after Fritz tossed them, Alyea also filmed the discovery and fingerprint dusting of the rifle found on the sixth floor.

Alyea was the only newsman to join the initial police search of the Book Depository. He told *Dallas Times Herald* reporter Connie Kritzberg;

"I was the first newsman into the building and the only newsman to accompany the search team as they went from floor to floor searching for the person who fired the shots. At this time, we did not know the president had been hit, I rushed in with a group of plain clothesmen and a few uniformed officers. . . . [I followed] the search team that was on its way to the rear elevator, to start the floor by floor search. We searched every floor, all the way to the roof. The gunman could have still been in the building. Finding nothing they started back down. After approximately eighteen minutes, they were joined by Captain Fritz, who had first gone to Parkland Hospital. . . . The barricade [of boxes, the 'sniper's nest,] on the sixth floor ran parallel to the windows extending in an 'L' shape that ended against the front wall between the first and second twin windows. The height of the stack of boxes was a minimum five feet. I looked over the barricade and saw three shell casings laying on the floor in front of the second window in the two-window casement. They were scattered in an area that could be covered by a bushel basket. They were located about half way between the inside of the barricade and the low brick wall under the windows. No shell casings were touching the wall or the inside of the barricade. I set my lens focus at the estimated distance from the camera to the floor and held the camera over the top of the barricade and filmed them before anybody went into the enclosure. I could not position my eye to the camera's view finder to get the shot. After filming the casings with my wide-angle lens, from a height of five feet, I asked Captain Fritz, who was standing at my side, if I could go behind the barricade and get a close-up shot of the casings. He told me that it would be better if I got my shots from outside the barricade. He then rounded the pile of boxes and entered the enclosure. This was the first time that anyone walked between the barricade and the windows. Fritz then walked to the casings, picked them up and held them in his hand over the top of the boxes for me to get a close-up shot of the evidence. I filmed

about eight seconds of a close-up shot of the shell casings in Captain Fritz's hand. I stopped filming, and thanked him. I do not recall if he placed them in his pocket or returned them to the floor, because I was preoccupied with recording other views of the crime scene. I have been asked many times if I thought it was peculiar that the Captain of Homicide would pick up evidence with his hands. Actually, that was the first thought that came to me when he did it, but I rationalized that he was the homicide expert and no prints could be taken from spent shell casings. Therefore, any photograph of shell casings taken after this, is staged and not correct. It is highly doubtful that the shell casings that appear in Dallas police photos of the crime scene are the same casings that were found originally. . . . Police officers who claim they were on the sixth floor when the assassin's window was found have reported that they saw chicken bones at or near the site. One officer reported that he saw chicken bones on the floor near the location. Another said he saw chicken bones on the barricade boxes, while another reported that he saw chicken bones on the box that was laying across the window sill. Some of these officers have given testimony as to the location and positioning of the shell casings. Their testimony differs and none of it is true. I have no idea why they are clinging to these statements. They must have a reason. Perhaps it is because they put it in a report and they must stick to it. . . . One officer [Sergeant Gerald Hill] stated that he found the assassin's location at the sixth floor window. He went on to say that as he and his fellow officers were leaving the building, he passed Captain Fritz coming in. He said he stopped briefly to tell Captain Fritz that he had found the assassin's lair at the sixth-floor window. This seems highly unlikely because Captain Fritz joined us on the fifth floor and aided in the search. The chances are great that . . . these officers . . . heard . . . WFAA-TV's incorrect announcement that the chicken bones were found on the sixth floor. This officer or officers perhaps used this information to formulate their presence at the scene. There were no chicken bones found on the sixth floor. We covered every inch of it and I filmed everything that could possibly be suspected as evidence. There definitely were no chicken bones on or near the barricade of boxes at the window. I shot close-up shots of this entire area. The most outstanding puzzle as to why these officers are sticking to this story is the fact that they claim to have found the sniper's location, then left the building, as they said, to join the investigators at the Tippit shooting location. I have never seen a report that indicates they attempted to use any telephone in the building in an attempt to notify other investigators. They just left the scene to check another assignment, and by chance ran into Captain Fritz coming in the front door. They claim to have placed a detective at the location but they did not relay their finding to any other officer before they left the building. I presume that the alleged detective left at the scene was instructed to stand there until someone else stumbled upon the scene, or they found time to report it after investigating the Tippit scene. Sorry, it doesn't wash."

Alyea also filmed Lee Harvey Oswald, near death, being taken into Parkland Hospital on November 24, 1963. He later covered Jack Ruby's murder trial for WFAA and filmed a documentary called "A Day in the Life of Marina Oswald."

(See also CHICKEN BONES; FRITZ, WILL; HILL, GERALD.)

American Communist Party

Organization run by Gus Hall (born Arvo Kusta Halberg), who received an honorary membership card from Lee Harvey Oswald to Oswald's fictional New Orleans Fair Play for Cuba Committee. Hall was so fearful of being stigmatized by Oswald's paper trail—a trail designed to make the alleged assassin appear to have big Communist connections—Hall voluntarily testified for the Warren Commission that he had never associated with Oswald. Hall ran for president of the United States four times and though he never got as much as one percent of the vote, he did get 36,386 votes in the 1984 election. Hall served in the U.S. Navy in the Pacific during World War II. Soviet documents released in 1987 revealed that the American Communist Party had received $2 million from the Soviet government. Hall died on Friday, October 13, 2000, at age 90.

American Council of Christian Churches   See
ABUNDANT LIFE TEMPLE.

American Fact-Finding Committee   See "WELCOME, MR. KENNEDY" AD.

American Security Council

The organization that put forth the story that Oswald was an agent for the KGB, the Russian intelligence service, who had been trained to kill in Minsk. According to William W. Turner in *Power on the Right,* the ASC was an organization of lobbyists seeking increased American involvement in Vietnam, removal of Fidel Castro from Cuba, and a stronger military stance against the Soviet Union. Members included General Charles Willoughby and William Pawley. Contributors to the Council's anticommunist coffers included General Dynamics, Lockheed, General Electric, and other large corporations. Peter Dale Scott calls this organization "the largest p.r. lobby for the military-industrial complex."

Pawley committed suicide on January 7, 1977.

(See also WILLOUGHBY, CHARLES.)

Andrews, Dean

Dean Adams Andrews Jr. was a New Orleans attorney, asked by Oswald during the summer of 1963 to have his U.S. Marine Corps discharge changed to "honorable." On November 23, Andrews received a call from a lawyer named "Clay Bertrand" (see SHAW, CLAY) who asked him to represent Oswald in Dallas.

Andrews testified before the Warren Commission that on the day after the assassination, while a patient at Hotel Dieu Hospital, he received a call from a man identifying himself as "Clay Bertrand." The man asked him to fly to Dallas to represent Oswald—and, although Andrews said "Bertrand" was a client of his, he had never seen him in person.

Andrews, an overweight lawyer who spoke like a beatnik, met with New Orleans district attorney Jim Garrison in 1967 at Broussard's Restaurant in New Orlean's French Quarter, to explain his story—which kept changing. When first interviewed by the FBI following the assassination, Andrews said that Bernard was six-feet two inches tall. He told the Warren Commission that Bertrand was five-feet eight inches. Then he told Garrison that he'd never met Bertrand.

In the FBI interview, Andrews claimed that Bertrand had called him occasionally, always to request help getting a young male friend out of legal difficulties. This was how Andrews met Oswald. Bertrand had asked Andrews to help Oswald with problems concerning Marina Oswald's citizenship. Oswald, Andrews said, subsequently visited Andrews repeatedly in his office.

During the FBI interview, it became obvious that the FBI did not want to hear about Bertrand. This prompted Andrews to tell the Federal investigators that it was okay if they said he was nuts. They took him up on his offer. In the FBI report, it stated that Bertrand was a "figment of Andrews' imagination."

Garrison, in 1967, had known Andrews since the days when they attended Tulane Law School together, although they graduated in different years. Garrison said, "[Andrews] appeared to obtain much of his business from his regular presence in some of the more off-beat bars in [New Orleans]."

When Garrison asked Andrews about Bertrand in Broussard's Restaurant in 1967, Andrews was quoted by Garrison as saying: "God almighty, you're worse than the FeeBees (FBI). How can I convince you that I don't know this cat? I don't know what he looks like and I don't know were he's at. All I know is that sometimes he sends me cases. So, one day, this cat Bertrand's on the phone talkin' to me about going to Dallas and representing Oswald. Scout's honor, man. That's all I know about the guy. . . . Is this off the record, Daddy-o? In that case, let me sum it up for you quick. It's as simple as this. If I answer that question you keep asking me, if I give you that name you keep trying to get, then it's goodbye Dean Andrews. It's bon voyage, Deano. I mean like permanent. I mean like a bullet in my head—which would make it hard to do one's legal research, if you catch my drift."

Evidence exists that Andrews and Shaw knew one another. Edward Whalen, a professional criminal from Philadelphia, told Garrison that Shaw introduced him to Andrews in early 1967 in Shaw's apartment.

An NBC-TV special called *The Case of Jim Garrison*, which appeared hell-bent on destroying Garrison's credibility, featured an appearance by Andrews. The attorney claimed that Clay Shaw was definitely not Clay Bertrand, and that he wouldn't know Shaw if he "fell across him lying dead on the sidewalk." Andrews made that same statement to the New Orleans Grand Jury that indicted Clay Shaw for conspiracy to assassinate the president; Garrison filed perjury charges against Andrews. Andrews was convicted on the perjury charges but did not serve time in jail because of his failing health. Andrews died soon thereafter of complications from a longtime heart condition.

Actor John Candy was memorable playing Andrews in Oliver Stone's movie *JFK*.

Angleton, James Jesus

CIA counterintelligence chief who strongly pushed the Oswald-as-part-of-a-communist-conspiracy theory during the days following the assassination, using CIA memos out of Mexico City that Oswald had visited an assassination expert in the Soviet embassy there as his evidence. This push greatly helped Angleton's friend, Warren commissioner Allen Dulles, to sell the lone-gunman theory.

According to assassination researcher and theorist Peter Dale Scott, Angleton took charge of the CIA's investigation into the assassination and immediately pointed attention toward the Soviets. Angleton said he had received a cable from Winston Scott, station chief of the CIA's Mexico City headquarters, that warned of an association between KGB killer Kostikov—the same Kostikov who supposedly met with Oswald in Mexico City—and Rolando Cubela, the very agent who had been recruited by the CIA's Desmond FitzGerald to kill Castro. Angleton's office later became the liaison between the CIA and the Warren Commission, claiming that he got the job because of his expertise in the workings of the KGB and Kostikov's murderous Department 13.

According to former Nixon aide H. R. Haldeman, in his book *The Ends of Power,* "The CIA literally erased any connection between Kennedy's assassination and the CIA . . . in fact . . . Angleton . . . called Bill Sullivan of the FBI [number-three man under J. Edgar Hoover, who later died

of a gunshot wound] and rehearsed the questions and answers they would give to the Warren Commission investigators."

When KGB agent Yuri Nosenko defected to the United States on January 20, 1964, and told the CIA that he had handled the Oswald case during Oswald's stay in the Soviet Union, the CIA interrogated Nosenko for 1,277 days. By the time the interrogation was complete, Nosenko had lost all of his teeth. During that period Nosenko, though failing several lie-detector tests, maintained that the KGB had given Oswald two mental examinations. The tests showed that Oswald was not terribly intelligent and mentally unstable. Nosenko said Oswald was never used as an agent and had not been debriefed concerning his military background.

While J. Edgar Hoover and Richard Helms, the respective heads of the FBI and the CIA, believed Nosenko, Angleton did not. Along with the rest of the CIA's counterintelligence faction, Angleton believed Nosenko had been sent to the United States by the KGB, his assignment to stifle suspicions that the USSR had President Kennedy killed. Angleton believed that Nosenko had also been assigned to help maintain the cover of Soviet agents working within U.S. intelligence.

(See also CENTRAL INTELLIGENCE AGENCY.)

Anti-Castro Cubans

According to author William Manchester, during mid-April 1963 there was distributed among the Cuban exiles in Miami, source unknown, a leaflet which read: "Only through one development will you Cuban patriots ever live again in your homeland as free men . . . [Only] if an inspired Act of God should place in the White House within weeks a Texan known to be a friend of all Latin Americans."

(See also ALPHA 66; ARCACHA SMITH, SERGIO; D.R.E.)

Arcacha Smith, Sergio

Born January 22, 1923, in Havana, Cuba. Former leader of the anti-Castro Cuban exile group, the Cuban Revolutionary Front. Smith was also involved with the Cuban Revolutionary Council, the CIA-backed organization with offices at 544 Camp Street, the same building that housed Guy Banister Associates in New Orleans. Arcacha Smith was also an employee of Texas oil billionaire H. L. Hunt. Smith fled from New Orleans to Dallas during Jim Garrison's prosecution of Clay Shaw. While in Dallas, Smith was protected from extradition by Assistant District Attorney Bill Alexander and Governor John Connally. He died in 2000.

(See also CHERAMIE, ROSE.)

Arce, Danny Garcia

Texas School Book Depository employee who was standing out in front of the building at the time of the assassination. He later said that he did not think that the shots came from directly over his head, but rather that they sounded as if they had come from the railroad tracks near the parking lot to the west of the building.

(See also FLOOR-LAYING CREW, THE.)

Army Intelligence

U.S. Army Intelligence kept a file on Lee Harvey Oswald that it never showed to the Warren Commission and planted false clues that Oswald killed President Kennedy as part of a Communist conspiracy.

Lieutenant Colonel Robert Jones, operations officer for the 112th Military Intelligence Group, San Antonio, Texas, received a report from Dallas at 3:15 P.M. on November 22, 1963, that an "A. J. Hidell" had been arrested. Jones said there was no mention in the report of Oswald's real name. Jones claims he looked up Hidell in his files and found it cross-referenced to Oswald as an alias. This is interesting because the only time Oswald ever reportedly used Hidell as an alias was when he theoretically mail-ordered the guns that killed President Kennedy and J. D. Tippit.

An Army Intelligence cable from the Fourth Army Command in Texas to the United States Strike Command at McDill Air Force Base in Florida on November 22, 1963, stated, erroneously but perhaps not without purpose, that Oswald had defected to Cuba in 1959 and was a card-carrying member of the Communist Party.

Lieutenant Colonel George Whitmeyer, commander of the Army Intelligence unit in Dallas, rode in the presidential motorcade "pilot car" which preceded the president by one-quarter mile. The army's liaison with the Secret Service was Ed J. Coyle. Coyle had a meeting with the FBI agent in charge of Lee Harvey Oswald's case, James Hosty, and Treasury agent Frank Ellsworth, who had been investigating Oswald–look-alike John Thomas Masen, 45 minutes before the assassination in downtown Dallas. (After the assassination, Coyle was transferred to South Korea.)

Military intelligence agent James Powell was in Dealey Plaza at the time of the assassination and took a photo approximately 30 seconds after the assassination that appears to show a man in the "sniper's nest window." He was a special agent of Region II, 112th INTC, Army Intelligence Corps, with offices at 912 Rio Grande Building, Dallas. The military intelligence office in Dallas was only two blocks away from Dealey Plaza. Powell had been photographing the motorcade. Powell said he carried a Minolta 35mm camera loaded with Kodachrome X slide film, ASA 64, shutter speed 1/25th of a second, light aperture at f-11. He had taken pictures of the president at Love Field and took a photo of the Texas School Book Depository only seconds after the shots were fired. After the assassination he went into the Depository to look around and was trapped inside for an hour and a half when the Dallas police refused to believe his identification until they called his office. Powell's job was in surveillance, but it is unclear what his focus was on November 22, 1963.

Sam Kail, a Texan and an officer of Army Intelligence, worked closely with Oswald's friend George DeMohrenschildt after DeMohrenschildt left Dallas and moved to Haiti. According to Anthony Summers, "Kail specialized in Cuban intelligence operations involving Army intelligence and the CIA." Kail says that he met DeMohrenschildt at an Army intelligence meeting. At the time of the assassination, Kail was a resident of Dallas, a known acquaintance of CIA agent Maurice Bishop, and the military intelligence liaison to the anti-Castro group known as Alpha 66.

According to phone records, Lee Harvey Oswald attempted to make phone calls from the Dallas Police station following his arrest that are not mentioned in the *Warren Report*. Those records indicate that Oswald attempted to call (919) 834-7430 and (919) 833-1253. Both numbers are listed to John Hurt in Raleigh, North Carolina, at two separate addresses (415 New Bern Ave, and Old Wake Forest Road). The first was listed to a John D. Hurt and the second to John W. Hurt. A John D. Hurt from Raleigh, according to researcher Ira David Wood III, served with U.S. Military Intelligence during World War II. Wood contacted John David Hurt in Raleigh and discovered that he had been a U.S. counterintelligence officer during World War II. Hurt said that he had worked as an insurance investigator ever since, employed by the state of North Carolina. He claimed to have no idea why Lee Harvey Oswald would have wanted to contact him from his jail cell.

(See also SAUL; TEXAS SCHOOL BOOK DEPOSITORY.)

Arnold, Carolyn (Mrs. R. E.)

She worked in the Texas School Book Depository with Oswald. She said, "about a quarter of an hour before the assassination, I went into the lunchroom on the second floor for a moment. . . . Oswald was sitting in one of the booth seats on the right-hand side of the room as you go in. He was alone as usual and appeared to be having lunch. I did not speak to him but I recognized him clearly."

By 12:15 P.M., at the same time Arnold saw Oswald on the second floor, assassination witness Arnold Rowland was already watching a gunman on the sixth floor. Mrs. Arnold was standing in front of the Book Depository at the time of the shooting.

Arnold, Gordon

Soldier who claims he was in Dealey Plaza during the assassination and tried to film the presidential motorcade from behind the wooden fence atop the grassy knoll but was chased away by a man showing Secret Service credentials. Arnold instead filmed the assassination from in front of the fence, a fact unsupported by the photographs of other eyewitnesses.

Arnold claims the first shot "whistled by" his left ear. Arnold threw himself onto the ground and covered his head. He says the next shot went over him.

According to author Henry Hurt, Arnold says he felt "as if he were standing there under the muzzle." Arnold says he was confronted by a hatless man with dirty hands in a policeman's uniform who was "shaking and crying." The man kicked Arnold and took the film out of his camera.

Arnold told Earl Gotz of the *Dallas Morning News* in 1978, "The shot came from behind me, only inches over my left shoulder. I had just got out of basic training. In my mind, live ammunition was being fired. It was being fired over my head. And I hit the dirt . . . you don't exactly hear the whiz of a bullet, you hear just a shock wave. You *feel* it . . . you feel something and a shock wave comes right behind it."

Two days after the assassination, Arnold was transferred to Alaska and didn't return for several years.

Assassination Records Review Board

The Assassination Records Review Board was established by Congress in 1992 through the President John F. Kennedy Assassination Records Collection Act and signed into law by President George H. W. Bush on October 26, 1992. The five members of the board were appointed by President Clinton, confirmed by the U.S. Senate, and sworn in on April 11, 1994. The law gave the review board the mandate and the authority to identify, secure, and make available all records related to the assassination of President Kennedy. It was the responsibility of the board to determine which records were to be made public immediately and which ones were to have postponed release dates. The review board consisted of the following members: Honorable John R. Tunheim, Chair, U.S. District Court Judge, District of Minnesota; Dr. Henry F. Graff, Professor Emeritus of History at Columbia University; Dr. Kermit L. Hall, Dean, College of Humanities, and Professor of History at Ohio State University; Dr. William L. Joyce, Associate University Librarian for Rare Books and Special Collections at Princeton University; Dr. Anna K. Nelson, Distinguished Adjunct Historian in Residence at the American University.

Here are short biographies of the members:

The American Bar Association recommended the Honorable John R. Tunheim to the president. Judge Tunheim was a U.S. district court judge in the District of Minnesota, and, at the time of his nomination, was chief deputy attorney general of the state of Minnesota. Judge Tunheim worked in the Office of the Attorney General for 11 years as the solicitor general before his appointment as chief deputy. Earlier, he practiced law privately and served as staff assistant to U.S. senator Hubert H. Humphrey. He received his J.D. from the University of Minnesota Law School and his B.A. from Concordia College in Moorhead, Minnesota. The Review Board members elected Judge Tunheim to chair the review board.

Henry F. Graff was recommended to President Clinton by the White House staff. He is professor emeritus of history at Columbia University, where he held rank as instructor to full professor from 1946–1991. He served as the chairman of the History Department from 1961–1964. In the 1960s he served on the National Historical Publications Commissions, having been appointed by President Lyndon B. Johnson. Dr. Graff was also a Senior Fellow of the Freedom Forum Media Studies Center from 1991–1992. He received an M.A. and his Ph.D. from Columbia University, and a B.S.S. from City College, New York.

The Organization of American Historians nominated Kermit L. Hall, executive dean of the Colleges of the Arts and Sciences, dean of the College of Humanities, and professor of history and law at Ohio State University. Dean Hall was appointed by Chief Justice William Rehnquist to the Historical Advisory Board of the Federal Judicial Center and is a director of the American Society for Legal History. Dean Hall received his Ph.D. from the University of Minnesota, a Master of Study of Law from Yale University Law School, an M.A. from Syracuse University, and a B.A. from the University of Akron.

The Society of American Archivists recommended Dr. William L. Joyce to the president. Dr. Joyce is currently the associate university librarian for rare books and special collections at Princeton University. Joyce previously served as assistant director for rare books and manuscripts at the New York Public Library. Dr. Joyce has also held positions at the American Antiquarian Society, initially as the curator of manuscripts, and later as the education officer. He received his Ph.D. from the University of Michigan, his M.A. from St. John's University, and his B.A. from Providence College.

The American Historical Association recommended to the president Anna Kasten Nelson, the Distinguished Adjunct Historian in Residence at the American University. Dr. Nelson has been a professor of foreign relations at the American University since 1986. In 1975, she served on the staff of the Public Documents Commission. Dr. Nelson previously served as the director of the Committee on the Records of Government and a member of the Historical

Advisory Committee of the State Department. She was a Distinguished Visiting Professor at Arizona State University in 1992. She received her Ph.D. from George Washington University, and both her M.A. and B.A. from the University of Oklahoma.

Two members of the board, Henry F. Graff and Kermit L. Hall, were former U.S. Army intelligence officers. The A.R.R.B. released their final report in September 1998.

Atkins, Thomas Maurer

White House photographer who rode in the Dallas motorcade, in Camera Car 1, six cars behind President Kennedy's limousine. Atkins was born on March 24, 1934, in Mannington, West Virginia. He graduated from the University of Ohio in 1956. In 1963, Atkins was a naval officer on assignment as a photographer to the White House. At the time of the assassination, Atkins was carrying a German 16mm Ariflex-S movie camera.

In 1977, Atkins told *Midnight* magazine, "The shots came from below and off to the right from where I was. . . . I never thought the shots came from above."

In 1986, he told assassination researcher Richard B. Trask that Camera Car 1 was on Houston Street when the shooting began: "[We] were going directly at the Depository. . . . I remember looking at my watch, and it was 12:30, and just as I looked at my watch I heard an explosion. The thought that ran through my mind, 'Oh brother, somebody lit a cherry bomb. I bet the Secret Service are jumping out of their britches.' And then immediately following there were two more quick explosions and my stomach just went into a knot. The explosions were very loud, like they were right in front of me." Atkins described the cadence of the shots: "You know when kids play Cowboys and Indians and they go, 'Bam!—Bam! Bam!'? The last two clustered together." Atkins climbed out of Camera Car 1 as it headed downhill on Elm Street toward the mouth of the triple underpass, and he filmed the activity on the north side of Elm Street, much of it comprised of other photographers running around. Despite the fact that Atkins did not believe the shots came from high up but rather at ground level does not mean that he thought they came from the direction of the grassy knoll. Atkins said, "I had not even seen the grassy knoll at that point. If they were coming from anywhere, they were coming from that turn. If they had come from the grassy knoll, I don't think they would have been anywhere near as loud, because I think the buildings there tended to throw the sound at us."

Austin's Barbecue

Owned by Austin Cook, a member of the right-wing John Birch Society, the restaurant employed murder-victim patrolman J. D. Tippit part-time as a security guard on weekends. Cook once sold a business to Ruby's business partner Ralph Paul and, according to researcher Larry Harris, Tippit had a long affair with one of Cook's waitresses, a blonde, who was also married. At the time of Tippit's death, this waitress was pregnant, perhaps with Tippit's child.

The restaurant was closed for business in July 2000 and was subsequently torn down, with plans to replace it with an Eckerd drugstore.

(See also HARRIS, LARRY RAY.)

Autopsy of John F. Kennedy

According to Texas law, the autopsy following a Texas homicide must take place in Texas. But President Kennedy's body was forcibly removed from Parkland Hospital by members of the Secret Service and returned to Washington to be autopsied at Bethesda Naval Hospital in Bethesda, Maryland, under the supervision of the Pentagon.

The cloud of secrecy regarding President Kennedy's autopsy started from the very beginning. Indeed, the fact that it had even taken place was kept secret for days, but word eventually leaked out and the military was forced to admit that they had autopsied their slain commander in chief.

With the exception of the autopsy surgeons themselves, everyone in attendance seems to agree that there was something wrong with the autopsy. Bullets removed from the president's body disappeared, men in plain clothes ordered certain autopsy procedures not to be performed, and the photographs and X rays taken have had their authenticity questioned.

Here is a list of most of the military top brass who were present at the president's autopsy: Rear Admiral Edward C. Kenney; Admiral Calvin B. Galloway; Captain David Osborne, chief of surgery at Bethesda; Captain Robert O. Canada, commanding officer of the Bethesda Naval Hospital; Captain James H. Stover, commanding officer of the Naval Medical School; General Philip C. Wehle, commander in chief of the Military District of Columbia; Admiral George C. Burkley, JFK's personal physician; and General Godfrey McHugh, U.S. Air Force, an aide to President Kennedy. Following the autopsy Admiral Kenney ordered those present not to discuss what they had seen. Admiral Galloway issued a written order that any witness to the autopsy who spoke about what he had seen would be court-martialed.

Captain Stover received a memo on November 22 from autopsy attendees, FBI agents Francis O'Neill Jr. and James Sibert, reading, "We hereby acknowledge receipt of a missle [sic] removed by Commander James J. Humes, MC,

USN on this date." Robert Bouck had signed the receipt. Officially, no bullet was removed from President Kennedy's body at the autopsy or at any other time. The memo was released to attorney Mark Lane under the Freedom of Information Act. Both later said that, despite the fact that they wrote in their report that a "missle" had been removed from JFK's body at the autopsy, what they meant to say was "bullet fragments" had been removed.

Admiral George G. Burkley was President Kennedy's personal physician. He rode at the tail end of the motorcade and was the only physician present at both Parkland and Bethesda. He was never asked to sort out the discrepancies between descriptions of President Kennedy's wounds at those two locations. Autopsy witnesses say Burkley was, at least partially, responsible for the procedure's incompleteness, since he constantly interrupted and ordered that certain standard procedures not be performed because "the Kennedy family would not approve." Burkley's death certificate for President Kennedy (first made public in 1975) says simply that the president was "struck in the head." He also says that JFK was shot "in the posterior back at about the level of the third thoracic vertebra." This places the back wound well below where the Warren Commission insisted it had to be to preserve the "magic bullet" theory.

Autopsy witness Dennis David says that, immediately following the autopsy, a Secret Service agent had him type a memo stating that four pieces of lead were removed from President Kennedy during the procedure. These were not separate bullets but had ragged edges like shrapnel. "There was more material than would have come from one bullet," David said, "but not enough for two." David told assassination researcher David Lifton that the ornamented casket that arrived at Bethesda with the former First Lady was a decoy, and that President Kennedy's body was already in the hospital when it arrived, carried in the back entrance in a plain coffin.

Secret Service agent Roy Kellerman attended President Kennedy's autopsy and later told the Warren Commission, "A Colonel [Pierre A.] Finck—during the examination of the president, from the hole that was in his shoulder, and with a probe, and we are standing right alongside of him, he is probing inside the shoulder with this instrument and I said, 'Colonel, where did it go?' He said, 'There are no lanes for an outlet of this entry in this man's shoulder,'" This does not sound like the same autopsy that determined that the bullet had not entered President Kennedy's shoulder, but rather his neck, and that the bullet was not without outlet but rather exited through the throat.

Bethesda Hospital radiologist Dr. John Ebersole, a witness to the autopsy, told his hometown newspaper in 1978, "When the body was removed from the casket there was a very obvious horrible gaping wound in the back of the head." Dr. Ebersole also said that a large piece of occipital bone (that is, from the back of the president's head) arrived late at the autopsy. How is any of this possible when the autopsy photos show the back of JFK's head to be intact?

Laboratory Technologist Paul Kelly O'Connor was one of the major witnesses supporting David Lifton's theory that President Kennedy's body was altered somewhere between Parkland and Bethesda and made to appear as if it had been shot only from the rear. Lifton speculates that President Kennedy's body was taken off Air Force One and placed on a helicopter, which took it to another hospital, most likely Walter Reed, where the alterations were made. It was then delivered via helicopter to Bethesda for the autopsy. The casket that a worldwide television audience saw unloaded from Air Force One was actually empty, the theory states. O'Connor says that President Kennedy's body arrived at Bethesda in a commercial shipping casket as opposed to the bronze casket in which it left Dallas. He says that the body arrived in a military-type body bag, which differed from the sheet it was wrapped in at Parkland Hospital. The hole in President Kennedy's head, he says, was so large at Bethesda that it included parts of the back, side, top, and front. The weight of President Kennedy's brain on the autopsy report, he says, must be fiction, because the brain was gone by the time the body arrived at Bethesda.

There is evidence that the Secret Service, for security reasons, used two caskets and drove a decoy hearse up to the front of Bethesda, but this does not explain how President Kennedy's body switched caskets and wrappings.

O'Connor says that he heard helicopters (maybe two of them) outside of Bethesda landing on the helicopter pad there and several moments later saw six to eight men carrying a casket into the hospital. He says that the body was in a military body bag when it arrived at Bethesda. (It had been wrapped in a clear plastic mattress cover when it left Parkland.) (See also DECOY HEARSE.)

O'Connor says President Kennedy's brain had already been removed by the time it got to Bethesda, and that there was only "half of a handful" of brain matter left inside the skull, which would mean that the autopsists were lying when they said the brain was removed, weighed, and preserved, and that it yielded bullet fragments.

According to Nigel Turner, director of the 1988 British television documentary The Men Who Killed Kennedy: "There were mysterious men in civilian clothes at the autopsy. They seemed to command a lot of respect and attention—sinister looking people. They would come up and look over my shoulder or over Dr. [J. Thornton] Boswell's shoulder, then they'd go back and have a little conference in the corner. Then one of them would say, 'Stop what you're doing and go on to another procedure.'

We jumped back and forth, back and forth. There was no smooth flow of procedure at all."

Captain P. David Osborne (later admiral) originally said he had seen an "intact bullet . . . not deformed in any way" fall from President Kennedy's wrappings onto the autopsy table—but he later told the House Select Committee on Assassinations he was "not sure" he had seen this.

SURGEONS

Commander James J. Humes, now deceased, performed the autopsy on President Kennedy at Bethesda Naval Hospital in Maryland. Dr. Humes was unfamiliar with gunshot wounds. Hume's report bears little relation to the reports of doctors at Parkland Hospital in Dallas who saw the president's wounds immediately after the shooting. Humes's observations are further clouded by the fact that he destroyed his original notes taken at the autopsy. He said he did it so that the notes couldn't become a morbid curiosity, like Lincoln's chair in Ford's Theater. He says that his conclusions as to what happened to President Kennedy were changed after the autopsy when he learned for the first time that the tracheotomy incision in the president's neck had been put over a small and perfectly round wound that was already there and had been universally assumed to be an entrance wound. (It would later be concluded that this was actually the exit wound for a shot that struck Kennedy in the back.) The trouble with Humes's story is that there is evidence that he knew about the wound to the front of Kennedy's throat before the autopsy.

Dr. Robert Livingston—who had served with the U.S. Naval Medical Corps during the battle of Okinawa, which qualifies him as an expert on gunshot wounds—worked at Bethesda at the time of the assassination, and was following the story via radio and television before the president's body arrived at that hospital for autopsy. He claims he telephoned Dr. Humes and told him that it had been reported that President Kennedy had a small wound in the front of his throat, presumably one of entrance. This is important because Humes later claimed that much of the confusion at the autopsy was based on the fact that they did not know that President Kennedy had a bullet wound in the front of his throat, because this wound had been obliterated at Parkland Hospital during emergency treatment by a tracheotomy incision. Oddly, Livingston remembers that an FBI agent interrupted his conversation with Dr. Humes, and the conversation was never allowed to resume, which has since led Livingston to believe that there was a nonmedical control over President Kennedy's autopsy. Livingston claims that he emphasized to Humes that the throat wound should be tracked carefully since it indicated a shot from the front.

At the autopsy, Humes says he saw a large wound to the right front of Kennedy's head and a small entrance wound in the back of the head. He saw a small wound in Kennedy's back but failed to trace the path of this entrance wound upon the orders of an unnamed general who was in the autopsy room. When Humes learned that the wound in the throat was not just a tracheotomy but a bullet wound as well, he burned his original autopsy notes and rewrote his conclusions, saying that the throat wound was a wound of exit and had been caused by the same bullet that entered President Kennedy's back. Since the bullet, if fired from the sixth floor of the Texas School Book Depository had to have a downward slope to its path, Humes moved the back wound in his report up into the back of Kennedy's neck, thus setting the framework for the Warren Commission's infamous "Single Bullet Theory." To add further intrigue to the macabre discrepancies between the observances of doctors at Parkland and Bethesda, Humes's first impression was that "surgery" had been performed on Kennedy's head, leading some—in particular conspiracy theorist David Lifton—to believe that President Kennedy's body had been altered somewhere between Texas and Maryland.

Commander J. Thornton Boswell assisted Dr. James J. Humes in performing President Kennedy's autopsy. Dr. Boswell told author Josiah Thompson that the president's back wound was explored by Humes at the autopsy, who found only "a penetration of one or two inches." If this is true, then it is impossible for this wound to be caused by the same bullet that wounded the president's throat.

Lieutenant Colonel Pierre A. Finck, chief of the Wound Ballistics Pathology Branch of the Armed Forces Institute of Pathology and a doctor at Bethesda Naval Hospital, was the only one of the autopsists to have previous gunshot-wound experience. He told the Warren Commission that the "magic bullet" could not have caused Governor Connally's wrist wound since there was more metal in Connally's wrist than was missing from the bullet.

Testifying as a defense witness at the Clay Shaw trial that the autopsy "strongly" suggested President Kennedy had been killed by a lone gunman shooting from the rear and above, upon cross-examination, Finck revealed some illuminating facts about President Kennedy's autopsy: "I was called as a consultant to look at these wounds. . . . I heard Dr. Humes stating that—he said, 'Who's in charge here?' and I heard an Army general, I don't remember his name, stating, 'I am.' You must understand that in those circumstances, there were law enforcement officers, military people with various ranks and you have to coordinate the operation according to directions."

Finck then admitted that the army general in question was not, to his knowledge, a qualified pathologist. Finck continued: "The autopsy room was quite crowded. It is a small autopsy room, and when you are called in circumstances like that to look at the wound of the President of the United States who is dead, you don't look around too much to ask people for their names and take notes on who they are. I did not do so. The room was crowded with military and civilian personnel and federal agents, Secret Service agents, FBI agents, for part of the autopsy . . . there were [also] admirals, and when you are a lieutenant in the Army you just follow orders, and at the end of the autopsy we were specifically told—as I recall it, it was by Admiral K[e]nney, the Surgeon General of the Navy—this is subject to verification—we were specifically told not to discuss the case. . . . We did not dissect the neck. . . . I was told that the [Kennedy] family wanted an examination of the head, as I recall, the head and chest, but prosectors in this autopsy didn't remove the organs in the neck, to my recollection. . . . I looked at the trachea, there was a tracheotomy wound the best I can remember, but I didn't dissect or remove these organs. . . . I was told not to, but I don't remember by whom." Finck said autopsists did not dissect President Kennedy's neck wound because they were ordered not to, "perhaps" by an army general. He also said that it is essential in a firearms case to examine the victim's clothing, but in this case the doctors were ordered by "another official" not to examine President Kennedy's clothing.

PHOTOS

The first photographs reportedly taken at President Kennedy's autopsy to become public were traced back to James K. Fox, a former Secret Service agent who had given the photos to acquaintance Mark Crouch in 1981. Crouch got in touch with assassination researcher David Lifton, who eventually included the pictures in his book, *Best Evidence.*

Several years earlier, Robert Groden acquired a set of autopsy photographs while working as a photographic consultant to the House Select Committee on Assassinations. Even before the photographs became public, there were reasons to suspect that there was something wrong with them. They somehow didn't jibe with the memories of the autopsy eyewitnesses. For example, when asked by the House Select Committee on Assassinations if a certain spot on an autopsy photo was a wound, Finck replied, "I don't know what it is. How are these photos identified as coming from the autopsy of President Kennedy?"

Lieutenant Commander William Bruce Pitzer reportedly attended President Kennedy's autopsy (although his name does not appear on the official list of those present) and, according to several accounts, filmed the Bethesda autopsy. On October 29, 1966, Pitzer was found dead of a .45 caliber pistol wound in his Bethesda office. According to Harrison Edward Livingstone and Robert Groden, Pitzer was murdered as a warning to all autopsy witnesses not to talk about what they had seen. Pitzer was found

dead just before he was scheduled for retirement after 28 years in the service. Just before his death, Pitzer had been offered a job working for a "network television station" for $45,000 a year. Livingston and Groden continue, "His family was told that his death was a suicide, and no one in his family believes it. The government refuses to give up a copy of the autopsy report. . . . His widow stated . . . that Pitzer left . . . notes for the smallest thing and would have left a suicide note. . . . His widow said that his left hand was so mangled that they could not remove his wedding ring to give it to her, but he was right-handed. The question is, if he shot himself in his office with his right hand, how could his left hand be mangled?" According to the Waukegan, Illinois, *News-Sun* on May 1, 1975, Pitzer had taken the President Kennedy autopsy photos and had been repeatedly threatened because of what he had seen. According to Dennis David, a medical corpsman who officially attended the autopsy, "Pitzer filmed in detail the Kennedy autopsy."

Floyd Riebe photographed President Kennedy's autopsy. Riebe said President Kennedy had "a big gaping hole in the back of the head . . . like somebody put a piece of dynamite in a can and lit it off." Shown the official autopsy notes, Riebe said, "[It's] not what I saw that night. . . . It's being phonied someplace. It's make-believe."

According to Robert Groden, staff photographic expert for the House Select Committee on Assassinations, the autopsy photographs were foremost among his concerns after his appointment to the committee's staff. He told committee investigator Gaeton Fonzi: "One of the first things I did was ask to see the autopsy photographs in the National Archives. I wanted to find out how it was that the Warren Commission concluded the shots came from the rear when all the doctors at Parkland Hospital, every one of them, wrote in their reports that Kennedy's head was blasted out. When I saw the autopsy photographs I was shocked. After years in photo optic work I knew what I saw, and what I saw was a matte line in the photograph of the back of the President's head. That's when two photographic elements come together visually and there's an overlap. I saw a soft-edged matte insertion forgery of very high quality which made it appear as if there were a small wound of entry in the rear of the President's head." Groden says he wrote a report to Robert Blakey, head of the committee, stating that the photos were forgeries. According to Groden, Blakey suppressed the report.

The FBI agents who attended the autopsy agree that the photographs do not reflect their observations. O'Neill, when shown the autopsy photo of the back of President Kennedy's head by the Assassination Records Review Board, which shows the skull in that region to be intact, said "This looks to be doctored in some way." Sibert agreed: "I don't remember seeing anything that was like this photo. . . . I don't recall anything like this at all at the autopsy."

At the supplementary autopsy at which JFK's brain was removed and weighed, photos were taken by John Stringer. These photos have never been publicly revealed, but those who have seen them unanimously agree that the photos show the cerebellum to be intact—this, despite the fact that the surgeons at Parkland Hospital who saw the head wound agree that there was cerebellum tissue protruding from the wound. Stringer was shown the photos of the brain as they currently exist in the National Archives by the Assassination Records Review Board and he failed to recognize them as the photos he had taken. The type of film was different, the brain was shown from angles from which he had not taken photographs, and the identification cards he had used with each photograph were not on the current images.

Nurse Diana Bowden, when shown the reported autopsy photo of President Kennedy's back said, "This is not the back I saw."

X RAYS

Those who believe the President Kennedy autopsy X rays are forgeries have to deal with the statements of Dr. Clyde Snow, a forensic pathologist, who says he has verified the authenticity of those X rays by comparing them with pre-mortem X rays of President Kennedy's "sinus print," that is, the ridge of bone at the rear of the nose.

However, Dr. Humes, who died in 1999, was confused when shown the autopsy X rays that currently exist. Those X rays show a trail of metal through JFK's brain going from high up on the head in the back to low, about eye level, in the front. Humes remembered the trail of metal through the president's brain going from low in the back upward to a spot at about eye level in the front.

Jerrol F. Custer and Edward Reed are the two technicians who x-rayed President Kennedy's body at the autopsy. Custer insists that there was a massive wound in the back of President Kennedy's head. He said, "I could put both my hands in the wound." Describing President Kennedy's wounds to David Lifton via telephone on September 30, 1979, Custer said, "Let me tell you one thing. If you have ever gone hunting, you know as well as I do, when a bullet goes into a body, it goes in small and comes out big. Okay? Well, that is exactly how the skull looked. Okay? . . . from the front to the back." Custer says he never saw the small entrance wound in the back of President Kennedy's head visible in the autopsy photos. In a 1993 written statement, Custer said that the extant autopsy X rays "didn't match the X rays that I took and which were taken that night in the morgue."

(See also KENNEDY'S BRAIN; LIVINGSTON, DR. ROBERT; MAGIC BULLET; PARKLAND HOSPITAL.)

Aynesworth, Hugh

Local Dallas reporter who used the assassination to launch a national career as a reporter for *Newsweek*. Aynesworth couldn't have been luckier. He was repeatedly at the scene of the action during the assassination weekend. He was in Dealey Plaza when President Kennedy was shot, he was in the Texas Theatre when Oswald was arrested and he was in the basement of the Dallas Police Department headquarters when Oswald was murdered.

Aynesworth was the science editor for the *Dallas Morning News* in 1963 and became a part of the story because he happened to be in Dealey Plaza when it happened.

He was standing in the center of Elm Street, at the Houston Street intersection, where traffic had been cut off. He started out looking for a spot to watch the motorcade on Main Street but switched to Elm because the crowds were thinner.

Aynesworth told assassination researcher Larry A. Sneed, "The first shot I wasn't sure was a shot. I thought it might have been backfire from one of the motorcycles since there were several in the vicinity. When you hear one, you listen more closely, and when I heard a second and then a third very clearly, there was no doubt in my mind that they were shots and that they were from a rifle. . . . I remember one woman throwing up while others were screaming, shouting, and running to protect their children. It was just total chaos. . . . I remember hearing on the police radio the transmission, 'This is a citizen' or something to that effect. 'A policeman's been shot. He's been hurt pretty bad, I think.' . . . I remember seeing the regular police reporter, Jim Ewell. . . . I said to Ewell, 'Well, you've got one here. This is probably going to be a conspiracy situation.' A cop isn't shot three miles away from where the president is shot unless there's something connected. . . . So I said, 'Ewell, why don't you stay here and get this one and I'll go in the Channel 8 cruiser?' . . . The drive over to Oak Cliff where the officer was shot was precarious because the traffic was stopped in some areas, and not in others. . . . When we arrived, we talked with one of the eyewitnesses, Helen Markham, as well as to Callaway and a guy named Guinyard. We also talked to the Davis sisters who were either half-sisters or step-sisters or something. They lived in the house right there and had seen the suspect leave the scene. . . . I remember seeing Assistant District Attorney Bill Alexander at the scene. Bill's got a good nose, and after somebody had said, 'I think he ran in there,' we went into an old furniture store looking for the suspect. Furniture was stacked everywhere in this old ramshackled place. I was there with Bill and five or six officers; all had guns except me. All of a sudden someone fell through the second floor. I remember screaming, as I was scared to death! But it turned out to be nothing. He probably hadn't been there at all. . . . At any rate, I went back to an FBI car outside that place and heard an announcement: 'Suspect has entered the Texas Theatre.' I'm not sure how far that was, maybe four or five blocks, something like that, so I ran to the location. When I arrived at the Texas Theatre, I ran into Jim Ewell again. We decided that he'd go upstairs into the balcony since somebody had said that he'd gone there. So Jim went up while I decided to go down and under, and maybe I could see what was going on in the balcony. As luck would have it, I just got in there when I saw officers coming off the stage on both sides. . . . They paused and talked to some other people on the way up so that he wouldn't become alarmed and try to escape. But when one of the officers, Nick McDonald, got to Oswald, Oswald hit him as he came into the row. Had it not been for the other cops coming from behind and grabbing Oswald, I think that he would have probably pulled a gun and shot and killed him. But it was over in an instant. The thing that I remember most about that is that immediately, as soon as they got him, Oswald started screaming, 'I protest this police brutality!' . . . Then they whipped him out front and put him in the car."

Aynesworth reappeared in the assassination story during the prosecution of businessman Clay Shaw for conspiracy to assassinate the president by New Orleans parish district attorney Jim Garrison. Aynesworth either took it upon himself or was assigned to discredit Garrison, and thus to vindicate Shaw. In the May 15, 1967, issue of *Newsweek,* Aynesworth wrote, "Jim Garrison is right. There has been a conspiracy in New Orleans—but it is a plot of Garrison's own making." Aynesworth's mission to destroy the Garrison investigation seemingly overstepped his bounds as a journalist. There is evidence that Aynesworth was tampering with witnesses before Garrison could get them on the stand.

Aynesworth, no longer a science editor, went on to write five books about true crime. Aynesworth remained in Dallas, serving as the southwest bureau chief for the *Washington Times.*

(See also EWELL, JIM E.)

B

Babushka Lady

Figure visible for 21 frames in the Zapruder film, standing on the greensward between Elm and Main Streets, directly across Elm Street from Zapruder's position, also filming the motorcade. She gets her name because she is wearing a triangular kerchief. She also has on a buff raincoat.

For years, despite a "thorough" search, her identity was unknown. She was sought not just because she was one of the closest witnesses to the shot that killed President Kennedy, but also because photographic evidence (the Zapruder film, the Muchmore film, et al.) showed her filming the motorcade. Because of her location, it was suspected her film showed both the Texas School Book Depository and the grassy knoll at the time of the shots.

Beverly Oliver, 19 years old in 1963, claims she was the woman. Oliver came forward in the mid-1970s, telling her story to author J. Gary Shaw—a story so wild that it stretches the imagination: On November 22, 1963, she was an entertainer at the Colony Club, next door to Ruby's Carousel Club. She knew Ruby and many of the women who worked for him and says that on or about November 8, 1963, she met a man in the Carousel whom Ruby introduced as "Lee Oswald of the CIA." Oliver recognized Oswald later on television. She says assassination suspect David Ferrie was such a frequent Carousel visitor that she mistook him for the manager.

She says that she kept quiet about her eyewitness status for years because she was afraid she would be harmed if she spoke up. A friend of hers, she says, who knew of Ruby and Oswald's relationship had disappeared.

In 1970, Oliver married George McGann, a Dallas mobster. The best man at the wedding was Russell D. Mathews,

Beverly Oliver, the self-proclaimed "Babushka Lady," signs autographs at a Dallas assassination symposium during the early 1990s. *(MacIntyre Symms)*

a close friend of Ruby. In 1968, during the presidential campaign, Oliver and McGann met for two hours in a Miami Hotel with Richard Nixon.

In 1970, McGann became the victim of a gangland-style murder in West Texas. Oliver claims she never had an opportunity to see the film she took of President Kennedy's death with a Super-8 Yashica movie camera.

On November 25, 1963, Oliver says, she was approached by two men near the Colony Club. The men showed no identification, but she believed them to be U.S. government agents—FBI, CIA, or Secret Service. They told her they knew about the film and needed it for evidence. How they discovered her identity is a mystery to her. Oliver handed over the film to the men and never saw it again. After viewing many photos, she identified FBI agent Regis Kennedy as one of the men who had taken her film. Following the assassination, Agent Kennedy worked on the New Orleans part of the investigation and reportedly told FBI director J. Edgar Hoover that mobster Carlos Marcello was a "tomato salesman."

(See also CAROUSEL NIGHT.)

Backyard Photos

Among the early evidence used to convict Lee Harvey Oswald of JFK's assassination in the mind of the public, perhaps the most important was a set of photos reportedly taken by Marina Oswald on March 31, 1963, in the backyard of their Dallas home of Lee holding two leftist newspapers, a handgun, and a rifle.

The photos were found during a search of the home of Ruth Paine, where Marina had been living with her children at the time of the assassination. The image of Oswald with the guns that reportedly killed Tippit and Kennedy appeared on the cover of *Life* magazine, cementing in the mind of America that this was the man who did it.

There are problems with the photos, however. When Oswald himself was shown the photos while in custody he denied vehemently that they were real. He said that someone had pasted a picture of his face over someone else's body.

And, there is evidence that Oswald's diagnosis was correct. Despite the fact that the other shadows in the picture go off to the left, the shadow beneath his nose remains straight up and down. Despite the fact that the photos are taken at different distances from their subject, and the size of the body differs accordingly, the size of the head is exactly the same in each photo.

At first Marina said that she did not remember taking the photos, then she did but she only remembered taking one. Then she remembered taking more than one but said that the background in the photos was wrong because she took her photos facing in the other direction.

(See also OSWALD, MARINA; WHITE, ROSCOE.)

Photo purportedly taken by Marina Oswald showing her husband carrying leftist literature and the weapons that were reportedly later used to kill President Kennedy and Officer J. D. Tippit. *(Author's Collection)*

Badgeman   See MOORMAN PHOTO.

Baetz, Wilfred

On December 5, 1966, Baetz called Charles Batchelor, then the chief of police in Dallas, and told him that he had been an assassination witness. Baetz, who was calling from New York City where he lived, said that he had been on the grassy knoll at the time of the shooting. He said he saw smoke coming from the trees behind the wooden fence and thought the shots came from the direction of the triple underpass.

Baetz was not a good witness. He was deaf in his left ear so the fact that he thought the shots came from his right is not indicative of anything. He had been convicted of arson as a teenager and, at the time of the assassination, was married to a woman who worked for Time-Life. When contacted by the FBI, Baetz denied that he had called

Batchelor. A check of his phone records, however, showed that the call had come from his home.

Baker, Marrion L.

Patrolman Baker, who had been with the Dallas Police Department since 1954, was the man who first identified the Texas School Book Depository as the source of the shots.

"At the time [of the shooting]," he told researcher Larry A. Sneed, "I was approximately 150 feet south of Elm Street traveling north on Houston on the right hand side of the street. Suddenly, I heard these three shots. It was my impression that they came from directly in front of me and high. I just assumed that they came from the top of the Texas School Book Depository. The shots were very distinct. The first two were pretty evenly spaced and the last was a little closer."

Baker's attention was drawn to the School Book Depository because a flock of pigeons—maybe 50 to 100 of them, he estimates—flew up from the Depository roof following the report of the shots.

It was Baker who, along with Book Depository superintendent Roy Truly, encountered a composed Oswald in the building's second-floor lunchroom between 75 and 90 seconds after the assassination.

Baker rode a motorcycle in the motorcade and was assigned to flank the right rear of the press bus, well behind the presidential limousine. While other policemen were either confused about the source of the shots or were running toward the grassy knoll and the triple underpass, Baker alone made a beeline for Lee Harvey Oswald.

Unlike other earwitnesses to the assassination, Baker did not say that he thought the first report was a firecracker or a car backfiring. He had just returned from a deer-hunting trip, he says, and immediately recognized the sound of a powerful rifle.

At the sound of the shots, Baker rode toward the north curb of Elm Street, dragging his feet. With revolver drawn, he ran up the front steps of the building. He was met at the entrance by building manager Roy Truly, who identified himself. Baker instructed Truly to accompany him and Truly led Baker to the elevators, the cars for which were both on one of the upper floors.

Baker did not wait for the elevators to come down but rather ran up the stairs. Truly followed close behind him. On the second floor, Baker saw movement out of the corner of his eye and stopped. Through the glass door Baker could see an empty-handed man standing near a Coke machine in the building's lunchroom. Baker entered the room and said, "Come here." The man who was later identified as Oswald approached slowly.

Truly then entered the room. Baker asked the building manager, "Do you know this man?" Truly said yes. "Does he work here?" Baker inquired. "Yes, he works for me," Truly responded. With that, Baker and Truly left the lunchroom and continued up the stairs.

Since both Book Depository elevators were on the upper floors just after the assassination the official scenario one is compelled to envision is that Oswald must have used the stairs to get from the sixth to the second floor.

Baker's original written report to the FBI (dated November 23, 1963) said that Oswald was "drinking a Coke" at the time of the encounter. The words "drinking a Coke" were crossed out and the Warren Commission did not probe the matter. Moments after Baker's encounter with the alleged assassin, Oswald was also seen drinking a Coke by Mrs. Elizabeth Reid. Tests indicated that Oswald just barely had enough time to do what he was supposed to have done, and did not want to add that possibility that he had also purchased a Coke at a Coke machine between the shooting sequence and Oswald's encounter with Baker.

Baker's quick response to the shooting has troubled supporters of the lone-gunman theory since it is questionable whether Oswald had time to get from the sniper's nest on the sixth floor to the second-floor lunchroom in time to meet Baker and Truly without being out of breath or showing any outward signs of excitement.

Baker continued up the stairs after his encounter with Oswald, convinced from his first impression that the shots had come from the roof of the building. As soon as he got to the roof, however, he realized that it was an unlikely spot for a sniper. The parapet wall around the edge of the roof was too high.

Baker retired from the Dallas Police Department in 1977.

Baker, Mrs. Donald "Virgie" (née Rachley)

Texas School Book Depository bookkeeper who watched the motorcade from in front of the building. Following the shooting, Mrs. Baker ran 50 yards westward to see what was happening on the grassy knoll.

She says she knows the first shot missed because she saw it strike the southmost lane of Elm Street just behind President Kennedy's limo. In her Warren Commission testimony, Mrs. Baker said: "I thought it was firecrackers because I saw a shot or something hit the pavement . . . you could see the sparks from it and I just thought it was a firecracker." She said she thought the firecrackers came from "down below or standing near the underpass or back up here by the [Stemmons Freeway] sign." Mrs. Baker's statements that the first shot missed are corroborated by assassination witnesses Royce Skelton and Harry Holmes.

During Mrs. Baker's testimony, Warren Commission counsel Wesley Liebeler tried to talk her out of her belief that the shots had come from the front, explaining that "the shots actually came" from the Book Depository. Mrs. Baker refused to be swayed. "Well, I guess it could have been the wind, but to me it didn't [sound that way]," she told Liebeler.

(See also HOLMES, HARRY; SKELTON, ROYCE.)

Baker, Robert G. "Bobby"

Aide to Vice President Lyndon B. Johnson for eight years, but due to a scandal he resigned on October 7, 1963. During those eight years, Baker made $2 million. His influence peddling (including deals with the mob) were exposed by the *Washington Post*. Because of the scandal, it was rumored that President Kennedy would dump Johnson as vice president for the 1964 election.

Penn Jones Jr. reported in the *Midlothian Mirror* on July 31, 1969, "Bobby Baker was about the first person in Washington to know that Lyndon Johnson was to be dumped as the vice-presidential candidate in 1964. Baker knew that President Kennedy had offered the spot on the ticket to Senator George Smathers of Florida. . . . Baker knew because his secretary, Miss [Nancy] Carole Tyler, roomed with one of George Smathers' secretaries. Miss Mary Jo Kopechne had been another of Smathers' secretaries. Now both Miss Tyler and Miss Kopechne have died strangely."

Tyler died at age 26 in a plane crash on May 10, 1965, over the Atlantic Ocean near Ocean City, Maryland. Her body was recovered the following day. Kopechne died in Senator Edward Kennedy's car in 1969 at Chappaquidick.

(See also JOHNSON, LYNDON BAINES.)

Banister, William Guy

A politically right-wing former head of the Chicago FBI office whose association with the supposedly left-wing Oswald in New Orleans during the summer before President Kennedy's death makes him a key figure in the assassination.

Banister, who worked closely with the CIA and the Office of Naval Intelligence, was a member of the ultra-right-wing Minutemen, the John Birch Society, and Louisiana's Committee on Un-American Activities. He closely associated with assassination suspects David Ferrie and New Orleans mob boss Carlos Marcello. Banister incorporated his own anti-Castro group called Friends of a Democratic Cuba.

Banister died of a heart attack within 10 days of the final Warren Commission hearing. Jim Garrison's investigation revealed that Banister was seen in 1963 in his New Orlean's office having meetings with Ferrie and Oswald. Oswald used Banister's office address on his Fair Play for Cuba Committee leaflets.

Banister had been a deputy superintendent of police in New Orleans in 1963. With blue eyes and a ruddy complexion, Banister always wore a rosebud in his lapel. Garrison says Banister had an occasional drink but was not known to drink to excess. Other sources have called Banister an alcoholic. It is known that he drank to excess on November 22, 1963. When Banister learned that President Kennedy had been assassinated, he "made a noble effort to polish off all of the liquor in the Katzenjammer Bar."

Drinking with Banister was occasional private detective Jack Martin, who regularly visited Banister's Camp Street office. The pair returned to Banister's office after leaving the bar. There they got into a heated argument. According to New Orleans Police Department report number K-12634-63, dated November 22, 1963, Banister ended up pistol-whipping Martin so severely that Martin had to be hospitalized.

Soon thereafter, Martin started telling friends that he suspected David Ferrie, another frequenter of Banister's office, had "driven to Dallas on the day of the assassination to serve as the getaway pilot for the men involved in the assassination." The first batch of pro-Castro pamphlets that Oswald handed out in New Orleans had "544 Camp Street" stamped on them. This address was in the same structure as 531 Lafayette Street, the address of Guy Banister Associates. It was this fact that gave Garrison his first indication that Oswald might not have been a Marxist after all, but rather an agent provocateur whose flaky behavior might serve to discredit the entire Fair Play for Cuba Committee, an organization with which Oswald had no real relationship.

Oswald only put the 544 Camp Street address on his first batch of pamphlets. Thereafter, Oswald showed the address of the Fair Play for Cuba Committee as either his own address or as a New Orleans post office box number. The number on the pamphlets, however, matched no real post office box number. Oswald actually had rented a post office box, using both his own name and his Fair Play for Cuba "partner," Alec J. Hidell, as those who could receive mail there (just as he would later do in Dallas). Except when Oswald wrote the number down in his notebook, he transposed two of the numbers.

After Jack Martin was released from the hospital, Garrison interviewed him. Why had Banister beaten him? "I told him that I remembered the people I had seen around the office that summer," Martin said. "And that's when he hit me." Who were the people? "There were a bunch of them," Martin replied. "There were all those Cubans. . . . They all looked alike to me. . . . There was David Ferrie.

. . . He practically lived there . . . [Oswald] was there, too. Sometimes he'd be meeting with Guy Banister with the door shut. Other times he'd be shooting the bull with David Ferrie . . . [Banister] was the one running the circus." Martin then told Garrison that he should stop his investigation because he was going to "bring the goddamned federal government down on our backs."

Banister died, reportedly of a heart attack, nine months after President Kennedy's assassination. In 1967, Banister's widow told Garrison that, when cleaning out his office after his death, she found many leftover pamphlets, identical to those handed out by Oswald. She also told Garrison that, following Banister's death, she had gone to her late husband's office. She discovered that federal government representatives (FBI or Secret Service, she wasn't sure) had already been there. Banister's locked file cabinets had been removed.

Delphine Roberts, Banister's blue-haired secretary, corroborated Martin's statements that Oswald and Banister had repeatedly visited Banister's office where they had engaged in closed-door meetings during the summer of 1963. The secretary added that Banister allowed Oswald to use a third-floor office, one flight up from Banister.

Banister's partner Hugh Ward and New Orleans mayor Chep Morrison were killed in a plane crash within 10 days of Banister's death. According to Penn Jones Jr. in the *Midlothian Mirror* (January 23, 1969), Mayor Morrison's secretary at one time attempted to rent an apartment in New Orleans for Guy Banister's "business use." She tried to rent the apartment from a man named Rev. Abraham Khrushevski, who was the landlord of Nancy and Robert Lee Perrin (see PERRIN, ROBERT AND NANCY).

According to Anthony Summers, "Banister was an old-fashioned American hero who had refused to go gracefully. He had been a star agent for the FBI, a tough guy whose long career covered some of the Bureau's most famous cases, including the capture and killing of . . . John Dillinger. He was commended by FBI Director [J. Edgar] Hoover and rose to become Special Agent-in-charge in a key city, Chicago. In World War II—according to his family—he distinguished himself with Naval Intelligence [ONI], a connection he reportedly maintained all his life. Banister came to New Orleans in the Fifties, at the request of the mayor, to become Deputy Chief of Police. This was the high point of a flawed career. In 1957, at the age of fifty-eight, Banister was pushed into retirement after an incident in New Orlean's Old Absinthe House, when he allegedly threatened a waiter with a pistol."

Soon thereafter, Banister started Guy Banister Associates on Camp Street. He published a racist magazine called the *Louisiana Intelligence Digest* and helped to organize the anti-Castro organizations, Friends of a Democratic Cuba and the Cuban Revolutionary Democratic Front.

Banister supplied arms for the 1961 Bay of Pigs invasion. In 1963, he did investigative work for assassination suspect, New Orleans crime boss Carlos Marcello. A New Orleans crime commissioner said that it was not alcohol that caused Banister's downfall but rather a "serious brain disorder which led him increasingly into irrational, erratic conduct."

Also in the same building as Banister's offices were those of the Cuban Revolutionary Front. A member of this organization was Carlos Bringuier, whose summer-of-1963 street scuffle with Oswald led to Oswald's arrest. The Camp Street offices were also around the corner from the William Reily Coffee Company, where Oswald reportedly worked that summer.

(See also FERRIE, DAVID; 544 CAMP STREET; GARRISON INVESTIGATION; GAUDET, WILLIAM GEORGE.)

Barclay, Malcolm James (Mike)

Friend of Jack Ruby's roommate George Senator who was standing on the corner of Main and Houston Streets at the time of the assassination. Barclay heard "one or more" shots, he said, but couldn't determine their source.

Barker, Bernard

A possible assassination witness who worked with assassination suspects David Ferrie, E. Howard Hunt, and Frank Sturgis, as well as General Charles Cabell and Richard Nixon, in the CIA planning of the Bay of Pigs operation.

Barker was the leader of the Watergate burglars and was once associated with the Miami mob, headed by Santos Trafficante. Assassination-witness Seymour Weitzman identified a photo of Barker as the man on the grassy knoll who was showing Secret Service ID and ordering people out of the area.

Barnett, Welcome Eugene

Dallas Police Department officer who was in Dealey Plaza to witness the aftermath of the assassination. He was one of the first policemen to report that the shots had originated from the Texas School Book Depository, having heard this info from a construction worker, presumably assassination witness Howard Brennan.

Basinger, Rex Harding

During a stint in the Dallas city jail from December 14–17, 1963, for vagrancy, Basinger claims he was placed in the same jail cell as Jack Ruby. Basinger later told his brother—First Baptist Church of Lake City, Arkansas, minister John Basinger—that Ruby had told him that there was an invasion of Cuba scheduled for May 1, 1964. Some of the invasion forces were to gather in Mexico while others gathered in Key West, Florida. Ruby did not say who the leaders of the invasion were to be but implied that it was to be sponsored by the U.S. government. The FBI says that Basinger's story cannot be true. Although Basinger's arrest record and incarceration can be verified, Ruby had been transferred to the county jail before Basinger arrived in the city jail, therefore they could not have met.

Bayo, Eddie (a.k.a. Eddie Perez)

Brother-in-law of suspected MK/ULTRA subject Luis Castillo and a member of Alpha 66. According to authors Warren Hinckle and William Turner, Bayo was the leader of a "hit team."

(See also CASTILLO, LUIS.)

Bay of Pigs

On April 17, 1961, the CIA sponsored an attack on Cuba—which came to be known as the Bay of Pigs—in an attempt to get rid of Castro. Since the attack did not involve the U.S. Army, the attack needed soldiers. The CIA used Cuban exiles, those who had fled the Communist government and very much wanted to get their homeland back. The exiles were trained by the CIA in Guatemala, and they were supplied weapons and other supplies of war by the American military. The Cuban exiles also believed that they had been promised the support of the U.S. Air Force.

The new soldiers—1,300 of them—who had been trained rather quickly to fight went to Cuba by boat. They hit the beach at the Playa Girón, the Bay of Pigs.

The plan assumed that, once the Cuban people heard of the attack, they would rise up in revolt. Soon Castro would be out of power, they thought. It didn't work out that way. The invasion was a miserable failure. When the exiles landed they were given no air support. As it turned out, U.S. president John F. Kennedy had never promised U.S. military support, and he wasn't about to order in the U.S. Air Force at the last second because things were going poorly on the ground. Such a move, President Kennedy feared, might start World War III.

During the short battle at the Bay of Pigs many died. The freedom fighters who were not killed by Cuba's army were captured on the beach. No Cubans rose up in revolt in response to the invasion. The invasion was poorly planned and implemented on every level.

At first the embarrassed CIA said that it had nothing to do with the invasion, that it had been entirely planned and carried out by the Cuban exiles. But the truth quickly came out. President Kennedy speedily went on TV and took full responsibility for the invasion.

Many of the Cuban freedom fighters blamed President Kennedy for the failure of the invasion, feeling that the president had gone back on his word. The Cubans were not released from their prisoner-of-war cells until a few days before Christmas 1962, when President Kennedy made a deal with Castro. The United States gave Cuba food and medicine and, in exchange, the Cuban exiles were allowed to return to the United States.

Beers, Ira Jefferson "Jack," Jr.

Dallas Morning News photographer, born in 1923, who was in Dealey Plaza moments after the assassination. With William Allen of the *Dallas Times Herald* and Joe Smith of the *Fort Worth Star-Telegram*, Beers was one of three photographers who photographed the three "tramps" sometime after 2:15 P.M. on the afternoon of the assassination as they were led by Dallas police from a boxcar near Dealey Plaza to the nearby Dallas County Sheriff's Department headquarters.

On Sunday morning, November 24, 1963, Beers was in the basement of the Dallas police station where he took the second most famous photo of Jack Ruby shooting Lee Harvey Oswald for which he was later nominated for a Pulitzer Prize.

(See also JACKSON, ROBERT.)

Bell, Jack See SMITH, MERRIMAN.

Bell Film, The

Assassination witness F. M. "Mark" Bell was born on March 6, 1918, in Limestone County Texas. He saw combat with the First Marine Division during World War II. A letter carrier for the U.S. Postal Service, Bell worked out of the Terminal Annex Post Office on the south side of Dealey Plaza. When Bell went to see the motorcade he brought with him his movie camera, a one-lens Kodak 8mm. To take his film Bell stood on a four-foot pedestal that was east of Dealey Plaza's north peristyles. Bell exposed $15\frac{1}{2}$ seconds of film as the president passed by his position on Houston Street. Bell says he couldn't tell how many shots there were because of the echoes in Dealey Plaza—which probably means that he heard more than three. By the time the shooting started, Bell had jumped off of his pedestal and moved to where he had a view of Elm Street's approach to the triple underpass. He did not start filming again, however, until the presidential limousine was passing the motorcade's lead car just before disappearing into the tunnel. The remainder of his film shows the reactions of spectators and activity on the grassy knoll. Two days later Bell watched Jack Ruby shoot Lee Harvey Oswald live on television. Bell knew Ruby because his nightclub was on his mail route. Bell's film received no public attention until 1967 when frames from his film appeared in *LIFE* magazine.

Belli, Melvin   See RUBY, JACK.

Bennett, William   See BISHOP, WILLIAM C.

Betzner, Hugh William, Jr.

Twenty-two-year-old assassination witness who lived near the Lakewood Country Club in Dallas and worked at Railway Express Agency, Inc., at 515 South Houston Street. For the motorcade, Betzner was standing on the curb on the west side of Houston Street near the reflecting pool, 70 feet south of Elm Street. Betzner had with him his Kodak 120 camera with black-and-white film in it. Betzner took a photo as the presidential limousine passed his position, and then ran to the southwest corner of Elm and Houston. Betzner's photo of JFK's car turning onto Elm Street is ruined by three spectators who got in the way. His third photo, taken while JFK's car headed down Elm Street toward the triple underpass, shows a dark figure behind the concrete abutment on the grassy knoll, the figure who became known as "Black Dog Man." Abraham Zapruder, his receptionist Marilyn Sitzman, and a portion of the Umbrella Man's umbrella are visible. The House Select Committee on Assassinations concluded that this photograph coincided in time with frame number 186 of the Zapruder film. Betzner told the Dallas Sheriff's Department that there were "at least" four shots and that, during the shooting sequence, the limousine came to a stop. None of his photographs were used by the Warren Commission as evidence.

(See also BLACK DOG MAN; SITZMAN, MARILYN; ZAPRUDER FILM.)

Biffle, Kent

Dallas Morning News reporter who rode in the motorcade. Biffle climbed out of the car he was riding in on Elm Street and saw the immediate aftermath of the shooting.

Biffle told his own newspaper in 1981, "A rush of men and women swept by me. They were running away from the sound of the shots. A few of us ran towards the shooting. People were crouched behind the concrete structures in the plaza on the grassy slope that drops down toward the underpass, several figures were flat on the ground. . . . Some teenagers followed. One of them darted ahead and hit the fence [at the top of the knoll] before I did. I remem-

ber thinking, 'This nutty kid is going to get his head blown off and he's not even getting paid for it.' Puffing, I followed him."

According to WFAA newsman Tom Alyea, who had just entered the Texas School Book Depository moments following the shooting, "I turned to film the police rushing in the door behind me and saw Kent Biffle in my viewfinder as he passed in front of my lens. . . . Kent made it into the building only a second or two before a commanding voice yelled for the uniformed officers to close and lock the door."

To a Dallas assassination conference in 1993, Biffle picked up the story, "We went in with the first wave of policemen. They immediately sealed off the building so we had it all to ourselves at first, for two or three hours. . . . The crime lab people were investigating, and I remember I was worried when we first went in. I was afraid that a policeman was going to shoot me because these guys all had their guns out and they were nervous. I remember once stepping out of an office where I interviewed some office workers on the second floor. And there was a policeman at one end of the hall and another at the other end of the hall, and they both had riot guns and they both drew down on me when I stepped out into the hall. But I never worried too much about the assassin because I had a theory that with the last shot he had killed himself, and they would find the body in the building somewhere. And, in fact, when one of the detectives yelled at [Dallas police chief homicide investigator] Captain Fritz, I thought they had finally found the body, but it was the rifle. . . . You could see part of the muzzle and part of the butt plate sticking out from under a box of books. . . . And then a little later an officer came in and told Captain Fritz, 'We've got a man down in Oak Cliff.' They didn't immediately link this up with the assassination. It was like an altogether isolated incident. . . . They said his name is Tippit. At first, you know, they were all cast down, because there was an extroverted policeman named Tippit that everyone liked. And they were kind of relieved to hear that it was not him but the other Tippit who had been killed. Apparently J. D. was a quiet sort of man, and he was not well known to these detectives."

Bishop, Maurice   See PHILLIPS, DAVID ATLEE.

Bishop, William C. (a.k.a. Bennett, William)

Born on February 18, 1923, in Cherokee, North Carolina, under the name William Bennett, this man became a colonel in military intelligence who claimed he was in Dallas on November 22, 1963. Originally scheduled to cover the Trade Mart at the end of the motorcade, Colonel Bishop said he went to Parkland Hospital where he says he helped put President Kennedy's remains in a body bag. Bishop also claims that he was a member of William King Harvey's ZR/RIFLE CIA assassination team, and that he was personally responsible for the deaths of Teamsters leader Jimmy Hoffa and Dominican dictator Rafael Trujillo. According to Colonel Bishop, JFK's assassination was planned by General Edwin Walker, Richard Helms, General Charles Willoughby, and Cuban exile Felipe Vidal Santiago. See entries in this book for each of these individuals.

Black Dog Man

Visible in photos taken by Hugh Betzner and Phillip Willis, the "Black Dog Man" was a figure visible behind the concrete retaining wall, perhaps holding a weapon. The statements of Marilyn Sitzman, receptionist for Abraham Zapruder and the woman who was standing with him on a pedestal near the spot where "Black Dog Man" can be seen, tends to dispose of the notion that this figure is sinister. She says that a young couple was sitting on a park bench at that spot and that the woman stood up at the sound of the first shot. A gunman shooting from where "Black Dog Man" was would have been visible to many eyewitnesses.

(See also SITZMAN, MARILYN.)

Bogard, Albert Guy   See DOWNTOWN LINCOLN-MERCURY.

Bond, Wilma Irene

Assassination witness who was among those who photographed the assassination scene from the south side of Elm Street. Forty-two years old in 1963, Bond was a native of Indiana and worked as a bookkeeper. She was carrying with her a 35mm camera loaded with a roll of 36-exposure slide film. Bond was with assassination witness Mary Muchmore about 30 feet north of the northwest corner of Main and Houston. When the motorcade passed, Bond and Muchmore moved to a spot near Dealey Plaza's north peristyles to view JFK on Elm Street. Because of Bond's excitement, she failed to take any photos during the shooting sequence. She later told the FBI that she had heard "at least" three shots. She was not called as a Warren Commission witness but she was called as a prosecution witness at the Clay Shaw trial in New Orleans, Louisiana. Bond died at the age of 58 on January 8, 1980, at Baylor Hospital in Dallas.

Bonds, Joe (a.k.a. Locurto, Joe)

A former business partner of Jack Ruby who told the FBI that Ruby often "made women available to [police] officers."

Wilma Bond's photograph taken moments after the shooting shows the entire grassy knoll. The pergola is on the right. The Babushka Lady can be seen standing on the nearside of the street on the left, while witnesses Jean Hill and Mary Moorman crouch to her right. *(Collector's Archive)*

Boone, Eugene

Twenty-six-year-old Dallas deputy sheriff who, along with Deputy Constable Seymour Weitzman, discovered the alleged assassination weapon poorly hidden on the Texas School Book Depository's sixth floor. The rifle was identified by Boone at the scene as a German Mauser rather than as an Italian Mannlicher-Carcano. Born in Dallas, Boone had worked for eight years in the advertising department of the *Dallas Times Herald* before joining the Dallas Sheriff's Department in 1962.

Boone watched the assassination from in front of the sheriff's office and then ran into Dealey Plaza. First, he searched the railroad yards behind the grassy knoll. Then he moved to the Texas School Book Depository where he is given credit for being the first to discover the weapon that became the purported assassination weapon.

After the shooting, Boone, according to his Warren Commission testimony, "went on west across Houston Street, and then cut across the grass out there behind the large cement works there. Some of the bystanders over there seemed to think the shots came from up over the railroad in the freight yards, from over the triple underpass. So there was some city officer, I don't know who he was, motorcycle officer had laid his motorcycle down and was running up the embankment to get over a little retaining wall that separates the freight yards there. He went over the wall first, and I was right behind him, going into the freight yards. We searched out the freight yards. We were unable to find anything." After he got to the sixth floor, Boone "proceeded to the east end of the building, I guess, and started working our way across the building to the west wall, looking in, under, and around all the boxes and pallets, and what-have-you that were on the floor. Looking for the weapon. And as I got to the west wall, there were a row of windows there, and a slight space between some boxes and the wall. I squeezed through them. When I did—I had my light in my hand. I was slinging it around on the floor, and I caught a glimpse of the rifle, stuffed down between two rows of boxes with another box or so pulled over the top of it. And I hollered that the rifle was here. . . . Some of the other officers came over to look at it. I told them to stand back, not to get around close, they might want to take prints of some of the boxes, and not touch the rifle. And at that time Captain Fritz and an I.D. man came over. I believe the I.D. man's name was Lieutenant Day—I am not sure. They came over and the weapon was photographed as it lay. And at that time Captain Fritz picked it up by the strap, and it was removed from the place where it was. . . . [The rifle was] in the corner of the building, something like this, and there is a wall coming up here, making one side of the stairwell with the building acting as the other two sides. And from that, it was almost directly in front or about eight feet south, I guess, it would be, from that partition wall that made up the stairwell. . . . And at first, not knowing what it was, I thought it was 7.65 Mauser."

Bosch, Orlando Avila

Marita Lorenz, a former CIA and FBI undercover operative, told the *New York Daily News* that, a few days before the assassination, she drove from Miami to Dallas. Her companions on the trip were "Oswald," CIA contact agent Frank Sturgis, Cuban-exile leader Bosch and his fellow Cuban-exile Pedro Diaz Lanz, and two Cuban brothers named Novis. All of the men in her scenario were members, she said, of Operation 40, a CIA guerrilla group that had been formed three years earlier for the Bay of Pigs invasion. Lorenz also said that Operation 40 was an "assassination squad" that killed the president because they blamed him for the Bay of Pigs fiasco. She said she saw "Oswald" at an Operation 40 training camp in the Florida Everglades, and that he was at a meeting at Bosch's Miami home with the above-mentioned men. During the meeting, she said, the men spread out street maps of Dallas and studied them. Bosch was later tried and acquitted for allegedly blowing up a Cuban airliner in 1976, killing 73. He strongly denied that there was any truth in Lorenz's statements.

(See also HEMMING, GERRY PATRICK; LORENZ, MARITA; STURGIS, FRANK.)

Bothun, Richard O.

Assassination witness who was born May 31, 1921, in Albert Lea, Minnesota. He served with the Navy-Marine Air Corps in World War II and moved to Texas in 1949 when he took a job with the Fort Worth and Denver Railroad. Bothun enjoyed photography, both taking and developing his own photos.

As the presidential motorcade approached, Bothun was standing on the south side of Main Street, just east of Houston Street, carrying a Nikon or a Pentax camera—he doesn't remember which one he had. Bothun was using a 50mm lens and black-and-white film. He took two photos of the president's car approaching and passing his position. He then ran 220 feet toward Elm Street to take another picture as the presidential limousine went past the grassy knoll. Bothun can be seen in the Zapruder film, holding his camera at chest level, reaching a point 10 feet from Elm Street's south curb as Mrs. Kennedy crawls onto the back of the limousine. Although Bothun took no photographs during the shooting sequence, he did photograph the immediate aftermath, in particular activity on the north side of Elm Street. One of his photos gives us our best view of the face of the "Umbrella Man," seen in profile while sitting on Elm Street's north curb.

Bothun died January 5, 1981, at Saint Joseph's Hospital in Fort Worth, Texas, of a heart attack.

(See also UMBRELLA MAN.)

Bowen, Jack Leslie (a.k.a. Grossi, John Caesar)

Born in Paterson, New Jersey, August 5, 1925, police were drawn to Bowen by the fact that he had signed the Dallas Public Library card that was reportedly found in Oswald's wallet following his arrest. Bowen's real name, it was learned, was John Caesar Grossi and he had served time in several penitentiaries, once for bank robbery. He was interviewed by the FBI on December 7, 1963. Bowen said he was 38 years old and had known Oswald because they had been coworkers at Jaggars-Chiles-Stovall, where it was learned that the photographic work for the U.S. spy plane U-2 was done. Oswald worked there from October 12, 1962, until April 6, 1963, while Bowen had worked there from August 1961 until August 1963. Bowen admitted that he had allowed Oswald to use his name as a reference on his library card. Bowen later claimed that Oswald had brought his Mannlicher-Carcano rifle to work and showed it to him, unlikely as the rifle had not yet been ordered.

The FBI had done a previous interview of Bowen in 1956. The resulting memo listed Bowen as six-foot tall, 170 pounds, medium build, dark brown, wavy, thick hair, blue eyes, and a tanned complexion. His "peculiarities" are listed as "accomplished artist, caricaturist." His wife was listed as "Lucille Ryder Bowen (pregnant)."

Researchers have long noticed the similarity between the alias of John Caesar Grossi—Jack Leslie Bowen—and the alias of Albert Osborne, the man with whom Lee Harvey Oswald supposedly traveled to Mexico—John Howard Bowen.

(See also CENTRAL INTELLIGENCE AGENCY; CORSICAN MOB, OSBORNE, ALBERT.)

Bowen, John Howard   See OSBORNE, ALBERT.

Bowers, Lee E., Jr.

Bowers was the railroad towerman for the Union Terminal Company at the time of the assassination. He says he watched the assassination from a 14-foot tower behind the wooden fence atop the grassy knoll near the railroad tracks.

Of all of the assassination witnesses, Bowers reportedly had the best view of the spot from which the grassy knoll shots were theoretically fired. During the hour before the assassination, Bowers saw three cars enter the parking lot area behind the Texas School Book Depository and the knoll, one at a time. The first was a blue and white 1959 Oldsmobile station wagon with an out-of-state license plate. The car had a "Goldwater for President" sticker on the bumper and was splattered with dirt. It circled the area, then left. The second car, which also circled the area before leaving, was a black 1957 Ford, driven by a man who appeared to be speaking into a microphone. The third car, which also had a Goldwater sticker, was a Chevy and entered the area about 10 minutes before the shooting. At the time of the shooting, Bowers saw only two strangers in

Lee Bowers's 14-foot tower, from which he saw some suspicious activity behind the grassy knoll. *(MacIntyre Symms)*

the area, two men near the wooden fence—one middle aged and heavy set, the other in his mid-twenties wearing a plaid shirt. Bowers recognized everyone else he saw as railroad employees.

At the time of the shots, Bowers's attention was drawn to the area. He said there was a "flash of light or smoke or something." Bowers's description of the men behind the wooden fence corroborates the statement of assassination witness Julia Mercer.

Bowers told the Warren Commission, "I heard three shots. One, then a slight pause, then two very close together. Also reverberations from the shots. . . . The sounds came either from up against the School Depository Building or near the mouth of the triple underpass. . . . I had worked this same tower for some ten to twelve years . . . and had noticed at that time the similarity of sounds occurring in either of these locations. . . . There is a similarity of sound, because there is a reverberation which takes place from either location."

According to early assassination researcher Penn Jones Jr., Bowers received death threats after the assassination. Bowers died on August 9, 1966, in a one-car crash. Bowers apparently drove his car off the road into a concrete abutment in Midlothian, Texas. No autopsy was performed. His body was cremated.

(See also MERCER, JULIA.)

Braden, Jim   See BRADING, EUGENE HALE.

Brading, Eugene Hale

Following the assassination, a man named Jim Braden was arrested and taken in for interrogation because he had been in the Dal-Tex Building, overlooking Dealey Plaza, without a good excuse. He was wearing a light-colored trenchcoat and a hat with big X's on the headband.

According to patrol officer Roy Vaughn of the Dallas police, moments after the assassination, "I was standing there on the sidewalk amidst all this mass confusion when a security guard from [the Dal-Tex Building] brought a man down who he had found up in the building. I don't know what floor he was on, but he had no reason to be there. I talked to the man, got his I.D., and noticed that he was well dressed, nice expensive suit, and had on a hat. The one thing that caught my eye that I'll never forget was when he opened his billfold and showed me some identification. Of course, I don't remember his name, but he had a bunch of credit cards. I talked to him briefly and then carried him across the street to the sheriff's office, told them what I'd found and what the circumstances were, and they took custody of him." (At that time, having credit cards would have been an indication of wealth.)

Brading told the Dallas County Sheriff's Department after the assassination that he had been innocently walking down Elm Street when he heard from people on the street that the president had been shot. "I moved on up to the building that was surrounded," he said, "and I asked one of the girls if there was a telephone I could use and she said, 'Yes, there is one on the third floor of the building where I work.' I walked through a passage to an elevator where they were getting on [the elevator] and I got off at the third floor of the building with all of the other people. . . ." Later, the man who ran the elevator spotted Brading as a man who did not belong in the building and ran outside to tell an officer.

That officer was Deputy Sheriff C. L. "Lummie" Lewis who died in 1978 of natural causes before he could testify for the House Select Committee on Assassinations.

Lewis took the suspect to the sheriff's office around the corner and there Braden explained that he was in Dallas on oil business and had entered the building to make a phone call. He was released.

Although Braden said he had not entered the building until after the shooting, eyewitnesses said he was inside the building at the time of the assassination.

Braden visited the offices of Texas oil billionaire Lamar Hunt the day before the assassination (as would be appropriate if he were on "oil business"). Jack Ruby visited Hunt's offices on the same day.

The parallel movements of Braden and Ruby doesn't end there. The night of November 22, Braden stayed at the Cabana Hotel in Dallas. Ruby visited there, too, around midnight.

According to author Peter Noyes, Braden had an office in New Orleans at the time in Room 1701 of the Pere Marquette Building. Simultaneously, assassination suspect David Ferrie was working for organized crime boss Carlos Marcello's attorney G. Wray Gill on the same floor, in room 1707.

It was later discovered that Jim Braden was actually Eugene Hale Brading, a southern California mobster. He had had a new driver's license made for him on September 9, 1963, in the name of Jim Braden.

He was on parole at the time President Kennedy was shot. He had been arrested 35 times and had previously been convicted of burglary, bookmaking, and embezzlement. Some of Brading's arrest records later disappeared from the National Archives. Brading didn't testify at the 1967 Clay Shaw trial when his extradition was refused by later U.S. Attorney General Ed Meese III.

Brading was a charter member of Moe Dalitz's Teamster-financed La Costa Country Club, and once lived in a Palm Springs mansion that had, at one time, been owned by Bing Crosby.

Brading's traveling companion for his Dallas trip was Morgan Brown, who also stayed at the Cabana Hotel. Brown's cover story was that he was a successful oil man but he was later jailed for selling fake oil stock. Brown checked out of the Cabana at 2:00 P.M. on November 22, 1963.

In 1968, the Los Angeles Police Department interviewed Brading about his presence in Los Angeles, far from his home, on the night and in the vicinity of Robert Kennedy's murder.

Brading was a known associate of assassination suspect Loran Eugene Hall, as well as others who were members of the Minutemen and suspects in the assassinations of Robert F. Kennedy and Martin Luther King Jr.

(See also GEMSTONE FILES.)

Bradley, Edgar Eugene

California right-wing preacher who was identified in October 1967 by former deputy sheriff Roger Craig as a man he had seen in Dealey Plaza after the assassination posing as a Secret Service agent. During Jim Garrison's assassination investigation, Garrison wanted to charge Bradley with conspiring to kill the president, but then-California governor Ronald Reagan refused to extradite Bradley. Bradley gave Reagan an affidavit stating that he was in El Paso at the time of the assassination.

On December 20, 1967, Garrison filed a bill of information in New Orleans, charging that Bradley did "willfully and unlawfully conspire with others to murder John F. Kennedy."

According to Paris Flammonde, "Bradley was originally from Arkansas, moving to Los Angeles in 1936, after serving in the United States Navy. Five feet eight inches tall, with dark hair, graying a little at the temples," he was married with a grown son and daughter. Bradley had a "special assignment" during World War II about which nothing is known. The *New Orleans States-Item* (December 22, 1967) states Garrison's reply to Bradley's alibi: "Our evidence indicates that he was in Dallas. Furthermore, I think I can say with assurance that the federal government and the federal investigative agencies know he was in Dallas, and know precisely what he was doing." Garrison refused to discuss specifics. In Los Angeles, District Attorney Eville J. Younger ordered Bradley's arrest on December 26, 1967, adding "this does not indicate any opinion on our part as to the validity of the charge or the guilt or innocence of Mr. Bradley."

Contemporaneous to these events, Flammonde spoke with an unnamed source within the Garrison investigation, who said Bradley had been an Office of Strategic

Services—precursor to the CIA—officer, probably still had intelligence connections, and was a member of an elite Minuteman-like group. The source said that Bradley knew assassination suspect Loran Hall and had been involved in anti-Castro activities. Flammonde writes, "On January 15, 1968, Court Clerk Max Gonzales asserted he had observed 'meetings at New Orlean's Lakefront Airport in either June or July 1963 between . . . Bradley of North Hollywood and the late David W. Ferrie.'"

Garrison claimed to possess an affidavit from former Dallas County deputy sheriff Roger Craig, whom he did not name, stating that Bradley had impersonated a Secret Service agent in front of the Texas School Book Depository after the assassination.

While Bradley successfully fought extradition attempts, researcher Mark Lane said, in May 1968, that he had a copy of a letter written by Bradley to a young woman in which he had written that he knew "facts about the [assassination] that the public will never know about . . . ," that "his life had been threatened many times," and that "another patriotic friend of [his] has just been shot and killed." Lane reported in the *Los Angeles Free Press* (May 3–9, 1968) that the recipient of that letter had been asked by Bradley to lie, via a prepared affidavit, to provide him with an alibi for November 22, 1963. Lane claimed that the woman showed him her diary, and that it indicated that, although she had seen Bradley on the 20th, she had not seen him on the 22nd. That same month, Garrison interviewed Loran Hall, who told him that he knew Bradley, having met him at a "house that was noted for their anti-Semitic and paramilitary feelings and thinkings," and that, in his mind, he figured Bradley for a CIA man. By 1969 Bradley was a sheriff in Los Angeles and part-time assistant to the right-wing cold warrior, Reverend Carl McIntire. According to Penn Jones Jr., at this time, Bradley "hounded" Craig "almost daily." Apparently ignorant of the details, some assassination books claim that Garrison's interest in Bradley was based solely on his confusing his name with that of Eugene Hale Brading, a known criminal picked up by a sheriff's deputy in Dealey Plaza moments after the shooting.

(See also CRAIG, ROGER; HALL, LORAN EUGENE.)

Brehm, Charles

Brehm was standing on the south curb of Elm Street only 20 feet from President Kennedy at the time of the fatal shot. Brehm told attorney Mark Lane that he saw a portion of the president's skull fly toward the rear and left, indicating that the final shot came from in front and to the right.

Brehm was not called to testify before the Warren Commission.

Brehm was a veteran of World War II, who served in the Ranger battalions. He had hit the beaches of Normandy on D day and had seen action in Europe until he was wounded by rifle fire. At the time of the assassination Brehm was a carpet salesman for Montgomery Ward. He worked at the Wynnewood Shopping Center in the Oak Cliff section of Dallas.

Brehm told researcher Larry A. Sneed that the first shot was a "surprising noise." He continued, "The third shot really frightened me. It had a completely different sound to it because it had really passed me as anybody knows who has been down under targets in the army or been shot at like I had many times. You know when a bullet passes over you, the cracking sound it makes, and that bullet had an absolute crack to it. I do believe that that shot was wild. It didn't hit anybody."

Brehm appeared on television during the first hours after the shooting and his tearful descriptions of what he had seen were memorable. Brehm appeared on a British television documentary called *On Trial: Lee Harvey Oswald*, produced by LWT International in 1986. Brehm died in 1996.

Brennan, Howard L.

The Warren Report's star assassination witness, Brennan was standing on the southwest corner of Houston and Elm, facing the Texas School Book Depository when the shots were fired. Brennan claims to have seen Oswald in the "sniper's nest" window, 120 feet away. He was later found to have poor eyesight, but the Warren Commission took him at his word anyway. Although it was probably Brennan's description of the man in the window ("slender white male, 5'10", early thirties") that was broadcast over police radio minutes after the assassination, Brennan could not possibly have known how tall the man was, since any sniper in that window would have had to kneel to get into position.

Sandy Speaker, Brennan's job foreman, told assassination researcher Jim Marrs, "They took [Brennan] off for about three weeks. I don't know if they were Secret Service or FBI, but they were federal people. He came back a nervous wreck and within a year his hair had turned snow white. . . . He was scared to death. They made him say what they wanted him to say."

Brennan later wrote a book about his experiences in which he claimed that Earl Warren offered to introduce him to Jackie Kennedy.

Bringuier, Carlos   See D.R.E.

Bronson, Film, The

Charles Leslie Bronson, a witness to the assassination, who filmed Dealey Plaza just before the shooting, was born on February 28, 1918, in Centralia, Illinois. At the time of the assassination he was the chief engineer at Varel Manufacturing. He went to the presidential motorcade with his wife. They climbed atop one of the concrete abutments to Dealey Plaza's south peristyles to watch and film JFK. Frances Bronson tore a stocking while climbing.

Bronson carried two cameras. His still camera was a chrome-trimmed, black-bodied 35mm Leica Model III-a, serial number 259903, which he had purchased for $169.95 from Sears & Roebuck in 1938. The shutter speed was set at 1/100 of a second. Bronson's movie camera, only a week old, was an 8mm Keystone Olympic K-35, serial #774192, mounted with a three-lens turret. The camera was set to run at 12 frames per second. The f-stop was set at f8 for bright sun. The camera was loaded with Kodachrome Type-A film.

Bronson filmed the commotion at the corner of Elm and Houston where, six minutes before the assassination, an ambulance came to pick up a spectator who appeared to be having an epileptic seizure (see EPILEPTIC FIT).

Less than two days after the assassination, Bronson wrote a letter to his sisters in which he described what happened when the shooting began: "As they were half way down to the underpass. And then it happened! . . . I heard the first two shots ring out in rapid succession and a slight pause before the third shot rang out."

One of Bronson's still photos shows the presidential limousine during the shooting sequence, but because the car is so far away there is little detail. Bronson switched to his movie camera just before the president was hit in the head. He filmed only two seconds before he realized that the sounds he was hearing were gunshots and that it would be a good idea for he and his wife to get off their perch.

On November 24, 1963, Bronson had his film developed and took it to the FBI. But they were not interested in it, Bronson said, because the film did not show the Texas School Book Depository. However, that was not true. The School Book Depository did appear in the film. For 92 frames, during the early portion of the film, in which the ambulance is sitting at the corner of Elm and Houston, much of the Depository is visible, including the "sniper's nest" window. In the film, some independent researchers (including Robert Groden) say, one or more figures can be seen on the sixth floor. The House Select Committee on Assassinations called the movement "random photographic artifact." Groden told the committee, regarding the Bronson film, "You can actually see one figure walking back and forth hurriedly. I think what was happening there

is the sniper's nest was actually being completed just prior to the shots being fired."

In 1983, the film was analyzed by the Massachusetts photographic-interpretation firm ITEK, at the request of CBS television. ITEK concluded that the movement in the sixth floor windows was caused by "the movement of the film in the pate of Bronson's camera as the movie strip was being recorded."

Broshears, Reverend Raymond

Broshears gave New Orleans Parish district attorney Jim Garrison a statement in 1967 that, two years before, he had met and spoken to assassination suspects David Ferrie and Clay Shaw together and that, when Ferrie drank, he liked to talk about his role in President Kennedy's assassination. Broshears shared an apartment with Ferrie in 1965.

During August 1968, Broshears said on a Los Angeles television program that, "David admitted being involved with the assassins. There's no question about that. [Ferrie] was in Houston at the time. Mr. Garrison has him in Houston with an airplane waiting."

Broshears said that Ferrie's job was to pilot two of the actual assassins on the second stage of an escape flight that would eventually take them to South Africa via South America. Assassination researcher Paris Flammonde points out that the United States had no extradition treaties with South Africa, and that it was here that "the CIA front operation Permindex moved when it was asked to leave Europe." (See PERMINDEX.)

Broshears said that Ferrie told him the plan had fallen apart when the assassins, flying in a light plane, had decided to skip the Houston stop and "make it all the way to some point in Mexico nonstop." The assassins reportedly crashed off the coast of Corpus Christi, Texas, and died. Broshears has also said that Ferrie was murdered, since Ferrie had once told him that "no matter what," he would never commit suicide.

(See also FERRIE, DAVID.)

Brown, Earle V.

Dallas police patrolman who witnessed the assassination from the railroad trestle just north of the triple underpass. Brown told the Warren Commission, "The first I noticed [President Kennedy's] car was when it stopped [after turning onto Elm]." Brown saw the pigeons flying off the roof of the Texas School Book Depository when the shots were fired. Brown says he smelled gunpowder several minutes after the shooting.

Brown, Judge Joseph B. "Joe"

Presided over Jack Ruby's murder trial and eventual death sentence. Judge Brown eventually had to disqualify himself from the case when it was learned that he had been working on a book during the trial, the sales of which would have been enhanced by a quick conclusion of the proceedings. A retrial was ordered.

Brown granted columnist Dorothy Kilgallen permission to interview Ruby alone for 30 minutes during Ruby's murder trial, an interview that reportedly took place in complete privacy. Even Ruby's guards were said to have left the room during the interview. Kilgallen died before the interview with Ruby could be published.

(See also RUBY, JACK LEON.)

Brown, Madeleine Duncan

Former mistress to Vice President Lyndon B. Johnson, who claims to have fathered Johnson's child. Now an advertising businesswoman, Brown claims to have met Jack Ruby through one of Lyndon Johnson's lawyers.

In 1988, Brown told Jack Anderson, "In the fall of 1963 I was in the Carousel Club with other advertising people and Jack Ruby was saying that Lee Harvey Oswald had been in the club and he had been bragging that he had taken a shot at Major General Edwin Walker."

On A Current Affair (February 24, 1992) Brown said that Johnson had foreknowledge of the assassination but did nothing to stop it because of his intense desire to be president and hatred of President Kennedy. She said that LBJ was amoral and killed President Kennedy with the help of J. Edgar Hoover, Richard Nixon, Clint Murchison, H. L. Hunt, John McCloy, and others. Brown knew about the conspiracy, she said, because she had attended a party at the mansion of Clint Murchison on the night before the assassination and in attendance were the above-mentioned men, along with Bruce Alger, John Curington, and George Brown. At one point in the party the men went into another room to have a meeting and when LBJ came out, Brown says, he told her that "those goddamn Kennedys will never embarrass me again."

She has also said that Abraham Zapruder, who filmed the assassination, was a friend of oil billionaire H. L. Hunt, which has not been corroborated. She also said she saw Oswald at Jack Ruby's Carousel Club.

(See also JOHNSON, LYNDON BAINES.)

Brown, Maggie

Dallas Morning News employee who watched the assassination from the north side of Elm Street near the grassy knoll. She said the shots came from behind her and to the right—that is, from the direction of the knoll. She was not questioned by the Warren Commission.

Brown, Morgan

According to FBI agent Pal Rotherman, Brown—along with Roger Baumen and Eugene Hale Brading—visited the offices of oil billionaire Lamar Hunt on November 21, 1963. Jack Ruby visited those offices the same day. The next day Brown checked out of Dallas' Cabana Hotel at 2:00 P.M. while his colleague Brading was still being held by the Dallas Sheriff's Office for questioning because of suspicious behavior in Dealey Plaza.

(See also BRADING, EUGENE HALE.)

Brown Paper Sack

Dallas Police homicide detective L. D. Montgomery, who joined the department in 1954, is the man credited with finding the brown paper sack on the sixth floor of the Texas School Book Depository. This sack was alleged to have been the bag Oswald used to carry the rifle into the building.

The brown paper is not mentioned in many police reports and the paper that was introduced as evidence before the Warren Commission lacked any oil that would have been apparent if the paper had been used to transport a rifle.

Montgomery said, "I don't remember exactly where I found the brown paper that Oswald had wrapped the rifle in. It was probably close to 36 inches long with tape on it and no writing. I recall that it was stuffed between the boxes, not lying out open on the floor as were the shell casings. Since we were looking for the rifle, we figured it must have been used to wrap the rifle." Two days later, Montgomery was standing directly behind Oswald when he was murdered. Montgomery retired from the Dallas Police in 1980.

(See also HILL, GERALD.)

Bruneau, Emile (a.k.a. Bruno, Emile)

It was Bruneau—a former Louisiana boxing commissioner and alleged member of Carlos Marcello's New Orleans crime organization—who paid Oswald's bail after his arrest in New Orleans for disturbing the peace.

Bundy, McGeorge

Top aide to both JFK and LBJ and an architect of U.S. policy in Vietnam. According to Colonel Fletcher Prouty, Bundy radioed Air Force One while it was flying from Dallas to Washington carrying JFK's body and LBJ, saying that the assassination was not the result of a conspiracy but had been the act of a lone gunman. Prouty also claims that it was Bundy who ordered the air support for the Bay of Pigs invasion to be cancelled.

Bundy died on September 16, 1996, of a heart attack in Boston, Massachusetts, at the age of 77.

(See also MILITARY-INDUSTRIAL COMPLEX; NSAM 263; NSAM 273.)

Burroughs, Henry

Associated Press photographer who rode in the Dallas motorcade in Camera Car 2. He was born in 1918 in Washington, D.C. In the motorcade, Burroughs carried two Rolleiflex 35mm cameras loaded with Tri-X ASA 400 film. Burroughs later said he heard four shots.

Bush, George Herbert Walker

Possible CIA agent; later CIA director, U.S. president, and father of a U.S. president. While CIA director, on November 17, 1976, Bush wrote that a reported FBI memo stating that Oswald had been in touch with Cuba just before the assassination did not exist. Bush admitted that the CIA had been guilty in the past of "abuses of power" but said that there was no evidence the agency was involved in President Kennedy's assassination or its cover-up. He then reaffirmed his belief that an intelligence-gathering agency working in other countries was necessary.

Bush claims to have had no association with the CIA before he was named director in 1976. Yet, according to *The Nation* (July 1988), there is an FBI memo—acquired through the Freedom of Information Act—dated November 29, 1963, from J. Edgar Hoover, stating that "George Bush of the CIA" would be assessing reaction to the assassination by the Cuban-exile community.

Although there is no evidence that Bush was involved in the Bay of Pigs operation, there is a series of thought-provoking coincidences. According to Fletcher Prouty, who was the CIA/Pentagon liaison during the Bay of Pigs attack and in charge of ordering supplies for the invasion, "The CIA had code-named the invasion 'Zapata.' Two boats landed on the shores of Cuba. One was named *Houston,* the other *Barbara.* They were Navy ships that had been repainted with new names. I have no idea where the new names came from." At the time of the Bay of Pigs invasion, George Bush lived in Houston, was married to Barbara, and owned a company called Zapata.

In a memo dated September 15, 1976, from CIA director Bush to his deputy director of central intelligence, Bush stated, "A recent Jack Anderson story referred to a November 1963 CIA cable, the subject matter of which had some U.K. journalist observing Jack Ruby visiting [Santos] Trafficante in jail [in Cuba]. Is there such a memo? If so, I would like to see it."

In 1992, while visiting Australia, President Bush was asked by NBC News correspondent John Cochran whether or not he had ever gone back and read the CIA's findings regarding the assassination to satisfy his curiosity.

"No," Bush said, apparently forgetting about the memo he had written in 1976. "I didn't have any curiosity, because I believed the [Warren Commission]. . . . I saw no reason to question it. Still see no reason to question it."

(See also CENTRAL INTELLIGENCE AGENCY.)

Butler, Edward S.

Executive director of the Information Council of the Americas who appeared on the New Orleans WDSU radio debate arranged by William Stuckey and broadcast August 21, 1963, between Oswald and anti-Castro Cuban Carlos Bringuier. According to John Wilds and Ira Harkey, the biographers of Dr. Alton Ochsner, Butler was a former U.S. Army intelligence officer.

(See also INFORMATION COUNCIL OF THE AMERICAS.)

Butler, George

A witness to Oswald's murder, Butler was a lieutenant in the Dallas Police Department, and an extreme right-winger. He was in immediate charge of Oswald's aborted transfer from the Dallas Police Station to the Dallas County Sheriff's Office.

Butler is the one who gave the "all-clear" sign in spite of the fact that the car assigned to pick up Oswald had not yet completely backed into position. Butler was not called as a Warren Commission witness. Penn Jones Jr. wrote: "Butler is a speaker for the right-wing anti-Communist fighters. He was formerly head of the Policemen's Union for Dallas, and it is common talk that he is in the good graces of [Dallas oil billionaire] H. L. Hunt which makes him immune to pressure from anyone. . . . During 1961, Butler made talks in Midlothian and on one such occasion he approached this writer in *The Mirror* offices and wanted to know if we would print a region wide KKK [Ku Klux Klan] newspaper. . . . He claimed we did not have to bid on a competitive basis, but simply tell him how much we wanted for the job. His second statement was that half of the police force in Dallas were members of the KKK." According to the Warren Commission testimony of another man who was in the basement of the Dallas police headquarters when Oswald was shot, Thayer Waldo of the *Fort Worth Star-Telegram*, Butler seemed throughout most of the assassination weekend to be a man of extraordinary poise, who was constantly in on inside information and was willing to share it with the press. Butler's poise, however, deserted him on the morning of the 24th, as the transfer of Oswald became imminent. Waldo testified that

Butler "was an extremely nervous man, so nervous that when I was standing asking him a question after I had entered the ramp and gotten down to the basement area, just moments before Oswald was brought down, he was standing profile to me and I noticed his lips trembling as he listened and waited for my answer. It was simply a physical characteristic. I had by then spent enough time talking to this man so that it struck me as something totally out of character." In a bizarre statement, Butler told assassination investigators that Oswald was Ruby's illegitimate son and that Ruby was in Mexico City during the autumn of 1963 at the same time that Oswald was supposed to be there.

(See also OSWALD, MURDER OF.)

Byers, Bo

Byers was a reporter for the *Houston Chronicle* who rode in the press bus in the Dallas motorcade. Addressing a conference at Southern Methodist University on November 20, 1993, Byers said, "We were on Houston [Street]. I was looking across the plaza when we heard the shots. I remember three shots. I have always had a memory—as a matter of fact, I've had nightmares about it—of the sunlight on Kennedy, and the explosion, the car almost coming to a stop, almost to a dead stop, and then accelerating at tremendous speed." The Zapruder film, as it currently exists, shows the presidential limousine maintaining a steady speed throughout the shooting sequence.

Cabana Hotel

Larry Meyers, a sporting goods salesman from Chicago and known associate of Jack Ruby, checked into the Teamster-financed Cabana Hotel in Dallas for a series of business meetings on the eve of the assassination. With Meyers was Jean Aase, a.k.a. Jean West, who was described by the married Meyers as "a rather dumb but accommodating broad." Also staying at the hotel, checking in the same day, was assassination witness Eugene Hale Brading, traveling under the name of Jim Braden. Braden was arrested the following day for suspicious behavior in Dealey Plaza after the shooting. On the eve of the assassination, Meyers had a meeting in the Egyptian Lounge in Dallas with Ruby and Dallas mobster Joseph Campisi. According to her phone records, obtained by Jim Garrison, Aase received a phone call from assassination suspect David Ferrie two months before the assassination.

(See also BRADING, EUGENE HALE.)

Cabell, Charles P.

Brother of the Dallas mayor, former Air Force general and former deputy director of the CIA who was fired by President Kennedy on December 29, 1961, after the Bay of Pigs invasion. It is questionable just how far away from the CIA Cabell got, however, as his future employment seemed to be with firms that were known to cover for the CIA. He became a member of the Board of Directors for the Pacific Corporation, the parent company of Air America. He also worked for Howard Hughes and became involved with Robert Maheu in plots to kill Castro.

Cabell, Earle

Brother of Charles (see above) and Mayor of Dallas in 1963. Mayor Cabell rode in the motorcade beside his wife "Dearie." According to United Press International correspondent H. D. Quigg, Cabell was under police protection in the days following the assassination because of death threats.

When the Carousel Club and all of the buildings surrounding it were torn down, a skyscraper known as the Earle Cabell Federal Building was put in its place.

Cabell, Mrs. Earle (Elizabeth) "Dearie"

Wife of the Dallas mayor who presented Jackie Kennedy with the bouquet of red roses at Love Field. All the other ladies in the motorcade were given the traditional Texas yellow roses. Mrs. Kennedy held her roses right up until the shooting sequence.

Mrs. Cabell was in the motorcade, sitting next to her husband. Their car was still on Houston Street at the time of the shooting. She says she jerked her head toward the Texas School Book Depository on the sound of gunfire and saw something sticking out of one of the windows.

At Parkland Hospital, Dearie sat alone for a time in the backseat of the car she had been riding in. The car was in the parking area in front of the emergency room, and the other occupants of the car all got out to find out what was going on.

Calderón, Luisa

Cuban embassy official in Mexico City who, according to FBI agent James Hosty, was also a Cuban intelligence agent. Within hours of President Kennedy's death, a CIA wiretap inside the Cuban embassy picked up Calderón telling a friend that she had known beforehand of the assassination. Soon thereafter Calderón returned to Havana, Cuba. When the House Select Committee on Assassinations sent representatives to Cuba, Castro allowed certain employees of the Cuban embassy to talk to the Americans, but not Calderón.

Calvery, Gloria

Texas School Book Depository employee who witnessed the assassination while standing next to John Chism and Karen Westbrook near the "Stemmons Freeway" sign on the north side of Elm Street. She later said that the president was first shot when his limo was directly in front of her position. After the shooting she ran back toward the front entrance to her building screaming—"The president has been shot!"—since many people at the entrance to the building were initially unable to tell what had occurred.

Campbell, Allen and Daniel

Brothers and former Marines who were recruited by New Orleans private investigator Guy Banister during the summer of 1963 to help identify pro-Castro sympathizers among New Orleans college students.

In a 1979 interview, Daniel told Anthony Summers that Oswald entered Banister's offices on the day of his New Orleans arrest and used Daniel's desk phone to make a call.

In 1969, Allen told the New Orleans District Attorney's Office that Banister usually became furious when notified of communist activity, but when told about Oswald's pro-Castro demonstration, Banister just laughed.

Campbell, Ochus V.

Texas School Book Depository vice president who witnessed the assassination while standing in front of his building. Campbell said, "I heard shots being fired from a point which I thought was near the railroad tracks."

Cancellare, Frank

News photographer and assassination witness who was born in Brooklyn, New York, in 1910. Cancellare had photographed the building of the Burma Road during World War II. His most famous photograph was his "Dewey Defeats Truman" image of President-elect Truman holding up a copy of the newspaper that called the presidential election incorrectly. Cancellare rode in the Dallas motorcade in Camera Car 2. He carried around his neck two cameras, a Rolleiflex and a Nikon using black and white

Frank Cancellare's photo showing the south side of the triple underpass and south knoll. The man on the far left, on the opposite side of Elm Street, is carrying a sign that reads "S.O.B., Jack Kennedy." *(Collector's Archive)*

Tri-X ASA 400 film. He remembered: "Police ran their bikes up the bank toward the railroad overpass. I thought they were chasing the culprit and I think they thought so also." Cancellare got out of the car and took pictures of activities on the north side of Elm Street and the remainder of Dealey Plaza. One of his photos taken from the north side of Elm shows a man in a light jacket standing on the south side of the street carrying a sign that says, "S.O.B., Jack Kennedy," Researcher Edgar F. Tetro believes he can see an assassin with a rifle in the background of this photo on the *south* grassy knoll.

Cancellare died in July 1985.

Carlos

Pseudonym of a witness who testified anonymously to the House Select Committee on Assassinations. We know that Carlos is an explosives expert and that he was among those who volunteered his services to Jim Garrison's investigation.

The code name Carlos was also brought up by a Florida State Prison inmate (not named) who told an investigator from the House Select Committee that "Carlos" had been in Dealey Plaza at the time of the murder "posing as a photographer."

(See also CONEIN, LUCIEN; EASTERLING, ROBERT WILFRED; FERRIE, DAVID.)

Carousel Club

Strip club operated by Jack Ruby and owned by Ruby and his "Chicago friend" Ralph Paul. The club opened in 1960 and was located at 1312 1/2 Commerce Street, adjacent to the Adolphus Hotel.

The club was one flight up. Eight-by-ten-inch glossies of the striptease artists who were performing that night hung above the entrance. There was a two-dollar cover charge. The room was barn-like, and dark. The carpeting was dark red and the booths were made of black plastic. Beer cost 60 cents a glass.

The girls, when it wasn't their turn on stage, would work as "B-girls." That is, they would try to talk the customers into buying them champagne, which was purchased cheap and sold for as much as $17.50 a bottle.

The club was only a few doors away from its number-one competitor, Abe Weinstein's Colony Club at 1322 Commerce—a club that was bigger and did more business than the Carousel.

After Ruby shot Oswald, Ralph Paul kept the club open for a time but eventually the building that held the Carousel Club was torn down to make room for a sky-scraper called the Earle Cabell Federal Building, named after the mayor of Dallas at the time of the assassination.

(See also CAROUSEL CLUB EMPLOYEES; JACK'S GIRLS; RUBY, JACK.)

Carousel Club Employees (Male)

Here is information about some of the men who worked for Jack Ruby at the Carousel Club:

Norman Earl Wright worked as an emcee and comic in the Carousel Club during the autumn of 1963. He told the Warren Commission that Ruby was sensitive about Jewish jokes, his receding hairline, and his slight lisp—that Ruby was afraid people would think he was a homosexual. Wright said he was "out of town" on the day of the assassination and told the commission regarding the shooting of Oswald: "In my opinion, the police department is just as much to blame as Jack in a roundabout way, because there was no reason in the world, with all the police they had, for Jack to walk directly straight through that many people and . . . shoot him. . . . The Dallas Police shared at least fifty percent of the blame."

Billy Joe Willis was a former employee by the time of the assassination. He, like many other witnesses, said he saw a man resembling Oswald in the Carousel Club. According to the *Warren Report*, which went out of its way to avoid finding any connection between Ruby and Oswald, Willis "did not think the man was Oswald." Why bring it up then?

Wally Weston was the former Carousel Club emcee. He also believed he saw Oswald in the Carousel Club—and his memory was quite specific. In 1976, Weston told a national television audience that, in September or October of 1963, Oswald (or an Oswald look-alike) came into the Carousel. Weston and Oswald got into a verbal altercation, during which "Oswald" called Weston a communist and

Weston hit "Oswald." At that point Ruby interjected and bounced "Oswald" from the premises, saying, "I told you never to come in here again."

Another Carousel Club employee remembered a friendlier relationship between Ruby and Oswald. William D. Crowe Jr. (a.k.a. Bill DeMar) was a 22-year-old Carousel Club performer, ventriloquist, and "mind reader," whose repertoire consisted of a "memory act." (His performance can be seen in the exploitation film *Naughty Dallas*. The "nudie cutie" film, as they were called at the time, is now available on video, and contains several scenes shot in Ruby's Carousel Club.) Crowe said he remembered seeing Oswald and Ruby drinking and talking in the Carousel "a little more than a week" before JFK's death. "The face seemed familiar," he said. Crowe told a reporter on April 11, 1964: "I gave the FBI a statement about seeing Oswald in the club and that was it. I told them the same thing I'm telling you. I signed it and have heard nothing more about the incident to this day."

William F. Simmons was the Carousel Club piano player from September 17 until November 21, 1963. In their feigned attempt to locate links between Oswald and Ruby, the Warren Commission investigated Simmons, who lived at 2539 West 5th Street in Irving, Texas. This was interesting because Ruth Paine and Marina Oswald lived at that time at 2115 West 5th Street in Irving. Simmons testified that he didn't know Ruth, Marina, or Lee—and that his only relationship with Ruby was as an employee.

Mike "Mickey" Ryan (alias Roy William Pike; Mike Pike) was Ruby's bookkeeper. He also worked as the bartender at the North Park Inn in Dallas. He was the husband of Tuesday Ryan (a.k.a. Ramona Wagner), a Carousel stripper. Ryan left Dallas on November 30, 1963. Carousel employee Andrew Armstrong told the Warren Commission that Ryan had visited Ruby at the Carousel on the night before the assassination. Ryan, however, told the Warren Commission that he hadn't seen Ruby for two weeks before President Kennedy's death.

Thomas Stewart Palmer was an occasional fill-in comedian and magician at the Carousel Club, and the Dallas branch manager of AGVA, the union to which Ruby's performers were required to belong. Palmer told the Warren Commission that Ruby violated several AGVA rules, including the use of strippers as "B-girls," employees who teased men with the possibility of sexual favors in order to sell drinks. Both Janet "Jada" Conforto and Karen "Little Lynn" Carlin submitted affidavits to AGVA on this point. Other allegations against Ruby included physical abuse of employees. Palmer told the commission that Ruby had a high employee turnover, that he wouldn't permit racial or religious jokes "of an obviously dirty nature." Palmer said Carlin was living with a Dallas policeman at least six months before the assassination. If so, at least two Dallas policemen were co-habitating with strippers who worked for Jack Ruby at the time of the assassination, with Harry Olsen and Kathy Kay being the other couple.

Andrew Armstrong Jr. was an African-American ex-convict and the handyman at the Carousel Club. Armstrong originally told the FBI that he had called stripper Karen Carlin on Friday night, November 22, 1963, to tell her that, because of President Kennedy's death, Ruby's clubs would be closed for the next three nights. When testifying to the Warren Commission, Armstrong denied calling Carlin at all. Carlin told the commission that Armstrong called her on Friday night, but that he'd said the clubs would be closed only for one night. Armstrong told the House Select Committee on Assassinations that Ruby wasn't having the problems he said he was having with the AGVA, thus throwing further doubt on Ruby's cover story to explain his extraordinary number of pre-assassination long-distance phone calls.

Other employees helped establish the case that Ruby and the Dallas police had an extensive relationship. Joseph Weldon Johnson Jr., the bandleader at Carousel Club for six years, told attorney Mark Lane that Ruby knew at least half of the 1,200 Dallas policemen, and that cops visited the Carousel "all the time" and were "treated royally." James H. Rhodes, a Carousel Club bartender, told the FBI that Ruby once held a private party for 30 or 40 police officers at the Carousel, and that "the chief" was there. Rhodes noted that Ruby picked up the tab.

(For Jack Ruby's female employees, see JACK'S GIRLS. For information about Ruby-employee Larry Crafard, see OSWALD LOOK-ALIKES; see also PERRIN, ROBERT AND NANCY; SUSPICIOUS DEATHS; WHITE, ROSCOE.)

Carousel Night

Saturday night October 24, 1992, was Carousel night at the JFK Assassination Symposium at the Hyatt-Regency Hotel in Dallas, Texas. Assassination buffs wearing Oswald T-shirts were being given a night to let their hair down. With a disregard for those who might have found the proceedings in bad taste, the symposium conference room was done up like Jack Ruby's Carousel Club. A bar was set up. The film *Naughty Dallas* was shown repeated on a TV in the back. A band called Nick Naughty and the Naughty Ones played songs from 1963, including an unbelievably hot "Harlem Nocturne." Two strippers with 1963 hair took almost everything off but never got quite topless. The highlight of this evening was a performance by Beverly Oliver—the self-proclaimed "Babushka Lady"—who sang "Let's Twist Again," and "Summertime," while sitting in the laps of men in the front row. Also in attendance was Madeleine Brown, the woman who claimed that she was LBJ's lover, that she was an acquaintance of Jack Ruby, and

that LBJ had foreknowledge of the assassination. In between songs, Nick Naughty made assassination jokes. Referring to Ruby's most famous stripper, Nick said, "That Jada, what a muff she had! Dave Ferrie could have made three wigs out of it!"

(See also BABUSHKA LADY; JACK'S GIRLS.)

Carr, Richard Randolph

Assassination witness who watched from high above Dealey Plaza. Carr was perched on a girder on the Courts Building then under construction at the northeast corner of Main and Houston streets.

Carr could see into the sixth floor of the Texas School Book Depository and before the shooting looked through the sixth-floor windows and saw a heavy-set man wearing a hat, a tan sportscoat, and horn-rimmed glasses. After the shooting, Carr climbed down from his perch, and saw the man in the tan sportscoat, along with two others, hurrying away from the scene on Commerce Street.

Carr told the FBI, "This man, walking very fast, proceeded on Houston Street south to Commerce Street to Record Street, which is one block from Houston Street. The man got into a 1961 or 1962 gray Rambler station wagon which was parked just north of Commerce Street on Record Street. The station wagon, which had Texas license and was driven by a young Negro man, drove off in a northerly direction."

Carr's observances corroborate those of Roger Craig, Carolyn Walther, and James R. Worrell. According to Carr, the FBI told him, "If you didn't see Lee Harvey Oswald in the School Book Depository with a rifle, you didn't see it."

Carr received phone threats, ordering him to leave Texas or else. Carr moved to Montana. There, Carr once found dynamite taped to his car ignition. Carr was about to testify in the New Orleans trial of Clay Shaw when someone took a shot at him. Carr captured the gunman with help from a policeman neighbor.

Carr went through with his testimony in New Orleans, by this time confined to a wheelchair because of a construction accident, and he was later attacked again by two men in Atlanta. This time he was stabbed but managed to kill one of his attackers by shooting him three times. After being shot, the assailant said, "Doodle Bug, he has killed me."

In 1975, as the House Select Committee on Assassinations was gearing up, Carr again received phone threats.

(See also CRAIG, ROGER; NASH RAMBLER STATION WAGON; WALLACE, MALCOLM.)

Carr, Waggoner

Texas attorney general who reported to the Warren Commission that Oswald was an FBI undercover agent assigned number 179 and received $200 a month for the final 14 months of his life. J. Edgar Hoover denied the allegation, and the Warren Commission believed him.

Carr testified to the commission that at 8:00 or 9:00 P.M., November 22, 1963, he received a phone call from a person at the White House. ("I can't for the life of me remember who it was," Carr claimed.) The caller asked Carr if it was true that Oswald's indictment for the president's murder was to include the allegation that Oswald was part of an "international conspiracy."

Carr testified: "the concern of the caller was that because of the emotion or the high tension that existed at that time that someone might thoughtlessly place in the indictment such an allegation without having the proof of such a conspiracy. . . . There was no talk or indirect talk or insinuation that the facts, whatever they might be, should be suppressed. It was simply that in the tension someone might put something in an indictment for an advantage here or a disadvantage there, that could not be proved, which would have a very serious reaction, which the local person might not anticipate since he might not have the entire picture of what the reaction might be."

(See also ALEXANDER, WILLIAM.)

Carter, John
Carter provides a possible pre-assassination link between Lee Harvey Oswald and Jack Ruby. Carter was both a boarder at 1026 North Beckley in Oak Cliff (where Oswald lived) and friends with Wanda Joyce Killam, who was a longtime friend and ex-employee of Ruby's. Carter worked with Wanda's husband Hank as a house painter.

Casas Saez, Miguel
According to CIA memos, a private Cubana Airlines flight, scheduled to leave from Mexico City for Havana at 6:20 P.M. on November 22, 1963, did not leave until 10:30 P.M. because a passenger was late in arriving. The passenger was Casas, and when he did arrive he was allowed to board without going through customs.

Casas entered the cockpit upon boarding the plane and stayed there for the duration of the flight so that none of the other passengers had an opportunity to see him.

According to CIA documents, Casas, who spoke Russian, had entered the United States at the beginning of November, perhaps on an espionage assignment, using the name Angel Dominguez Martinez.

The House Select Committee on Assassinations looked into this matter and, using airport records, determined that the incident had not occurred, but the committee

never considered the question of why CIA internal communications would discuss a fabricated incident.

(See also LOPEZ, GILBERTO.)

Castillo, Luis (a.k.a. Eloriaga, Antonio Reyes; Gradjeda, Ignacio Gonzales; Hernandez, Razo; Rodriguez, Angelo; Rodriguez, Mario)
Castillo, then 24 years old, was arrested on March 2, 1967, by the Philippine National Bureau of Investigation. He was charged with suspicion of conspiring to assassinate President Ferdinand Marcos in Manila. He had been sought since February, when the NBI learned that he had made contact with a guerrilla group known for its constant plotting to kill Marcos and overthrow the Filipino government. During his interrogation he requested that he be given truth serum and be hypnotized. This was done and Castillo told the NBI that four years earlier, on November 22, 1963, he had been involved in the assassination in Dallas, Texas, of a man riding in an open car whose identity he did not know. He asked for political asylum in the Philippines. Castillo told reporters from the *Manila Times,* "I am afraid to go anywhere anyway. I am as good as dead now. . . . I don't know how I got into Dallas and how I got out, but I am sure I did not carry a gun."

Castillo told the NBI that his "instructions" in Dallas had come from a woman he knew as "Mrs. Kreps," who spoke with a German accent. She had been one of many people who had hypnotized him, preparing him for his "job." Mrs. Kreps, he recalled under hypnosis, took him repeatedly to a factory "way outside of Chicago." During certain portions of the interview he admitted a romantic interest in the woman, and at other times he said that he despised her.

Castillo said that he had been involved in an assassination that had taken place "before noon." He was with a man named "Lake" (tall, 190 lbs., hawk-nosed, Asian eyes, and black hair), whom he had met along with four or five other men—both Americans and foreigners, one of whom might have been Spanish—at an airport. They drove together in a black car to a building and went to a second-floor room filled with packing crates. Lake opened a "bowling bag" with a lock on it and pulled out the parts of a rifle, which he assembled. Castillo said that the rifle might have been Russian. Lake gave Castillo the rifle and told him that he was going to shoot a man riding in the backseat of a car, riding in the middle of a caravan. When he saw two flashes from a mirror in a window in a building "across the street" he was to shoot the man in the next car to come into view. Before Castillo could shoot, however, Lake ran in and said that the intended victim had already been shot. Lake took the gun away, disassembled it, put it back in the bag, and together the men fled the building.

They got into a car that was waiting for them. Two men were already in the car. After turning a corner, they stopped and picked up a bald and skinny man. A few blocks later they picked up a second man. He "remembered" getting an injection in the backseat of the car. The next thing he recalled he was in a Chicago hotel room with Mrs. Kreps. Later that day he learned that President Kennedy had been assassinated.

During one interrogation, Castillo said he had been a private in the Cuban militia known as the Segunda Organizacion Defensiva which operated out of Santiago, Cuba. While with the militia, he said he had been trained by a communications expert named Karnovsky. His "needs" had been taken care of, both in Cuba and later in the United States, by an American he knew as "James Smith."

During another session he said that his name was Manuel Angel Ramirez, a sergeant assigned to the Strategic Air Tactical Command in South Vietnam. Stationed in Saigon in January 1966, his superior officer was named Colonel Summers and he had flown B-26 missions over Haiphong and Hanoi. In this hypnotic state, he confessed that he came to Manila to murder Marcos in June during one of the president's public speeches.

A news blackout on Castillo was declared by the Filipinos, and Castillo faced a series of further hypnotic sessions, now at the request of the FBI, who had taken an interest in Castillo. One of these session, three-and-a-half hours long, spawned this report from the hypnotist, "Initially, the subject indicated an admixture of desired susceptibility to hypnosynthesis but deep-seated resistance due to the presence of a posthypnotic block. This block appeared to have been connected with the presence—nightmarish—of a Mrs. Kreps. The total removal of this block may pave the way for maximum results."

Tiny scars were discovered on Castillo's fingers, forehead, chest, and stomach. When asked about the scars, Castillo explained that he had gotten them in a car accident when he was being chased, attempting to deliver a package.

The psychiatrists began to think that Castillo was a genuine "programmed agent," and discovered that he had four distinct personalities that would emerge during hypnosis, and they designated these states ZOMBIE I, II, III, and IV.

In one trance, Castillo was handed an empty pistol and a picture of President Marcos. He repeatedly pulled the trigger. When Castillo heard his own name, he put the gun to his own head and pulled the trigger. He pulled the trigger again each time his name was repeated.

Attempting to get responses with different verbal cues, a psychiatrist said the letter "X" aloud. Castillo, bizarrely, replied, "Mauricio."

Just after awakening from one trance, Castillo was informed of the psychiatrist's suspicions. He said that "Papa" didn't know anything about that and that, while in one of his zombie states, he feared he would kill "Papa." Asked who "Papa" was, Castillo explained that he was referring to his real father, a man who worked for the "Agency," had a moustache, smoked a pipe, the initials. A.D. and the first name Allen—an obvious reference to Allen Dulles, former director of the Central Intelligence Agency.

The summary report by the NBI psychiatrists reads: "The Zombie phenomenon referred to here is a somnambulistic behavior displayed by the subject in a conditioned response to a series of words, phrases and statements, apparently unknown to the subject during his normal waking state. While under the influence of such a Zombie state, the subject closed his eyes, rose bodily, walked, triggered a pistol, stared blankly, and fell to the floor with no apparent sense of physical pain. As far as could be determined experimentally, the Zombie behavior had for its objective the assassination of . . . Marcos. . . ."

According to assassination researcher Peter Dale Scott, there exists a CIA document from station JM/WAVE dated July 26, 1963, that states that Castillo is the brother-in-law of Eddie Perez (Bayo), who led a three-man assassination team sent to Cuba to kill Castro. According to Scott, the document says that the team had hoped that Castillo would be included in the "hit."

Castillo was returned to the United States later in 1967 and, while being questioned by the FBI, said that he had made up the story of his participation in the Kennedy assassination while he was in Manila.

Castillo has been missing since 1974, after serving 37 months in prison in Missouri for robbery.

Castro, Fidel

Cuban premier who, before President Kennedy's assassination, said that, if CIA attempts on his life did not cease, U.S. leaders should expect payback in kind. Some Cuban Nationalists, as well as CIA agents, who attempted to overthrow Castro's government—through both assassination attempts and the botched Bay of Pigs invasion—are suspects in the assassination. They blamed Kennedy for the failure at the Bay of Pigs and may have turned on the president because they felt betrayed.

Associated Press correspondent Daniel Harker interviewed Fidel Castro at a reception at the Brazilian embassy in Havana on September 7, 1963. According to Harker, Castro said President Kennedy was "a cretin . . . the Batista of his times . . . the most opportunistic American president of all time. . ."

Regarding Cuban exile invasions such as the Bay of Pigs (and to attempts on his own life) Castro said, "We are prepared to fight them and answer in kind. United

Cuban premier Fidel Castro. *(Author's Collection)*

States leaders should think that if they are aiding terrorist plans to eliminate Cuban leaders, they themselves will not be safe."

Castro told Lou Stokes of the House Select Committee on Assassinations, "You see, it was always very much suspicious to me that a person who later appeared to be involved in Kennedy's death would have requested a visa from Cuba. Because, I said to myself—what would have happened had by any chance that man come to Cuba—visited Cuba—gone back to the States and then appeared involved in Kennedy's death? That would have really been a provocation—a gigantic provocation. . . . That is why it has always been something, a very obscure thing, something suspicious, because I interpreted it as a deliberate attempt to link Cuba with Kennedy's death."

Castro told the House Select Committee, regarding the fact that some people thought he was responsible for John F. Kennedy's death: "That was insane. From the ideological point of view it was insane. And from the political point of view, it was a tremendous insanity. I am going to tell you here that nobody ever had the idea of such things. What would it do? We just tried to defend our folks here, within our territory. Anyone who subscribed to that idea would have been judged insane. . . . Never in twenty years of revolution, I never heard anyone suggest or even speculate about a measure of that sort, because who could think of the idea of organizing the death of the President of the United States. That would have been the most perfect pre-

text for the United States to invade our country which is what I have tried to prevent for all these years, in every possible sense. Since the United States is much more powerful than we are, what could we gain from a war with the United States? The United States would lose nothing. The destruction would have been here." According to Castro, the attempts on his life did not stop with JFK's death.

Castro never believed that it was possible for one man to have killed JFK and, to prove this to himself, the Cuban president—who fancied himself a sharpshooter—"used a high-powered rifle with a telescopic sight to re-create the assassination." Evidently he did not hit his target two out of three times, because he hasn't changed his belief that "about three" people killed JFK.

Cellar, The

Fort Worth, Texas, nightclub (1001 Main Street) where members of the Secret Service drank the night before the assassination. The Cellar's owner was Pat Kirkwood, a soldier of fortune, former champion stock-car driver, confidential informant for the U.S. Customs Service, and licensed pilot who owned a twin-engine plane and flew to Mexico hours after President Kennedy's death.

Some Secret Service men partied until 3:00 A.M. (one until 5:00 A.M.) on the eve of the assassination.

The Cellar was a "beatnik" establishment with a sign on the wall that read, "Evil Spelled Backwards Is Live."

Kirkwood told the *Fort Worth Star-Telegram:* "After midnight the night before, some reporters called me from the Press Club, which didn't have a license to sell drinks after midnight. Said they had about 17 members of the Secret Service and asked if they could bring them to my place. I said sure. About 3:30 in the morning, these Secret Service men were sitting around giggling about how the firemen were guarding the president over at the Hotel Texas. . . . Ruby used to come over on Friday nights and steal my girls. . . . Oswald washed glasses for two nights at the San Antonio Cellar. . . . We didn't say anything, but those [Secret Service] guys were bombed. They were drinking pure Everclear [alcohol]."

According to Dallas reporter Jim Marrs, Kirkwood was the sort of nightclub owner who had friends in powerful places. Among his acquaintances were organized crime figures (Meyer Lansky, Dino Cellini), big money oil men (H. L. Hunt, Clint Murchison), and politicians (Lyndon Johnson, John Connally). Several of the women serving liquor to the Secret Service agents on the night before the assassination were strippers from Jack Ruby's Carousel Club.

Kirkwood died of lung cancer at age 73 on February 9, 2001.

(See also JOHNSON, LYNDON; HUNT, H. L.; SECRET SERVICE.)

Central Intelligence Agency

The Central Intelligence Agency is the premier overseas spy organization in the United States, established to gather information about enemies and potential enemies. On the morning of the assassination, Desmond FitzGerald—the CIA chief of the Far Eastern Division from 1957–62, chief of the Cuban Task Force in Mexico City, 1962–64, and who, by March 1964, would be the CIA's chief of the Western Hemisphere Division—met with Rolando Cubela (code named AM/LASH) in Paris. FitzGerald gave Cubela a weapon that resembled a pen but was actually a hypodermic needle with poison inside. The weapon was to be used to assassinate Fidel Castro. FitzGerald promised that, following Castro's death, the United States would fully support the overthrow of Castro's government.

Dallas' top CIA man in 1963 was J. Walton Moore, a close friend of Oswald's mentor, George DeMohrenschildt. After DeMohrenschildt completed his "walking tour" of Central America he was completely debriefed by Moore. In his Warren Commission testimony, DeMohrenschildt said that he had discussed Oswald with Moore. Moore denied this conversation ever took place. DeMohrenschildt later wrote that Moore had talked to him about Oswald while Oswald was still in the Soviet Union. Moore told DeMohrenschildt that Oswald would be returning to Dallas and that it might be a good idea to keep an eye on him. DeMohrenschildt assured him that he would. Moore died in 1993.

The CIA did have an "assassination unit" in 1963. The operation was called ZR/RIFLE, and it was the brainchild of ex-FBI agent William King Harvey. Earlier in his career with the CIA, Harvey had exposed three double agents who had been spying for the Soviets: Guy Burgess, Donald McLean, and Kim Philby. Before the Bay of Pigs Harvey had been handler of Cuban exiles in charge of CIA-Mafia plots to kill Fidel Castro. Harvey, a man with bad habits, had been more or less banished by the CIA to Sardinia, Italy, at the time of the assassination. Two members of the ZR/RIFLE team have been identified by the CIA's Richard Helms by their cryptonyms, WI/ROGUE and QJ/WIN. WI/ROGUE, according to the Church Committee Report, was "an 'essentially stateless' soldier of fortune, a forger and a former bank robber. The CIA sent him to the Congo after providing him with plastic surgery and a toupee." The report went on to say that WI/ROGUE could distinguish between right and wrong, but could choose not to distinguish if his work called for him to do so. He was, in other words, a professional sociopath. About QJ/WIN, Helms told the Church Committee, "If you need somebody to carry out murder, I guess you had a man who might be prepared to carry it out." According to recently released CIA documents, QJ/WIN's employment with the CIA began in 1958 and that, at that time, the agency thought of him as an "agent provocateur" or "double agent" against the USSR. CIA documents also show that their business relationship with QJ/WIN ended on February 14, 1964, following the shelving of his "operation." CIA documents from 1962 reveal that QJ/WIN had at one time worked for the Bureau of Narcotics under the supervision of Charles Siragusa—later to be involved with the CIA mind-control program known as MK/ULTRA. Assassination researcher Peter Dale Scott has theorized that Siragusa himself might have been QJ/WIN. Other researchers believe that WI/ROGUE might have been Corsican assassin Christian David.

Harvey hated the Kennedys. He felt he had been "browbeaten" by Attorney General Robert Kennedy and felt that his "banishment" to the CIA's Rome office in January 1963 was the ultimate insult. While supposedly on duty in Rome, Harvey is said to have attended meetings in the Florida Keys at anti-Castro camps, with David "El Indio" Sanchez Morales, David Atlee Phillips (a.k.a. Maurice Bishop), and Johnny Roselli. Harvey's comment upon hearing of President Kennedy's death was, "This was bound to happen, and it's probably good that it did." When Harvey learned that his assistant was spending time receiving condolences from local well-wishers, Harvey fired him for inefficient sentimentality. Harvey died at the age of 60 of a heart attack on June 9, 1976.

According to soldier of fortune Gerry Patrick Hemming, Harvey was a mole in the CIA placed by the FBI, and that he never stopped reporting to J. Edgar Hoover. Hemming says that CIA mole-hunter James Jesus Angleton suspected this to be the case.

The largest CIA installation outside of its headquarters in Langley, Virginia, in 1963 was JM/WAVE, headquartered in a secluded and heavily wooded tract of land in Miami that had formerly been a naval air station and part of the University of Miami's south campus. The headquarters for JM/WAVE were in a building that overtly housed Zenith Technical Enterprises Inc. It was from here that the CIA headquartered its anti-Castro activities. The D.R.E. student anti-Castro organization of Carlos Bringuier was under the wing of JM/WAVE.

Was Lee Harvey Oswald a CIA agent? According to *The Assassination Chain* by Sybil Leek and Bert R. Sugar, there is a former CIA agent named Ronald Lee Augustinovich who claims that Lee Harvey Oswald was an undercover agent for the CIA who used the code name "Tom Kane."

John Scelso was the pseudonym used by a high-ranking official of the CIA who testified before the House Select Committee on Assassinations. A total of 192 pages of Scelso's testimony was released to the Assassination Records Review Board on October 1, 1996. Here is a synopsis of what Scelso said: Scelso was chief of the CIA branch responsible for Mexico and Central America.

Scelso wrote a report to President Lyndon Johnson two days after JFK's assassination stating that there was nothing in Oswald's visit to Mexico City to indicate that there were other assassins involved in President Kennedy's death. Scelso was critical of James Jesus Angleton whom he stated was hell-bent on blaming the assassination on a communist conspiracy, and of William King Harvey, whom he called a "wacko" and accused of killing San Giancana. He also stated that Angleton had mob ties. According to assassination researcher David Lifton, Scelso is actually a man named John Whitter.

(See also ANGLETON, JAMES JESUS; BOWEN, JACK LESLIE; COLBY, WILLIAM; DULLES, ALLEN; MK/ULTRA; HELMS, RICHARD.)

Chaney, James M.
Dallas police motorcycle patrolman who rode to the side and just behind the presidential limo during the motorcade. The first shot, Chaney said, came from over his right shoulder—that is, from the direction of the Texas School Book Depository.

Describing the fatal shot, Chaney said President Kennedy was "struck in the face." On November 23, 1963, Chaney told reporters the first shot missed.

Chapman, Al
One-armed man with a crippled leg who apparently tried to shake down Texas oil billionaire H. L. Hunt for money, which he said would go to the struggling Garrison investigation, perhaps in exchange for withdrawing the names of members of the Hunt family from Garrison's public list of suspects. No deal was made.

Cheek, Bertha
Cheek was connected to the assassination in a number of ways. She was the sister of Oswald's housekeeper, Earlene Roberts. She once considered investing in Ruby's Carousel Club and visited the club on November 18, 1963, four days before the assassination. She was also the former landlady of Officer Harry N. Olsen, the only member of the Dallas Police Department on record who doesn't remember precisely where he was at the time of the assassination (although his best guess places him in close proximity to the scene of the Tippit killing). Cheek met Ruby through Olsen, who later married Kathy Kay, one of Ruby's strippers. Dallas County Records show that Cheek purchased 13 apartment buildings in 1963. In 1968, Cheek purchased a hotel in Dallas for more than $900,000.

At the time of the assassination Cheek had a younger boyfriend named Wilburn Waldon Litchfield, who witnessed her November 27, 1963, interrogation by the FBI.

On December 2, 1963, Litchfield approached the FBI on his own and told them that he had seen a man resembling Lee Harvey Oswald at the Carousel Club.

(See also OLSEN, HARRY; ROBERTS, EARLENE.)

Cheramie, Rose (a.k.a. Marcades, Melba Christine)
A prostitute and drug addict who once worked for Ruby—and also one of a handful of people known to have publicly discussed the assassination before it happened. During the early morning hours of November 20, 1963, Cheramie was found battered lying next to a road near Eunice, Louisiana. She was taken to East Louisiana State Hospital (near Jackson, Louisiana) where she hysterically told doctors that President Kennedy was to be killed.

According to Dr. Victor Weiss, in a deposition for the House Select Committee on Assassinations, Cheramie said after the assassination weekend that she had been headed toward Dallas in the company of two "Latin" men and that "the word in the underworld" was that President Kennedy would be hit. She claimed that it had been two of Jack Ruby's employees who had dumped her on the road the previous night. She also said that Oswald and Ruby had been "bedmates".

On September 4, 1965, Cheramie was reportedly struck and killed by a car near Big Sandy, Texas. The driver said that Cheramie was lying in the road and, although he tried, he couldn't avoid running over her skull.

Although her death certificate reads "DOA," official hospital records indicate she was operated on for eight hours after she arrived on a "deep punctate stellate" wound to her right forehead, which could indicate a gunshot wound at point blank range.

Mac Manuel, owner of the Silver Slipper Lounge in Louisiana, who saw Cheramie and her two Latin companions before her November 1963 "accident," later identified one of the men to Lieutenant Francis Fruge of the Louisiana State Police as Sergio Arcacha Smith of the anti-Castro Cuban exile group known as Alpha 66.

(See also ALPHA 66; ARCACHA SMITH, SERGIO; JACK'S GIRLS.)

Chicken Bones
When police found the "sniper's nest" on the sixth floor of the Texas School Book Depository building, some said they found the remains of a bag lunch—chicken bones, an apple core, etc.—nearby, and it was at first assumed that this was the assassin's lunch. Later, they said the lunch belonged to Bonnie Ray Williams, one of the floor-laying crew who had been putting a new floor down on the sixth floor on the morning of the assassination. Since Williams said that he finished his lunch at 12:20, only 10 minutes

before the assassination, and the sniper's nest, with its walls of heavy boxes, must have taken some time to create, the uncomfortable thinking was that, either these two events were going on at the same time or Williams was eating his lunch only a few feet away from a concealed assassin at the corner window. However, there are some eyewitnesses to events in the School Book Depository during the moments following the assassination who claim that the brown bag with the chicken bones was not there at all. "Police officers who claim they were on the sixth floor when the assassin's window was found have reported that they saw chicken bones at or near the site," said reporter Tom Alyea. One officer reported that he saw chicken bones on the floor near the location. Another said he saw chicken bones on the barricade boxes, while another reported that he saw chicken bones on the box which was laying across the window sill. Some of these officers have given testimony as to the location and positioning of the shell casings. Their testimony differs and none of it is true. I have no idea why they are clinging to these statements. They must have a reason. Perhaps it is because they put it in a report and they must stick to it. Alyea, when addressing a conference of journalists who had covered the Kennedy assassination at Southern Methodist University in Dallas, Texas, on November 20, 1993, said that the reason he knows the chicken bones were not on the sixth floor was that he was there when they were discovered on the *fifth* floor. He said, "On the fifth floor . . . I was walking with this officer, plainclothesman, and we see a sack on the floor. And a Dr. Pepper bottle. . . . He hit it with his toe. Some chicken bones came out of it."

Chism, John Arthur and Mary

Husband and wife who witnessed the motorcade, with their three-year-old son, directly in front of the "Stemmons Freeway" sign on the north side of Elm Street. Immediately after the assassination, both Chisms looked behind them toward the grassy knoll to see if they could see the shooter.

Civello, Joseph

A reputed crime boss, who was reportedly a liaison between his friend Jack Ruby and his employer, New Orleans crime boss Carlos Marcello, Civello served six years of a 15-year sentence on a narcotics conviction during the 1930s and got a pardon in 1937 after Sheriff Bill Decker—the same man who was in charge of the Dallas Sheriff's Department at the time of the assassination—testified for him as a character witness. Civello was also arrested at the famous Apalachin meeting of organized crime bosses.

Civello was also reportedly friendly with Sergeant Patrick Dean of the Dallas Police who was one of those responsible for security when Ruby shot Oswald.

Clark, Ramsay

U.S. attorney general under President Lyndon B. Johnson who, in March 1967, told reporters that the Garrison case had no merit and that Clay Shaw had been investigated by the FBI in 1963 and no connection found between Shaw and the assassination. Clark did not offer, and he was not asked for, an explanation as to why Shaw was investigated in 1963 by the FBI in connection with the assassination.

Clifton, Major General Chester V. "Ted"

Military aide to President Kennedy who rode in the Dallas motorcade in a station wagon with Godfrey McHugh. Clifton was still on Main Street at the time of the shooting and reportedly said to McHugh, "That's crazy, firing a salute here."

Author William Manchester describes Clifton as a "realist" who adjusted quickly to the change in power rendered in Dallas.

Clinton, Louisiana, Incident, The

William Dunn, a member of the Clinton, Louisiana, Congress of Racial Equality [CORE], organized a voter registration drive that drew only one white man: Lee Harvey Oswald. Dunn saw Oswald arrive in a black Cadillac. One of the car's passengers was identified by eyewitnesses as David Ferrie.

According to Anthony Summers, "some of the Clinton witnesses thought [Clay Shaw] could have been the driver. . . . In the light of all the other evidence, many investigators [theorize it was] Guy Banister."

The question of the white-haired man's identity was answered when the House Select Committee on Assassinations interviewed Clinton town marshall John Manchester on March 14, 1978. Manchester said that he had approached the black Cadillac after Oswald had gotten out of it and had asked the driver to identify himself. The marshall said that the man gave the name Clay Shaw and produced a driver's license that matched. Manchester's testimony was taken in executive session, and it didn't become public until after the passing of the JFK Assassination Materials Act of 1992. Manchester said the driver of the black car identified himself as "a representative of the International Trade Mart in New Orleans."

Other citizens of Clinton who saw and identified Oswald were Corrie Collins, the local CORE chairman; Edwin McGehee, the town barber who testified at Clay

Shaw's trial that Oswald came in for a haircut, showed his Marine discharge card, and told him that he was seeking a job at the hospital in nearby Jackson. Oswald appeared shocked when McGehee informed him that this was a mental hospital but continued to express interest in the job; and Reeves Morgan, the state representative for Clinton. McGehee referred Oswald to Morgan. Oswald visited Morgan at his home and Morgan told him he would have a better chance of getting the job if he were a registered voter in the parish. Morgan testified for the prosecution at the Clay Shaw trial, telling the jury that he called the FBI after the assassination and the FBI told him they already knew about Oswald's visit to Clinton.

In September 1963 in Elizabethtown, New Jersey, someone resembling Oswald was seen as a lone white man in a CORE demonstration. The Elizabethtown sightings were called to the attention of the FBI immediately following Oswald's fame, and before the Clinton incidents received any press.

Cody, Joseph R.

Cody, a burglary and theft detective with the Dallas Police Department and a licensed pilot assigned to the Counter-Intelligence Corps during the Korean War, said he had known Ruby for 13 years. Cody was born in Dallas and joined the military in January 1944. He completed advanced infantry training at Camp Roberts, California. He was shipped to San Francisco, where he applied for CIC. He says that 70,000 applied and only nine were accepted, and that he was one of the nine. He worked as a plainclothes warrant officer investigating treason, sabotage, and subversion. After the Korean War, he attended North Texas State University. He played professional hockey and joined the Dallas Police Department in 1950.

Cody worked as a patrol officer for four years and then became a detective in the Narcotics and Vice Division. Before Cody, Dallas police did not work undercover. Along with Dallas policeman Red Souter, Cody is responsible for the formation of the Criminal Intelligence Section.

Cody says he arrived in Dealey Plaza about 10 minutes after the shooting and while searching the plaza found "a bone lying in the gutter that apparently came out the back of the president's head." He also says that when Lee Harvey Oswald was first brought into the Dallas Police Station following his arrest in the Texas Theatre Cody was left alone in the interrogation room with Oswald.

According to Warren Commission Exhibit 1736, Cody says he ran into Ruby repeatedly at the Fair Park Skating Rink in Dallas, as they shared an interest in skating. (Cody and Ruby weren't the only two people interested in skating. Remember, assassination suspect David Ferrie—

another pilot—had an unquenchable urge to go skating with several of his young friends during the hours following the assassination.)

Ruby, apparently, wore racing skates and knew what he was doing. After seeing Jack skate, Cody arranged to meet him so that they could skate together on Wednesday and Thursday afternoons. Cody was called by Dallas reporter Seth Kantor, one of Ruby's "special pals." According to assassination investigators Sybil Leek and Bert R. Sugar, Cody was the nephew of Ruby's friend from Chicago, Allen Cody.

According to Cody, New Orleans Parish district attorney Jim Garrison thought he had been a getaway pilot and had his plane warmed up and ready to go at Redbird Airport at the time of the assassination. Cody says his plane wasn't even at Redbird Airport as they charged too much money for storage and instead he kept his plane at Grand Prairie Airport.

Cody was not in Dallas on November 24 because "while flying low, had hit a high wire with the wing of the plane and had been forced down on Lake Bisteneau near Shreveport, Louisiana." He had been on his way to a gar rodeo in Lake Bisteneau, Louisiana. The .38 Colt Cobra with an aluminum frame, metal barrel, and steel cylinder that killed Oswald had been purchased in Cody's name. Cody told Ruby that it was legal for him to carry a gun as long as it was only to and from work or to and from the bank, when, as a nightclub owner, he might be suspected by bandits of carrying lots of cash. Ruby wasn't carrying much cash when it came to buying the gun, however. It cost $62.50 and Ruby did not have the money so Cody purchased the gun for him under the agreement that Ruby would pay him back later when he could.

In one of the notebooks kept by Lee Harvey Oswald seized after the assassination is the name of Kenneth Cody, Joe's uncle. According to Joe, Kenneth was a bus driver whose regular route was between Dallas and Shreveport, Louisiana. His uncle Kenneth, he said, lived in Oak Cliff behind the Redline Apartments about a block and a half from Methodist Hospital.

Cody retired from the Dallas Police Department in 1980 and has worked since as a private investigator.

Coffin, President Kennedy's

According to U.S. Defense Department documents released from the National Archives in 1999, the coffin used to transport President Kennedy's body from Love Field in Dallas to Andrews Air Force Base in Washington, D.C., was disposed of in a most bizarre way.

By orders of the Kennedy family, the coffin was drilled full of holes and filled with 240 lbs. of sand and then was dropped into the sea via helicopter in 1966. The documents revealed that the Defense Department had sought the advice of a submarine officer on the best way to get the coffin to the ocean floor.

The coffin was bronze and lined with brushed satin. It had been purchased from undertaker Vernon O'Neal in Dallas. According to historian William Manchester, this casket was damaged by clumsy Secret Service men trying to get it out of the hearse at Love Field.

President Kennedy was buried in a mahogany coffin purchased in Washington, D.C.

The first coffin had been stored in a basement at the National Archives in Washington until Robert Kennedy, then a senator from New York, ordered it to be destroyed.

Kennedy family spokesperson Melody Miller said that the disposal of the coffin was "in keeping with the tradition of President Kennedy's naval service and his love of the sea."

A U.S. Air Force van picked the coffin up at the National Archives and transported it to Andrews Air Force Base where it was put aboard a C-130 airplane. The plane took off at 8:38 A.M. and flew to a spot 131 miles off of the Maryland-Delaware coast.

The pilot descended to 500 feet. At 10:00 A.M. the plane's tail hatch was opened and the coffin was pushed out. To further ensure that the coffin would sink, heavy metal bands had been wrapped around it. Parachutes were attached to the coffin so that it wouldn't break up upon impact with the water.

Colby, William E.

Future director of the Central Intelligence Agency who, as late as 1976, insisted that the CIA had no contact with Oswald after his return from the Soviet Union. Colby disappeared on April 27, 1996, while on a solo canoe trip at night in rough waters on the Wicomico River, near the confluence of the Wicomico and Potomac Rivers in Rocky Point, Maryland, 40 miles south of Washington, D.C.

Oddly, Colby had called his wife—who was in Houston, Texas, at the time—earlier in the evening and had complained that he wasn't feeling well.

Colby began his spy career during World War II, parachuting into France to fight the Nazis. He joined the CIA in 1950 and served in Saigon, Vietnam (where he headed Operation *Phoenix*, which included the torture and execution of thousands of Vietnamese), Stockholm, and Rome before becoming director in May 1973 during the Watergate scandal. He remained as director until 1976.

Collins Radio   See WHITE, T. F.

"Comrade Kostin" Letter

On November 9, 1963, while staying in Irving, Texas, at the Paine home, Lee Harvey Oswald allegedly typed the following letter on Ruth Paine's typewriter. Despite the fact that Ruth had a Russian alphabet typewriter, Oswald is said to have used the English alphabet typewriter when typing this letter. Ruth later read the letter and hand-wrote a copy for herself, she says. All spelling and typographical errors are transferred from the original. The letter read:

From Lee H. Oswald, P.O. Box 6225, Dallas, Texas, Marina Nichilayeva Oswald, Soviet Citizen To: Consular Division, Embassy U.S.S.R., Washington, D.C., November 9, 1963 . . . Dear Sirs: This is to inform you of recent events since my meetings with comrade Kostin in the Embassy of the Soviet Union, Mexico City, Mexico. . . . I was unable to remain in Mexico indefinily because of my mexican visa restrictions which was for 15 days only. I could not take a chance on requesting a new visa unless I used my real name, so I returned to the United States. . . . I had not planned to contact the Soviet embassy in Mexico so they were unprepared, had I been able to reach the Soviet Embassy in Havana as planned, the embassy there would have had time to complete our business. . . . Of corse the Soviet embassy was not at fault, they were, as I say unprepared, the Cuban consulate was guilty of a gross breach of regulations, I am glad he had since been replced. . . . The Federal Bureau of Investigation is not now interested in my activities in the progressive organization "Fair Play For Cuba Committee," of which I was secretary in New Orleans (state Louisiana) since I no longer reside in that state. However, the F.B.I. has visited us here in Dallas, Texas, on November 1st. Agent James P. Hosty warned me that if I engaged in F.P.C.C. activities in Texas the F.B.I. will again take an "interest" in me. . . . This agent also "suggested" to Marina Nichilayeva that she could remain in the United States under F.B.I. "protection," that is, she could defect from the Soviet Union, of course, I and my wife strongly protested these tactics by the notorious F.B.I. . . . Please inform us of the arrival of our Soviet entrance visa's as soon as they come . . . Also, this is to inform you of the birth on October 20, 1963 of a daughter, Audrey Marina Oswald in Dallas, Texas, to my wife. . . . Respectfully, (signed) Lee H. Oswald.

According to researcher Michael H. B. Eddowes, whose writings always have a decided anticommunist bias, Kostin was Valeri Dmitrevich Kostin, a clandestine KGB officer possibly a member of Department 13, made up of professional killers. The man whom Oswald met at the Russian embassy according to the official record is Valeri Vladimirovich Kostikov, and it is to this man that the Warren Commission concluded Oswald was sending his Comrade Kostin letter. Eddowes believes that Kostin and Kostikov are separate individuals and that both were undercover KGB agents.

Conein, Lucien

Fought with the Corsican Brotherhood during World War II, which was then part of the Resistance Movement. According to assassination researcher Gordon Winslow, Conein, who is said to have given the green light to the murders of the Diem brothers in Vietnam on November 1, 1963, worked with the man code-named Carlos and Mitch WerBell, who was accused by Gerry Patrick Hemming of supplying the Dealey Plaza hit team with silenced weapons.

(See also "CARLOS.")

Connally, Governor John Bowden, Jr.

Severely wounded in the assassination, Governor Connally was sitting directly in front of the president when the shots were fired. During the shooting sequence Connally reportedly said, "My God, they are going to kill us all!"

He was wounded in the back, chest, thigh, and wrist. In order for the Warren Commission to pin the assassination on Oswald as the lone assassin, all of Connally's wounds had to be caused by the same bullet that supposedly caused the wounds to Kennedy's back and neck (the so-called magic bullet).

This theory is supported neither by the Zapruder film, which shows Connally holding onto his Stetson hat after Kennedy has been hit and after he supposedly had his wrist bone shattered, nor by Connally himself, who claims he heard the first shot and responded to it before he was hit.

Connally said, "They talk about the 'one-bullet' and the 'two-bullet theory,' but as far as I am concerned, there is no 'theory.' There is my absolute knowledge, and my wife's too, that one bullet caused the president's first wound, and that an entirely separate shot struck me."

If Kennedy's and Connally's wounds were caused by separate bullets, then more than one gunman had to have been firing from the rear. This likelihood, along with eyewitness evidence of shots coming from the front, would indicate at least three shooters.

Many researchers feel the shot or shots that struck Connally were fired from the roof of the Dallas County Records Building at the southeast corner of Elm and Houston Streets.

Metal traces in the threads of Governor Connally's coat at the point of entry may have helped to determine the source of the shots. Unfortunately, the coat was cleaned and pressed before it was delivered to the Warren Commission.

In 1969, as Jim Garrison was trying Clay Shaw in New Orleans for conspiracy to kill the president, he sought to question Sergio Arcacha Smith, who was in Dallas. Connally refused to extradite Smith.

Connally's first campaign manager, Eugene Locke, was also Mrs. J. D. (Marie) Tippit's attorney before the assassination.

Connally died on June 15, 1993, at age 76 at Methodist Hospital in Houston, Texas, from complications of pulmonary fibrosis. A day later, several assassination researchers—including James H. Lesar, the head of the nonprofit Assassination Archives and Research Center, and Cyril Wecht, a forensic pathologist and longtime vocal critic of the "magic bullet" theory—asked the U.S. Justice Department to try to recover the bullet fragments from Connally's wrist before the body was buried. They asked that neutron activation analysis and other tests be performed on the bullets to determine conclusively whether or not the fragments came from Warren Commission Exhibit 399 (the magic bullet). If the fragments did not come from that particular bullet, there would be proof for the first time that more than one gunman fired upon the Dallas motorcade. U.S. Attorney General Janet Reno forwarded the request to the FBI's Dallas field office for a determination.

On June 17 in what must have been a bizarre scene, the FBI—after determining that it favored the removal of the bullet fragments—decided to approach the Connally family about the matter *during* the funeral.

The FBI was angrily rejected by the family, who told the press through a representative that it was deeply offended by the FBI's methods. Connally's burial was held as planned.

The following day the FBI requested permission to exhume Connally's body. Again they were rejected by the family, who promised to "resist vigorously any efforts to disturb the body of John Connally."

Conservatism, U.S.A.   See "WELCOME, MR. KENNEDY" AD.

Corsa, Robert C.   See NAGELL, RICHARD CASE.

Corsican Mob

Christian David, a jailed French mobster, has publicly named fellow French gangster Lucien Sarti, now deceased, as one of the men who shot President Kennedy. David admits to being involved in CIA efforts in 1960–61 in the Congo to kill President Patrice Lumumba. David denies that he has ever received plastic surgery but says that all photos of him have been faked. David said Sarti was bald but always wore a wig when having his photo taken. Sarti was blind in his left eye from a car accident. According to David, all three gunmen in Dealey Plaza were Corsicans.

French mobster turned U.S. government informant Michel Nicoli corroborates these statements that three Corsican assassins killed JFK, one of whom was Lucien Sarti. Nicoli, who has been given a new identity by the U.S. government, made his statements on the 1988 television documentary *The Men Who Killed Kennedy,* produced by Nigel Turner. According to Nicoli, Sarti had wanted to shoot from the triple underpass but found it guarded on the morning of the assassination and so, instead, moved behind the wooden fence atop the grassy knoll. Nicoli says that Sarti fired the fatal shot using a frangible bullet. Nicoli and David agree that the assassins were paid in heroin. Nicoli converted the heroin into cash in his Buenos Aires apartment, not knowing what the payment was for. He says that the assassination was Mafia-sponsored and that, when the Corsican Mafia was thrown out of Cuba by Castro, they moved to Montreal where they established a heroin smuggling ring. According to Nicoli, it was the U.S. Mafia that hired Sarti. Sarti was reportedly killed by the Mexican police in 1972. According to assassination researcher Noel Twyman, Sarti met with General Edwin Walker during the spring of 1963 to discuss the training of anti-Castro Cubans.

On Nigel Turner's documentary, David said there were three Corsican assassins in Dealey Plaza but only mentioned Sarti by name because he is dead. He has written his entire knowledge of the assassination on a piece of paper and has sealed it inside an envelope. He gave the envelope to his lawyer, who is not to open it until David has been given his freedom. The information revealed in the documentary was originally discovered by assassination researcher Steve Rivele.

David says the three assassins were all members of the Corsican Mafia, hired in Marseilles in the fall of 1963. They were flown from Marseilles to Mexico City where they spent two or three weeks in the house of a contact. They were then driven from Mexico City to Brownsville, Texas, where they crossed the border and were picked up in Texas by a representative of the Chicago Mafia, with whom they conversed in Italian. They were then driven to Dallas and put up in a safe house. They spent several days photographing Dealey Plaza, carefully planning a crossfire.

He says two of the assassins were in buildings to the rear of the president, one high and one low (almost on the horizontal). There were four shots, the first from the rear striking Kennedy in the back, the second from the rear causing Governor Connally's wounds, the third shot, fired by Sarti from behind the wooden fence atop the grassy knoll, caused the president's fatal wound, and the fourth shot, fired from the rear, missed the car entirely. Earwitnesses heard only three shots because two of the shots were fired almost simultaneously.

In the panic that followed the assassination, David says, the three gunman had no trouble getting out of Dealey Plaza. They returned to their safe house where they remained for 10 days, before flying from Dallas to Montreal. From Montreal they returned to Marseilles.

David claims the assassins were paid in heroin. David's publicly disclosed information has been corroborated by former mobster turned U.S. government informant Michel Nicoli, who says he and David contemporaneously received the information.

Another Corsican suspect is Jean Rene Souetre, a French Secret Army Organization (OAS) terrorist who was in the area, according to a CIA document (no. 632-796) obtained in 1977 by independent researcher Mary Ferrell through the Freedom of Information Act, dated April 1, 1964. French Intelligence claimed Souetre was in Fort Worth, Texas, during the morning of November 22, 1963, and in Dallas that afternoon. According to French intelligence, Souetre was picked up by U.S. authorities in Texas within 48 hours of JFK's death and was immediately expelled from the country. Some theorize that Souetre's code name was QJ/WIN, and that he was a foreign national with Mafia connections recruited by the CIA to be part of its "assassination unit." According to Souetre's dentist, Souetre was about 35 years old at the time of the assassination, a ladies' man of ultra-right political persuasion. He stood six foot one and weighed 175 pounds. According to the late assassination investigator Bud Fensterwald, Souetre became head of OAS in Algeria during the summer of 1963 and is alleged to have been involved in a plot to kill President Charles de Gaulle in August 1962. Souetre's name games have rendered his trail muddy. Souetre used the pseudonym Michel Mertz and Michel Roux, both of which were the names of real people whose activities sometimes paralleled those of Souetre, at least in terms of location. Roux, in fact, was in Fort Worth, Texas, only a few miles from Dallas on the day of the assassination. When Souetre was asked what he was doing in Dallas on November 22, 1963, he said that it wasn't he but Michel Mertz, who was using his name.

(See also CONEIN, LUCIEN.)

Corso, Philip J.

U.S. Army colonel and former member of General Douglas MacArthur's intelligence staff following the Korean War. Corso was a witness to the famous Roswell UFO incident and claimed to have seen an alien body in a cargo hold in July 1947.

Corso retired from the U.S. Army in August 1963, and was, according to author Dick Russell, one of the first to spread rumors that Oswald had been working for a communist sect within the CIA.

Along with General Charles Willoughby, security chief for oil billionaire H. L. Hunt at the time of the assassination, Corso was a member of a right-wing fraternal organization known as The Sovereign Order of Saint John of Jerusalem, more popularly known as the "Shickshinny Knights," because they were headquartered in Shickshinny, Pennsylvania. The group claimed to be the original Knights of Malta, a fraternal order that dated back to the Crusades.

Regarding the Roswell incident, Corso described seeing a small body with pronounced eyes and almost no mouth floating in an unidentified liquid inside a box. Corso, in his book *The Day After Roswell*, claimed that much of today's state-of-the-art technology was back-engineered from materials confiscated at the site of the Roswell crash. These technologies included velcro, the microchip, and fiber optics. Corso claimed that, while he was working on the Army Research and Development's Foreign Technology Desk at the Pentagon, his boss—Lieutenant General Arthur G. Trudeau—put Corso in charge of artifacts from the Roswell crash. Corso said that the weapons buildup of the cold war was actually intended to defend the Earth against an invasion from outer space, and that the Strategic Defense Initiative was designed for the same purpose. He said that aliens were responsible for mutilating cattle, spying on military bases, human abductions, and the buzzing of manned space missions. The team of Corso and Birnes were said to be working on a book called *The Day After Dallas: Inside the Warren Commission*. Before that could be accomplished, however, Corso died at age 83 on July 16, 1998, of a heart attack in Palm Beach, Florida.

(See also WILLOUGHBY, CHARLES.)

Couch, Malcolm O.

WFAA-TV cameraman who rode in the motorcade in Camera Car 3, which was still on Houston Street, during the shooting. Couch was born in 1938 in Dallas, Texas. He began work for WFAA in 1955. He, and his fellow photographer with whom he was riding, Robert Jackson, saw a rifle barrel being withdrawn from the "sniper's nest" window.

The Warren Commission found six witnesses who said they saw a rifle protruding from a Texas School Book Depository window. Couch told the commission that Wes Wise, a KRLD employee, saw Ruby near the Book Depository soon after the assassination.

The Warren Commission refused to consider this testimony because it was hearsay, yet members didn't call Wise as a witness.

(See also POOL OF BLOOD.)

Courson, James W.

Dallas police motorcycle patrolman who rode a Harley-Davidson in the motorcade. Courson, a Marine who had served in Korea, told researcher Larry A. Sneed that at the time of the shooting he was on his motorcycle in the left lane on Houston Street facing the Texas School Book Depository.

Courson says he heard three shots but had difficulty determining their source because of the echoing. Despite this, he says he believes that they all came from the same location.

Courson says the first two shots were closer together with the second and third being further apart. He told Sneed that the presidential limousine came to a stop when Mrs. Kennedy climbed onto the back.

The stoppage allowed Secret Service agent Clint Hill to climb onto the limousine and push Mrs. Kennedy back into the limo's rear seat. The limo at that point, Courson observed, "took off at a high rate of speed."

Courson recalled the horrific scene at Parkland Hospital: "Two other officers and I helped take the President out of the car and put him onto the stretcher. From what I was able to see of the wound, the damage seemed to be in the right rear of his head, but it was hard to tell because there was so much blood. The back part of the skull seemed to be laying over the forehead. I didn't actually see an exit wound since I saw only the back part of the head."

Courson retired from the Dallas Police Department in 1979.

Crafard, Curtis LaVerne   See OSWALD LOOK-ALIKES.

Craig, Roger

Dallas County deputy sheriff Roger Craig filed this "supplementary Investigation Report" on November 23, 1963: "I was standing in front of the Sheriff's Office at 505 Main Street, Dallas, Texas, watching President Kennedy pass in the motorcade. I was watching the rest of the motorcade a few seconds after President Kennedy passed where I was standing when I heard a rifle shot and a few seconds later a second and then a third shot. At the retort of the first shot I started running around the corner and Officer Buddy Walthers and I ran across Houston Street and ran up the terrace [grassy knoll] on Elm Street and into the railroad yards. We made a round through the railroad yards and I returned to Elm Street by the Turnpike sign at which time Officer Walthers told me that a bullet had struck the curb on the south side of Elm Street. I crossed Elm with Deputy C. L. Lummie Lewis to search for a spot where a shell might have hit. About this time I heard a shrill whistle and saw a white male running down the hill from the direction of the Texas School Book Depository Building and I saw what I think was a light-colored Rambler station wagon with luggage rack on top pull over to the curb and this subject who had come running down the hill get into this car. The man driving this car was a dark complected white male. I tried to get across Elm Street to stop the car and talk with subjects, but traffic was so heavy I could not make it. I reported this incident at once to a secret service officer, whose name I do not know, then I left this area and went at once to the building and assisted in the search of this building. . . . Later that afternoon, I heard that the City had a suspect in custody and I called and reported the information about the suspect running down the hill and getting into the car to Captain Fritz and was requested to come at once to City Hall. I went to the City Hall and identified the subject they had in custody as being the same person I saw running down this hill and get into the station wagon and leave the scene."

Craig's observations are corroborated by an eyewitness to the aftermath of the assassination named Marvin C. Robinson, who was driving east on Elm Street through Dealey Plaza a few minutes after the shooting. In an FBI summary of his interview dated November 23, 1963, Robinson said that as he was driving past the Texas School Book Depository Building a "light-colored Nash station wagon suddenly appeared before him. He stated this vehicle stopped and a white male came down the grass-covered incline between the building and the street and entered the station wagon after which it drove away in the direction of the Oak Cliff section of Dallas."

The man running down the knoll, Craig said, was Oswald. Craig positively identified the man as Oswald after the alleged assassin's arrest. Craig told Captain Fritz his story, and Fritz asked Oswald, "What about the car?"

Oswald replied, "That station wagon belongs to Mrs. Paine [Marina Oswald's housemate, and the woman who got Oswald his job at the Texas School Book Depository]. Don't try to tie her in with this. She had nothing to do with it."

Ruth Paine did own a station wagon with a luggage rack on top, but it was not a Nash Rambler. When Craig testified before the Warren Commission, he was questioned by David Belin. Later Craig was shocked to find his testimony changed 14 times in the Warren Commission Hearings and Exhibits.

Craig was also with Deputy Sheriff Eugene Boone and Deputy Constable Seymour Weitzman when a rifle was found on the sixth floor of the School Book Depository. Craig, like the other two, said the rifle was a 7.65 Mauser. Craig became persona non grata after testifying for the Warren Commission about what he saw, including the Nash station wagon. He was eventually fired from the Dallas Sheriff's Department. In 1967, Craig traveled to New Orleans to serve as a prosecution witness at Clay Shaw's

assassination-conspiracy trial. Later that year, back in Dallas, a bullet grazed his head while he was walking to a parking lot. In 1973, a car forced Craig's car off the road and he severely injured his back. In 1974, he was shot again, this time by a shotgun in Waxahachie, Texas. Craig was told that the Mafia had put a price on his head. He died May 15, 1975, soon after appearing on a series of radio talk shows to discuss the assassination, of a "self-inflicted" gunshot wound. Shortly before his death, he was seriously injured when his car engine exploded.

When Craig first had an opportunity to read his Warren Commission testimony in the 26 volumes he was shocked to find that what was there differed from what he had said. He wrote down precisely what those differences were: "1) Arnold Rowland told me that he saw two men on the sixth floor of the Texas School Book Depository 15 minutes before the President arrived: one was a Negro, who was pacing back and forth by the southwest window. The other was a white man in the southeast corner, with a rifle equipped with a scope, and that a few minutes later he looked back and only the white man was there. In the Warren Commission: Both were white, both were pacing in front of the southwest corner and when Rowland looked back, both were gone. 2) I said the Rambler station wagon was light green. The Warren Commission: Changed to a white station wagon. 3) I said the driver of the Station Wagon had on a tan jacket. The Warren Commission: A white jacket. 4) I said the license plates on the Rambler were not the same color as Texas plates. The Warren Commission: Omitted the 'not' omitted but one word, an important one, so that it appeared that the license plates were the same color as Texas plates. 5) I said that I got a good look at the driver of the Rambler. The Warren Commission: I did not get a good look at the Rambler. 6) [In Captain Fritz's office] I had said that Fritz had said to Oswald, 'This man saw you leave' (indicating me). Oswald said, 'I told you people I did.' Fritz then said, 'Now take it easy, son, we're just trying to find out what happened', and then [to Oswald], 'What about the car?' to which Oswald replied, 'That station wagon belongs to Mrs. Paine. Don't try to drag her into this.' Fritz said 'car'—station wagon was not mentioned by anyone but Oswald. (I had told Fritz over the telephone that I saw a man get into a station wagon, before I went to the Dallas Police Department and I had also described the man. This is when Fritz asked me to come there). Oswald then said, 'Everybody will know who I am now;' The Warren Commission: Stated that the last statement by Oswald was made in a dramatic tone. This was not so. The Warren Commission also printed, 'Now everybody will know who I am', transposing the 'now.' Oswald's tone and attitude was one of disappointment. If someone were attempting to conceal his identity and he was found out, exposed—his cover blown, his reaction would be dismay and disappointment. This was Oswald's tone and attitude—disappointment at being exposed!"

(See also NASH RAMBLER.)

Craniotomy

According to Paul Groody, the undertaker who buried Lee Harvey Oswald, the top of Oswald's head had been sawed off at his autopsy when a craniotomy was performed. Groody also buried Oswald after his exhumation and claims that 1. the grave had been previously opened, and 2. the head had been severed from the body, and the head that was there had not received a craniotomy. Groody says that someone had dug up the body of Lee Harvey Oswald, if that was indeed who had been buried in the grave, and had switched heads. Questions about who is buried in Oswald's grave persist.

Craven, Thomas Joseph

CBS television cameraman who rode in the Dallas motorcade in Camera Car 1, a station wagon, which was the seventh vehicle in the motorcade. Craven was born in August 1930 in Queens, New York, and began to work for the Columbia Broadcasting System in February 1955. During the motorcade Craven held a 16mm FILMO Bell & Howell 70 DL movie camera with a three-turret lens system. The camera was loaded with Dupont 936 negative film with an ASA of 250. In 1985, Craven described what he saw and heard to researcher Richard B. Trask: "It was just as we were making the turn [onto Houston Street]. We thought it was a motorcycle backfiring." Regarding the number of shots, Craven said, "To tell the truth, I wouldn't be really positive. I could have sworn they were backfires."

Crawford, James N.

Assassination witness who stood on the southeast corner of Elm and Houston with fellow Dallas County deputy district clerk Mary Ann Mitchell. According to the *Warren Report:* "After the President's car turned the corner, Crawford heard a loud report which he thought was a backfire coming from the direction of the Triple Underpass. He heard a second shot seconds later, followed quickly by a third. At the third shot, he looked up and saw a 'movement' in the far east corner of the sixth floor of the Depository, the only open window on that floor. He told Miss Mitchell, 'that if those were shots they came from that window.'"

Asked to describe the "movement" by the Warren Commission, Crawford testified, "I would say it was a profile, somewhat from the waist up, but it was a very quick movement and rather indistinct and it was very light colored.

. . . When I saw it, I automatically in my mind came to the conclusion that it was a person having moved out of the window."

Crawford, John M.   See REDBIRD AIRPORT.

Crisman, Fred Lee (a.k.a. Gold, Jon)

Like Philip Corso, Crisman is another spooky figure that shows up both in the Kennedy assassination literature and in UFO tales. In the spring of 1947, Crisman, a former Army Air Corps captain who had flown during World War II, became a supervisor for the Puget Sound Harbor Patrol. On June 21 of that year, a man who worked for Crisman, Harold Dahl, reported seeing six "doughnut-shaped" UFOs above Maury Island that spewed silvery foil-like flakes along with a hot slag-like material along a beach over a wide area. The craft resembled designs seen on Nazi drawing boards and, according to *UFO* magazine, those designs were perhaps brought to the United States via Operation *Paperclip* (the recruitment, immediately following World War II of Nazi scientists, many considered war criminals, to carry out cutting edge scientific research in the United States). Three days later, on June 24, similar craft were spotted by U.S. marshall Kenneth Arnold flying near Mt. Rainier.

Crisman and Dahl got in touch with Arnold, told him about Dahl's sighting, and showed him a sample of the "slag." Arnold, according to researcher Jerome Clark, excitedly turned the material over to an Air Force Intelligence officer, who claims he recognized the material immediately as common aluminum.

In 1966–67, Crisman was subject to an Atomic Energy Act applicant investigation. The investigation turned up an FBI report regarding Crisman and an unnamed second man who, on August 7, 1947, only six weeks after Harold Dahl's UFO sighting, had picked up a "strange rock formation" on Maury Island, put it in a shoebox, and turned it in for chemical analysis, saying that it came from a "flying disk." The January 5, 1967, FBI report went on to say, "the applicant admitted that this statement was entirely false. . . . It is noted that a B-25 Army aircraft had crashed during the night of July 31, August 1, 1947, near Kelso, Washington, killing the pilot and co-pilot. It was also noted that the pilot and co-pilot had left McCord Field, Tacoma, and that they had called upon (name deleted) and CHRISMAN [sic] the preceding day and talked about the flying disk. Subsequent newspaper stories hinted that this B-25 was carrying fragments of the flying disk to Hamilton Field, California, and it was believed that this information had come from (name deleted) and the applicant."

The pilot and co-pilot killed in the August 1, 1947, crash, Capt. William L. Davidson and Lt. Frank M. Brown, were en route to Wright-Patterson Air Force Base. The army admitted that "classified" material had been aboard the plane. News reports hinted that the plane had crashed due to sabotage.

In August 1967, UFO researcher Gary Lesley claims to have received a letter from Dahl that read: "Crisman has been in the deep South for a long time . . . certain government agencies are very interested in his movements at all times. He sometimes drops out of sight for months on end and returns just as quietly. I do not know how he supports his manner of living, but he never lacks for money."

Crisman's name next became public on October 31, 1968, when he was subpoenaed by New Orleans Parish district attorney Jim Garrison to testify for the grand jury that would eventually send Clay Shaw to trial for conspiracy to assassinate President Kennedy. Garrison issued a press release along with the subpoena that read in part: "A Grand Jury subpoena was issued today . . . for . . Fred Lee Crisman from Tacoma, Washington. . . . Mr. Crisman has been engaged in undercover activity for a part of the industrial warfare complex for years. His cover is that of a 'preacher' and a person 'engaged in work to help gypsies.' . . . Our information indicates that since the early 1960's he has made many trips to the New Orleans and Dallas areas in connection with his undercover work for that part of the warfare industry engaged in the manufacture of what is termed, in military language, a 'hardware'—meaning those weapons sold to the U.S. Government which are uniquely large and expensive."

Jobs that Crisman held since the Maury Island UFO sighting include right-wing talk-show host, KAYE radio, Puyallup, Washington (using the name Jon Gold); president of a car lot; an official of six companies, none of which had an office; "industrial psychologist" for Boeing; bishop in the Universal Life Church (which also counted among its members another figure in the President Kennedy case, David Ferrie).

The precise reason why Garrison subpoenaed Crisman is open to conjecture. Crisman told the *Tacoma News Tribune* that he thought he had been subpoenaed because Garrison thought he knew something about fund raising for anti-Castro causes, money which Garrison suspected had been diverted to fund President Kennedy's assassination. A better theory is that Garrison suspected Clay Shaw, the man whom he eventually unsuccessfully prosecuted, and Crisman of being Office of Strategic Services agents involved in Operation *Paperclip*.

Judging from Crisman's involvement in the Maury Island sighting, it is possible that some of the technologies recruited in *Paperclip* remain secret to this day.

In the 1960s Crisman changed his story about Maury Island, now claiming that the tale was his way of reporting radioactive waste being dumped into the harbor by military aircraft. Crisman died December 10, 1975.

Croft, Robert Earl

Assassination witness who filmed the motorcade with an Argus C3 35mm camera loaded with a roll of 36-exposure Kodachrome-X daylight color slide film. Croft was a missionary from the Church of Jesus Christ of Latter-day Saints from Salt Lake City, Utah. During the late morning of November 22, 1963, Croft was waiting for a train at the Union Terminal a few blocks from Dealey Plaza. He said he went to see the parade on an impromptu basis, not knowing what was going on. After checking his bags into a locker in the terminal he walked to Dealey Plaza and took up a spot at the northwest corner of Main and Houston Streets. After the presidential limousine passed his position, he moved north to the south curb of Elm Street, across the street from the walkway and steps on the east side of the pergola.

Croft told researcher Richard B. Trask in 1988, "I can't tell you at this point anything about the shots, numbers, or where they were. I was on my way back, as I remember, before the car ever got—it was kind of going down a hill and under a railroad track. And I noticed what time it was and took off because I was going to be late for the train. I kind of jogged back to the station and got my baggage out of check and took off."

He boarded a train bound for Denver. The following day, realizing what he had filmed, Croft turned his film over to the Denver FBI. Croft believed that he had taken a photo during the shooting sequence, but when the FBI had the film developed at the Kodak laboratory, frame number 18, the photo taken during the shooting sequence, was blank. Only photos taken before and after the shooting came out.

Cuban Revolutionary Council

The Cuban Revolutionary Council was housed in the same building as Guy Banister Associates. One-time secretary for Publicity and Propaganda for the Cuban Revolutionary Council was Carlos Bringuier, who once got into a street scuffle with Oswald.

(See also ALPHA 66; ARCACHA SMITH, SERGIO; D.R.E.)

Curry, Jesse Edward "Jay"

Curry was the chief of police for the Dallas Police Department at the time of the assassination. He appeared on local TV on the morning of the assassination and said that he wanted no incidents during JFK's visit. He asked the good citizens of Dallas to notify the police if they heard of anyone threatening to create an unpleasant demonstration.

Curry drove the lead car, an enclosed sedan, at the head of the motorcade at the time of the shooting. Moments after the shooting, he called into his microphone, "Get a man on that overpass and see what happened up there."

Curry accompanied Lyndon Johnson from Parkland Hospital to Love Field, and stayed by the new president's side through LBJ's swearing in on Air Force One.

Curry was a political animal more than a law enforcement officer. He had been an all-state football player at Crozier Tech High School in Dallas and reportedly chose his drinking buddies carefully, being chummy with those who could get him ahead in the world.

Rumored to have had a drinking problem at the time of the assassination, Curry could not be reached on the night following the assassination because his home phone had been taken off the hook, reportedly by his wife.

The next day, Curry told reporters he could tell by the sound of the shots that they had come from the Texas School Book Depository, a reversal of his original opinion. This was not the last time Curry was forced to flip-flop, as the evidence seemed to change beneath him. He later wrote that the *Warren Report* had "yielded to political pressure." Curry, after viewing the Zapruder film, agreed with Governor Connally that Connally and JFK had been struck by separate bullets.

Curry attended the meetings that determined the motorcade route and later wrote that most of the decisions were made by Secret Service agent Winston G. Lawson.

Just before Ruby shot Oswald, Curry was taken out of the security picture. "I was called to take a phone call from Dallas Mayor Cabell in my office," Curry wrote.

Curry's book about the assassination (*JFK Assassination File,* American Poster and Publishing Co., 1969) was the first to publish photos of an FBI agent picking something up out of the grass in Dealey Plaza following the shooting (a bullet perhaps) and marks made on curbstones by bullets that are officially unaccounted for.

Curry did not believe that Oswald acted alone, or acted at all, for that matter. "We don't have any proof that Oswald fired the rifle, and never did. Nobody's yet been able to put him in [the Texas School Book Depository] with a gun in his hand," he once said to interviewer Tom Johnson. In his own book, Curry wrote that "the physical evidence and eyewitness accounts do not clearly indicate what took place on the sixth floor . . . the testimony of the people who watched the motorcade was much more confusing than the press or the Warren Commission seemed to indicate."

Curry joined the Dallas police on May 1, 1936. He retired under pressure at age 52 on March 10, 1966. He suffered a stroke in 1978, and died in his sleep on June 22, 1980.

Curtain Rods   See FRAZIER, BUELL WESLEY.

Curtis, Willard   See SCOTT, WINSTON.

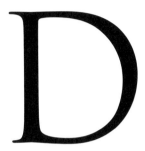

Dale, Bobby Joe

Dale, who had served in the U.S. Navy during the Korean War, was a nine-year veteran of the Dallas Police Department in 1963. Dale rode a solo motorcycle in the presidential motorcade.

Dale recalls that he had just turned off Main Street and had proceeded perhaps 30 feet onto Houston when he heard the first loud report. He says his motorcycle was in the right lane on Houston and at first it didn't occur to him that the loud sound was a shot.

"At first I thought it was a backfire," he told researcher Larry A. Sneed. "But then I heard rapid succession. . . . It just wasn't possible to tell where they were coming from."

Dale recalled the scene at Parkland Hospital, "I went over to the limousine and saw a Secret Service man starting to put the top up. 'Help me secure this,' he said, since it was heavy and in sections. Blood and matter was everywhere inside the car including a bone fragment which was oblong shaped, probably an inch to an inch and a half long by three-quarters of an inch wide. As I turned it over and looked at it, I determined that it came from some part of the forehead because there was hair on it which appeared to be near the hairline. There were other fragments around, but that was the largest piece that grabbed my attention. What stood out in my mind was that there was makeup up to the hairline. Apparently he had used makeup for the cameras to knock down the glare."

Dale retired from the Dallas Police Department in 1981, and he went on to become an assistant chief with the Dallas County Sheriff's Department, a position from which he retired in 1985.

Dal-Tex Building

Building at the northeast corner of Elm and Houston Streets, directly across Houston from the Texas School Book Depository. When it was built in 1902 it was known as the Kingman-Texas Implement Company Building. The building was owned at the time of the assassination by Morris J. Russ and D. R. Weisblat. The sixth floor of the Dal-Tex Building housed the offices of Dallas Uranium and Oil. Abraham Zapruder's offices were on the fourth and fifth floors. This is the building where assassination suspect Eugene Hale Brading was found by a security guard "in the building without a good reason." The building is currently known by its address, 501 Elm Street.

(See also BRADING, EUGENE HALE; DEALEY PLAZA; ZAPRUDER, ABRAHAM.)

Davidson, Alfred Jr.

Self-confessed assassin Luis Castillo claimed that he was the man who shot President Kennedy from the Texas School Book Depository and that he was instructed to shoot the man sitting next to the woman with red roses. Although it is true that Jackie Kennedy was the only woman in the motorcade carrying red roses—all of the others were given yellow ones—considering the fact that the First Lady was wearing a shocking pink dress and pillbox hat designed by New York fashion designer Oleg Cassini to be seen from far away, the color of the flowers she was carrying seems irrelevant. A sniper, probably not Luis Castillo, would only need to know the color of Jackie's dress to identify immediately which car contained President Kennedy and Governor Connally.

But how would the conspirators know the color of the dress in advance?

This leads us to Alfred Davidson Jr., a representative of Cassini's, who happened to be an acquaintance of Jack Ruby. Davidson and Ruby met in September 1963 through the credit manager at the Neiman-Marcus Department Store in Dallas. Davidson, who visited Dallas to promote Cassini's radio show *The World of Fashion,* was given a tour of the city by Ruby and even visited Ruby's Carousel Club. Davidson told the FBI that Ruby called him on the telephone a day or two before the assassination. Davidson was not asked if the color of Jackie's dress was discussed. Davidson also volunteered that Ruby had told him that he had friends and financial interests in Las Vegas and Los Angeles, he had a press pass on his car, carried a "police pass," and carried a revolver in his glove compartment for which he had no permit.

Davis, Bruce Frederick

According to a document approved for release in the 1994 CIA Historical Review Program: In August 1960 Davis deserted his Marine unit, left his car and belongings on the Bavarian-East German border, and crossed over, intending to defect to the Soviet Union. As his motive he stated racial prejudice and America's insincere attempts to make peace. He was described as an "unstable and insecure drifter type who, though likable, could never get ahead." Davis was taken to East Berlin and kept there for five weeks at which time he was allowed to enter the Soviet Union as a student at Kiev Institute of National Economy. He did not renounce his U.S. citizenship and did not legally expatriate himself. He was classified a "stateless resident." In October 1960, Davis was attending school, had a free dormitory room, and was receiving 900 old rubles per month, which was three times what Soviet students received but normal for non-Soviet students. During October 1960 several Soviet newspapers printed stories saying Davis had defected because of his disillusionment with U.S. military policy. In the spring of 1961 Davis made several unauthorized trips to Moscow, flying there and back, and was finally caught and reprimanded by his school. That summer he tried to hitchhike to the Crimea but was picked up by police. In February 1962 he made an eight-day unauthorized trip to Yalta and was not caught. In April 1962 he made an unauthorized weekend trip to Zhitomir and was not caught.

Is there, or was there a document monitoring Lee Harvey Oswald's "unauthorized" travels in the Soviet Union?

Davis, Thomas Eli, III

Davis ran guns and jeeps to Cuba with Ruby. He first approached Ruby to make pornographic films. Just before the assassination, Davis had been running guns in Algeria. In December 1963, Davis was jailed in Tangiers for running guns. While in jail, Davis said that he had information regarding Lee Harvey Oswald and Lyndon Johnson. He was soon thereafter released through the efforts of a CIA agent code-named QJ/WIN, who was working under the auspices at the time of William King Harvey and his ZR/RIFLE (assassination) operation. After Ruby's arrest, his lawyer asked Ruby if there was anyone who could hurt his defense that he killed Oswald spontaneously. Davis's was the only name Ruby mentioned. Davis died in September 1973, electrocuted while stealing wire from a warehouse.

(See also CENTRAL INTELLIGENCE AGENCY.)

Davison, Captain Alexis

Captain in the U.S. Air Force and reported contact man for at least one alleged U.S. spy within the Soviet Union. In 1962, Captain Davison was the assistant air attaché and doctor at the U.S. embassy in Moscow. In that capacity he gave Marina Oswald a physical as part of the preparation for her to go to the United States. Davison admitted to the FBI that he spoke to Lee and Marina Oswald at the end of May 1962, just before they left the USSR. He said that he befriended the couple and told them that, when they returned to the United States, they should visit his mother in Atlanta, Georgia. Perhaps coincidentally, when the Oswalds did return to the United States, their flight from New York to Dallas made a stopover in Atlanta, although only to drop off and pick up passengers. After Oswald's death, the name and address of Davison's mother were found in Oswald's address book. The story is made more intriguing by the fact that, on October 22, 1961, when Colonel Oleg Penkovskiy was arrested by the Soviets and charged with spying for the United States and Great Britain, a list of Penkovskiy's contacts included the name Alexis Davison. Some have theorized that the Oswalds were actually delivering packages to "Davison's mother" when they stopped in Atlanta, noting that the couple had seven pieces of luggage when they arrived in New York, but only two when they arrived in Dallas.

Day, J. Carl

Dallas police lieutenant in the Crime Scene Search Section who joined the department in 1940. Day spent three years in the U.S. Navy during World War II before returning to the Dallas Police Department. Day says he saw "just three" spent shells near the window through which the assassin theoretically fired. Day put fingerprint powder on the shells. In a move that defies all police procedure, Day says that he gave one of the shells to one of Captain Will Fritz's detectives and kept the other two. He marked only the two he kept. He does not explain why he separated the evidence, but this supposedly explains the fact that there were early reports that only two shells had been found. Day says that he was the first to actually touch the rifle that had been discovered on the Texas School Book Depository's sixth floor. Day took photographs of the rifle, noted its serial number (C-2766), and marked the evidence by scratching his name on the stock. Day later said that he saw no identifying marks on the rifle and did not identify it as a Mauser or anything else. Back at police headquarters, at the Identification Bureau where there was a room for locking up evidence, Day locked up the rifle in a box to which only he and Captain Doughty had a key. After locking up the rifle, Day returned to the Book Depository's sixth floor, where he saw the boxes stacked like a sniper's nest. Day is careful to point out that he cannot vouch for the fact that this was the configuration of the boxes at the time of the shooting. As Day notes, "There had been a lot of prowling around up there."

While testifying to the Warren Commission about the palm print reportedly found on the rifle, Day said, "No, sir, I could not make a positive identification of these prints."

Day retired from the Dallas Police Department in 1977.

(See also MANNLICHER-CARCANO.)

Dead Secret Service Agent

From moments following the assassination to the present, there has persisted, especially in Dallas, a rumor that a Secret Service agent was killed in Dallas on November 22, 1963, but that the death for some reason has been covered up. Here is the evidence.

Reporter Seth Kantor told the Warren Commission that, while he was at Parkland Hospital during the hour after JFK was shot, he heard a nurse ask a Western Union man if the rumors of a Secret Service man being killed were true. The Western Union man, who had been traveling with the press, said that it was.

On February 21, 1968, a woman who signed her name Amy Britvar of Turtle Creek Boulevard in Dallas wrote a letter to New Orleans district attorney Jim Garrison that said: "A Mr. Robertson, Assistant Director of the Dallas or Fort Worth Secret Service Office confided to [deleted] in 1963 that a plot to kill President Kennedy was planned and he did not want any part of it. On November 22, 1963, my friend was in the office of Mr. Robertson when all phones began to ring, about the time Kennedy was arriving at [Fort Worth's] Carswell Air Force Base, Mr. Robertson then said, 'Well, this is it,' and left the office. Since that time Mr. Robertson's family of seven children and wife have not seen or heard from him, yet his paychecks continue to be mailed to his home."

Investigating the rumor in 1965, assassination researchers J. Gary Shaw and Penn Jones Jr. found that a man named Robertson had been in Dallas in 1963 posing as a postal inspector. Their report continues: "We also learned from newsmen that something unusual did happen [in the motorcade] on Harwood [Street] shortly before the turn to Main Street. No one wanted credit for this, but we were told by reliable newsmen that a man jumped in front of Kennedy's car on Harwood shouting 'Stop, I must tell you.'" The man, according to their report, "was promptly wrestled to the ground and hustled away."

On November 17, 1980, Joseph G. Forrester of the U.S. Customs Service sent a letter to Attorney General Benjamin R. Civiletti that read, in part: "My interest in the Kennedy murder started in 1966 when I met an Air Force Master Sergeant at St. Albans Naval Hospital, Queens, N.Y. This sergeant, an elderly man, was suffering from terminal cancer. He stated on November 22, 1963 he was attached to Air Force One as an electronics technician. He further stated that after the President was shot a message was received over a military frequency that multiple assassins had attacked the President . . . a Secret Service agent, Mr. Robertson, stationed in the Dallas-Fort Worth area disappeared on November 22, 1963 yet his family still receives his paychecks. The disappearance of an individual is not unusual except that it has been said that Mr. Robertson became aware of an assassins' plot against the President. An assassin plot had been unearthed in Chicago a short time before President Kennedy's Dallas trip."

On January 31, 1967, assassination researcher Vince Salandria interviewed a U.S. Navy nurse named Rita Rollins, who said, "The name of the person in Dallas . . . is Inez Robertson. Chuck Robertson, her husband, was at the post office. . . . Inez [who had knowledge of an assassination plot] actually saw them make a breakdown of the rifles. This tall man with long grey or white hair, he was in the station wagon. It was a Rambler station wagon. This fellow with the mixed grey hair carried [the armed men] to the airport. . . . This tall man had been around Dallas the day before the assassination. . . . This episode has caused friction between Chuck Robertson and Inez Robertson. He is not in Dallas now."

(See also NASH RAMBLER STATION WAGON.)

Dead Witnesses   See SUSPICIOUS DEATHS.

Dealey Plaza

Landscaped plaza at the western edge of downtown Dallas, 3.07 acres in size—named after George Bannerman Dealey (1859–1946), founder of the *Dallas Morning News*—where President Kennedy was assassinated.

The land that would later become the site of JFK's death was originally claimed by John Neely Bryan, a Tennessee-born lawyer, as part of a bluff overlooking the "three-forks" area of the Trinity River. Bryan sold the land nine years later when he headed west in search of gold.

The "Old Red" Courthouse, just southeast of the plaza, was completed in 1892. The land was the site of the first fraternal lodge in Dallas. The Dal-Tex Building at 501 Elm was built in 1902 by the John Deere Plow Company. The Dallas Criminal Courts Building was constructed in 1913 and the Dallas County Records Building was erected in 1922.

In 1916, the Trinity River was dredged and its course was altered by a mile. Railroad tracks were built to accommodate the Dallas Union Terminal Building, just south of the site of the plaza.

The plaza was designed in 1939 by the landscape architecture firm of Hare and Hare. It was built in 1940 by Works Progress Administration workers. Main and Commerce Streets, which formerly went straight, curved inward and joined Main Street in the middle.

Earth was dug out so that the three streets could go under a single railroad bridge called the "triple underpass." Officially known as the Union Terminal Company Underpass, the triple underpass was built by the Texas Highway Department with the Austin Road and Bridge Company as contractors. The hole dug to create the triple underpass created two landscaped slopes—grassy knolls—on the north and south side. The assassination occurred on the north side.

Each grassy knoll had a pergola. Opposite the Texas School Book Depository Building on the north and the Post Office Annex on the south were peristyles, each with a nearby pool.

To prevent flooding under the triple underpass a storm sewer system was constructed. One storm drain leads from a point at the northeast corner of the triple underpass. That drain leads to a spot on the south side of Commerce Street.

On November 22, 1993, the 30th anniversary of the assassination, Dealey Plaza, including the triple underpass and the railroad tracks north of the yard, were dedicated as a National Historic Landmark District.

At the ends of the triple underpass, on either side, hard up against the east side of the bridge, were storm-drain openings large enough for a man to crawl inside. The opening on the south side has been paved over since the assassination. But assassination researcher Jack Brazil has climbed down into the opening on the north side of the bridge, at a location very close to where some thought shots originated. The drain pipe led Brazil under Elm, Main, and Commerce Streets and returned him above ground southwest of Dealey Plaza not far from the location

of the car dealership known in 1963 as Downtown Lincoln-Mercury.

(See also DAL-TEX BUILDING; DOWNTOWN LINCOLN-MERCURY; TEXAS SCHOOL BOOK DEPOSITORY.)

Dean, Harry (a.k.a. Fallon, Harry)

Dean was an undercover FBI operative from 1960–65. His assignment was to infiltrate the John Birch Society, which he came to view as a subsidiary of an evil empire known as The Church of Jesus Christ of Latter-day Saints.

During his undercover assignment Dean discovered several John Birch Society operations, including a planned assassination of President Kennedy in Mexico City in 1962 that did not occur and the assassination in Dallas.

Dean claims that all three plots involved John Rousselot, then the western director of the John Birch Society and later a Republican congressman representing San Marino. The meeting place for all anti-Kennedy activities was at a residence on San Pierre Street in El Monte, California, headquarters of the Covina Birch Society.

Plans were carried out with the cooperation of anti-Castro Cubans, with whom the Birchers interfaced through the "Drive against Communist Aggression," an organization funded by the John Birch Society, which held meetings both in California and Mexico.

The Mexican director was Guy "Gabby" Gabaldin. The U.S. director was Ray Flieshman of Whittier, California. Other active members, according to Dean, were Dave Robbins, then a high-ranking official of the Fluor Corporation, headed by J. Robert Fluor, a known political ally of John Rousselot.

During his undercover stint Dean observed on many occasions the activities of Loran Hall and Lawrence Howard, and knew them to be close associates of General Edwin Walker, the right-winger at whom Lee Harvey Oswald is alleged to have taken a shot. (See ODIO INCIDENT.)

Dean says that Walker, Rousselot, Hall, Howard, and Dean planned to frame Lee Harvey Oswald, whom they believed to be a communist, as President Kennedy's assassin. The men last met in October 1963 at the San Pierre Street home, each carrying arms, medicines, and the plans to implicate Oswald.

Other men Dean claims were involved in the plans to assassinate President Kennedy were Ed Peters and Ed Butler.

According to assassination researcher W. R. Morris: "[Dean's] knowledge of the true facts behind the president's assassination has caused him and his family to live in constant hell. . . . Born in Cuba, Dean joined

Castro's guerrillas in the revolution against Batista and kept U.S. Intelligence informed as to the Cuban leader's activities. On returning to the United States he monitored the Fair Play for Cuba Committee, becoming secretary of local committees in Chicago, Detroit, and Los Angeles. Later, he joined the John Birch Society where, in 1962, he learned of a conspiracy to assassinate the president."

Dean told Morris—and later Tom Snyder, host of NBC-TV's *The Tomorrow Show*, on an episode that never aired—that two of the gunmen hired by the John Birch Society to kill President Kennedy were Eladio del Valle and Loran Hall.

Dean said in a 1977 interview that the John Birch Society had a heavily armed network of citizen soldiers ready to take to the streets in 1963 and early 1964 if President Johnson attempted a thorough investigation of President Kennedy's assassination.

(See also HALL, LORAN; SUSPICIOUS DEATHS.)

Dean, Patrick Trevore

Dallas Police sergeant who interviewed Jack Ruby on November 26, 1963. Dean later told the Warren Commission that Ruby had told him he had entered the Dallas police headquarters basement to shoot Oswald via the Main Street ramp and that he had decided to kill Oswald two days before the event. This second statement is in direct contrast to Ruby's later claim (and the Warren Commission's conclusion) that Ruby had spontaneously decided to shoot Oswald—a decision the commission made in part because it did not want to interfere with Ruby's defense at his murder trial, then underway. Dean said that all the basement entrances were locked and guarded, so that—contrary to some claims—Ruby must have entered via the ramp.

A longtime friend of Ruby, Dean failed a polygraph examination regarding Lee Harvey Oswald's death, despite the fact that he got to write his own questions.

According to Anthony Summers, "Years earlier [Dean] had been on good terms with Joe Civello, the Dallas Mafia figure widely acknowledged to have been the Texas representative for [assassination suspect] Carlos Marcello."

According to Dallas police accident investigator Edgar L. Smith, a colleague of Dean's, Dean was known as a lady's man and quite a drinker. Smith says that, although Dean spent time in the Carousel Club enjoying the striptease acts, he doubted that this translated into any connection with organized crime.

Following Ruby's murder trial, Ruby's lawyers asked for a retrial on the grounds that Dean had perjured himself when he testified that Ruby had admitted to premeditating Oswald's killing.

Dean, Ruth

Bookkeeper and cashier for the MacMillan Company with offices on the third floor of the Texas School Book Depository. She watched the shooting from the front steps of the Depository.

She told researcher Larry A. Sneed, "The view from where we were was very good. But the motorcade went a little bit beyond us before the shooting started. I heard three shots with two being close together and one a little further apart. . . . When the President was hit, apparently I wasn't able to see because some of the tree trunks were at that point. I wasn't able to tell where the shots were coming from. The sounds seemed to reverberate from the buildings around that particular location. . . . We continued to stand there because it was so quick when all three had been fired, and then we decided we needed to hurry on because the bank was going to be closing. So we went on to the bank, made the deposit, had our lunch, and came back."

"Dear Mr. Hunt" Letter

Dated "Nov. 8, 1963", the note read, in its entirety: "Dear Mr. Hunt, I would like information concerding [sic] my position. I am asking only for information. I am suggesting that we discuss the matter fully before any steps are taken by me or anyone else. Thank you. [signed] Lee Harvey Oswald."

This letter, apparently sent to Texas oil billionaire H. L. Hunt, can be traced back only to John Curington, an aide to H. L. Hunt who is alleged by LBJ's mistress Madeleine Brown to have had foreknowledge of JFK's assassination. Curington, it is said, gave the letter to assassination researcher Penn Jones Jr. The letter, it is said, bears a Mexican postmark.

According to FBI handwriting experts the letter was, in fact, written by Lee Harvey Oswald.

According to former KGB officer Vasily Mitrokhin, in his book *The Sword and the Shield*, written with Christopher Andrew, the letter was a KGB plant designed to incriminate CIA agent E. Howard Hunt.

(See also HUNT, E. HOWARD; HUNT, H. L.)

Decker, J. E. (Bill)

Legendary Dallas County sheriff—it was Decker's tip that resulted in the police ambush on bank robbers Bonnie Parker and Clyde Barrow in East Louisiana on May 23, 1934. He was once described in 1946 as an "old bootlegger."

Decker rode in the backseat of the motorcade's lead car. With him were the driver, Police Chief Jesse Curry, Winston G. Lawson, sitting in the front passenger seat, and Forrest Sorrels, who sat to Decker's right in the backseat.

After the shooting, Sheriff Decker ordered "move all available men out of my office into the railroad yard . . . and hold everything secure until Homicide and other investigators should get there."

Dallas police captain Will Fritz's first questioning of Oswald on the afternoon of the 22nd was interrupted by a phone call from Sheriff Decker. Whatever Decker needed to talk to Fritz about, it couldn't be discussed on the phone. Fritz left Dallas police headquarters and walked 15 blocks to Decker's office. After the pair had their meeting, topic unknown, Fritz returned to resume the questioning.

According to Penn Jones Jr., crack shot and Deputy Sheriff Harry Weatherford, who, Jones writes, had received a custom-made silencer for his rifle several weeks before the assassination, had been ordered by Sheriff Decker to stand atop the Dallas County Jail during the presidential motorcade—which is very suspicious indeed since this location is suspected by some as having been the source of the shots that struck Governor Connally.

On the morning of the 22nd, Decker ordered his deputies to "take no part whatsoever in the security of the presidential motorcade."

Decker, who had a glass eye, died on August 29, 1969, of emphysema.

Decoy Hearse

It has long been the contention of assassination researcher David Lifton and others that the coffin removed from Air Force One and placed in a waiting ambulance at Andrews Air Force Base on the evening of November 22, 1963, was empty. The president's body, he theorized, was taken off the jet out of the television camera's view. Confirmation of this portion of Lifton's theory comes from a House Select Committee on Assassinations report of an interview of Lieutenant Richard A. Lipsey on January 18, 1978, by committee staff members Donald Andrew Purdy Jr. and T. Mark Flanagan Jr. in which Lipsey reportedly said that, in his capacity as aide to General Wehle, he had met President Kennedy's body at Andrews Air Force Base. The report stated that Lipsey "placed [the casket] in a hearse to be transported to Bethesda Naval Hospital. Lipsey mentioned that he and Wehle then flew by helicopter to Bethesda and took the President's body into the back of Bethesda. A decoy hearse had been driven to the front." A decoy hearse carrying an empty casket.

Del Valle, Eladio   See SUSPICIOUS DEATHS.

DeMohrenschildt, Sergei "George" S.
A White Russian count with a background in intelligence, DeMohrenschildt and his wife befriended Lee and Marina Oswald following the Oswalds' return from the Soviet Union. He had been employed in 1956 by Pantetic Oil Company, owned by the family of William Buckley. DeMohrenschildt, who said he enjoyed ice skating, was involved in CIA training for the Bay of Pigs invasion in Guatemala. He lived in Haiti at the time of President Kennedy's death.

Getting in touch with Oswald, DeMohrenschildt later wrote, was the idea of J. Walton Moore, the head of the CIA's Dallas office. When George and his wife went on an extended "walking tour" of Central America, in particular to Guatemala, he was debriefed by Moore upon his return. Late in life, DeMohrenschildt claimed Moore had told him about Oswald while Oswald was still in the Soviet Union. Moore told him, DeMohrenschildt said, that Oswald was an ex-Marine working in a Minsk electronics factory. Moore said he was interested in Oswald. Moore told DeMohrenschildt that Oswald would be returning to Dallas and asked him to "keep an eye on him" when he did. During the summer of 1962 an associate of Moore's gave DeMohrenschildt Oswald's address in Fort Worth. DeMohrenschildt approached the Oswald home first when Lee was not there. Talking to Marina alone, the story goes, he told Marina his memories of Minsk, where they had both lived. Marina was very drawn to DeMohrenschildt so, when George met Lee, Marina was hoping they would become friends. DeMohrenschildt convinced Lee to write a "detailed memoir" of his experiences in the Soviet Union, and when Oswald did so, DeMohrenschildt turned it over to the CIA.

DeMohrenschildt urged the Oswalds to move to Dallas, which they did, and to mingle with the Dallas Soviet emigré community, many of whom were right-wing "solidarists" who had sided with the Nazis against the communists. Before seriously befriending Oswald, DeMohrenschildt later said that he again talked with Moore. Moore had said that Oswald was okay. "He is just a harmless lunatic," DeMohrenschildt quoted Moore as saying.

DeMohrenschildt even encouraged the Oswalds to move in briefly with his daughter Alexandra and 23-year-old son-in-law, Gary E. Taylor. Marina and June Oswald lived with the Taylors for three days (October 8–10, 1962) while Lee looked for work. This was the first of many times Lee and Marina Oswald would live apart during their marriage. Gary Taylor told the Warren Commission of DeMohrenschildt's tremendous influence over Oswald, adding "If there was any assistance or plotters in the assassination . . . it was, in my opinion, most probably the DeMohrenschildts." Taylor also said that DeMohrenschildt was in Guatemala while the Bay of Pigs troops were being trained there. The Taylors were of interest to the Warren Commission because, when Alec Hidell ordered the

Mannlicher-Carcano that was allegedly used in the assassination, he gave the address of the Taylors as his own.

Two members of the Russian-speaking community in Dallas—Igor and Natasha Voshinin—said that during DeMohrenschildt's last days in Dallas before moving to Haiti, he told the other Russians that Oswald had a rifle and had taken a "potshot" at General Edwin Walker. The DeMohrenschildts moved to Haiti on April 19, 1963. Five days later Marina Oswald moved into Ruth Paine's home in Irving, Texas.

The count, who apparently worked for the Nazis during World War II, said that Oswald spoke "almost flawless Russian." He wrote that Oswald's handgun was a "Beretta," not at all like the gun reportedly found on him in the Texas Theatre.

DeMohrenschildt once worked for a Murchison oil company, Three States Oil and Gas, and was reportedly friends with Ruth Paine's father. He knew oil billionaire H. L. Hunt and future director of central intelligence and U.S. president George Bush through his oil business.

The fact that DeMohrenschildt was an educated man of foreign nobility who has been linked to the Bay of Pigs operation, had ties with the Bouviers, Jacqueline Kennedy's family, has been suspected of being a spy, and was a close friend of Oswald casts serious doubt on the Warren Commission's portrait of Oswald as a "lone nut."

According to Cindy Adams in the *New York Post* (February 12, 1992), DeMohrenschildt was once engaged to Jacqueline Bouvier's Aunt Michele, and "nearly married [Jackie's mother] Janet Auchincloss. . . . President Kennedy's widow called him Uncle George."

Jackie's first cousin Edie Beale is quoted by Adams as saying, "We all knew George. He was a regular visitor. As a child Jackie played on the lawn with Uncle George."

According to Adams, Jackie's brother Jack said, "George took Janet out during the time she was divorcing Jackie's father. George was very much a potential stepfather to Jackie. He wanted to marry Janet, but Janet wanted a very rich man."

In 1976 he wrote a manuscript, called *I Am a Patsy! I Am a Patsy!*, which he claimed named names. Later he said, "That's when disaster struck. You see, in that book I played devil's advocate. Without directly implicating myself as an accomplice in the assassination I still mentioned a number of names, particularly of FBI and CIA officials who apparently may not be exposed under any circumstances. I was drugged surreptitiously. As a result I was committed to a mental hospital." On the day he agreed to an interview with the House Select Committee on Assassinations, he was found dead of a gunshot to the mouth, an apparent suicide. George's wife Jeanne said that, before he was committed to Parkland Hospital for mental problems, he was under the medical care of Dr. Charles

George DeMohrenschildt. *(AP/Wide World Photos)*

Mendoza, a "shadowy" Dallas doctor who gave him two or three hours of therapy at a time that included injections.

Jeanne, who in the early 1950s had worked for Abraham Zapruder, believed her husband was a mind-control experiment victim, and that his suicide death was triggered by a phone call command. He was forced to spend eight weeks in a mental institution and was given electroshock treatments. Near the end, he was ranting and raving about his World War II experiences, saying, "The Jews have finally caught up with me."

A Dutch journalist named Willem Oltmans claimed that DeMohrenschildt, during the last days of his life, confessed to him that he had been part of an unnamed "Dallas conspiracy" comprised of oil billionaires and anti-Castro Cubans. The conspiracy had had "a blood debt to settle," and that Lee Harvey Oswald took commands from DeMohrenschildt as part of the conspiracy.

DeMohrenschildt died on March 30, 1977, in Palm Beach, Florida, of an apparent suicide just after he was located by reporters and investigators from the House Select Committee on Assassinations.

(See CENTRAL INTELLIGENCE AGENCY; MK/ULTRA; OSWALD, LEE HARVEY; WHITE RUSSIANS; ZAPRUDER, ABRAHAM.)

Dillard, Thomas Clinton

Assassination witness Dillard was born in Fort Worth, Texas, on October 26, 1914. In 1963 Dillard was chief photographer for the *Dallas Morning News*. He rode in a motorcade press car, five cars behind President Kennedy's limo. He carried two cameras, a small Leica F with wide-angle 28mm lens, and a 35mm Yashica.

Years later, Dillard remembered, "The sad thing news-wise was the custom always was that a selected group of press people—photographers—were to ride a flatbed truck in front of the president. That was standard procedure in all presidential parades. I was one of the selected photographers. I was the head man at my paper. . . . It was understood the flatbed was going to be there. But at the last moment it was canceled. We bounced around and ended up on one of those Chevrolet convertibles." That was the car known as Camera Car 3.

Dillard told the Warren Commission, "We had an absolutely perfect view of the School Depository from our position in the open car and Bob Jackson said, 'There's a rifle barrel up there.' I said, 'Where?' I had my camera ready. He said, 'It's in that open window.' Of course, there were several open windows and I scanned the building. . . . He said it was the second from the top on the right-hand side, and I swung to it, and there were two figures below. . . . We were getting a reverberation which made it difficult to pinpoint the actual direction, but my feeling was that it was coming into my face and that I was facing north towards the School Depository. . . . I very definitely smelled gunpowder when the car moved up at the corner (of Houston and Elm)." Dillard was about 50 yards away from the Texas School Book Depository on Houston Street at the time of the shooting sequence. Dillard said he heard three shots, equally spaced. Dillard took two pictures of the Texas School Book Depository after the third shot. Dillard's photo of the sniper's nest window immediately after the shooting shows boxes and shadows in that window. Comparing this photo with one taken 30 seconds later by James Powell gives the impression that the boxes in the sniper's nest window were rearranged after the shooting. Because Oswald was seen 90 seconds after the shooting on the second floor of the Book Depository composed and not out of breath, this photographic evidence supports the implausibility of Oswald's lone guilt.

Dillard worked for the *Dallas Morning News* until 1977 and currently lives in Henderson County, Texas.

Dobbs House Snack Bar

Mary Adda Dowling—a former waitress at Dobbs House Snack Bar, located at 1221 North Beckley—told FBI agent Kenneth B. Jackson on December 6, 1963, that Lee Harvey Oswald had occasionally come into the restaurant between 7:00 and 7:30 A.M. on weekdays to have breakfast. There is no reason to doubt this as Oswald lived only three blocks south of the snack bar at the time.

Dowling told the FBI agent that Oswald had asked her what her name was a couple of times but that she had refused to give it to him. Dowling's story was corroborated by waitress Dolores Harrison who told the FBI that Oswald didn't talk much and was usually reading while he ate. The manager of the Dobbs House, Sam Rogers, agreed that he remembered serving Oswald coffee. Dowling remembered in particular that Oswald had come in for breakfast on Wednesday morning, November 20, 1963, two days before the assassination and that he had been in a foul mood. Oswald, she recalled, had ordered eggs over light and then cursed and complained when his eggs arrived that they were too hard. Oswald later cursed again when his coffee cup was not refilled quickly enough. Dowling said that at the time Oswald was making a nuisance of himself Officer J. D. Tippit was also in the restaurant and that he "shot a glance" at Oswald. Dowling had known Tippit for five years so she would not have been mistaken about his identity. Dowling told the FBI that no words had been exchanged between Oswald and Tippit.

Dodd, Richard C.

Dodd watched the assassination from atop the triple underpass. Later Dodd told Dallas reporter Jim Marrs that he, like other triple-underpass witnesses, saw smoke coming out from the bushes atop the grassy knoll after the shots were fired.

Dodd, Senators Thomas and Christopher

Thomas Joseph Dodd was born in Norwich, Connecticut. He graduated from Providence College and received his law degree from Yale University. A former FBI agent, Dodd prosecuted Nazi war criminals in 1945. He served two terms in the U.S. Senate as a Democrat from Connecticut, 1959–71. At the time of the assassination, Senator Dodd was chairman of a congressional subcommittee—Juvenile Delinquency Subcommittee of the Senate Judiciary Committee—seeking to establish greater control over the mail-ordering of guns. Among the gun outlets under investigation were Seaport Traders in Los Angeles, California—where "A. Hidell" reportedly mail-ordered his .38 revolver allegedly used in the murder of J. D. Tippit—and Klein's Sporting Goods in Chicago, Illinois—where "Hidell" supposedly mail-ordered the Mannlicher-Carcano allegedly used in JFK's assassination. Senator Dodd opened his subcommittee hearings on January 29, 1963, two days after Lee Harvey Oswald theoretically ordered his .38.

Adrian Alba, who knew Oswald in New Orleans, said that Oswald's "special interest seemed to be in how one goes about ordering guns by mail." The subcommittee's concern with dangerous "junk guns" might explain why Oswald chose to order a Mannlicher-Carcano. Senator Thomas Dodd's son was Christopher Dodd, born on May 27, 1944. Like his father he received his B.A. at Providence College (1966). From 1966–68 he served in the Peace Corps in the Dominican Republic. He received his J.D. from the University of Louisville Law School in 1972. As a member of the House of Representatives (1975–81), Christopher served on the House Select Committee on Assassinations.

The elder Dodd died in Old Lyme, Connecticut, on May 24, 1971.

Donaldson, Ann

A *Dallas Morning News* employee who watched the motorcade "from the grassy knoll area" (i.e., from the north side of Elm Street west of the Texas School Book Depository) with coworkers Mary Woodward, Maggie Brown, and Aurelia Lorenzo. She, like her companions, said the shots came from the knoll.

Dorman, Elsie

A Texas School Book Depository employee who watched the motorcade from an open window on that building's fourth floor, second window from the west. Dorman was born in 1906 in Pembroke, Maine. She witnessed the assassination with co-workers Victoria Adams, Sandra Styles, and Dorothy May Garner.

As the motorcade passed, Dorman sat on the floor and took photographs of the parade with her husband's movie camera. At the sound of the shots she became excited and didn't take any more movies. She told the FBI on November 24, 1963, that she "thought at the time that the shots or reports came from a point to the west of the building," perhaps the Dallas County Records Building.

Assassination researcher Richard Sprague visited Mrs. Dorman in 1967 and watched her movie. Contrary to her memory, she did film right through the shooting sequence, however, she aimed high in her excitement and filmed "mostly trees."

Mrs. Dorman died in 1983.

Downey, Mr. and Mrs. William

A married couple who testified to the Warren Commission that George Senator, Jack Ruby's roommate, called them on the morning of Sunday, November 24—the morning that Ruby shot Oswald—saying that Jack had left their apartment. Senator then offered to visit their home and make them breakfast. Mr. Downey declined the offer and Senator said he would probably go downtown for breakfast.

Senator firmly denied ever making this phone call, explaining that he and the Downeys were no longer friends.

Downtown Lincoln-Mercury

An auto dealership just southwest of Dealey Plaza that shows up in the assassination investigation multiple times and in various ways. Albert Guy Bogard, a salesman there, said that on November 9, between 1:30–2:00 P.M., a man claiming to be "Lee Oswald" came in and test drove a Mercury Comet recklessly on Stemmons Freeway. After the test drive, "Oswald" said he would have to come back in two or three weeks to put a down payment on the car as "he had some money coming in." Many feel this "Oswald" was a fake. The real Oswald did not know how to drive a car. After testifying for the Warren Commission, Bogard was beaten so badly by a group of men that he required extensive hospitalization. Bogard was found dead at the age of 41 in his car in a Hallsville, Louisiana, cemetery on February 14, 1966. A hose had been connected to his exhaust pipe and run into the car, which had all of its windows rolled up. Officials called Bogard's death a suicide. Eugene M. Wilson and Frank Pizzo, other salesmen, corroborated everything Albert Bogard said. Wilson added to speculation of impersonation by telling the Warren Commission that the man he saw was "only about five feet tall."

Jack Lawrence, another employee, was the one who called the FBI to report that incident, against the wishes of his coworkers. According to J. Gary Shaw, Lawrence borrowed a car from the dealership on the eve of the assassination and then did not show up for work that Friday morning. The next time his fellow employees saw him was when "30 minutes after the assassination, Lawrence, muddy and sweating profusely, came running into the dealership and was overcome by nausea. His abandoned vehicle was later found parked behind the wooden fence on the Grassy Knoll . . . [After his co-workers called the police] Lawrence was arrested later that afternoon and held in jail for 24 hours." Lawrence's story is that he was late for work because of a hangover and he parked his car where he did because of the traffic jam caused by the assassination. Lawrence quit his job the next day. It was later learned that he had used a phony story to get his job in the first place. According to Beverly Oliver ("The Babushka Lady"), Lawrence was a regular at Ruby's Carousel Club and close friends with George Senator, Ruby's roommate. According to Shaw, Lawrence was an "ardent right-wing speaker" and had moved to Dallas from Los Angeles. Records show that Lawrence, during his stint in the military, had been an expert marksman. The FBI was told that

Lawrence was an ardent Castro supporter and had received a dishonorable discharge. Charles and Sam Giancana, in their book *Double Cross,* name Lawrence as a member of the assassination team. Lawrence stayed at the same YMCA as Oswald in Dallas. Before coming to Dallas, he worked in an auto agency in New Orleans. There was also a Jack Lawrence in Gerry Patrick Hemming's anti-Castro soldier-of-fortune group called INTERPEN, but it is not known if this is the same man.

Assassination witness Phillip L. Willis also worked at Downtown Lincoln-Mercury.

According to the Warren Commission, seven of the cars in the presidential motorcade were supplied by Dick Fischer of Downtown Lincoln-Mercury, including Vice President Johnson's gray 1964 Lincoln convertible.

(See also DEALEY PLAZA; HEMMING, GERRY PATRICK; YMCA.)

D.R.E. (Directorio Revolucionario Estudiantil)

Militant anti-Castro student organization subsidized by the CIA, William Pawley—an oil millionaire who had been the U.S. ambassador to two South American countries during the Eisenhower administration—and Clare Boothe Luce, wife of mega-publisher Henry Luce.

Its members included Carlos Bringuier, who was born in Havana, Cuba, in 1934, and who fled his island home in 1960. It was with Bringuier that Oswald had a "street scuffle" in New Orleans.

Another member was Manuel Rodríguez Orcarberro, who was also a leader of Alpha 66 and was "violently anti-Kennedy," according to Warren Commission document 853a.

On August 5, 1963, Oswald visited the store in New Orleans that anti-Castro activist Bringuier managed. Oswald expressed interest in joining the anti-Castro struggle. Oswald was arrested in New Orleans on August 9, 1963, for disturbing the peace. Oswald had been handing out pro-Castro Fair Play for Cuba Committee leaflets. Bringuier was notified that Oswald was passing out the leaflets by a man named Celso Hernandez. Oswald got into an argument with Bringuier. Oswald reportedly told Carlos to hit him. Carlos did. Oswald was arrested and was later released after speaking with FBI agent John Quigley.

On August 21, 1963, Bringuier argued the anti-Castro viewpoint in a New Orleans debate on a radio show called *Conversation Carte Blanche.* His opponent, representing the Fair Play for Cuba Committee, was Oswald. Some assassination researchers suspect that Oswald and Bringuier were actually playing on the same team and "staged" their confrontations.

Here is how Bringuier described his association with Oswald in his Warren Commission testimony: "on August 9 [1963], three months before the assassination, I was sure that [Oswald] was a pro-Castro and not an FBI. . . . [O]n August 5, . . Oswald came into the store. . . . He told me that he was against Castro and that he was against communism . . . that he will bring to me next day one book as a present, as a gift to me, to train Cubans to fight against Castro . . . August 6, Oswald came back . . . and he left with my brother-in-law a Guidebook for Marines . . . on August 9, one of my two friends, Miguel Cruz . . . told me that the guy [Oswald] was another time in Canal Street . . I was surprised when I recognized that the guy [outside Ward Discount House] with the sign hanging on his chest, said 'Viva Fidel' and 'Hands Off Cuba' was Lee Harvey Oswald. . . . I became angry . . . he recognized me . . . immediately he smiled at me and he offered the hand to shake hands with me. I became more angry . . . with what face was he doing that, because he had just come to me four days ago offering me his service and that he was a Castro agent, and I start to blame him in the street. . . . The people in the street became angry and they started to shout to him. 'Traitor! Communist! Go to Cuba! Kill him!'"

Oswald and Bringuier's shoving match took place on Friday, August 9, 1963, at 4:45 P.M., amid hurried commuters, anxious to start their weekend.

Bringuier continued, "When we were in the first District of Police . . . some of the policemen start to question Oswald as if he was a Communist, what was he doing that . . . and Oswald at that moment . . . was really cold blood. He was answering the questions that he would like to answer, and he was not nervous, he was not out of control, he was confident in himself. . . . On August 16, another friend of mine left a message in the store that Oswald was another time handing out pro-Castro propaganda for the Fair Play for Cuba Committee, this time in front of the International Trade Mart. . . . The leaflet [on] August 9 didn't have his name of Oswald . . . they have the name A. J. Hidell and one post office box here in New Orleans and the address and leaflets that he was handing out on August 16 have the name L. H. Oswald, 4907 Magazine Street . . . my friend [Carlos Quiroga] asked to me if I think it would be good that he would go to Oswald's house posing as a pro-Castro and try to get as much information as possible from Oswald. I told him yes; and that night [August 16] he went to Oswald's house . . . My friend . . . was talking to Oswald for about one hour . . . in the porch of the house, and there was where we found that Oswald had some connection with Russia . . . because the daughter came to the porch and Oswald spoke to her in Russian, and my friend . . . asked Oswald if that was Russian and Oswald told him yes, that he was attending Tulane University and that he was studying the language . . . my friend came back from Oswald's house and told me what had happened over there . . . We also discussed this conversation in front of Ed Butler . . . [of] the Information Council of the Americas . . The last day that I saw Oswald was August 21, the day of the debate. I went to WDSU radio. . . . They were already there—[broadcaster] Bill Stuckey and Lee Harvey Oswald . . . before the debate started. I was trying to be as friendly to him as I could. I really believe that the best thing I could do is get one Communist out of the Communist Party and put him to work against communism. He smiled to me . . . he answered that he was in the right side . . . and that I was in the wrong side and that he was doing his best . . . he saw my guidebook for the Marines that I was carrying . . . and he told me, 'Well, listen Carlos, don't try to do an invasion with that guidebook for the Marines, because that is an old one and that will be a failure.' That was his joke in that moment."

The House Select Committee on Assassinations discovered that Bringuier had reported his contact with Oswald to D.R.E.'s headquarters in Miami and that this information had, in turn, been given to the CIA. A CIA document exists that admits the agency had had "past contact with . . . Bringuier . . . Contact was limited to Domestic Service activities."

Bringuier gave a letter to the FBI that he had written to a friend (identified as José Antonio) sometime after the assassination. It read, in part: "The police here are looking for a certain 'Clay Bertrand' who is a pervert. They say Ruby is also a pervert. One of these individuals that was distributing handbills with Oswald has a face that appears to me to indicate that he is also a pervert. . . . I advised the Secret Service that one of those who was distributing handbills with Oswald was working in Pap's Supermarket located on Mirabeau Avenue and who, last year, had attended Delgado Trade School. He mentioned that his name might possibly be Charles and that he regularly got off of the bus at Paris Avenue and Filmore Street. I am given to understand that this was correct but I have learned nothing more. I have given them other information, for example, that Oswald was on one occasion after his difficulty with me, at the Habana Bar, which is just two doors from my store. Oswald asked for a lemonade and when they collected for it he said that surely the owner had to be a Cuban capitalist. On that occasion Oswald was accompanied by a Mexican. After that the Mexican returned with another Mexican to the Habana Bar. The FBI was making inquiries for them and left word that if they saw them again, to call there. A few days later the brother of the owner of the Habana Bar appeared and asked me to call the FBI because he had seen two Mexicans in an automobile and he had noted the license number but not the state. I called the FBI on that occasion and gave them the information by telephone. This occurred between August fifteenth and August thirtieth, 1963, approximately."

Bringuier is the author of *Red Friday: November 22, 1963* (C. Hallberg, 1969), which, predictably enough, puts forth the theory that the assassination of President Kennedy was the result of a communist conspiracy.

(See also INFORMATION COUNCIL OF THE AMERICAS; PHILLIPS, DAVID ATLEE.)

Droby, C. A.
The Dallas attorney who arranged the meeting between Ruby's roommate George Senator, Ruby's lawyer Tom Howard, and two journalists, Bill Hunter and Jim Koethe, in Ruby's apartment on the evening of November 24, 1963, the day Ruby shot Oswald. The meeting is noteworthy because Howard, Hunter, and Koethe all died soon thereafter.

The *Dallas Times Herald* of November 25, 1963, said that Droby's life had been threatened. The paper said that Droby was "one of several lawyers who called at police headquarters to consult with Jack Ruby . . . [He] told police his wife had received two 'threatening' telephone calls. Both times, Droby said, his wife was warned that they 'would be next' if he defended Ruby."

Years later, Droby recalled that the threats became even worse. "I was at my office at Main and Lamar," Droby told Dallas reporter Bill Sloan, "when I got a call from the police. They told me an anonymous caller had threatened to blow up my car. When I went down to where the car was parked, they had the whole street cordoned off, and there were cops and demolition experts everywhere. They didn't find any bomb, but that was enough for me. I used to represent Jack all the time, but I decided I didn't want any part of this damned mess. My wife was so scared that she left town for a while, and I got out of it right then. I got out and stayed out."

Dudley Hughes Funeral Home
Not just a funeral home but also the number-one dispatch of ambulances on the south side of Dallas. Amazingly, the call that a police officer was shot came into the Dallas police at 1:18 P.M. on November 22, 1963. Police dispatch called the funeral home and the ambulance was sent to the site, arriving less than a minute after the first call from the murder scene. Two employees of the funeral home, Clayton Butler and Eddie Kinsley, put Tippit's body into the ambulance with the help of witness T. F. Bowley.

Dulles, Allen W.
Former U.S. director of the Central Intelligence Agency who was fired by JFK after the Bay of Pigs fiasco and who, perhaps ironically, became a member of the Warren Com-

mission. Dulles was a master spy during World War II. Dulles supervised the penetration of the Abwehr (Hitler's military intelligence agency) and the subsequent incorporation of many of its undercover agents into the CIA. During Jim Garrison's assassination probe, Garrison subpoenaed Dulles. The subpoena was ignored. According to Dulles's deputy director of central intelligence, Richard Bissell, the CIA-sponsored attempts on the life of Castro were so secret that only Dulles received reports about them.

(See also ANGLETON, JAMES JESUS; CASTILLO, LUIS; CENTRAL INTELLIGENCE AGENCY; PAINE, RUTH AND MICHAEL R.)

E

Easterling, Robert Wilfred (a.k.a. Taylor, George; "Hardhat")

All indications are that this man, diagnosed 10 years after the assassination as a psychotic and schizophrenic, is a false confessor, but his tale remains compelling. Easterling called author Henry Hurt on September 29, 1981, and offered a detailed confession of his involvement in a plot to kill JFK.

Before calling Hurt, Easterling had attempted to confess to the FBI and the Secret Service—but both organizations had ignored him. Easterling said he was confessing to clear his conscience because he believed he was dying.

This is Easterling's story. In February 1963, Easterling was a mechanic working near New Orleans. One of his favorite drinking places at the time was the Habana Bar (117 Decatur Street, New Orleans), where Easterling claimed to have met a CIA/Castro double agent whom Hurt calls "Manuel." Easterling described Manuel as being of medium height, with a stocky build, heavy body hair, a receding hairline, and a birthmark on the side of his neck.

Manuel enlisted Easterling in a plot to kill JFK. His group, Manuel explained, wanted President Kennedy dead because they felt betrayed at the Bay of Pigs. Other members of the conspirational group, Manuel explained, were David Ferrie and Clay Shaw, whom he also saw in the same bar. A third member of the group was a Cuban named Joe who had a deformed hand and sometimes tended bar. (The owner of the bar, Orest Pena, admits that Ferrie and Shaw had both been known to drink there, but denies ever hiring a bartender with a deformed hand.)

Manuel, who drove a gray Volkswagen, explained that President Kennedy was going to be shot with a 7mm Czech weapon. Manuel further claimed that he had personally supervised the design of the assassination weapon, which fired bullets that disintegrated on impact, thus leaving no ballistic evidence. The cover story, Manuel said, would involve a patsy (Oswald), fake ballistic evidence (magic bullet), and a cover weapon (a Mannlicher-Carcano). To create the phony ballistic evidence, Manuel went to a field behind Easterling and his wife's home. He fired the weapon into a barrel of water and collected the shell casings and the fired bullets. These were subsequently planted to incriminate Oswald.

Easterling claims that Manuel then lined up three coconuts and fired his Czech weapon into each of them, to show off. This story is partially corroborated by Easterling's wife (now remarried and requesting anonymity). She recalled that, before the shooting started, Easterling came into their trailer to borrow dishcloths. When Hurt reminded Easterling of this, Easterling recalled that he and Manuel had tried for a time to suspend the dishcloths in the barrel so the bullets could be retrieved without emptying the barrel. Mrs. Easterling also recalled that, later that day, she had made coconut pie because her husband had brought her three coconuts with bullet holes in them.

In late February, Easterling claims, a large white car containing several angry Cubans parked outside his trailer. Easterling hurriedly telephoned Manuel who told him that the Cubans were afraid he would talk and planned to kill him. Manuel showed up and talked the Cubans out of it. This story is also corroborated by Mrs. Easterling, as well as a neighbor, both of whom clearly remember the incident.

Later, while blindfolded, Easterling claims, he was taken to the group's headquarters. There, Manuel showed Easterling a wooden box with a false bottom, in which to hide a rifle. The box would be placed at the assassination site. After the assassination, the Czech weapon would be hidden in the box while false evidence was planted. The box, then, could be retrieved at some later date.

Easterling claims to have met Oswald, who spoke little. Manuel explained that he met Oswald in Czechoslovakia, where the weapon was built, while Oswald was officially in the Soviet Union.

Easterling says that he knew a New Orleans businessman who laundered cash for a Dallas oilman and that one of the legmen for this operation was Jack Ruby. The Dallas oilman was paying for the assassination.

On the morning of September 24, 1963, Manuel assigned Easterling to pick up Oswald and sneak him from New Orleans to Houston. The mission was difficult because Oswald was under FBI surveillance. According to Easterling, the conspirators started a fire in a "wooden church in a black neighborhood," then used the confusion to get Oswald out of town. The FBI was still on their tail, Easterling says, and it took a 100 m.p.h. chase through New Orleans streets to lose their pursuers.

Hurt checked on this story and found that there was a suspicious fire in a wooden building (2011 Melpomene) in a black neighborhood (albeit an apartment building across the street from a church) that was reported at 9:22 A.M. on September 24.

In Houston, says Easterling, he and Manuel stayed in the car while Oswald got out at the bus station. When Oswald returned, he was with a man introduced as "Carlo," who greatly resembled Oswald.

On November 19, Easterling called Manuel, and David Ferrie answered the phone. Ferrie told him that Manuel had gone on to Dallas. Ferrie gave Easterling his next assignment, which was to pick up Oswald at 10:30 A.M. on November 22 at the Greyhound Bus Station in Dallas. From there they were to go to Mexico City to meet Manuel.

It was at this point that Easterling's conscience (as well as his fear that he would be rubbed out for knowing too much) began to get the better of him. He called the FBI and explained his situation. He says the FBI told him, "You're in too deep. You're going to get killed. We have lines open to Dallas now. . . We know all about it. We're going to catch them red-handed. . . . Whatever you do, don't go to Dallas."

Easterling didn't go to Dallas. Instead, he tried to rob a store on the day of the assassination. He was eventually caught and was sentenced to five years in the Louisiana State Penitentiary in Angola. He was later told by Manuel's brother that the conspirators didn't get around to retriev-

ing the Czech weapon out of the Texas School Book Depository until June 1964.

Edison, Edele

Edison claimed at the 1993 JFK Assassination Symposium in Dallas to have had foreknowledge of a plot to assassinate JFK because, for reasons unknown, she was a victim of mind control. She claims to have been repeatedly drugged and hypnotized by a man she knew as "Dr. José Rivera," although she later learned that he had no doctorate under that name.

Dr. Rivera was a science administrator who taught at Loyola University and was the editor of a published book about Syria. At the time Edele knew him, he was 48–50 years old, five-foot two, and obese.

"He wasn't pretty," Edele said. "He had thick glasses and waddled when he walked."

Her story—which she tells with a slight accent, her first language being Finnish—begins in November or early December 1962 when Edele was a married neurophysiology major and a third-year post op at the National Health Institute [NHI], a few blocks from Tulane University, where she was studying the synapses of monkeys—a splendid occupation for a future mind-control victim.

Dr. Rivera, whom she had never heard of before, called her on the phone and told her that she had received an NHI fellowship. She was to receive an award at a huge convention in Atlantic City, and he was looking forward to meeting her at that time.

She delivered her speech about the synaptic inhibition in a cat's spinal cord and all went well. Later, she met Dr. Rivera at the Atlantic City Convention Center. His conversation was professional and comfortably casual so she accepted when he offered her a lifesaver candy. The lifesaver made her feel dizzy and light-headed. He told her that, when she came to Washington, he would give her a tour of the city—which she thought was a funny thing to say because she had no plans of going to Washington. After a while he gave her another lifesaver and she took it.

Then he said to her, "If you see anything unusual, please give me a call."

She did visit Washington in the near future, just as Dr. Rivera had predicted, arriving on April 22, 1963. She called him as soon as she got there and he invited her to lunch. After a quick lunch, he invited her to dinner that night with his wife. She accepted and told him where she was staying: the Kenwood Golf and Country Club outside of Washington, D.C. He said he would pick her up.

As soon as she got in the car he gave her a lifesaver and soon thereafter she began to feel euphoric. He took her to Marky's House of Beef where he announced that, having been called away to the hospital, his wife would not be able to make it. Apparently she was a "doctor" too. Over dinner he intermingled with pedestrian conversation several topics that would later stick in her mind.

"The next time you go to Dallas, you should visit the Carousel Club. It's a nice club . . ."

"Have you ever heard of Lee Oswald? . . ."

At first Edele thought maybe Dr. Rivera was referring to Fred Oswald, with whom she had gone to high school.

"Oswald lived in the Soviet Union and has a nice wife. He is coming to New Orleans. You should get to know him."

Edele began to feel woozy as she sat in Marky's House of Beef listening to this. Woozy and a little nauseous.

"Have you ever heard of the Walker incident? They think Oswald did it."

Edele thought perhaps Oswald was a scientist of some sort, and perhaps Dr. Rivera had friends in the FBI.

"Tonight you are not going to be able to sleep all night. You are going to be kept awake by a terrible storm."

He returned her to her hotel and that night, just as he had said, a horrible storm crashed down, with thunder and lightning and strong winds. The storm lasted all night long and was so noisy that she didn't get a moment's rest.

In the morning, when Edele went outside to see what damage the storm had caused, she discovered that it hadn't even rained. Everything was dry.

She began to feel very strange and she knew Dr. Rivera was responsible. She developed a constant feeling of *deja vu*. She was determined to stay away from him. The last thing she wanted to do was see or hear from him . . . so she called him up. He picked her up and drove her into Washington, and he gave her a lifesaver. Again he said his wife was indisposed so it would just be the two of them again. He stopped the car and showed her a list of "foreign visitors." He wanted to know if she had heard of any of them. She said no.

They drove around Washington for a while and he parked near the back of the White House.

"Caroline has a pony named Pony Macaroni. Do you see Caroline on her Pony Macaroni?"

"No."

So he drove her around Washington again, and again came to a rest behind the White House.

"Do you see Caroline on her Pony Macaroni?"

"No."

Again they drove a big circle through Washington, and again returned to the same spot.

"Do you see Caroline on her Pony Macaroni?"

She still didn't but she knew that this would continue until she said she did.

"Yes, I see her."

"Good, now we can talk."

He then took her to a Marriott Hotel and got them a room. Again, he said weird things to her:

"Tell Winston Demontreberg to call Dr. Rivera when leaving New Orleans."

"I wonder what the chief would think if he knew what Lee was going to do?"

"Write down this number: 889-4244 . . ."

She says her handwriting was very shaky and it took her a long time to write the number down.

"Now write this down: Lee Harvey Oswald. Call him up. Tell him to kill the chief."

"What does it mean?" Edele asked.

"We are playing a joke on him," Dr. Rivera said. "I wonder what Jackie will do when her husband dies."

"The chief's best friend will jump out of a window because of his grief."

[Who does this refer to? RFK? Edele did a lot of research and learned that a man by the name of Grant Stockdale did jump out of a window and kill himself after hearing that JFK had been assassinated—but this might have happened to any man that day, providing he had invested heavily enough in the stock market, which took it's largest single-day plummet on November 22, 1963, since 1929.]

Dr. Rivera then drew a rough diagram on a piece of paper. She says she still has the paper today, and on it there is a diamond with an x near it.

"This is where it will happen, on the fifth floor . . There will be some men up there."

"Every time I travel to New Orleans, I arrive before I leave."

"The Director of the International Trade Mart will be directly involved."

"It will happen right after the Shriner [sic] Circus." She probably means the Shrine Circus.

"I have an office at Foggy Bottom."

This being the days before the CIA moved to Langley, she learned that CIA agents often referred to their headquarters as Foggy Bottom.

[This is true, however, this could also mean generically that his office was in Washington, D.C.]

In early May she called the phone number that Dr. Rivera had given her and an older man answered. She asked if Lee was there and he said that no one lived there by that name.

A short time later she called the number again and the same man answered. This time, when she asked for Lee, the man said he wasn't there but his wife was. Edele told the man to put her on. He did but she couldn't talk to the wife, because the wife only spoke Russian. The third time she called the number she finally got a man who said he was Lee Harvey Oswald.

"Do you know a Colonel or a Doctor Rivera?" she asked.

"No."

"Where is this phone located?"

"This is a house of Magazine Street."

She thanked him and hung up.

She later assumed that she must have spoken to Oswald's landlord at first and checked to see who owned the Magazine Street property. She found that it was a man named McLaney.

"I don't know if it was Mike or William," Edele said, assuming that this McLaney must be the same family as the Mike McLaney who was involved in the Lake Pontchartrain paramilitary training camps.

In August 1963 Dr. Rivera gave her so much of the drug that—she is now convinced that it was LSD—she thought she was going to die. Her husband told her that she just sat there and stared. She told him all of the details she could remember about Dr. Rivera and he said that it all sounded as if there was a plot to assassinate the president. They told no one. She and her husband talked to a lawyer about suing Dr. Rivera, but learned that this was impossible without a toxicology report.

When Oswald was passing out procommunist leaflets, Edele says she heard about it on television, but that they referred to the man as Leon Oswald, so she was relieved that it wasn't the same man she had spoken to.

She says she went to the FBI, still before the assassination, and spoke to special agent Oran Bartlett. She told him the whole story and thought that he believed her. After the assassination, she spoke to the Secret Service and thought they believed her too—so much so that she was surprised when she wasn't called to testify before the Warren Commission.

Edele says that she only saw Dr. Rivera once after the assassination (and after her near overdose), and—though they did not speak—he looked at her with wide eyes, as if looking at a ghost.

(See also CASTILLO, LUIS; MK/ULTRA.)

El Indio   See MORALES, DAVID SANCHEZ.

Ellis, Starvis "Steve"

The Dallas police motorcycle sergeant who was in charge of the presidential motorcade's motorcycle escort. The sergeant rode alongside the lead car in the motorcade and later told the House Select Committee on Assassinations that he looked back and "saw" a bullet bounce off the Elm Street pavement.

Ellis was born in 1918 in Laredo, Texas, and joined the Dallas Police Department in 1946.

Although it was customary for the press bus to be close to the president during motorcades, the press bus in Dallas was well back in the motorcade. According to Ellis, it was Chief Jesse Curry's idea to keep the bus back away from the presidential limousine. Ellis told this story to researcher Larry A. Sneed: "At the airport, Chief Curry told me, 'Look, you see that double-deck bus up there? That's full of news media. Now they've got to get to the Mart out there where the president is going to talk, but we don't want them messing up this motorcade. Just give them one of your men back there and tell him to escort them there on time but to keep them out of the motorcade and not to mess with us. So I got M. L. Baker and told him exactly what the chief had told me. That put him behind us quite a bit."

Baker was the motorcycle patrolman who ran directly into the Texas School Book Depository instead of turning onto Elm Street with the rest of the motorcade.

Ellis said that he was riding between Jesse Curry's lead car and President Kennedy's car during the motorcade and the last thing he remembers before the shooting started was waving to Bill and Gayle Newman who were standing on the north side of Elm Street. The Newmans were Ellis's wife's niece and nephew.

Ellis told Sneed, "I turned around and the first shot went off . . . I could see where the shot came down into the south side of the curb. It looked like it hit the concrete or grass there in just a flash, and a bunch of junk flew up like a white or gray color dust or smoke coming out of the concrete. . . . I turned around and rode up beside the chief's car and bang! Bang! Two more shots went off—three shots in all. The sounds were all clear and loud and sounded about the same. From where I was, they sounded like they were coming from around where the tall tree was in front of [the Texas School Book Depository]. But all the time I was moving up, I still didn't know it was shots, until [James M.] Chaney rode up beside me and said, 'Sarge, the president's been hit!' I asked him how bad and he replied, 'Hell, he's dead. Man, his head's blown off!'"

At Parkland Hospital, Ellis says that he, along with several other motorcycle police from the motorcade were looking at what appeared to be a through-and-through bullet hole in the windshield of the presidential limousine. Even then, Ellis claims, Secret Service agents were trying to convince the Dallas police that the windshield had merely been struck by "a fragment."

Ellis retired from the Dallas Police Department in 1976.

Ellsworth, Frank

Agent for the Internal Revenue Service's Division of Alcohol and Tobacco Tax who was present on the Texas School Book Depository building's sixth floor when the rifle was found. Ellsworth was allegedly involved in Oswald's interrogation. In 1976, Ellsworth told *Village Voice* writer Dick

Russell that he had knowledge of an "Oswald double" who had been associating with the right-wing Dallas Minutemen in 1963. Ellsworth told Russell that the Oswald double was still alive and resided in Dallas. He said that this was the man mistaken for Oswald repeatedly in and around Dallas during the months before the assassination. Said that this "twin" was a frequent traveler to Mexico, had associations with the family of oil billionaire H. L. Hunt, and had been convicted of a federal arms violation. (According to a Warren Commission memo, the member of the Minutemen whom Ellsworth had been investigating was a "local gun shop owner.") Ellsworth said that the "twin" associated with anti-Castro Cuban exiles, was associated with the anti-Castro group known as Alpha 66, and had admitted to supplying arms to a terrorist Cuban organization. Among the "twin's" other associates was General Edwin Walker. Ellsworth told Russell that he had gone undercover, posing as a criminal involved in Mexican smuggling, to track the Oswald twin—and had eventually gotten the twin convicted on a gun violation.

At the time of the assassination, Ellsworth was working undercover as a gunrunner. He had arranged with gunshop owner John Thomas Masen to sell him a large cache of military weapons recently stolen from the Texas National Guard armory in Terrell, Texas. (Interestingly, Jack Ruby had traveler's checks on him when he shot Oswald that were traced to a soldier stationed in Terrell.) On November 18, 1963, Ellsworth's operation was accidentally disrupted by the Dallas police. The police busted the gunrunners before Ellsworth could and, in the process, allowed the man Ellsworth wanted most, Masen, to get away. The Dallas police did recover the guns and did capture two of the men who were delivering the weapons to Ellsworth. The arrests came after a car chase, which ironically passed the Texas School Book Depository building, that ended when the gun-carrying Thunderbird crashed into a utility pole. The driver of the Thunderbird was Donnell Darius Whitter, who suffered severe abdominal injuries and the passenger, Lawrence Reginald Miller, whose severely smashed face had to be sewn together at Parkland Hospital before he could be taken to police headquarters where he and Whitter were charged with violation of the National Firearms Act. Because of the foul-up with the Dallas Police Department, Ellsworth did not get an opportunity to arrest Masen. But this scenario becomes pertinent to the assassination when we take into consideration that 1. The only gun shop that sold ammunition for an Italian Mannlicher-Carcano rifle belonged to Masen; 2. After JFK's shooting, Frank Ellsworth was among those who first searched the sixth floor of the School Book Depository; 3. When Ellsworth first saw the accused assassin in the Dallas Police headquarters, he thought that it was Masen who had been arrested, such was the resemblance between

Oswald and Masen. Lawrence Miller received four years in the federal penitentiary in Texarkana, while Whitter was sent to the U.S. Medical Center for Federal Prisoners in Springfield, Missouri—where General Edwin Walker had received treatment and where, years later, Albert Bolden and Richard Case Nagell were sent. Miller drank himself to death at the age of 43 in 1974. At the time of his death he lived at 5917 Gaston in Dallas, an apartment building owned by Bertha Cheek, who was negotiating with Jack Ruby to invest in the Carousel Club a few days before the assassination and whose sister was Earlene Roberts, who tended the rooming house where Lee Harvey Oswald lived on November 22, 1963.

Ellsworth told the Warren Commission: "The organization known as the Minutemen is the right-wing group most likely to have been associated with any effort to assassinate the president. . . . The Minutemen are closely tied to General [Edwin] Walker and H. L. Hunt."

According to FBI agent James Hosty's House Select Committee on Assassinations testimony, Ellsworth had "indicated that he had been in the grassy knoll area for some reason and had identified himself as a Secret Service agent."

(See also ELROD, JOHN FRANKLIN; HOSTY, JAMES P., JR.; MASEN, JOHN THOMAS; POWELL, JAMES W.)

Eloriaga, Antonio Reyes   See CASTILLO, LUIS.

Elrod, John Franklin

Elrod walked into the Shelby County Sheriff's Office on August 11, 1964, with a sawed-off shotgun. He said that he had been contemplating killing his wife and he thought it might be better if he came to the sheriff's office for a talk. A check of Elrod's record revealed that he had been arrested twice in Dallas for drunk driving, and the second time he had been sentenced to three days in the city jail. There had also been an arrest on November 22, 1963, when Elrod was rounded up by Dallas policemen, who were picking up suspicious characters. Elrod told the sheriff's deputies the story of his arrest that day. It was several hours after the assassination and Elrod had been walking along a railroad track near Harry Hines Boulevard. There had been an earlier report broadcast over police radio that a man with a rifle had been seen walking near railroad tracks near Harry Hines Boulevard. Elrod had no rifle, but he was the only man around. He was arrested for "investigation of conspiracy to commit murder." While in his cell, Elrod said, a man with a smashed-up face was led down the hall outside the cell. He recognized the battered man as a gunrunner who drove a Thunderbird whom he'd met in a meeting in a motel with four other men, one of whom was

Jack Ruby. His cellmate, Elrod said, had been Lee Harvey Oswald.

Having heard Elrod's story, the Sheriff's Office called the FBI, and the FBI came to interview Elrod. The FBI ran a check and found no record of an arrest on November 22, 1963.

However, there was a man with a smashed face. The man was named Lawrence Miller and had been picked up after crashing his Thunderbird. Oswald, Elrod said, told him stories of being in a meeting with Miller and Ruby in a motel, at which money exchanged hands and the smuggling of guns was discussed. Apparently Miller had gotten into a car chase with the police in his T-Bird that ended in a car crash. Also in the car when it cracked up was a man named Donald Whitter, who just so happened to be Jack Ruby's car mechanic. Assassination researcher Peter Dale Scott says, "No one ever asked Whitter about this, but there are documents concerning Whitter that remain classified and have not been released."

(See also ELLSWORTH, FRANK.)

Epileptic Fit

Fifteen minutes before the motorcade passed through Dealey Plaza a very strange thing happened in front of the Texas School Book Depository building. Jerry B. Belknap, dressed in army fatigues, seemingly had an epileptic seizure, which managed to draw everyone's attention. Because of the timing, the seizure resembles a diversion. Belknap later claimed to have had a history of seizures since childhood. One eyewitness in Dealey Plaza claims Belknap simply got up and walked away. But other evidence indicates that he was picked up in Dealey Plaza by an ambulance and taken to Parkland Hospital's Emergency area where he was subsequently forgotten because of the mass hysteria and confusion caused by the arrival of President Kennedy and Governor Connally. Without saying anything to anyone, Belknap left Parkland and took a bus back to downtown Dallas. Dennis McGuire was the attendant in the ambulance that picked up Belknap in front of the School Book Depository. Belknap died in 1986.

Euins, Amos Lee

Fifteen-year-old witness to the assassination who was standing across Elm Street from the Texas School Book Depository. Euins, black himself, said he saw a black man with a rifle in the southeast corner window before the shooting. After his family received threatening phone calls, Euins said he "couldn't tell" if the man was white or black.

In his testimony before the Warren Commission, Euins left out his description of the shooter altogether: "I seen this pipe sticking out of the window. I wasn't paying too much attention to it. Then when the first shot was fired, I started looking around, thinking it was backfire . . . Then I looked up at the window, and he shot again. . . . I got behind this little fountain . . . and then, after he shot again, he pulled the gun back in the window."

Ewell, Jim   (a.k.a. Well, Jim E.)

Full-time day-side crime-beat reporter for the *Dallas Morning News*. Ewell covered President Kennedy's arrival at Love Field, then returned to downtown Dallas via the Stemmons Freeway. He passed the motorcade going the other way after the assassination, strung out and speeding toward Parkland Hospital. Ewell drove through Dealey Plaza where he noticed a crowd of people congregated near the triple underpass—and then went to the Dallas police station basement, where two days later Oswald would be shot. There he parked his own car in the press parking lot and ran into Sergeant Gerald Hill who told him the president had been shot. Ewell told assassination researcher Larry A. Sneed: "He then ran around and jumped into a black and white squad car. There was a uniform officer behind the wheel already. So, I just ran over there and got in the back seat. . . . We were back there at the School Book Depository in less than two minutes. . . . [While I stayed in the street,] Jerry Hill worked his way up to the sixth floor, leaned out an open window, and he had what was thought to be Oswald's little fried chicken lunch. . . . About that time there was a commotion around one of the squad cars, and we could hear a radio saying that an officer had been shot in Oak Cliff. . . . There had only been one other Dallas policeman killed in the line of duty in the previous twelve years or so . . . I left the location at the School Book Depository and jumped into a car driven by Captain Westbrook with Sergeant Stringer. I rode in the back seat as we sped across into Oak Cliff. . . . When we arrived in Oak Cliff, I got a chance to go into a convenience store . . . I did get to make a phone call to the city desk asking them to send me a photographer. They didn't know what I was doing in Oak Cliff. . . . As I stepped out of this convenience store, next door to it was a two-story boarding house, and there I saw Bill Alexander with an automatic pistol stalking across the balcony very carefully. . . . From there we proceeded to a side street down there where they said J. D. Tippit had been shot . . . There was another police car there as they were examining a jacket next to the curb . . . I remember it as being a light tan windbreaker. . . . They were discussing it when the report came in that the person they thought might be the police officer's assailant had gone into the Texas Theatre. . . . When we arrived at the Texas Theatre, we parked right in front and everybody jumped out and went into the lobby. There were other police cars getting there, too. I was very familiar with the

Texas Theatre, having lived close by . . . Somebody kept shouting, 'Turn on the house lights!' . . . I went up these stairs to the balcony. And there, there must have been 15 to 20 high school age boys up there watching. . . . Then there was a commotion. I stepped to the railing so that I could look down onto this. Just about that time the house lights came up and Nick McDonald made his move on Oswald. . . . First, Nick was shouting, and then there was a swarm of officers that came in. . . . Someone was trying to hold the barrel of a shotgun, or train a barrel of a shotgun down among the heads of these officers. I thought, 'What's he going to do with the shotgun?' . . . The officers bringing Oswald out of the theater . . . kind of separated the crowd and made an aisle for him to come through to get to the car. I'd say that I was about ten to twelve feet away from Oswald at the time. . . . A teenage girl . . . shouted, 'Kill the son of a bitch!' . . . Oswald then took my place in the back-seat of the same car that I arrived in. So when they left with him, I stood there, stranded. I then hitchhiked a ride with a man in a pickup truck. . . . I was probably the only reporter that I remember who was at the Texas Theatre. However, Hugh Aynesworth, who was a member of our staff, said he arrived at the Texas Theatre also. I didn't see Hugh."

Ewell left the *Dallas Morning News* to become the public information director for the Dallas County Sheriff's Department.

(See also AYNESWORTH, HUGH; CHICKEN BONES.)

Factor, Loy

Confessed assassination conspirator who claimed to have been on the sixth floor of the Texas School Book Depository building at the time of the shooting. According to his brother, Loy had a plate in his head due to a shrapnel wound he received during World War II. Factor, a Chickasaw Indian, also had his right leg removed below the knee in June 1964 because of an infection from a seven-year-old copperhead bite that had never healed. He said that he was supposed to be one of the shooters but at the last second didn't pull the trigger. He claimed that he had known a man was to be killed, but it didn't occur to him until the last moment who the victim was to be. Among his co-conspirators, Factor said, was Malcolm Wallace, the same man whom Lyndon Johnson-associate Billy Sol Estes named in grand jury testimony as a professional killer who had worked for LBJ. Factor described Wallace as being between 40 and 45 years old and dark-skinned. Factor said he met Wallace at the November 1961 funeral for 79-year-old Speaker of the House Sam Rayburn. Wallace befriended Factor. Factor, as their friendship grew, found occasion to show off his impressive marksmanship skills to Wallace. Factor said that Wallace offered him $8,000 to kill a man and Factor took him up on it. On the morning of the assassination, Factor said, he was picked up at his house by an attractive young woman and a young man, both of whom looked Hispanic. The woman's name was Ruth Ann. They drove Factor to the School Book Depository, where he learned he was to be one of three shooters, the other two being Wallace and Lee Harvey Oswald. Jack Ruby was also involved in the conspiracy, Factor said.

(See also WALLACE, MALCOLM.)

Fair Play for Cuba Committee

On April 19, 1963, Oswald wrote a letter to the Fair Play for Cuba Committee headquarters in New York that read: "Dear Sirs, I do not like to ask for something for nothing but I am unemployed. Since I am unemployed, I stood yesterday for the first time in my life, with a placard around my neck, passing out fair play for Cuba pamphlets, etc. I only had fifteen or so. In 40 minutes they were all gone. I was cursed as well as praised by some. My home-made placard said: HANDS OFF CUBA! VIVA FIDEL! I now ask for 40 or 50 more of the fine basic pamphlets. Sincerely, Lee H. Oswald."

Oswald is said to have used the reportedly factitious name Alec Hidell on some Fair Play for Cuba Committee materials, in order to, theoretically, create the appearance that the New Orleans chapter of the organization had more than one member.

It has been theorized that Oswald's mission in associating himself with a known organization was to discredit that organization with his unwanted association. The last thing that the Fair Play for Cuba Committee national director V. T. Lee wanted was to be associated with an ex-Marine who had deserted to the Soviet Union. If this theory is correct, then Oswald's mission was a success, as the Fair Play for Cuba Committee was forced to disband following the assassination because of their unwanted and unwarranted notoriety.

Faulkner, Jack

Deputy sheriff in the Criminal Investigation Division of the Dallas County Sheriff's Department, Faulkner was Bill

Decker's next-door neighbor in 1948 when Decker was elected sheriff of Dallas County and Faulkner joined Decker's department a year later.

Faulkner was standing outside the sheriff's offices on Houston Street at the time of the shooting. He says he heard three shots with a pause between the first and second shot, but with the second and third shots very close together. "At that time, I actually thought that someone had attempted to shoot the president and possibly the Secret Service had shot back. It was that fast!"

Along with fellow deputy sheriff A. D. McCurley, Faulkner moved after the shooting to the grassy knoll where there were people pointing back to the rail yards. When crossing Elm Street, McCurley picked up a piece of bone on the street, but threw it back down because it didn't have any blood on it.

Realizing their error, Faulkner says, they later went back to look for the bone, which Faulkner now believes was a portion of President Kennedy's skull, but they could not find it.

After searching the parking lot behind the grassy knoll and finding nothing, Faulkner went to the sixth floor of the Texas School Book Depository where he noticed that a new floor was being put in. "There were still saws and plywood lying around," he said.

Faulkner retired from the Sheriff's Department in 1989 and died in October 1996.

(See also FLOOR-LAYING CREW.)

Featherston, Jim

Dallas *Times Herald* courthouse reporter who was standing at the corner of Main and Houston Streets at the time of the assassination. Featherston was assigned to pick up film thrown to him by *Times Herald* photographer Robert Jackson, and to call in to the *Times Herald* rewrite desk with information regarding crowd reactions to JFK's visit.

Featherston told reporter Connie Kritzberg: "Bob Jackson was in the photographers' car, which was seventh in the procession. As the [photographers' car] drew abreast of me, Bob threw the film at me. It was in a little paper sack, however, and a gust of wind caught it and blew it toward the other side of the street . . . I ran through the motorcade to retrieve the film and then heard the shots. I really didn't recognize the shots as gunfire. I thought what I heard might be fireworks. However, I quickly realized that something catastrophic had happened from the reaction of the crowd. One woman was hysterical. . . . I spotted a young lawyer named Frank Wright. 'What happened?' I shouted. 'I don't know, but a woman down there has taken a picture of whatever happened,' Wright said, pointing toward nearby Dealey Plaza. . . . I ran to Dealey Plaza, a few yards away, and this is where I first learned that the president

had been shot. I found two young women, Mary Moorman and Jean Lollis Hill, near the curb on Dealey Plaza. Both had been within a few feet of the spot where Kennedy had been shot, and Mary Moorman had taken a Polaroid picture of Jackie Kennedy cradling the president's head in her arms. It was a poorly focused and snowy picture, but, as far as I knew then, it was the only such picture in existence. I wanted the picture and I also wanted the two women's eyewitness accounts of the shooting. . . . I told Mrs. Moorman that I wanted the picture for the *Times Herald* and she agreed. I then told both of them that I would like for them to come with me to the courthouse pressroom so I could get their stories and both agreed. . . . Mrs. Hill told her story over and over again for television and radio. Each time, she would embellish it a bit until her version began to sound like Dodge City at high noon. She told of a man running up toward the now-famed grassy knoll pursued by other men she believed to be policemen. In the meantime, I had talked to other witnesses and at one point I told Mrs. Hill she shouldn't be saying some of the things she was telling television and radio reporters. I was merely trying to save her later embarrassment but she apparently attached intrigue to my warning. . . . As the afternoon wore on, a deputy sheriff found out that I had two eyewitnesses in the pressroom, and he told me to ask them not to leave the courthouse until they could be questioned by law enforcement people. I relayed the information to Mrs. Moorman and Mrs. Hill. . . . All this time I was wearing a lapel card identifying myself as a member of the press. It was also evident we were in a pressroom and the room was so designated on the door. . . . I am mentioning all this because a few months later Mrs. Hill told the Warren Commission bad things about me. She told the commission that I had grabbed Mrs. Moorman and her camera down on Dealey Plaza and that I wouldn't let her go even though she was crying. She added that I 'stole' the picture from Mrs. Moorman. Mrs. Hill then said I had forced them to come with me to a strange room and then wouldn't let them leave. She also said I had told her what she could and couldn't say. Her testimony defaming me is all in Volume VI of the Warren Commission Hearings and Exhibits. Why Mrs. Hill said all of this has never been clear to me. I later theorized that she got swept up in the excitement of having the cameras and lights on her and microphones shoved into her face. She was suffering from a sort of star-is-born syndrome, I later figured."

Speaking at the "Reporters Remember Conference" in Dallas on November 20, 1993—and later telecast by C-SPAN—regarding the Moorman photo, Featherston said: "I wanted that picture, period. At the time I thought that was the only photo in existence. Mary Moorman agreed to give me the film. I asked both of them (Moorman and Hill) to come back to the press room with me, which they did. I interviewed them, called the rewrite desk. In their own words they said what they had seen. Later, Jean Hill told the Warren Commission I was down there and I grabbed her. Mary Moorman, she was crying, and I wouldn't let her go, and I took them to a strange room. Of course, that was the press room. It was a very strange room at that time. She also told them they couldn't leave. That's all nonsense."

Federal Bureau of Investigation

The FBI is the U.S. domestic federal police force. Though it is no longer true, at the time of JFK's death murdering a U.S. president was not a federal crime. Therefore, the FBI had no jurisdiction to investigate this case, a fact which did not stop them. FBI agents were involved in the investigation from the beginning, and, after Oswald's death, they took control of the investigation. The head of the FBI was J. Edgar Hoover, an enemy of the Kennedys who was approaching the age of mandatory retirement. Hoover was also good friends with Lyndon Johnson. The FBI was involved with the assassination in several ways, including: 1. the fact that Oswald's killer, Jack Ruby, was recruited as an FBI informant; 2. evidence that Oswald was used as an FBI informant; 3. the fact that the FBI had Oswald under surveillance during the weeks and months before the assassination; and 4. evidence that the FBI had foreknowledge of a conspiracy to kill the president in Dallas and did not act upon it.

Here is a rundown of the FBI agents who had noteworthy associations with the Dallas crimes or those accused of those crimes.

Dallas FBI agent Charles W. Flynn, starting in March 1959, had a series of meetings with Jack Ruby to recruit him as an informant. According to William Scott Malone (*New Times,* January 23, 1978), "After the first FBI contact Ruby went on an electronic shopping spree. He purchased . . . a wrist watch with a built in microphone, a telephone bug, a wire tie clip and bugged attaché case." Ruby spent more than $500 on sophisticated spy equipment.

According to the *Warren Report,* FBI agent Milton R. Kaack ran the first FBI background check on Oswald after Oswald's return from the Soviet Union. Kaack gave his assembled information to agent James Hosty in Dallas, who was in charge of Oswald's case. In this manner, Hosty learned that Oswald had lied to the FBI in New Orleans on a number of points: his wife's maiden name was not Prossa and he and Marina had not been married in Fort Worth, Texas. Kaack's report also revealed that Oswald had lied when he told his arresting officers in New Orleans that he had been born in Cuba.

According to Nina Gardner, Oswald's landlady in New Orleans, she was questioned about Oswald by Kaack less than three weeks after Oswald's arrival in New Orleans. Kaack, according to Anthony Summers, "did indeed investigate Oswald," but refuses to discuss his investigation. FBI director J. Edgar Hoover told the Warren Commission that he had submitted an affidavit from every FBI agent who had contacted Oswald—yet there was none from Kaack.

On August 9, 1963, when Oswald was arrested on Canal Street in New Orleans and jailed for disturbing the peace by the police, he requested a meeting with an FBI agent. Agent John Lester Quigley was sent to interview him. According to the *Warren Report*, the police had not given the FBI Oswald's name when they summoned Quigley on August 10. Therefore, Quigley had not had an opportunity to do a background check on Oswald—and didn't know Oswald had attempted to defect to the Soviet Union and had already been interviewed by the FBI since his return to the United States. Quigley testified that Oswald was cooperative when answering questions about his general background—but not so cooperative when asked about the Fair Play for Cuba Committee.

Quigley said, "When I began asking him specific details with respect to his activities in the Fair Play for Cuba Committee in New Orleans as to where meetings were held, who was involved, what occurred, he was reticent to furnish information, reluctant and actually as far as I was concerned, was completely evasive on them . . . [Oswald] was probably making a self-serving statement in attempting to explain to me why he was distributing this literature, and for no other reason, and when I got to questioning him further than he felt that his purpose had been served and he wouldn't say anything further." Quigley burned the notes he took during the Oswald interview.

On November 17, 1963, FBI night clerk William S. Walter of the New Orleans office received a memo via telex warning of a plot to kill President Kennedy. Walter told five agents of the memo and considered his job done.

Walter's story was authenticated in 1976 when researcher Mark Lane successfully invoked the Freedom of Information Act to get a copy of the telex.

It reads:

URGENT: 1:45 AM EST 11-17-63 HLF 1 PAGE. TO: ALL SACS. FROM: DIRECTOR, THREAT TO ASSASSINATE PRESIDENT KENNEDY IN DALLAS TEXAS NOVEMBER 22, DASH THREE NINETEEN SIXTY THREE. MISC INFORMATION CONCERNING. INFORMATION HAS BEEN RECEIVED BY THE BUREAS [sic] BUREAU HAS DETERMINED THAT A MILITANT REVOLUTIONARY GROUP MAY ATTEMPT TO ASSASSINATE PRESIDENT KENNEDY ON HIS PROPOSED TRIP TO DALLAS TEXAS NOVEMBER TWENTY TWO DASH TWENTY THREE NINETEEN SIXTY THREE. ALL RECEIVING OFFICES

SHOULD IMMEDIATELY CONTACT ALL CIS, PCIS LOGI-CAL RACE AND HATE GROUP INFORMANTS AND DETERMINE IF ANY BASIS FOR THREAT. BUREAU SHOULD BE KEPT ADVISED OF ALL DEVELOPMENTS BY TELETYPE. OTHER OFFICES HAVE BEEN ADVISED. END AND ACK PLS.

FBI agent Regis Kennedy worked on the New Orleans part of the assassination investigation and reportedly told FBI director J. Edgar Hoover that assassination suspect Carlos Marcello was nothing more than a "tomato salesman." Kennedy is described in *High Treason* as being "deeply involved in this case." He refused to testify before the New Orleans grand jury investigating the assassination, citing "executive privilege"—that is, LBJ gave him permission not to testify. Penn Jones Jr. wrote at the time, "It is inconceivable to us that every Federal cop in the country can refuse to talk to a secret grand jury on grounds that he works for the President; therefore can remain silent." Kennedy died in 1978, not long after testifying before the House Select Committee on Assassinations. (For more on agent Kennedy, see the entry for the BABUSHKA LADY.)

A special agent who has drawn fire from conspiracy theorists is Warren DeBrueys, who, according to the assassination researcher who wrote under the name William Torbitt, was a White Russian and a member of the anticommunist Solidarists. (See also TORBITT DOCUMENT.) According to Jim Garrison, DeBrueys was heavily involved in the activities of Guy Banister, David Ferrie, and anti-Castro Cubans during the summer of 1963. According to Anthony Summers, DeBrueys also monitored Oswald's activities during that same period. He was also the agent who took Oswald's possessions from Dallas to Washington for analysis. Garrison subpoenaed DeBrueys but he pleaded executive privilege and refused to testify at Clay Shaw's conspiracy trial under instructions from the Justice Department. Garrison said in his October 1967 *Playboy* interview: "I'd like to find out the exact nature of DeBruey's relationship with Lee Oswald. As long as Oswald was in New Orleans, so was DeBrueys. When Oswald moved to Dallas, DeBrueys followed him. After the assassination, DeBrueys returned to New Orleans. This may all be coincidence, but I find it interesting that DeBrueys refuses to cooperate with our office—significant and frustrating, because I feel he could shed considerable light on Oswald's ties to anti-Castro groups."

On the day of the assassination, the FBI immediately moved in on the scene—sometimes with hostile results. Doyle Williams, the senior criminal agent in the Dallas FBI office, minutes after the assassination had been ordered by FBI director J. Edgar Hoover and U.S. attorney general Robert Kennedy to go to Parkland Hospital and determine what was happening. While looking for a phone in the emergency room area of Parkland, Williams was knocked down by a punch to the nose from a Secret Service agent. It turned out that Williams was about to pull back a curtain that would have revealed Lyndon Johnson's hiding place.

One of the methods used to link Oswald with the Mannlicher-Carcano rifle that purportedly killed JFK was a palm print found inside the rifle by Dallas Police lieutenant J. C. Day, several days after the assassination—and not found by FBI experts immediately following the assassination. On August 28, 1964, FBI assistant to the director Alan H. Belmont received a memo that expressed FBI doubts as to the authenticity of the palm print. The memo, from the supervisor of the Latent Fingerprint Section of the Identification Division of the FBI, Sebastian Francis Latona, read: "[Warren Commission General Counsel J. Lee] Rankin advised because of the circumstances that now exist there was a serious question in the minds of the Commission as to whether or not the palm print impression that has been obtained from the [Dallas Police] is a legitimate latent palm impression removed from the rifle barrel or whether it was obtained from some other source."

Special agent Vincent Drain transported the Mannlicher-Carcano rifle from Dallas to Washington on November 23, 1963, for examination by the FBI Laboratory. In a 1984 interview with researcher Henry Hurt, Drain said that he didn't think the discovery, by the Dallas Police, of Oswald's palm print on the Mannlicher-Carcano rifle was legitimate. Drain said, "All I can figure is that [the print] was some kind of cushion because they [the Dallas Police] were getting a lot of heat by Sunday night. You could take the print off Oswald's card and put it on the rifle." The FBI examined the rifle, found no prints, then sent it back to Dallas where the palm print was discovered.

The FBI might not have been able to find a palm print, but they nonetheless developed evidence from the rifle that would have been incriminating to Oswald. FBI hair and fiber expert Paul Morgan Stombaugh was among those who examined "Oswald's" Mannlicher-Carcano rifle at the FBI Laboratories. According to the *Warren Report*: "In a crevice between the butt plate of the rifle and the wooden stock [of the Mannlicher-Carcano rifle] was a tuft of several cotton fibers of dark blue, gray-black and orange-yellow shades. On November 23, 1963, these fibers were examined by . . . Stombaugh . . . [who] compared them with the fibers found in the shirt Oswald was wearing when arrested in the Texas Theatre. This shirt was also composed of dark blue, gray-black and orange-yellow cotton fibers. Stombaugh testified that the colors, shades and twist of the fibers found in the tuft on the rifle matched those in Oswald's shirt."

The FBI also assisted in linking Oswald to the Tippit killing. It was FBI firearms identification expert Charles L. Killion, who examined the four cartridges reportedly found at the scene of the Tippit killing and determined that they came from the revolver reportedly found on Oswald at the time of his Dallas arrest.

Nancy Fenner was the receptionist at FBI's Dallas office. On November 6, 1963, Oswald left a note with Fenner for agent James Hosty. Hosty was at lunch when Oswald left the note. According to Fenner, the note read: "Let this be a warning. I will blow up the FBI and the Dallas Police Department if you don't stop bothering my wife. (signed) Lee Harvey Oswald." The note was destroyed by Hosty after the assassination and the existence of the note did not become public knowledge until 1975. Hosty remembers a more mildly worded note, and has described Fenner as "excitable" and "unreliable." There was definitely a note, however. The FBI agent in charge of the Dallas office was J. Gordon Shanklin. Shanklin ordered FBI agent James Hosty to destroy the note he had received from Oswald before the assassination.

Hosty maintains that Oswald was never an FBI informant. However, according to Jim Garrison, FBI agent Carver Gaten told Milwaukee-resident Jim Gechnour that he knew James Hosty (the FBI agent in charge of Oswald's case following Oswald's return from the USSR) and Hosty told him that "Oswald had been paid regularly for information but provided little." Hosty, it was said, expressed bitterness because he had been criticized by his superiors for not prying more out of Oswald.

The Houston reporter who first published the story about Oswald being an FBI informant was Alonzo Hudkins, a former engineer for Hunt Oil. His story said that Oswald had been paid $200 a month and had the code number 179.

Another FBI agent who said Oswald was "definitely an [FBI] informant" was Will Hayden Griffin. Griffin also interviewed Oswald's housekeeper, Earlene Roberts, on November 29, 1963. She told him that the Dallas Police car that honked its horn outside her rooming house about a half hour after the assassination—while Oswald was in his room putting on his jacket—was no. 207. Griffin died in August 1982 of cancer.

Bardwell D. Odum, FBI agent, was the assassination investigator who interviewed many of the witnesses to the President Kennedy and Tippit murders. Marguerite Oswald (Lee's mother) says she was interrogated by Agent Odum on November 23, 1963, the day before Ruby shot her son. At the time, she claimed, Odum showed her a photo and asked her if the man looked familiar. She later came to believe it was a photo of Ruby. (Julia Ann Mercer also claimed she was shown Ruby's photo by law enforcement officials before Ruby became famous.) According to

the Warren Report, "In the course of Marguerite's testimony, the Commission asked the FBI for a copy of the photograph displayed by Odum to her. When Marguerite viewed the photograph provided the Commission, she stated that the picture was different from the one she saw in November, in part because the 'top two corners' were cut differently and because the man depicted was not Jack Ruby." The Warren Report then explains Mrs. Oswald's confusion this way: "On November 22 the CIA had provided the FBI with a photograph of a man who, it was thought at the time, might have been associated with Oswald. To prevent the viewer from determining precisely where the picture had been taken, FBI Agent Odum had trimmed the background . . by making a series of straight cuts which reduced the picture to an irregular hexagonal shape." The FBI says this was the same photo as supplied to the Warren Commission, except the commission's version had been trimmed of all background so that only a silhouette image of the man remained. (See SAUL.) The Warren Report concluded, "Neither picture was of Jack Ruby. The original photograph had been taken by the CIA outside of the United States sometime between July 1, 1963 and November 22, 1963, during all of which time Ruby was within the country." The Warren Report seems to be referring to a photo taken in September 1963 in Mexico City of a man whom the CIA allegedly at the time believed to be Oswald, exiting the Russian embassy there. The man didn't look like Ruby or Oswald.

Robert P. Gemberling was among the FBI agents who interviewed assassination witnesses on November 22, 1963. When on November 23, 1963, he submitted a list of names found in Oswald's notebook, he deleted the name of FBI agent James P. Hosty—which had been misspelled "Hasty." The FBI report to the Warren Commission on the case was known as the Gemberling Report, written by Gemberling, who had supervised the interviewing of assassination witnesses in Dealey Plaza and at Parkland Hospital. Interestingly, the Gemberling Report's conclusions differ from those of the Warren Commission. The FBI, unlike the Warren Commission, did not need a magic bullet. That's because they chose to ignore the fact that James Tague was also wounded in the attack. Without having to account for a missed shot that wounded a bystander, the FBI was able to say that one shot struck JFK in the head, one hit him in the back, and a third caused all of Governor Connally's wounds.

Special agent James W. Bookhout interrogated Oswald after his Dallas arrest. Bookhout said Oswald told him that the pictures of him holding the murder weapons were composites, with Oswald's face superimposed over someone else's body.

The FBI agents in charge of keeping track of Oswald immediately after his return from the Soviet Union were

Special agents B. Thomas Carter, Arnold J. Brown, and John Fain. Carter and Fain interviewed Oswald on June 26, 1962, in the Fort Worth FBI office. The interview dealt with Oswald's experiences while in the Soviet Union. Oswald denied any dealings with the KGB and refused to take a polygraph. Brown and Fain interviewed Oswald in the back seat of Fain's car (which was parked outside Oswald's home) on August 16, 1962. Brown said Oswald was arrogant and evasive.

After Oswald was arrested for the shooting of Officer Tippit, a number of FBI agents attempted to participate in his interrogation. Among them were Manning C. Clements, who interrogated Oswald during the evening of November 22, 1963. Clements described Oswald as "angry," particularly hostile toward FBI agents, for whom he refused to answer questions.

Cortlandt Cunningham was the FBI ballistics expert who told the Warren Commission that it was impossible to ballistically match the bullets recovered at the scene of the Tippit shooting with the gun allegedly belonging to Oswald, but that he could match the four shell casings found near the scene with "Oswald's" handgun, "to the exclusion of all other weapons."

Assistant Director Cartha D. "Deke" DeLoach wrote an internal memo to J. Edgar Hoover's close friend and assistant Clyde Tolson that "the President [Lyndon Johnson] felt the CIA had something to do with this plot."

Firearms identification expert Robert A. Frazier testified, following the Warren Commission's re-creation of the assassination in Dealey Plaza (supposedly based on the Zapruder film), that in regards to the damage attributed to the "magic bullet": "They [President Kennedy and Governor Connally] both are in direct alignment with the telescopic site at the ['sniper's nest'] window. The Governor is immediately behind the President in the field of view." His testing with the Mannlicher-Carcano rifle determined it took a minimum of 2.3 seconds to work the bolt and refire. Therefore, a lone assassin could have only fired three shots during the shooting sequence, thus creating the necessity for the "magic bullet." Frazier also testified at the Clay Shaw trial on February 22, 1969.

FBI photography expert Lyndal L. Shaneyfelt told the Warren Commission that, after examining the photos of Oswald holding the alleged murder weapons (supposedly taken by Marina Oswald), that he could not determine if the rifle in the photo was the same as the one found on the Texas School Book Depository's sixth floor. Despite Shaneyfelt's testimony, the Warren Commission stated point blank that the rifle in the photo was the alleged murder weapon. Shaneyfelt also examined the Zapruder film and determined that the "rifleman" supposedly visible at frame 413 couldn't be a man, since the tree the man seems to be hiding behind was only six feet tall and was only five feet from Zapruder. Shaneyfelt also verified Oswald's handwriting on the Oswald diary and the mail-order forms used to order the "murder weapons."

Following Oswald's murder, the FBI investigated that crime as well. Agent C. Ray Hall interviewed Ruby following Oswald's murder. Ruby told him that he was able to sneak down the Main Street ramp to the basement of police headquarters unmolested because he waited until Officer Roy Vaughn, who was guarding that entrance, was busy watching traffic while helping to guide the patrol car of Officer Rio Pierce.

FBI agent Nat A. Pinkston gave Warren Commission testimony regarding "Oswald's clipboard" found many days after the assassination on the Texas School Book Depository's sixth floor. Since the clipboard was not found when that floor was initially searched, either that search was not thorough or the clipboard was planted later to further incriminate Oswald.

Agent Ivan D. Lee photographed the rear of Major General Edwin Walker's home for comparison with similar photos found among Oswald's belongings. He conducted the post-assassination interview with mob figure Joseph Civello, assassination-suspect Carlos Marcello's number-one Dallas lieutenant, which appeared in the Warren Commission Hearings and Exhibits files devoid of references to organized crime and with Civello's name spelled incorrectly (Cirello).

Inspector James R. Malley was in charge of all FBI agents assigned to the case in Dallas as of 6:00 P.M., November 22, 1963. At that time, the FBI had no jurisdiction, since President Kennedy's assassination was not a federal crime. Malley told the Warren Commission that the CIA would not release the photo purportedly of Oswald leaving the Cuban embassy in Mexico City in September 1963 unless all background data was trimmed away. What remained was a silhouetted photo of a man (decidedly not Oswald) that could have been taken by anybody, anywhere, at any time. (See SAUL.) As we now know, the background had to be trimmed because it would have revealed the location of the camera.

According to James Hosty's book *Assignment: Oswald*, agents from both Division 5 (Security) and Division 6 (Criminal) of the FBI were involved in the investigation of the assassination. Briefings were held under the direction of Deputy Associate Director Alan Belmont and they would start out with agents from Divisions 5 and 6 together. At some point, however, in every briefing, the Division 6 agents would be asked to leave while the briefing continued for the agents of Division 5 alone. From this information Hosty assumed that sensitive security or espionage matters were being discussed in connection with the assassination.

Almost every agent who had contact with Oswald or was in charge of Oswald's files before the assassination was punished by J. Edgar Hoover. Some received pay cuts or transfers to less desirable cities. Others retired rather than accept their punishment.

(See also AUTOPSY OF JOHN F. KENNEDY; GEMSTONE FILE; HOOVER, J. EDGAR; HOSTY, JAMES P., JR.; WALTER, WILLIAM S.)

Ferrell, Mary

The number-one independent assassination archivist, Ferrell has kept her files on the assassination since the day it occurred and has functioned as a document repository for other researchers. She has never published anything about the assassination herself. She is the so-called keeper of the keys.

Before the assassination she was the longtime employee of John Connally's best friend Eugene Locke, who had been the deputy ambassador to South Vietnam in 1967 under Henry Cabot Lodge. Locke's firm helped organize the motorcade and later represented Mrs. J. D. Tippit.

Ferrie, David William (a.k.a. Ferris, David)

The most bizarre character associated with President Kennedy's assassination. Ferrie knew Lee Harvey Oswald. He was a CIA pilot famous for his journeys into Castro's Cuba to deliver ammunition and weapons to anti-Castro forces, and, at the time of the assassination, he was working as a private detective for New Orleans crime boss and assassination suspect Carlos Marcello.

Born in 1918 in the middle-class suburbs of Cleveland, Ohio, his father was James H. Ferrie, a captain in the Cleveland Police Department who later became an attorney. Raised as a Catholic, Ferrie graduated from St. Ignatius High School in Cleveland in 1935. From 1935–38 he attended John Carroll University but dropped out during his senior year to become a priest. He studied for three years at St. Mary's Seminary but suffered a nervous breakdown, which both prevented him from achieving the priesthood and serving in World War II. Deciding to become a teacher, Ferrie attended Baldwin-Wallace College in 1940 and during 1940–41 was a student teacher at Rocky River High School. In August 1941 he again tried to become a priest, entering St. Charles Seminary in Carthagena, Ohio. In 1944, as he was about to achieve his goal, the school kicked him out because of an "element of instability" in his character. In 1945, Ferrie taught English and aeronautics at Benedictine High School and began to work for the Civil Air Patrol. His record of misconduct with the Civil Air Patrol began in 1948 when he took a couple of students to a house of prostitution and impersonated an air force officer in order to appropriate a squadron airplane. Although it is unclear where he learned to fly, by 1950 Ferrie was a top-notch pilot. In 1951, Ferrie moved from Ohio

to New Orleans. In the early 1950s Ferrie got a job as a pilot flying for Eastern Airlines. During the time he was a commercial airline pilot Ferrie studied biochemistry, hypnotism, and psychology. He began to list himself in the telephone book as Dr. David Ferrie. It was during the late 1950s that Ferrie 1. first met Lee Harvey Oswald in the Civil Air Patrol; 2. lost his hair, and 3. began to moonlight as a pilot for the CIA. In 1961 Ferrie moved into a three-level house near New Orleans International Airport. Ferrie said his mother lived on the first floor and he lived on the second and the third floors in order to conduct his scientific research. Not long thereafter, Ferrie got drunk with a teenaged boy, borrowed a plane, and flew it at tree-top level around New Orleans. The boy apparently claimed that he had had sex with Ferrie on the plane because when they landed Ferrie was arrested on "decency charges," which eventually cost him his job with Eastern Airlines and his role in the Civil Air Patrol. In 1961 Ferrie joined the Apostolic Orthodox Old Catholic Church of North America. He attempted to become a bishop of the church but was rejected when the archbishop learned he had been chastised in the past for unnatural sexual behavior. By 1963 Ferrie was attempting to become a clergyman for another religious sect, this time the Orthodox Catholic Church of Washington, D.C. Ferrie's final attempt to become a man of the cloth was sabotaged by the same man who told New Orleans district attorney Jim Garrison that he should look into Ferrie's activities immediately following the assassination: Jack Martin (a.k.a. Jack Shuggs). Although Ferrie's plans were once again foiled, Rev. George A. Hyde, the head of the Orthodox Catholic Church, was one of only three names listed in Ferrie's handwritten will (along with Ferrie's brother and his friend Alvin Beauboeuf).

Ferrie died on February 22, 1967, of a "brain hemorrhage" just before he could be indicted and tried by Jim Garrison for conspiracy to assassinate the president. With Ferrie, right up until the time of his death, was *Washington Post* reporter George Lardner Jr. Ferrie's close friend Eladio del Valle, who has also been implicated in the assassination, was murdered the same hour Ferrie died. Ferrie's autopsy revealed contusions on his gums and the insides of his cheeks.

Ferrie first met Oswald in the New Orleans Civil Air Patrol in 1955. According to Marguerite Oswald, Lee's mother, the teenaged Lee was visited in 1955 by a man in a uniform whom she believed was trying to recruit him for the Marines. In October 1956 Oswald wrote to the Socialist Workers Party asking for information concerning their "Youth Program." In the letter, Oswald states that he had been studying socialist ways for longer than 15 months, which dates back approximately to the time he met Ferrie.

Ferrie once wrote, in a letter to the commander of the United States First Air Force, "I want to train killers. There is nothing I would enjoy better than blowing the hell out of every damn Russian, Communist, Red or what-have-you."

Beverly Oliver, the self-proclaimed "Babushka Lady," who worked next door to Ruby's Carousel Club, claims she saw Ferrie in the Carousel so often she thought he was one of the managers. This statement, however, is not corroborated by any of the many Carousel Club employees who were questioned following the assassination. The House Select Committee on Assassinations developed strong evidence that Ferrie once accompanied Oswald to an anti-Castro training camp in Lacombe, Louisiana.

Ferrie was reportedly hairless from head to toe, reportedly because he suffered from alopecia praecox, and wore a piece of rug for a toupee, along with painted-on eyebrows. After he was fired by Eastern Airlines for his pedophiliac homosexuality, he sued the airlines. During his testimony in his lawsuit against Eastern Airlines, Ferrie cast doubt across his entire biography—is it just a legend?—when he said that all of his attempts to be ordained were to assist Jack Martin in a Department of Health, Education, and Welfare investigation into "the sale of phony certificates of ordination and consecration."

Ferrie's appearance was so strange that he would have been a perfect master of disguise. All he would have to do was make himself up to appear "normal" and no one would recognize him. Conversely, all someone would have to do was paint on eyebrows and wear a goofy wig and they could pass themselves off as Ferrie.

Ferrie was once arrested with three blank passports in his possession.

Ferrie helped bring attention to himself as a suspect when, days after the assassination, he knocked on the door of Lee Harvey Oswald's former landlady in New Orleans and asked if he could come in and look for the library card he had lent Lee. Of course, Oswald had moved out months before.

According to assassination researcher Harold Weisberg, two days after the assassination, on the day Ruby shot Oswald, the FBI asked Marina Oswald if she knew a "David Farry." She said no.

As Captain David Ferrie of the Civil Air Patrol, Ferrie counted among his students Oswald and the son of Mary Bledsoe, Oswald's one-time landlady, who told the Warren Commission that she recognized Oswald on a city bus moments after the assassination.

When Jim Garrison began his assassination investigation, he had met Ferrie only once, a meeting Garrison calls in *On the Trail of the Assassins,* "casual but unforgettable." The incident took place in 1962, as Garrison was walking across Carondelet Street in New Orleans. "Just then, a man grabbed me by both arms and stopped me cold. The face grinning ferociously at me was like a ghoulish Halloween mask. . . . The traffic was bearing down on us as he gripped me, and I hardly could hear him amidst the din of the horns . . . he was shouting congratulations on my recent election [to New Orleans Parish district attorney]. As I dodged a car, at last escaping his clutch, I recall his yelling that he was a private investigator . . . I remembered Ferrie's reputation as an adventurer and pilot . . . the legend that he could get a plane in and out of the smallest fields . . . his involvement in the abortive 1961 Bay of Pigs invasion of Cuba, his anti-Castro activities, and his frequent speeches to veterans' groups about patriotism and anti-communism . . . [Ferrie's] name . . . was well known in New Orleans."

Ferrie's mother, who had been living with him in New Orleans, died in March 1962 and, according to Ferrie's friend John Erion, this is when Ferrie began to take drugs. Ferrie was also, after this time, known to make pornographic films with an African-American woman named Wanda.

Garrison first became interested in Ferrie during the initial stages of his investigation, prompted by Oswald's presence for much of the summer of 1963 in New Orleans, within Garrison's jurisdiction. Garrison learned that Oswald and Ferrie had been seen together that summer.

The district attorney later learned that Jack Martin—who remained hospitalized from a pistol-whipping he had received from Guy Banister on November 22, 1963—was telling friends that Ferrie had been involved in the assassination plot. Ferrie's role, Martin claimed, was to go to Houston to serve as a "getaway" pilot for the assassins. Banister had done some work for G. Wray Gill, the lawyer for Carlos Marcello who also employed Ferrie, and Ferrie had worked as a go-between for Marcello and Banister. Jack Martin had been trying to hurt Ferrie in any way possible, including writing letters that suggested that he be fired from his job, ever since June 1963 when Ferrie kicked Martin out of Wray's office.

Garrison called Ferrie into his office on November 25, 1963. Ferrie, Garrison wrote, appeared as if "he'd been shot by cannon through a Salvation Army clothing store." At that time, Ferrie said he did not know Oswald but admitted to a strange "ice-skating" trip to Houston on the day of the assassination.

Garrison's staff learned that Ferrie had deposited more than $7,000 in cash to his bank accounts during the weeks leading up to the assassination. (Around the same time, Carlos Marcello, as a gift, gave Ferrie a successful gas-station franchise.)

Garrison first linked Ferrie to Clay Shaw (whom Garrison later unsuccessfully prosecuted for conspiracy to assassinate the president), through statements made by right-wing fanatic Jules Kimble. Kimble told Garrison that Ferrie had introduced him to Shaw in 1960 or 1961.

Ferrie's relationship with Shaw was corroborated by David Logan, who had been introduced to Shaw by Ferrie in a Bourbon Street bar, and Nicholas and Mathilda Tadin, who met Shaw through Ferrie when arranging to have Ferrie give their son flying lessons.

But the most damaging link between Ferrie and Shaw was provided by Raymond Broshears, who told Garrison in 1965 that he had seen and talked to Ferrie and Shaw on a number of occasions together. Broshears said that Ferrie, when drunk, liked to discuss his role in the assassination. Ferrie told Broshears that his job was to pick up two members of the assassination team in Houston—one of whom Ferrie knew fairly well and was named Carlos. The assassins were to arrive from Dallas via a single-engine plane. Ferrie would then fly the men to a never-specified distant location. Ferrie did as he had been instructed but Carlos and his companion didn't show up.

Ferrie told Broshears that Carlos was a Cuban exile, as were the other members of the assassination team, who believed that President Kennedy had "sold them out to the communists."

Professional criminal Edward Whalen—from Philadelphia, Pennsylvania—told Garrison's staff in 1967 that recently Ferrie and Shaw (who was using his usual alias, Clay Bertrand) had met him in a Bourbon Street bar and had offered him $25,000 to "hit" Garrison. Ferrie had told Whalen that "Bertrand had done a lot for . . . Oswald and it was only because Oswald had fouled up that he had been killed."

On February 22, 1967, Garrison was about to arrest Ferrie when he discovered that Ferrie had died. He was found in his apartment lying on the sofa with a sheet pulled over his head. Photos taken of the scene, with the sheet pulled back, reveal that Ferrie died with his wig on.

By the time Garrison received the news, the coroner had already picked up the body. Garrison did not actually see Ferrie's corpse, but he was shown a photo of it. The photo showed the scar on Ferrie's stomach caused by a knife wound while working as a soldier-of-fortune pilot in Cuba.

In Ferrie's apartment, Garrison found two typed suicide notes, many empty cages that still reeked of white mice, stacks of books, a big map of Cuba, and overall filthy conditions. The bathroom's medicine cabinet mirror was covered with globs of purple glue—perhaps used to hold on Ferrie's wig.

The suicide notes read, in part, "To leave this life is, for me, a sweet prospect. I find nothing in it that is desirable and on the other hand, everything that is loathsome," and "When you read this I will be quite dead and no answer will be possible."

In the medicine cabinet were several empty bottles of Proloid, a thyroid medicine, with their covers off.

Regarding Ferrie's suspicious post-assassination activities, registration cards at the Alamotel in Houston, an inn owned by assassination suspect Carlos Marcello, show that D. W. Ferrie, and his young companions Melvin Coffey and Alvin Beauboeuf, checked into room no. 19 at 4:30 P.M. on November 23, 1963, and checked out the following day.

Oddly, records at the Driftwood Motel in Galveston, Texas, show that the same trio checked in there at 11:00 P.M. on November 23 and checked out at 10:00 A.M. on November 24. Why did the trio need two hotel rooms? In both establishments, registration indicates the trio were traveling in a Louisiana licensed car, plate no. 784-895.

FBI reports regarding Ferrie—which fell into the hands of David Lifton through Warren Commission staff member Wesley Liebeler—indicated that Ferrie flew to Guatemala aboard Delta Airlines twice during the fall of 1963, evidence that Ferrie's detective work for G. Wray Gill was directly related to his defense of Carlos Marcello's immigration-fraud charges.

Ironically, Marcello was acquitted of those charges on November 22, 1963, the same day that President Kennedy died. Ferrie said that he was in court when the president was shot.

While being cross-examined at the assassination-conspiracy trial of Clay Shaw, Ferrie's friend, prosecution witness Perry Russo, said: "Dave Ferrie talked about so many things. When he would talk to me, he would give me advice or make statements and he would refer to certain books—certain pages—and advise that I read them . . . there was some talk of the assassination last summer, but we talked about many things. He talked about a cure for cancer. You name it, he talked about it. I learned not to argue with him. I knew that he knew everything. I believed him. People say to me about Ferrie, 'What was he like?' To me, he was a walking encyclopedia . . . he knew it all . . . all the answers . . . why should I question him?"

Earlier, during direct examination at the Shaw trial, Russo described the meeting he had attended in September 1963 in Ferrie's apartment. Present were Russo, Ferrie, Shaw (using the name Clem Bertrand), and a man who was introduced as "Leon Oswald": "Ferrie took the initiative in the conversation, pacing back and forth as he talked . . . [He said] an assassination attempt would have to involve diversionary tactics . . . there would have to be a minimum of three people involved. Two of the persons would shoot diversionary shots and the third . . . would shoot the 'good shot.' . . . [You would have to create] a triangulation of crossfire . . . If there were three people, one of them would have to be sacrificed."

Paris Flammonde writes: "A low requiem mass was said for David William Ferrie at St. Matthias' Church on March 1, 1967. Only two mourners attended. Interment followed in near solitude at St. Bernard's Memorial Cemetery. His body was claimed by Parmalee T. Ferrie of Rockford, New York, understood to be a brother. [There is no Rockford in New York.] Two weeks later the press reported in an isolated three-inch item that attorney John P. Nelson Jr., representing J. T. Ferrie of Rockford, Illinois, also identified as a brother [the same or another?] had petitioned for a search for a will . . . Among Ferrie's final possessions were found four rifles, an assortment of shotgun shells and .22 rifle blanks, a radio transmitter tuning unit, two Signal Corps field telephones, a 100-pound aerial-type practice bomb and—a sword."

In a *Playboy* magazine interview (October 1967), Jim Garrison said: "I had nothing but pity for Dave Ferrie. . . . From the moment he realized we had looked behind the facade and established Lee Oswald was anything but a Communist, from the moment he knew we had discovered the role of the CIA and anti-Castro adventurers in the assassination, Ferrie began to crumble psychologically . . . yes, I suppose I may have been responsible for Ferrie's death. If I had left this case alone, if I had allowed Kennedy's murderers to continue to walk the streets unimpeded, Dave Ferrie would be alive today. I don't feel personally guilty about Ferrie's death, but I do feel terribly sorry for the waste of another human being. In a deeper sense, though, David Ferrie died on November 22, 1963. From that moment on, he couldn't save himself, and I couldn't save him."

The name "Ferris," a known David Ferrie alias, appears in Jack Ruby's last address book.

For those interested in looking Ferrie up in the Warren Commission's 26 volumes of hearings and exhibits, look at Volume VIII, pages 14, 29–31; and at Warren Commission Document 3119.

Files, James E. (a.k.a. Sutton, James)

Another confessed assassin, born January 1942, who is assumed by most experts to be lying. Tipped off by an FBI agent, assassination researcher Joe West found Files in Joliet State Penitentiary in Illinois.

Files is serving a life sentence for shooting a policeman. West interviewed Files on videotape on March 22, 1994. The tape was later sold commercially as *Confession of an Assassin* (1996, Bob Vernon, UTL Productions/MPI Video).

On the tape, Files told the following story: He had been an employee of organized crime boss Charles Nicoletti. Up until late in 1963 his name had been James Sutton, but he had been given a new identity by the government because of his work with an anti-Castro group and the Bay of Pigs operation.

He worked out of No Name Key under the control of David Atlee Phillips. He served with the 82d Airborne for 14 months in Laos. Returning to civilian life he became a professional race-car driver and was recruited at that time by Nicoletti to be the personal driver for the crime boss.

Initially the conspirators had wanted to assassinate President Kennedy in Chicago, but they weren't comfortable with the plan and regrouped in Dallas.

Files drove the weapons for the operation to Mesquite, Texas, one week before the assassination. A day or two later Lee Harvey Oswald came to him and gave him a tour of the area, including spots where he could practice with the weapons Files had brought.

Files says he first met Oswald in early 1963 in connection with gun-running operations. Files believes Oswald didn't know what the plan was.

On the day of the assassination, Files met Johnny Roselli at the Cabana Hotel at 7:00 A.M. Together they went to a pancake house in Fort Worth where they met Jack Ruby. Files was the lookout at the meeting. Ruby handed Roselli an envelope and left. The envelope, which they opened in the car, contained Secret Service identifications and an updated version of the motorcade route. The only update in the route was the turn onto Elm Street.

They returned to the Cabana and then Nicoletti and Files arrived at Dealey Plaza at 10:00. It was only then that Nicoletti asked Files to be a backup shooter—only if needed.

Files said okay. Files suggested to Nicoletti that he shoot from the Dal-Tex Building, and Files himself took up a spot behind the fence on the grassy knoll. Nicoletti had a rifle. Files was carrying a briefcase with a Remington Fireball inside.

When it came his turn to shoot President Kennedy, he could see that he was going to have to shoot because Kennedy had merely been wounded to the body. He could also see that it was going to be very difficult to shoot without shooting Jackie, and he had been instructed to be very careful not to hit anyone in the car other than the president, *especially* Jackie.

Files fired, he claims, just after Nicoletti, and both of their shots struck the president in the head. Files's shot struck Kennedy in the right temple (he originally said left temple but corrected himself).

As a calling card, Files bit the shell and left it sitting on top of the fence. He returned his weapon to his briefcase and turned his coat inside out so that it went from plaid to gray, then walked to Houston Street, taking the Elm Street extension that ran in front of the Texas School Book Depository.

Two men in suits took up a position at the top of the stairs and turned people away. Files says he did not see Abraham Zapruder and says that is a lucky thing because he might have shot him, fearing that he had seen too much.

Files says he was also unaware that Mary Moorman had taken a photo of his position at the moment he had fired. As he walked toward Houston, he says he saw Frank Sturgis and Eugene Brading in the crowd.

He saw Jack Ruby at the bottom of the grassy knoll. At Houston Street, Files got into a 1963 Burgundy-colored Chevy. Roselli was in the back seat and Nicoletti was in the front passenger seat.

They drove for five or six blocks to another car and separated. Files returned to his room in Mesquite, washed himself thoroughly, then cleaned both his gun and the one used by Nicoletti.

The next day Files claims he drove to Illinois. Sometime later, he was paid $30,000 for the job. Files says the man who killed J. D. Tippit had been assigned to kill Oswald but had messed up.

Fischer, Ronald B.
Dallas County auditor who witnessed the assassination while standing on the southwest corner of Elm and Houston. Ten minutes before the shooting, Fischer saw a man in a white T-shirt or a light sport shirt leaning out of a Texas School Book Depository window, surrounded by boxes, staring "transfixed" toward the triple underpass.

Fischer later said he thought the shots came from "just west" of the Book Depository. Fischer's observations are corroborated by his companion at the time, Robert Edwards. At the sound of the first shot, both men laughed, thinking it was a backfire.

Fischer later told researcher Larry Harris that he didn't think the man in the window was Oswald, insisting that the man he saw had "light-colored hair."

544 Camp Street (a.k.a. The Newman Building)
Run-down three-story building at the corner of Camp and Lafayette Streets in New Orleans. This address, 544 Camp Street, was stamped on the first set of pro-Castro Fair Play for Cuba Committee pamphlets distributed by Lee Harvey Oswald. (Later sets listed a post office number or Oswald's address at 4907 Magazine Street.)

The building also housed the offices of the anti-Castro Cuban Revolutionary Council, which was in 1963 the organization of assassination suspect Sergio Arcacha Smith. The council was also the former organization of Carlos Bringuier (before he joined the student anti-Castro organization D.R.E.), the man with whom Oswald got into a street scuffle over the distribution of a later version of his Fair Play for Cuba Committee leaflets.

Perhaps most interestingly, 544 Camp Street is part of the same structure as 531 Lafayette Street, with an entrance around the corner, which housed the offices of Guy Banister, the anticommunist ex-FBI man who was seen by several witnesses having meetings with both Oswald and assassination suspect David Ferrie during the summer of 1963. New Orleans Parish district attorney Jim Garrison claimed that both entrances led to the same area, but this is not true. The only way to have gotten from 544 Camp Street to the offices of Guy Banister Associates was to go through a window. The proximity of the two addresses remains fascinating, however.

See also ARCACHA SMITH, SERGIO; BANISTER, WILLIAM GUY; D.R.E.; FERRIE, DAVID.)

Floor-Laying Crew, The
On the day of the assassination, six employees of the Texas School Book Depository were laying a new tile floor. The crew started their work on the west side of the floor and worked their way eastward, that is toward the side of the floor that held the so-called sniper's nest. As the new floor was put down, boxes were moved eastward to be out of the way. Oswald was not a member of the floor-laying crew but he was on the sixth floor that morning filling orders for books published by Scott Foresman and Co. The crew broke for lunch at 11:45 on the morning of the assassination and, while racing downstairs to their lunches, noticed Oswald on the fifth floor waiting for an elevator.

According to assassination witness Bonnie Ray Williams, the floor-laying crew consisted of himself, Oswald look-alike Billy Lovelady, Harold Norman, Charles Givens, William Shelley, and Danny Arce.

Florer, Lawrence Huber "Larry"
Twenty-three-year-old man who was apprehended by Dallas County sheriffs 10 to 15 minutes after the assassination while exiting the Dallas County Records Building. A pudgy man wearing black horned-rim glasses, Florer appeared drunk and claimed that he had been on the third floor of that building not long after the assassination looking for a pay telephone. Florer told the Dallas Sheriff's Department that he was at a barbeque place on Pacific Street during the assassination and heard about it on the radio.

The "looking for a telephone" excuse was the same one used by suspect Eugene Hale Brading, who was picked up by a sheriff's deputy across the street at the Dal-Tex Building under similar circumstances.

Flynt, Larry
Publisher of the raunchy men's magazine *Hustler*, who offered, in the January 1978 issue of that periodical, a $1 million reward to anyone who could solve the JFK assassination mystery. On March 5, 1978, Flynt was shot by an

Publisher Larry Flynt. *(Author's Collection)*

unknown assailant and was left paralyzed from the waist down. The shooting was blamed on right-wingers who objected to Flynt's publishing pornography. In February 1979, Flynt published a heavily edited version of *The Gemstone File,* an alternative history that portrays Greek shipping magnate Aristotle Onassis as the mastermind behind JFK's death—as well as many of the modern world's ills.

(See also GEMSTONE FILE.)

Ford, Gerald   See WARREN COMMISSION.

Foster, J. W.
Dallas police accident investigator who joined the department in 1955. Foster was stationed atop the triple underpass during the motorcade. He checked the railroad employees standing on the triple underpass for identification and says that he tried to get them to leave that restricted area but they paid no attention to him. Since the land belonged to the railroad, they felt they had a right to be there.

Foster says that there were seven or eight people standing on the triple underpass at the time of the shooting.

Foster told assassination researcher Larry A. Sneed: "Just prior to the shots, a three engine locomotive went by, so there wasn't a lot you could see or hear from up there even though the locomotive had already passed and just the boxcars were going by at the time the motorcade passed through."

Photographic evidence indicates that the train had cleared the triple underpass by the time the motorcade arrived in Dealey Plaza.

Foster says he heard three evenly spaced shots. He says that an officer came running up toward the triple underpass just after the shooting saying that the shots had come from up there. "I told him they didn't," Foster said. "Then I moved around to the end of the viaduct (triple underpass) where somebody said some man had run up the railroad track from that location. So I proceeded up to the yards maybe ten to fifteen minutes looking in the cars, but I didn't find anything."

Foster then moved to a spot where he thought a bullet might have struck, in the turf near a manhole cover on the south side of Elm Street—very close to where assassination witness Jean Hill had been standing at the time.

"The plaza had been freshly mowed," Foster told Sneed. "Thus I noticed this clump of sod that was laying there and was trying to find out what caused that clump of grass to be there. That's when I found where the bullet had struck the concrete skirt by the manhole cover and knocked that clump of grass up. Buddy Walthers, one of the sheriff's deputies, came up and talked to me about it, and discussed the direction from which the bullet had come. It struck the skirt near the manhole cover and then hit this person (Tague) who had stood by the column over on Commerce Street. It appeared to come from the northeast . . . but we were never able to find the slug." Foster does not mention that, as documented in photographs of the scene, an unidentified man, who seemed official, came by and joined Walthers and Foster. The man in the suit, according to the photos, appears to have picked something up out of the grass and put it in his pocket.

Foster retired from the Dallas Police Department in 1976.

(See also HOLLAND, SAM; WALTHERS, BUDDY.)

Fowler, Billy
Dallas police officer who says that, two weeks after the assassination, he was cruising in his patrol car along Fort Worth Avenue just west of downtown Dallas when he pulled over a Volkswagen Beetle because it had only one

headlight working. The driver was a middle-aged man of average height who seemed extremely nervous. When he asked the driver to show his license he saw that it was an apparently valid Texas driver's license but the address showed that the driver lived in Mexico City. Fowler searched the car and found in the trunk a suitcase filled with official-looking documents. One of the documents he saw was a letter addressed to Jack Rubenstein at the Dallas County Jail. The letter said something to the effect of "We are sorry about your current difficulties and we promise we will do whatever we can to help you." Fowler arrested the man and took him in. Several days later, when he checked to see what had happened, he found that the nervous man had been released almost immediately without any charges. "Don't worry about him," Fowler was told. "He's just some kind of nut."

Franzen, Mrs. Jack

A woman who was standing with her small son on the south side of Elm, across from the Texas School Book Depository at the time of the assassination. Mrs. Franzen said that she thought the first shot was a firecracker. She says she saw "dust or small particles of debris" fly from President Kennedy's limo. She later saw blood come from the president's head.

Frazier, Buell Wesley

Buell Wesley Frazier was Lee Harvey Oswald's Texas School Book Depository coworker and a neighbor of Ruth Paine (Marina Oswald's housemate). Frazier often gave Oswald a ride to work on Monday morning after Lee spent the weekend with his family in Irving. The only time Frazier ever gave Oswald a ride to work on a Friday was the day of the assassination. Frazier, along with his sister, Linnie Mae Randle, were the only two Warren Commission witnesses who saw Oswald carry a "long and bulky package" to work that day, which Oswald claimed contained curtain rods. It was raining that morning. Both Frazier and Randle testified that the package was too short to contain a rifle, even if broken down.

Garland G. Slack, who testified seeing an Oswald look-alike practicing with a rifle at a firing range on November 10, 1963, told the commission that the man had been driven to the range by "a man named Frazier from Irving." The first broadcasts about the assassination said the weapon found in the Texas School Book Depository was a British .303 rifle, the type of rifle Frazier owned. Frazier's lifelong friend was John M. Crawford, who was also a friend of Jack Ruby.

Irving (Texas) police detective J. A. McCabe arrested Frazier at the Irving Professional Center, where Frazier had been visiting his father on the evening of November 22, 1963. Frazier was sought by the Dallas Police as a material witness because he was a neighbor of Marina Oswald and it was he who gave Oswald a ride to work that morning.

Dallas police detective R. D. Lewis administered a polygraph examination to Wesley Frazier on the evening of November 22, 1963. The procedure lasted approximately 50 minutes, and, although Frazier seemed anxious, the exam indicated he was telling the truth when he said Oswald brought "curtain rods" with him to work that morning.

After he was arrested, Oswald said he never told Frazier anything about curtain rods and that the only bag he took to work with him on Friday morning contained his lunch.

Freeman, H. D.

Dallas police motorcycle patrolman who rode in the Dallas motorcade. As the motorcade came north on Houston Street and prepared to make the 120-degree turn onto Elm Street, it appears on the Zapruder film as if one of the lead motorcycles peeled off from the motorcade and went straight, heading north on Houston, behind the Texas School Book Depository, rather than making the turn with the rest of the vehicles.

According to researchers Harrison Edward Livingstone and Robert Groden, this motorcycle was "apparently" being ridden by Freeman. Although, later, the same authors write, "No-one to this day knows for sure who it was or why it happened."

Frenchy   See THREE TRAMPS.

Fritz, John Will

Dallas police captain who interrogated Oswald after his arrest. Captain Fritz was also leading the procession to transfer his prisoner on the morning of November 24, 1963, when Oswald was murdered in the basement of the Dallas Police station.

Fritz was one of the first men to see the sniper's nest and the rifle found on the Texas School Book Depository's sixth floor. Just after Oswald was brought in for interrogation, Fritz was called away from the prisoner by Sheriff Bill Decker for a private meeting (they didn't want to use the phone) a mile away, despite the fact that they'd just seen each other.

Officially, Fritz "kept" no tapes or transcripts of Oswald's interrogation. He says he based his written report on rough notes that were written several days after Oswald was shot. Those notes were not available to the public until the Assassination Records Review Board made them so on November 20, 1997.

They read:

1st 11–22
B.O. & James P. Hosty
Jame W Bookout

3:15 p.m.
Didn't own rifle saw
one at Bldg M. True & 2 others
home by bus changed britches

Ans Hosty adm going to Russia
adm wrighting Russian
Embassy & to Hosty
says lived Russia 3 yrs.

Does write over then now
school in Ft W—to Marines
says got usual medals
claims no politicial belief
belongs Fair Pl
Hdqts NY off N.O.
says supports Castro Rev.
claims 2nd floor Coke when
off came in
to 1st floor had lunch
out with Bill Shelley in
front
lft wk opinion nothing be
done that day etc.
? punch clock
8-4-45 wre not
rigid abt time
wked reg 1st Fl
but all over
speaks Russian

?Why live O.H. Lee
says landlady did that

Terminate interview
with line up
4:15
4 man left to right as #2

Time of filing 11:26 pm Johnson Pres 22nd Precinct 2 F154
Received evidence 1st then filed

2nd interview 23rd
Present 10:35–11:34
T. J. Kelly Robt Nash

Grant??
B. O. & myself
Boyd & Hall

Says 11-22-63 rode bus
got trans same out of pocket
says 1 p.o. box denied bringing
package to wk. Denied telling Frazier
purpose of going to Irving—denied
curtain rods—got off bus after seeing
jam got cab etc .85 fare told you wrong before
at apt. Changed shirts & tr. Put in dirty clothes—long sleeve
red sh & gray tr.

morning 23rd
says 11-21-63 say two negr came in
one Jr. & short negro—ask? for lunch says cheese
sandwiches & apple

says doesn't pay cash for wife staying with Mrs. Payne
denied owning rifle in garage or elsewhere admits other
things these
Came there 63—N.O.
Says no visitors at apt. Claims never order
owns???? for gun
denies belonging to Com party
says bgt gun 7 mo Ft. W. didn't know what Place.
arms to grest abt questioning
Arv. July 62 from U.S.S.R. Int. by F.B.I. Ft. W
says Hard & Soft meth etc. Buddy
says on interview of Payne by F.B.I. He thought she was
intimidated
Decires to talk to Mr. Abt. I ask who
says Smith act att,
Says did live N.O. 4706 Magazine St. From Apt.
Wked Wm R, Riley Co 640
says nothing against Pres does not want to
talk further-No Poly at time in past had
refused
Oswald A.C.L.U. member he says says
Mrs. Payne was too. I ask abt organization
he says to pay lawyer fees when needed
B.O. asks about Heidel selective s. Card—adm having
would not admit signature—wouldn't say
why he had it. Says add. Book has names of Russian
Emigrants he visits—denies shooting Pres says didn't know
Gov. shot
3rd 11-23—6:35

Shows photo of gun. Would not discuss photo
denies buying gun from Kleins.
Comp I made picture super imposed

arr 10-11:15
4th11-24 Insp Holmes—Sorrels—Kelley et al

Chief

Assassination archivist Mary Ferrell says that Fritz later told a friend at a luncheon that, the day after the assassination, he received a phone call from Lyndon Johnson, the new president, saying, "You've got your man, the investigation is over."

On June 9, 1964, Fritz wrote a letter to the Warren Commission regarding the spent shells found on the sixth floor of the Texas School Book Depository. That letter is now missing.

Garner, Darrell Wayne "Dago"

Warren Reynolds, a witness to the Tippit killing, originally stated that he couldn't identify the shooter as Oswald, despite the fact that he followed the man for a block after the shooting. Before Reynolds could testify to this effect, on January 23, 1964, he was shot through the head in the darkened basement of his used car lot office. Reynolds survived the attack, and later told the Warren Commission that the man he saw was Oswald.

The primary suspect to the Reynolds shooting was 23-year-old Garner, who was arrested after drunkenly admitting that he shot Reynolds. Garner later said that Reynolds "got what he deserved" and confessed to being on the scene at the time of Reynolds's shooting. Garner was released after an alibi witness came forward.

The witness was Nancy Jane Mooney, and in yet another amazing Dallas coincidence, she turned out to be an ex-employee of Jack Ruby at the Carousel Club. She said she was with Garner at the time of Reynolds's shooting.

Miss Mooney was arrested for "disturbing the peace" by Dallas Police eight days after providing the alibi. She was later found hanged in her cell with her toreador pants tied around her neck, presumably a suicide.

Garner died at the age of 30, during January 1970, of a heroin overdose, in Metairie, Louisiana.

Garner, Dorothy Ann

She watched the assassination from the Texas School Book Depository's fourth floor with coworkers Victoria Adams, Elsie Dorman, and Sandra Styles. Garner said the shots "came from the west."

Garner, Jesse J. and Nina

The Garners were neighbors and landlords of the Oswalds when they lived at 4905 Magazine Street in New Orleans beginning May 10, 1963. Mrs. Garner told researcher Anthony Summers: "FBI agent Milton Kaack questioned her about Oswald within three weeks of his arrival in New Orleans." She later learned that her lodger was under heavy surveillance by "FBI" men in "a car which used to park there at night and watch him and the house, round the corner by the drugstore." Mrs. Garner told the Warren Commission she had seen "a Cuban" looking for Oswald when he wasn't home. (See D.R.E.) Mr. Garner told the commission that when Oswald moved out, he skipped out on 15 days rent.

Garrick, J. B.

Dallas police motorcycle patrolman who, according to the Warren Commission, was one of the three patrolmen who rode directly in front of President Kennedy's limo during the Dallas motorcade.

Garrison Investigation, The

New Orleans district attorney Earling Carothers "Jim" Garrison, the man who indicted and unsuccessfully prosecuted Clay Shaw for conspiracy to assassinate President Kennedy, was born 1920 in Denison, Iowa. He moved to New Orleans in 1930 and during World War II was an artillery observation pilot in Europe, 1944–45. Discharged in 1952, he became a graduate of Tulane University Law School and spent four months as an FBI agent.

Garrison was elected New Orleans Parish district attorney in 1961.

In 1967, a man named Emilio Santana—a friend and former employee of Clay Shaw's, and a former CIA employee—told Garrison that Shaw and Jack Ruby had once gone together to Havana, reasons unknown, soon after the Castro takeover. By the time Shaw went to trial, Santana was nowhere to be found.

That same year, Garrison spoke with a former employee of Guy Banister named David Lewis. Rosemary James and Jack Windlaw wrote in their book *Plot or Politics?*, "the Lewis story is that late in 1962, he was drinking coffee with Banister's secretary, Delphine Roberts, in Mancuso's Restaurant, when Carlos Quiroga, a Cuban exile, came in with a fellow he introduced as *Leon* Oswald . . . Lewis was working for Banister at the time. Then, a few days later, Lewis entered Banister's office and there was a meeting in progress of Banister, Quiroga, Ferrie, Leon Oswald, and another person. Lewis was asked to leave." Lewis told the *New York World Journal Tribune* (February 22, 1967) that the New Orleans conspiracy investigation was "not a hoax on anyone's part. There was a plot. I know about it and I know the people involved." When Lewis was asked by the *New York Post* (February 20, 1967) why he was telling Garrison things that he hadn't told the FBI, he replied, "The FBI didn't ask me about it."

Many of Garrison's problems came in selecting his staff. The district attorney's investigators all-too-often turned out to be spies for the defense or turncoats. For example, William C. Wood, also known as Bill Boxley, was a member of Jim Garrison's investigation. He was a square-jawed reformed alcoholic who had told Garrison that he had worked for the CIA until he was fired because of his drinking. Wood worked for Garrison on a volunteer basis. Garrison wrote: "Because of the curiosity of the news media . . . we kept it quiet that we had a former Agency man aboard. So we used the name 'Boxley' instead of Wood. Bill Boxley became a familiar figure in and out of the office. He always carried a loaded 45 automatic pistol, which he kept in a holster under his armpit. This indicated to me that his original intelligence service had been in the U.S. Army, because all of the other American intelligence services used the .38 caliber revolver. He also always carried with him a large rectangular black briefcase. He was an indefatigable worker, and it was apparent that he was dedicated to our effort." Garrison learned later that there was nothing dedicated whatsoever about Wood's work for the effort, and there was nothing ex-about his relationship with the federal government. Philadelphia attorney Vincent Salabria told Garrison that Wood was working for the Feds, reporting on the investigation and conspiring to discredit Garrison. When Wood eventually disappeared, he took many of Garrison's files with him.

New Orleans Parish district attorney Jim Garrison. *(Author's Collection)*

FBI agents Warren DeBrueys and Regis Kennedy were both subpoenaed by Garrison but refused to testify, citing executive privilege—that is, they had permission from President Lyndon Johnson not to testify.

One of the reasons Clay Shaw was acquitted by his jury so rapidly was that many of the witnesses and suspects subpoenaed by Garrison were not extradited. Garrison commented on this problem in a *Playboy* magazine interview (October 1967): "The reason we are unable to extradite anyone connected with the case is that there are powerful forces in Washington who find it imperative to conceal from the American public the truth about the assassination. And as a result, terrific pressure has been brought to bear on the governors of the states involved to prevent them from signing the extradition papers and returning the defendants to stand trial. I'm sorry to say that in every case, these Jell-O-spined governors have caved in and 'played the game' Washington's way."

Witnesses disappeared and died. Those that showed up sometimes turned out to be kooks, embarrassing Garrison and his case. After Shaw's acquittal, it was revealed that he actually had done work for the CIA, and it was perhaps this fact that caused the official backlash against Garrison's efforts. Eerily, it was also revealed that Shaw had been on the Board of Directors of an organization, Permindex, which had been linked to an assassination attempt on French president Charles de Gaulle.

On May 24, 1968, Garrison was quoted by the *Los Angeles Free Press* as saying, "The assassination of President Kennedy . . . was precipitated by the Fascists and the rightist anarchists [who] are one and the same. I firmly believe that the rightist anarchists and the CIA can take over our country right now and it would be a Fascist state except for two things. They would have to demolish and destroy the conservative movement by the radical right. They would have to destroy organizations such as the John Birch Society . . . [and] the other thing that is in their way is . . . Jim Garrison."

Garrison became an appeals judge and ironically played Chief Justice Earl Warren in the 1991 Oliver Stone film *JFK*, which was partially based on Garrison's second book. He died in 1992 at the age of 71 of heart failure.

(See also BANISTER, WILLIAM GUY; FERRIE, DAVID; NOVEL, GORDON; PERMINDEX; SHAW, CLAY; SUSPICIOUS DEATHS; THORNLEY, KERRY WENDELL.)

Gaudet, William George

Gaudet received a visa to go to Mexico City at the same time as someone reported to be Lee Harvey Oswald received a similar visa. Gaudet's and Oswald's entry papers into Mexico dated September 17, 1963, have consecutive serial numbers.

Gaudet confirmed in a November 27, 1963, FBI interview that he had picked up his travel permit on the same day as Oswald. Gaudet admitted to working for the CIA but denied any contact with Oswald south of the border.

Bizarrely, Gaudet admitted in 1978 to assassination researcher Anthony Summers that he had seen Oswald on several occasions in New Orleans, sometimes in the company of Guy Banister and once handing out leaflets. Gaudet said he thought Oswald's distribution of leaflets and subsequent street scuffle with Carlos Bringuier was a "P.R. operation" designed by right-wing propagandist Ed Butler. Gaudet told Bernard Fensterwald in a May 13, 1975, interview, "I don't think (Oswald) knew exactly what he was distributing . . . The Fair Play for Cuba deal . . . was nothing but a front and was one of the dreams of—I think Guy Banister."

Gaudet was a CIA operative, a public relations expert, a one-time editor of a journal, supported by the United Fruit Company, called the *Latin-American Report,* sponsored by Dr. Alton Ochsner, and a consultant to the U.S. Air Force. Gaudet is deceased.

(See also BUTLER, EDWARD; OCHSNER, DR. ALTON.)

Gemberling Report See FEDERAL BUREAU OF INVESTIGATION.

Gemstone File, The

Apparently written by a man named Bruce Roberts (born October 27, 1919, in New York State; died July 30, 1976, in San Francisco, California, of lung cancer), the "Gemstone File" is a document written in the form of a timeline that combines historical facts with wild conjecture, resulting in an intricate alternative history in which the MacGuffin for world power in the 20th century is the formula to create fake rubies (they're called "jack rubies" in the trade), which would go on to become the basis for laser technology. The formula, according to the story, had been developed by Roberts himself. In this "history" the Greek billionaire Aristotle Onassis is the most evil man in the world. He is deeply involved in international opium and narcotics trade. He has taken control of Howard Hughes fortune by kidnapping him and replacing him with a double in 1957. When JFK tried to stop Onassis, Onassis had him killed. The plot was devised by Hughes aide Robert Maheu, and the shooters were Lee Harvey Oswald, Eugene Hale Brading, Johnny Roselli, and Jimmy Frattiano. (Frattiano died on July 2, 1993 at age 79.) Oswald's job was to shoot Governor Connally, and he did. Brading fired from Dealey Plaza's south pergola and missed. Roselli shot from the grassy knoll and fired the head shot. Frattiano shot from the second floor of the Dal-Tex Building and hit President Kennedy twice, in the back and in the back of the head. E. Howard Hunt was also in Dealey Plaza at the time. Onassis later married Jackie Kennedy to complete his evil plan. Historians are fascinated with *The Gemstone File* because, on several levels, it is difficult to disprove. *The Gemstone File*, even though it is not fact, has—as does all good fiction—the undeniable feel of a template for fact.

(See also FLYNT, LARRY; HUGHES, HOWARD; JARNAGIN, CARROLL.)

Giancana, Momo Salvatore "Sam"

Chicago mob boss and alleged assassination conspirator. Giancana had been talking to a Senate Intelligence Committee. He died on June 19, 1975, at age 67 while under police protection, shot with a .22 pistol once in the back of his head and six times around his mouth—mob symbolism for "talks too much." The murder weapon was later found on the bank of the Des Plaines River. It was a silenced Suramatic semi-automatic .22 pistol.

In the early 1960s, Giancana helped the CIA (with money and personnel) in covert operations within Cuba to rid that country of Castro. For a time, Giancana and JFK shared a mistress, Judith Exner. In 1988, Exner told *People* magazine, "I lied when I said that President Kennedy was unaware of my friendship with mobsters. He knew everything about my dealings with Sam Giancana and Johnny

Roselli because I was seeing them for him." According to Anthony Summers, "For 18 months in 1960 and 1961, Exner said, she repeatedly carried envelopes from the President to Giancana and Roselli. There were, she calculated, some ten meetings between the President and [Giancana], one of them in the White House." Exner offered her opinion on why these meetings were held: "I was probably helping Jack orchestrate the attempted assassination of Fidel Castro with the help of the Mafia." Exner died on September 24, 1999, of breast cancer at age 65 in Duarte, California.

Giancana wasn't known for his ability to keep a secret. When the CIA/Mafia teams were planning to assassinate Castro in 1960, J. Edgar Hoover got wind of the plan because Giancana "told several friends."

According to Giancana's half-brother Charles (Chuck) and his nephew Sam in their book *Double Cross*, President Kennedy was murdered by a team of Chicago hitmen sent to Dallas by Giancana. The fatal shot, they claim, was fired by Giancana-lieutenant Richard Cain, from the Texas School Book Depository's sixth floor. Cain himself was murdered in 1973, "gangland style." The book states that the assassination was orchestrated by Lyndon Johnson, Richard Nixon, and others, and funded by Texas oil money. The book also claims that Giancana ordered the murder of his mistress Marilyn Monroe, who was killed by Giancana henchmen with a poison suppository. Giancana

San Giancana, a reputed leader in the Chicago crime syndicate, is shown in a 1965 photo. *(AP/Wide World Photos)*

had been talking to a Senate Intelligence Committee when he was murdered.

Giesbrecht, Richard

A 35-year-old Mennonite businessman and father of four, Giesbrecht told the FBI in 1964 of a conversation he had overheard in the Horizon Room cocktail lounge at Winnipeg International Airport on February 13, 1964.

The conversation was between a man he later came to believe was David Ferrie and a man in his middle or late 40s. The second man had reddish blond hair, a badly pock-marked neck and jaw, wore a hearing aid, and spoke with an accent, possibly Latino.

Giesbrecht said that, from listening to their conversation, it didn't take him long to realize that these men had knowledge of the plot to assassinate President Kennedy. Both men, he said, wore light tweed suits and loafers. He assumed that both were homosexuals.

The man Giesbrecht came to believe was Ferrie said he was troubled over how much Oswald had told his wife about the plot to kill Kennedy. The two men also discussed a man named Isaacs, who apparently knew Oswald. The men thought it odd that Isaacs would become involved with a "psycho" like Oswald. Apparently Isaacs had been at Love Field when President Kennedy arrived in Dallas and had inadvertently gotten himself filmed by news cameras. At the time of the airport conversation, Isaacs was being followed by a man whose name was either Hoffman or Hochman—Giesbrecht couldn't be sure of what he heard. Hoffman or Hochman was to "relieve" Isaacs and destroy a 1958 car that Isaacs had. According to Giesbrecht, "Ferrie" said: "We have more money at our disposal now than at any other time."

Giesbrecht also heard the pair in the airport discussing a meeting scheduled for March 18, 1964, at the Townhouse Motor Hotel in Kansas City, Missouri. A rendezvous, they said, would be registered under the name of the textile firm.

The men said that no meeting had been held since November 1963, presumably meaning since President Kennedy's assassination. "Ferrie" said that an "aunt" was to fly in from California for the meaning. Best guess is that "aunt" in this case is slang for an older homosexual.

Giesbrecht also heard a name that sounded like "Romeniuk" mentioned several times. "Ferrie" asked about merchandise coming from Nevada. The other man said the risks were too great and that the "shop at Mercury had been closed down." He then added that a "good shipment" had been successfully delivered from Newport to Caracas.

Giesbrecht, as he eavesdropped, realized that there was a third man—35 years old, light-haired, six-foot tall, 200 pounds, red-cheeked with a "slightly deformed" nose and a scar or a tattoo on his left hand. Extremely frightened at this point, Giesbrecht left his spot and headed for the airport's Royal Canadian Mounted Police office. He was followed and his entrance to the RCMP was blocked by two men.

Giesbrecht ran to a phone booth and tried to call the RCMP but was forced to hang up when his pursuers approached. He finally lost the men and called his lawyer, who called the U.S. consulate, who called the FBI.

At first the FBI was enthusiastic about Giesbrecht's information. "This looks like the break we've been waiting for," agent Merryl Nelson reportedly told him.

Within two months, however, the bureau had cooled considerably. They told him to forget what he had heard. "It's too big," an agent told him. "We can't protect you in Canada."

Who was Isaacs, the man who got too close to JFK at Love Field? There were several men with that name who cropped up in the various assassination-oriented investigations. The first was Chuck Isaacs, the best suspect, whose name was found in Jack Ruby's notebook [Warren Commission Exhibits: Armstrong Exhibit, No. 5309-A]. Chuck was Charles R. Isaacs, who worked as an American Airlines ticket agent at Love Field. Isaacs's wife reportedly made costumes for Ruby. Later associates of Isaacs theorized that Isaacs's relationship with his wife might have been one of convenience. Isaacs later moved to San Francisco, where he was reportedly "somewhat of an operator." In 1992, Isaacs was reportedly suffering from Alzheimer's disease in Louisiana.

Social worker Martin Isaacs's name was found in Lee Harvey Oswald's notebook. It turned out that Martin had helped arrange for the Oswalds' relocation to Texas following their return from the Soviet Union. He said that he had never been to Dallas or Winnipeg.

When assassination researcher William Turner began to vigorously investigate Chuck Isaacs, he was told that he was on the wrong trail by William Wood, formerly of the Garrison investigation, and assassination-archivist Mary Ferrell, who strongly suggested that he investigate Dr. Harold R. Isaacs instead, who was mentioned in Warren Commission Document 1080. He was a professor at M.I.T. with intelligence connections. He was also possibly an associate of Oswald's globetrotting cousin Marilyn Murret.

(See also FERRIE, DAVID; GARRISON INVESTIGATION; MURRET, CHARLES AND LILLIAN.)

Givens, Charles Douglas "Slim"

According to author Josiah Thompson, Givens, a middle-aged employee of the Texas School Book Depository, was one of the last to see Oswald before the assassination.

Givens says Oswald was on the sixth floor with a clipboard at 11:55 A.M. Oswald's clipboard was later (much later) found on the sixth floor, not far from where the Mannlicher-Carcano rifle had been hidden.

According to Penn Jones Jr., Givens originally said that he had seen Oswald on the first floor of the Book Depository about a half hour before the assassination, but—by the time he testified for the Warren Commission—he had changed his story. Now he said he saw Oswald on the sixth floor.

Givens was considered a suspect immediately following the assassination. He was missing from the building after the shooting—contradicting the official story that Oswald was the only Depository employee to miss a roll call taken after the assassination. In addition, Givens had a police record (narcotics).

According to Book Depository colleague Roy E. Lewis, Givens was known to "tease" Oswald.

Gonzalez, Henry B.

The representative in Congress from San Antonio, Texas, who rode in the Dallas motorcade. Gonzalez says he warned President Kennedy "not to come to Dallas." In early 1977, Gonzalez replaced Congressman Thomas Downing as the chairman of the House Select Committee on Assassinations—and then was subsequently replaced himself by Louis Stokes.

Gradjeda, Ignacio Gonzales   See CASTILLO, LUIS ANGEL.

Grant, Donald Lincoln "Clint"

A Dallas Morning News staff photographer, born in 1916 in Nashville, Tennessee, who rode in the Dallas motorcade in Camera Car 2 carrying two cameras, both Nikon F single-lens reflex cameras, one with a 105mm lens and one with a 35mm lens. He had worked for the newspaper since 1941. Grant told researcher Richard B. Trask in 1985 that the presidential limousine was out of his view at the time of the shooting because it had turned onto Elm Street while Camera Car 2 was still on Houston Street. Grant said that his first inkling that something was wrong was when he saw a Secret Service agent with his automatic weapon raised. Grant knew that the Secret Service never displayed their weapons unless it was an emergency. Grant said, in a letter to researcher Richard B. Trask dated December 1, 1985, that he heard four shots all together: one shot followed by a pause and then three in quick succession. Eight years later, on November 20, 1993, addressing a conference at Southern Methodist University, Grant said that he had heard only three shots.

Great Southwest Corporation

According to assassination researcher and theorist Peter Dale Scott, the Great Southwest Corporation was a real-estate venture headquartered in Dallas and under the control of the family of Bedford Wynne and the Rockefellers. Employees and representatives of this corporation took charge of Marina Oswald's life following her husband's arrest and death. One such employee, James Herbert Martin, became her manager and negotiated her sale of the backyard photos. Two of the witnesses who saw Oswald or an Oswald look-alike practicing with a rifle were employees of Great Southwest. George DeMohrenschildt was represented by Morris Jaffe, who was Bedford Wynne's law partner. Former vice president Richard Nixon had been in Dallas the day before the assassination because of an impending land deal between Great Southwest and Pepsico, the soft-drink manufacturer for whom Nixon worked at the time. Beverly Oliver, the self-proclaimed assassination "Babushka Lady," worked at the Great Southwest–owned Inn of the Six Flags in 1961, the same hotel where, two years later, Marina Oswald was taken, ostensibly to keep her away from a theoretically hostile public.

Greener, Charles W.   See IRVING SPORTS SHOP.

Groden, Robert J.

Photographic consultant to the House Select Committee on Assassinations. Groden, using a self-created computer photographic enhancement technique known as Groden-scoping, has created new versions of the assassination's photographic evidence. Groden "Groden-ized" the Zapruder film and the Nix film by "enhancing and stabilizing" them frame by frame. It was Groden's optically enhanced version of the Zapruder film that, after being shown on national television, was instrumental in the formation of the House Select Committee.

It has concerned some researchers, however, that so much of the photographic evidence now must be viewed through the filter of Groden-scoping, for every enhancement is an alteration. It is of particular concern that the original Nix film can no longer be found, which means that all existing versions have been Groden-ized.

If Groden accidentally covered something up or deleted an image during the execution of his process, that information is now gone forever. Of course, some have hinted that Groden's job is to cover up information—but, before that accusation can be made, we must show one instance of useful information that existed before a photo was Groden-ized that was missing after the process was completed—or evidence that a Groden-ized image contains seemingly important information that wasn't there in the original. No such evidence has been found.

Grossi, John Caesar   See BOWEN, JACK LESLIE.

Haas, R. E. "Buster"

Desk editor for the *Dallas Morning News* who witnessed the assassination with his wife and son, and then returned to his office where he was told to "get every picture and every story into the paper no matter how many pages it takes." Haas passed away on March 24, 1996, of a heart attack at age 70.

Hall, Loran Eugene (a.k.a. Hall, Lorenzo; Pascillio, Lorenzo; Skip)

Anti-Castro Cuban activist who was thought by the Warren Commission to be one of the three men who visited Cuban exile Silvia Odio (one of whom was identified as Leon Oswald) on either September 25 or 26, 1963, when, officially, Oswald was on his way by bus to Mexico City.

The FBI said Hall was "Leon Oswald." J. Edgar Hoover offered that there was enough "phonetic resemblance" between the two names to cause the confusion. Hall, however, wore a full beard when supposedly visiting Odio and couldn't have been mistaken for Oswald. (And, of course, if the Odio incident never took place at all, as some believe, the point is moot.)

It says in the *Warren Report:* "On September 16, 1964, the FBI located Loran Eugene Hall in Johnsandale, Calif. . . . He told the FBI that in September of 1963 he was in Dallas, soliciting aid in connection with anti-Castro activities. He said he had visited Mrs. Odio. He was accompanied by Lawrence Howard, a Mexican-American from East Los Angeles and one William Seymour from Arizona. He stated that Seymour is similar in appearance to Lee Harvey Oswald; he speaks only a few words of Spanish, as

Mrs. Odio had testified one of the men did . . . [T]he Commission has concluded that Lee Harvey Oswald was not at Mrs. Odio's apartment in September of 1963."

Both Howard and Seymour denied visiting Silvia Odio when traced and questioned by the FBI. According to former undercover agent Harry Dean, President Kennedy's assassins were Hall and Eladio del Valle. Dean claims the pair had been hired by the John Birch Society.

Hall admits to being jailed and released in Cuba in 1959 at the same time as assassination suspect Santos Trafficante. Hall worked with a Cuban-exile/CIA anti-Castro group called INTERPEN (Intercontinental Penetration Force) with Marine-veteran Gerry Patrick Hemming—who in turn was identified under oath by Marita Lorenz as one of the men who rode in a gun-toting caravan from Miami to Dallas, arriving on the eve of the assassination.

Hall and Hemming also worked together in the International Anti-Communist Brigade, a group which included suspects David Ferrie and Frank Sturgis, and reportedly maintained a paramilitary training camp on Lake Pontchartrain near New Orleans where Oswald had reportedly been seen with Ferrie.

According to the *Dallas Morning News* (September 17, 1978), Hall claims that, one month before President Kennedy's death, he was approached by ultra-right-wing activists working with CIA operatives. These men, Hall claims, wanted him to take part in the president's murder.

When testifying for the House Select Committee on Assassinations, Hall refused to divulge his whereabouts before and at the time of the assassination until he was granted immunity from prosecution.

House Select Committee on Assassinations chief counsel G. Robert Blakey writes: "In September 1963 Hall and

Howard drove from Los Angeles for Miami with a trailer-load of arms, but they were forced to leave the trailer in Dallas for lack of a hiding place in Florida. In October Hall and Seymour, back in Dallas to retrieve the trailer, were arrested for possession of drugs; but with the help of an influential financial supporter, they were released. They took the arms back to Miami, but the mission for which they were intended, Hall told us, was aborted in late October when he, Howard, Seymour, and some Cubans were arrested by customs officials as they were driving to their embarkation point south of Miami. No charges were filed, but their arms and equipment were confiscated so they returned to Miami, frustrated, and in early November, headed west. All three swore they were at their respective homes—Hall and Howard in California, Seymour in Arizona—on November 22, 1963."

According to Paris Flammonde, however, Seymour "claimed—with some proof—to have been in Miami at the time [of JFK's death]."

After Jim Garrison concluded a long interview with Hall in connection with his assassination investigation, Garrison issued a press release: "It is apparent that Hall is in no way connected with the events culminating in the assassination . . . it is equally apparent that other individuals and agencies caused Mr. Hall's name to be injected into [Warren Commission] exhibits . . . so that any effort to investigate the assassination would cause his name to appear . . . Hall proved to be a helpful witness for our inquiry."

At the time of the assassination Hall appeared Mexican. He was dark-skinned and balding, six-feet tall, between 40 and 45 years old. He was also, according to one FBI report, a "loud mouth."

(See also DEAN, HARRY; HEMMING, GERRY PATRICK; ODIO INCIDENT.)

Hall, Lorenzo   See HALL, LORAN EUGENE.

Hamblen, C. A.
Hamblen was the early night manager at the Dallas Western Union Telegraph Co. The *Warren Report* states: "Five days after the assassination . . . Hamblen . . . told his superior that about two weeks earlier he remembered Oswald sending a telegram from the office to Washington, D.C., possibly to the Secretary of the Navy, and that the application was completed in an unusual form of hand printing. The next day Hamblen told a magazine correspondent . . . that he remembered seeing Oswald in the office on other occasions collecting money orders for small amounts of money. Soon thereafter, Hamblen signed a statement . . . specifying two instances in which he had seen the person he believed to be Oswald in the office; in each instance the

man behaved disagreeably and one other Western Union employee had become involved in assisting him." Federal investigators could find no record of any of the telegrams or money orders. The coworker implicated in Hamblen's story denies it happened. During his Warren Commission testimony, Hamblen became uncertain about his story's details. The *Warren Report* says: "Hamblen's superiors have concluded 'that this whole thing was a figment of Mr. Hamblen's imagination,' and the Commission accepts this assessment."

Hardee, Jack, Jr.
Dallas numbers operator who told the FBI that J. D. Tippit was "a frequent visitor to Ruby's nightclub" during a December 26, 1963, deposition at the Mobile (Alabama) County Jail, where Hardee was incarcerated. The FBI reported: "Hardee stated that he has spent some time in Dallas, Texas, and he had met Jack Ruby during the course of his contacts in Dallas. He stated that approximately one year ago, while in Dallas, Texas, he attempted to set up a numbers game, and he was advised by an individual, whom he did not identify, that in order to operate in Dallas it was necessary to have the clearance of Jack Ruby. He stated that this individual . . . told him Ruby had the 'fix' with the county authorities, and that any other fix being placed would have to be done through Ruby . . . Hardee also stated that the police officer whom Harvey Lee Oswald [sic] allegedly killed after he allegedly assassinated the president was a frequent visitor to Ruby's night club, along with another officer who was a motorcycle patrol in the Oaklawn [sic] section of Dallas. Hardee stated from his observation there appeared to be a very close relationship between these three individuals . . . Hardee stated that he knows of his own personal knowledge that Ruby hustled the strippers and other girls who worked in his club. Ruby made dates for them, accepting the money for the dates in advance, and kept half, giving the other half to the girls. The dates were filled in the new hotel in downtown Dallas and the Holiday Inn in Irvington, where Ruby had an associate, whom Hardee could only identify as a Negro who drove a big Cadillac."

Hardie, Julius
He claims to have been in Dealey Plaza on the morning of the assassination and, at that time, saw three men with rifles or shotguns standing atop the triple underpass.

Hargis, Bobby W.
The Dallas police motorcycle patrolman who rode just behind and to the left of President Kennedy's limo during

the motorcade and was splattered with blood and brain tissue by the final shot, indicating that the final shot came from the right front.

Hargis was struck by so much bodily material that he thought at first that he, himself, had been shot. He was horrified to discover a piece of the president's brain and skull clinging to his lip.

According to William Manchester, Hargis was "doused in a red sheet." Hargis parked his motorcycle immediately following the shooting and ran up the grassy knoll in search of the shooter.

(See also ROBINSON, MIKE.)

Harkness, David V.

Dallas police sergeant who joined the department on July 8, 1946. Harkness was in Dealey Plaza before, during, and after the assassination. He was a three-wheel motorcycle officer supervising point control and three-wheel officers, assigned to keep the motorcade route open from the corner of Main and Field to the corner of Elm and Houston. It was Harkness who summoned an ambulance to the front of the Texas School Book Depository moments before the assassination to help Jerry B. Belknap, who seemingly was having an epileptic seizure. Some have suspected the "seizure" was meant as a diversion. (See also EPILEPTIC FIT.)

Harkness says that he saw Jack Ruby poking around Dealey Plaza on the morning of the assassination, and he had to tell him to move on because pedestrians were not being allowed on the grass south of Elm Street. "I don't recall whether he said anything, but he left," says Harkness.

Harkness estimated that he was between 150 and 200 feet away from the presidential limousine when the shooting began. He was standing at the edge of the median between Main and Elm, only a few feet from his motorcycle, which was parked at the intersection of Elm and Houston. He says he heard three shots and that there was a longer gap between the first two than the last two, saying the final two shots were "pretty close together." He said he could not determine the source of the shots.

Immediately following the assassination, Harkness searched "the area behind" the Texas School Book Depository. He then moved to the front of the building where he overheard witness Howard Brennan telling policemen that he had seen a man shooting from an upper floor of the Book Depository. (See also BRENNAN, HOWARD.)

Harkness then spoke to Amos Euins, a "little colored boy," who had also seen a rifleman (although not one who was alone) in the Depository. At that point Harkness began to seal off the building. (See also EUINS, AMOS.)

Moving back to the building's rear Harkness saw two men "lounging." The men verbally identified themselves as Secret Service agents, and Harkness did not ask for written identification.

According to the Secret Service, all real Secret Service agents accompanied the motorcade to Parkland Hospital. This is not the only report of spurious Secret Service agents on the assassination scene.

Following this encounter, Harkness moved into the railyards behind the grassy knoll where he discovered and arrested "six to eight" hoboes. He says that many tramps were arrested in the area, and that the three whose pictures appeared in the magazine—none of whom were tramps whom he arrested—were just the three "famous ones." (See also THREE TRAMPS.)

Harkness never did seal off the Texas School Book Depository. The building was not sealed until seven full minutes after the shooting under the orders of Inspector Herbert Sawyer.

Harkness testified at Ruby's murder trial that at approximately 3:00 P.M. on November 23, 1963, he saw Ruby in the crowd while clearing the entrance to the Dallas police Station in preparation for a planned transfer of Oswald at 4:00 P.M. The transfer was eventually postponed until the following morning.

Harkness retired from the Dallas Police Department in 1973 and worked for the Probation Department until 1991.

Harper Fragment, The

William "Billy" Harper, a witness to the assassination, found a piece of President Kennedy's skull 25 feet southeast of the presidential limousine's position at the time of the fatal shot.

Harper turned the bone (commonly referred to as the "Harper fragment") over to the chief pathologist at Methodist Hospital, who identified it as bone from the back of the president's head. The fragment was then transported from Dallas to Washington where, on the night of November 22, it was turned over to the FBI laboratory.

The fragment is significant because, officially, the back of President Kennedy's skull was left intact by the shooting.

Harrelson, Charles V.

Professional killer who, upon capture, confessed and then retracted his confession to killing President Kennedy. Columnist Jack Anderson, among others, has suggested that the "tall tramp" photographed in Dealey Plaza after the assassination, was, in fact, Charles Harrelson, an organized crime hitman.

Harrelson has been serving a life sentence in Federal Prison in Marion, Illinois, since 1979 for the murder of U.S. District Court judge John H. Wood Jr. He is the only prisoner in the United States currently incarcerated for killing a federal official with a rifle.

Harrelson told British documentary filmmaker Nigel Turner (*The Men Who Killed Kennedy,* 1988), "On November 22, 1963, at 12:30, I was having lunch with a friend in a restaurant in Houston, Texas . . . I did not kill John Kennedy."

Independent forensic anthropologists, using the photographic evidence, have stated that there is a 90 to 95 percent chance that Harrelson is the "tall tramp."

According to a statement given in Dallas in 1992 by researcher Phillip Rogers: "Harrelson was born near Huntsville, Texas. As a young man he went on to California, where he became the salesman of the year as an encyclopedia salesman and soon turned to a life of crime. He was convicted of armed robbery in 1960. He turned probation and was cleared of probation in 1965. This is kind of a shady period of his life. Not too much is known about where he went or what he did during that time. In 1968 he became a public figure when he faced several trials, two of which he was acquitted for, then, at a re-trial he was convicted of his first murder for hire in South Texas. He served time and was released. He then quickly became involved in the Judge Wood assassination. He went on the run and ended up in El Paso. A funny thing happened: He borrowed a Corvette. He was high on cocaine, when he thought the muffler was making too much noise. He shot out the back tires trying to remove the muffler with a .44 magnum. He was arrested after a six-hour stand-off during which time he held a gun to his head and confessed to shooting President Kennedy. He later recanted that, saying that he was high at the time—although he continued to drop hints about the matter for awhile."

Harrelson is the father of film and television star Woody Harrelson.

(See also THREE TRAMPS.)

Harris, Jones

Assassination researcher who did work for the investigation into conspiracy to assassinate JFK conducted by New Orleans district attorney Jim Garrison. Harris stated publicly that he believed the Japanese killed JFK.

It was Harris who first spotted the suspicious shape—it looked like a man shooting from beside a car at the top of the grassy knoll—in the background of frames from the film taken by Orville Nix. The shape, later analysis theorized, was actually caused by the shape of the light shining through the trees.

Harris, Larry Ray

Harris was the coauthor, with J. Gary Shaw, of *Cover-up.* Harris was a JFK assassination fanatic who once took a job

at the Texas School Book Depository for a few weeks, just so he would have access to the sixth floor.

On Friday afternoon, October 23, 1992, Harris gave a workshop on the Tippit killing at which he stated his conclusion that J. D. Tippit's life and death had nothing to do with JFK's death. He said he believed that it was merely a matter of coincidence that he was murdered on the same day in a location that is the center of a small triangle formed by the alleged assassin's home, the place where Oswald was arrested, and Jack Ruby's home. Harris called Tippit an "East Texas farm boy" who didn't swing with the same crowd as Ruby, no matter what others might say. Tippit's death, Harris believed, was the result of a love triangle.

Apparently Tippit was having an affair with a married woman named Jonny Maxi Thompson (later Witherspoon). Harris interviewed Mr. Thompson in west Texas and said that he answered questions freely, admitting that Jonny Maxi's last child was Tippit's. The Thompsons were divorced in April 1963. They reconciled for a time in September 1963. Mr. Thompson says that the reconciliation didn't take place until November 23, the day after Tippit was killed. The woman may be telling this particular lie to protect her child, since it was born seven months after Tippit's death, and she no doubt did not want the child to know Tippit was not its father.

Although Harris would have us believe Thompson is a suspect in this crime, he also stated that Thompson was a ne'er do well whose own infidelity hardly put him in a position to criticize his wife's behavior. Jonny Maxi, for the record, did not marry Witherspoon until the mid-1970s. Here are seven other items regarding Tippit's murder that Harris felt were important:

1. Tippit was in the "Top Ten Record Store" next to the Texas Theatre at 1:00 P.M., less than 15 minutes before his death. According to one witness, he pushed his way to a pay phone, made a call, got no answer, hurried out, and screamed off in his car. Another source said that this was an accurate description of his actions in the store, but that they occurred at nine that morning, not at one in the afternoon. (See also TOP 10 RECORD STORE.)

2. Mrs. Helen Markham, the confused witness to the Tippit killing who became the Warren Commission's star witness, was a waitress at the Eat Well Cafe on Main Street in downtown Dallas, an establishment that was admittedly frequented by Jack Ruby.

3. When Oswald was finally searched, several hours after his arrest in the Texas Theatre, one half of a Cox's department store box top was found in his pocket. Harris led us to believe that this was evidence of secret agent activity, as men meeting in a clandestine fashion often carry half of the same item (like a dollar bill) to prove to each other that they are the real article. This

seemed fascinating until it was revealed later in the day under unrelated circumstances that Oswald's mother worked at Cox's department store in Ft. Worth. Still, one half of a box top seems like an odd thing to carry.

4. The FBI agent who was with the Dallas police at the Texas Theatre at the time of Oswald's arrest was Special Agent Bob Barrett. Why would the FBI be involved in the apprehension of a man suspected of sneaking into a movie theater without paying?

5. Harris spoke to many of the shop owners near the theater along Jefferson Blvd. and they agreed that they had never seen so many cop cars in all their life as they did before and during Oswald's apprehension. Another indication that the fix was in?

6. This not from Harris but rather in spite of him: Just before the Dallas police received a call that a suspicious man had entered the Texas Theatre without paying for his ticket, they had a good identification on an armed perpetrator entering the Abundant Life Temple, a church just one block from 10th and Patton. (See also ABUNDANT LIFE TEMPLE.)

7. Virginia Davis was an eyewitness to the Tippit shooting, and it was on her front lawn that several shell casings were found. Now it comes out that Davis's phone number was in Jack Ruby's notebook. This together with the fact that Mrs. Markham probably knew Ruby gives rise to even more questions about the incident.

Harris died in October 1996 in a car accident.
(See also TIPPIT, MURDER OF.)

Hartman, Wayne and Edna

The Hartmans were standing on Main Street, east of Houston Street (around the corner from Dealey Plaza). After hearing shots, Mr. and Mrs. Hartman ran onto the grassy area on the south side of Elm.

Edna told reporter Jim Marrs, "There were not many people in this area at the time, but a policeman was there. He pointed to some bushes near the railroad tracks on the north side of the street and said that's where the shots came from. . . . Then I noticed these two parallel marks on the ground that looked like mounds made by a mole. I asked, 'What are these, mole hills?' and the policeman said, 'Oh no, ma'am, that's where the bullets struck the ground.'"

Edna told a gathering at the JFK Assassination Symposium in Dallas on November 15, 1991, that the bullet mark she had seen pointed southeast, consistent with a shot from the grassy knoll.

Harvey, William King   See CENTRAL INTELLIGENCE AGENCY.

Hathaway, Philip B.

During the late morning of November 22, 1963, Hathaway was walking with coworker John Stevens Rutter Lawrence on Akard Street toward Main Street to find a place to watch the motorcade. Hathaway told Dallas reporter Jim Marrs that he saw a big man in a gray business suit—six-foot-five, 250 pounds—dirty blond hair in a crew cut, with thick chest hair, carrying a rifle in a leather and cloth case. Presumably, the man was not wearing a tie or the quantity of his chest hair would have remained unknown. Lawrence, who saw the man but, because of the crowd, not the gun, said the man resembled a "professional football player." Both witnesses assumed the man was a Secret Service agent.

(See also HEMMING, GERRY PATRICK.)

Haygood, Clyde A.

Dallas police motorcycle patrolman who was assigned to protect the right rear of President Kennedy's limousine during the motorcade. Haygood, however, "straggled" before the shots were fired. Immediately following the shooting, Haygood parked his motorcycle and ran up the grassy knoll and into the parking lot behind the wooden fence. While there, he says, he saw "nothing suspicious."

Haygood was then told by an unidentified witness that the shots had come from the Texas School Book Depository. Haygood then radioed in (using the code number 142) and called for the Book Depository to be sealed off.

The patrolman went on the air at 12:35, five minutes after the shooting sequence, saying, "I just talked to a guy up here who was standing close to it and the best he could tell it came from the [Depository]. It is believed the shots came from there. If you're facing it on Elm Street looking toward the building, it would be the upper-right-hand window, the second window from the end."

Helms, Richard McGarrah

Born in Pennsylvania, March 30, 1913, Helms graduated from Williams College in 1935. He was a United Press International staff correspondent for a time and then became a reporter for the *Indianapolis Times* in 1937, staying with the paper until 1942 when he was assigned by the U.S. Navy to work with the Office of Strategic Services. Helms stayed with the OSS after the war, and still later when it became the CIA. Helms was deputy director of plans at the time of the assassination and then director of central intelligence during the Vietnam era (1965–73). MK/ULTRA, the CIA mind-control program, has been called Helms's brainchild. Helms became a controversial figure in 1971 when it was revealed that the CIA was waging a clandestine war in Southeast Asia. A congressional hearing into the assassination squads and secret armies that performed CIA-sponsored functions in the former Indochina and elsewhere under Helms's watch resulted in new laws necessitating presidential approval of all covert operations. Helms served as ambassador to Iran, 1973–76.

(See also CENTRAL INTELLIGENCE AGENCY; MK/ULTRA.)

Hemming, Gerry Patrick

Born March 1, 1937, in Los Angeles, California, Hemming served in the U.S. Marine Corps from April 1953 until 1958. An Office of Naval Intelligence agent, he fought in Fidel Castro's Revolutionary Army from February 1959 until August 1960. He stood six-foot-six and weighed 230 pounds. During 1961 and 1962, Hemming trained Cubans and Americans in guerrilla warfare as the leader of a sol-dier-of-fortune group known as INTERPEN (the International Penetration Force) at a location known as No Name Key in the Florida Keys.

Hemming was named by former Castro mistress Marita Lorenz under oath as one of the men who participated in a gun-toting caravan from Miami to Dallas that arrived on the eve of the assassination. Others in the caravan, accord-ing to Lorenz, were assassination suspects Frank Sturgis and Lee Harvey Oswald (who, according to all other accounts, was working at the Texas School Book Deposi-tory at that time). Hemming also worked for the Interna-tional Anti-Communist Brigade that trained anti-Castro Cuban-exile paramilitary troops at a camp on Lake Pontchartrain near New Orleans, where Oswald had reportedly been seen repeatedly in the company of assas-sination suspect David Ferrie. Hemming's association with INTERPEN and the International Anti-Communist Brigade, where he worked with assassination suspect Frank Sturgis, would have made him a coworker of assas-sination suspect Loran Hall.

Hemming claims that he met Oswald three times: 1. at the Cuban consulate in Monterrey Park, California, while Oswald was in the Marines and stationed at Santa Ana, California. Hemming says Oswald tried to enlist his aid in getting to Cuba, where he wanted to fight on Castro's side; 2. In Cuba, where Oswald came to see him (although the Cubans, according to Hemming, did not allow Oswald to stay for very long); 3. On December 6, 1962, in Miami. This final meeting was very brief.

Hemming says that the real Lee Harvey Oswald was never in Mexico City and that the illusion of his visit there was completely manufactured.

Hemming says that he met Jack Ruby in September or October of 1959 at a house in Cuba. Ruby was there, he says, trying to sell "inferior jeeps" to the Cuban air force.

Hemming says that he was approached by Guy Banister to "do the Dallas hit" but turned it down. That offer came

during March or April 1962 and took place at Luis Rabel's home in Matairie, Louisiana.

In a strange coincidence, Hemming once worked at Klein's Sporting Goods store in Chicago, the same store from which Lee Harvey Oswald was alleged to have mail-ordered the rifle that is supposed to have killed the presi-dent. Hemming, in fact, used Klein's as a reference on his CIA job application form.

Hemming told assassination researcher Noel Twyman that there were several assassination teams in Dallas on November 22, 1963, including one on the other side of the triple underpass from Dealey Plaza with an explosive-laden automobile. Hemming says that the shots from behind came from Abraham Zapruder's offices in the Dal-Tex Building. He says that the assassins in Dealey Plaza used sonic silencers that were purchased through Mitchell WerBell. Hemming says he thinks J. Edgar Hoover and General John Magruder of military intelligence were the masterminds behind the plot with Charles Siragusa and William K. Harvey also involved.

(See also CENTRAL INTELLIGENCE AGENCY; HALL, LOREN; HATHAWAY, PHILIP B.; LORENZ, MARITA; STURGIS, FRANK; WER-BELL, MITCHELL.)

Hendrix, Ruth

Employee of Allyn and Bacon Publishers, with offices on the third floor of the Texas School Book Depository, who watched the assassination from the north side of Elm Street, near a lamppost about even with the west edge of the Depository. As did many assassination witnesses, she thought the first shot was a firecracker.

Hendrix told researcher Larry A. Sneed, "In all, I heard three shots, and it seemed to me that there was more time between the first and second and less between the second and third shots. I wasn't sure where they were coming from, but I knew they were coming from over my head from a high location."

She worked in that building until retiring at the age of 65 in 1977.

Hernandez, Razo   See CASTILLO, LUIS ANGEL.

Hester, Charles and Beatrice

Assassination witnesses who were sitting on the grass on the north side of Elm Street just in front of the north per-gola. The Hesters heard two shots that they thought came from the Texas School Book Depository. At the sound of the shots Charles threw Beatrice down to the floor of the pergola and then got down with her. The couple, con-cerned that so many policemen were running toward the grassy knoll, triple underpass, and railroad yard, then told John Wiseman of the Dallas County Sheriff's Department to check out the Book Depository.

Hicks, James

A surveyor from Enid, Oklahoma, Hicks was in Dealey Plaza during the assassination and reported seeing a bullet hole in the Elm Street "Stemmons" traffic sign—the same sign that obscures our view of President Kennedy first being wounded in the Zapruder film—soon after the shooting. The sign was removed almost immediately by men he presumed to be members of the Dallas police.

According to the January 12, 1968, edition of the *New Orleans Times-Picayune,* on the day before he was to testify for New Orleans district attorney Jim Garrison before the grand jury to indict Clay Shaw, Hicks was pushed through a plate glass window and severely beaten.

According to author Paris Flammonde, "In the early morning prior to his grand jury appearance [in the Clay Shaw case], Hicks reported, his hotel room was invaded by two Negro men who roughed him up and tossed him through French doors leading to a balcony outside his sixth-floor room. However, the witness said he did not believe the assault was related to the investigation."

Hicks is believed by assassination researchers Bernard Fensterwald and Robert Sam Anson to be the radio communications coordinator for the Dallas assassins. Photographs taken following the assassination appear to show Hicks in Dealey Plaza with some sort of radio.

Hidell, Alec J.

Allegedly an alias for Lee Harvey Oswald and the name under which the accused assassin is believed to have mail ordered the weapons with which he supposedly killed JFK and Officer J. D. Tippit. Oswald is said to have first used the name as an alias on January 27, 1963, when he reportedly ordered a .38 revolver from Seaport Traders in Los Angeles under that name—although Oswald's official bio tells us that he had been called "Alik" in the Soviet Union. An identification card with a photo of Oswald and the name Alec J. Hidell was, according to the official scenario, found in the wallet Oswald had on him when he was arrested in the Texas Theatre.

However, there was no public announcement of Oswald's alias—or even a suggestion that the alias existed—until after Oswald was murdered on November 24, 1963. Private mentions of the name are claimed but none can be verified. The alias was not used over the police radio during the minutes following Oswald's arrest. Up until Oswald's death it was said repeatedly that Oswald had used an alias and that it was O. H. Lee, the name under which he was registered at his rooming house.

Detective Jim Leavelle, famous as the man who was handcuffed to Oswald when Ruby shot him, saw Oswald's wallet in the interrogation room in the Dallas police station—probably the wallet found on Oswald at the time of his arrest. Leavelle says he remembers seeing the Oswald ID but not the Hidell ID. The original Dallas police inventory of the contents of Oswald's wallet makes no mention of the Hidell identification card.

Army intelligence had a file on Hidell, cross-referenced to Oswald as an alias. This is interesting since, although Oswald was associated with the name Hidell on pamphlets in New Orleans and various job applications, the only time he reportedly ever used it as an alias was when mail-ordering the guns that theoretically killed Tippit and Kennedy.

(See also ARMY INTELLIGENCE.)

Hill, Clinton J.   See SECRET SERVICE.

Hill, Gerald Lynn

Former *Dallas Times Herald* crime-beat reporter who joined the Dallas Police Department in 1955 and three years later was promoted to sergeant. Hill was a witness to the aftermath of the assassination in Dealey Plaza, was among the first to search the sixth floor of the Texas School Book Depository, was among the first police to reach the scene of the Tippit killing and handled key evidence there, then was among those who went to the Dallas theater for the arrest of Lee Harvey Oswald. Hill found—or was in the vicinity of—much of the hard evidence that would have been used against Oswald had he gone to trial.

According to Hill's Warren Commission testimony, he was at the Dallas police station, working in plain clothes in the personnel department, when he heard about the assassination. Hill rode from the police station to the Texas School Book Depository in car no. 207, which was driven by officer Jim M. Valentine. Also in the car was *Dallas Morning News* reporter Jim Ewell. KRLD-TV news footage of Dealey Plaza repeatedly shows car no. 207 with Hill, Valentine, and Ewell inside, arriving at the Texas School Book Depository at 12:55, 25 minutes following the shooting.

Hill briefly searched the Book Depository's sixth floor. Hill told assassination researcher Dale K. Myers in 1986 his version of how the search of the sixth floor went: "Officer Mooney from the Sheriff's office, took the northeast corner and I took the south side of the building. And we started working toward the middle. Mooney found where the shots had been fired from, found three spent shells on the floor—and hollered at me and I went to that location. I told him to stay there and make sure nobody fools with anything, and I went over to another window and tried to yell down six floors, over sirens and fire trucks and everything else, and I wasn't sure they heard me on the ground. So, I left there, and I went back down to the ground floor to make sure that the Crime Lab had been notified to come to the sixth floor of the Depository Building." Hill went down to the street to communicate his message in person, just as Captain Will Fritz was arriving. Fritz, according to the *Warren Report*, arrived at the Book Depository "shortly before 1:00 P.M."

While outside the Depository, Hill encountered Assistant District Attorney Bill Alexander, and together they heard the call on the police radio that an officer was down in Oak Cliff. This call came at 1:18. Hill does not account for the missing 20 minutes.

Hill rode from the Texas School Book Depository to Oak Cliff with Sergeant Owens, Bill Alexander, and an unidentified fourth man. Once in Oak Cliff, this car approached the Tippit murder scene by going south on Beckley, the street where Oswald's rooming house was. It is not specified in which car they went. He was in the second car to arrive at the scene of the Tippit killing—yet Tippit's body had already been removed. In fact, Hill told assassination researcher Larry A. Sneed that while he was traveling south on Beckley at the corner of Colorado, the ambulance carrying Tippit passed in front of them on its way to Methodist Hospital.

Hill was familiar with the Oak Cliff streets. He had attended W. H. Adamson High School, only a few blocks from the corner of Tenth and Patton where J. D. Tippit was murdered.

Only eight minutes elapsed between the time the first call for help came from the corner of Tenth and Patton and Hill's first call-in from the area. At 1:26 P.M., Hill broadcast, "I'm at 12th and Beckley now. Have a man in the car that can identify the suspect if anyone gets him."

Upon arriving at the Tippit scene Hill told Myers that he was immediately approached by a male witness who said, "'The man that shot him was a white male about five-feet, ten-inches, weighing 160 to 170 pounds, had on a jacket and a pair of trousers, and brown bushy hair.' I turned this man over to Officer Joe Poe who had just arrived. I didn't even get [the witness's] name. I told Officer Poe to stay on the scene and guard the car and talk to as many witnesses as they could find to the incident, and that we were going to start checking the area."

Soon after arriving, Hill, Owens, and Alexander, now joined by Officer C. T. Walker, left the scene of the Tippit murder to chase the shooter and "shake down vacant houses on the north side of Jefferson." Among the buildings that Hill searched was the Abundant Life Temple a block west of the crime scene where a witness said he had

seen the assailant flee. It was near the rear door of the temple in a gas-station parking lot where the jacket reportedly worn by the assailant fleeing the scene was discovered.

They did not find anything so they returned to Tenth and Patton, where officer J. M. Poe gave Hill an empty Winston cigarette pack containing shells—which apparently had been ejected from the murder weapon.

Hill says he was talking to accident investigator Bob L. Apple when a call came in that a suspect had been seen entering the Texas Theatre. Hill and Apple traveled together in Apple's car to the Texas Theatre.

Hill told researcher Larry A. Sneed, "I went into the lobby and immediately went upstairs into the balcony. There was very little light in the theater. All they had on was a clean-up light. So I went over and kicked the fire doors open on the balcony to flood the place with light. We determined that there wasn't anybody that fit the description that we had up in the balcony. Basically it was kids shooting hooky from school."

Hill went downstairs and was among those who helped escort Lee Harvey Oswald to a Dallas Police car waiting at the curb on Jefferson outside the theater. The weapon said to be the Tippit murder weapon was seized at the time of Oswald's arrest.

After the arrest, in Hill's presence—again, according to Hill—identification for "Alec Hidell" was found in Oswald's wallet, thus linking Oswald to the two reported murder weapons. Hill later said, "I never did have the billfold in my possession."

(This scenario is thrown into question by reports that Oswald's wallet had actually been found earlier at the scene of the Tippit killing—see OSWALD'S WALLET—and by the fact that there was no public mention of the Hidell alias while Oswald was still alive.)

With the exception of the "magic bullet" found on a stretcher at Parkland Hospital, ballistic evidence found in President Kennedy's limousine and the seemingly doctored photos of Oswald holding the murder weapons found at the Paines' home following the assassination, Hill found or was near every piece of Oswald-incriminating evidence.

Oswald's housekeeper Earlene Roberts first said that it was Dallas Police car no. 207 that stopped outside when Oswald was in his room around 1:00 P.M., tooted the horn twice, and then drove off. After further interrogation, Mrs. Roberts changed her mind about the number, but no. 207 was the first number she mentioned, which coincidentally is the number of the car Hill had been in when he arrived in Dealey Plaza.

Hill was given plenty of opportunity to mention the Hidell identification card in Oswald's wallet during the hours following Oswald's arrest, but Hill behaved as if that ID card did not exist.

Hill was interviewed on the afternoon of November 22, 1963, by NBC-TV and asked to comment on the arrest. He said, "Oswald did not volunteer any information to us at all. . . . The only way we found out what his name was to remove his billfold and check it ourselves. He wouldn't tell us what his name was." Hill said the billfold's ID revealed that the suspect's name was "Oswald. O-S-W-A-L-D."

According to the FBI, this wallet contained only one photo identification of the man and that ID bore the name "Alek James Hidell," although there were nonphoto identification cards in the wallet that bore Oswald's true name.

While Hill sat in the front seat of a patrol car outside the Texas Theatre, it was Officer Bentley, in the back seat with the suspect, who reached into Oswald's pocket to pull out his wallet.

Hill testified to Warren Commission counsel: "the name Lee Oswald was called out by Bentley from the back seat and he also made the statement that there was some more identification in this other name, which I don't remember, but it was the same name that later came in the paper that he bought the gun under."

It is remarkable that these men distinguished so rapidly between the suspect's real name and pseudonym, especially considering the fact that the best identification, the only one with a photo of the suspect, was under the pseudonym.

Hill spelled the real name for reporters later that day, yet forgot about the pseudonym all together. Then months later, while testifying under oath, he still couldn't remember the pseudonym, although on this occasion he remembered that there was one.

A witness to the Tippit killing named Domingo Benavides claims to have picked up two shells at the scene of the crime, in shrubbery on the southeast corner lot at Tenth and Patton. Benavides placed them in an empty cigarette pack and handed them to a police officer, apparently Officer J. M. Poe.

Hill later testified to Warren Commission counsel, "Poe showed me a Winston cigarette package that contained three spent jackets from shells . . . I told Poe to maintain the chain of evidence as small as possible, for him to retain these at that time, and to mark them for evidence." If Benavides found two shells, how come there were three in the cigarette pack when Hill saw it?

In a radio interview with Hill recorded only hours after the assassination, Hill says: "[The Tippit murder weapon was] a .38 snub nose that was fired twice, and both shots hit the officer in the head."

Shells three and four were found one at a time by the Davis sisters, Barbara and Virginia, alongside their house and next to the sidewalk leading to their front door.

Hill wrote in his arrest report, "When the pistol was given to me, it was fully loaded and one of the shells had a hammer mark on the primer." The hammer mark supposedly indicated that Oswald had attempted to shoot one of his arresting officers.

Hill refers to the gun on November 22 as a pistol when it was actually a .38 revolver—a distinction Hill first made at 1:40 P.M., about a half hour after Tippit was murdered. At that time Hill broadcast over the police radio, "Shells at the scene indicate the suspect is armed with an automatic .38 rather than a pistol."

Among the items the Warren Commission says were found on the Book Depository's sixth floor was a paper sack. This was the sack in which Oswald allegedly brought his rifle into the building. The sack appears in none of the photographs taken by police photographers on the sixth floor. Hill told the commission that he saw a chicken leg bone and a paper sandwich bag on top of the cartons near the "sniper's nest." Hill said, "That was the only sack I saw. If it [the long paper bag] was found up there on the sixth floor . . . I didn't see it."

Oswald was arrested before he was officially a suspect in the assassination. Hill described for the Warren Commission what happened after Oswald was brought to police headquarters for questioning: "Captain Fritz walked in. He walked up to [Detectives] Rose and Stovall and made the statement to them, 'Go get a search warrant and go out to some address on Fifth Street . . .' and '. . . pick me up a man named Oswald.' And I asked the captain why he wanted him, and he said, 'Well, he was employed down at the Book Depository and he had not been present for a roll call of the employees.' And we said, 'Captain, we will save you a trip,' or words to that effect, 'because there he sits.'"

Hill retired from the Dallas Police Department in 1979.

(See also ABUNDANT LIFE TEMPLE; ACOUSTIC EVIDENCE; ALYEA, TOM.)

Hill, Jean Lollis

A Dallas schoolteacher, Mrs. Hill was one of the most public witnesses to the assassination. Easily identifiable in the Zapruder film because of her long red coat. Hill stood on the south side of Elm Street across from the grassy knoll with her friend Mary Moorman as the motorcade passed.

She later said, "I frankly thought [the shots] were coming from the knoll . . . I did think there was more than one person shooting." Using photographs and films of Dealey Plaza taken during the moments following the assassination, we can follow Mrs. Hill's movements. We see her run across Elm Street and up the grassy knoll to watch the chase of the assailants behind the wooden fence toward the railroad yards. She claims she was later intimidated by the FBI because she insisted on giving a story that didn't conform with the official scenario.

Hill told Dallas reporter Jim Marrs that, before the assassination, she had seen a van with writing on the side that said "Uncle Joe's Pawn Shop." (This van's presence on the scene has been corroborated. See entry for HONEST JOE'S PAWN SHOP.) The van drove past police lines and down the service road in front of the Texas School Book Depository, and behind the pergola atop the knoll just east of the wooden fence.

She told Marrs, "I saw a man fire from behind the wooden fence. I saw a puff of smoke and some sort of movement on the grassy knoll where he was. Then I saw a man walking briskly in front of the Texas School Book Depository building. He was the only person moving." That Sunday, after Oswald was shot, Hill recognized Ruby as the man she had seen walking in front of the Book Depository.

In November 1991, Mrs. Hill told her story in Dallas: "In 1963 I was a teacher in the Dallas school system, having recently moved here from Oklahoma City. I didn't yet know my way around Dallas, so a friend of mine, Mary Moorman, had said that we should play hooky that day and head down to the motorcade. There were some policemen in that motorcade that we were particularly interested in, so we went to see the President as well. The [policeman] friend of mine was riding on the President's wheel and I think that is one reason that Mary got the picture she got at the moment of the headshot. (See also MOORMAN PHOTO.) We had gotten down to the area in Dealey Plaza about an hour before the motorcade came around. We had been on the opposite side of the street, just out in front of the School Book Depository and people were filing in and it was getting—there were too many people there, and we were afraid that these policemen weren't going to see us. We started across the street toward the triangle. We were stopped by a policeman on the corner and he told us that there was no one allowed in that area. After some flirting, though, Mary and I got him to let us go down there. Mary was rather short and we wanted to get a picture of this police officer's motorcycle as it came around. That area is sloping so when Mary reached up to take the picture, we did get a picture of the School Book Depository. We knew that, because we had a Polaroid camera, we were going to have to be quick if we wanted to take more than one picture. So what we planned was, Mary would take the picture, I would pull it out of the camera, coat it with fixative and put it in my pocket. That way we could keep shooting. When the head shot came, Mary fell down and the film [i.e., the famous photograph] was still in the camera. When the motorcade came around, there were so many voters on the other side [of Elm Street] that I knew the President was never going to look at me, so I yelled, 'Hey Mr. President, I want to take your picture!' Just then his hands came up and the shots started singing out. Then, in half the time it takes for me to tell it, I looked across the street and I saw them shooting from the knoll. I did get the impression that day that there was more than one shooter, but I had the idea that the good guys and the bad guys were shooting at each other. I guess I was a victim of too much television, because I assumed that the good guys always shot at the bad guys. Mary was on the grass shouting, 'Get down! Get down! They're shooting! They're shooting!' Nobody was moving and I looked up and saw this man, moving rather quickly in front of the School Book Depository toward the railroad tracks, heading west, toward the area where I had seen the man shooting on the knoll. So, I thought to myself, "This man is getting away. I've got to do something. I've got to catch him." I jumped out into the street. One of the motorcyclists was turning his motor, looking up and all around for the shooter, and he almost ran me over. It scared me so bad, I went back to get Mary to go with me. She was still down on the ground. I couldn't get her to go, so I left her. I ran across and went up the hill. When I got there a hand came down on my shoulder, and it was a firm grip. This man said, 'You're coming with me.' And I said, 'No, I can't come with you, I have to get this man.' I'm not very good at doing what I'm told. He showed me ID. It said Secret Service. It looked official to me. I tried to turn away from him and he said a second time, 'You're going with me.' At this point, a second man came and grabbed me from the other side, and they ran their hands through my pockets. They didn't say, 'Do you have the picture? Which pocket?' They just ran their hands through my pockets and took it. They both held me up here [at the shoulder near the neck] someplace, where you could hurt somebody badly—and they told me, 'Smile. Act like you're with your boyfriends.' But I couldn't smile because it hurt too badly. And they said, 'Here we go,' each one holding me by a shoulder. They took me to the Records Building and we went up to a room on the fourth floor. There were two guys sitting there on the other side of a table looking out a window that overlooked 'the killing zone,' where you could see all of the goings on. You got the impression that they had been sitting there for a long time. They asked me what I had seen, and it became clear that they knew what I had seen. They asked me how many shots I had heard and I told them four to six. And they said, 'No you didn't. There were three shots. We have three bullets and that's all we're going to commit to now.' I said, 'Well, I know what I heard,' and they told me, 'What you heard were echoes. You would be very wise to keep your mouth shut.' Well, I guess I've never been that wise. I know the difference between firecrackers, echoes and gunshots. I'm the daughter of a gameranger and my father took me shooting all my life."

Mrs. Hill died November 7, 2000, of a heart attack.

(See also FEATHERSTON, JIM.)

Hine, Geneva L.

Texas School Book Depository employee who was looking out a second-floor window toward the motorcade during the shooting sequence. Hine told the Warren Commission that she heard three shots and that they made the Book Depository "vibrate."

Hoffa, James Riddle "Jimmy"

Assassination suspect who was president of the Teamsters Union from the late 1950s to the mid-1960s. Hoffa's closest ties in organized crime were with Santos Trafficante and Carlos Marcello, both listed by the House Select Committee on Assassinations as suspects in President Kennedy's death.

At the time of the assassination, Hoffa had been under investigation for six years by Attorney General Robert

Teamsters leader Jimmy Hoffa, in 1973. *(AP/Wide World Photos)*

Kennedy and was under indictment. Hoffa once threatened to break Robert Kennedy's back.

Hoffa later said President Kennedy would make a better target since "when you cut down the tree, the branches fall with it." Hoffa vanished in July 1975 while on his way to meet Anthony Provenzano, a mob-connected Teamster official.

For 27 years Frank Ragano was the lawyer for Florida mob boss Santos Trafficante and for 15 years he represented Hoffa. In the January 14, 1992, *New York Post*, Ragano revealed knowledge of a plot involving Hoffa, Trafficante, and New Orleans Mob boss Carlos Marcello to assassinate the president. Now all three are dead. (See MARCELLO, CARLOS for more details on Ragano's story.)

During the weeks before the assassination Jack Ruby's number of long-distance phone calls increased dramatically, with a disproportionate number of them placed to representatives of the Teamsters.

The House Select Committee concluded, "the former Teamsters Union president had the motive, means and opportunity for planning an assassination attempt upon the life of President Kennedy."

Hoffman, Ed

Self-proclaimed assassination witness who claims he was standing on the shoulder of the Stemmons Expressway, 200 yards west of the Texas School Book Depository parking lot and the railroad tracks behind the grassy knoll.

Twenty-six years old at the time of the assassination—and deaf and dumb—Hoffman claims he witnessed men behind the fence atop the grassy knoll with a rifle moments after the shots were fired.

The first man, who wore a dark suit and a tie with an overcoat, ran west (toward the triple underpass) along the wooden fence with a rifle, tossed it to a second man who was dressed as a railroad worker.

The second man hid behind a railroad switchbox, disassembled the rifle, and put it in a soft brown bag. When last seen by Hoffman, the "railroad worker" was walking toward the tower in which Lee Bowers was posted.

Hoffman says he tried in vain to tell to authorities what he had witnessed. His story was not made public until 1985, when he related his tale to Dallas reporter Jim Marrs. In 1991, Hoffman claimed the FBI tried to pay him not to say anything more about what he had seen.

(See also BOWERS, LEE; MERCER, JULIA.)

Holland, Sam M.

Union Terminal Company employee who was standing atop the triple underpass directly in front of J. W. Foster at the time of the assassination. Holland says he heard four shots, one of which, he said, hit President Kennedy on "part of his face."

After the shooting, Holland says he saw "a puff of smoke" come from "six or eight feet above the ground right out from under those trees" near the wooden fence at the top of the grassy knoll. Holland watched as "12 or 15 policemen and plainclothesmen" looked for "empty shells" behind the wooden fence.

He said there was a station wagon parked near the fence and it looked like somebody had been standing between it and the fence for some time. He said there was "mud up on the bumper" of the station wagon "in two spots."

Holland said the footprints "didn't extend further than from one end of the bumper to the other. That's as far as they would go. It looked like a lion pacing a cage. . . . Just to the west of the station wagon there were two sets of footprints. . . They could've gotten in the trunk compartment of this car and pulled the lid down, which would have been very, very easy."

The trunks of the parked cars were never searched. In the 1966 film *Rush to Judgment* (later released as *The Plot to Kill JFK*), Holland said, "I know where the third shot came from—behind the picket fence. There's no doubt whatsoever in my mind."

Holmes, Harry D.

Born July 2, 1905, in the Indian Territory of Oklahoma, the son of a goatherder. Holmes went to school, including dental college, in the Kansas City area. At age 18 he went to work with the U.S. Postal Service, where he was employed until his retirement in 1966. At the time of the assassination, he was the Dallas postal inspector, yet his multiple involvements in the case would suggest that there is a part of Holmes's bio to which the public is not privy.

Prior to the assassination, Holmes worked as an FBI informant, keeping the Feds updated on who had rented post office boxes in the Dallas area. Authors Sylvia Meagher and George Michael Evica say that Holmes's informant number was T-7. Warren Commission Exhibit 1152 states information learned through informant T-7, and it includes all of the material known to have been supplied by Holmes. Holmes admitted in his Warren Commission testimony that he was "feeding change of address as bits of information to the FBI and the Secret Service."

Holmes was also a witness to the assassination, watching the motorcade from his office on the fifth floor of the Terminal Annex Building, across Dealey Plaza from the Texas School Book Depository Building at the corner of Houston and Commerce Streets, and perhaps the only assassination witness to have watched the shooting sequence through binoculars, 7 1/2 X 50 power. In an early

statement, Holmes said he saw a man in the grassy knoll area trying to "take a gun away" from a woman.

Immediately following Oswald's arrest, Holmes began to investigate the case on his own. He heard from the FBI that the Mannlicher-Carcano rifle had been purchased through mail order from Klein's Department Store in Chicago on March 20, 1963. Holmes searched in vain for the money order used in the transaction. Holmes arranged 24-hour surveillance on Oswald's post-office box (box 6225), despite the fact that Oswald was in jail. He sent his secretary out to buy men's magazines in hopes of finding exactly where Oswald had found the order blank to order the "assassination rifle."

On Sunday morning, November 24, 1963, Holmes was invited by Captain Will Fritz to join in that morning's interrogation of Oswald. According to Holmes, he had driven to church with his wife that morning and, instead of going inside, he had dropped his wife off and then gone to the Dallas police station, where he walked in. Inside he ran into Fritz who said, "We are getting ready to have a last interrogation with Oswald before we transfer him to the county jail? Would you like to join us?" Holmes said he would. Also present at that interrogation were Secret Service agents Thomas J. Kelley and Forrest V. Sorrels (agent-in-charge of the Dallas office). Holmes took extensive notes of the interrogation. Those notes appear three times in the Warren Commission Hearings and Exhibits (Vol. XXIV, WCE 2064, pp. 488–492; Vol. XX, pp. 177–181; and in the *Warren Report*, Appendix XI, pp. 633–637). Holmes did not just listen but also asked many questions about Oswald's use of post-office boxes, thus delaying the transfer of the prisoner. The interrogation did not end until Chief Curry was "beating on the door."

In his Warren Commission testimony, Holmes also provided details on Oswald's use of post office box 2915 at the post office at the corner of Bryan and North Ervay Streets in Dallas, the same building in which the Warren Commission interrogators took testimony from their Dallas-based witnesses. There are indications that Holmes was not entirely truthful while testifying for the commission. He stated, for example, that the card that listed who was authorized to receive mail in Oswald's post office box had been destroyed routinely when that box was closed by Oswald on May 14, 1963. In actuality postal regulations specify that all information contained on a post office box application be retained for two years after the box is closed.

Holmes died October 14, 1989.

Honest Joe's Pawn Shop

Joe Goldstein was another guy said to be "best friends" with Jack Ruby. Goldstein was known as a "Dallas extrovert," an eccentric who advertised himself as "Honest Joe Goldstein, the Loan Ranger." Goldstein owned a gaudily painted Edsel with a plugged .50 caliber machine gun mounted on the top that, according to Secret Service agent Forrest Sorrels, was parked outside the Dallas police station on Commerce Street during the early evening of Saturday, November 23.

Reporter Tony Zoppi, who watched the motorcade on Main Street, recalls, "We all said, here comes the parade, and it was Honest Joe in his station wagon about two minutes before the parade. And everybody says, aw hell."

A. J. Millican, an assassination witness, told sheriff's deputies he saw "a truck from 'Honest Joe's Pawn Shop' park close to the Texas School Book Depository, then drive off five to ten minutes before the assassination."

Assassination witness Jean Hill told Dallas reporter Jim Marrs that, before the assassination, she had seen a van with writing on the side that said "Uncle Joe's Pawn Shop." The van drove past police lines and down the service road in front of the Texas School Book Depository, and behind the pergola.

Assassination witness Marilyn Willis told FBI special agent A. Raymond Switzer on June 19, 1964, that, 30 seconds before the parade, "there was an old loan truck called 'Honest Joe.' He was a pawn shop operator and his old black car was painted with all kinds of signs on it and it had a great big gun mounted on top of that car. And he drove up Houston towards the Depository and pulled in behind somewhere back there and turned around and came back."

(See also BOWERS, LEE.)

Hoover, J. Edgar

Longtime director of the Federal Bureau of Investigations, the United States' "top cop" at the time of the assassination, and friend of Lyndon Johnson. On May 14, 1964, Hoover told the Warren Commission: "When President Johnson returned to Washington [from Dallas] he communicated with me within the first twenty-four hours, and asked the Bureau to pick up the investigation of the assassination. It is not a Federal crime to kill or attack the President or the Vice President or any of the continuity of officers who will succeed to the Presidency. However, the President has a right to request the Bureau to make special investigations, and in this instance he asked that this investigation be made. I immediately assigned a special force headed by the special agent in charge at Dallas, Texas, to initiate the investigation, and to get all the details and facts concerning it, which we obtained, and then prepared a report which we submitted to the Attorney General for transmission to the President. . . . I have read all of the requests that have come to the Bureau from

this Commission, and I have read and signed all of the replies that have come to the Commission. In addition, I have read many of the reports that our agents have made and I have been unable to find any scintilla of evidence showing any foreign conspiracy or any domestic conspiracy that culminated in the assassination of President Kennedy. . . . I, personally, feel that any finding of the Commission would not be accepted by everybody, because there are bound to be some extremists who have very pronounced views, without any foundation for them, who would disagree violently with whatever findings the Commission makes. But I think it is essential that the FBI investigate the allegations that are received in the future so it can't be said that we ignored them or that the case is closed and forgotten . . . [T]here are at present at least fifty or sixty men giving their entire time to various aspects of the investigation, because while Dallas is the office of origin, investigation is required in auxiliary offices such as Los Angeles or San Francisco, and even in some foreign countries like Mexico. We have representatives in Mexico City."

Later in his testimony, Hoover added, "the President decided to form a Commission, which I think was very wise, because I feel the report of any agency of Government ought to be reviewed by an impartial group such as this Commission. And the more I have read these reports, the more I am convinced that Oswald was the man who fired the gun; and he fired three times; killed the President and wounded Governor Connally. And I am further con-

America's longtime "top cop" J. Edgar Hoover with President Kennedy, his bitter enemy.

vinced that there is absolutely no association between Oswald and Ruby. There was no such evidence ever established . . . There was suspicion at first that this might be a Castro act."

According to Peter Dale Scott: "Hoover, more than any other individual, was a major architect within the government of the lone-assassin cover-up." The question is, did Hoover cover up with or without foreknowledge of the assassination? Dr. Scott believes Hoover even went so far as to leak to the press hints of a communist conspiracy in the hours after the assassination—with paranoid whispers of nuclear holocausts—just to frighten U.S. politicians into craving the lone-nut scenario.

Despite evidence to the contrary (Waggoner Carr, the attorney general of Texas, said he had information that Oswald was an FBI "undercover" agent), Hoover denied that Oswald was ever an agent or a paid informant for his agency. According to author John Davis, "Hoover had no interest in uncovering the truth behind the assassination or in bringing the guilty to justice; he was only interested in protecting his reputation and that of the FBI."

According to Hoover biographer Mark North: "In September 1962, as a result of data obtained through covert surveillance programs against the Mafia, . . . Hoover learned that a subcomponent of that organization, the Marcello family of New Orleans . . . had, in order to prevent its own destruction . . . put out a contract on the life of President Kennedy . . . Hoover did not inform his superiors within the Justice Department [i.e., Robert Kennedy] or warn the Secret Service . . . He withheld the data in part because he felt Kennedy was an indecisive, immoral liberal who . . . would destroy the nation. But most important, he did this because JFK . . . intended . . . to retire the Director and replace him with a man of his own, more liberal political philosophy . . . [B]y the fall of 1962 [Hoover] held sufficient information to control Lyndon Johnson, a longtime friend, were he to become President. Through data gleaned (and withheld from the Justice Department) from investigations of the Billy Sol Estes and soon-to-break Bobby Baker/Mafia scandals, Hoover had hopelessly compromised Johnson. Johnson, a man tremendously dissatisfied with his position in government, knew this. . . . As a result of Hoover's traitorous act, [JFK] was assassinated, Johnson became President, and the Director obtained an Executive Order, on May 8, 1964, waving his compulsory retirement."

According to Penn Jones Jr., who got his information from a chauffeur who dropped off a guest outside the event, a conference was held November 21, 1963, at the home of Texas oil billionaire Clint Murchison. Present were Richard Nixon and J. Edgar Hoover. Jones writes, "Hoover, the task force commander, was present to confer with his troops, to issue last-minute instructions, to review

the final plans and to give the word to 'go' or to cancel as necessary."

The existence of the party and Hoover's presence there was corroborated by Madeleine Brown, Lyndon Johnson's mistress. (See BROWN, MADELEINE.)

On November 24, 1963, Hoover wrote in a memo to President Johnson. "The thing I am concerned about . . . is having something issued so we can convince the public that Oswald is the real assassin." Hoover's FBI would, soon thereafter, become the Warren Commission's primary source of information.

On November 29, 1963, in a phone conversation, Hoover explained to President Johnson that three shots had been fired and all three shots had been fired at the president. In the transcript to the taped conversation, Hoover said, "Two of the shots fired at the President were splintered . . . but they had characteristics on them so that our ballistics experts were able to prove that they were fired by this gun. . . . The President . . . was hit by the first and the third . . . second shot hit the Governor. The third shot is a complete bullet . . . and that rolled out of the President's head . . . it tore a large portion of the President's head off . . . and in trying to massage his heart at the hospital, on the way to the hospital . . . they apparently loosened that and it fell on to a stretcher." This statement agrees in almost no way with the eventual official scenario.

The House Select Committee on Assassinations found that the FBI's initial assassination investigation was conducted improperly and that it had issued a distorted report of its results. For example, while arguing that Ruby was, like Oswald, a lone nut, they omitted Ruby's role as an FBI informant in the late 1950s.

Obviously, the need for a magic bullet had not yet occurred to any one, since the FBI did not recognize the small wound to the face of James Tague as having been caused by an individual shot.

Hoover died on May 1, 1972.

Hopson, Mrs. Alvin

Texas School Book Depository employee who witnessed the assassination through the glass of a fourth-floor Depository window (the window would not open). She says she heard "two or more loud sounds" and thought they were firecrackers that had "been set off on the street below." She told the FBI that the shots "did not sound to her like [they] were coming from her building."

Hosty, James P., Jr.

Hosty, now retired, was FBI agent in charge of Lee Harvey Oswald's case in Dallas. According to the *Warren Report,* on November 6, 1963, Oswald wrote a note to Hosty, which

Hosty later ripped up and flushed down the toilet, under the orders of FBI office chief J. Gordon Shanklin. According to Hosty, the note read, in effect, "Dear Mr. Hasty (sic): If you want to talk to me, talk to me. Do not talk to my wife when I am not around. If you do not cease and desist, I will have to take the matter up with the proper authorities."

Hosty was involved in the early interrogation of Oswald following Oswald's arrest in the Texas Theatre. Oswald, according to Captain Will Fritz, became angry when Hosty entered the interrogation room, saying that Hosty had "accosted" his wife. According to Hosty, and only Hosty, Oswald apologized to him soon after he arrived in the interrogation room, saying, "I'm sorry for blowing up at you, and I'm sorry for writing that letter to you."

Hosty was seen in the company of Army Intelligence agent James Powell, the army's liaison to Secret Service agent Ed J. Coyle, and Treasury agent Frank Ellsworth, who had been investigating Oswald look-alike John Thomas Masen, on Main Street 45 minutes before the presidential motorcade passed.

Hosty's name (spelled "Hasty") and license plate number appear in Oswald's notebook.

Researcher Penn Jones Jr. wrote that Hosty was the bridge-playing partner of General Edwin Walker's aide Robert Surrey. The *Warren Report* tells us that Surrey was the printer and distributor of the anti-JFK "Wanted for Treason" leaflets prevalent in Dallas on November 22, 1963.

In a 1988 interview Hosty said, "I feel there was, based on what I know now, a benign cover-up. [The government] was concerned about Oswald's connections to the Soviet Union and to Castro. They were fearful that, if the public were to find this out, they would become so incensed that it could possibly have led to an atomic war."

Hosty also said on that documentary that he was told by an FBI counterintelligence agent not long after the assassination that he was to halt all FBI investigations of Oswald and all cooperation with the Dallas police regarding Oswald's background. Hosty said, "I have since determined that those orders came directly from Assistant Director William Sullivan who was in charge of foreign counterintelligence and direct liaison to the National Security Council."

According to Harold Weisberg's book *Oswald in New Orleans*, Hosty supplied the Warren Commission with a memo regarding an October 1963 meeting of Carlos Bringuier's D.R.E. organization, at which both General Edwin Walker and Lee Harvey Oswald were in attendance. The memo read, in part: "EDWIN L. STEIG, 713 Winifred Street, Garland, Texas, advised he attended a meeting of the Student Directorate of Cuba held on a Sunday evening at 8:00 P.M. some time during . . . October, 1963. There

were about seventy-five persons present at this meeting which was held at the First Federal Savings and Loan Association Conference Room in the North Line Shopping Village in Dallas, Texas. [Steig said that he] sat in the back of the room and listened to several speakers who talked about the situation in Cuba . . . Steig stated that another individual sat in the back of the room who he believes is identical with . . . Oswald. This individual spoke to no one but merely listened and then left."

Hosty says in his book *Assignment: Oswald* that he was briefed by his superior Gordon Shanklin on November 23, 1963, that FBI agents, during their investigation of Oswald, were not to ask questions regarding the "Soviet aspects of the case" because "Washington does not want to upset the public."

Hosty's book contained the first published reports that a wallet belonging to Lee Harvey Oswald and containing identification for Alek J. Hidell was found in the street near the body of Officer J. D. Tippit by Captain W. R. Westbrook of the Dallas police. Another different wallet was reportedly found on Oswald after he was arrested in the Texas Theatre. Hosty learned of the wallet found at the Tippit murder scene from FBI agent Robert Barrett who was there and had seen both the wallet and the ID. Film taken at the scene by news cameramen tends to support this claim.

The official explanation as to why Hosty's license plate number was found in Oswald's notebook is that Marina Oswald jotted it down during one of the times Hosty came to the Paines' house looking for Lee. This does not explain how Marina knew which car belonged to the FBI agent.

(See also OSWALD'S WALLET.)

House, Donald Wayne

On the day of the assassination, according to researcher Dr. Walt Brown, Secret Service agent Roger Warner was called away from his post at Love Field guarding Air Force One to interview a suspect named Donald Wayne House at 404 Lula St., Ranger, Texas. Sometime later, according to transcripts of police radio (Warren Commission Exhibit 1974) a call was put out to tow the suspect's car from the parking lot of Cobb Stadium, which was along the motorcade route between Dealey Plaza and the Trade Mart. It is unknown if this "suspect" is House, or another individual.

House Select Committee on Assassinations

The House Select Committee on Assassinations was created on September 17, 1976, when the U.S. House of Representatives passed House Resolution 1540. The Select Committee was expected to "conduct a full and complete investigation and study of the circumstances surrounding the assassination and death of President John F. Kennedy."

The committee ended up spending $5.5 million in taxpayers' money, but a "full and complete" investigation was never even attempted.

According to Peter Dale Scott, the House Select Committee, which had been assigned to investigate both the President Kennedy and Martin Luther King assassinations, had a "resistance to the proposition that President Kennedy was murdered by forces operating within and through our social system, rather than by external forces."

Therefore, whereas the Warren Commission was not willing to admit that Jack Ruby had any noteworthy connections with anyone, the House Committee is willing to recognize Ruby's associations with gangsters, but systematically underplays his "links to law enforcement, the judicial system, and politics."

The committee worked out of a building called House Annex 2, formerly known as the FBI Records Building. The building was undergoing renovations during the time the committee worked out of it, and rats scurrying in the hallways were a constant problem.

Chairman G. Robert Blakey, at the time of his appointment, was a 41-year-old criminal law professor at Cornell University. To head his Kennedy investigation task force, Blakey named Gary Cornwell, who had been chief of the anti-mob Federal Strike Force in Kansas City. Cornwell had been a prosecutor for the U.S. Department of Justice Organized Crime and Racketeering Section.

The committee report came to a very vague conclusion regarding who killed President Kennedy. It said, "The Committee believes, on the basis of evidence available to it, that the national syndicate of Organized Crime, as a group, was not involved in the assassination of President Kennedy, but that the available evidence does not preclude the possibility that individual members may have been involved." Elsewhere in the report it contradicts itself by letting the prime suspects off the hook: "It is unlikely either [Carlos] Marcello or [Santos] Trafficante was involved in the assassination of the president." The report, therefore, left the reader with the impression that organized crime had been behind the assassination, without ever actually accusing anyone.

Blakey insisted that the committee conclude that Oswald's participation in the assassination was due to his leftist leanings.

The committee also differed from the Warren Commission in its conclusion as to how Jack Ruby had managed to enter the basement of police headquarters in Dallas in order to shoot Lee Harvey Oswald. The Warren Commission concluded that Ruby had come down the Main Street ramp while a police guard at the entrance had his back turned. The committee postulated that Ruby had probably entered the building through an unlocked door in the alley. That door led to a staircase that led down to the basement.

The House Select Committee's report and its accompanying 12 volumes of evidence were published in March 1979. A disproportionate number of those scheduled to be interviewed by the committee died before they could testify.

(See also SUSPICIOUS DEATHS; and APPENDIX D: CONCLUSION OF THE HOUSE SELECT COMMITTEE ON ASSASSINATIONS.)

Hudson, Emmett Joseph

Dealey Plaza groundskeeper who was standing on the steps leading up to the top of the grassy knoll at the time of the assassination. With Hudson, according to photographic evidence, were two unidentified men.

Hudson told the Warren Commission: "Well, there was a young fellow, oh, I would judge his age in his late twenties. He said he had been looking for a place to park . . . he finally [had] just taken a place over there in one of them parking lots, and he came on down there and said he worked over there on Industrial [Boulevard] and me and him both just sat down there on those steps. When the motorcade turned off of Houston onto Elm, we got up and stood up, me and him both . . . and so the first shot rung out and, of course, I didn't realize it was a shot . . . the motorcade had done got further on down Elm . . . I happened to be looking right at the President when that bullet hit him—the second shot . . . it looked like it hit him somewhere along about a little bit behind the ear and a little above the ear . . . this young fellow that was . . . standing there with me . . . he says, 'Lay down, Mister, somebody is shooting the President.' . . . he was already lying down one way on the sidewalk, so I just laid down over on the ground and was resting my arm on the ground . . . when that third shot rung out . . . you could tell that the shot was coming from above and kind of behind."

Hudson was standing with his back to the picket fence atop the grassy knoll when the shots began. No mention of the third man on the steps (visible in photographs and film) is made by Hudson in his testimony.

Huff, Larry

Huff's wife told the House Select Committee on Assassinations that her husband had learned of a team investigating the assassination of President Kennedy sponsored by the military and run out of Camp Smith in Hawaii.

The man in charge of the investigation was reportedly Lieutenant General Carson A. Roberts. Huff's claims, seemingly benign, are interesting because no record of such an investigation exists.

According to the House Select Committee: "Huff stated under oath on December 14, 1963 that he departed Kaneohe Base in Hawaii in a C-54-T aircraft, serial number 50855, for Wake Island, with Chief Warrant Officer Morgan as pilot . . . Huff stated that there were ten to twelve CID military investigators on that flight [for which Huff was navigator] . . . Huff said that he learned the purpose of the trip by the CID investigators through conversations on the plane during the flight . . . On the return flight, he had spoken with the investigators about their work in Japan and was told that they had spent the entire stay investigating Oswald. Huff said that during that flight he was allowed to read the report prepared by the investigators. He described the report as being typewritten, about twenty pages, and classified 'Secret—For Marine Corps Eyes Only.' Huff recollected that the substance of the report dealt with interviews of individuals and that it contained a psychological evaluation of Oswald. Huff remembered the conclusion being that Oswald was incapable of committing the assassination alone."

The Defense Department told the Committee that it had no record of any such flight or any such investigation. The department said that Huff was confusing his story with an actual military investigation of John Edward Pic, Oswald's half-brother. Why was the military investigating Oswald's half-brother?

Huggins, Hugh   (a.k.a. Howell, Hugh; "The Chameleon")

Huggins claims that, from 1955 until 1965 he was a hit-man for the CIA, killing 37 people during that time. Most of the killings were in foreign countries, but some, he said, were in the United States. Because of his expertise, Huggins claims, he was contacted by Attorney General Robert Kennedy minutes after the shooting and was sent to Dallas to investigate. Huggins went to Dealey Plaza and talked with the medical personnel who had treated JFK at Parkland Hospital. Huggins determined that between seven and 10 shots were fired by four different assassins. Huggins says that he investigated the assassination for two years and came to the conclusion that the shooters were Charles Harrelson, Frank Sturgis, Charles Rogers, and a fourth shooter whose identity he did not learn.

(See also HARRELSON, CHARLES; STURGIS, FRANK; THREE TRAMPS.)

Hughes, Howard Robard, Jr.

Born December 24, 1905, at 11:00 P.M. in Houston, Texas, Hughes was one of the richest men in the world. He became a famous aviator, a movie producer, and, in his later years, an eccentric recluse. Hughes's money came

from his father who had patented a drill bit for oil wells and received in return, a percentage of the world's oil income. On February 25, 1977, Jack Anderson wrote in the *New York Times* that, according to mobster Johnny Roselli (who was later murdered for talking too much), the first CIA plot to kill Castro was hatched when the CIA "spoke secretly to Howard Hughes' chief honcho in Las Vegas, Robert Maheu, about the project. Maheu recruited Roselli, then the Chicago Mob's debonair representative in Las Vegas . . . Roselli looked upon the assassination mission as an opportunity to gain favor with the U.S. Government." Maheu, who worked closely with Oswald-associate Guy Banister and "figured prominently" in the Watergate scandal, was the intermediary between CIA security director Sheffield Edwards and crime boss Sam Giancana to discuss "several clandestine efforts" in Cuba during the early 1960s.

Hughes also employed Charles P. Cabell, the brother of the Dallas mayor who was a former Air Force general and former deputy director of the Central Intelligence (until he was fired by President Kennedy following the Bay of Pigs). According to Livingstone and Groden, Cabell was involved with Robert Maheu in plots to kill Castro.

During the mid-1950s, Hughes reportedly suffered a second mental breakdown (the first had taken place in 1944) and, after that, he was never publicly seen. He lived in Las Vegas for most of that time, where he reportedly only made physical contact with Mormons because they

Howard Hughes. *(Author's Collection)*

were clean. Robert Maheu, Hughes "right-hand man," admits that he never actually met Hughes, although he did see him briefly from afar on two occasions. Hughes reportedly developed a serious drug habit. Hughes was pronounced dead on arrival at Methodist Hospital in Houston, Texas, on April 5, 1976. His fingerprints were checked by the FBI to make sure that the dead man was actually Hughes. At the time of his death, Hughes had not been seen publicly or photographed for 20 years.

Fletcher Prouty wrote in his book *The Secret Team,* "Howard Hughes . . . had a huge empire which largely lived on CIA money. He was their chief cover in many operations." According to Harrison Edward Livingstone and Robert J. Groden in their book, *High Treason,* President Kennedy's assassination was the result of "the Dallas-Hughes-CIA-Mafia-Anti-Castro Cuban connection."

(See also CENTRAL INTELLIGENCE AGENCY; GEMSTONE FILE, THE; ROSELLI, JOHNNY.)

Hughes Film, The

Assassination witness Robert Joseph Elmore Hughes was born on April 15, 1938, in Mount Pleasant, Iowa, but had lived in Dallas since 1959. In 1963 he was employed at the Terminal Annex Post Office on the south side of Dealey Plaza. He went to see the presidential motorcade and brought with him his Bell & Howell 8mm movie camera loaded with Kodachrome film. Hughes stood at the southwest corner of Main and Houston. He filmed 16 seconds of the presidential limousine approaching on Main Street and then turning onto Houston Street. His film shows the lower floors of the County Court, County Records, and Dal-Tex buildings, as well as the facade of the Texas School Book Depository. The "sniper's nest" window is visible for 88 frames. Hughes turned off the camera and watched in confusion during the shooting sequence.

On November 28, 1963, Hughes told the *Record Herald and Indianola Tribune:* "About five seconds after I quit taking pictures, we heard the shots. . . . Some of the people dropped to the ground with the first shot, but most of us just stood where we were. Nobody knew for sure who had been hit. My first reaction was that somebody was shooting firecrackers. Then the lady standing next to me said, 'They're shooting at him.' The car had just turned the corner to go under the triple underpass beneath the railroad tracks. I saw Mrs. Kennedy then. She seemed to be in about a half-standing position with her arm behind her on the back of the car. I couldn't see the President. After a minute's hesitation, the car roared off through the underpass and the crowd began to run from the scene. Almost half-way through all that, I realized what had happened and began taking pictures again. I may have some movies of the car leaving the scene, but there was so much confu-sion that I don't really remember. However, I know I have shots of the crowd as the first reaction set in. The people ran toward where the shooting took place, and also toward where the shots seemed to come from."

Later on in the same film, there are scenes of the near-stampede of eyewitnesses running up the grassy knoll to see what is going on back by the railroad yards. Hughes filmed the scene on the grassy knoll, then took more film in the parking lot behind the grassy knoll fence. He then filmed a panorama of the buildings around Dealey Plaza and the last shot is of the milling crowd in front of the Texas School Book Depository building.

Hughes took the film to the Dallas FBI office on November 25, 1963. The film appears to show two silhouettes in the "sniper's nest" window. *Life* magazine requested that the Massachusetts photographic interpretation firm ITEK, which also analyzed the Nix film, study the "sniper's nest" window in the Hughes film.

According to ITEK, "A rectangular shape with the long dimension vertical can be seen slightly to the right of center in the half-open, right-hand window of the Texas School Book Depository . . . the shape appears to change in size as the car approaches the corner of Houston and Elm. It seems to decrease in size from left to right and from top to bottom."

ITEK said that there was motion but they could not identify what was causing it. The House Select Committee on Assassinations concluded that the movements in the window in the Hughes film "are attributable to photographic artifact."

Hughes died during the autumn of 1985.

Hunt, E. Howard (a.k.a. Hamilton, Edward J.; St. John, David; Warren, Edwards)

Assassination suspect and CIA agent who later became a Nixon henchman arrested and convicted in connection with the Watergate burglary. Hunt was the acting chief of the CIA station in Mexico City at the time of Lee Harvey Oswald's reported visits there in September–October 1963. Hunt worked closely with General Charles Cabell, who was fired by JFK in the aftermath of the Bay of Pigs fiasco. Hunt's "good friend and idol" was Richard Helms, the man who created the CIA's mind-control program. He was also close friends with former CIA director and Warren commissioner Allen Dulles, who had also been fired by President Kennedy following the Bay of Pigs. Hunt even ghost-wrote the book *The Art of Intelligence* for Dulles.

Hunt was the political officer for the Bay of Pigs operation, in charge of coordinating the Cuban-exile warriors. He worked for many years for Richard Nixon—and not just prior to the Watergate break-in. Hunt had, according to researchers Robert Groden and Harrison Edward Livingstone, "helped run operations for Nixon against Aristotle Onassis in the late 1950s, when Nixon was Vice President under Eisenhower."

Nixon aide Charles Colson ordered Hunt to break into Arthur Bremer's apartment after Bremer was arrested for the attempted assassination of Alabama governor Wallace in 1972. Those orders were withdrawn after Hunt objected. (Nixon then ordered the FBI to seal off Bremer's apartment.)

In 1975, the *Washington Post* reported, "E. Howard Hunt, the former CIA agent who helped engineer the Ellsberg and Watergate burglaries, told associates that he was ordered to kill [Jack] Anderson with an untraceable poison obtained from a former CIA doctor, but that the scheme was dropped at the last minute." If Hunt and the doctor were "former" CIA agents, then who was giving them their orders?

Hunt's lawsuit against A. J. Weberman and Michael Canfield (which he lost), authors of *Coup d'Etat in America,* stems from their publication of a memo allegedly written by Tom Karamessines, an aide of Richard Helms, stating that Hunt was in Dallas on the day of the assassination. The memo allegedly expresses fear that this fact will be discovered. House Select Committee chief counsel Robert Blakey, who later wrote a book about the assassination that points a guilty finger at organized crime, defends Hunt, saying that the Karamessines memo does not exist. Weberman and Canfield were the first two to name Hunt and CIA-colleague Frank Sturgis as two of the "tramps." Photographs of the "three tramps" who were arrested in a railroad car behind the grassy knoll minutes after the assassination show that one of the three somewhat resembles Hunt. Disclosures in 1992 by the Dallas police and FBI—that those tramps were actually tramps—would seem to indicate, however, that Hunt was not one of the photographed tramps.

Among other dirty tricks that Hunt might have pulled in his career include the possible forging of cables accusing President Kennedy of ordering the murder of South Vietnamese president Diem.

Hunt's wife, Dorothy Wetzel Hunt, who also had a background in intelligence work, was killed when the airliner she was riding in blew up over Chicago on December 8, 1972. Sabotage was never proven.

According to Sturgis, "Howard was in charge of other CIA operations involving 'disposal' [i.e. assassination] and . . . some of them worked."

Tad Szulc, Hunt's biographer, writes that Hunt was acting CIA station chief in Mexico City for a brief time during 1963, in particular during the time when Oswald was supposed to have been there. Hunt has denied this, but suspected conspirator David Atlee Phillips said Hunt was in Mexico City at the time.

E. Howard Hunt, who served three years in federal prison for his role in the Watergate break-in, shown in 1982. *(AP/Wide World Photos)*

According to Jim Hougan in his Watergate exposé, *Secret Agenda,* Hunt was a GS-15 CIA staff officer in 1969 when he began to pester Nixon staff member and fellow Brown University alumnus, Charles Colson, to get him a consultancy with the Nixon White House.

Hunt's career began as a *Life* magazine war correspondent in 1943. He joined the Office of Strategic Services that same year, serving in Kunming and Shanghai, China, with the 202 detachment. After the war, Hunt tried to resume his writing career. He wrote a novel in Mexico then attempted screen plays in Hollywood. In 1948 he became the press aide for U.S. ambassador Averell Harriman—although it has been suggested by journalist Tad Szulc that this position was, already, a cover for Hunt's CIA activities.

Attorney Mark Lane, who was retained by Marguerite Oswald to defend the memory of her son Lee, considers Hunt his top suspect in the assassination. Lane's book *Plausible Denial* (Thunder's Mouth Press), which, according to Lane's hyperbole, "definitely proves" that the CIA killed President Kennedy, arises from his successful defense of the right-wing Washington tabloid *The Spotlight* against a $1 million lawsuit by Hunt. The newspaper published an article by former CIA agent Victor Marchetti placing Hunt in Dallas on November 22, 1963. The article strongly suggested that a CIA memo indicated that Hunt had played a substantial role in the president's killing. Hunt claimed that allegations against him were causing his family stress, that his children were starting to doubt his innocence. However, when asked under oath where he was when President Kennedy was shot, Hunt said he was home watching TV with his children. This obvious discrepancy cost Hunt his case—and "proved" Lane's. Of course, the fact that a CIA agent cannot disclose his whereabouts at a certain time is not an indication of guilt but rather an indication that he really was a secret agent. The jury at the trial ruled against Hunt and ordered him to pay the publisher of *The Spotlight,* the ultra-right wing Liberty Lobby, $25,000 in court costs. In Lane's book, the strongest piece of evidence against Hunt involves the statements of Marita Lorenz, who, according to Lane, "placed Hunt in Dallas days before the assassination with a group of people, one of whom [Frank Sturgis] subsequently admitted to her that he'd been involved in the assassination."

(See also LORENZ, MARITA; OSWALD IN MEXICO; PHILLIPS, DAVID ATLEE; THORNLEY, KERRY WENDELL.)

Hunt, Haroldson Lafayette

Right-wing Dallas oil millionaire who was friends with Oswald-associate George DeMohrenschildt. H. L. Hunt, who would become perhaps for a time the richest man in the world, was born in 1889, the youngest of eight children of Haroldson Lafayette and Ella Rose (Myers) Hunt. He was born in Carson Township, Fayette County, Illinois, on February 17, 1889, and was educated at home. H. L. traveled through Colorado, California, and Texas in 1905 and by 1912 he had settled in Arkansas. He operated a cotton plantation that was flooded out by 1917. In 1921 he became a lease broker and promoted his first well, Hunt-Pickering No. 1 in El Dorado, Arkansas. By 1925, Hunt was worth $600,000. That year he purchased an entire block of land in El Dorado and built upon it a three-story mansion for his family. Then bad investments caught up with him—as they did to so many after the stock market crash of 1929, and, by 1930, he was broke. Two years later he was once again thriving, operating 900 oil wells. In 1935 H. L. Hunt, Incorporated, was superseded by Placid Oil Company. Shares to the stock were divided into trusts for Hunt's six children. In late 1936 Hunt acquired the Excelsior Refining Company in Rusk County and changed the name to Parade Refining Company. It was residue gas from this company's lines that caused the New London Explosion on March 18, 1937. Most of the people involved in that catastrophe were Hunt employees. In 1937 or 1938 the family moved to Dallas. On April 5,

1948, *Fortune* magazine called Hunt the richest man in the United States. It estimated the value of his oil properties at $263 million and the daily production of crude from his wells at 65,000 barrels.

Hunt married Lyda Bunker on November 26, 1914, in Arkansas. They had six children. But Hunt's life was a lot more complicated than that. On Armistice Day 1925 a Franklin Hunt married Frania Tye (probably short for Tiburski) in Florida. They had four children. On November 11, 1975, after H. L. Hunt had died, Mrs. Frania Tye Lee filed a civil complaint against Hunt in which she revealed they had married in 1925 and lived together in Shreveport until 1930, when they moved to Dallas. In May 1934, when "Franny" discovered Hunt's other marriage, Hunt sent her to New York and in 1941 provided trusts for her four children. A friend of his, John Lee, married her and gave his name to the children. Lyda Bunker Hunt died in 1955. In November 1957 Hunt married Ruth Ray and adopted her four children, who had been born between 1943 and 1950. Ruth Hunt admitted in an interview that H. L. Hunt had, in fact, been their real father. H. L. and Ruth Hunt became Baptists.

During the 1950s and 1960s Hunt spent much of his money fighting communism. He was quick to lend a financial hand to anything that he thought would hurt the communist cause. He funded two radio shows, *Facts Forum* and *Life Line,* which he supported from 1951 to 1963. In 1952 *Facts Forum* endorsed Senator Joseph McCarthy. In 1960 Hunt published a romantic utopian novel, *Alpaca.*

Hunt was frequently escorted to public engagements by extreme right-winger Lieutenant George Butler of the Dallas Police, the man who prematurely gave the "all clear" to transfer Oswald, moments before Jack Ruby shot him. According to an Earl Golz report in the *Dallas Morning News,* Hunt reportedly financed the publication of the book *Khrushchev Killed Kennedy* (KKK) by Michael Eddowes. Hunt was a long-time financial backer of Richard Nixon and had pushed to have former Warren Commissioner Gerald Ford run as Nixon's vice presidential candidate in 1968.

Hunt's personal bodyguards were comprised almost entirely of ex-FBI men, and he employed his own intelligence staff. Hunt's intelligence department was run by General Charles Willoughby, the former chief of intelligence for General Douglas MacArthur during the Korean War.

Through his riches, Hunt was able to subsidize many of the men in Congress, including Lyndon Johnson. Hunt was the financial backer of witch-hunter Senator Joseph McCarthy, whose attempt to purge the United States of predominantly imaginary communists became a national disgrace. Through McCarthy, Hunt hired cutthroat attorney Roy Cohn. During the 1950s, Hunt was spending

Dallas businessman and millionaire H. L. Hunt, in a 1965 photo. *(AP/Wide World Photos)*

upwards of $2 million a year for an anticommunist broadcast campaign.

And Hunt's son Lamar's offices were visited on the day before the assassination by two assassination suspects: Eugene Hale Brading and Jack Ruby. Hunt's son Nelson Bunker donated $1,465 toward a full-page ad that ran in the *Dallas Morning News* on the day of JFK's visit. The ad denounced JFK for having "scrapped the Monroe Doctrine in favor of 'The Spirit of Moscow.'"

According to Hunt aide Paul Rothermel Jr., Nelson Bunker Hunt put together a "paramilitary operation" and for a while was interested in a tube-shaped gas gun capable of inducing untraceable heart attacks.

Hunt's private intelligence network, headed by General Charles Willoughby, according to Peter Dale Scott, "entered into play with other, better established networks, such as the Gehlen Organization."

President Kennedy incurred the wrath of Big Oil when he moved to repeal a tax loophole, the 27 1/2 percent oil-depletion allowance.

Hunt watched the motorcade go down Main Street toward Dealey Plaza from the seventh floor of the Mercantile Building.

Hunt told United Press International after the assassination, "Every American, whatever the faith of his views or his political affiliations, suffers a personal loss when a President dies . . . freedom is in fearful danger when a President dies by violence."

According to Penn Jones Jr., "The FBI, who could not protect the President, could take the time and effort to hustle H. L. Hunt out of Dallas on Delta Flight 44 on that November 22 afternoon."

According to a former aide to Hunt, John Curington, Hunt left Dallas hours after the assassination and moved into the Mayflower Hotel in Washington, D.C., presumably so he could be close to the new president in case LBJ needed his advice. Hunt then sent Curington to Dallas police headquarters to check out the security in the building, in particular in the elevators used to transport prisoners. Curington told researcher Harrison Edward Livingstone in 1992: "I thought this was rather strange, but I did so, and even ended up in the same elevator with Oswald and his police escort, quite by accident. I could easily have killed Oswald right then. Hunt was right glad to learn that the elevators had no security. I walked in and out of the building three times and nobody ever checked me or my briefcase."

Hunt died on November 29, 1974.

(See also ABUNDANT LIFE TEMPLE; BUTLER, GEORGE; DEMOHRENSCHILDT, GEORGE; OSWALD, MURDER OF; RUBY, JACK; TEXAS SCHOOL BOOK DEPOSITORY; WILLOUGHBY, CHARLES; ZAPRUDER, ABRAHAM.)

I

Information Council of the Americas (INCA)
Right-wing organization designed to spread anticommunist propaganda in Latin America; run by Ed Butler, who appeared on the New Orleans WDSU radio debate arranged by William Stuckey and broadcast August 21, 1963, between Oswald and anti-Castro Cuban Carlos Bringuier. Apparently a disproportionate number of INCA employees were also on the payroll of Standard Fruit, and at least one resigned to join the staff of William B. Reily Company where Oswald was given a "job," now suspected of being a cover for other activities.

(See also OCHSNER, DR. ALTON, SR.)

International Anti-Communist Brigade (IAB)
See HEMMING, GERRY PATRICK.

Irving Sports Shop
The Irving Sports Shop in Irving, Texas, gained attention on November 25, 1963, when an undated repair tag was found bearing the name "OSWALD" in the handwriting of Dial D. Ryder, an employee. The proprietor of the shop was Charles W. Greener. Irving was the same Dallas suburb where Marina Oswald was living with Ruth Paine at the time of the assassination, and where Lee Oswald had been spending his weekends. The tag indicated that three holes had been drilled in an unspecified type of rifle and a telescopic sight had been mounted on the rifle and bore-sighted. Since the alleged assassination weapon already had a telescopic sight when it was shipped, this indicated the work was done for another "Oswald," or that Oswald had another rifle. Neither Greener nor Ryder recalled Oswald coming into the store.

Isaacs, Charles R.   See GIESBRECHT, RICHARD.

Isaacs, Harold R.   See GIESBRECHT, RICHARD.

Isaacs, Martin   See GIESBRECHT, RICHARD.

Jacks, Hurchel

Texas highway patrolman who drove the Dallas motorcade's fourth car, a four-door Lincoln convertible containing Vice President Lyndon Johnson. After the shooting, at Parkland Hospital, Jacks was assigned to guard President Kennedy's limousine.

Jacks said on November 28, 1963. "We were assigned by the Secret Service to prevent any pictures of any kind to be taken of the President's car on the inside," he stated.

Jack's Girls

Many of the strippers, barmaids, and waitresses employed by Jack Ruby have had experiences, or made statements, that are pertinent to this case. We suspect, however, that many of them have only discussed a fraction of what they know. A disproportionate number of them have died violently, and the trend has been enough to make the rest keep their mouths shut.

Nancy Monnell Powell, whose professional name was Tammy True, was the so-called girlfriend of Ruby's business associate Ralph Paul. (See also TAGUE, JAMES.) On the weekend of the assassination, Powell had many unnamed houseguests from out of town. (See also SANTANA, EMILIO.) Immediately following the shooting, she, like Ruby, drove from her Fort Worth home to Parkland. During the evening of November 23, 1963, Powell drove coworker Karen Carlin ("Little Lynn") and her husband from Fort Worth to Dallas. The threesome went to the Colony Club, one of the Carousel's competitors (where self-proclaimed assassination witness Beverly Oliver reportedly worked), and from there Karen Carlin called Ruby to ask for money.

This is significant since wiring money to Carlin the following morning would be part of Ruby's alibi that he murdered without malice.

Kay Helen Olsen was a British woman and one of the most interesting of Ruby's strippers. She lived on Ewing Street in Oak Cliff, only a few blocks from Ruby's residence. According to the *Warren Report,* Olsen—then single but attached to Dallas policeman Harry Olsen—the only member of the department who couldn't remember precisely where he was at the time of the assassination—saw Ruby on the night of the assassination for one hour outside a parking garage at Jackson and Field Streets in Dallas. Kay says she told Ruby, regarding Oswald, "In England they would drag him through the streets and would have hung him." Kay, again accompanied by Harry Olsen, saw Ruby outside the Carousel Club on Saturday evening as well, but, according to the *Warren Report,* only to exchange greetings. The Olsens were married in either December 1963 or January 1964 and soon thereafter moved to California. Kathy Kay was born in 1936 as Lillian Helen Harvey. Her AGVA application lists her occupation as "Exotic Snake Act." She met her first husband, Kenneth Joseph Coleman, at a U.S. Air Force base in Essex, England. Harry Olsen, her second husband, told the FBI in 1978 that she had left Dallas soon after the assassination because of something Ruby had told her. When asked, Coleman said that he knew what Ruby had said but he refused to divulge it. By 1978, Kathy and Olsen were also divorced.

Nancy Jane Mooney (a.k.a. Betty MacDonald) was a former Carousel Club stripper at the time of the assassination. She comes into the story through the murder of

Officer J. D. Tippit. A witness to the Tippit killing, Warren Reynolds, was shot in the head before he had a chance to testify that he couldn't identify the fleeing assailant as Oswald. He survived the attack, miraculously, and later made a positive identification of Oswald. The man accused of shooting Reynolds was Darrell Garner, who had bragged of the shooting while drunk. Garner was released by Dallas police after receiving an alibi from Nancy Jane Mooney, who said she was with him elsewhere at the time of the shooting. Eight days after Garner's release Mooney was arrested for "disturbing the peace" and died in jail on February 13, 1964. According to Dallas police, she hanged herself in her cell with her own toreador trousers.

Marilyn April Walle (a.k.a. Marilyn Magyar Moon, Delilah), who was stripping at the Carousel Club at the time of the assassination, planned to write a book about the assassination and was murdered September 1, 1966, by her husband of 24 days.

Karen Bennett Carlin (a.k.a. "Little Lynn," Karen Bennett, Theresa Norton) was Ruby's youngest stripper at 20 years old. It was Carlin to whom Ruby reportedly wired money a scant three minutes before he shot Oswald. This split-second timing helped Ruby convince the Warren Commission that he murdered without malice. On November 24, 1963, Secret Service agent Roger C. Warner interviewed Carlin. His written report reads in part, "Mrs. Carlin was highly agitated and was reluctant to make any statement to me. She stated to me that she was under the impression that Lee Harvey Oswald, Jack Ruby and other individuals unknown to her, were involved in a plot to assassinate President Kennedy and that she would be killed if she gave any information to the authorities." Carlin reportedly died in August 1964 of a gunshot wound in Houston, Texas. She was going by the name Theresa Norton at the time. According to Harrison Edward Livingstone, Carlin's death may have been staged and she may still be alive.

The most famous of Ruby's strippers at the time was the oft-married Jada, whose real name was Janet Adams Bonney Cuffari Smallwood Conforto. Twenty-seven years old at the time, she reportedly told reporters that Jack Ruby knew Lee Harvey Oswald the day before Ruby shot Oswald.

Jada and Ruby had a tumultuous relationship, according to Criminal Investigation detective Bill Courson of the Dallas County Sheriff's Department, who arrested Ruby on a threats warrant that Jada had filed on him. Jada's contract stated that she received a $2,000 bonus if she fulfilled her end of the contract. To avoid paying the $2,000, Ruby had threatened her, hoping she would quit. According to Jada, Ruby said he would cut up her wardrobe—which she claimed to be worth $40,000—if she didn't get out. Publicly Ruby was stating that Jada's act was too raunchy—her appearance in the film *Naughty Dallas* reveals that she pulls off her G-string a nanosecond before disappearing off-stage—and that she was going to get his beer license taken away. The judge, when their hearing came up, questioned Jada's figure regarding the value of her wardrobe since "G-strings were all he'd ever seen her in."

Ruby hired Jada in June 1963 in New Orleans, where she was working in a club run by Harold Tanenbaum and at least partially owned by assassination suspect Carlos Marcello. Seth Kantor called Jada "supercharged with animalism." According to G. Robert Blakey, Jada got Ruby into "considerable trouble with her 'x-rated' act." Reportedly, Ruby once asked Jada to live with him platonically, to help stifle rumors he was homosexual—a proposition that infuriated the libidinous dancer. According to Beverly Oliver, Conforto died a mysterious death.

The Carousel waitresses who spoke to the FBI offered insights into Ruby's character and what life was like around the Carousel Club. Marjorie R. Richey was a twenty-year-old Carousel Club waitress from June 1963 until the assassination. She said stripper Kay Olsen ("Kathy Kay") lived with a policeman (probably Harry Olsen) and that Ruby would not tolerate stripper Janet "Jada" Conforto "popping her G-string" in her act, a move that violated Texas obscenity laws.

Janice N. Jones told FBI that Ruby never charged policemen who came into his club and sometimes gave them bottles of liquor. Esther Ann Mash told Jack Anderson on television in 1988, "One night Jack [Ruby] had a meeting with several other men, there were seven men at the table with Oswald being the seventh and they were there [in the Carousel] until about 1:00 A.M." Mrs. Edward J. Pullman, a hostess, told the Warren Commission that Dallas police members were always served on the house. Mrs. Pullman added that, although Dallas policemen frequented the club, they never drank alcoholic beverages while on duty.

(See also CHERAMIE, ROSE; PERRIN, ROBERT AND NANCY; SUSPICIOUS DEATHS.)

Jackson, C. D.

Life magazine publisher, cold warrior, and alleged CIA propagandist who purchased and suppressed the Zapruder film. Jackson served with the Office of Strategic Services during World War II and is said to be responsible for the setting up of the anticommunist broadcast known as Radio Free Europe. When *Life* magazine originally published frames from the Zapruder film, the order of those frames was reversed so that President Kennedy's head appeared to snap forward rather than rearward with the final shot.

Jackson died less than a year after the assassination, on September 18, 1964, of cancer.

Jackson, Murray James

Dallas policeman and friend of murder-victim J. D. Tippit for 20 years. Jackson was the radio dispatcher who instructed Tippit to patrol the Oak Cliff section of Dallas—where Tippit met his death—while virtually all other patrol cars had been ordered to Dealey Plaza.

Jackson, Robert Hill

The only person to win a Pulitzer Prize because of events surrounding the assassination, Jackson was born on April 8, 1934, in Dallas, Texas. A *Dallas Times Herald* photographer, Jackson rode in Camera Car 3, six cars behind JFK. In the car with him were fellow photographers Malcolm Couch and Tom Dillard.

Jackson told the *Dallas Times Herald* on November 23, 1963, "As I looked up to window above, I saw a rifle being pulled back in the window. It might have been resting on the window sill. I didn't see a man. I didn't even see if it had a scope on it. . . . I looked to my left and I could see both cars speeding off . . . the President's car and the car behind him carrying the Vice-president. They disappeared under the underpass. Then I could see a colored family covering up their child on the grass. A policeman was down on his knee. I couldn't tell if he were hit. I thought the child was dead or something. Then the Negro parents picked up the boy and ran."

Jackson later told the Warren Commission that he heard three shots, with a longer space of time between the first and second shots than there was between the second and third shots.

Jackson was criticized by Warren Commission counsel David Belin for not immediately contacting a policeman, so that the Book Depository could have been sealed off before Oswald had a chance to escape.

Jackson was also in the basement of the Dallas City Hall when Jack Ruby shot Oswald. Jackson's photo of the grimacing Oswald taken a fraction of a second after the shot was fired won Jackson a Pulitzer Prize. He remained with the *Dallas Times Herald* until 1974.

Jada   See JACK'S GIRLS.

Jaggars-Chiles-Stovall

Small photographic laboratory in Dallas known to do work for the Army Map Service, as well as "highly secret" work for the Pentagon. As unlikely as it seems, this is where Lee Harvey Oswald—who in theory should have been strongly suspected of treason due to his behavior while in the Soviet Union—gained employment through the Texas Employment Commission, starting work on October 12, 1962, within days of the Cuban Missile Crisis—a crisis reportedly started when spy plane surveillance photographs were developed, revealing nuclear missiles in Cuba.

Another employee at Jaggars wouldn't seem like the type to pass a security check. He was 38-year-old John Caesar Grossi who was an ex-con with an FBI file. Grossi was working at Jaggars under the pseudonym Jack Leslie Bowen, which is too close for some conspiracy theorists to John Howard Bowen, the alias of Albert Osborne, the 75-year-old man with a spooky background who supposedly accompanied Lee Harvey Oswald on his bus trip to Mexico City in late September 1963.

Some feel it is too much of a coincidence that a radar operator who tracked the U-2 spy plane would later be hired to work in the photographic lab where work was done on photographs taken by the U-2 spy plane. (Those who are even further conspiratorial minded will say that it is too much of a coincidence to believe that Oswald threatened to divulge secrets he had learned in the U.S. Marine Corps soon before the Soviet Union gained the capability for the first and only time to shoot down a U-2 spy plane, and that Oswald was hired at Jaggars just in time for the Cuban missile crisis, the start of which came when missiles were discovered in photographs taken by a U-2 spy plane. It is as if Oswald is being controlled by some international force to disrupt détente—and, indeed, disrupting détente is just what he was supposed to be doing on November 22, 1963, as well.)

In Oswald's phone book, beneath the name and address of Jaggars-Chiles-Stovall, he wrote the word "microdots."

Jarman, James, Jr. ("Junior")

One of three men, all employees of the Texas School Book Depository, who reportedly watched the assassination from the Book Depository's fifth floor—from directly below the alleged "sniper's nest."

When Oswald was interrogated following his arrest later that day, he said that he was in the Depository lunchroom at the time of the shooting, having lunch with a short fellow called Junior.

Photos of the Depository taken seconds after the shooting show Jarman's two friends looking out the window, but Jarman is nowhere to be seen.

When Jarman heard the shots his first reaction was that they had come from below, although he eventually changed his tune and claimed, as did his friends, that the shots came from directly above, causing plaster dust to shower down upon them.

Jarnagin, Carroll

Dallas attorney, with offices at 511 North Akard Building, Room 428. On December 5, 1963, the FBI received the following message from Jarnagin:

Dear Mr. Hoover: On Oct. 4, 1963 I was in the Carousel in Dallas Texas and while there I heard Jack Ruby talking to a man using the name H. L. Lee. These men were talking about plans to kill the Governor of Texas. This information was passed on to the Texas Department of Public Safety on Oct. 5, 1963 by telephone. On Sunday Nov. 24, 1963 I definitely realized that the picture in the Nov. 23, 1963 Dallas Times Herald of Lee Harvey Oswald was a picture of the man using the name of H. L. Lee, whose conversation with Jack Ruby I had overheard back on Oct. 4, 1963. I thereafter attempted to recall as much of the Oct. 4, 1963 conversation with as much accuracy as possible, and to reduce it to writing. The enclosed original and two copies of this report are true to the best of my personal knowledge and belief; and this report is sent to you for whatever use it may be in assisting the FBI in your current investigation. If and when you see fit, I have no objection to the copies of this report being sent by you to the District Attorney of Dallas County and to the Attorney General of Texas, and to any other officials to whom you may see fit to disclose this information. My only request is that my identity remain undisclosed as long as possible.

Respectfully submitted. Yours Very Sincerely, Carroll Jarnagin

[Attached] Report of events which took place in the Carousel Club 1312 1/2 Commerce Street, Dallas, Texas on Friday October 4, 1963 about 10 P.M. until about 11:45 P.M. The club is located on the second floor, and is entered by a stairway leading up from the sidewalk on the South side of Commerce Street.

Witness, who is an attorney, and a client [of his], who is an "exotic dancer," walk up the stairs to the Carousel Club Oct. 4, 1963 at about 10 P.M., on business, the dancer, stage name "Robin Hood," desires to talk with Jack Ruby, the owner of the club, about securing a booking for employment. The witness and the dancer enter the club, and sit down at the second table on the right from the entrance; the dancer faces the stage, which is against the East wall and to the left, North of the passage way which leads East from the second floor entrance door; the ticket booth is at the South end of the landing at the top of the stairs, and the entrance door of the second floor is to the left coming off the landing, that is East is the direction a person would be facing entering the club. Several minutes after the witness and the dancer are seated, the witness notices a man appear in the lighted entrance area and tell the girl in the ticket booth: 'I want to see Jack Ruby.' In a short period of time the bouncer appears and with a flashlight shines a beam of light upon the ceiling on the inside of the club at the entrance

area. The man who has asked to see Jack Ruby is dressed in a tan jacket, has brown hair, needs a haircut, is wearing a sport shirt, and is about 5'9" or 10" in height, his general appearance is somewhat unkempt, and he does not appear to be dressed for night-clubbing; he, the new arrival, sits with his back to the wall at the first table to his right from the entrance area; after a few minutes he orders and is served a bottle of beer; he continues to sit alone and appears to be staring at the dancer; the dancer [waitress?] leaves the table and the new arrival stares intently at the witness; the witness notices that the new arrival's eyes are dark, and his face is unsmiling; after some minutes a man dressed in a dark suit, about 45–50 years of age, partially bald, medium height and medium to heavy build, dark hair, and more or less hawk-faced in appearance from the side, joins the new arrival at the table; the new arrival appeared to be about 25 years of age; (the older man dressed in the dark suit was later indicated by the dancer to be Jack Ruby); and the following conversation was overheard:

JACK RUBY: "—(some name not clearly heard or not definitely recalled by the witness)—what are you doing there?"

MAN WHO HAD BEEN SITTING ALONE: "Don't call me by my name . . ."

JACK RUBY: "What name are you using?"

MAN WHO HAD BEEN SITTING ALONE: "I'm using the name H.L. Lee."

JACK RUBY: "What do you want?"

LEE: "I need some money."

JACK RUBY: "Money?"

LEE: "I just got in from New Orleans. I need a place to stay, and a job."

JACK RUBY: "I noticed you hadn't been around in two or three weeks, what were you doing in New Orleans?"

LEE: "There was a street fight and I got put in jail."

RUBY: "What charge?"

LEE: "Disturbing the peace."

RUBY: "How did you get back?"

LEE: "Hitchhiked, I just got in."

RUBY: "Don't you have a family, can't you stay with them?"

LEE: "They are in Irving, they know nothing about this; I want to get a place to myself; they don't know I'm back."

RUBY: "You'll get the money after the job is done."

LEE: "What about half now, and half after the job is done?"

RUBY: "No, but don't worry, I'll have the money for you, after the job is done."

LEE: "How much?"

RUBY: "We've already agreed on that . ." (Ruby leans forward, and some of the conversation following is not heard by the witness.)

RUBY: "How do I know that you can do the job?"

LEE: "It's simple, I'm a Marine sharpshooter."

RUBY: "Are you sure that you can do the job without hitting anybody but the Governor?"

LEE: "I'm sure, I've got the equipment ready."

RUBY: *"Have you tested it, will you need to practice any?"*

LEE: *"Don't worry about that, I don't need any practice; when will the Governor be here?"*

RUBY: *"Oh, he'll be here plenty of times during campaigns . . ." (distraction . . .)*

LEE: *"Where can I do the job?"*

RUBY: *"From the roof of some building."*

LEE: *"No, that's too risky, too many people around."*

RUBY: *"But they'll be watching the parade, they won't notice you."*

LEE: *"But afterwards, they would tear me to pieces before I could get away."*

RUBY: *"Then do it from here (indicating the North end of the Carousel Club) from a window."*

LEE: *"How would I get in?"*

RUBY: *"I'll tell the porter to let you in."*

LEE: *"But won't there be people in the place?"*

RUBY: *"I can close the place for the parade, and leave word with the porter to let you in."*

LEE: *"But what about the porter . . ."*

RUBY: *"I can tell him to leave after letting you in, he won't know anything."*

LEE: *"I don't want any eyewitnesses around when I do the job."*

RUBY: *"You'll be alone."*

LEE: *"How do I get away, there won't be much time afterwards."*

RUBY: *"You can run out the back door."*

LEE: *"What about the rifle, what do I do if the police run in while I'm running out?"*

RUBY: *"Hide the rifle, you just heard the shot and ran in from the parade to see what was going on; in the confusion you can walk out the front door."*

LEE: *"No, they might shoot me first; there must be time for me to get out the back way before the police come in; can you lock the front door after I come in, and leave the back door open?"*

RUBY: *"That would get me involved, how could I explain you in my club with a rifle and the front door locked?"*

LEE: *"You left the front door open, and it was locked from the inside when somebody slipped in while you were outside watching the parade."*

RUBY: —*(distraction—)*

LEE: *"But what about the money, when do I get the money?"*

RUBY: *"I'll have it here for you."*

LEE: *"But when? I'm not going to have much time after the shooting to get away."*

RUBY: *"I'll have the money on me, and I'll run in first and hand it to you, and you can run out the back way."*

LEE: *"I can't wait long, why can't you leave the money in here?"*

RUBY: *"How do I know you'll do the job?"*

LEE: *"How do I know you will show up with the money after the job is done?"*

RUBY: *"You can trust me, besides, you'll have the persuader."*

LEE: *"The rifle, I want to get away from it as soon as it's used."*

RUBY: *"You can trust me."*

LEE: *"What about giving me half of the money just before the job is done, and then you can send me the other half later?"*

RUBY: *"I can't turn loose of the money until the job is done; if there's a slip up and you don't get him, they'll pick the money up immediately; I couldn't tell them that I gave half of it to you in advance, they'd think I double-crossed them. I would have to return all of the money. People think I have a lot of money, but I couldn't raise half of that amount even by selling everything I have. You'll just have to trust me to hand you the money as soon as the job is done. There is no other way. Remember, they want the job done just as bad as you want the money; and after this is done, they may want to use you again."*

LEE: *"Not that it makes any difference, but what have you got against the Governor?"*

RUBY: *"He won't work with us on paroles; with a few of the right boys out we could really open up this State, with a little cooperation from the Governor. The boys in Chicago have no place to go, no place to really operate; they've clamped down the lid in Chicago; Cuba is closed; everything is dead, look at this place, half empty; if we can open up this State, we could pack this place every night, those boys will spend, if they have the money; and remember, we're right next to Mexico; there'd be money for everybody, if we can open up this State."*

LEE: *"How do you know that the Governor won't work with you?"*

RUBY: *"It's no use. He's been in Washington too long, they're too straight up there; after they've been there awhile they get to thinking like the Attorney General. The Attorney General, now there's a guy the boys would like to get, but it's no use, he stays in Washington too much."*

LEE: *"A rifle shoots as far in Washington as it does here, doesn't it?"*

RUBY: *"Forget it, that would bring the heat on everywhere, and the Feds would get into everything, no, forget about the Attorney General."*

LEE: *"Killing the Governor of Texas will bring the heat on too, won't it?"*

RUBY: *"Not really, they'll think some crackpot or communist did it and it will be written off as an unsolved crime."*

LEE: *"That is if I get away."*

RUBY: *"You'll get away. All you have to do is run out the back door."*

LEE: *"What kind of door is there back there, it won't accidentally lock on me will it?"*

RUBY: *"No, you can get out that way without any trouble..."*
LEE: *"There's really only one building to do it from, one that covers Main, Elm and Commerce."*
RUBY: *"Which one is that?"*
LEE: *"The School Book Building, close to the triple underpass."*
RUBY: *"What's wrong with doing it from here?"*
LEE: *"What if he goes down another street?"*

The FBI sent a copy of Jarnagin's document to Dallas County district attorney Henry Wade, who dismissed it with the statement: "It didn't ring true to me."

Jefferson Branch Library

Minutes after police cars left Dealey Plaza and headed toward the site of the Tippit murder at 1:18, someone called the police to say that the gunman had just run into the Jefferson Branch Library, on the south side of Jefferson only two blocks from the shooting. The library was located at East Jefferson Boulevard and Marsalis Avenue, only one block from Jack Ruby's apartment. This was Oswald's library and he was known to go there three to four times a week.

Dallas police lieutenant Elmo L. Cunningham, a seven-year Marine veteran, describes what happened: "When we got there, there must have been in the neighborhood of thirty to forty armed people there, most of them being civilians, though some could have been deputies or constables in plain clothes. I thought we were going to have another Little Big Horn right there. I don't know where they all came from."

The person running across the library lawn turned out to be a 19-year-old Arlington State University student named Adrian D. Hamby. Hamby had a part-time job at the library. He was wearing a gray sweater and gray pants that day. He had driven to work and had been told by a policeman that he should inform everyone inside the library that a policeman had been shot in the area and that they should lock the doors and not come out until the area was secured. Hamby ran across the lawn to do as he was told and thus caused the police call that the assailant was in the library.

Jiffy Store

On December 2, 1963, special agent David Barry of the FBI interviewed Fred Moore, a store clerk at the Jiffy Store at 310 South Industrial Boulevard, who told him that a person he believed to be Lee Harvey Oswald had entered the Jiffy Store at 8:30 A.M. on the morning of the assassination. Moore said that identification of this individual arose when he asked him for identification as to proof of age for purchase of two bottles of beer. The man looked to be older than 21 to Moore, but he asked for identification anyway because he had had trouble with authorities about serving beer to minors. Moore said that the man showed him a Texas driver's license and that his name was Lee Oswald or possibly H. Lee Oswald. He said that the year of birth had read 1939 and he thought it might have been the 10th month. Perhaps Lee and Buell Wesley Frazier stopped off for a couple of beers before starting their work day at the Texas School Book Depository building. But Oswald, according to the official story of his life, did not have a driver's license.

JM/WAVE   See CENTRAL INTELLIGENCE AGENCY.

John Birch Society

Professor Revilo P. Oliver, a John Birch Society Council member whose name is a palindrome, was a bizarre Warren Commission witness. Although he had nothing relevant to say about the assassination, he managed to fill over 150 pages (all published) with neo-Nazi ravings. He was dismayed over the fact that some people mourned JFK's death but nobody mourned Hitler's death. He believed the assassination was part of a communist conspiracy. (They killed him, he said, because they were afraid he was about to "turn American.") The Warren Commission gave Oliver more room in their 26 volumes of hearings and exhibits than it did to Jackie Kennedy, Governor Connally, and Nellie Connally combined.

Johnson, Arnold Samuel

Director of the Information and Lecture Bureau of the U.S. Communist Party. The *Warren Report* says that, in 1962, "Oswald . . . attempted to initiate . . . dealings with the Communist Party USA [with regard to his New Orleans chapter of the Fair Play for Cuba Committee] . . . the organization was not especially responsive . . . [Johnson informed Oswald] that although the Communist Party had no 'organizational ties' with the Fair Play for Cuba Committee, the party issued much literature which was 'important for anybody who is concerned about developments in Cuba.' In September 1963 Oswald inquired how he might contact the party when he relocated to the Baltimore-Washington area, as he said he planned to do in October, and Johnson suggested in a letter of September 19 that he 'get in touch with us [in New York] and we will . . . [get] . . . in touch with you in [Baltimore].' However, Oswald had also written asking whether, 'handicapped as it were, by . . . [his] past record' he could 'still . . . compete with anti-progressive forces, above ground or whether in your opinion . . . [he] should always remain in the background, i.e. underground,' and in the September 19 letter received the reply that 'often it is advisable for some people to remain in the background, not underground.'"

Oswald wrote in one letter to Johnson, "On October 23, I had attended a ultra-right meeting headed by General Edwin a. Walker, who lives in Dallas. . . . This meeting preceded by one day the attack on a.e. Stevenson at the United Nations Day meeting at which he spoke. . . . As you can see, political friction between 'left' and 'right' is very great here."

Johnson—along with Gus Hall and Benjamin J. Davis, who were also officials in the U.S. Communist Party—were mailed by Oswald "honorary membership cards" to his New Orleans Fair Play for Cuba Committee.

Johnson, Clemon Earl

Johnson was standing atop the triple underpass at the time of the assassination. Johnson told researcher Larry A. Sneed, "It was pretty hard for people to get up on that [triple underpass] because police would run them off. But since we worked there, they let us up with no questions asked. . . . I was standing with a man named [James L.] Simmons, who was a [railroad] car man. A policeman was also there. . . . The President was headed toward the underpass at the time the shots went off. First, you think of firecrackers going off, then, when you see all of the motorcycles buzzing around, falling down, turning around, and running into one another, then you could see plainly that the President's head was shot off. . . . I heard maybe three shots. I know two plainly. After the second shot went off, you could tell distinctly that it wasn't a 'Baby John' firecracker. You could tell that it was a rifle. . . . You could see [JFK's limo] speed up and then stop, then speed up, and you could see it stop while they threw Mrs. Kennedy back up in the car. Then they just left out of there like a bat of the eye and were just gone. . . . A fellow by the name of [Richard C.] Dodd, and at that time our boss [Sam M.] Holland, went running round to some bushes. They kept saying, 'The shots came out of those bushes!' . . . I didn't have any idea where the shots came from, not even a guess. . . . Later, they were digging around down there where a woman and a little child were sitting. I think the woman said, 'It's a wonder we didn't get shot because the bullet went right in there.' They kept digging and they finally found the bullet. I never saw the bullet dug out of the ground but I heard a lot of people talking about it."

He had been hired by the Union Terminal Railroad on April 16, 1946. He retired from the railroad in 1966 and later worked as a maintenance man in an apartment complex. He died at age 90 in 1996.

Johnson, Clyde

A Kentwood, Louisiana, preacher who once ran for Louisiana governor on an anti–John F. Kennedy platform. The day before Reverend Johnson was scheduled to testify in New Orleans against Clay Shaw (February 18, 1969) regarding his knowledge of a relationship between Shaw and Oswald, Johnson was severely beaten up. He never testified.

Previously Johnson had told Jim Garrison that he had, on September 2, 1963, from 2:00 P.M. to 9:00 P.M., spoken with Ruby, Shaw, and Oswald at the Jack Tar Capital House in Baton Rouge, Louisiana.

On July 23, 1969, Johnson was killed at age 37 in a shotgun attack near Greensburg, Louisiana, by his wife's second cousin.

Johnson, Guy P.

Attorney and Office of Naval Intelligence (ONI) reserve officer who became the first attorney to defend Clay Shaw after his arrest in New Orleans for conspiracy to kill President Kennedy. Johnson also knew former FBI agent and Oswald-associate Guy Banister, and successfully recommended Banister's services to the ONI.

Johnson, Lyndon Baines

Attorney Craig I. Zirbel, author of *The Texas Connection: The Assassination of John F. Kennedy* (1991), argues that Vice President Lyndon Johnson was behind the assassination.

Here are the major points of evidence Zirbel uses:

1. Before the shooting, Johnson confided to his longtime mistress, Madeleine Brown, that Kennedy would be killed in Dallas.
2. Johnson was head of the team that planned the president's route—which took him past the Texas School Book Depository.
3. Johnson desperately tried to get his pal, Texas governor John Connally, out of the Kennedy limousine—and put in his place a political enemy (Senator Ralph Yarborough) who would be directly in the line of fire.
4. After Oswald was killed, Ruby smuggled a letter out of prison in which he named Johnson as the brains behind the assassination. Ruby wrote, "They alone planned the killing. By they I mean Johnson and the others."

In 1984, Billy Sol Estes told a grand jury that Johnson had ordered the murder of Department of Agriculture official Henry B. Marshall, who could have testified that LBJ and Estes were generating $21 million per year through illegal cotton allotments. Estes testified that the man who killed Marshall was assassination suspect Malcolm Wallace.

President Lyndon Baines Johnson: The Man Who Gained the Most. *(Author's Collection)*

According to JFK's personal secretary Evelyn Lincoln, President Kennedy told her three days before the assassination, due to LBJ's involvement in the Bobby Baker financial scandal, that Lyndon Johnson would not be his running mate in 1964.

(See also BAKER, ROBERT G. (BOBBY); BROWN, MADELEINE DUNCAN; HOOVER, J. EDGAR; WALLACE, MALCOLM "MAC.")

Johnson, Speedy

Houston aircraft broker and manufacturer's agent who met Jack Ruby in June or July 1963 in the Carousel Club. Johnson told the Warren Commission that Jack Ruby picked up his tab despite never having met him before.

Johnson, who legally had his name changed to Speedy, saw Ruby at Sol's Turf Bar on November 23, 1963. At that time Ruby complained about the anti-Kennedy ad that had run the previous day in the *Dallas Morning News,* and about the "IMPEACH EARL WARREN" sign Ruby had photographed the previous night.

Ruby reportedly said, "We ought to shoot all of them sons-of-bitches." Johnson was under the impression Ruby was advocating the shooting of Earl Warren.

Johnston, Judge David L.

Dallas justice of the peace who presided over the 7:10 P.M. (November 22, 1963) arraignment of Lee Harvey Oswald for the Tippit murder. The procedure took place in Captain Will Fritz's office on the third floor of the Dallas police station.

Judge Johnston also presided over the 1:30 A.M. (November 23, 1963) arraignment of Oswald for the assassination (murder with malice) held in the Dallas police station's fourth-floor identification bureau.

The judge later said, "Oswald was very conceited. He said sarcastically, 'I guess this is the trial,' and denied everything."

Jones, Paul Rowland

In 1946, Jones, Chicago mobster, attempted to bribe the Dallas Sheriff's Department and the Dallas district attorney into turning a blind eye while a mob-operated gambling casino opened in Dallas. Jones offered the Dallas officials $1,000 a week—and was promptly arrested and charged with attempted bribery. According to former Dallas sheriff Steve Guthrie in a 1963 statement, the man the mob planned to have operate their casino was Jack Ruby, who arrived in Dallas in 1947 and promptly set up the operation of a nightclub. Jones later became known as the mob's "paymaster in Dallas," and met with Ruby only days before the assassination.

Jones, R. Milton

The Warren Commission believed Lee Harvey Oswald got on a Dallas city bus immediately following the assassination partially because of the statements of bus driver Cecil McWatters.

McWatters said that Oswald was on his bus following the shooting and that Oswald grinned when told of the assassination. The next day, McWatters was driving his bus along the same route when Milton Jones got on.

McWatters immediately realized that it was Jones and not Oswald who had been on his bus the previous day. He tried to withdraw his previous statements, but he was ignored—probably because his previous statements had been corroborated by a passenger on the bus, and the appropriate bus transfer was reportedly found in Oswald's pocket hours after his arrest.

Jones, William Penn, Jr.

Editor of the *Midlothian Mirror* (Midlothian, Texas, circulation less than 1,000), author of *Forgive My Grief* (Volumes I–IV), and a breakthrough researcher concerning the mysterious deaths that followed the assassination. Jones was born on October 14, 1914, in Annona, Texas. He became an army brigadier general who served in Europe during World War II.

Jones claims to have taken a photograph that shows Ruby on the grounds of Parkland Hospital immediately following the assassination of President Kennedy. This is difficult to verify since the photo, unfortunately, shows the man's back.

For many years, as long as his health allowed, on the anniversary of the assassination, Jones held a memorial service in Dealey Plaza. Jones died on January 25, 1998, in Alvarado, Texas.

(See also ACOUSTIC EVIDENCE; MAGIC BULLET.)

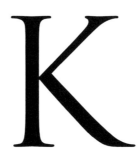

K

Kaiser, Frankie

Texas School Book Depository employee who found Oswald's work clipboard on December 2, 1963, on the Book Depository's sixth floor. The clipboard was found in the corner near the stairs—not far from where a rifle had been discovered 10 days earlier.

The question is: Why wasn't the clipboard found sooner? How thorough could the initial search of the sixth floor have been? Perhaps the clipboard had been placed there sometime after the assassination to further incriminate Oswald.

Kantor, Seth

Dallas reporter who rode in the presidential motorcade as a reporter for the Scripps-Howard newspapers. Kantor told the Warren Commission that he saw and *spoke to* Jack Ruby at Parkland Hospital around 1:28 P.M., just before President Kennedy's death was announced. Kantor and Ruby knew one another and referred to each other by name.

The commission had testimony from Ruby himself that he had not gone to Parkland Hospital following the assassination so decided that Kantor must have been mistaken. The commission probably wasn't worried about Ruby's presence at Parkland nearly as much as the fact that he had been there but felt compelled to lie about it.

Had Ruby been up to something he didn't care to discuss? If he was at Parkland he may have been in a position to plant the "magic bullet" (Commission Exhibit 399).

Kantor wrote one of the best books about Ruby: *Who Was Jack Ruby?* (Everest House, 1978), reissued as *The Ruby Cover-Up* (Zebra, 1992). Kantor died on August 17, 1993, of a heart attack in a Washington, D.C., hospital at the age of 67.

Katzenbach, Nicholas deB.

United States deputy attorney general who, during the weeks following the assassination, became the acting attorney general because Robert Kennedy was reportedly incapacitated by grief. On November 25, 1963, Katzenbach wrote a memo to President Lyndon Johnson's press secretary Bill Moyers. The memo said: "It is important that all of the facts surrounding President Kennedy's assassination be made public in a way which will satisfy people in the United States and abroad that all of the facts have been told and that a statement to this effect be made now. 1) The public must be satisfied that Oswald was the assassin; that he did not have confederates who are still at large; and that the evidence was such that he would have been convicted at trial. 2) Speculation about Oswald's motivation ought to be cut off, and we should have some basis for rebutting thought that this was a Communist conspiracy or (as the Iron Curtain press is saying) a right-wing conspiracy to blame it on the communists. Unfortunately, the facts on Oswald seem too pat—too obvious (Marxist, Cuba, Russian wife, etc.) The Dallas police have put out statements on the Communist conspiracy theory, and it was they who were in charge when he was shot and thus silenced. 3) The matter has been handled thus far with neither dignity nor conviction. Facts have been mixed with rumor and speculation. We can scarcely let the world see us totally in the image of the Dallas police when our

President is murdered . . . I think this objective may be satisfied by making public as soon as possible a complete and thorough FBI report on Oswald and the assassination. This may run into the difficulty of pointing to inconsistencies between the report and statements by Dallas police officials. But the reputation of the Bureau is such that it may do the whole job."

Kennedy, Jacqueline Bouvier (later Onassis)

The First Lady, dressed in pink, was sitting to the left of President Kennedy at the time of the assassination. According to earwitnesses, she said immediately following the shooting, "No, no, they've killed Jack, I'm holding his brains in my hand."

After the shooting, Mrs. Kennedy crawled onto the back of the presidential limousine. At the time some thought that she was trying to escape the car. The Zapruder film, however, tends to support the conclusion that she was actually attempting to retrieve a portion of her husband's head. She claimed to have had no recollection of doing this.

America's First Couple 1960–63: President John F. and Jacqueline Kennedy. *(Author's Collection)*

During the hours after her husband's death, she refused to change her clothes, appearing in public in the blood-stained outfit at Andrews Air Force Base in Washington, D.C., and then at Bethesda Medical Center in Bethesda, Maryland. She reportedly explained this refusal to change by saying, "I want the world to see what they did to Jack."

Mrs. Kennedy's brave manner following the assassination, at the various ceremonies and the funeral, helped heal a torn nation.

She testified to the Warren Commission: "[T]here is always noise in a motorcade and there are always motorcycles beside us, a lot of them backfiring. So I was looking to the left, I guess there was a noise, but it didn't seem like any different noise, motorcycles and things. But then Governor Connally was yelling, "Oh, no, no, no." . . . I was looking . . . to the left, and I heard these terrible noises. You know. And my husband never made a sound. So I turned to the right. And all I remember is seeing my husband, he had this sort of quizzical look on his face, and his hand was up, it must have been his left hand. And just as I turned and looked at him, I could see a piece of his skull and I remember it was flesh colored. I remember thinking he just looked as if he had a slight headache. I just remember seeing that. No blood or anything . . . And then I just remember falling on him and saying . . . "Oh my God, they have shot my husband," and "I love you, Jack." I remember I was shouting. And just being down in the car with his head in my lap . . . There must have been two [shots] because the one that made me turn around was Governor Connally yelling. And it used to confuse me because first I remembered there were three and I used to think my husband didn't make any sound when he was shot. And Governor Connally screamed. And then I read the other day that it was the same shot that hit them both . . . But I used to think if I only had been looking to the right, I would have seen the first shot hit him, then I could have pulled him down, and then the second shot would not have hit him. But I heard Governor Connally yelling and that made me turn around, and as I turned around, my husband was doing this [holds hand to neck]. He was receiving a bullet. And those are the only two I remember."

(See also GEMSTONE FILE.)

Kennedy, John Fitzgerald

Thirty-fifth president of the United States who became an assassination victim on November 22, 1963. During his 100 days as leader of the free world, Kennedy had made a lot of enemies. Much of this case's fascination stems from the fact that many of the most powerful men in the world, in theory, had reasons to want Kennedy dead.

President John F. Kennedy (right) with his brothers Edward (center) and Robert. *(Author's Collection)*

In his presidential election, in which he defeated Republican Richard Nixon by a very small margin, John Kennedy, through the machinations of his father, the powerful and ruthless Joseph Kennedy, had allowed organized crime to "help" him win votes in Chicago—votes which gave Kennedy Illinois' electoral votes and thus the election. Instead of paying those crime figures back for their favor, John Kennedy's brother, Attorney General Robert Kennedy, aggressively hunted down and prosecuted mobsters. To aggravate matters, the president slept with a woman named Judith Exner, who was the mistress of Chicago crime boss Sam Giancana.

President Kennedy had decided to dump Vice President Lyndon Johnson from his campaign ticket for the 1964 elections, which would have left LBJ to crash and burn in a political scandal that was about to unfold. So Lyndon Johnson theoretically had a very strong reason to want JFK dead.

LBJ's good friend J. Edgar Hoover, the longtime head of the Federal Bureau of Investigation, was approaching the age of mandatory retirement and JFK planned on enforcing the rule. Hoover knew that, with Lyndon Johnson in the White House, he had every reason to believe he would remain the head of the FBI until his death.

The U.S. Central Intelligence Agency, an organization that routinely resorted to political assassination to effect change, was angry at Kennedy because of his failure to back up their play at the Bay of Pigs. Kennedy, in response to the rogue nature of the Bay of Pigs plan, threatened to

tear the CIA into a thousand pieces and scatter it to the winds. So members of the CIA, both high-ranking and otherwise, had a theoretic reason to want Kennedy dead.

The Bay of Pigs had also incurred the wrath, for JFK, of the militant anti-Castro exiles who were being trained and funded in paramilitary activities by the CIA and other U.S. and private groups. These men were anxious to kill for their cause, and Kennedy had betrayed them on the beaches, and with his refusal to allow the U.S. military to attack Cuba.

At the same time the Pentagon and their defense contractors were gearing up for a war in Southeast Asia, a war that Kennedy at times seemed determined to leave up to the Southeast Asians. The war was "South Vietnam's to win or lose," JFK said. Billions of dollars were made by a small group of people during the years following the assassination because of the Vietnam War, a war that might not have happened as it did if JFK had remained president into 1964. And so that conglomerate of military and materiel manufacturers known as the military-industrial complex had a theoretical reason to want JFK dead.

Kennedy, Regis   See BABUSHKA LADY; FEDERAL BUREAU OF INVESTIGATION.

Kennedy, Robert Francis

Attorney General of the United States, appointed by his older brother, the president. Robert had devoted much of his energy as Attorney General to a war on organized crime, a crime syndicate that J. Edgar Hoover, the longtime head of the FBI, said did not exist. Robert's war on mob-

Attorney General Robert Kennedy. Less than five years after his brother's death, he too would die violently. *(Author's Collection)*

sters was acutely dangerous for himself and his family because organized crime in Illinois had helped John Kennedy win that stage against Richard Nixon in the 1960 presidential election. Matters were further complicated by the fact that President Kennedy was having an affair with Chicago mob boss Sam Giancana's mistress. Five years after the president's assassination, Robert was running for president himself when he was gunned down in Los Angeles, California.

Kennedy's Brain

Following President Kennedy's "autopsy" on November 22, 1963, his brain was transferred to the Secret Service at the White House in a stainless steel box. On April 26, 1965, the box was transferred to President Kennedy's secretary, Evelyn Lincoln, who was then working at the National Archives. The box was in a footlocker, along with other materials from the autopsy. After about a month, Lincoln, in turn, sent the entire footlocker to Angela Novello, Robert Kennedy's personal secretary. On October 31, 1966, the footlocker was again sent to the National Archives. Ms. Novello had a key and the footlocker was opened and it was discovered that the brain along with sample slides of JFK's tissues were missing.

Kimble, Jules Ricco (a.k.a. Kimble, Jules Ron; Kimble, Jules Rocco)

Ku Klux Klan pilot who told Jim Garrison in 1963 that he had been introduced to Clay Shaw by David Ferrie in 1960 or 1961. Kimble says that he drove a KKK official named Jack Helm to Ferrie's apartment on the day after Ferrie's death and that Helm removed from the apartment a valise full of papers, which Helm then put into a bank deposit box.

Kimble has also been connected with the 1968 killing of Martin Luther King, Jr. According to researchers John Edgington and John Sergeant in their article "The Murder of Martin Luther King Jr." (*Covert Action Information Bulletin,* Summer 1990), Kimble—who is currently serving a life sentence for murder in the El Reno Federal Penitentiary in Oklahoma—has admitted being involved in a widespread conspiracy that resulted in King's death: "Kimble, a shadowy figure with ties to the U.S. intelligence community and organized crime . . . alleges that [convicted King assassin James Earl] Ray, though involved in the plot, did not shoot King and was in fact set up to take the fall for the assassination . . . Kimble, in implicating the mob and the CIA in the assassination, claims to have introduced Ray to a CIA identities specialist in Montreal, Canada, from whom Ray gained four principle aliases . . .

Kimble cannot be dismissed out-of-hand. For a start he has a long record of mob activity and violence, often with political overtones . . . He has proven links to the Louisiana mob empire of Carlos Marcello . . . and admits to having done mob related work in New Orleans, Montreal and Memphis during the late sixties . . . Investigative records from the period confirm Kimble to have been involved with the underworld and the KKK, to have been in Montreal in the summer of 1967, and to have been called in for questioning in connection with the Kennedy assassination by then-New Orleans Parish District Attorney Jim Garrison. During this questioning, Kimble admitted being linked to the local FBI and CIA and Garrison accepted this admission as true . . . Kimble had been living in Crescent City, California, during the early 1960s and was associating with gangsters, segregationists, the FBI and, he forcefully asserts, the CIA. He is known to have been in contact with David Ferrie, the dead CIA flier who has been repeatedly implicated in the assassination of John Kennedy."

During the summer of 1963, Kimble maintained a New Orleans post office box in the same building as Lee Harvey Oswald, assassination suspect David Ferrie, and suspected Oswald impersonator Kerry Thornley.

According to Garrison-expert James DiEugenio, Kimble was a former CIA agent who "had been on a mysterious plane flight to Montreal in 1963 with David Ferrie and Clay Shaw."

King, Otis "Karl"

Prisoner of war during World War II in the Philippines who was news director for KBOX in Dallas at the time of the assassination, and who also provided audio submissions to United Press Audio. King may have been the first person on the air with news of the shooting in Dealey Plaza. He was fired on the day of the assassination for helping the competition but was hired immediately by KLIF.

He also covered Jack Ruby's murder trial. When King asked Ruby "what this was all about?" Ruby replied, "Ask the man who is up there now," meaning Lyndon Johnson.

When King returned from the war after years in a P.O.W. camp, he was given a parade in Dallas and treated as a hero. Some time after that King went to Ruby's club and was treated like a hero there as well. Ruby offered him three bottles of whiskey and a date with the famous stripper known as Candy Barr. Since King was neither married nor dating anyone, he took Ruby up on it.

Knight, Russell Lee   See WEIRD BEARD.

Komitet Gosudarstvennoy Bezopasnosti (KGB)

Foreign intelligence agency for the Soviet Union, the equivalent to the United States' CIA. Yuri Nosenko was the KGB officer stationed at the KGB Center in Moscow, Russia from 1959–64. Two months after the assassination, Nosenko, then 36 years old, was attending Geneva disarmament talks when he sent a coded message to CIA headquarters in Virginia stating that he wished to defect. He was a member of the senior rank of the KGB's counterintelligence department within the USSR, with a background in post-war naval intelligence. He was suspected of specializing in the recruitment and blackmailing of foreigners—especially British and Americans. Even before his coded message, he had sold information to the CIA for small sums of money. When the CIA first received the coded message from Nosenko, they tried to discourage him from defecting—thus leaving his wife and children behind—telling him he would be a far greater asset to the United States as an informant in Moscow. Nosenko insisted, saying he had reason to believe Soviet officials already knew he wanted to defect. A return to Moscow would be fatal. (Nosenko later admitted that this claim of defection was false, a story invented to make sure the United States accepted him.) The CIA removed Nosenko from Switzerland, by this time aware of the potentially frightening importance of his information. Nosenko claimed to have been in charge of Oswald's file while Oswald lived in the USSR. He claimed the KGB had never heard of Oswald until the ex-Marine requested to become a permanent Russian resident. At that point, Nosenko claimed, the KGB did not know about Oswald's U.S. Marine Corps background, secret status, and U-2 knowledge—and, astoundingly, Nosenko claimed that they would *not* have been interested in Oswald even if they *had* known. Nosenko said the KGB, when they did investigate Oswald, found him unintelligent and unstable. He was never debriefed on his military background and they never considered his usefulness as an agent. Nosenko said, "the interest of KGB headquarters in Oswald was practically nil."

The KGB, Nosenko continued, was not even concerned when Oswald married a Russian girl and returned to the United States with her. They had done a quick check on Marina and had discovered that she wasn't terribly bright either. After the assassination, the KGB conducted an "urgent" investigation into Oswald's Soviet activities. Nosenko remained in charge of the case. The large report sent to Khrushchev stated that Soviet intelligence was innocent of any malevolent connections to Oswald or the assassination.

The question of whether or not to believe Nosenko's angelic tale created a rift in the CIA that affected the company's functioning for more than a decade. For the following four years, Nosenko was held in solitary confinement by the CIA and subjected to "hostile interrogation." The CIA built a special building—likened to a bank vault—to hold his single-room cell. Although Nosenko became increasingly uncertain of the details of his past during the interrogation, his story never changed. When Nosenko was finally released he was given a new identity and a yearly salary for the rest of his life—a reward for his services.

One of the reasons people in the United States became so upset about Lee Harvey Oswald's reported trip to Mexico in September–October 1963 was that, while in the Soviet Embassy in Mexico City, Oswald or someone impersonating Oswald met with Valeri Vladimirovich Kostikov, who, according to U.S. intelligence, was then the head of the Western Hemisphere Sabotage and Subversion Division of the KGB. According to Michael Eddowes's book *Khrushchev Killed Kennedy,* "[Kostikov was a] clandestine KGB officer stationed at the Soviet Embassy in Mexico City, Mexico." He was believed to be a member of Department 13, the sabotage and assassination squad of the KGB during September and October 1963. If the meeting between Oswald and Kostikov never occurred, it is an indication that the "dirty little secret" that perhaps caused the Warren Commission whitewash was wholly false. Kostikov was believed by the commission to be the "Comrade Kostin" mentioned by Oswald as the man he met in Mexico City in a letter Oswald, according to Ruth Paine, wrote to the Soviet embassy in Washington, D.C., on November 9, 1963. Eddowes claims Kostin and Kostikov are separate individuals. Kostikov, likewise, says that he is a separate individual, and he laughs at the suggestion that he was the head of any division in 1963, citing the fact that he was only 30 years old at the time of the assassination.

Oleg Danilovich Kalugin was a former Russian major general who headed the KGB's foreign counterintelligence service. In 1990, Kalugin denounced the KGB where he had been employed for 32 years. He told the *New York Times* (January 20, 1992) that Oswald was not recruited by the KGB in the USSR because he was viewed as a CIA plant.

Vitality Gerasimov was an employee at the Soviet embassy in Washington, D.C., in 1962 and, according to CIA records: "known to have participated in clandestine meetings in [the U.S.] and to have made payments for intelligence information of value to the Soviets." In July 1962, Marina Oswald wrote Gerasimov, informing him and the embassy of her U.S. address. The letter was intercepted and read by the FBI. According to FBI agent James Hosty, Gerasimov was in charge of KGB deep-cover or "sleeper" agents in the United States. Hosty also says that Marina Oswald was not the only one to write to Gerasimov. Lee, Hosty says, wrote to Gerasimov while living in Fort Worth, New Orleans, and Dallas.

Colonel Oleg Maximovich Nechiporenko is a retired KGB agent who, on January 9, 1992, called a press conference in Moscow and claimed that he had "new data" concerning JFK's death. Nechiporenko urged "the creation of a joint Russian-U.S. investigatory commission" and said that his "historical information" would cast new light on the events of November 22, 1963. He refused to give details but made it clear that he intended to be paid for the information and added, "If I gave it out now, it would be unfair to the other people who took part and it would be premature." According to the Associated Press (AP), Nechiporenko was a senior KGB agent before his retirement, had been kicked out of Mexico in 1971 for purportedly scheming to topple its government. The AP wrote: "Nechiporenko said he and two other agents met Oswald on Sept. 27–28, 1963, at the Soviet Embassy in Mexico City, where Oswald was [unsuccessfully] trying to get a visa to re-enter the Soviet Union . . . There was no immediate way to verify Nechiporenko's claim to have met Oswald in Mexico City. The KGB and Russian Foreign Ministry could not be reached for comment . . . But Nechiporenko is known to have been a spy in Mexico in this period. He said he was twice posted at the Soviet Embassy in Mexico City, from 1961 to 1965 and from 1967 until 1971. He later was sent to Vietnam . . . He said his name never came up in connection with the assassination because Oswald never used it during bugged telephone conversations." Nechiporenko subsequently wrote a book called *Passport to Assassination* (Birch Lane Press, 1993), which said that the real Oswald had gone to Mexico City and had visited the Soviet embassy there. He wrote that Oswald had a handgun with him during one of his visits and that he became very anxious and wept when told that he would not immediately be granted a visa. According to Nechiporenko, Oswald, at one point, screamed, "For me, it's all going to end in tragedy!"

(See also CENTRAL INTELLIGENCE AGENCY.)

Kostin, Valeri Dmitrevich   See COMRADE KOSTIN LETTER.

Kounas, Dolores A.

Assassination witness who was standing near the southwest corner of Elm and Houston. Although directly across the street from the Texas School Book Depository, she thought "the shots came from a westerly direction in the vicinity of the viaduct [triple underpass]."

Kramer, Joseph   See NAGELL, RICHARD CASE.

Lacombe

A training camp for anti-Castro paramilitary operations situated on land owned by Bill McLaney, a business associate of Jack Ruby's. The camp, near Lake Pontchartrain, was northwest of New Orleans. One of the trainers there was assassination suspect David Ferrie.

Lambchop

Assassination witness Jean Hill started telling her story about a man shooting from the grassy knoll immediately following the assassination. In her first version of the story, which she told to a television reporter only minutes after the shooting, she noted that Jackie was looking at a "little white dog" in the back seat of the limousine just before the shooting sequence began. Since there was no dog in the car, supporters of the official scenario, in particular Warren Commission counsel David Belin, took great delight in bringing up Mrs. Hill's comment about the dog whenever her testimony came up. Obviously the woman was hallucinating at the time of the assassination. If there was no dog, then there probably wasn't anyone shooting from the grassy knoll either.

Then, in 1992, an analysis of film taken at Love Field on the morning of the assassination revealed that Jackie Kennedy had been handed a "Lambchop" puppet along with flowers by an admirer in the crowd, which could have resembled a small white dog. What happened to the puppet after the assassination is unknown.

Lane, Mark R.

An attorney, Lane was retained by Marguerite Oswald soon after her son's death to defend his memory. The result was the book *Rush to Judgment*. If the *Warren Report* is the case for the prosecution against Oswald, then *RTJ* is the case for the defense.

Lane gathered evidence that Oswald was framed, and he did his best to refute all evidence of Oswald's guilt. While promoting his book, Lane became one of the most visible critics of the *Warren Report*.

Lane later worked on the Garrison investigation and successfully defended the Washington tabloid, *The Spotlight,* published by the ultra-right-wing Liberty Lobby, against a $1 million lawsuit brought by assassination suspect E. Howard Hunt for defamation.

The suit was over an article published in *The Spotlight* by former CIA agent Victor Marchetti. The article had claimed Hunt played a substantial role in President Kennedy's assassination. Lane wrote a book about the libel suit called *Plausible Denial* (Thunder's Mouth Press, 1991). The book claims to "definitely prove" that the CIA killed Kennedy—Hunt being Lane's top suspect.

Lane's role in the uncovering of an assassination conspiracy is made murkier by the fact that Lane was a lawyer for Jim Jones's People's Temple in Jonestown, Guyana. Lane managed to escape the bizarre community just before the massacre.

Lawrence, Jack   See DOWNTOWN LINCOLN-MERCURY.

Lawrence, John Stevens Rutter   See HATHAWAY, PHILIP B.

Levine, Isaac Don

Ex-CIA agent who coached Marina Oswald before she gave her Warren Commission testimony. According to assassination analyst Peter Dale Scott, Levine allegedly spent an "intensive week with Marina before she first testified on February 3, 1964, and, as a representative of Time-Life, Inc., helped to arrange for Marina to receive a $25,000 advance for a book that was never written." Levine planned to write that Marina was probably a KGB spy. When John J. McCloy got wind of the impending publication he had Allen Dulles speak to Dulles's friend Henry Luce and the story was "spiked."

Levine's background is exemplified by the fact that he collaborated with *Life* Magazine's C. D. Jackson and Director of Central Intelligence Allen Dulles on a psychological warfare response to Soviet leader Joseph Stalin's death.

(See also DULLES, ALLEN; JACKSON, C. D.; *LIFE* MAGAZINE.)

Lewis, C. L. "Lummie"   See BRADING, EUGENE HALE.

Lewis, Roy E.

Texas School Book Depository employee who watched the motorcade from the building's front steps. Lewis told researcher Larry A. Sneed, "As the motorcade came by, I remember seeing Kennedy brushing back his hair. That's when all hell broke loose. I heard, 'Boom! Boom! Boom!' With the second and third shots being closer together. The people down in front of me hit the ground then everybody started running toward the grassy knoll. Apparently the people assumed that whoever was doing the shooting might have been over there so I followed them. But before we could get far, a policeman stopped us and told us to go back into the building and wait. . . . I didn't see any smoke or smell any gunpowder, nor could I tell the direction of the shots . . . But no way did I suspect anything coming from the Texas School Book Depository . . . Having seen what happened at the time, too that's what made me think about the grassy knoll when we ran toward that direction. I thought that maybe there was something or someone there. . . . I'll never be convinced that Oswald did it or that he acted alone." Lewis worked for the Texas School Book Depository until 1966 when he became a truck driver.

About Oswald, Lewis continued: "Usually he brought his own lunch, hardly ever went out, and he almost never played dominos or talked with the rest of us. We all thought he was very odd. He never wanted to get a haircut. We would tease him about it because hair would be growing down his neck. We told him a week or two before the assassination that we were going to throw him down and cut it ourselves, but he just smiled."

Life Magazine

Top-selling U.S. weekly magazine published by Henry Luce, whose wife Clare Boothe Luce was involved in militant anti-Castro activities. Richard B. Stolley, Los Angeles bureau chief was instrumental in *Life*'s purchase of the Zapruder film. In *Entertainment Weekly* (January 17, 1992), Stolley—at that time the editorial director of Time Inc. magazines—told how *Life* came to purchase the film.

At about 6:00 P.M. on November 22, Stolley received a phone call from one of *Life*'s part-time reporters, Patsy Swank, who was at Dallas police headquarters speaking in a whisper. She told him that Oswald was being interrogated in an office nearby and that the corridors in the building were a mob scene of police and reporters. She had received a tip that the assassination had been filmed by a local garment manufacturer named Zapruder. Stolley looked up Zapruder's phone number in a phone book and called him every 15 minutes until he received an answer at 11:00 P.M. that night. Stolley writes: "It was Zapruder himself. He had been driving around trying to calm his nerves. After photographing the shooting, he had literally stumbled back to his office nearby, muttering, 'They killed him, they killed him.' . . . Incredibly, nobody in authority was much interested in [the film]. Zapruder had contacted the Dallas police, but by mid-afternoon they had Oswald in custody and the film seemed of marginal importance. Both the Secret Service and the FBI said it was his property to dispose of as he saw fit but that they would like copies. Zapruder took his 8mm film to a Kodak lab, and by evening had the original and three copies in hand." Stolley viewed the film for the first time the following day. He purchased the original and a copy for $50,000 and agreed, according to Zapruder's wishes, that the film would never be used to ghoulishly exploit the president's death. Stolley defends charges that *Life* had covered up evidence by holding the film without allowing it to be seen: "*Life* did not bury the Zapruder film for twelve years as [film director Oliver] Stone charges. All the relevant images were printed immediately except for frame 313. We felt publishing that grisly picture would constitute an unnecessary affront to the Kennedy family and to the President's memory. Today, that may seem a strange, even foolish, decision. But this was 1963, a few years before Vietnam brought carnage into American living rooms . . . *Life* decided not to sell the Zapruder film for TV or movie showing for reasons of both taste and competition . . . There have been charges that *Life* tampered with the film, removed or reversed frames, diddled with it to confound the truth. Nothing like that ever happened. I have inspected the film many times, as have others; the frames are all there, in proper order."

Despite Stolley's statement, the magazine twice showed that it was not above misrepresenting facts in order to sell the story that Oswald had acted alone. On one occasion frames from the film were published out of order to make it appear as if JFK's head had moved forward when hit by a bullet, thus indicating that the shot had come from behind. In another issue it was explained that the Zapruder film showed that the first shot had been fired while the president was looking back over his shoulder, thus explaining the entrance wound in his throat. The film, as we now know, shows no such thing.

Wife of *Life* publisher Henry Luce, Clare Boothe Luce, was reportedly a lover at one time of both former director of central intelligence Allen Dulles, and the head of H. L. Hunt's private intelligence gathering service, General Charles Willoughby. Following JFK's death, she also funded disinformation efforts designed to blame the assassination on Fidel Castro.

(See also PHASE-ONE COVER-UP.)

Lincoln, Evelyn
President Kennedy's private secretary. She rode in V.I.P. bus at the rear of the motorcade. On October 7, 1994, Lincoln wrote a return letter to a Virginia schoolteacher in which she wrote that she thought there were five groups or people involved in President Kennedy's death. "These five conspirators were," she wrote: "Lyndon B. Johnson, J. Edgar Hoover, the Mafia, the CIA and the Cubans in Florida." She died on May 11, 1995, at the age of 86.

(See also KENNEDY'S BRAIN.)

Livingston, Dr. Robert   See AUTOPSY OF JOHN F. KENNEDY.

Long, Max Allen
An FBI memo dated August 24, 1977, states that an unnamed police source told Lieutenant James E. Hobbs, Intelligence Division, Dallas Police Department, that Long was a drinking buddy of his and had told him that Oswald was on his way to 324 East Tenth Street when he encountered and fatally shot Officer J. D. Tippit. This is the address where Long lived with his mother. Long told the source that, at the time of the assassination, the house was a "safe house" and that allowing Oswald to stay there would wipe out a longstanding debt Long had with "some people in New Orleans." The house is only a block away from the site of Tippit's death. Long, who had been a rated boxer during the 1940s, told his drinking companion that he was acquainted with several figures pertinent to the assassination, including Oswald, Jack Ruby, David Ferrie, and Clay Shaw. Long reportedly showed the source a poor-quality photo that supposedly showed Long in the company of Oswald, Shaw, Ferrie, and Ruby. The source said

that he recognized Ruby in the photo but failed to recognize any of the others. Long, who had 28 arrests on his record, mostly for drunk and disorderly conduct, died in December 1980 of throat cancer.

Lopez, Gilberto Policarpo
According to the report of the House Select Committee on Assassinations: "in early December 1963, CIA headquarters received a classified message stating that a source had requested 'urgent traces on U.S. citizen Gilberto P. Lopez.' . . . Lopez had arrived in Mexico in November 1963 and had disappeared with no record of his trip to Havana. The message added that Lopez had obtained tourist card No. 24553 in Tampa on November 20, that he had left Mexico for Havana November 27 on Cubana Airlines, and that his U.S. passport number was 310162 . . . [On the same day] the FBI had been advised that Lopez entered Mexico on November 27 at Nuevo Laredo . . . Two days later these details were added: Lopez had crossed the border at Laredo, Texas, on November 23; registered at the Roosevelt Hotel in Mexico City on November 25; and departed Mexico on November 27 on a Cubana flight for Havana. Another dispatch noted that Lopez was the only passenger on Cubana flight 465 on November 27 to Havana. It said he used a U.S. passport and Cuban courtesy visa."

The Lopez in question, it was determined, was born January 26, 1940. He was a different person from the pro-Castro Gilberto Lopez who lived in Los Angeles.

CIA headquarters received a message in March 1964 from an unnamed source. The message said that a U.S. citizen named Gilberto Lopes (sic) "had been involved in the Kennedy assassination."

According to the House Select Committee, the message stated "that Lopes had entered Mexico on foot from Laredo, Texas, on November 23 carrying U.S. passport 319962, which had been issued July 13, 1960; that he had been issued Mexican travel form B24553 in Nuevo Laredo; that Lopes had proceeded by bus to Mexico City 'where he entered the Cuban Embassy'; and that he left the Cuban Embassy on November 27 and was the only passenger on flight 465 for Cuba."

The CIA paid no attention to the March 1964 message. They said that there were too many discrepancies in details between it and the December 1963 information the CIA had received.

This move prompted the House Committee to ask: "Why [hadn't] the CIA . . . taken more aggressive investigative steps to determine whether there had been a connection between Lopez and the assassination?"

The FBI filed a report on August 26, 1964, regarding an interview with Lopez's cousin, Guillermo Serpa Rodriguez, conducted in Key West, Florida. According to Rodriguez, Lopez came to the United States after Castro took over in Cuba, had returned to Cuba after about a year because he was homesick, then returned to the United States to avoid the Cuban draft in 1960 or 1961.

Oddly, Lopez had earlier used a similar excuse. Lopez had told Rodriguez of his plans to return to Cuba in November 1963, saying that he was afraid of getting drafted into the U.S. military.

Lopez, according to Rodriguez, was passionately pro-Castro but politically inactive. Reminiscent of Oswald's "street scuffle," Lopez did once get into a fistfight because of his pro-Castro beliefs.

The August 26, 1964, FBI report also contained an interview with Lopez's wife. In the interview, she listed Lopez's places of employment. The list included "a construction firm in Tampa."

Lopez's wife also said her husband was hospitalized at Jackson Memorial Hospital in early 1963 in Miami, suffering from epileptic attacks. He had been treated for the condition by doctors in Key West and Coral Gables. Lopez's wife said that she thought his seizures were brought on by worry for his family in Cuba.

Lopez, she claimed, had written her since his return to Cuba. He told her his trip had been made with financial assistance from "an organization in Tampa." The woman verified that Lopez wouldn't have been able to afford the trip on his own.

According to the FBI, Lopez attended a Fair Play for Cuba Committee meeting in Tampa on November 20, 1963. During March 1964, the FBI changed the date of that meeting to November 7, 1963.

The House Select Committee on Assassinations reported that, at that meeting, "Lopez had said he had not been granted permission to return to Cuba but that he was awaiting a phone call about his return to his homeland."

The March 1964 FBI report said a Tampa Fair Play for Cuba Committee member claimed that she had called a friend in Cuba on December 8, 1963, and was assured of Lopez's safe arrival. She said that Lopez had made the trip via Mexico because he lacked a passport and that he had been given $190 by the FPCC for the trip.

But Lopez *did* have a passport. It was #310162 and had been issued in January 1960. The FBI verified that Lopez's Mexican tourist card was #M8-24553, issued November 20, 1963, in Tampa.

Lopez entered Mexico, according to the FBI, via automobile on November 23 at Laredo, Texas, and was flown to Havana, Cuba, November 27 as the plane's lone passenger.

The House Select Committee called Lopez's association with the Fair Play for Cuba Committee and his suspicious behavior "a troublesome circumstance that the committee was unable to resolve with confidence."

The Cuban government officially denies that the incident involving the delayed flight from Mexico City to Havana ever happened.

(See also CASAS SAEZ, MIGUEL.)

Lorenz, Marita

CIA and FBI undercover operative and former mistress to Fidel Castro who once attempted to assassinate Castro with a poison pill under CIA orders. A professional mistress of sorts, she was also former mistress to CIA asset and assassination suspect Frank Sturgis. According to the *New York Daily News* (November 3, 1977), Lorenz says "that she accompanied . . . Oswald and an 'assassin squad' to Dallas a few days before President Kennedy was murdered there . . . [Lorenz] told the *News* that her companions on the car trip from Miami to Dallas were Oswald, CIA contact agent Frank Sturgis, Cuban exile leaders Orlando Bosch and Pedro Diaz Lanz, and two Cuban brothers whose names she did not know. She said that they were members of Operation 40, a secret guerilla group originally formed by the CIA in 1960 in preparation for the Bay of Pigs invasion . . . Ms. Lorenz described Operation 40 as an 'assassination squad' consisting of about thirty anti-Castro Cubans and their American advisors. She claimed the group conspired to kill Cuban Premier Fidel Castro and President Kennedy, whom it blamed for the Bay of Pigs fiasco . . . She said Oswald . . . visited an Operation 40 training camp in the Florida Everglades. The next time she saw him, Ms. Lorenz said, was . . . in the Miami home of Orlando Bosch, who is now in a Venezuelan prison on murder charges in connection with the explosion and crash of a Cuban jetliner that killed seventy-three persons last year [1976; Bosch was acquitted]. Ms. Lorenz claimed that this meeting was attended by Sturgis, Oswald, Bosch and Diaz Lanz, former Chief of the Cuban Air Force. She said the men spread Dallas street maps on a table and studied them . . . She said they left for Dallas in two cars soon after the meeting. They took turns driving, she said, and the 1,300-mile trip took about two days. She added that they carried weapons—'rifles and scopes'—in the cars . . . Sturgis reportedly recruited Ms. Lorenz for the CIA in 1959 while she was living with Castro in Havana. She later fled Cuba but returned on two secret missions. The first was to steal papers from Castro's suite in the Havana Hilton; the second mission was to kill him with a poison capsule, but it dissolved while concealed in a jar of cold cream. . . . Informed of her story, Sturgis told the *News* yesterday: 'To the best of my knowledge, I never met Oswald.'"

According to assassination investigator Harrison Edward Livingstone, "A few days after his story came out, Sturgis was arrested in Lorenz' apartment, where he had gone to discuss matters with her."

Lorenz later testified for the House Select Committee on Assassinations, where she named Frank Sturgis as one of the men who had fired upon the president. The House Select Committee, by this time determined to conclude that the "Mafia" killed JFK, dismissed Lorenz's testimony, since they "found no evidence" to support it.

In January 1985, Lorenz testified for the defendant in the case *E. Howard Hunt* v. *Liberty Lobby*. Lorenz repeated her story—but this time with greater detail. She now recalled that the two Cuban brothers were surnamed Novis. The new information she offered at that time was:

1. On November 21, 1963, while staying in a Dallas motel, the group was visited by E. Howard Hunt and Jack Ruby. Hunt delivered a package of money.
2. Among those at Orlando Bosch's home while assassination plans were discussed was CIA-employee Alexander Rorke, Jr.—who officially was already missing and presumed dead at the time.

Dunne asked Lorenz why she had waited so long to speak out about what she knew. Lorenz said that, soon after the assassination, she had told everything she knew, including the names she had just named, to the FBI, adding, "They didn't want to go into it. They were CIA activities, not FBI."

According to Lorenz, soon after the assassination, Sturgis said to her: "[You missed] the really big one [in Dallas]. We killed the President that day. You could have been part of it—you know, part of history. You should have stayed. It was safe. Everything was covered in advance. No arrests, no real newspaper investigation. It was all covered, very professional."

Predictably, Sturgis and Hunt deny there is any truth to Lorenz's statements. Obviously, the real Oswald couldn't have ridden in the caravan since he was steadily employed at the Texas School Book Depository at the time.

When told of Lorenz's accusations, Orlando Bosch replied, "I've never been farther west than New Orleans."

(See also CASTRO, FIDEL; STURGIS, FRANK.)

Lorenzo, Aurelia

Dallas Morning News employee who was standing on the north side of Elm Street, "in the grassy knoll area," with three of her coworkers—Mary Woodward, Maggie Brown, and Ann Donaldson—at the time of the assassination. All four said the shots came from behind them and to their right, that is, from the direction of the knoll.

Lovelady, Billy   See ALTGENS PHOTO; OSWALD LOOK-ALIKES.

Lumpkin, George L.

Dallas police assistant chief who rode one of the lead motorcycles during the Presidential motorcade. Lumpkin was a former aircraft electrician for General Dynamics who joined the Dallas Police Department in 1953. Lumpkin was riding in front of JFK's car by a quarter mile during the shooting and at first says he thought the shots were a motorcycle backfiring. He says he heard three shots and that they were evenly spaced. Lumpkin told the Secret Service during the motorcade's planning stages that the Elm Street to Stemmons Freeway route was preferable to a Main Street to Industrial Boulevard route. The Industrial course, Lumpkin noted, was "filled with winos and broken pavement."

Lumpkin retired from the Dallas Police Department in 1981.

Mabra, W. W. "Bo"

Deputy sheriff who joined the Dallas County Sheriff's Department in March of 1950 after 10 years of working in a machine shop. Deputy Sheriff Mabra was a witness to the assassination's immediate aftermath and later served, along with Nell Tyler, as a bailiff at Jack Ruby's murder trial.

Mabra was standing with fellow deputy Orville Smith in front of the Main Street side of the Old Criminal Courts Building, around the corner from Dealey Plaza. Mabra says the first shot, to him, sounded like a car backfiring down near the triple underpass. Mabra says he heard three shots with a longer pause between the second and third than between the first and second—a different cadence than the one more commonly reported. Recognizing the reports as rifle fire, the men ran into the plaza in the direction of the grassy knoll, where Mabra could see what looked like "a whirl of smoke." But by the time they reached the top of the incline the smoke had disappeared. Mabra says he knew about the wooden fence and the parking lot behind it because he parked his car there. While searching the parking lot behind the wooden fence, Mabra says he was approached by a Dallas policeman. "I don't know what's going on," Mabra quotes the unknown officer as saying. "But there hasn't been a thing move back here in a hour or more because I've been here all that time." Hearing that, Mabra searched the area no further.

McHugh, Godfrey

Presidential aide who both rode in the Dallas motorcade and witnessed President Kennedy's autopsy at Bethesda. McHugh was among those who helped carry JFK's coffin from the ambulance into Air Force One at Love Field in Dallas.

McHugh told assassination researcher David Lifton on November 19, 1967, that he had participated in the photography of Kennedy's body during the autopsy.

"I was holding his body several times when they were turning it and photographing it," McHugh said. "[P]eople keep on saying that his face was demolished and all; he was in absolute perfect shape, except the back of the head, top back of the head, had an explosive bullet in it and was badly damaged . . . and that had blown part of his forehead, which was recuperated and put intact, back in place . . . so his face was exactly as it had been alive . . . I think they took photographs before, during and after [the autopsy]; they kept on taking photographs."

McKenzie, William

It's a small world. McKenzie was the attorney who represented Marina Oswald after the assassination. McKenzie's office-mate was Pete White, who represented Jack Ruby before the assassination.

McKinnon, Cheryl

Assassination witness who later became a *San Diego Star News* reporter. McKinnon wrote in 1983, "On November 22, 1963, I stood . . . on the Grassy Knoll in Dealey Plaza . . . Suddenly three shots in rapid succession rang out. Myself and dozens of others standing nearby turned in horror toward the back of the grassy knoll where it seemed the shots had originated. Puffs of white smoke still hung in the air in small patches. But no one was visible."

McLain, H. B.

Dallas solo motorcycle officer who rode approximately 150 feet behind JFK's limo. McLain offered these recollections to researcher Larry A. Sneed, "I had stopped right by the side of the entrance of the old jail, which is about midway between Main and Elm streets on Houston. I heard one very clear shot. Evidently I must have felt like it was coming from straight ahead because at that instant I was looking down, and when I heard the shot, threw my head up and it appeared that about 5,000 pigeons flew up from behind the Texas School Book Depository. . . . As I sped through Dealey Plaza, the only thing I noticed was [motorcycle patrolman Bobby W.] Hargis with his motorcycle laid down crawling on his hands and knees across the knoll."

Here's what McLain told Sneed about his experiences at Parkland Hospital: "I parked my motorcycle and came back to the limousine about fifteen feet away. As the hospital workers approached to take him out of the car, Mrs. Kennedy was still laying over him, covering his head, and wouldn't get up. So I took it upon myself, reached over and caught her by the shoulder, pulled her and said, 'Come on, let them take him out.' Somebody threw a coat over him just as she raised up, and they took him out on the right side of the car. She then stepped out on the left, stunned, and walked with me in a daze into the emergency room."

When the House Select Committee on Assassinations was accepting so-called acoustic evidence that a fourth shot had originated from behind the wooden fence atop the grassy knoll but had missed, it was supposedly McLain's motorcycle microphone that had stuck in the open position, thus allowing the tape of the events in Dealey Plaza to be recorded. McLain says that it couldn't have been his mike because he turned his siren on immediately following the shooting and there is no siren audible on the Dictabelt recording. New research seems to indicate that the stuck microphone was actually some distance away from Dealey Plaza at the time of the shooting and that, in fact, there are no shots on the tape.

McLain joined the Dallas Police Department in 1953 and retired in 1980. After that McLain went to work for the Dallas County Sheriff's Department where he became a sergeant in the Warrants Division before retiring again in 1996.

(See also ACOUSTIC EVIDENCE.)

McLendon, Gordon

Dallas journalist and operator of KLIF radio in Dallas who was an acquaintance of Jack Ruby. Ruby said he tried to call McLendon around midnight, on November 23, 1963, the night before he shot Oswald, but he couldn't get through. During his testimony to Chief Justice Earl Warren, Ruby asked, out of the blue, if Warren had heard of McLendon. Warren replied that he hadn't. McLendon was co-owner, with Clint Murchison Jr. of the Dallas Cowboys. During the 1960s McLendon co-founded the Association of Former Intelligence Officers with conspiracy suspect David Atlee Phillips.

McLendon was also the top radio personality on his own station. Known as "The Old Scotchman," which referred to liquor as much as ethnicity, he was known for his on-the-air re-creation of baseball games.

MacNeil, Robert

NBC news correspondent who rode in the Dallas motorcade. After hearing the shots and seeing the commotion in Dealey Plaza, MacNeil jumped out of his car. First he ran up the grassy knoll and got all the way to the triple underpass before determining that there was nothing to see there. He then ran back toward the Texas School Book Depository's front entrance.

At the door he asked a man where he could find a phone and the man pointed inside. (Later MacNeil was told that the man who gave him directions at the door may have been Lee Harvey Oswald, but MacNeil isn't the only one who came into the Book Depository at approximately that time looking for a phone, and Tom Alyea claims that it was he to whom Oswald spoke. MacNeil himself has never

Like many other eyewitnesses, NBC correspondent Robert MacNeil (fifth from left, facing camera) ran to the corner of the triple underpass and the grassy knoll to see what had happened. *(Collector's Archive)*

claimed that the man he spoke to was Oswald.) MacNeil says that, after making a phone call, he then ran down to Elm Street from the Texas School Book Depository building and hailed down a citizen's car as one might a cab. The driver stopped, let him in, and gave him a ride to Parkland Hospital. (See also CRAIG, ROGER.)

At Parkland, MacNeil relayed the message that the president had died via telephone to anchor Frank McGee, who in turn informed NBC television's viewers of the president's death. MacNeil later became co-host of the long-running PBS program *The MacNeil-Lehrer Report*.

Maddox, Al

Deputy sheriff (b. 1930, Limestone County, Texas) who would later become the brother-in-law of assassination witness Malcolm Summers. An 11-year U.S. Navy veteran, Maddox joined the Dallas County Sheriff's Department only months before the assassination.

Maddox says that, the night before the assassination when he was returning from work, he saw a man in a policeman's trenchcoat standing in front of the Dal-Tex Building at the Oak Cliff bus stop. He offered the man a ride and the man, after looking inside Maddox's car, said no thanks.

The next day Malcolm Summers was told to get away from the grassy knoll by a man who was hiding a weapon. (See SUMMERS, MALCOLM.) and the two men are now convinced that they both saw the same man. They admit that 25 years passed before they made the connection.

Maddox retired from the Sheriff's Department in 1978. He ran for Dallas County sheriff in 1980 and lost.

Magic Bullet, The

Officially known as Commission Exhibit 399, the "magic bullet" is so called because, for the lone-gunman theory to remain feasible, that bullet had to account for all of the nonfatal wounds suffered in the presidential limousine—that is, the president's back wound, throat wound, and all of Governor Connally's wounds.

The governor's body was littered with metal fragments from the bullet that struck him, yet CE 399 is missing very little metal, and appears almost pristine, although it is slightly flattened.

An FBI memo states that, among the evidence gathered, is a metal fragment that was removed from Governor Connally's arm at Parkland Hospital. If this fragment exists, or ever existed, then the lone gunman theory becomes impossible. The bullet that must have caused all of Connally's wounds was theoretically recovered practically intact and could not have left a fragment behind.

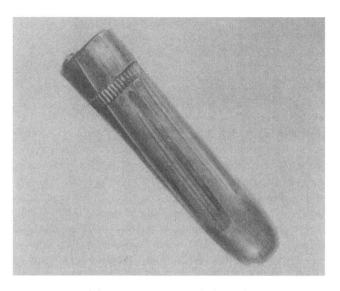

Commission Exhibit 399, the "magic bullet," does not appear to have struck anything. *(Author's Collection)*

Darrell C. Tomlinson, a Parkland Hospital senior engineer, discovered the "magic bullet" jammed into a corner of a stretcher in the hallway in the emergency area of the hospital between 1:00 and 2:00 P.M. on November 22. The bullet was given by Tomlinson to Officer O. P. Wright.

Wright gave the bullet to Secret Service agent Richard Johnsen, who took it to Washington and handed it over to Secret Service chief James Rowley in the Executive Office Building. Rowley, in turn, sent the bullet to the FBI laboratory at 8:50 P.M. on November 22, 1963.

Darrell Tomlinson says that CE 399 does not look anything like the bullet he found.

According to Elizabeth Goode Wright, in a 1993 interview with researcher Wallace Milam, Mrs. Wright's husband, O. P. Wright, the head of security at Parkland Hospital, now deceased, told her that he handled two bullets that day: the bullet that became known as the "magic bullet," and an unfired .38 marked ".38 SP WCC" that he found on a hospital gurney. The bullet's casing was identical to two of the four shell casings found at the scene of J. D. Tippit's murder.

Tomlinson claimed the bullet was found on a stretcher used by neither Governor Connally nor President Kennedy. The Warren Commission concluded that Tomlinson must be mistaken.

The bullet was the only ballistic evidence found that was sufficiently intact to link the shooting to the Mannlicher-Carcano rifle that was discovered on the sixth floor of the Texas School Book Depository.

Dr. Milton Helpern, former New York City chief medical examiner, told assassination researcher Josiah Thompson: "The original pristine weight of this bullet before it was fired was 160–161 grains. The weight of the bullet recovered on the stretcher at Parkland Hospital was reported by the Commission as weighing in at 158.6 grains. The bullet wasn't distorted in any way. I cannot accept the premise that this bullet thrashed around in all of that bony tissue and lost only 1.4 to 2.4 grains of its original weight."

The magic bullet theory was not part of the FBI's original official scenario. The FBI did not acknowledge that James Tague had been wounded by a shot that missed the presidential limousine and therefore had an extra bullet to work with. The FBI stated that one shot hit Kennedy in the back and came out his throat, another wounded Connally, and a third killed Kennedy. Only after the Warren Commission decided that it could not ignore James Tague the way J. Edgar Hoover had that CE 399 needed to be given magic capabilities.

The magic bullet theory was invented by Warren Commission counsel Arlen Specter, a former stand-out on the Yale debating team. Specter said that the single-bullet theory was the only way to explain what happened to the bullet that came out of the front of Kennedy's throat, since the bullet was not found in the car.

Specter's theories, understandably enough, never allow for the possibility that the wound to President Kennedy's throat was one of entry, or that there were bullets found in Parkland Hospital or during the autopsy at Bethesda that were never publicly acknowledged. To entertain the possibility that Kennedy's throat wound was one of entry would have been to concede that there might have been more than one shooter, and the Warren Commission was not about to do this.

The possible effects of "souvenir-hunting" on the assassination investigation were considered after investigator Penn Jones Jr. reported that, at Parkland Hospital, one hospital employee had the nerve to ask Mrs. Kennedy if he might keep the president's T-shirt. Assassination investigator Josiah Thompson has suggested that this souvenir hunting may have been responsible for the location of the "magic bullet" at the time it was discovered. Perhaps, Thompson suggests, someone picked up the bullet and then, realizing its importance, placed it in the nearest inconspicuous place—in this case, the nearest empty gurney.

Maheu, Robert   See HUGHES, HOWARD.

Mannlicher-Carcano

The alleged assassination weapon, an Italian Mannlicher-Carcano rifle, marked serial number C2766, was reportedly found at 1:22 P.M., approximately 52 minutes after the assassination, on the sixth floor of the Texas School Book

Depository building, partially hidden between two boxes. The rifle was originally identified as a 7.65mm German Mauser. Deputy Sheriff Seymour Weitzman was so positive of his identification that he signed an affidavit to the effect that the gun was a Mauser on November 22, 1963. Dallas police photographer Robert Lee Studebaker took photos of the alleged assassination rifle still in its hiding spot.

According to assassination authors Stanley J. and Ethel M. Marks, the proof of a conspiracy is in the simple fact that the Mannlicher-Carcano rifle found on the sixth floor of the Texas School Book Depository was not in firing condition when discovered. The rifle, built in 1940, was found by the FBI to have "wear and rust." More dangerously, the ammunition for the gun was made in 1944. Most weapons experts would say that using ammunition that was almost 20 years old was foolishly dangerous.

Following the assassination, the rifle reportedly found on the sixth floor was sent to the Infantry Weapons Evaluation Branch of the Ballistics Research Laboratory of the Department of the Army. Before the rifle could be test fired, some repairs had to be made. The telescopic sight, which had been mounted for a left-handed person (and Oswald was right-handed), had to be rebuilt, and three light metal shims had to be added to correct deficiencies in the sight's azimuth and elevation. The rifle was found to have a rusty firing pin and test riflemen were afraid to fire the weapon because they feared the firing pin would break.

It should be noted that, even when it is in prime condition, a Mannlicher-Carcano rifle is not considered a very good weapon. During World War II it was known as the "humanitarian" rifle because it had never been known to hurt anyone intentionally. In a book called *Rifle Book* by Jack O'Connor, the weapon is described as "terrible." The October 1964 issue of *Mechanix Illustrated* stated that the rifle was "crudely made, poorly designed, dangerous and inaccurate."

According to the Markses: "The FBI informed the Warren Commission that the Italian rifle's barrel had to be rebored, or re-machined, so that bullets could be discharged through the barrel. In other words, if Oswald had tried to discharge three bullets from the Italian rifle it could have burst in his hands or face. The FBI riflemen refused to fire the Italian rifle until it had been completely re-bored."

The rifle, according to the Warren Commission, was 40.2 inches long and weighed eight pounds. It was a model 91/38, whereas the advertisement in the *American Rifleman*, from which Oswald supposedly ordered the rifle, was for a Model 41, which was 36 inches long and weighed only five and a half pounds. Klein's Sporting Goods, the store from which the rifle had been ordered, later explained that they had run out of Model 41, so sent "A. Hidell" the Model 91/38 instead. No ammunition was ordered for the rifle, and no ammunition for the rifle was found among Lee Harvey Oswald's possessions at the time of his Dallas arrest.

To link the Mannlicher-Carcano rifle found on the sixth floor of the Texas School Book Depository with the crime, it was necessary to test the rifling marks left on the intact bullet found in Parkland Hospital. With the exception of CE399, the magic bullet, no other bullets or bullet fragments were found of sufficient size to link them with the gun found on the sixth floor.

According to the official scenario the ammunition used in the Mannlicher-Carcano were standard military full-metal jacket bullets. These bullets are designed not to come apart and are not the type that would leave fragments throughout the president's brain as we are told happened here.

(See also DAY, J. CARL; MAGIC BULLET, THE.)

Marcades, Melba Christine   See CHERAMIE, ROSE.

Marcello, Carlos

Marcello was born Calogero Minacero and became the boss of America's oldest Mafia family, based in New Orleans, Louisiana. He was a crime boss during the 1950s, 1960s, and 1970s.

During that time, Marcello's power spread from New Orleans westward and by the time of the assassination encompassed Dallas.

Marcello was furious with the Kennedys after Attorney General Robert Kennedy had him deported in April 1961. Marcello was "kidnapped" and flown to Guatemala without being allowed to even make a phone call.

While in Latin America, Marcello had a hellish experience, wandering several days in the jungle with a broken rib. He was flown back to the United States four months later, according to the U.S. Border Patrol, by CIA pilot (and assassination suspect) David Ferrie. After his return, Marcello reportedly said of the Kennedys, "Take the stone out of my shoe."

On November 22, 1963, Ferrie was working for Marcello's lawyer G. Wray Gill on Marcello's defense against immigration fraud charges. (Marcello was acquitted of these charges on the day of the assassination.)

FBI reports indicate that Ferrie flew to Guatemala aboard Delta Airlines twice during the fall of 1963, evidence that Ferrie's detective work for G. Wray Gill was directly related to his defense of Carlos Marcello's immigration-fraud charges. Ferrie and Marcello saw each other frequently in the days leading up to the assassination as Marcello's trial was taking place and Ferrie was doing investigative work for Marcello's lawyer. Marcello and Ferrie were together on the weekends of November 9–10 and November 16–17 at Churchill Farms, Marcello's 6,000-acre estate.

As part of an FBI sting called BRILAB, the FBI made 1,350 tapes of Marcello's conversations between February 1979 and February 1980. Agents Mike Wacks, Larry Montague, and Joseph Hauser made the tapes. The tapes were sealed by Judge Morey Sear at the start of Marcello's bribery and conspiracy trial in 1981. The judge ordered them permanently sealed, ruling that they would prejudice the jury against Marcello.

According to former chief counsel of the House Select Committee on Assassinations G. Robert Blakey, Marcello "implicated himself in the assassination on three of those tapes . . . On one tape, Marcello asked the other person to leave the room and resume the conversation in the secrecy of his car when the assassination came up. Marcello said something like, 'We don't talk about that in here.'"

Assassination researcher John Davis, who believes that organized crime was behind President Kennedy's death, writes that the tapes amount to a veiled "admission of complicity" by Marcello and his brother Joe. Though Davis filed a 1988 Freedom of Information Act suit for the release of the tapes, the tapes remain sealed.

Las Vegas private investigator Ed Becker says Marcello told him in September 1962 about a plan to assassinate President Kennedy, which included the using of a "nut" to deflect blame from the mob. Becker says he told the FBI about the plot a year before the assassination. In 1978, Becker repeated the story to the House Select Committee, who found him credible.

Reputed Mafia boss Carlos Marcello in 1980. *(AP/Wide World Photos)*

Some feel the assassination, as executed, was beyond the scope of mobsters. According to Harrison Edward Livingstone, "There is no way Carlos Marcello [and other mobsters] . . . could have done all this alone or covered any of it up. Neither these Mafia bosses nor the men who work for them had this kind of access to the evidence."

Frank Ragano was, for 27 years, the lawyer for Florida mob boss Santos Trafficante. For 15 of those years he also represented Teamster president Jimmy Hoffa. In 1992, Ragano revealed knowledge of a plot involving Hoffa, Trafficante, and Marcello to assassinate the president. All three men are dead now, but at the time of Ragano's statement Marcello was still alive, in jail, where he reportedly was suffering from Alzheimer's disease. Ragano said he became an "unwitting intermediary" to the plot when he met with Hoffa at Teamsters headquarters in Washington in January or February 1963. Ragano, who was about to fly to New Orleans for a meeting with Trafficante and Marcello, says Hoffa told him, "Tell Marcello and Trafficante they have to kill the president."

Ragano continued, "Hoffa said to me, 'This has to be done.' Jimmy was ranting and raving for a long time. I didn't take it seriously because I knew Jimmy was a hothead with a short attention span. Marcello and Trafficante never met Hoffa. I had lawyer-client privilege with Hoffa and Trafficante and so I was designated intermediary. Marcello and Trafficante were extremely cautious. They always wanted to be able to truthfully tell a grand jury that they never met Hoffa." A few days later Ragano claims he met with Trafficante and Marcello at the Royal Orleans Hotel. Ragano continued, "I told them, 'You won't believe what Hoffa wants me to tell you. Jimmy wants you to kill the president.' They didn't laugh . . . Their looks scared me. It made me think they already had such a thought in mind." Ragano says he returned to Washington, told Hoffa he had delivered the message, and Hoffa reportedly replied, "It is going to be done." On November 22, 1963, Hoffa called Ragano three or four minutes after the first news bulletins.

"Have you heard the good news?" Hoffa asked. "They killed the S.O.B. This means Bobby is out as Attorney General."

Marcello gave immunized testimony to the House Select Committee on Assassinations on January 11, 1978. At that time Marcello expressed "a deep dislike" for Robert Kennedy. Marcello stated that he had been "illegally kidnapped" by government agents during his deportation. He admitted that David Ferrie worked for his lawyer G. Wray Gill. Marcello denied, however, that Ferrie worked directly for him—or that he had a close relationship with Ferrie.

The House Select Committee concluded that "Marcello had the motive, means and opportunity to have President John F. Kennedy assassinated, though [the Committee] was unable to establish direct evidence of Marcello's complicity . . . In its investigation of Marcello, the committee identified the presence of one critical evidentiary element that was lacking with the other organized crime figures examined by the committee: credible associations relating both Lee Harvey Oswald and Jack Ruby to figures having a relationship, albeit tenuous, with Marcello's crime family or organization."

Lee Harvey Oswald's uncle, Dutz Murret, worked for Marcello. Oswald's mother had dated men who worked for Marcello. Both Guy Banister and Ferrie had done work for Marcello.

The House Committee also established "associations between Jack Ruby and several individuals affiliated with the underworld activities of Carlos Marcello. Ruby was a personal acquaintance of Joseph Civello, the Marcello associate who allegedly headed organized crime activities in Dallas . . . [and] a New Orleans nightclub figure, Harold Tanenbaum with whom Ruby was considering going into partnership in the fall of 1963."

Jim Garrison's assassination investigation has been criticized because it didn't include the possibility of Marcello's involvement. Garrison, when questioned about this, always said that he had seen no evidence that Marcello was a member of organized crime.

Garrison's blind spot toward Marcello may have been explained by a *Life* magazine article (September 8, 1967), which noted that Garrison knew Marcello-aide Mario Marino and that Marino "picked up a couple of hotel bills" for Garrison on visits to Las Vegas.

FBI agent Joseph Hauser went undercover in 1979 to investigate Marcello's crime organization. According to Hauser, Marcello admitted to knowing Oswald and his uncle, Charles "Dutz" Murret, and that Oswald worked for him in 1963 as a runner for his betting operation. This is corroborated by an independent report from an FBI informant that Oswald received money from Carlos Marcello's crime lieutenant Joe Poretto in the New Orleans Town and Country Restaurant managed by Marcello's brother Anthony.

In 1980, Hauser talked to Carlos's brother Joseph about the way the Kennedys had hassled him and his brother during the early 1960s. Joseph Marcello reportedly replied, "Don't worry, we took care of them, didn't we?"

According to an FBI teletype dated March 3, 1989, Marcello—who had been in prison in Minneapolis, Minnesota, since 1983 for conspiracy to bribe a judge—mistook his prison guards for personal bodyguards while apparently suffering from dementia. Marcello told the men that he had just driven back to New Orleans from New York City where he had had a meeting with Tony Provenzano, a captain in the Genovese crime family and a Teamsters International vice president. He and Provenzano, Marcello said, had decided to "get Kennedy in Dallas."

Mark on the Curb

In most scenarios of the shooting sequence, a shot missed. How else to explain the scratch on the cheek of assassination witness James Tague who was standing at the mouth of the triple underpass other than that he was hit by debris from a missed shot? In addition to a multitude of eyewitness testimony to the effect, other evidence supporting the fact that at least one shot missed is a mark on a curb on the south side of Main Street about 20 feet from the entrance to the triple underpass. On November 23, 1963, cameramen Tom Dillard and Jim Underwood photographed the mark on the curb. On August 5, 1964, a section of the curb was removed by special agent Lyndal Shaneyfelt and transported to the FBI lab in Washington, D.C. The mark was measured before it was moved and was determined to be 23 feet and four inches from the triple underpass. The mark was analyzed spectrographically and was found to consist of lead with a trace of antimony. No copper was found. This meant that, if a bullet from the Mannlicher-Carcano rifle had struck that curb, it must have completely lost its jacket.

Martin, John, Jr.

An assassination witness born in 1905 in Minnesota, Martin watched the motorcade from the north end of the reflecting pool near Elm Street and filmed it with an 8mm DeJur movie camera. Martin worked in 1963 at the Terminal Annex Post Office at 207 South Houston Street, on the south side of Dealey Plaza directly across from the Texas School Book Depository Building. Martin told assassination researcher David Hawkins in 1979: "The shot came over my head . . . Then a few seconds later there were two more shots . . . Thinking that perhaps the person who fired the shots had left the building and was being pursued by police . . . I ran over there and asked a man I found later was [from the] Treasury Department. I said, 'Why are you running up here?' He says it seems like someone was chasing someone up here. When I saw him he was right on top of the hill behind the gang that was running up there. I walked up part way and then turned around and came back, and told a policeman that they ought to surround the building [School Book Depository] there."

Martino, John

Born in 1911, in Atlantic City, New Jersey, Martino started out as a numbers runner and casino operator for organized crime and was arrested in Cuba by Castro in 1959 while working for mob boss Santos Trafficante. Martino spent three years in prison and returned to Miami in the fall of 1962, where he became involved in anti-Castro activities. He was given the military rank of captain by the

CIA and worked together with assassination suspects Frank Sturgis and Gerry Patrick Hemming, who admits foreknowledge of a plot to kill JFK. Six months before his death Martino admitted to having some knowledge about the assassination himself, stating that he knew for certain that there had been two shooters in Dealey Plaza and that neither of them had been Oswald. The accused assassin, he said, went to the Texas Theatre because he was supposed to meet an anti-Castro Cuban there. Oswald, according to Martino, was to be killed while leaving the country. Martino reportedly told Texas businessman Fred Claasen in 1975, "The anti-Castro people put Oswald together. Oswald didn't know who he was working for—he was ignorant of who was really putting him together. Oswald was to meet his contact at the Texas Theatre. . . . There was no way we could get to him. They had Ruby kill him." According to Fred Claasen, Martino said that the assassins knew the motorcade route before they went to Dallas.

Martino said that he worked in 1959 with Jack Ruby to smuggle casino cash profits into the United States from Havana. In 1963, as part of a "book tour" sponsored by the John Birch Society, Martino gave a series of anti-Castro talks to Cuban exiles.

According to Martino's wife Robbyn, Martino and she were at their home in Miami, Florida, when a news item came over the radio during the autumn of 1963 regarding JFK's visit to Dallas. Martino reportedly told his wife, "They're going to kill him when he gets to Dallas."

Martino died on August 3, 1975.

(See also MATHEWS, RUSSELL D.)

Masen, John Thomas   See OSWALD LOOK-ALIKES.

Mastoidectomy

When Lee Harvey Oswald was six years old he came down with acute mastoiditis, an infection of the bone behind his left ear. He was taken to the hospital and a mastoidectomy was performed. That is, the bone was removed. The operation usually leaves a scar between one and two inches long behind the ear, where of course it is rarely noticed. According to the Warren Commission Hearings and Exhibits (Volume 19, pp. 582–590) Oswald's mastoidectomy scar was noted in his U.S. Marine Corps health records both in 1956 and 1959.

However, when the body of Oswald was autopsied at Parkland Hospital in Dallas on November 24, 1963, by Dallas County medical examiner Dr. Earl Forrest Rose, together with Dr. Sidney Stewart, no mastoidectomy was noted. (The autopsists did note the scar on the inside of Oswald's left wrist, which seemingly establishes that this was the same man who attempted suicide in the Soviet Union in October 1959.)

Mather, Carl

On December 4, 1963, the FBI received a report from a KRLD-TV reporter in Dallas named Wes Wise (later, mayor of Dallas). The report stated that at 2:00 P.M., November 22, 1963, a mechanic named T. F. White had spotted a man who "looked like Lee Harvey Oswald" sitting in a *red* 1957 Plymouth with the Texas license plate number PP 4537 in the parking lot of the El Chico Restaurant, not far from the site of the Tippit slaying. (The real Oswald was already under arrest). White wrote down the license plate number and told his boss, who told Wise.

Mather, a close friend of J. D. Tippit, lived in Garland, Texas, and he owned a *blue* four-door 1957 Plymouth with the Texas license plate number PP 4537.

According to Mather's wife, Mather worked until 2:00 P.M. on the day of the assassination. After work, he returned home to take his family to the Tippit home to pay their condolences.

Mather's wife said the family had never owned any type of red car. Mrs. Mather was interviewed twice by the FBI, but the federal agents never spoke to Carl. Wes Wise had dinner with the Mathers and said that, although Carl was too nervous to eat, his wife was "cool, very cool."

At the time of the assassination, Mather worked for the Collins Radio Company in Richardson, Texas, where he had been employed for 21 years. He had once worked for that company at Andrews Air Force Base in Washington, D.C.

While working in the nation's capital, he had been assigned to do electronic repairs on Vice President Lyndon Johnson's Air Force II. According to Harrison Edward Livingstone, "From this evidence, it would appear that someone borrowed the license plates from Mather's Plymouth then returned them."

Mathews, Russell D.

Mathews has a number of connections to the assassination. He was a friend of Jack Ruby, an "idol" of assassination suspect Charles Harrelson, the best man at the wedding of "Babushka Lady" Beverly Oliver and George McCann. McCann was later murdered. Mathews was a coworker of John Martino at the Hotel Deauville, and he was living in Dallas at the time of the assassination.

The Warren Commission found that the only substantiated rumor of Ruby being involved in pro- or anti-Castro activities involved the time in January 1959 when Ruby

"made preliminary inquiries, as a middle-man, concerning the possible sale to Cuba of some surplus jeeps located in Shreveport, Louisiana, and asked about the possible release of prisoners from a Cuban prison." One of these prisoners is alleged to have been assassination suspect Santos Trafficante.

The *Warren Report* says this about Mathews: "During the period of the 'jeep sale,' R. D. Mathews, a gambler and a 'passing acquaintance' of Ruby, returned to Dallas from Havana where he had been living. In mid-1959, he returned to Cuba until mid-1960. On October 3, 1963, a telephone call was made from the Carousel Club to Mathews's former wife in Shreveport. No evidence has been uncovered that Mathews was associated with the sale of jeeps or the release of prisoners or that he knew of Oswald prior to the assassination. Mathews's ex-wife did not recall the phone call in October of 1963, and she asserted that she did not know Jack Ruby or anyone working for him."

(See also BABUSHKA LADY; HARRELSON, CHARLES; MARTINO, JOHN; RUBY, JACK.)

Medical Evidence   See AUTOPSY OF JFK; PARKLAND WITNESSES.

Mentesana, Ernest Charles

A 45-year-old owner of a Dallas grocery store who filmed the aftermath of the assassination in Dealey Plaza, including police officers removing a rifle from the roof of the Texas School Book Depository. The weapon has no sling and no scope, so it is obviously not the Mannlicher-Carcano. In the next sequence filmed by Mentesana, the rifle is being examined on the ground. Thayer Waldo, a reporter for the *Fort Worth Star-Telegram,* says that he interviewed a secretary from the Depository and she said she had been told by Dallas police that a rifle had been found on the roof of the building. Mentesana was at the nearby Katy Railroad Freight Depot at the time of the shooting and did not learn of the assassination until several minutes later.

Mentesana died of a heart attack in 1969.

Mercer, Julia Ann

Shortly before 11:00 A.M. on the day of the assassination, 23-year-old Mercer was driving west on Elm Street through Dealey Plaza when she was temporarily forced to stop by a green Ford pick up.

The truck had a Texas license plate and was parked on the right side of Elm Street, closest to the grassy knoll. There was, Mercer says, a heavy-set, middle-aged man sitting behind the wheel. There was another man, in his late-twenties and wearing a plaid shirt, who was outside the truck pulling a gun case from over the tailgate. Just as she was pulling away, she saw the second man carrying the gun case up the grassy slope.

In the early morning of November 23, she was shown many photographs and asked if any resembled the men she had seen. She picked out two photos which resembled the man behind the wheel. She turned over one of the photos and read the name "Jack Ruby." If Mercer's memories are correct, this means that authorities considered Ruby a suspect in the assassination one day before he shot Oswald.

Mercer is one of several witnesses who were interviewed by the Warren Commission who claim that the published version of her testimony has been drastically altered.

See also BOWERS, LEE; HOFFMAN, ED; MURPHY, JOE.

Mertz, Michel   See SOUETRE, JEAN.

Meyer, Mrs. Mary Pinchot

Mistress of President Kennedy who was murdered in Washington, D.C., in 1964 while jogging along a canal in the Georgetown section of the city. Mrs. Meyer, the divorced wife of CIA agent Cord Meyer, was a "stunning 43-year-old bohemian aristocrat."

According to author Leo Damore, President Kennedy had planned on dumping Jackie and marrying Mary, who reportedly had introduced Kennedy to marijuana and LSD in 1962.

Damore was quoted in the *New York Post* in 1991 as saying, "She had access to the highest levels. She was involved in illegal drug activity. What do you think it would do to the beatification of Kennedy if this woman said, 'It wasn't Camelot, it was Caligula's court'?"

After Meyer was murdered, her diary and letters were obtained by top CIA officer James Angleton. Angleton claimed that he burned them, but Damore is convinced they still exist.

Raymond Crump Jr. was tried and acquitted for the 1964 murder of JFK-mistress Mary Pinchot Meyer, whose body was found along a towpath that paralleled a canal on one side and the Potomac River on the other. She had been shot to death during the noon hour. A police detective responded to the scene where an eyewitness told him that Crump, a black man who had just consumed a six-pack of beer, had been seen bending over the body of Mrs. Meyer. Crump accounted for his presence in the area by saying he had been fishing in the river. His clothing was water-soaked, a result, he claimed, of falling in the river. No fishing gear or gun was found in the area. Says author Leo

Damore, "Two shots were fired within eight seconds—one behind her ear so that it traversed her brain, and one behind her shoulder blade so it severed her aorta." These are earmarks of a professional hit.

Military-Industrial Complex

Term for the powerful coalition between the Pentagon and the defense contractors who provide billions of dollars worth of military materiel. During Dwight D. Eisenhower's last speech as president of the United States, on January 17, 1961, he said, "The conjunction of an immense military establishment and a large arms industry is new to the American experience. We must guard against the acquisition of unwarranted influence, whether sought or unsought, by the military-industrial complex."

Miller, Austin L.

Miller was standing on the triple underpass at the time of the assassination. Miller stated in a November 22, 1963, affidavit: "One shot apparently hit the street past the car . . . I saw something which I thought was smoke or steam coming from a group of trees north of Elm off the railroad tracks."

Strangely, Miller said he thought shots came from "right there in the car."

Millican, A. J.

Millican was standing on the north side of Elm midway between Houston and the triple underpass at the time of the assassination. He later told sheriff's deputies he saw "a truck from 'Honest Joe's Pawn Shop' park close to the Texas School Book Depository, then drive off five to ten minutes before the assassination." This truck was also spotted by assassination witnesses Jean Hill and Marilyn Willis.

According to Millican: "Just after the President's car passed, I heard three shots from up toward Elm right by the Texas School Book Depository, and then immediately I heard two more shots come from the arcade between the Texas School Book Depository and the underpass, then three more shots came from the same direction only sounded further back. It sounded approximately like a .45 automatic, or a high-powered rifle."

Millican was never questioned by the Warren Commission or the House Select Committee on Assassinations.

(See also HONEST JOE'S PAWN SHOP.)

Milteer, Joseph

On November 9, 1963, in the downtown Miami apartment of Miami police informant Willie Somersett, Milteer was taped as he said that it was "in the working" that President Kennedy would be killed from an office building with a high-powered rifle, and that someone was going to be arrested within an hour of the shooting, just to throw the public off.

Since Kennedy was scheduled to be in a motorcade on November 18 in Miami, that motorcade was canceled and the president instead traveled to and from his speaking engagement by helicopter.

Milteer was interviewed by the FBI after they received the tape, and released. He died on February 9, 1974, when a Coleman stove blew up in his mansion in Quitman, Georgia.

Milteer went to the hospital following the accident and his condition was reportedly improving for two weeks when he suddenly died. According to assassination researcher Harrison Edward Livingstone: "The mortician preparing the body examined the wounds from the explosion and felt that the damage was not severe enough to have caused Milteer's death." A man resembling Milteer can be seen in photographs watching the Dallas motorcade from the sidewalk in Dealey Plaza.

Milteer was a wealthy, politically active racist from Georgia, who was the organizer for the National States Rights Party, and the organizer for the Constitution Party. Milteer attended an April 1963 meeting of the Congress of Freedom, Inc. held in New Orleans.

Minox Spy Cameras

Four days after the assassination, members of the Dallas police, while searching Ruth Paine's home, found a German-made Minox spy camera in Oswald's seabag. It was three inches long and resembled a cigarette lighter. It was designated in the Dallas police inventory as item no. 375. When that inventory was published in the Warren Commission's 26 volumes, the piece of equipment was listed as a "Minox light meter."

"I know a camera when I see it," rebutted Dallas police detective Gus Rose, who was involved in the inventory of Oswald's possessions. *Dallas Morning News* reporter Earl Golz contacted the Minox Corporation and found that the company did not sell light meters at that time. They also said that the serial number on Oswald's camera was not a valid serial number.

"It was a little bitty thing," Rose said, referring to the camera. "And the way you rolled the film, you just pulled it apart and the film advanced. . . . I didn't know much about it but when I opened it there was film in it. The FBI later asked me to change my report to say that it was a Minox light meter, but I never did."

FBI agent Vincent Drain says that he was involved in the itemization of all of Oswald's possessions seized in the searches of his Beckley Street rooming house as well as the search of the Paines' home in Irving, and says that he remembers no Minox camera—and, he adds, he would have recognized one because the FBI used them.

Interestingly, Ruth Paine told the FBI that her husband had a Minox camera that he kept in the garage, the same garage where Oswald reportedly kept his Mannlicher-Carcano, but that it didn't work because Michael had soaked the camera in a can of kerosene. Kerosene is not known as a cleaner of cameras, but it is known to remove fingerprints. Ruth gave the FBI Michael's camera and the pictures on the film in it showed scenes of Third World countries, tankers off shore, etc. Ruth says that those photographs were taken in Korea, when Michael was in the U.S. Army.

(See also PAINE, RUTH AND MICHAEL R.)

Minsk Espionage School

J. Edgar Hoover testified before the Warren Commission that: "[On May 12, 1964,] information came to me indicating that there is an espionage training school outside Minsk—I don't know whether it is true—and that [Oswald] was trained at that school to come back to this country to become what they call a 'sleeper,' that is a man who will remain dormant for three or four years and, in case of international hostilities, rise up and be used. I don't know of any espionage school at Minsk or near Minsk, and I don't know how you would find out if there ever was one because the Russians won't tell you if you ask them. They do have espionage and sabotage schools in Russia and they do have an assassination squad that is used by them but there is no indication he had any association with anything of that kind."

The rumor that there was an espionage school outside Minsk originated from a CIA memo, in response to a Warren Commission query, stating that an earlier defector had reported the existence of the school in 1947.

Mintkenbaugh, James

According to retired FBI agent James Hosty, Mintkenbaugh was an American who emigrated to the Soviet Union during the late 1950s. In 1959, however, Mintkenbaugh, who had been attracted to Russia by an idealistic image of communism, became disillusioned by life there and decided that he wanted to return to the United States. Mintkenbaugh later told the FBI that, soon after he made his wishes to return to the United States known, he was approached by agents of the KGB who requested that he marry a Russian woman and return with her to the United States. Mintkenbaugh said no. The possible parallels to the experiences of Lee and Marina Oswald are obvious.

Mitchell, Mary Ann   See CRAWFORD, JAMES.

Mitchell, Willie
Inmate at the Dallas County Jail on the east side of Houston Street whose window overlooked Dealey Plaza. Many inmates watched the assassination, but none were officially asked about what they saw.

MK/ULTRA
CIA mind-control program, the brainchild of CIA deputy director of plans Richard Helms. The original concept was to test the use of different drugs in conjunction with interrogation techniques. Helms believed that the USSR was working on these techniques, so the United States had to also in order to avoid being victimized by the Soviets. The study dosed innocent people, many of them CIA agents, with LSD without their consent. Prostitutes and their clients were given LSD in rooms equipped with surveillance cameras. It is feared that these mind-control experiments were also attempting, through drugs and hypnosis, to create a robotic killer, a Manchurian Candidate, who could perform tasks and commit crimes without remembering these activities.

Dr. Louis Jolyan West was referred to by former U.S. Naval Institute Intelligence Briefing Team member William Cooper as one of "the government's premiere experts in mind control." Dr. West was the last psychiatrist to see Ruby before his death to an amazingly fast-working cancer. Dr. West said that Ruby "was neither an irresponsible hoodlum nor a criminal conspirator, but an emotionally liable and impulsive man. . . . Jack shot Oswald in a moment of blind passion during which he was capable neither of premeditation nor judgment of his consequences . . . [Jack was in] a paranoid state. The delusion manifested itself in his belief that President [Lyndon] Johnson, who Jack Ruby thought was behind the assassination, arranged a cover-up by finding a scapegoat. In this case, as with Adolph Hitler, it was the Jews. Jack Ruby was very sensitive about religion. In his mind, he believed that every person of the Jewish faith was systematically being brought into Dallas and killed. Dallas to him had become Johnson's concentration camp." The late Dr. West was involved in illegal experiments upon human guinea pigs during the 1950s. These experiments involved drugs and hypnosis. Sadly, Dr. West once killed an elephant by giving it an overdose of LSD. Dr. West was also the psychiatrist who treated Ruby after he was arrested for shooting Oswald. Dr. West concluded that Ruby was in a "paranoid state, manifested by delusions, visual and auditory hallucinations and suicidal impulses." Ruby's number-one delusion was his belief that Dallas had been transformed by Nazis into a giant concentration camp where Jews were being systematically exterminated. Dr. West prescribed medication.

MK/ULTRA's New York City supervisor was George White, an Office of Strategic Services agent during World War II. He also worked for the Federal Bureau of Narcotics, making heavy use of mob informants along the way.

(See also CASTILLO, LUIS; EDISON, EDELE.)

Molina, Joe Rodriguez
Texas School Book Depository credit manager who was standing on the front steps of that building at the time of the assassination. Molina told the FBI that he thought the shots came from the west of the building.

Molina was treated as a suspect by the Dallas police during the first 24 hours following the shooting. He was a Dallas-born Navy veteran who had worked at the Book Depository since 1947. Molina became a suspect, according to the *Warren Report*, because of his employment—and because he was a member of the Latin American Veterans Organization and a veterans' group called the American G.I. Forum, which the Dallas Police considered "possibly subversive."

According to Roy Westphal, a detective with the Dallas Police Criminal Intelligence Division, the American G.I. Forum was an exclusively Hispanic organization that had been determined to be capable of "causing problems." Westphal said that one of the memos he had received even mentioned Molina by name and this was enough to get a search warrant.

The *Warren Report* says, "Dallas policemen searched Molina's home with his permission, at about 1:30 A.M., Saturday, November 23. During the day Molina was intermittently interrogated at police headquarters for six or seven hours . . . He was never arrested, charged or held in custody . . . According to Molina, he had never spoken to Oswald . . . Molina lost his job in December. He felt that he was being discharged because of the unfavorable publicity he had received."

Monroe, Marilyn
Mistress of President Kennedy as well as of Attorney General Robert Kennedy. At the time of her death in 1962 she was the world's number-one movie star. Monroe was reportedly murdered via a drug-laden suppository by employees of assassination suspect Sam Giancana, according to Charles and Sam Giancana (the mobster's nephew) in their book *Double Cross*. The reason: she knew too much. Monroe's autopsy revealed a bruised colon. Her death was officially called a suicide.

Marilyn Monroe: Was she murdered with a poison suppository? *(Author's Collection)*

Montgomery, L. D.   See BROWN PAPER SACK.

Mooney, Luke

A veteran of the 764th Amphibious Tank Tractor Battalion during World War II, who had been a Dallas deputy sheriff in the Writ and Execution Division since 1958. Mooney was standing on Main Street just north of the old courthouse at the time of the shooting. After the shots were fired, Mooney ran across Dealey Plaza, up the grassy knoll, and into the railroad yards. After looking into several cars and finding nothing, Mooney went to the Texas School Book Depository where he became involved in the search of the sixth floor. While searching the floor he claims to be the first to find the spent shells in the "sniper's nest" area. Mooney says that he carefully avoided leaving fingerprints as he called out the window down to the ground to Sheriff Decker or Captain Fritz who were both in the street downstairs to send up the Crime Lab. When Fritz arrived at the southeast corner of the sixth floor, Mooney searched the northwest corner of the building with sheriff's deputy Eugene Boone. Boone noticed the partially hidden rifle first. Mooney said years later that he did not know what kind of weapon it was, although it

reminded him of the bolt-action carbines he had used while in the army. A few minutes after seeing the alleged assassination weapon, Mooney says he returned to the Sheriff's Department and had nothing further to do with the assassination investigation. Mooney reported at the time that he thought the weapon was a 7.65 German Mauser.

Mooney retired from the Sheriff's Department in 1980.

Mooneyham, Mrs. Lillian

A 95th District Court clerk who viewed the assassination from windows in the Dallas Criminal Courts Building on the east side of Houston Street. Mooneyham said that she heard three shots. She thought the first was a firecracker and said second and third shots came close together.

According to a January 10, 1964, FBI report, "Mrs. Mooneyham estimated that it was about four and a half to five minutes following the shots . . . that she looked up towards the sixth floor of the Texas School Book Depository and observed . . . a man standing in the . . . window behind some cardboard boxes. The man appeared to Mrs. Mooneyham to be looking out the window, however, the man was not close up to the window but was standing slightly back from it, so that Mrs. Mooneyham could not make out his features."

By this time, Oswald, by most accounts, had already left the building.

Moore, Russell Lee   See WEIRD BEARD.

Moore, T. E.

Assassination witness who watched the motorcade from in the middle of Elm Street, where traffic had been blocked off at the corner of Houston Street. Moore, who saw action in the South Pacific during World War II, was a clerk for Bill Shaw, the district clerk for Dallas County, with offices in the Dallas County Records Building Annex.

Moore told researcher Larry A. Sneed, "There was a highway marker sign right in front of the Book Depository, and as the President got around to that, the first shot was fired. . . . You couldn't tell exactly where the shots were coming from . . . I fell certain that there were three shots and they were spaced at regular intervals."

Moore died in January 1994 in Dallas.

Moorman Photo, The

Assassination witness Mary Ann Moorman was, in 1963, the 31-year-old wife of a plumber. She went to see the presidential motorcade with her friend Jean Hill, and took along her Polaroid Highlander camera, a Model 80 that used series 30 film. The camera had a 100mm focal lens with shutter speeds from 1/25 to 1/100 of a second. She and Hill were standing on the south side of Elm Street across from the grassy knoll. Her first photo, which showed the Texas School Book Depository in the background, was taken of Moorman's friend, Officer Glen McBride, who was riding his motorcycle in the motorcade. One of her photos has become famous because it shows a clear view of the knoll during the shooting, and—if one uses a lot of imagination and/or "computer enhancement"—appears to show a man on the other side of the picket fence firing a rifle. This figure has come to be known as Badgeman because, after much enhancement, the figure appears to be wearing a policeman's uniform, with badge showing.

A more compelling image exists in the photo. This one, known as "number-five man," was first discovered in 1965 by assassination researcher David Lifton. Lifton called the image that because it was the fifth man-like image he had found in the small Polaroid photo, and by far the easiest to see. Number-five man is visible from the waist up and appears to be holding a long slender object in a horizontal manner in front of him. Soon after discovering the image, Lifton shifted the focus of his research and the cause of publicizing number-five man's existence was taken up by researcher Raymond Marcus.

Mary Moorman testified for the prosecution at Clay Shaw's conspiracy trial.

(See also HILL, JEAN LOLLIS.)

Morales, David Sanchez (a.k.a. El Indio; Pancho)

Morales was born in 1925 in Phoenix, Arizona. He stood five-feet-eleven and weighed upwards of 250 pounds. He attended college at Arizona State, the University of Southern California, and the University of California at Los Angeles.

Morales was recruited by the Office of Strategic Services in Germany at the end of World War II and had been used to train Cuban exiles before the Bay of Pigs operation.

Morales is said to have been close friends with CIA/mobster Johnny Roselli. He ran CIA assassination programs in South America, Vietnam (Operation *Phoenix*), Bolivia, and Chile. Morales was the chief of operations at JM/WAVE, the CIA operation out of Miami designed to get rid of Castro.

During a drunken tirade in 1973 he said, regarding President Kennedy, "Well, we took care of that son of a bitch, didn't we?"

During his investigation into the assassination, New Orleans Parish district attorney Jim Garrison received an anonymous letter postmarked from Miami, Florida, which stated that one of the hitmen in Dealey Plaza was code-named Indio. El Indio was Morales's nickname.

Morales died in 1978 of a heart attack.

Morningstar, Robert

Photographic expert who claimed at the "Web of Conspiracy Symposium" in New York City on October 18, 1992, that the Zapruder film is a "radically altered document" and has never been publicly viewed in its original form. Morningstar's conclusions have received support in recent years from others who have found their own reasons to believe that the Zapruder film is an altered document, yet the effectiveness of Morningstar's methods remains unconfirmed.

Although FBI photographic expert Lyndal Shaneyfelt told the Warren Commission that only three frames were missing from the Zapruder film due to an error in processing (during a section of the film when JFK is hidden behind the "Stemmons Freeway" sign; Shaneyfelt said they were frames #208-210), Morningstar believes that, because of the altering he has discovered, as many as 24 frames may be missing. "It was a purposeful destruction of history," Morningstar says.

Everyone who has seen the film has noticed the jump in the film while the presidential limousine is behind that sign. The edit here, according to Morningstar, was done with blue splice glue and was purposefully sloppy, not only to force the viewer to disregard the image at that point but also to distract the viewer from a subliminal edit which immediately follows.

Before the subliminal edit, one notices the right side of the Stemmons Freeway sign lines up vertically with the corner of the concrete wall on the far side of Elm Street (see Z-202, 203, 204). After the edit, the right side of that sign lines up with a tree trunk approximately 30 feet to the right of the wall's corner. Since we know that Zapruder remained stationary while filming—he was standing on a concrete pedestal and couldn't have moved if he had wanted to—this shift in perspective is impossible. The entire background of the photo, that is, everything on the far side of Elm Street, has been shifted to the left, while the foreground has remained stationary.

"The reason this editing technique is so difficult to distinguish from reality is that the editors of the film used gestalt perception techniques. The tree trunk lines has been juxtaposed to replace another vertical reference, formerly associated by the viewer's eye with the corner of the concrete wall. The edit creates the illusion that the vehicle has accelerated once under fire, an illusion belied by the fact that the American flag on the front of the limousine is drooping, motionless [unlikely if the car was accelerating]. The blue glue used in the sloppy edit has been used as paint, not only to force the viewer to disregard the image as being devoid of information, but through vertical lines in the splice glue, to prepare the viewer for the transposition of the wall into a new space drastically to the left. You can't imagine the sophisticated technology that would have been needed to accomplish this effect with 8mm film in 1963."

The unspoken implication is that the presidential limousine stopped for perhaps more than a second once under fire. Whatever other information the edit obliterated may never be known.

Morningstar also claims that bullet paths caused by shots fired on the presidential limousine, but which missed the president, are visible on the film, and that—using sophisticated infrared and laser technology—it is possible to determine the source of the shots. The laser experiments were conducted in Dealey Plaza by assassination researcher and nutritionist Dr. Gary Null and revealed that there were two shooters in the Texas School Book Depository and a third on the third floor of the Dal-Tex Building across the street. Null's research has led him to believe that at least two shots came from the Dal-Tex Building, specifically from an empty office on the third floor, equipped only with a telephone, which belonged to a "Texas oil magnate with a penchant for [American] football."

Morningstar and Null believe this to be the office occupied that day by a man calling himself Jim Braden. (See BRADING, EUGENE HALE.) who was arrested by the Dallas police immediately after the assassination for "being in the building without a good excuse." Brading admitted to being on the third floor.

It is Morningstar and Null's opinion that JFK and Governor Connally were struck by 5.56mm bullets such as those fired by the M-15 and M-16 rifles.

"In 1963, the M-16 was the world's most advanced high-tech firearm, and was available only to the [U.S.] military and high government agencies," says Morningstar.

Why are the bullets' paths visible on the film?

"The path of a bullet creates an atmospheric distortion. There are four different signatures for each bullet fired," Morningstar says. "The first two are in the body of the bullet due to the tremendous friction produced by its acceleration against the rifling in the muzzle and the explosion of the cartridge which makes the tail end of the bullet hotter than the front. The third would be found in micro-ionization of air particles around the bullet leaving a micro-vapor trail in the air. The fourth signature would come from the glint of the bullets in the heat of the sun, which was at an optimal position [the assassination took place at 12:30 P.M.], above, forward, and to the right of Zapruder."

"We know that these are not scratches on the film. A scratch would have obliterated all visual information. The tracer's turbulence mottles the background, but does not obliterate it," says Morningstar. "The tracers appear in all versions of the film, with the exception of the 1978 Secret Service version, which was—according to some—fed to researcher Robert Groden when he was the photographic consultant to the House Select Committee on Assassinations."

Morrow, Robert D.

A former CIA operative who has written two books about President Kennedy's assassination from a seemingly privy first-person point of view. He has written that Jack Ruby was one of President Kennedy's killers, and that there were Oswald look-alikes involved in the plot.

Morrow writes that the assassination took place because of Kennedy's failure to fully back the Bay of Pigs invasion.

Morrow writes: "Oswald, who went to Russia for the CIA and was an FBI informant by the summer of 1963, was brought into an assassination plot led by CIA consultant Clay Shaw, using right-wing CIA operatives and anti-Castro Cubans headed by Jack Ruby in Dallas and Guy Banister in New Orleans. This group, operating outside Agency control, manipulated events to insure Oswald being named as the assassin. They also used an Oswald lookalike to incriminate the ex-Marine by firing shots from the [Texas School Book Depository] . . . Tippit was killed by this Oswald substitute when he failed to go along with the group's scheme to have Tippit kill the real Oswald in the Texas Theatre. With the capture of Oswald, Ruby was compelled to stalk and finally kill the accused assassin."

On August 3, 1976, a United Press International (UPI) dispatch announced that Representative Thomas Downing was distributing a 79-page booklet by Morrow entitled *Motivation Behind the Assassination of John F. Kennedy.* According to UPI: "The material . . . alleged that Vice President Richard Nixon was the 'CIA action man in the White House in earlier stages of planning for the Bay of Pigs attack.' Morrow alleged that a recognized right-wing leader of Cuban exiles, Mario Garcia Kohly Sr., told him a year ago [1975] he had an understanding with the CIA that top left-wing Cuban exiles 'would be eliminated after a successful invasion of the Bay of Pigs' . . . Nixon, while a lawyer in the 1960s, served Kohly, apparently without fee . . . Downing would not vouch for [the booklet's] authenticity, but he said that the material 'does raise a number of questions which I believe need to be answered. I would like to know what was behind the intense interest shown by President Nixon and his staff in the Bay of Pigs' [as revealed in the Watergate White House tapes]."

Motorcade Route

On November 16, 1963, the *Dallas Morning News* published a report that said President Kennedy's motorcade would go straight on Main Street when it came to Houston Street. The report said that the motorcade would go through the center of Dealey Plaza. On November 19, the route was again published in the newspaper and this time the item included the turn from Main Street onto Houston and then onto Elm Street, the route that was eventually used. But, on November 20, 1963, the same newspaper published a map of the motorcade route, which once again showed the parade going straight on Main through the center of the plaza. Officially, the route was changed to include the turn onto Houston and then Elm because the only way to access the Stemmons Freeway was from Elm Street. To get onto the expressway from Main Street would have meant that every vehicle in the parade would have had to drive over a small concrete curb.

Muchmore Film

Assassination witness Maria Muchmore was an Oklahoma native who was living in the Farmer's Branch section of Dallas in 1963. She went to the motorcade with her friend Wilma Bond. Muchmore took along her Keystone K-7 zoom lens 8mm movie camera, serial number 20648. The camera had cost $150. Bond was taking still photos. The women first stood 30 feet north of the northwest corner of Main and Houston. When the motorcade passed, they moved to a spot near Dealey Plaza's north peristyles to view JFK as he went down Elm Street toward the triple underpass. Muchmore filmed more than three seconds of the shooting sequence from the center of the greensward on the south side of Elm Street. Her film shows the fatal shot, Jackie Kennedy's crawl onto the back of the limousine and the motorcade's disappearance into the tunnel. Muchmore then stopped filming and looked for a place to hide. Muchmore apparently became so ill because of what she had seen that she called in sick for the next four work days.

Muchmore sold her film to United Press International. She was not called as a Warren Commission witness.

Mudd, F. Lee

Mudd was standing on the "north curb of Elm," 75 to 100 feet west of the Texas School Book Depository at the time of the assassination and later told author Josiah Thompson "one or more of the shots came from the direction of the Dal-Tex Building."

Mudd fell prone when he heard the shots, his eyes looking toward the corner of Elm and Houston. Earlier, Mudd's story had been reported differently. He reportedly told the

Dallas Sheriff's Department that he had heard two shots, thought they came from the Texas School Book Depository, and that the shots were "less than a second apart."

Murchison, Clint, Sr.

Texas oil millionaire who—according to Lyndon Johnson's mistress Madeleine Brown, who claims to have been there—held a party at his home on the evening before the assassination. In attendance were Johnson, H. L. Hunt, Richard Nixon, and J. Edgar Hoover, among others.

Murchison's son Clint, Jr. was a Marine during World War II, and attended Duke University and M.I.T. An engineer, Murchison designed the widening of the Panama Canal and the Saint Lawrence Seaway. He created the Dallas Cowboys and designed their home, Texas Stadium, in Irving, Texas. Murchison made and lost $350 million.

Right after the assassination, Silvia Odio, whose story contradicts the official facts, was hidden in the home of Ralph Rogers, president of Murchison's company, Texas Industries.

According to assassination analyst Peter Dale Scott, "A good part of the Murchison fortune derived from the mob-dominated Teamster's Pension Fund, at a time when corrupt Teamster locals played a prominent part in bringing heroin (and cocaine) into the United States."

Murchison Jr. died in 1987 of divopontine cerebellar atrophy, a rare degenerative nerve disease.

(See also BROWN, MADELEINE DUNCAN; TORBITT DOCUMENT.)

Murphy, Joe E.

Dallas police patrolman who joined the department in 1942 after playing a year of professional baseball in the West Texas–Mexican League. At approximately 11:00 A.M. on the morning of the assassination, Murphy radioed in from Dealey Plaza, "Could you send a city wrecker to the triple underpass, just west of the underpass on Elm, to clear a stalled truck from the route of the escort?"

A few minutes later, Murphy again radioed in, saying, "Disregard the wrecker at the triple underpass. We got a truck to push him out of here."

This incident took place at approximately the location and time of suspicious activities reported by witness Julia A. Mercer. At the time of the assassination, Murphy was stationed atop the Stemmons Freeway overpass, west of the triple underpass, and further from the Texas School Book Depository. His job was to keep traffic moving and to make sure no one parked their car along the shoulder on the Freeway.

He says that he saw men on the triple underpass, whom he could tell were railroad employees and one police officer. He says he heard three evenly spaced shots, that he could not see the president's limousine at the time because there were trees in the way.

At the sound of the shots he saw pigeons fly and start to circle. After the shooting he was assigned to search the area behind the Depository where he says there were reports of people running.

Murphy retired from the Dallas Police Department in 1986 and is deceased.

(See also MERCER, JULIA.)

Murphy, Thomas J.

Murphy was standing on the triple underpass at the time of the shooting and told assassination researcher Stewart Galanor in May 1966 that the shots came from behind the "hackberry and elm trees . . . on the hill up there." Like other eyewitnesses who viewed events from that position, Murphy said that he saw smoke coming out from those trees after the shots were fired. Murphy said he "heard two shots [that] came from a spot just west of the Depository."

Murray, Jim

Assassination witness born September 9, 1929, in Rockland, Illinois, who watched the Dallas motorcade through a window on the first floor of the Criminal Courts Building. Murray, a Blackstar Photo Service photographer, said that he heard three shots with a longer pause between the first and second shots than there was between the second and third shots. After the shooting his attention was drawn to the grassy knoll where he saw teenagers running and wondered if perhaps they had thrown firecrackers. He then ran to his car and put two loaded cameras around his neck. He began to photograph the aftermath to the assassination in Dealey Plaza, starting with a spot close to the entrance of the Texas School Book Depository Building. By 10 minutes after the assassination, Murray was on the greensward between Elm and Main Streets, taking a photo of Dallas deputy sheriff Buddy Walthers, Dallas police patrolman J. D. Foster and an unidentified and neatly dressed blond man with a plastic radio receiver clipped to his ear looking at something in the grass on the south side of Elm. Was it a bullet? The blond man is seen apparently picking up and putting the object in his pocket. Officer Foster later told the Warren Commission that he had been looking "where one shot had hit the turf there at that location."

Murret, Charles and Lillian

Charles "Dutz" Murret was Lee Harvey Oswald's 63-year-old uncle. Dutz had strong organized crime ties and reportedly was a father figure to his nephew. Dutz is alleged to have been a New Orleans bookmaker, working for the Carlos Marcello crime family. Dutz testified before the Warren Commission, who never asked him what he did for a living. He told the commission that Oswald used to raise his voice when he spoke to his mother, but that was about all he could remember. The House Select Committee on Assassinations determined that Murret was "a minor underworld gambling figure," that he, "who served as a surrogate father of sorts throughout much of Oswald's life in New Orleans, was in the 1940s and 1950s and possibly until his death in 1964 an associate of significant organized crime figures affiliated with the Marcello organization. The committee established that Oswald was familiar with his uncle's underworld activities and had discussed them with his wife, Marina, in 1963."

Dutz's wife was Lillian Murret, who was the sister of Marguerite Oswald, Lee's mother. She told the Warren Commission that Lee was a loner and uncomfortable with his peers. Oswald stayed with the Murrets for a few weeks during the summer of 1963, just before he got his job at the Reily Coffee Company.

The Murrets had a son named John Martial Murret, who was nicknamed "Boogie." He was 29 at the time of the assassination and told the Warren Commission that he once tried to teach Oswald to drive, with no success.

The Murrets had a daughter name Marilyn Dorothea Murret who told the commission that Lee's junior high school friend Ed Voebel was the one who convinced Oswald to join the Civil Air Patrol when he was a teenager. She said that Carlos Marcello associate Emile Bruneau was the person who got Oswald out of jail after he was arrested in New Orleans for disturbing the peace.

According to Marilyn, Lee "was just a darling child." Marilyn was known as a world traveler, a fact which has led some assassination researchers to speculate that she may have been a member of the intelligence community.

(See also VOEBEL, EDWARD.)

Nagell, Richard Case (a.k.a. Corsa, Robert C.; Kramer, Joseph; Nolan, Robert C.)

Nagell was born August 5, 1930, in New York City. He entered the U.S. Army in 1948 and, fighting in Korea, he became the youngest American of that war to receive a battlefield commission to captain. He was the only survivor of a plane crash near Andrews Air Force Base in Washington, D.C., on November 28, 1954. He survived by bailing out and was unconscious for 27 days in the army's Walter Reed Hospital. Nagell was assigned to the Army's Counter-Intelligence Corps in May 1955. (It is interesting to note that the army began to train Nagell to be a spy *after* his serious head injury.) On May 5, 1956, he was assigned to Field Operations Intelligence in the Far East under the command of General Charles Willoughby, who was Douglas MacArthur's chief of intelligence and went on to become the head of security for Hunt Oil. Nagell's duties with Field Operations Intelligence involved working in Japan classifying postwar counterintelligence documents.

Nagell said that he met Oswald in 1957 or 1958 with Dr. Chikao Fujisawa, a Tokyo University professor, who later tried to recruit Nagell to work for Soviet intelligence. Like Oswald, Nagell had a girlfriend at the ritzy Queen Bee bar in Tokyo.

A document from Nagell's military intelligence file states that Nagell worked as an "informant and/or investigator" for the CIA from August 1962 through October 1963 and was assigned in April 1963 to investigate Marina Oswald's reported desire to return to the Soviet Union. Nagell's duties were, the file said, "primarily concerned with investigating activities of Anti-Castro organizations and their personnel in the United States and Mexico." In that capacity he had reportedly conducted an inquiry into Lee Harvey Oswald and the Fair Play for Cuba Committee.

Nagell said the plot to kill JFK was domestic, and not CIA—although he did not rule out the possibility that ex-employees of the CIA might have been involved.

Nagell told New Orleans Parish district attorney Jim Garrison that he had been a "federal intelligence agent" who, in mid-1963, discovered a plot to kill President Kennedy. The body of Warren Commission Document 197, regarding Nagell, says in its entirety, "For the record he would like to say that his association with Oswald was purely social and that he had met him in Mexico City and in Texas."

At a clandestine meeting in an open field in New York's Central Park with Garrison during Garrison's Clay Shaw investigation, Nagell reportedly said that in 1963 he had been assigned by a federal agency (he wouldn't say which one) to find out about "a project" involving Oswald and others. During his investigation, he learned that a "large operation" was underway to kill JFK, but he did not know where or when. At this time, Nagell's direct contact was moved to another part of the country so Nagell wrote a letter reporting what he knew to J. Edgar Hoover. When he received no reply, he feared he was being suckered into a trap. Nagell figured his best bet was to be in prison whenever the hit took place, so that he couldn't be charged with the crime. Pursuing a criminal mischief charge, he entered an El Paso, Texas, bank, fired two shots into the ceiling, and then went outside and sat on the curb. But Nagell was not charged with mischief, but rather with armed robbery. He was convicted and served three years of a 10-year sentence. Years later, Nagell told Garrison the other men who were working with Oswald were "Guy Banister, Clay Shaw and David Ferrie." Although Nagell was willing to testify at Shaw's trial, Garrison chose not to put him on the stand, feeling that he would have been "eaten alive" during cross-examination because he refused to name his employer.

Nagell claimed that he first met Oswald in the Far East. Nagell said that in late 1957, the CIA had a defection plan to get a Soviet colonel to defect, and that the plan was headed by Desmond FitzGerald. (This notion is similar to that of Robert Morrow who says in his book *First Hand Knowledge* that the Russian the CIA was trying to get out was Marina Oswald's uncle.) According to Nagell, Oswald was photographed by the Russians meeting with this colonel in the Soviet embassy in Tokyo. Nagell said that was why Oswald was suspected of being an agent when he defected. (Although it would seem that this suspicion would have existed anyway since no one in their right mind would defect to Russia.) Nagell said that, if Oswald was an agent while in Russia, his reports would have gone to John Paisley, a man who later died mysteriously, disappearing off his yacht. Paisley, Nagell claims, was suspected of being a high-level KGB mole working within the CIA.

On November 21, 1975, in Los Angeles, Nagell said, in a sworn affidavit: "In September 1963, the exact day of which I am capable of verifying, I dispatched a letter via registered mail addressed to 'Mr. John E. Hoover, Director, Federal Bureau of Investigation, United States Department of Justice, Washington 25, D.C.' The envelope in which this letter was enclosed bore the same address, in addition to the return address 'Joseph Kramer, Apdo. Postal 88-Bis, Mexico, D.F., Mexico,' and was mailed within the United States. The letter was neatly typewritten and composed in the style and format used by operational personnel of the Central Intelligence Agency in writing their reports; that is, it was clear and concise, with the names of persons and organizations typed in caps.

"In the aforesaid letter, I advised Mr. Hoover of a conspiracy (although I did not use the word 'conspiracy') involving Lee Harvey Oswald 'to murder the Chief Executive of the United States, (President) John F. Kennedy.' I indicated that the attempt would take place 'during the latter part of September (1963), probably on the 16th, 27th, 28th, or 29th,' presumably at Washington, D.C. I furnished a complete and accurate physical description of Mr. Oswald, listing his true name, two of his aliases, his residence address and other pertinent facts about him. I disclosed sufficient data about the conspiracy (citing an overt act which constituted a violation of federal law) to warrant an immediate investigation if not the arrest of Mr. Oswald. I revealed something about myself which incriminated me

on another matter. I stated 'by the time you receive this letter, I shall have departed the USA for good.' I signed the letter with the name 'Joseph Kramer,' an alias of a known Communist (Soviet) agent then residing in Canada, and also an alias I had used during my meetings with two FBI agents in January 1963 at Miami, Florida, who in turn used the name 'The Tacos.' I am willing to undergo a polygraph examination relative to any and all statements made herein."

Nagell said that there had been assassination attempts planned on JFK for Miami during the winter of 1962–63 and in Los Angeles for the premiere of the movie *PT-109*.

Nagell reportedly died November 1, 1995, age 65, of heart disease at his triplex apartment on a dead-end street near a freeway overpass, where he lived alone, in the rundown neighborhood of Silver Lake, near Hollywood, California. His obituary didn't appear in the *Los Angeles Times* until November 10 and it mostly talked about Dick Russell's book. Nagell promised—falsely, it would seem—to leave behind material when he died that would be illuminating for assassination researchers: a photo of himself and Lee Harvey Oswald in New Orleans, an audio tape of Oswald and two Cubans talking about the Kennedy hit. Nagell's death coincided with the arrival of a subpoena to testify before the Assassination Records Review Board.

The November/December 1995 issue of *Probe* magazine published a letter Nagell wrote to his friend Arturo Verdestein dated October 8, 1967, which describes elements of the coup cabal in a comedic code. Hairy DeFairy=Dave Ferrie; Dirty Dick=Richard Helms, Big Mother Busher=Castro, etc. The text contains this phrase: "ZIP!ZIP!ZIP! BANG! ZIP!BANG!ZIP!BANG!" or five silenced shots and three loud reports.

Nash Rambler

Marvin C. Robinson in an interview with the FBI the day after the assassination corroborated Sheriff's Deputy Roger Craig's eyewitness report. Robinson said he was driving west on Elm Street about 10 minutes after the shooting when a "light-colored Nash station wagon stopped in front of him. A man ran down the incline in front of the Texas School Book Depository and got into the car, which then sped off." With Robinson in the car was Roy Cooper. Cooper was also interviewed the day after the assassination and he also remembered the running man. He said that he and Robinson had been traveling south on Elm when they got to the corner of Elm and Houston but otherwise his story is the same. He said that he "observed a white male somewhere between 20 and 30 years of age wave at a Nash Rambler station wagon, light colored, as it pulled out real fast in front of the Cadillac [Robinson was driving]." Cooper said that Robinson had to slam on the brakes to keep from hitting the station wagon. Another corroborating witness was interviewed by researcher Michael L. Kurtz for his book *Crime of the Century*. She was Mrs. James (Helen) Forest who was standing in the crowd at the base of the grassy knoll 10 minutes after the shooting when she saw the man run from the rear of the Texas School Book Depository and down to Elm Street where he got into the station wagon. She said, "If it wasn't Oswald, it was his identical twin."

(See also CRAIG, ROGER; DEAD SECRET SERVICE AGENT.)

Naughty Dallas   See APPENDIX C.

Nechiporenko, Col. Oleg   See KOMITET GOSUDARST-VENNOY BEZOPASNOSTI (KGB).

Nelson, Sharon
Twenty-year-old Texas School Book Depository employee who watched the assassination while standing on the north side of Elm Street mid-way between the Book Depository and the triple underpass.

Nelson said she never returned to work following the assassination, disproving the Warren Commission's claim that Lee Harvey Oswald was the only Depository employee missing at a roll call held after the assassination.

Nelson stated that she did not see Oswald at the time of the shooting and encountered no strangers in the building that morning during work.

Newman, Jean
Twenty-one-year-old manufacturing company employee who witnessed the assassination while standing on the north curb of Elm between the Texas School Book Depository and the Stemmons Freeway sign. She said she thought the shots came from her right—that is, from the direction of the grassy knoll and the triple underpass.

Newman, John
Dr. Newman spent 20 years as a military intelligence officer and has written of the disturbing signs that the military was preparing for the change in U.S. foreign policy toward Vietnam while President Kennedy was still alive and before Lyndon Johnson had endorsed that policy.

At the 1993 Assassination of John F. Kennedy Symposium at the Regency-Hyatt Hotel in Dallas, Newman gave a presentation based on his study of official files recently declassified. Since there were so many pages of released documents and so many of the pages have been so severely edited that they no longer actually say anything, Newman has approached them via their marginalia. Each file, he discovered, had a cover sheet, upon which everyone who read the file has initialed it and placed small code letters in the margins.

Newman said that Oswald's CIA 201 file consisted of two four-drawer safes and that he suspected he was the first human being to overtly go through it all.

"Neither Robert Blakey nor Gerald Posner looked at the entire thing," Newman said.

The "third agency" files on Oswald, Newman noted, have yet to be released. These would consist of Office of Naval Intelligence, FBI, etc. reports to the CIA regarding Oswald.

Using marginalia, keeping track of who looked at what and which files were given the strictest security, Newman came to the conclusion that James Jesus Angleton took over the Lee Harvey Oswald investigation immediately following the assassination and that the most highly restricted files concerned Oswald's relationship with the Soviet Union and Cuba. Newman found a note in a margin that stated that Oswald had been debriefed upon his return from the USSR by a man named Andy Anderson. This is contrary to the CIA's official claim that it never debriefed Oswald at any time. Newman verified that a CIA official by the name of Andy Anderson did exist.

Newman pointed out, "There is nothing conspiratorial about the CIA debriefing Oswald. One would expect them to. The suspicious thing is that they denied doing it." One memo stated that the CIA had an "operational" interest in Oswald. "The Agency claimed to not care about Oswald. Oswald, who worked in Atsugi, who defected and announced his intention to commit treason, received no interest from the CIA. They launched no counter-intelligence program—and this is totally unsatisfactory. If we are to believe what they say, for fourteen months they are asleep at the switch. I can accept Murphy's Law . . . on occasion. The trouble is, as I go through the files, I keep bumping into Mr. Murphy every time I turn the corner." There is an indication that Oswald was picked up by the HT/LINGUAL program, namely, that his mail from the USSR to the United States was intercepted and read, but there was no file indicating that he was a threat and in need of investigation. Those who looked at reports on Oswald before the assassination consisted of the CIC (Counter-Intelligence Corps, i.e., molehunters), the Soviet Russian Division (SR), and, in September 1963, the Special Affairs staff. Within SR, SR-6 most frequently signed off. The SR-6 people's job was to paint legends, to gather everything that is authentically Russian. Also frequently signing off were the SR-9 people who ran agents inside

Russia from Moscow, and the SR-10 people, known as "Legal Travellers," who run agents in the Soviet Union from Washington. With the latter, communications between agents within the USSR and their control had to be accomplished through secret writing and microdots. These facts don't prove that Oswald was an agent, but they don't discourage that kind of thinking either.

Newman said, "There are indications that Oswald was receiving packages from outside the USSR during the time (1960–1) when he officially fell off the map."

Newman is the author of *JFK and Vietnam* (Warner Books, 1992) and *Oswald and the CIA* (Carroll and Graf, 1995).

Newman, William J. and Gayle

William, a twenty-two-year-old design engineer, was standing with his wife Gayle and their two children on the north side of Elm Street just west of the Stemmons Freeway sign at the time of the assassination.

Newman apparently named a very important piece of real estate when, during a TV interview within minutes of the assassination, he was asked where he thought the shots had come from. "Back up on the, uh, knoll," Newman said.

The Newmans were standing directly in front of assassination witness and filmmaker Abraham Zapruder during the shooting sequence, and at first thought that Zapruder might be the assassin.

Bill later told a reporter: "For a second I thought it was firecrackers, but then I saw Kennedy raise his arms toward his face, and I knew it was shots. Then, just as the car came abreast of us, a third shot hit and blood went everywhere. It seemed to me that the shooting was coming from directly behind me, and I thought we must be right in the line of fire. That's when we turned around and hit the grass . . . We heard the first two shots as the car was coming toward us and still some distance from us. But when the last shot hit, we were probably no more than eight feet away. . . . I believe Kennedy's car came to a complete stop after the final shot. One of the two men in the front seat had a telephone to his ear, as though he were awaiting instructions. Then suddenly, the car took off. A car filled with Secret Service men was just behind the President's car, and when it was right beside us, it paused, and I saw several men with what looked like Thompson submachine guns get out of the car. I have a strong impression that these men were left behind when the motorcade went on, but I've never heard anyone confirm that."

At the Clay Shaw trial, William testified for the prosecution that he strongly believed that the shot that killed President Kennedy did not originate from the Texas School Book Depository.

The Newmans were photographed repeatedly in the seconds following the shooting as Bill and Gayle lay atop their children to protect them. Bill could be seen seconds after the shooting, prone on the grass, slamming his fist into the ground.

Newnam, John

Jack Ruby's alibi witness, Newnam was a member of the advertising staff for the *Dallas Morning News*. As of 12:20 on the afternoon of the assassination, 10 minutes before the shooting, Ruby was sitting across from Newnam's desk, submitting his weekend ads for the Carousel Club. The *Dallas Morning News* building is only two blocks from Dealey Plaza.

Newnam left Ruby alone to tend to his job and returned 10 minutes following the assassination. Ruby was sitting right where he had been. At that point, according to Newnam, neither man knew that the assassination had occurred.

When the news that JFK had been shot came in, Newnam says Ruby seemed stunned, but no more so than anyone else. Ruby reportedly said, "John, I will have to leave Dallas."

Newnam testified at Ruby's murder trial that, just before the assassination, Ruby had been complaining bitterly about the full page ad in that day's *Morning News* accusing President Kennedy of treason. Ruby was very interested in who Bernard Weissman was, since his name, with a post office box, appeared in the ad, and sounded Jewish.

Nix Film

Orville Orheal Nix Sr., born April 1911, was an air conditioning repairman for the U.S. General Service Administration in the Dallas Secret Service building. He was friends with the special agent-in-charge of the Dallas District Office of the Secret Service, Forrest V. Sorrels. Nix went to Dealey Plaza to see the presidential motorcade and brought his camera, a Keystone Auto-Zoom Model K-810 8mm loaded with Kodachrome II Type A Tungsten film—a film better suited for indoor filming. Nix stood near the curb at the southwest corner of Main and Houston. After the presidential limousine passed his position, he moved to a point 20 feet west of Houston on the south side of Elm Street. It was later determined that this spot was 200 feet from the president's position at the moment of the fatal head shot. Nix's film, taken facing the grassy knoll, lasts for 122 frames. It graphically shows a piece of Kennedy's head flying off of his head and landing on the back of the limousine. The film shows what Dallas reporter Jim Marrs refers to as "suspicious flashes of light" on the grassy knoll. The film also shows clearly that the limousine's brake lights are on after shots have been fired although the limousine appears to maintain a steady speed. Nix sold the film to United Press International in 1963 for $5,000.

During the 1990s, Nix's granddaughter Gayle Nix Jackson fought to get the film back in the family's possession. She told the *Village Voice* (March 31, 1992) that the film brought her grandfather nothing but heartache. She said: "The FBI had issued a dictum to all of Dallas' film labs that any assassination photos had to be turned over to the FBI. The lab called my granddad first and, like the good American he was, he rushed it to the FBI. They [the FBI] took the camera [as well] for five months. They returned it in pieces." In 1967, Nix participated in a CBS News re-creation of the assassination. Each time he told the interviewer that he thought the shots came from the grassy knoll, the director shouted, "Cut!" Finally, according to Ms. Jackson, the producer informed Orville that the Warren Commission had determined the shots came from the Texas School Book Depository, and that was what they wanted to hear—so that was what Nix told them.

Orville Nix's film, which is of very poor quality, was turned over, along with the camera he used, to Special Agent Joe B. Abernathy of the FBI on December 1, 1963. Although he requested that it be copied and returned immediately, the FBI did not return the film to him until December 4. His camera, however, was not returned until June 2, 1964, at which time footage indicator was broken and it was missing a spool. Later, the Nix family revealed that Orville had been suspicious at the time that something had been done to alter the film he took. Although the Nix film does show the presidential limousine maintaining a steady speed, like the Zapruder film, despite eyewitness reports that the limousine slowed practically to a stop during the shooting sequence, studies have shown that the Nix film shows the limousine traveling 22 percent slower than in the Zapruder film.

For the first 77 of the film's 122 frames, an image appears just above the concrete abutment beside the stairs leading to the top of the grassy knoll at the west end of the pergola, which appears to be a figure sighting a rifle from atop a car. Between January and May 1967, the film was studied by ITEK, which released a 55-page analysis on May 18, 1967. The figure, ITEK concluded, was sunlight and shadows caused by the trees and the pergola.

According to assassination researcher Harrison Edward Livingstone, the original of the Nix film was lost while in the possession of the House Select Committee on Assassinations and that all extant copies of the film have been "enhanced using a computer technique by Robert Groden."

Orville Nix died of a heart attack at age 60 on January 17, 1972.

(See GRODEN, ROBERT.)

Nixon, Richard M.

Nixon, who later became president of the United States, lost the 1960 presidential election to John Kennedy. Nixon was vice president of the United States under Dwight Eisenhower from 1952 to 1960 and, in that capacity, he ran the CIA.

Of course, Nixon's presidency ended in disgrace after the Watergate scandal. Among the Watergate conspirators are assassination suspects Frank Sturgis and E. Howard Hunt.

A 1947 FBI memo states, "It is my sworn statement that one Jack Rubenstein of Chicago, noted as a potential witness for hearings of the House Committee on Un-American Activities, is performing information functions for the staff of Congressman Richard Nixon, Republican of California. It is requested Rubenstein not be called for open testimony in the aforementioned hearings." That same year Rubenstein changed his name to Ruby and moved to Dallas.

Nixon was in Dallas from November 20–22, 1963, for a soft-drink bottlers convention (he was counsel for Pepsico) and left Dallas only three hours before the assassination.

According to former Counter-Intelligence Corps agent Russell Bintliff (and reported by the *Washington Star* on

President Richard M. Nixon. He was in Dallas that morning. *(Author's Collection)*

December 5, 1976), Pepsi set up a bottling plant in Vientiane, Laos, that didn't produce any soft drinks. Instead, it manufactured heroin.

(See also BABUSHKA LADY; BROWN, MADELEINE; CENTRAL INTELLIGENCE AGENCY; HUNT, E. HOWARD; RUBY, JACK; STURGIS, FRANK.)

Norman, Harold

One of three Texas School Book Depository employees who reportedly watched the assassination from the building's fifth floor, one floor below the "sniper's nest." Norman told the Warren Commission that he heard the action of a rifle bolt and the sound of shells hitting the floor coming from above. At 10:00 A.M. on the day of the assassination, Norman—along with colleague Junior Jarman—were on the first floor of the building looking out the windows toward Elm Street. Norman said, "Oswald walked up to us and asked us, 'What is everybody looking for? What is everybody waiting on?' So we told him we were waiting on the President to come by. He put his hand in his pocket and laughed and walked away. I thought maybe he's just happy this morning or something."

For the Warren Commission, Norman said that he heard the sounds of the shots and the rifle being cocked come from directly over his head as he watched the motorcade from the southwest corner of the Depository's fifth floor. He said the sequence sounded like this: "Boom, click-click, boom, click-click, boom."

Norman continued to work at the Depository, despite its changes in name, ownership, and usage, for another 30-plus years following the assassination.

(See also JARMAN, JAMES; WILLIAMS, BONNIE RAY.)

Norton, Donald P.

According to assassination investigators Sybil Leek and Bert R. Sugar, Norton was a CIA agent who was sent in September 1962 from Atlanta to Mexico with $50,000 for an anti-Castro group. Leek and Sugar wrote: "He registered at the Yamajei Hotel in Monterrey where he was told he would be contacted by 'Harvey Lee.' The man arrived, and Norton said he looked like Lee Harvey Oswald, except that his hair seemed to be thicker. Lee took the money and gave Norton a briefcase containing documents, which he delivered to a contact in an American oil company based in Calgary, Alberta, Canada."

Novel, Gordon

A CIA employee who was living in New Orleans in 1963. According to assassination researcher Paris Flammonde,

Novel was questioned by the FBI on five separate occasions following JFK's assassination.

Flammonde writes, "Novel was a buddy of [assassination suspect David] Ferrie's who had been working with the CIA since 1959 . . . [Novel] worked through the Double-Chek Corporation and the Evergreen Advertising Agency and he had carried out several missions in the Caribbean, was involved with arms purchases, and knew both Ruby and Oswald."

Jim Garrison subpoenaed Novel in 1967 but Novel fled to Ohio where Garrison failed to obtain his extradition. According to Garrison, "we . . . learned from . . . Novel . . . that David Ferrie, one of the leaders of the [New Orleans] Cuban Revolutionary Front, and a handful of others from [Guy] Banister's office drove one night to the blimp air base at Houma, a town deep in southern Louisiana. They entered one of the Schlumberger Corporation's explosive bunkers and removed the land mines, hand grenades, and rifle grenades stored there."

While Garrison was attempting to extradite Novel from Ohio in April 1967, principally to testify about the Schlumberger affair, Novel said that he had been working in his capacity as a CIA agent when robbing the bunker, gathering "war materiel" for the Bay of Pigs invasion. Novel told the *New Orleans States-Item* that all of the men involved in the "pickup" were "Company" [CIA] men and they included Ferrie and Sergio Arcacha Smith.

Garrison later found a letter written by Novel, confirmed to be authentic by a handwriting expert and Novel's lawyer, written in January 1967 to Novel's CIA contact "Mr. Weiss." The letter stated that, because several men involved in the Schlumberger affair were also suspected by Garrison of being assassination conspirators, the company should take "counteraction" against Garrison. Novel even suggested that it might be a good idea, since Garrison had ready reserve status in the Louisiana Army National Guard, to call the D.A. into active duty. Novel was hired as a consultant by NBC for their anti-Garrison special.

(See also UMBRELLA MAN, THE.)

NSAM 263

The last of JFK's National Security Action Memoranda concerning Vietnam, ambiguously worded:

NATIONAL SECURITY ACTION MEMORANDUM NO. 263
TO: Secretary of State
    Secretary of Defense
    Chairman of the Joint Chiefs of Staff

SUBJECT: South Vietnam

At a meeting on October 5, 1963, the President considered the recommendations contained in the report of Secretary

[Robert] McNamara and General [Maxwell] Taylor on their mission to South Vietnam.

The President approved the military recommendations contained in Section I B (1–3) of the report, but directed that no formal announcement be made of the implementation of plans to withdraw 1,000 U.S. military personnel by the end of 1963.

After discussion of the remaining recommendations of the report, the President approved the instruction to Ambassador Lodge which is set forth in State Department telegram No. 534 to Saigon. [signed] McGeorge Bundy

Copy furnished: Director of Central Intelligence Administrator, Agency for International Development 11/21/63

DRAFT
TOP SECRET
NATIONAL SECURITY ACTION MEMORANDUM NO

The President has reviewed the discussions of South Vietnam which occurred in Honolulu, and has discussed the matter further with Ambassador [Henry Cabot] Lodge. He directs that the following guidance be issued to all concerned:

1. It remains the central object of the United States in South Vietnam to assist the people and Government of that country to win their contest against the externally directed and supported Communist conspiracy. The test of all decisions and U.S. actions in this area should be the effectiveness of their contributions to this purpose.

2. The objectives of the United States with respect to the withdrawal of U.S. military personnel remain as stated in the White House statement of October 2, 1963.

3. It is a major interest of the United States Government that the present provisional government of South Vietnam should be assisted in consolidating itself in holding and developing increased public support. All U.S. officers should conduct themselves with this objective in view.

4. It is of the highest importance that the United States Government avoid either the appearance or the reality of public recrimination from one part of it against another, and the President expects that all senior officers of the Government will take energetic steps to insure that they and their subordinate go out of their way to maintain and to defend the unity of the United States Government both here and in the field. More specifically, the President approves the following lines of action developed in the discussions of the Honolulu meeting of November 20. The office or offices of the Government to which central responsibility is assigned is indicated in each case.

5. We should concentrate our own efforts, and insofar as possible we should persuade the government of South Vietnam to concentrate its efforts, on the critical situation in the Mekong Delta. This concentration should include not only military but political, economic, social, educational and informational efforts. We should seek to turn the tide not only of battle but of belief, and we should seek to increase not only our control of land but the productivity of this area whenever the proceeds can be held for the advantage of anti-Communist forces. (Action: The whole country team under the direct supervision of the Ambassador.)

6. Programs of military and economic assistance should be maintained at such levels that their magnitude and effectiveness in the eyes of the Vietnamese Government do not fall below the levels sustained by the United States in the time of the Diem Government. This does not exclude arrangements for economy on the MAP accounting for ammunition and any other readjustments which are possible as between MAP and other U.S. defense sources. Special attention should be given to the expansion of the import distribution and effective use of fertilizer for the Delta.
(Action: AID and DOD as appropriate.)

7. With respect to action against North Vietnam, there should be a detailed plan for the development of additional Government of Vietnam resources, especially for sea-going activity, and such planning should indicate the time and investment necessary to achieve a wholly new level of effectiveness in this field of action.
(Action: DOD and CIA)

8. With respect to Laos, a plan should be developed for military operations up to a line up to 50 kilometers inside Laos, together with political plans for minimizing the international hazards of such an enterprise. Since it is agreed that operational responsibility for such undertakings should pass from CAS to MACV, this plan should provide an alternative method of political liaison for such operations, since their timing and character can have an intimate relation to the fluctuating situation in Laos.
(Action: State, DOD and CIA.)

9. It was agreed in Honolulu that the situation in Cambodia is of the first importance for South Vietnam, and it is therefore urgent that we should lose no opportunity to exercise a favorable influence upon that country. In particular, measures should be undertaken to satisfy ourselves completely that recent charges from Cambodia are groundless, and we should put ourselves in a position to offer to the Cambodians a full opportunity to satisfy themselves on this same point.
(Action: State.)

10. In connection with paragraphs 7 and 8 above, it is desired that we should develop as strong and persuasive a case as possible to demonstrate to the world the degree to which the Viet Cong is controlled, sustained and supplied from Hanoi, through Laos and other channels. In short, we need a more contemporary version of the Jordan Report, as powerful and complete as possible.

(Action: Department of State with other agencies as necessary.)

[signed] McGeorge Bundy

(See also MILITARY-INDUSTRIAL COMPLEX; NSAM 273.)

NSAM 273

The first of President Lyndon B. Johnson's National Security Action Memoranda concerning Vietnam:

THE WHITE HOUSE
WASHINGTON
November 26, 1963
NATIONAL SECURITY ACTION MEMORANDUM NO. 273
TO: The Secretary of State
    The Secretary of Defense
    The Director of Central Intelligence
    The Administrator, AID
    The Director, USIA

The President has reviewed the discussions of South Vietnam which occurred in Honolulu, and has discussed the matter further with Ambassador [Henry Cabot] Lodge. He directs that the following guidance be issued to all concerned:

1. It remains the central object of the United States in South Vietnam to assist the people and Government of that country to win their contest against the externally directed and supported Communist conspiracy. The test of all U.S. decisions and actions in this area should be the effectiveness of their contribution to this purpose.

2. The objectives of the United States with respect to the withdrawal of U.S. military personnel remain as stated in the White House statement of October 2, 1963.

3. It is a major interest of the United States Government that the present provisional government of South Vietnam should be assisted in consolidating itself and in holding and developing increased public support. All U.S. officers should conduct themselves with this objective in view.

4. The President expects that all senior officers of the Government will move energetically to insure the full unity of support for established U.S. policy in South Vietnam. Both in Washington and in the field, it is essential that the Government be unified. It is of particular importance that express or implied criticism of officers of other branches be scrupulously avoided in all contacts with the Vietnamese Government and with the press. More specifically, the President approves the following lines of action developed in the discussions of the Honolulu meeting, of November 20. The offices of the Government to which central responsibility is assigned are indicated in each case.

5. We should concentrate our own efforts, and insofar as possible we should persuade the Government of South Vietnam to concentrate its efforts, on the critical situation in the Mekong Delta. This concentration should include not only military but political, economic, social, educational and informational effort. We should seek to turn the tide not only of battle but of belief, and we should seek to increase not only the control of hamlets but the productivity of this area, especially where the proceeds can be held for the advantage of anti-Communist forces.

(Action: The whole country team under the direct supervision of the Ambassador.)

6. Programs of military and economic assistance should be maintained at such levels that their magnitude and effectiveness in the eyes of the Vietnamese Government do not fall below the levels sustained by the United States in the time of the Diem Government. This does not exclude arrangements for economy on the MAP account with respect to accounting for ammunition, or any other readjustments which are possible as between MAP and other U.S. defense resources. Special attention should be given to the expansion of the import, distribution, and effective use of fertilizer for the Delta.

(Action: AID and DOD as appropriate.)

7. Planning should include different levels of possible increased activity, and in each instance there should be estimates of such factors as:
    A. Resulting damage to North Vietnam;
    B. The plausibility of denial;
    C. Possible North Vietnamese retaliation;
    D. Other international reaction.
Plans should be submitted promptly for approval by higher authority.

(Action: State, DOD, and CIA.)

8. With respect to Laos, a plan should be a developed and submitted for approval by higher authority for military operations up to a line up to 50 kilometers inside Laos, together with political plans for minimizing the international hazards of such an enterprise. Since it is agreed that operational responsibility for such undertakings should pass from CAS to MACV, this plan should include a redefined method of political guidance for such operations, since their timing and character can have an intimate relation to the fluctuating situation in Laos.

(Action: State, DOD, and CIA.)

9. It was agreed in Honolulu that the situation in Cambodia is of the first importance for South Vietnam, and it is therefore urgent that we should lose no opportunity to exercise a favorable influence upon that country. In particular a plan should be developed using all available evidence and methods of persuasion for showing the Cambodians that the recent charges against us are groundless.

(Action: State.)

10. In connection with paragraphs 7 and 8 above, it is desired that we should develop as strong and persuasive a case

as possible to demonstrate to the world the degree to which the Viet Cong is controlled, sustained and supplied from Hanoi, through Laos and other channels. In short, we need a more contemporary version of the Jorden Report, as powerful and complete as possible.

(Action: Department of State with other agencies as necessary.)

s/ McGeorge Bundy
McGeorge Bundy

cc:
Mr. Bundy
Mr. Forrestal
Mr. Johnson
NSC Files

Number-Five Man   See MOORMAN PHOTO.

Ochsner, Dr. Alton, Sr.

Born in 1896 in Kimball, South Dakota, Ochsner attended the University of South Dakota and received his medical training at Washington University in St. Louis, Missouri. Before the age of 30, Dr. Ochsner became known as the premier expert on blood transfusions in Europe. In 1936, Ochsner became one of the first to link cigarette smoking with lung cancer. In 1949, he became president of the American Cancer Society, and sat on the Board of Directors for that organization at the same time as the founder of the Office of Strategic Services, William Donovan. The Ochsner Clinic and Foundation Hospital opened in 1942, catering from its inception to the elite and wealthy of Latin America. Juan Perón, president of Argentina received treatment there. In 1946, Ochsner received a citation from the U.S. War Department commending him for the medical research he had done for the government. In 1959 Ochsner served on the Board of Directors of the Foreign Policy Association of New Orleans, at the same time assassination suspect Clay Shaw was on that board.

Ochsner formed the Information Council of the Americas (INCA) in 1961. This was an organization dedicated to the liquidation of communism. Ed Butler, who debated Lee Harvey Oswald on radio station WDSU on August 21, 1963, was the executive director of INCA. During the Clay Shaw trial, Ochsner helped attack New Orleans Parish district attorney Jim Garrison by digging up his military medical records which revealed that Garrison's combat-caused mental difficulties resulted in his discharge. He also reportedly attempted to discredit attorney and assassination investigator Mark Lane, then working on Garrison's staff, as a communist and as a sexual deviate.

Dr. Ochsner knew Guy Banister, according to a one-time Banister investigator named Allen Campbell, and the pair had been known to have dinner together in the French Quarter. He was also a friend of Clay Shaw, whom a New Orleans Grand Jury indicted for conspiracy to assassinate JFK.

Ochsner received clearance for a sensitive position with the U.S. government by the FBI in October 1959. It is unknown what that position was. Ochsner died in 1981.

(See also SHERMAN, DR. MARY.)

Odio Incident, The

Silvia Odio was born on May 4, 1937, to Sara del Toro and Amador Odio-Padron. Her father was a trucking magnate in Havana and very rich. Silvia attended Mercy Academy in Havana, the Eden Hall Convent of the Sacred Heart in Philadelphia, Pennsylvania, and then Villanova University, also in Philadelphia. At Villanova, she majored in pre-law. In 1957 she married Guillermo Herrera, also from a rich Cuban family. By 1963, Silvia was a beautiful young Cuban exile living in Dallas, attending both the top society parties in Dallas, and meetings of anti-Castro Cubans. She belonged to the anti-Castro organization known as J.U.R.E. (Junta Revolucionaria Cubana). Meetings at which running guns to Cuba was discussed were held in Silvia's Dallas apartment.

Odio's parents were imprisoned by the Castro government for purchasing anti-Castro arms. Silvia's story is well known: While the "real" Oswald was supposedly en route to Mexico during the last week of September 1963, Odio received a visit from two Latin men, and a white man introduced as "Leon Oswald." Later, one of the Latin men called Odio on the phone and said that Oswald thought "the Cubans had no guts and should shoot the President." Her story was corroborated without elaboration by her younger sister Annie.

However, this was not Odio's original story. According to her "social worker," Lucille Connell, in a Warren Commission document, Odio spoke to her on November 28, 1963, and said "she knew Lee Harvey Oswald and that he had made some talks to small groups of Cuban refugees in Dallas in the past. Odio stated she considered Oswald brilliant and clever, and that he had captivated the groups to whom he spoke . . . A call had been made in recent months by a Cuban associate of hers to an unknown source in New Orleans, Louisiana, requesting information on Lee Harvey Oswald . . . Oswald was considered by that source in New Orleans to be a 'double agent.' The source stated Oswald was probably trying to infiltrate the Dallas Cuban group, and that he should not be trusted." Odio's story that Oswald was attempting to infiltrate Cuban groups was corroborated by Edwin Steig, who, according to Warren Commission Document 205, reported seeing Oswald at a D.R.E. meeting in October 1963.

Odio's story did not last long and was quickly replaced with the tale of the three men at the door. The Warren Commission not only forgot completely that her first story ever existed but they went out and found three men who, briefly anyway, were willing to allow themselves to be suspected of being the three men: William Seymour, Larry Howard, and Loran Hall.

Odio was a friend of Carlos Bringuier. So, when Oswald ended up in court following his street scuffle with Bringuier in New Orleans, Silvia's uncle, Dr. Agustin Guitart, was in the courtroom.

According to Penn Jones Jr., "Right after the assassination Mrs. Odio was hidden in the home of Jack Rogers of Dallas, whose father, Ralph Rogers, is president of Texas Industries, one of the many firms controlled by the Murchison people."

Silvia Odio's parents had been arrested for harboring Reynol Gonzalez, who was wanted by the Cuban police for plotting to assassinate Castro in 1961. The chief organizer of that Castro assassination plot had been Alpha 66 founder Antonio Veciana, the man who claims to have seen Lee Harvey Oswald in the company of a CIA man code-named Maurice Bishop.

(See ALPHA 66; D.R.E.; HALL, LORAN; MURCHISON, CLINT; OSWALD LOOK-ALIKES; PHILLIPS, DAVID ATLEE.)

Odom, Lee

In Clay Shaw's address book, there was written the following notation: "LEE ODOM, P.O. BOX 19106, Dallas,

Texas." The number "19106" was also found in Oswald's notebook, preceded by Russian characters.

In 1967 the *New Orleans States-Item* discovered that there really was a Lee Odom living in Irving, Texas. Odom was interviewed and said that he had been in touch with Shaw repeatedly regarding the possibility of promoting a bullfight in New Orleans.

New Orleans Parish district attorney Jim Garrison, who was then prosecuting Shaw for conspiracy to kill President Kennedy, responded, "That is not the point. The point is that Clay Shaw and Lee Oswald have the same post office box number in their address books and this is, in coded form, the unpublished phone number of Jack Ruby in 1963." For unknown reasons, Garrison often mixed real revelations with bizarre claims.

(See also GARRISON INVESTIGATION; SHAW, CLAY.)

O'Donnell, Philip Kenneth "Ken"

Special assistant to President Kennedy and coordinator of the Texas swing of the president's trip who urged a motorcade through the heart of Dallas, so that the president and First Lady could be seen by as many people as possible.

O'Donnell rode in the motorcade. According to a CIA liaison man's 1975 statement to congressional investigators, O'Donnell originally thought the shots came from elsewhere than the Texas School Book Depository, but he altered his statements to conform to the official version of the facts following a "warning" from FBI director J. Edgar Hoover.

O'Donnell told the Warren Commission: "I remember the underpass and then the shots occurred—which, at the time, I did not know were shots. But as fast as that realization occurred, I saw the third shot hit. It was such a perfect shot—I remembered I blessed myself."

He later told Tip O'Neill, "I testified the way they wanted me to. I just didn't want to stir up any more pain and trouble for the family."

O'Donnell died at age 53 in Beth Israel Hospital in Boston, Massachusetts.

Olsen, Harry N.

Of all of the Dallas police officers who knew Jack Ruby, Olsen was one of the closest. Olsen was on restricted duty at the time of the assassination because of a broken kneecap he had suffered earlier in the year. Olsen dated (and later married) stripper Kay Helen Coleman, who worked under the name Kathy Kay at Ruby's Carousel Club.

It has been said that everyone alive in 1963 remembers where he or she was when they first learned of the assassination. Not Olsen. Olsen told the Warren Commission that on November 22, 1963, he worked the entire day as a security guard at an Oak Cliff estate whose owner and address he could not remember.

As can best be pinpointed from his vague testimony, he was on Eighth Street someplace, about five or six blocks from the Thornton expressway. This location would put him in an elevated section of Oak Cliff, possibly in a position to monitor the movements of Officer J. D. Tippit and Tippit's assailant below. (Tippit last radioed in his location as Eighth Street and Lancaster.) Olsen would also have been only a few blocks away from Ruby's apartment.

Dallas police chief Jesse Curry wrote that Olsen had a reputation for being "unstable." Olsen was known to carry an illegal gun and brass knuckles. Officially, Olsen was in the Carousel Club, which was closed, visiting Kay at 11:00 P.M. on November 22. At that time, according to Olsen, Ruby bragged about having seen Oswald at the Dallas police station. Olsen asked Ruby what he thought of the prisoner. Ruby said, "He looked just like a little rat. He was sneaky looking, like a weasel."

(See also JACK'S GIRLS.)

Onassis, Aristotle   See GEMSTONE FILE.

Operation *Paperclip*

At the end of World War II, 5,000 Nazis, many of whom should have been tried as war criminals, were recruited by the United States to work for U.S. intelligence, the thinking being that their expertise would come in handy fighting the new enemy, the Soviet Union. However, according to some conspiracy theorists, the influx of fascist thinking had a trickle down effect on all U.S. intelligence, an effect that can still be felt today.

Reinhard Gehlen was the Nazi commander in charge of German military intelligence throughout the Soviet Union and Eastern Europe during World War II. Allen Dulles, second in charge at the Office of Strategic Services at the time, foresaw Nazi defeat and the upcoming cold war with the Soviets. So instead of dismantling Gehlen's organization, he incorporated it. Gehlen surrendered to the U.S. forces in Europe during May 1945 and later became the chief of intelligence for the new Federal Republic of Germany.

(See also PAINE, RUTH AND MICHAEL; DULLES, ALLEN.)

Orr, Maurice

Orr was standing on the north side of Elm Street between the Texas School Book Depository and the steps to the pergola, one of the closest eyewitnesses to the president at the time of the fatal headshot. Orr was interviewed by the press a few minutes after the shooting and said he heard five shots. He was never interviewed by any official body.

Osborne, Albert (a.k.a. Bowen, John Howard; Owen, J.H.)

Supposedly the man with whom Oswald rode on the bus to Mexico City during late September 1963. Who Osborne is changes drastically depending on the source. According to researcher Michael H. B. Eddowes, who believes that President Kennedy was assassinated by a Soviet conspiracy, Osborne was a 75-year-old British confederate who for a long time had appeared to be a Russian agent. The FBI, Eddowes said, had an "Internal Security" file on him, but under the name John Howard Bowen. He had traveled all over North America under a variety of names, posing as a minister, a gardener, and a collector of rare books.

Other sources say Osborne was a fervent Nazi supporter, a member of the American Council of Christian Churches who reportedly ran an anticommunist missionary school for orphans in Puebla, Mexico. The school allegedly served as a cover for training marksmen.

Osborne reportedly accompanied "Oswald" by bus from New Orleans to Mexico City on September 26, 1963. On the bus, Oswald was heard to say he was "going to Havana." Osborne told the Warren Commission that it wasn't Oswald next to him on the bus, saying that the man was "Mexican or Puerto Rican." The Warren Commission, citing Osborne's shady past, refused to believe him. According to a Garrison aide who wrote under the name William Torbitt, Osborne and 10 of his professional killers were living at 3126 Harlendale in the Oak Cliff section of Dallas on November 22, 1963.

Osborne was interviewed twice by the FBI following the assassination. The first occurred on February 20, 1964, in Laredo, Texas. At that time Osborne denied being Osborne and claimed to be Bowen. On March 5, 1964, he was interviewed again, this time in Nashville, Tennessee. He admitted to being Osborne and claimed that he took the Bowen name from an acquaintance whom he resembled. He said that he was born on November 12, 1888, in Grimsby, England. He, however, denied riding on the bus to Mexico City with Oswald in September 1963.

In 1952, the accused murderers of Jake Floyd, the son of a district court judge, testified that they were hired by Albert Osborne, who, they said, ran a school for marksmen in Oaxaca, Mexico, reportedly since 1934. It was verified by the FBI that Osborne did have a school in Mexico for "boys," but that he taught "religious instruction."

As Bowen, the FBI had investigated him in 1942 because he was the head of a pro-Nazi camp for boys known as "Campfire Council" in Henderson Springs, Tennessee.

(See also BOWEN, JACK LESLIE; TORBITT DOCUMENT.)

O'Sullivan, Frederick Stephen Patrick

Born in 1937 in New Orleans, Louisiana, O'Sullivan was, at the time of the assassination, a vice detective for the New Orleans Police Department who had known Lee Harvey Oswald as a teenager in the Civil Air Patrol. O'Sullivan attended Beauregard Junior High School with Oswald as well. O'Sullivan told Warren Commission staff member Wesley J. Liebeler on April 7, 1964, in New Orleans that he himself had recruited Oswald into the Civil Air Patrol since Oswald carried himself so erect that O'Sullivan thought he would make a fine addition to the Civil Air Patrol marching unit. Liebeler questioned O'Sullivan at length about his knowledge of a possible relationship between Oswald and David Ferrie, who was a captain in the Civil Air Patrol in New Orleans at the time Oswald joined. O'Sullivan said that he knew Ferrie and Ferrie certainly *could* have known Oswald but that he had no independent recollection of a relationship between the two.

(See also VOEBEL, EDWARD.)

Oswald, Lee Harvey (a.k.a. Hidell, Alek J.; Lee, O. H.; Osborne, Lee)

Historically recognized as the murderer of JFK and Officer J. D. Tippit, but thought by many to be the subject of a frame-up for one or both of those crimes. Oswald was born in New Orleans on October 18, 1939, two months after his father's death. He was named Lee after his father and Harvey after his paternal grandmother's maiden name. He had one older brother, Robert, born in 1934, and a half-brother from his mother's previous marriage, John Edward Pic, born in 1931. Lee was born into a home among vice-ridden bars in a section of New Orleans' French Quarter called Exchange Alley.

Once divorced, once widowed, Lee's mother was both an overbearing yet self-absorbed mother. Marguerite's lack of nurturing instincts spawned familial dysfunction. All three sons fled the family as soon as they could and joined the military.

Marguerite's life was nomadic, carefree. She changed men and location easily, hardly cognizant of motherhood's responsibilities. Finally, she hooked one. Marguerite married a geologist named Edwin A. Ekdahl in May 1945.

Ekdahl was a man in whom Lee found a father figure. However, Marguerite's third marriage was not very old before it became filled with troubles. Marguerite and Ekdahl were divorced in June 1948.

Single again, Marguerite bought a small house in Benbook, Texas, a suburb of Fort Worth. The house was so small that Lee's older brothers slept on the porch, while Lee and his mother slept together. This remained the family sleeping arrangement until Lee was almost 11 years old.

By August 1952, both John Pic and Robert Oswald were in the service—John in the U.S. Coast Guard, Robert in the U.S. Marines. Lee and Marguerite moved to New York City, because John was stationed there.

At first Lee and his mother moved in with John and his wife, a tough living arrangement under the best of circumstances—and Marguerite and her daughter-in-law didn't get along. By September 1952, Marguerite had moved herself and her youngest son into their own apartment in the Bronx.

Lee only briefly went to school that fall and quickly developed a truancy problem. Instead of going to school, he often went to the nearby Bronx Zoo. He was caught skipping school and was remanded to a detention home called Youth House where he was evaluated from April 16 to May 7. While there, he was examined by Dr. Renatus Hartogs, the institution's chief psychiatrist. According to the *Warren Report,* Hartogs found Oswald to be a "tense, withdrawn and evasive boy who intensely disliked talking about himself and his feelings. [Hartogs] noted that Lee liked to give the impression that he did not care for other people but preferred to keep to himself, so that he was not bothered and did not have to make the effort of communicating. Oswald's withdrawn tendencies and solitary habits were thought to be the result of 'intense anxiety, shyness, feelings of awkwardness and insecurity.'"

Oswald was further quoted as saying, "I don't want a friend and I don't like to take to people . . . I dislike everybody." Hartogs wrote that Oswald had a "vivid fantasy life, turning around topics of omnipotence and power, through which he tries to compensate for his present shortcomings and frustrations."

Hartogs concluded: "This thirteen-year-old well-built boy has superior mental resources and functions only slightly below his capacity level in spite of chronic truancy . . . No findings of neurological impairment or psychotic mental changes could be made. Lee has to be diagnosed as 'personality pattern disturbance with schizoid features and passive-aggressive tendencies.' Lee has to be seen as an emotionally quite disturbed youngster who suffers under the impact of a really existing emotional isolation and deprivation, lack of affection, absence of family life and rejection by a self-involved and conflicted mother."

John Carro was Oswald's probation officer while he was at Youth House. According to the *Warren Report,* "Carro reported that Lee was disruptive in class after he returned to school on a regular basis in the fall of 1953. He had refused to salute the flag and was doing very little, if any, work." Carro reported that when questioned about his mother, Lee said, "Well, I've got to live with her, I guess I love her." Another social worker who interviewed Lee and his mother Marguerite, while Lee was detained in Youth House was Evelyn Siegel. In her report, she wrote: "[Lee] confided that the worst thing about Youth House was the fact that he had to be with other boys all the time, was disturbed about disrobing in front of them, taking showers with them, etc." She also noted that Lee was a "seriously detached, withdrawn youngster . . . a rather pleasant, quality about this emotionally starved, affectionless youngster [appears] which grows as one speaks to him." She felt that he was detached because "no one in [his life] ever met any of his needs for love . . . [he] withdrew into a completely solitary existence where he did as he wanted and he didn't have to live by any rules or come into contact with people . . . [He] just felt that his mother never gave a damn for him. He always felt like a burden that she simply just had to tolerate . . . Despite his withdrawal, he gives the impression that he is not so difficult to reach as he appears and patient, prolonged effort in a sustained relationship with one therapist might bring results. There are indications that he has suffered serious personality damage but if he can receive help quickly this might be repaired to some extent." In describing Marguerite, Mrs. Siegel wrote that she was "a smartly dressed, gray haired woman, very self-possessed and alert and superficially affable, [yet essentially] a defensive, rigid, self-involved person who had real difficulty in accepting and relating to people." Mrs. Siegel noted that Lee's mother had "little understanding" of "the protective shell he has drawn around himself."

Dr. Irving Sokolow—another psychologist at Youth House—administered a human figure-drawing test, and later reported: "The Human Figure Drawings are empty, poor characterizations of persons approximately the same age as the subject. They reflect a considerable amount of impoverishment in the social and emotional areas. He appears to be a somewhat insecure youngster exhibiting much inclination for warm and satisfying relationships to others. There is some indication that he may relate to men more easily than women in view of the more mature conceptualization . . . He exhibits some difficulty in relationship to the maternal figure suggesting more anxiety in this area than in any other." Tests showed a boy with no neurological impairment or psychotic changes. Oswald, the reports said, had a "personality pattern disturbance with schizoid features and passive-aggressive tendencies." The evaluation continued, "Lee has to be seen as an emotionally, quite disturbed youngster who suffers the impact of really existing emotional deprivation, lack of affection, absences of family life and rejection by a self-involved and conflicted mother."

Among the tests Oswald was given was an I.Q. test. He scored 118 on the Wechler Intelligence Scale for Children, putting him in the "upper range of bright normal intelligence." Oswald also scored above average on his reading and arithmetic exams. He was released from the institution on probation. The probation stated that Lee was not to leave town. Defying both court orders and psychologist's advice, Marguerite and Lee moved on January 10, 1954, to New Orleans, before Lee's probation had expired.

Oswald's writing shows greater difficulties than one would expect from someone of his intelligence. Today, with knowledge of learning disabilities, we might guess that Oswald was dyslexic. This learning disability would explain Oswald's trouble in school.

In New Orleans, Marguerite and Lee moved in with Marguerite's sister Lillian and her husband, Charles "Dutz" Murret. Murret promoted New Orleans prize-fighters and was known as a gambler with ties to the Carlos Marcello gambling syndicate. He quickly became Lee's newest father figure.

Marguerite also had connections with Marcello. She had once dated Clem Sehrt, Marcello's attorney, and was also friends with Louisiana crime figure and former Marcello bodyguard Sam Termine.

In the early summer of 1955, when Oswald was between the ninth and tenth grade, he attended several meetings of the Civil Air Patrol—a student aviation organization—at the Lakefront Airport. Oswald's commander was the freakish David Ferrie, who—along with being a pedophilic homosexual—was a crack pilot and fervent anticommunist. Ferrie claimed to be devoid of body hair because of a rare disease.

According to Ferrie's legend, he painted on his eyebrows and wore a crude reddish wig. With a Svengali-like presence, Ferrie was known to practice hypnosis. Ferrie was kicked out of the Civil Air Patrol in late 1955 when it was discovered by his superiors that he had been holding nude drinking parties with his boys.

In October 1955, when Oswald was just 16, he was as anxious to get away from his mother as his brothers had been. He attempted to enlist in the U.S. Marine Corps. He was turned down because he was too young.

According to his mother, Lee spent the entire following year waiting until he turned 17 so that he could be a marine. Oswald enlisted on October 24, 1956, six days after his 17th birthday.

From almost the instant that he became a Marine, Oswald began to brag about his prolific reading of communist literature. During the height of the cold war, nothing could make less sense. (See also OSWALD IN THE MARINES.)

It is suspected that Oswald, whether sponsored or on his own, was already preparing himself for a life in the world of counterintelligence. His mother confirmed that Lee's favorite television series during his teen years was *I Led Three Lives*, about an FBI agent who had infiltrated the Communist Party. Two weeks before Oswald enlisted, he wrote a letter to the Youth League of the Socialist Party of America, seeking information.

Oswald's treatment by the Marine Corps was unique. According to Oswald's legend, he had below-average scores on the rifle range, indicating below-average hand/eye control. Oswald's pattern analysis and arithmetic were well below average, yet he was assigned as a radio operator to the Marine Air Control Squadron at Atsugi Air Force Base in Japan, 20 miles west of Tokyo.

During this time, Oswald continued to talk publicly about his obsession with communist literature. Despite Oswald's seeming leftist leanings, he was granted a "confidential" clearance.

Oswald's clearance was a necessity for his job. Atsugi, Japan, where Oswald was to be stationed, was the home of the U-2 spy plane. The U-2 was used to take aerial surveillance photos of the Soviet Union from an altitude so high that the Russians, in theory, could not shoot it down.

During Oswald's marine career he would repeatedly spend large periods of his free time away from his fellow marines.

(It has been alleged that, during one of these times "away," Oswald was replaced by a man named Alek James Hidell. Hidell, it is said, lived out the rest of Oswald's life for him as an agent—either an American agent or a Soviet agent, depending on whose theory you are following. None of the theorists speculate about what happened to the real Oswald after the switch was made.)

At Atsugi, Oswald's fellow marines called him "Oswaldskovich." Oswald continued to be interested in everything Soviet—and was good-natured, unashamed, about the nickname.

Oswald effortlessly retained his security clearance despite the fact that he subscribed to Russian language newspapers. Oswald said that he needed the newspapers because he was teaching himself the Russian language.

The Marine base in Atsugi, Japan, was also alleged to be the home of a CIA mind-control program code-named MK/ULTRA, which was said to have used LSD and other drugs. The experiments, it is said, were designed to turn men into robots, fogging their ability to distinguish right from wrong and question authority. (see also MK/ULTRA.)

On September 16, 1958, while in Japan, Oswald was, according to his medical records, treated for a venereal disease that originated "in the line of duty, not due to his own misconduct." However, in a separate report, between September 8 and October 17, 1958, Oswald was reportedly on Taiwan with a new pay status and a new unit.

Oswald's fellow marines believed that he was teaching himself the Russian language. The best guess is that this was not the case. The marines tested him on his Russian proficiency on February 25, 1959. It is unlikely that they would have tested him if they not been teaching him as well.

According to Oswald's official records, he was court-martialed twice in 1957, once for possession of an unau-thorized weapon—a .22 pistol with which Oswald supposedly shot himself accidentally in the arm.

The other court martial followed an incident that would have been easy to stage had an excuse been needed to get Oswald away from his fellow marines. In a bar, Oswald poured a drink on a noncommissioned officer (a sergeant). Oswald's combined punishment was 40 days in confinement and a fine of $105.

Oswald was obliged to serve in the Marine Corps until December 7, 1959—two years from his induction plus time of confinement. Oswald, however, couldn't wait that long. He had himself honorably discharged early because, he claimed, his mother was ill and needed him. (She had dropped a box on her toe at work.) Oswald's family-hardship discharge wasn't changed to "undesirable" until after his "defection" to the Soviet Union.

Marguerite's illness, all evidence suggests, was nonexistent. The accident had laid her up for a time, but she had fully recovered by the time her son applied for his early discharge. The lack of logic in the situation is further noted by Lee's brothers, both of whom said it was doubtful that Lee would have gone out of his way to help his mother regardless of the circumstances.

On September 4, 1959, seven days before he was discharged, Oswald applied for U.S. passport. He stated on his application that he planned to attend the Albert Schweitzer College and the University of Turku in Finland.

The application further noted that Oswald also planned to travel to Cuba, the Dominican Republic, England, France, Germany, and Russia. Forgotten was Oswald's "sick mother" and her need for care.

Oswald's passport was issued on September 10. He was discharged from the Marines on September 11. On September 14, he arrived in Fort Worth, Texas, where his mother was living. He gave Marguerite $100 and stayed with her for three days. On September 17, Oswald left Fort Worth for New Orleans. This was the first step in his "attempted" defection to Russia.

Tracing Oswald's movements in the Soviet Union presents problems. No source of information, whether it be KGB files, the statements of Russians who claim to have known Oswald, or entries from Oswald's own "Historic Diary," can be verified.

The diary purports to have been written in a day-by-day fashion, covering the period Oswald was in the Soviet Union. Experts who have analyzed the diary, however, state that it appears to have been written in one or two sittings.

Another source is Marina Oswald, the Russian woman Lee met and married in the Soviet Union. Her story was told only after federal authorities had threatened her with deportation unless she cooperated.

Another source is Yuri Nosenko, a former KGB agent who defected to the United States with his primary goal to convince the CIA that the KGB had never had an interest in Oswald.

None of the sources are the best. To further confuse matters, the paper trail left by Oswald seems hopelessly nonsensical. According to the official record, Oswald used his Department of Defense identification card to get his passport on September 4, 1959. However, he was not issued his Department of Defense identification card until September 11, and the card reportedly found on Oswald's person at the time of his arrest in Dallas bore a photo of Oswald taken in Minsk, where he hadn't yet been when he received the card.

So this, as best as can be pieced together, is what happened to Oswald after he left the Marines Corps and planned to defect to the Soviet Union:

Oswald made travel arrangements through a New Orleans travel agency. He filled out the appropriate "Passenger Immigration Questionnaire." When it asked his occupation, he wrote "shipping export agent," which is a common cover for intelligence agents working abroad. His travel agent was Louis Hopkins. Hopkins said Oswald wasn't well-versed in European travel—surprising, considering the sophisticated and efficient manner in which he penetrated the Iron Curtain. (The Warren Commission later discovered that Hopkins' address—as of December 3 and 4, 1963, when he was interviewed by the FBI—was Travel Consultants, Inc., International Trade Mart, 124 Camp Street, New Orleans, La. The director of the International Trade Mart at that time was Clay Shaw, the man indicted, tried, and acquitted for conspiracy to assassinate JFK.)

Oswald paid $220.75 for his ticket and, on September 19, 1959, he embarked—one of only four passengers—aboard the SS Marion Lykes from New Orleans to Le Havre, France. The other passengers were Colonel and Mrs. George B. Church and Billy Joe Lord.

The ship arrived in France on October 8 and Oswald was in Russia a week later. He expertly avoided delays and red tape with a well-conceived route through Great Britain and Finland. While in Finland, Oswald stayed in two hotels, the Hotel Helsinki and the Hotel Torni. These were two of the best hotels in the city, known for their usage by intelligence. It is unlikely that Oswald would have stayed at either of these places unless someone else was paying the bills.

The official version of Oswald's movements presents several physical impossibilities and bureaucratic improbabilities. He flew when no flights were scheduled and received his visa at the Russian consulate in Helsinki, Finland, in two days. A full work week was considered the minimum.

Even the Soviet consul in Helsinki, Gregory Golub, who has been suspected by U.S. intelligence of being a KGB agent, seemed to want to make things easier for the young ex-marine. It's been said the only way to get into the USSR as fast as Oswald did was through Golub. Most assassination researchers feel someone was steering Oswald in the proper direction. It was Golub who issued Oswald a tourist visa in 48 hours, which represents record time. Golub, unlike other Soviet consuls, had the authority to grant visas without checking first with Moscow, if he thought the individual was "all right." Oswald applied for his visa on October 12, 1959, received it on October 14.

On October 16, Oswald was met by a Russian tourist agent at the Moscow railroad station and driven to the Hotel Berlin. She was Rima Shirokova, who had been assigned to Oswald by Intourist. He told her that he was a student. Not long after his arrival, Oswald wrote a letter to the Supreme Soviet requesting Soviet citizenship.

According to Oswald's diary, this is where his knack for cutting through red tape and getting what he wanted came to a halt. Oswald received a message from the Soviet Passport and Visa Department stating that his visa had expired. He had two hours to get out of the country.

Oswald returned to his room and slashed his left wrist. According to his diary, he was trying to end it all because of his despair and disappointment at not being allowed to stay in the USSR. According to the story, he might have bled to death but was discovered by his Intourist guide, Rima Shirokova. Oswald was taken to Botkinskaya Hospital for three days in the psychiatric ward and four days in the "somatic" ward, before getting released. The deadline for his expulsion from the country had come and gone.

After Oswald's release from the hospital, he was technically living in the country illegally. He checked out of his room at the Hotel Berlin and checked into another hotel called the Metropole. He did not behave suspiciously. He wasn't hiding from anyone. If he believed his movements were surreptitious, he was wrong. Russian officials knew just where to find him when they wanted him. Later that same day, October 28, he was contacted by the Pass and Registration Office. They asked him if he was still interested in becoming a Soviet citizen. He said he was. They told him that it would take at least 72 hours before their office could come to a decision.

On October 31, as the 72 hours had passed and still no word, Oswald apparently became impatient. He took a taxi to the American embassy in Moscow and tossed his passport on a worker's desk. He demanded to "dissolve his American citizenship." Oswald was speaking to Richard Edward Snyder, the foreign service officer at the U.S. embassy. Snyder refused to accept his renunciation and told Oswald that he would have to return "to complete the necessary papers." Before he left, Oswald gave Snyder his passport and a handwritten statement requesting that his U.S. citizenship be revoked. During that first 40-minute conversation, Oswald told Snyder that he had been a USMC radar operator and intimated that he might know things that were of value to the USSR. Oswald, however, never did file a formal renunciation. (Two years later, on July 10, 1961, when Oswald was attempting to leave the Soviet Union, he again had to deal with Snyder—who, of course, remembered him. Because Oswald had not officially expatriated himself, he was given his passport back at that time. According to the *Warren Report*, Snyder testified that he could "recall nothing that indicated Oswald was being guided or assisted by a third party when he appeared in the Embassy in July 1961. On the contrary, the arrogant and presumptuous attitude which Oswald displayed in his correspondence with the Embassy from early 1961 until June 1962, when he finally departed from Russia, undoubtedly hindered his attempts to return to the United States. Snyder . . . testified that although he made a sincere effort to treat Oswald's application objectively, Oswald's attitude made this very difficult.") Also present at the U.S. embassy on the day Oswald first visited there was Vice Consul John A. McVickar. McVickar corroborates Snyder's statement that Oswald had threatened to reveal military secrets. Later, McVickar said Oswald appeared to be "following a pattern of behavior in which he had been tutored by person or persons unknown." McVickar and Snyder's statements that Oswald threatened to divulge U.S. military secrets constitutes strong evidence that Oswald was working in some capacity for the U.S. government. If he were not a U.S. agent, he would have been arrested for treason upon his return to the United States.

During the next several days, Oswald gave interviews to the Soviet-based Associated Press and United Press International correspondents, as well as several other reporters. Aline Mosby of UPI spoke to Oswald soon after he arrived in Moscow in 1959. Oswald told Mosby that he had financed his trip with $1,500 he had saved out of his U.S. Marine Corps salary.

Priscilla Johnson (later Priscilla Johnson McMillan) interviewed Oswald on November 16, 1959, for the North American Newspaper Alliance. She was impressed that, while Oswald was outspoken about his desire to renounce his American citizenship, he never bothered to follow through with the necessary paperwork. Many years later, this same woman lived for a time with Oswald's widow Marina and wrote the book *Marina and Lee* (Harper and Row, 1977).

He told the reporters he loved communism. He said that he did not want to end up in "poverty" as his mother had. The interviews were published back in the United States. This was how Marguerite Oswald first learned that her youngest son was in the Soviet Union. Lee's mother

became immediately convinced that he was an undercover agent working for the United States.

According to the official version of the story, Snyder's stalling technique worked and Oswald never did follow through on his intense request to dissolve his U.S. citizenship. If Oswald was on a mission, however, he and Snyder had successfully left for Oswald a window of escape. When time came for him to return, things would go much easier for him if he were still a U.S. citizen.

In a letter to his brother Robert and in an interview with a United Press International correspondent on November 8 and 13, Oswald said he'd been told by Soviet officials that he'd been given the okay to stay.

In his "Historic Diary," however, Oswald says that he did not learn until later that temporary permission to stay in the Soviet Union had been granted—perhaps as late as November 16.

Oswald was called to the Soviet Passport Office on January 4, 1960. He was informed that he was being sent to Minsk, where he would live in a rent-free apartment and work at a well-paying job at the Belorussian Radio and Television Factory.

His starting salary at the factory was the same as that of the factory's foreman. He lived extravagantly for the next year. Popular because he was different, he became a playboy bachelor and dated many women. We now suspect that Oswald was not doing nearly as well with the ladies as he thought he was. Declassified KGB files state that *all* of his dates were government agents or informants. Because Lee's Russian friends thought his first name sounded Chinese, they called him "Alik." While in Minsk, Oswald's best friend was Pavel Golovachev, the son of Hero of the Soviet Union General P. Y. Golovachev. Pavel reportedly traveled in Minsk's highest social circles.

Seven months after Oswald arrived in the USSR, on May 1, 1960, Francis Gary Powers, piloting a U-2 spy plane, was shot down over the Soviet Union. Powers later said that he thought it was Oswald's knowledge of the new U.S. "MPS sixteen-inch height-finding radar," which he theoretically revealed to the Soviets, that gave them the capability of shooting down the spy plane.

The Soviet Passport Office summoned Oswald again in January 1961 and asked if he still wanted to become a Soviet citizen. Oswald said no, but—considering how fun life was—he wouldn't mind staying for another year.

On February 13, 1961, the American embassy received a letter from Oswald postmarked in Minsk on February 5. Oswald wrote that he wanted to return to the United States.

Snyder wrote back stating that Oswald would have to appear in person at the American embassy. On March 5, Oswald wrote again, explaining that without permission he was not allowed to leave Minsk. The letter, however, did not arrive at its Moscow destination until March 20. The Warren Commission theorized that the Soviets must have intercepted the second letter, because soon thereafter Oswald's aid from the Soviet Red Cross ceased.

Oswald met the woman he was to marry on March 17, 1961. She was 19-year-old Marina Nikolyevna Prusakova. They met in Minsk at a dance at the Palace of Culture for Professional Workers. Like Lee, she never knew her father. Her mother had died in 1957. She had lived for a time with her step-father but they had quarreled. When she met Lee, she was living with her aunt and uncle, Mr. and Mrs. Ilya Vasilyevich Prusakov. Her uncle, according to Marina, was a top official in the Minsk MVD. (Some have written that Marina's uncle was a KGB agent, which of course may be true, but Marina strongly denies it, insisting that he was a minister of domestic affairs, or the Russian equivalent to an FBI agent.)

Soon after meeting Marina, Lee was once again hospitalized—this time reportedly to have his adenoids removed. Marina visited Lee in the hospital and it was at this time, she says, that their love grew.

That same month, Oswald encountered some fellow Americans in Minsk. Katherine Mallory later told the Warren Commission that, during the second week in March 1961, she was in Minsk touring the Soviet Union with the University of Michigan Symphonic Band. She found herself encircled at one point by curious Russians whose questions she did not understand. A young man, she says, who told her he was an ex-marine and a Texan, stepped out of the crowd and offered to be her interpreter. She gladly accepted his offer and he translated for her for the next 15 or 20 minutes. She and the young man continued to speak even after the small crowd's curiosity had been appeased. He told her he despised the United States, that he wanted to stay in Minsk forever. She stated that she couldn't swear that the man was Oswald but that she was "personally convinced."

Sometime before April 11, 1961, Oswald asked Marina to marry him. They filed their intent-to-marry notice with the registrar by April 20 and had received all necessary permission for a Russian woman to marry an alien. Marina told the Warren Commission that when she married Lee she had no idea that he intended to leave the Soviet Union and return to the United States. In fact, she said, she had no idea that he would have been able to return to the United States even if he had wanted to. There were many people in the USSR who wanted to leave. That didn't mean they could. It was called "living behind the Iron Curtain" for a reason. By the end of May 1961, the Oswalds were nonetheless making plans to come to the United States. Oswald's diary says that he didn't tell Marina that they were going to the United States until "the last days of June," but the American Embassy in Moscow received a letter from Oswald on May 25, asking for assurances that he would not be prosecuted upon his return.

As might be expected, making the arrangements to return to the United States proved problematic. Most of the delays stemmed from Marina's difficulties getting a visa and her pregnancy.

In August 1961, Oswald was photographed—accidentally, according to the story—by Mrs. Marie Hyde, an elderly American tourist who was visiting Minsk. She said this was coincidence. Assassination researcher Anthony Summers argues that Hyde could have been an American agent sent to the USSR to check up on Oswald. For one thing, she told her traveling companions—Rita Naman and Monica Kramer, whom she'd just met—that she had gotten separated from her tour group and was seeking company—an unlikely scenario considering Intourist's tight restrictions on Americans traveling in the USSR at that time.

During December 1961, according to KGB files, Oswald started to build bombs. He built two pipe bombs with fuses designed to last about two seconds. The reports said that Oswald eventually threw the bombs away and it is unknown what he intended, if anything, to do with them.

June Oswald was born on February 15, 1962. On June 1, the Oswalds boarded a train bound for the Netherlands. They left Holland via the SS *Maasdam* on June 4 and arrived in Hoboken, New Jersey, on June 13.

They were met at the pier by a member of the Traveler's Aid Society (see also RAIKIN, SPAS T.) and were put up overnight in a Times Square hotel by a representative of the New York State Department of Welfare, who also loaned them money.

On June 14, the same representative put them on a commercial flight bound for Fort Worth, Texas, with a brief stopover in Atlanta, Georgia. (See also DAVISON, CAPTAIN ALEXIS.)

All in all, the Oswalds were treated very well upon their arrival in the United States, especially considering that Lee had defected to a communist country and, while there, offered to divulge the military secrets he knew.

Although the quantity of information regarding Oswald's activities after his return to the United States is much greater than that of when he was in the USSR, we still have difficulty at times determining the historical truth.

The biggest problem we have in gauging the quality of information regarding Oswald's movements after his return to the United States stems from evidence of several men impersonating Oswald, laying down a false trail for reasons unknown.

There is evidence that Oswald was being impersonated as early as 1961. There were certainly Oswald impersonators working in Dallas during the weeks leading up to the assassination.

Hysteria must be taken into consideration when regarding eyewitness testimony taken after the assassination. Shock set in. People did peculiar things and later forgot all about them. Some saw innocent behavior and altered it in their minds until they were convinced they were privy to part of the plot. Many people remembered having seen Ruby and Oswald in the past, sometimes together. Maybe they did and maybe they didn't—but understand that, a certain number of people would have said that even if Ruby and Oswald had never met until they came together in the basement of the Dallas police station.

Lee and Marina went to Fort Worth to live with Lee's brother Robert, who had sent Lee a letter in the Soviet Union inviting Lee's family to come stay with him. The Lee who came back from the USSR looked very different from the Lee who had enlisted in the Marines, leading some assassination theorists to believe that there had been a substitution somewhere along the line. Certainly Lee's family members noticed the change.

Robert noticed immediately that Lee had lost much hair and that he was thinner. There is also evidence that Lee was two inches shorter upon returning to the United States than he had been when he left. At the time of Oswald's arrest, he was five feet nine inches tall. His Defense Department identification card, found in his wallet following his arrest, lists his height as five feet eleven inches tall.

On June 18, 1962, Oswald contacted a public stenographer named Pauline Virginia Bates in Fort Worth, Texas, to transcribe some notes he "smuggled out of Russia." After eight hours together over three days, Oswald ran out of money to pay her. During that time she typed the first 10 pages of an intended article entitled "Inside Russia." Bates was later called to testify before the Warren Commission because of reports that Oswald had told her that "he had become a 'secret agent' of the U.S. Government and that he was going back to Russia 'for Washington.'" She testified that none of this was true, but admitted that she had a thought when she first learned Oswald had been in the USSR that "maybe he was going under the auspices of the State Department—as a student or something."

The FBI says it interviewed Oswald for the first time on June 26, 1962. Oswald, they said, was "arrogant" during the interview. Oswald, however, later said that he thought the interview went "just fine." The interrogations by the FBI became a regular thing, causing friction at Oswald's places of employment, something he didn't need because he had a hard enough time keeping jobs as it was. Then the FBI attempted to question Marina when Lee was not around, and Lee became increasingly hostile toward federal agents.

Lee, Marina, and June Oswald lived with Robert for about a month, during which time Lee's mother moved to Fort Worth. Lee, with wife and child, moved into Mar-

guerite's apartment at 1501 West Seventh Street sometime in July.

Lee and his mother did not get along. If this was a new Lee, the substitute didn't like Marguerite any more than the original had. Around the middle of August, the Oswalds moved to their own one-bedroom apartment at 2703 Mercedes Street. The apartment was described by visitors as "poorly furnished" and "decrepit."

Oswald got a job as a sheet-metal worker at the Leslie Welding Company—a division of the Louv-R-Pak Weather Company—during the third week in July 1962. Oswald was recruited by Tommy Bargas, the superintendent, through the Texas Employment Agency. Oswald interviewed for the job on July 17, 1962, got the job, and worked there until October 8, 1962, when he stopped coming to work.

Through Lee's efforts to publish an article about his experiences in the Soviet Union, and perhaps through machinations beyond their control, the Oswalds became acquainted with the Dallas–Fort Worth Russian-speaking community—a small but tight-knit group with language and anticommunist politics in common. (See also WHITE RUSSIANS.)

Most of these people—a disproportionate number of whom were geologists or had degrees in geology—liked Marina and disliked Lee. They became convinced that Lee was abusing his wife. When Marina acquired a black eye, most likely because Lee hit her, some of her Russian-Dallas friends tried to convince her that it would be in her best interests to get away from Lee for awhile. This recommendation put Marina in a very difficult position. Lee was all she had. Without him she was half way around the world from home without much hope of ever getting back.

The one Texas Russian who took a liking to Lee was George DeMohrenschildt, a White Russian count with an intelligence background. Given their differences in background, it is suspected that DeMohrenschildt's interest in Oswald was in some sort of official capacity. (See also DEMOHRENSCHILDT, SERGEI "GEORGE" S.)

The Oswalds still lived in Fort Worth when they were first visited by DeMohrenschildt on October 7, 1962. Because most of their Russian-speaking friends lived in Dallas, they should move there, he said.

The Oswalds took DeMohrenschildt's advice and moved. While in Dallas, DeMohrenschildt urged Lee to mingle with the Soviet émigré community, many of whom were right-wing "Solidarists" who had sided with the Nazis against the communists during World War II. (There is evidence that DeMohrenschildt worked for the Nazis during World War II, as well.)

After Oswald became the accused assassin, DeMohrenschildt spoke out in Lee's defense. Oswald, according to DeMohrenschildt, spoke nearly flawless Russian and owned a Beretta handgun totally unlike the one reportedly found on him at the time of his arrest.

The FBI interviewed Oswald again on August 16, 1962, this time in the back seat of a car parked in front of Oswald's Mercedes Street home. The questions reportedly covered the same ground as the first interview. Oswald again told them that he had not tried to become a Russian citizen and had never talked to anyone from the KGB, etc.

Oswald made it increasingly clear to the FBI agents that he felt he was being harassed. He became livid toward the interviewers, seemingly unable to understand why they couldn't leave him alone.

In October, Marina agreed to move with the baby into the Fort Worth home of Mrs. Elena Hall. Mrs. Hall was a woman of Russian heritage born in Iran. Marina and the baby, it was agreed, would be more comfortable there until Lee could get another job.

Here is another instance in which the official version of the facts stretches credibility. Officially, Lee was then recommended through an employment agency—and perhaps George DeMohrenschildt—for a job at Jaggars-Chiles-Stovall Company, which the *Warren Report* referred to as "a graphic arts company."

The company, however, also did photographic work, much of it highly secret, for the U.S. government. This would seem like the last place Oswald would be hired, considering his background, Marxist leanings, and questionable allegiance. But Lee got a job there nonetheless on October 11 as a photoprint trainee.

The timing of Oswald's hiring is interesting, since the Cuban Missile Crisis began on October 18, 1962, reportedly started by U-2 photographs of Russian missile sites on Cuba.

It is unclear where Lee lived during October 1962. He lived in a YMCA from October 15–19 and rented an apartment at 605 Elsbeth Street in Dallas on November 3. For two weeks, it is unknown where Oswald spent his nights.

Oswald rented Post Office Box 2915 in Dallas from October 9, 1962, until May 14, 1963. It was to this box that a Mannlicher-Carcano rifle and a .38 caliber pistol were delivered.

After Lee rented an apartment and secured a job, he and Marina were reunited. The couple got along no better than before. Marina and the baby lived in the Elsbeth Street apartment for only a few days when they again moved out and went to live with various Russian-speaking friends. Within a few weeks—after Oswald, according to Marina, cried and begged—Marina and the baby moved back in with him.

Samuel B. Ballen—a self-employed financial consultant and senior officer for several corporations including High Plains Natural Gas Company and Electrical Log Services Inc., studied geology and petroleum engineering as well as banking—met Oswald in autumn 1962 through Oswald's friend George DeMorenschildt. Ballen interviewed Oswald for a job doing photo reproduction with Electrical Log, but later said "he was too much of a hardheaded individual . . . and probably wouldn't fit in." Ballen claims DeMohrenschildt told him "this is a fellow with no hatred." Ballen said that DeMohrenschildt befriended "another stray dog" around the same time, this one from Hungary or Bulgaria, who disappeared after being around DeMohrenschildt for five or six weeks. Ballen told the *Washington Post* (December 1, 1963) that Oswald was "the kind of person I could like . . . He had a kind of Gandhi, far off look about him." (See also DEMOHRENSCHILDT, SERGEI "GEORGE" S.)

The day after he rented the post office box, Oswald was referred to a job opening at Harrell and Huntington Architects by Helen P. Cunningham, an employment counselor for the Texas Employment Commission. Oswald was not hired. Cunningham then referred him to the photo job at Jaggars-Chiles-Stovall, where Oswald started work on October 15, 1962. (See also JAGGARS-CHILES-STOVALL.)

On Thanksgiving 1962 Lee and his brothers John Pic and Robert Oswald got together for the last time. Those who think the Lee Oswald who returned from the Soviet Union was a different man from the one who had been a marine note John Pic's comments about that Thanksgiving get-together. Pic noted a "drastic change" in Lee's appearance and was struck by the fact that Lee referred to him, when introducing him to Marina, as his "half-brother," when Lee had always previously called him simply his "brother."

As if this were the object of the exercise, Oswald continued to lay out paperwork that would implicate him as a communist activist. He subscribed to communist literature and wrote to the American Communist Party, asking, considering his background, if it was a good idea for him to "continue the fight" for the communist cause.

According to the Warren Commission, Oswald mail-ordered a Wesson 38 revolver from Los Angeles on January 27, 1963, using the name A. J. Hidell. On March 12, 1963, again according to the commission, Oswald ordered a Mannlicher-Carcano bolt-action rifle from Klein's Sporting Goods in Chicago, this time using the name A. Hidell.

Again, creating the paper trail would seem to be the goal. A Texan who mail-orders weapons from out of state is akin to an Alaskan sending to California for ice cubes. If we assume for a moment that Oswald was guilty, we must figure he is unbelievably stupid. If Oswald had bought the weapons at a gun shop and had discarded them at the scenes of the crime, there would have been no way to trace those weapons to him. Instead, he created a situation in which law enforcement was guaranteed to link him to the weapons and thus to the crimes.

The timing of the mail orders also adds to suspiciousness of the situation. Despite the difference in the ordering dates for the revolver and the rifle, mail records show that both weapons arrived in Dallas at Oswald's post office box on the same day, March 20.

According to his interrogators, Oswald admitted to owning the handgun reportedly taken away from him in the Texas Theatre—although there is a report that Oswald's initial claim, upon arriving at the police station, was that a policeman had planted a gun on him in the movie theater.

But, throughout his questioning, he steadfastly denied that he had *ever* owned a rifle.

The Oswalds moved from their Elsbeth Street apartment to an upstairs apartment only a few blocks away at 214 West Neely Street on March 3, 1963. It was the backyard of this apartment that appears in the infamous "Backyard Photos," which Marina claims she took of Lee holding his weapons and communist literature. The photos, however, appear to be phonies. Soon thereafter, Lee and Marina learned that they were expecting their second child.

Oswald lost his job at Jaggars-Chiles-Stovall on April 6, 1963. His employer said that "he could not do the work." Later, Stovall refused to give a recommendation for employment to Oswald, making note of Lee's "communistic tendencies."

Someone took a shot with a rifle at the celebrated right-wing Texan, Major General Edwin Walker, on April 10, 1963, at about 9:00 P.M. General Walker was a man who had been forced to retire from the U.S. Army in 1961 because of the intense right-wing films he had been showing to the troops under his command.

According to police reconstructions of the crime, the assailant had apparently leaned a rifle against the top of a fence behind the Walker home and fired through a window, "barely missing" Walker.

Police believed that the shooting was the work of several men. Eyewitnesses reported a small group of men behaving suspiciously around the Walker home before the shot was fired.

But there were no suspects, at least not until after Lee's death when Marina said her husband had done it. Marina further incriminated her husband after his death by stating that he had also contemplated taking a shot at Richard Nixon. There, in a nutshell, is all of the existing evidence showing that Oswald had a capacity for violence.

The Warren Commission claimed that there was other evidence that Oswald was involved in the attempt on Walker's life—if indeed that was what the shooting was. According to the commission, there was a "firearm identification" of the bullet found in the Walker home with the Mannlicher-Carcano rifle that Oswald theoretically owned.

Among Oswald's belongings, after his arrest, was "found" a photo of the Walker home taken from the alley behind the house. In the picture there is a car parked in the driveway. By the time the photo was made public by the FBI, however, someone had cut a hole in it so that one couldn't read the car's license plate number. (A photo of evidence in the custody of the Dallas police shows that the photo was intact at that time so claims that the photo already had a hole in it when found are false.)

Also found was a note to Marina telling her what to do in case he was caught. The note does not specify what he might be caught doing. Experts have testified that the note was written in Lee's handwriting.

By the time the *Warren Report* was published, the suspicious activities of groups of men around the Walker home before and during the evening of the shooting had been forgotten, and the shooting, like the assassination, was said to have been the effort of a "lone nut."

Oswald reportedly decided that there was no chance of getting any work in Dallas on April 24, 1963. At that time, his wife suggested he look for work in New Orleans since that was his birthplace.

Marina told her interrogators after the assassination that she actually wanted Oswald to get out of Dallas because of the Walker incident. Oswald took Marina's advice and rode a bus to New Orleans. Marina moved in for the first time with Ruth Paine, her dear friend and a member of the Dallas Russian-speaking community.

When Oswald arrived at the New Orleans bus station he called his aunt, Lillian Murret, and asked if he could stay with her and Uncle Dutz for awhile. The last Lillian had heard Lee was in Russia. She had no idea that he was married with a baby. But, since he was alone and had not shown up with his entire family, she said okay.

According to the *Warren Report,* on Thursday, May 9, 1963, in response to a newspaper ad, Oswald secured employment at the William B. Reily Coffee Company located at 640 Magazine Street in New Orleans. (Oswald listed as one of his references Sgt. Robert Hidell on his job application.) The next day Oswald got an apartment at 4907 Magazine Street where his neighbors and landlords were Jesse J. and Nina Garner. According to Anthony Summers, Mrs. Garner said, "FBI agent Milton Kaack questioned her about Oswald within three weeks of his arrival in New Orleans." She later learned that her lodger was under heavy surveillance by "FBI" men in "a car which used to park there at night and watch him and the house, round the corner by the drugstore." Mrs. Garner told the Warren Commission she had seen "a Cuban" looking for Oswald when he wasn't home. (See D.R.E.) Mr. Garner told the commission that when Oswald moved out, he skipped out on 15 days rent.

Deputy Constable Charlie Kertz evicted Oswald from his Magazine Street apartment. "I'll never forget it," Kertz said to *New Orleans Times-Picayune* columnist Angus Lind in 1991. "It was a Friday afternoon, and it was very unusual to evict someone on a Friday afternoon."

According to Lind, "Kertz said he confronted Oswald with the order to evict, showed him his credentials and told him to get his personal belongings out of the furnished apartment; otherwise they would be placed on the sidewalk, routine eviction procedure."

"The guy was so weird," said Kertz. "He didn't say a word. There was a woman with him who had a child. He came down the steps, took a right, and headed toward Audubon Park." After that, Kertz never saw him again. According to Lind, "[Kertz] and another constable went in, put a baby bed and some clothes on the sidewalk, then opened a closet and found three rifles. They unloaded them and put them out on the sidewalk. They then removed about thirty paperbacks from the closet . . . and underneath them were two handguns, which they unloaded and put under the mattress of the baby bed. Kertz said he figured Oswald was 'some kind of hunter.'" Oswald's Magazine Street neighbors remember him as an odd duck who was often seen walking backward.

While looking for a job in New Orleans, just before he found one at Reily, Oswald applied for a job at S. K. Manson Marble and Granite Company. On his application he listed as a reference Charles Harrison, which bears a strong phonetic resemblance to assassination suspect Charles Harrelson.

On May 29, a thousand Fair Play for Cuba Committee leaflets were ordered from the Jones Printing Company, which was located directly across the street from the William Reily Coffee Company where Oswald was reportedly working at the time. The leaflets were ordered by a man named "Osborne," who, according to the owner of the printing company, was a husky fellow. "Osborne's" handwriting does not resemble Oswald's.

Was the Reily job a real one or a cover for other activities? An eyewitness has said that Oswald never seemed to do any work for the coffee company. Then there is the unsettling fact that four of his Reily coworkers (Emmet Barbee, John Branyon, Alfred Claude, and Dante Marachini) quit within weeks of his leaving—and all four went to work for NASA. One of them, Marachini, was a friend and neighbor of assassination suspect Clay Shaw.

Also on May 9, Oswald rented an apartment at 4905 Magazine Street with the help of Myrtle Evans, a woman who had known him as a child. Lee immediately called Marina and asked her to rejoin him. She quickly agreed.

Oswald moved into the Magazine Street apartment on May 10. Marina and June, driven by Mrs. Paine, arrived the following day. Ruth toured the city for several days and returned to Irving on May 14.

Lee was again employed and had his family with him. This condition lasted until July 19. On that day Lee was fired from his job for laziness. Around this time, according to Marina, Lee began to talk about going to Cuba.

Oswald became involved in a New York pro-Castro organization known as the Fair Play for Cuba Committee (FPCC) during May and June of 1963. He opened up his own chapter in New Orleans, of which he was the only member. The only other name associated with the New Orleans chapter of the FPCC was A. J. Hidell, who was listed as another officer of the organization separate from Oswald. According to the official story, Hidell is not a separate individual but rather an alias for Oswald. As noted, a batch of printed circulars for the FPCC was ordered by someone using the name Osborne.

At first, Oswald listed the address for his "Committee" as 544 Camp Street, which was a building adjacent to the offices of right-wing intelligence agent Guy Banister, who in turn was working with David Ferrie, the strange hairless man who'd been Oswald's Civil Air Patrol supervisor. By this time, Ferrie was a CIA pilot and private investigator for New Orleans crime boss Carlos Marcello.

On July 26, 1963, someone signed the guest log at the Atomic Energy Museum in Oak Ridge, Tennessee "Lee H. Oswald, USSR, Dallas Road, Dallas, Texas." The handwriting is not Oswald's. He was reportedly in New Orleans at the time.

During the summer of 1963, Oswald was seen meeting with Banister and Ferrie. Only Oswald's first batch of FPCC pamphlets had the Camp Street address stamped on them.

After that, Oswald listed the address as post office box number 30016, an unfortunate error since the box he had actually rented (under his name, his wife's name, and the Hidell alias) was 30061. He inverted the last two numbers on the pamphlets, as well as when he wrote the number in his notebook. It is doubtful if he ever received any mail that might have been recruited through this method. Perhaps this was to make sure that no actual applications were received.

It is still an assumption that the Hidell name was no more than an alias that Oswald used. Oswald had actually known a man called "Hidell" in the U.S. Marine Corps. Rene Heindel, whose nickname was Hidell, was reportedly living in New Orleans during the summer of 1963. (See also OSWALD IN THE MARINES.)

If one believes that Oswald was framed, the post office box system and the Hidell alias were used as a paper trail linking Oswald with the murder weapons of President Kennedy and Officer Tippit.

Allen and Daniel Campbell were former marines recruited by New Orleans private investigator and Oswald-associate Guy Banister during the summer of 1963 to help identify pro-Castro sympathizers among New Orleans college students. Daniel told Anthony Summers in 1979 that Oswald came into Banister's offices on the day he was arrested and used Daniel's desk phone to make a call. Allen told the New Orleans District Attorney's Office in 1969 that Banister usually had a temper tantrum when notified of communist activity, but when he was told about Oswald's pro-Castro demonstration, he just laughed. (See also BANISTER, WILLIAM GUY.)

Longtime New Orleans French Quarter resident Barbara Reid told New Orleans Parish district attorney Jim Garrison that Oswald's old marine buddy, Kerry Thornley, lived in New Orleans during the summer of 1963. She said she knew both Thornley and Oswald and had seen them together on several occasions. (See also THORNLEY, KERRY WENDELL.)

Oswald visited a New Orleans store managed by the fiercely anti-Castro Cuban-exile Carlos Bringuier on August 5, 1963. (See also D.R.E.) The *Warren Report* says that Oswald and Bringuier chatted about the struggle against Castro. The Warren Commission put forth the theory that this was an act on Oswald's part—but it may be a brief glimpse of the real Lee. There is evidence that Oswald and Bringuier were in cahoots about something. Two 16-year-old boys—Vance Douglas Blalock and Philip Geraci, III—came into Carlos Bringuier's store while Oswald was there "pretending" to be a right-wing activist. According to Geraci, one of Oswald's comments about rightist activism at that time was: "the thing he liked best of all was learning about how to blow up the Huey P. Long Bridge." That bridge spans the Mississippi River outside New Orleans, and, according to assassination researcher Paris Flammonde, "may have been used by Cuban exiles as a training run for actual sabotage within Cuba." Blalock says Oswald offered to give him and his pal a copy of the marine manual.

On August 9, 1963, Oswald stood on a street corner in New Orleans and handed out FPCC leaflets. Carlos Bringuier happened along. Small world. The two appeared to get into an argument—which some spectators later said seemed staged—and Bringuier finally struck Oswald. According to one eyewitness, Oswald said, "Go ahead and hit me," just before Bringuier struck him. The police came and only Oswald was arrested.

Oswald was in jail for only one night before he was bailed out by a representative of New Orleans crime boss Carlos Marcello. While Oswald was jailed, he asked to be visited by an FBI agent. His request was granted.

If we are to believe the official story of the assassination, it would seem that the FBI would be the last people whom Lee Harvey Oswald would want to see while he was in a jail cell.

By August 16, Oswald was back on the New Orleans streets handing out his FPCC leaflets carrying the headline "HANDS OFF CUBA!" This time he worked in front of the International Trade Mart in New Orleans. The director of the International Trade Mart was Clay Shaw, a man who would four years later be indicted, tried, and acquitted of conspiracy to kill JFK by New Orleans district attorney Jim Garrison.

This time someone notified the media that Oswald was handing out the controversial leaflets. That night the television news showed everyone in town how the ex-Soviet defector was handing out commie literature.

The publicity, as one might expect, did nothing for Oswald's ability to find a job. For the second session of leaflet distribution, Oswald even went so far as to get help from a casual labor pool, so Oswald and his employees handed out the leaflets together—a peculiar move for a man who was, in theory, broke.

Oswald drew attention to himself in a variety of situations. Orest Pena, owner of the Habana Bar in New Orleans, told the FBI that Oswald came into his bar in August 1963, accompanied by a man who appeared Latin American and who spoke Spanish. He said Oswald ordered a lemonade, immediately vomited it back up onto his table, and then left.

The end of September was nearing. Lee was again out of work. Marina was very pregnant. It was decided that Marina and June would again move in with Ruth Paine, at least until the baby was born.

According to Marina's Warren Commission testimony, Lee had been talking about going to Cuba via Mexico for much of the summer, and, according to the commission, Marina and Ruth left New Orleans for Irving on September 23.

The next day, again according to the Warren Commission, Oswald was on his way to Mexico. As is the case with the Walker shooting, we have little evidence that Oswald planned to go to Mexico beyond his wife's testimony.

The truth is, we don't know where Oswald went, but there is strong evidence that an imposter (or several), and not Oswald himself, went to Mexico City, ostensibly as the first step in a defection to Cuba. (See also OSWALD IN MEXICO.)

Mrs. Lee Dannelly, an employee of the Selective Service System in Austin, Texas, later said that on September 25, 1963, a man calling himself "Harvey Oswald" came to her asking if it were possible to have his "other than honorable" discharge upgraded. He told her he lived in Fort Worth. She couldn't find a Harvey Oswald listed in her files and suggested that he try the Fort Worth office. He left. Officially, Oswald was on his way from New Orleans to Mexico City on that date.

According to the *Warren Report,* Oswald returned to Dallas from Mexico on the afternoon of October 3 and spent the night at the YMCA. The next day he applied for a job at Padgett Printing Company but was rejected when his job superintendent, Robert Stovall, at Jaggars-Chiles-Stovall refused to recommend him, saying he had "communistic tendencies."

On October 4, Oswald visited Marina at the Paine home. He returned to Dallas on October 7. He rented a room at 621 Marsalis St. from Mrs. Mary Bledsoe, who later would become an eyewitness to Oswald's alleged "getaway" from the Texas School Book Depository on the afternoon of the assassination.

Oswald remained a tenant of Mrs. Bledsoe for only one week. She refused to rent the room to him for another week because she did not like him. After spending a weekend at the Paines' home, Oswald took a room on October 14 at 1026 North Beckley where he registered under the name O. H. Lee. This was to be his last address.

Oswald was still being watched. James D. Crowley, a State Department intelligence specialist, stated in an affidavit (WCH XI, 482) that, "The first time I remember learning of Oswald's existence was when I received copies of a telegraphic message from the [CIA] dated October 10, 1963, which contained information pertaining to his current activities." Crowley said he briefly reviewed Oswald's file on November 14, 1963, but offered no further details regarding this potentially fascinating message.

Also on October 14, Ruth mentioned to her neighbor, Mrs. Linnie Mae Randle, that Lee was looking for work. Mrs. Randle said that her younger brother, Buell Wesley Frazier, with whom she lived, had recently gotten a job at the Texas School Book Depository. Maybe Lee should try there.

Ruth called the Book Depository superintendent Roy Truly. She explained Lee's situation, and Truly said Lee should come down to the building in person for a job interview. Oswald made a favorable impression and began work as an order-filler on Wednesday, October 16. Lee continued to spend weekends at the Paines'. He now received rides to and from Irving with his new coworker Frazier.

Marina gave birth to her second daughter on October 20. The child was named Rachel. On November 1, Oswald rented Dallas post office box 6225 at the terminal annex, across Dealey Plaza from the Book Depository. He noted on his application that the box would be used to receive mail for the Fair Play for Cuba Committee and the American Civil Liberties Union.

On November 10, a Sunday, both Carousel Club employee Billy DeMar and Carousel patron Harvey L. Wade claim to have seen Oswald in Ruby's club and that Oswald participated in DeMar's "memory act." That same day, while the real Oswald was supposedly in Irving, Texas, at the Paines' house, Hubert Morrow, manager of the All-right Parking Systems, claims to have seen him in Dallas. A man identifying himself as "Oswald" applied for a job as a parking attendant and asked Morrow if the Southland Hotel, adjacent to the parking lot, provided a good view of downtown Dallas.

On Thursday, November 21, Oswald asked Frazier to take him to Irving, the first time he had made such a request on any day other than a Friday. It was also the first time that Oswald had made plans to go to the Paines' house without calling Marina first.

Frazier asked Oswald about this and Lee reportedly told him that he had to go out to the Paines to pick up some curtain rods he needed for his room. That night, Lee and Marina fought.

Marina had learned that Lee was living in Dallas under an assumed name, O. H. Lee, and this angered her. He went to bed early. In the morning, he left Marina some money (which he normally did) and put his wedding ring in a cup in her room (which he normally did not) and went to Mrs. Randle's house to meet Frazier.

Both Mrs. Randle and Frazier saw Oswald carrying a "long and bulky package" that they said he slipped onto the backseat of Frazier's car. After his arrest, Oswald denied carrying such a package.

Oswald maintained during his post-assassination interrogation that he had brought only his lunch to work with him that morning. Frazier says Oswald told him the package contained the curtain rods he had told him about the previous day. Jack Edwin Dougherty, a School Book Depository employee, said he saw Oswald enter the building on the morning of the assassination and that he didn't think Oswald was carrying anything.

During their testimony before the Warren Commission, both Frazier and Mrs. Randle made it clear that they thought the package was too short to have contained a rifle—even one that was broken down. Commission counsel tried very hard to get both of them to say that the package might have contained a broken down rifle, but neither of them would do it. Besides Mrs. Randle and Frazier, no one else saw Oswald carrying a package of any sort.

By his own account, Oswald left the Book Depository approximately three minutes after the assassination by the front entrance and walked seven blocks east. The most notable dissenting eyewitness is Deputy Sheriff Roger Craig, who says Oswald left the building 15 minutes after the assassination and entered a Nash station wagon on Elm Street. There is corroboration that a man did enter a Nash station wagon on Elm Street at this time and that he resembled Oswald. (See also CRAIG, ROGER; NASH RAMBLER.) If an Oswald look-alike was involved in the assassination both versions could be correct.

He apparently boarded a southbound Marsalis Street bus at the corner of Elm and Murphy that was headed west, back in the direction of the Book Depository.

Though the eyewitness testimony of Oswald being on this bus is shaky, a transfer from this bus was found in Oswald's pocket after his arrest. Oswald took the Marsalis Street bus, which came within only seven blocks of his roominghouse at 1026 North Beckley, instead of the Beckley bus, which would have dropped him off right outside his home. Perhaps he was not headed home. Oswald reportedly purchased a 23-cent ticket when boarding the bus. That ticket would have taken him two blocks from Jack Ruby's apartment. However, Oswald was no doubt in a hurry and may have gotten on the first bus to come along that headed toward the Oak Cliff section of Dallas.

The bus was driven by Cecil J. McWatters. The bus became caught in traffic and Oswald got off the bus two blocks or so after getting on, at the corner of Elm and Lamar Streets. McWatters was taken to a lineup the night after the assassination and said that the number-two man (Oswald) "resembled" the man on his bus. The man, he remembered, had grinned when hearing that the president had been shot. The following day, Milton Jones got on McWatters's bus and the bus driver realized that it was this man, and not Oswald, who had gotten on and grinned inappropriately. McWatters attempted to rescind his earlier statement but was ignored.

Mrs. Mary Bledsoe was on the bus, the same woman who had kicked Oswald out of her rooming house because she didn't like him. Oddly, when Mrs. Bledsoe described Oswald's appearance on the bus, she described the mussed

OSWALD MOVEMENTS BETWEEN 12:33 AND 12:48 P.M.

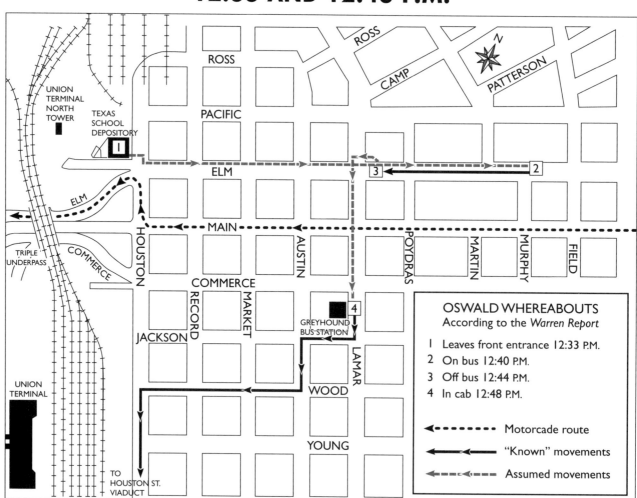

and beaten man who appeared on TV later in the day after his arrest. Oswald was on the bus for approximately four minutes.

Oswald theoretically walked two blocks south from Elm and Lamar, to the Greyhound bus station at Commerce and Lamar. He was still only two blocks from Dealey Plaza.

At the bus station, he got into the front passenger seat of a taxicab driven by William Whaley. This apparently is the only time in his life that he had ridden in an American taxicab.

Oswald acted neither nervous nor in a hurry. According to Whaley, he offered to give up the cab to a woman, who declined his offer and asked Whaley to call the dispatcher for a cab for her.

Attorney Mark Lane noted that Whaley listed this cab ride in his log as beginning at 12:30, which was the time of the assassination. Whaley later said that he often rounded off the times in his log book to the nearest quarter hour.

Oswald rode in Whaley's cab to the Oak Cliff section of Dallas. The *Warren Report* says that Oswald directed Whaley "to a point twenty feet north of the northwest corner of the intersection of Beckley and Neely . . . on the 700 block of Beckley."

Earlene Roberts, Oswald's housekeeper, says Oswald entered the rooming house at about 1:00 P.M. He seemed in a hurry. He went directly to his room. After three or four minutes, he emerged zipping up a jacket. (See also ROBERTS, EARLENE.)

While Oswald was in his room, Mrs. Roberts said, a Dallas police car pulled up in front of the house containing two uniformed officers. The car honked twice and then drove off.

Mrs. Roberts's first statement regarding the police car was that it was car number 207. After interrogation on the matter, she later expressed doubt as to what the number was. She says Oswald left the house at about 1:04.

Mrs. Roberts last saw Oswald standing at a bus stop. Officer Tippit was shot and killed about 11 minutes later near the corner of Tenth Street and Patton Avenue. The location of the murder was only $3/10$ of a mile from Jack Ruby's apartment. If Oswald had caught the bus that Mrs. Roberts says he was waiting for, he would not have gone in the direction of the Tippit murder.

The only eyewitness who identified Oswald as the man who shot Tippit was Helen Markham and her identification was extremely shaky. There were other witnesses in the area who identified Oswald, but only as a man they had seen fleeing the area.

The *Warren Report* says that, after shooting Tippit, Oswald reloaded his gun. He threw the empty shells into some bushes at the corner of Tenth and Patton. He then ran south on Patton one block to Jefferson Boulevard, and took a right. Heading west, he stopped briefly in a parking lot behind a gas station where he allegedly threw his jacket. He then continued west and allegedly sneaked into the Texas Theatre where he was arrested. Only six minutes after he entered the theater, he was under arrest and on his way to the Dallas police station.

According to the official scenario, Oswald entered the theater at 1:45. It has never been explained why it theoretically took Oswald only 11 minutes to get from his rooming house to the site of the Tippit murder, a distance of 10 blocks, yet from the murder site to the Texas Theatre, only seven blocks, it took him more than 30 minutes. (See also TEXAS THEATRE.)

When Oswald was first brought into the Dallas police station it was solely as a suspect in the Tippit killing. It wasn't until minutes later, when it was realized that Oswald was missing from the Texas School Book Depository, that Captain Will Fritz took over the case.

So the first few questions to be asked Oswald were by Detective Gus Rose, who asked Oswald why he had been arrested. Oswald reportedly said, "Oh, I was just sitting in the theater and officers came in and planted a gun on me and accused me of shooting somebody. I know nothing about that."

Between Oswald's arrest on November 22 and his death on November 24, Oswald was interrogated for approximately 12 hours. Captain Fritz of the Dallas Police Department, Homicide and Robbery Division, did most of the questioning.

The *Warren Report* says that Fritz "kept no notes" of the interrogation. He did write down notes later, after Oswald's death, regarding the statements he remembered Oswald making. (See also FRITZ.) There were no stenographic or tape recordings made. All reports on what Oswald said come from the memories of the law enforcement officials who were present.

Oswald was given a paraffin test on the evening of November 22 to determine if Oswald had fired a gun during the previous 24 hours. Officially, the results were positive for Oswald's hands yet negative for his right cheek. This would indicate that Oswald had not fired a rifle.

It is much easier to get a false positive than a false negative with a paraffin test, since it is almost impossible to fire a gun and not come up positive on the test, but there are many substances that will cause a positive result; therefore, firing a gun is hardly necessary.

Oswald denied until his death ever shooting anyone. He said he neither owned a rifle nor stored one in the Paines' garage. He said he had seen Roy Truly showing some Book Depository coworkers a rifle a few days before. He admitted to owning a pistol, but said that he had bought it in Fort Worth. On the 23rd (and again on the 24th), Oswald was shown photographs of himself holding a rifle and wearing a handgun in a holster.

OSWALD MOVEMENTS BETWEEN 12:54 AND 1:50 P.M.
OAK CLIFF SECTION, DALLAS

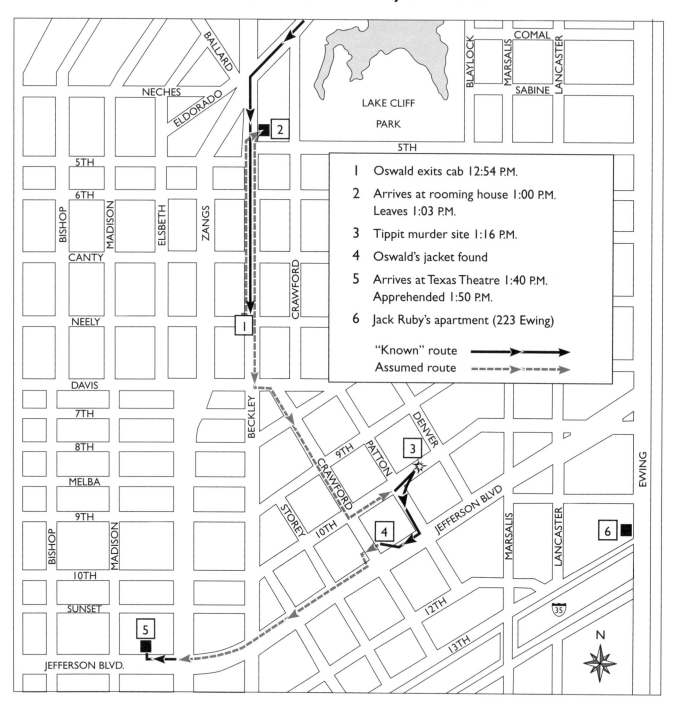

1 Oswald exits cab 12:54 P.M.

2 Arrives at rooming house 1:00 P.M.
   Leaves 1:03 P.M.

3 Tippit murder site 1:16 P.M.

4 Oswald's jacket found

5 Arrives at Texas Theatre 1:40 P.M.
   Apprehended 1:50 P.M.

6 Jack Ruby's apartment (223 Ewing)

"Known" route →→→
Assumed route ⇢⇢⇢

The *Warren Report* says, "Oswald sneered, saying that they were fake photographs, that he had been photographed a number of times the day before by the police" and that the photos were composites. He refused to comment in any way on the "Alek Hidell" identification found in his wallet. Referring to the ID card, Oswald reportedly told Fritz, "You know as much about it as I do." (Fritz disagrees with this quote, saying that Oswald told him he had picked up the Hidell name while working for the FPCC in New Orleans that summer.) He admitted to renting post office box 2915 in Dallas—where the weapons were allegedly sent—but denied that A. J. Hidell ever received a package through that box. When asked about post office box 30061 in New Orleans, which he also reportedly rented under both names, Oswald said, "I don't know anything about that." He said that he never allowed anyone—except for perhaps his wife—to use his post office boxes. He was asked why he had rented his room under the name O. H. Lee. He said that the landlady had simply made a mistake. He said he never told Frazier anything about curtain rods and that the only bag he took to work with him on Friday morning contained his lunch. He said that when JFK was shot he was eating lunch in the Texas School Book Depository building's first-floor lunch room and that he was with a short black man named "Junior." (See JARMAN, JAMES.) He admitted to the encounter with Roy Truly and Officer Marrion Baker about 90 seconds after the shooting on the second floor, saying he had gone there to get a Coke. He said that he then walked out the front door of the building and talked to coworker Bill Shelley for five to 10 minutes. Shelley told him that there probably wasn't going to be anymore work that day, so he went home. (Shelley denied seeing Oswald at any time after noon, although he admitted to being out in front of the building at the appropriate time.) Oswald reportedly confirmed that he had taken a bus and a cab to his rooming house. He said he went directly from his home to the movies.

During his interrogation, Oswald was asked what he had thought of President Kennedy. Oswald replied, "My wife and I like the President's family. They are interesting people. I have my own views on the President's national policy. I have a right to express my views but because of the charges I do not think I should comment further. I am not a malcontent; nothing irritated me about the President."

Witnesses to Oswald's questioning agree that the accused assassin remained calm throughout the interrogation sessions. The only exception to this was when FBI agent James Hosty entered the room. At that point, Oswald flared up with anger and accused Hosty of accosting his wife. (See also HOSTY, JAMES P., JR.)

Oswald said that he wanted New York City attorney John Abt, a lawyer known for handling political conspiracy cases, to serve as his attorney. He was allowed to call Abt, but Abt was away for the weekend.

No attorney ever stepped forward to assist Oswald, who died without legal representation. Oswald was arraigned for the Tippit murder at 7:10 P.M., November 22, and for JFK's murder at 1:35 A.M., November 23—both before Judge David Johnston. The judge later said, "Oswald was

very conceited. He said sarcastically, 'I guess this is the trial,' and denied everything."

The gun taken from Oswald in the Texas Theatre was reportedly ordered by mail from Seaport Traders, Inc. of Los Angeles, California, on January 27, 1963. The revolver was a .38 Special Smith & Wesson Victory model, serial number V510210. The gun's .38 chambers had been converted to .38 Special. Cases fired in such weapons tend to bulge and split, but there was no bulging or splitting in the shells reportedly found at the scene of Officer Tippit's murder. The revolver cost $29.95. There was a line on the order blank for a witness and in this spot was written "D. F. Drittal." The name of the purchaser was listed as "A. J. Hidell, aged 28." Handwriting experts have said that both the Hidell and Drittal signatures were in Oswald's handwriting. It was shipped on March 20, 1963, to A. J. Hidell at post office box 2915 in Dallas. Ten dollars in cash had been included with the order, which meant that $19.95 plus a $1.27 shipping charge were paid by "Hidell" when he picked up the gun at the post office.

Meanwhile, Marina Oswald was taken into custody also, "for her own protection." A great portion of the evidence that convicted the dead Lee Harvey Oswald of the assassination in the minds of the public was provided by his widow, who would not have been allowed to testify against him had he lived to go to trial. Since Marina was in a precarious position after Lee's arrest in Dallas, it is suspected that she was used, threatened with deportation if she didn't tell law enforcement officials precisely what they wanted to hear. Without Marina's testimony the case against Oswald as the assassin, even outside the judicial system, is considerably weakened. (See also OSWALD, MARINA.)

Oswald, Leon   See EDISON, EDELE; GARRISON INVESTIGATION, THE; HALL, LORAN EUGENE; ODIO INCIDENT, THE; OSWALD LOOK-ALIKES; RUSSO, PERRY RAYMOND.

Oswald, Marguerite Claverie

Mother of the alleged assassin, she claimed after the assassination that her son was a patsy and had been working as an agent for the U.S. government. After the House Select Committee on Assassination's 1979 conclusion that JFK was "probably assassinated as a result of a conspiracy," Oswald's mother commented to reporters, "The committee members have made a first step in the right direction . . . I hope and know the future will vindicate my son entirely. It took us 15 years to come this far. It may take another 15 years or longer . . . but the world will know that Lee Harvey Oswald was innocent of the charges against him."

Her opinion of the Warren Commission is clearly expressed in this letter she wrote to several congressmen in 1973: "Because I was critical of the commission, I was asked, 'Mrs. Oswald, are you implying that the Chief Justice would whitewash evidence or hide information so that the American people, as well as the whole world, would never learn the truth?' I answered yes, in the name of security, men of integrity . . . who have the welfare of the country at heart, would be most likely to do what the White House wanted and thought necessary."

Grinning as if pleased by all of the attention she was getting, she said during a filmed interview during the 1960s, "The only thing I know for sure is that I did not kill the president—and there's another thing I am sure of, I did not raise my sons to kill."

United Press International photographer Jerry McNeill remembered: "Within a couple of weeks of her son having been accused of committing the assassination of the President and himself being killed we went over to do a TV and word interview . . . Her first reaction was . . . the electricity, I can hardly pay the bill, and a twenty-dollar bill would help pay her electric bill. It got us inside, and then she was talking about no food in the house and the cameraman got

in his car and went down to the Seven-Eleven [convenience store] and bought a sack of groceries and that got us an interview with Marguerite Oswald. . . . It was something that I don't think was quite normal for a mother who had just lost a son under those circumstances."

The House Select Committee reported that Marguerite "was acquainted with several men associated with lieutenants in the [assassination suspect Carlos] Marcello organization. One such acquaintance, who was an associate of [Marguerite's brother-in-law] Dutz Murret, reportedly served as a personal aide or driver to Marcello at one time." (See also MURRET, CHARLES AND LILLIAN.)

According to the Warren Commission testimony of Oswald-witness Peter Paul Gregory, a member of Dallas' Russian-speaking community, Marguerite signed up for and attended his Russian language classes before the assassination, presumably so that she would better be able to communicate with her daughter-in-law Marina. (See also WHITE RUSSIANS.)

Following the assassination Marguerite retained attorney Mark Lane to defend the memory of her son. (See also LANE, MARK.)

Marguerite died of cancer in January 1982.

Marguerite Oswald, mother of alleged Kennedy assassin Lee Harvey Oswald, at home in 1964. *(AP/Wide World Photos)*

Oswald, Marina (née Prusakova, Marina Nikolyevna; later Porter, Marina)

Wife of the alleged assassin, Marina was a Russian woman whom Oswald met while living in the USSR. The pair returned together but were estranged at the time of the assassination. Marina's Warren Commission testimony damned Lee but was full of contradictions. It would not have been allowed in a court of law.

According to her official biography, Marina was born on July 17, 1941, in Severodvinsk (formerly Molotovsk), Russia, the child of Klavdiya Vasilevna Prusakova, an unwed mother. (Marina later told journalist Priscilla Johnson McMillan that her real father had been a Russian traitor named Nikolai Didenko.) A few years later her mother married Aleksandr Ivanovich Medvedev, an electrician who became Marina's stepfather. While still very small, Marina went to live with her maternal grandparents, Tatyana Yakolevna Prusakova, her grandmother, and Vasiliy Prusakov, her grandfather. Marina's grandfather died when she was four and she continued to live with her grandmother. At age seven, Marina moved back in with her mother and stepfather in Zguritva, Moldavia. The family moved to Leningrad in 1952 when Marina's stepfather got a job at a power station. After completing seventh grade, Marina entered pharmacy school, from which she graduated in 1959. Marina's mother died in 1957 and for a time she lived with her stepfather, although they did not get along. Following her graduation, Marina was given a

Lee Harvey Oswald's wife, Marina, and daughter Rachel, at their home in Richardson, Texas. *(AP/Wide World Photos)*

job preparing prescriptions at a pharmaceutical ware-house in Leningrad. She quit this job after one day and went to live with a childless aunt and uncle, also named Prusakov, in Minsk. Her uncle, Colonel Ilya Vasilyevich Prusakov, worked for the Soviet Ministry of Internal Affairs (the equivalent of our FBI). Because of his job, his apartment was nicer than any of the others Marina had lived in. In October 1960 Marina began to work in the pharmacy of the Third Clinical Hospital in Minsk. At that time she became a member of Komsomol, the Communist youth organization. Marina had been living in Minsk for approximately seven months and had dated many men during that time when she met Lee Harvey Oswald at a trade union dance at the Palace of Culture in Minsk on March 17, 1961. According to the *Warren Report:* "The dance followed a lecture by a Russian woman who had

just returned from the United States. Marina . . . arrived too late to hear the lecture but was at the dance. Oswald noticed her and asked Yuriy Merezhinskiy, the son of the lecturer and a friend of both Oswald and Marina, to intro-duce him to her. Oswald asked her to dance." On April 30, 1961, Lee and Marina were married. Still according to the official story, Lee told Marina about his intentions to return to the United States only days after their wedding. It is possible that this entire biography is a fiction, how-ever, supplied to her as a new identity. Assassination researcher Edward Jay Epstein notes that the birth certifi-cate Marina used to get her visa to come to the United States was dated July 19, 1961, yet she would have needed a birth certificate to get married the previous April. Why would she need two different birth certificates in four months?

Among Marina's uncorroborated claims used to convict her husband in the public's mind were that: 1. She took the photos of Oswald holding the alleged murder weapons, although she said that the backgrounds on the extant pictures were wrong since she was pointing the other way when she took the actual photos. 2. Oswald had confessed to her that he had taken a shot at right-winger General Walker. 3. Oswald had planned to shoot Richard Nixon. 4. Oswald owned a rifle which he kept wrapped in a blanket in Ruth Paine's garage.

Critics of the *Warren Report* say Marina was threatened with deportation by U.S. government officials and, out of fear, told them what they wanted to hear. There would have been no evidence that Oswald had a capacity for violence without Marina's testimony.

Marina believes that there *were* people impersonating her and her husband in the weeks and months leading up to the assassination. She told journalist Jack Anderson in 1988, regarding eyewitness reports that she and her husband had been seen in a rifle repair shop/furniture store seeking to have a scope for a gun repaired, "I thought at first that maybe I just didn't recall being there, that maybe I was losing my mind. The FBI took me there and I knew I had never been there before in my life."

On February 22, 1963, George and Jeanne DeMohren-schildt invited Marina to a dinner party and it was there that she met Mrs. Ruth Paine, with whom she was living without paying rent at the time of the assassination.

Mrs. Paine, who had a "difficult to define" separation from her husband Michael, found everything about the Soviet Union fascinating. Ruth, the story goes, was a housewife with children who was trying to learn Russian.

During the summer of 1963, Marina requested repatriation for herself, along with visas for Lee and her children. The KGB asked Marina's stepfather if he would give them a home and he said no. Her request was refused October 7, 1963, by the Soviet Ministry of Internal Affairs.

Jeanne DeMohrenschildt, wife of George, testified extensively regarding her opinion of Marina before the Warren Commission. Mrs. DeMohrenschildt testified: "Marina doesn't fit at all my . . . feeling about Soviet Youth." She said that she imagined the young people in Russia to be wholesome, healthy, active in sports, and "collecting things." Marina, on the other hand, liked to talk about her experiences with "these sort of orgies, you know, wild parties, and things like that." Mrs. DeMohren-schildt added, "She was promiscuous but not malicious." She also added that she thought it was strange that Marina was a trained pharmacist yet seemed to know nothing about hygiene when it came to taking care of her baby daughter.

After her husband was arrested in Dallas, an interpreter was needed to interrogate Marina. The first translator for Marina's questioning by the Dallas Police Department was Ilya Mamantov, a man recommended by U.S. Army Intelligence. Mamantov was picked up by a Dallas patrol car and taken to the Dallas police station.

Marina later married a man named Porter, raised her two daughters, and stayed in Texas. She still occasionally makes public appearances in connection with the assassination.

(See also WHITWORTH, MRS. EDITH.)

Oswald, Murder of

While Oswald was being held prisoner there, the Dallas police station was a madhouse, jam-packed with reporters who shouted questions to Oswald each time the prisoner was moved from one place to another. Oswald told the press that he hadn't shot anybody, that he was a patsy—and he asked for someone to step forward and give him legal assistance. No one did. Lurking in that madhouse throughout the weekend was Dallas nightclub owner Jack Ruby, with a gun in his pocket.

According to criminal investigation detective Bill Courson of the Dallas County Sheriff's Department, there are written transcripts of Sheriff Decker discussing the threats against Oswald that had been called in, indicating a need for security far beyond anything provided to Oswald by the Dallas Police Department.

At 11:21 A.M., November 24, 1963, Oswald was being transferred from the Dallas police station to the county jail, and was being led from the station through the basement parking lot. Cameraman George Phenix was filming the scene for KRLD-TV in Dallas. On Oswald's right was Homicide Detective James R. Leavelle, who was handcuffed to the alleged assassin at the wrist. On the other side was Homicide Detective L. C. Graves, who was not handcuffed to Oswald.

Ruby stepped out from behind a plain-clothes police officer and fired a single bullet into Oswald's abdomen. Oswald was rushed via ambulance to Parkland Hospital, the same hospital where JFK and Governor Connally had been taken—and there he died at 1:13 P.M.

Oswald had the benefit of the world's fastest ambulance. Michael Hardin, a Dallas City ambulance driver, drove the dying Oswald from the Dallas police station to Parkland. Hardin told the Warren Commission that he received the call that Oswald had been shot at 11:21, arrived on the scene at 11:23, and was at Parkland by 11:30.

Dallas police detective Leslie D. Montgomery, who was standing just behind Oswald at the time he was shot, testified that Oswald had to slow up, making him an easier target, because the car that was supposed to receive him had not yet backed into place.

BASEMENT LAYOUT, DALLAS POLICE STATION
DALLAS, TEXAS

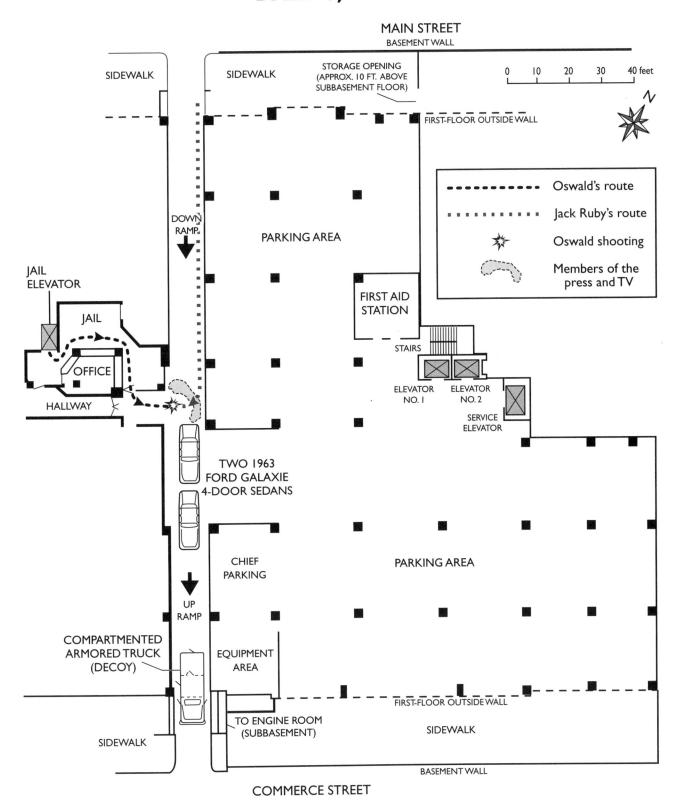

In a quote worthy of Yogi Berra, Graves, the man on Oswald's left, told researcher Larry A. Sneed that it was a good thing that Ruby had killed Oswald because, "Had Oswald been allowed to live, they would have made a martyr out of him." Graves, unlike Homicide Detective James R. Leavelle on Oswald's other side, was not handcuffed to Oswald. It was Graves who, during the scuffle following the shooting, took Ruby's gun away from him. After that Graves, who was a policeman until 1970 when he retired, climbed into the ambulance that had just pulled up and accompanied the victim to the hospital. Graves, who passed away in February 1995, also stood guard outside the operating room at Parkland Hospital while Oswald was being treated.

Leavelle—who had served on board the USS *Whitney* in the Pacific during World War II and who had joined the Dallas Police Department in 1950—estimates that it was about a second and a half between the time that Ruby first stepped out from behind reporters and policemen and when he pulled the trigger. Leavelle, who retired from the Dallas Police Department in 1974 and is still active speaking to those interested in the assassination, told researcher Larry A. Sneed, "Billy Combes, another detective who was standing behind us, picked up one arm and leg, and I got the other arm and leg on the right hand side, and we carried him back into the jail office and laid him down. I gave Billy my handcuff keys and told him to unlock the hand-

Dallas Police Homicide detective James R. Leavelle describes to a Dallas assassination symposium during the early 1990s what it was like to be handcuffed to Lee Harvey Oswald when he was shot. *(MacIntyre Symms)*

cuffs. We laid him down on the floor because we knew the officers weren't going to let anybody down that hallway, so we knew he was safe there. Meanwhile, the intern that was stationed was summoned and started artificial respiration." Artificial respiration can be fatal to a patient with extreme internal bleeding such as that being suffered at that moment by Oswald.

In charge of the investigation into Oswald's murder was the Forgery Bureau's captain Orville A. Jones, a member of the department since 1942. The inquiry focused on how Jack Ruby made it into the basement when security was supposed to be so stringent. Six-feet-four Dallas police patrol officer Roy Vaughn was the sole guard of the Main Street ramp at Dallas police headquarters on the morning Oswald was shot. Ruby, according to the Warren Commission, gained entrance to that building via the Main Street ramp, yet Vaughn denies seeing him pass. Others have testified that a man did walk by Vaughn unquestioned two or three minutes before the shooting and that the man could have been Ruby. Vaughn said on the 1988 British TV documentary *The Men Who Killed Kennedy,* "Ruby did not come down that ramp. I'll go to my grave saying that man did not come down that ramp."

According to the official scenario, Vaughn missed seeing Ruby's entrance into the building because he had stepped out onto the street to help a car driven by Dallas police lieutenant Rio Sam Pierce, which had just come up the ramp, turn into traffic on Main Street. Pierce, who retired from the force in January 1974, says he didn't see Ruby. Because of the aftermath to this situation, it isn't unusual that no one will admit seeing Ruby enter the building. Vaughn felt he was being made a scapegoat in the situation. He retired from the Dallas Police Department in 1980 and went on to become the chief of police in Midlothian, Texas—the same town in which assassination researcher Penn Jones, Jr. edited the local newspaper.

One of the eyewitnesses to Oswald's murder was Dallas policeman Donald Flusche who joined the department in 1954 and retired in 1986. His presence was unusual because he was not on duty. "I went there myself," he says. "I had no assignment. Like everybody else, I was curious." Flusche saw Pierce's car pull out onto Main Street and believes that it was not enough of a distraction to keep Vaughn from seeing Ruby's entrance. "I knew Jack Ruby on sight," Flusche said. "And he did not go down that sidewalk and into that ramp . . . I saw Vaughn barely step off the curb. He never really got into the street. He just stepped to the curb to check the traffic to see if they needed any help. They did not. The traffic was very light and they pulled on out. Vaughn then stepped back over into position there by the ramp."

Another eyewitness was KLIF reporter Gary DeLaune, who said, "I walked down the ramp and there was no secu-

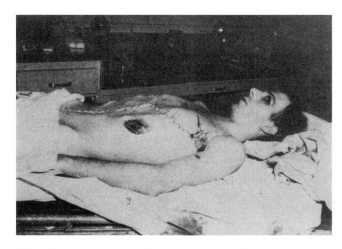

Photo from the autopsy of Lee Harvey Oswald. *(Author's Collection)*

rity. . . . There was a half-moon-shaped cordon of press and police officers, and I was looking almost across the room at Ike Pappas and Tom Pettit. I was directly across from them. And I was standing right next to Bob Jackson and Jack Beers."

Citing incidents of poor communication within the Dallas Police Department, the Warren Commission notes, "Several officers recalled that . . . [Dallas police lieutenant Woodrow] Wiggins was directed to clear the basement jail office, but Wiggins testified that he received no such assignment."

It has been argued by steadfast lone-nut theorists such as the late David Belin and Gerald Posner that Ruby's murder of Oswald *had* to be spontaneous. They argue that, because Ruby had arrived only seconds before Oswald was brought out into the basement, any delay in traffic or at the Western Union office would have caused him to miss his opportunity. Therefore, they say, a conspiracy in the death of Oswald is impossible. These arguments are ridiculous, of course, because they refuse to consider the possibility that Oswald was not going to be brought into the basement until Ruby was in place, whenever that occurred.

(See also APPENDIX B; RUBY, JACK.)

Oswald in Mexico

The question of whether or not the real Lee Harvey Oswald went to Mexico from September 26 to October 3, 1963 is one of ultimate importance. If an imposter went to Mexico City, then someone or some group was apparently attempting to set up Oswald as a patsy in the assassination, with the goal being to implicate either Cuba or the Soviet Union in the assassination.

A pair of British passengers on the bus to Mexico City with "Oswald" on September 26, 1963, were Dr. John Bryan and Mrs. Meryl McFarland. Dr. and Mrs. McFarland told the Warren Commission that they saw Oswald riding alone on their bus from Houston to Laredo, Texas, when they awoke on that bus at 6:00 A.M. on September 26, 1963.

Also aboard was Pamela Mumford, originally from Australia, with her friend Patricia Winston. Mumford said that her friend and Oswald were the only two English-speaking people on the bus, except for the McFarlands, and an older English gentleman in his 60s who sat with Oswald. Mumford told the Commission that Oswald chatted with her and her girlfriend throughout the trip, described Russia, showed them his passport, and recommended to them the Hotel Cuba in Mexico City. The old man who was reportedly sitting next to Oswald was named Albert Osborne. (See OSBORNE, ALBERT.) But Osborne denied sitting next to Oswald on the bus.

While in Mexico City, "Oswald" is reported to have visited both the Cuban and Soviet embassies where his brash manner and outrageous requests made him memorable to all he encountered. Oswald's first visit to the Soviet embassy was reported to be on September 27, 1963, at 12:30 P.M.

Oswald reportedly showed acceptable identification and announced he was seeking a visa to Cuba in transit to Russia—behavior which leaves the impression that Oswald was a bitter, desperate man—always living in a place where he felt he didn't belong, a man who felt his greatness and divine mission in life were universally and frustratingly unrecognized.

His requests were denied and he returned to the United States as he had come, by bus. (Although it should be noted that, according to assassination researcher James DiEugenio, Mexican border records for October 3, 1963, show Lee Harvey Oswald heading for New Orleans by car.)

The problem with this scenario is that there is much evidence that it is fake. Photographs, claimed by the CIA to be taken of Oswald in Mexico City, show an entirely different man.

Sound recordings, now reportedly destroyed, of "Oswald" speaking with a Soviet official are of a man with a rudimentary knowledge of Russian, when the real Oswald was fluent.

Witnesses in Mexico City who saw Oswald have described a different man from the one who was arrested in Dallas less than two months later. At the same time, we find persistently positive identifications of Oswald in the United States, when officially he is said to have been in Mexico.

If Oswald did not go to Mexico—and he denied doing so after his arrest—someone or some group tried to make it appear as if he did. If the story is fake, it adds immeasurable credence to Oswald's claim that he was patsy and casts considerable doubt on the remainder of the official story.

CIA cable sent from the Mexico City Station to the director of the Central Intelligence Agency on October 9, 1963:

TO: DIRECTOR
FROM: MEXICO CITY
ACTION: [DEDACTED]
INFO: [DEDACTED]
SECRET 0920432
DIR CITE MEXI [DEDACTED]
[DEDACTED]

1. ACC [DEDACTED] 1 OCT 63, AMERICAN MALE WHO SPOKE BROKEN RUSSIAN SAID HIS NAME LEE OSWALD (PHONETIC). STATED HE AT SOVEMB ON 28 SEPT WHEN SPOKE WITH CONSUL WHOM HE BELIEVED BE VALERIY VLADIMIROVICH KOSTIKOV. SUBJ ASKED SOV GUARD IVAN OBYEDKOV [DEDACTED] IF THERE ANYTHING NEW RE TELEGRAM TO WASHINGTON. OBYEDKOV UPON CHECKING SAID NOTHING RECEIVED YET, BUT REQUEST HAD BEEN SENT.

2. HAVE PHOTOS MALE APPEARS BE AMERICAN [DEDACTED] 1 OCT. APPARENT AGE 35, ATHLETIC BUILD, CIRCA 6 FEET, RECEDING HAIRLINE. BALDING TOP. WORE KHAKIS AND SPORT SHIRT.

The following day the CIA sent a cable to the FBI, the Office of Naval Intelligence, and the U.S. State Department advising them of the Oswald information. In that cable, the subject is referred to as Lee Henry Oswald, the same name mistake that Dan Rather made when first identifying the man arrested for the assassination. In fact, CBS reporters were referring to Oswald as Lee Henry right up until the time of his death. (Years later, in an attempt to determine if Lee Henry Oswald in Mexico City was the same man who was later arrested for the assassination, the House Select Committee on Assassinations asked the CIA if they had taken any photos of Oswald as he entered the Soviet embassy, as it was known by this time that the CIA had the Soviet embassy under photographic surveillance in 1963. The CIA told the committee that no such photos existed because the camera had broken that day. Three former CIA agents told the committee that they had seen a right-hand profile shot of Oswald as he was entering the Soviet embassy, but no such photo has seen the light of day.) That cable read:

SUBJECT: LEE HENRY OSWALD . . . 1. ON 1 OCTOBER 1963 A RELIABLE AND SENSITIVE SOURCE IN MEXICO REPORTED THAT AN AMERICAN MALE, WHO IDENTI-FIED HIMSELF AS LEE OSWALD, CONTACTED THE SOVIET EMBASSY IN MEXICO CITY INQUIRING WHETHER THE EMBASSY HAD RECEIVED ANY NEWS CONCERNING A TELEGRAM WHICH HAD BEEN SENT TO WASHINGTON. THE AMERICAN WAS DESCRIBED AS APPROXIMATELY 35 YEARS OLD, WITH AN ATHLETIC BUILD, ABOUT SIX FEET TALL, WITH A RECEDING HAIRLINE. . . 2. IT IS BELIEVED THAT OSWALD MAY BE IDENTICAL TO LEE HENRY OSWALD, BORN ON 18 OCTOBER 1939 IN NEW ORLEANS, LOUISIANA, A FORMER U.S. MARINE WHO DEFECTED TO THE SOVIET UNION IN OCTOBER 1959 AND LATER MADE ARRANGEMENTS THROUGH THE UNITED STATES EMBASSY IN MOSCOW TO RETURN TO THE UNITED STATES WITH HIS RUSSIAN-BORN WIFE, MARINA NIKOLAEVNA PUSAKOVA, AND THEIR CHILD.

On October 10, 1963, the director of Central Intelligence cabled his Mexico City Station:

LEE OSWALD WHO CONTACTED SOVEMB 1 OCT PROBABLY IDENTICAL LEE HENRY OSWALD (201-289248) BORN 18 OCT 1939, NEW ORLEANS, LOUISIANA, FORMER RADAR OPERATOR IN UNITED STATES MARINES WHO DEFECTED TO USSR IN OCT 1959. OSWALD IS FIVE FEET TEN INCHES, ONE HUNDRED SIXTY FIVE POUNDS, LIGHT BROWN WAVY HAIR, BLUE EYES.

Testifying in tandem before the Warren Commission, Director of Central Intelligence John A. McCone and Deputy Director of Plans Richard Helms originally called the subject "an alleged trip that Oswald made to Mexico City." Later, when asked if the CIA had investigated the Mexico trip, the pair replied, "We were aware that Oswald did make a trip to Mexico City and it was our judgment that he was there in the interest of ensuring transit privileges and that he made contact with the Cuban Embassy while he was there. We do not know the precise results of his efforts, but we assume, because he returned to the United States, he was unsuccessful. We have examined to every extent we can, and using all resources available to us, every aspect of his activity, and we could not verify that he was there for any purpose or that his trip to Mexico was in any way related to his later action in assassinating President Kennedy."

Edwin Juan Lopez was House Select Committee on Assassinations attorney who investigated Oswald's alleged trip to Mexico in September 1963 and concluded that an imposter had made the visits to the Soviet and Cuban embassies in Mexico City, posing as Oswald. He based this conclusion on CIA photos of "Oswald" in Mexico taken at three different sites, which show a man who is obviously not Oswald. Lopez's conclusion is supported by the fact that the Dallas FBI reportedly listened to tapes the CIA made of the alleged Oswald in Mexico City and rejected them as not being of Oswald's voice.

In 1989, Lopez wrote to Anthony Summers saying, "It was very obvious, from dealing with people at the CIA for approximately ten years, that the CIA was covering something up . . . I came away feeling that we could not trust our government, that what we had been told all along was a sham."

Eusebio Azcue was the Cuban consul in Mexico City in September 1963, at the time Oswald supposedly visited there. When Oswald (or an Oswald impersonator, hereafter referred to as Oswald) found out from consulate-employee Silvia Duran that it would take a week for him to get a visa to travel to Cuba, Oswald had a temper tantrum until Azcue, the consul himself, was forced to step in. According to Anthony Summers, Azcue "laboriously repeated the formalities, but still the stranger fumed. Now the consul lost patience too, finally telling the American that 'a person of his type was harming the Cuban revolution more than helping it.' That was still not the end of the saga. There was yet another visit and another row with the consul. Azcue and a colleague were suspicious of a card Oswald producing showing membership in the American Communist Party. It looked strangely new and unused. The officials were justifiably doubtful; Oswald had never joined the Party. According to Azcue, the final straw was when [Oswald] mocked him and his secretary Silvia Duran as 'mere bureaucrats.' At this the consul ordered him out of the building." Azcue was shown a photograph of Oswald and was asked if this were the man who visited him in September 1963. He said, "This gentleman . . . is not the person who went to the consulate . . . the man . . . was . . . over 30 years of age and very, very thin faced . . . He was . . dark blond . . . He had a hard face. He had very straight eyebrows, cold, hard, and straight eyes. His cheeks were thin. His nose was very straight and pointed." Azcue was not questioned by the Warren Commission. He did, however, testify before the House Select Committee. The committee showed Azcue photographs of Oswald and he said this was not the man at the consulate.

Silvia Tirado de Duran was the secretary at the Mexico City Cuban consulate when Oswald supposedly visited there in September 1963. She said the Oswald she saw was "35 years old." Duran was arrested twice in Mexico after the assassination, apparently on CIA orders, and told not to say anything more about "Oswald." The first order to arrest Duran (November 23, 1963) read, in part, "With full regard for Mexican interests, request you ensure that [Duran's] arrest is kept absolutely secret, that no information from her is published or leaked, that all such info is cabled to us." Duran was not released until she identified Oswald as the man she had seen. In a 1978 interview with

Anthony Summers, Senora Duran said the man she saw was only five feet three inches tall.

A November 23, 1963, cable, after discussing Oswald's reported visit to Mexico City, states:

SPECIAL AGENTS OF THIS BUREAU, WHO HAVE CONVERSED WITH OSWALD IN DALLAS, TEXAS, HAVE OBSERVED PHOTOGRAPHS OF THE INDIVIDUAL REFERRED TO ABOVE AND HAVE LISTENED TO A RECORDING OF HIS VOICE. THESE SPECIAL AGENTS ARE OF THE OPINION THAT THE ABOVE-REFERRED-TO INDIVIDUAL WAS NOT LEE HARVEY OSWALD.

According to transcribed tape of FBI director J. Edgar Hoover telephonically briefing the new president, Lyndon Baines Johnson, and, discussing the stories of Oswald in Mexico City, Hoover said, "We have up here the tape and the photograph of the man who was at the Soviet Embassy, using Oswald's name. The picture and the tape do not correspond to this man's voice, nor to his appearance. In other words, it appears that there is a second person who was at the Soviet Embassy down there."

On November 27, 1963, a CIA cable was sent to "Curtis"—perhaps Willard Curtis, a reported code name of [title] Winston Scott, from "Knight," a pseudonym frequently used by E. Howard Hunt, acting head of the Mexico City CIA station at the time of Oswald's reported visit there during the autumn of 1963. The cable read:

RE: MEXI-7101.

1. THIS INSTRUCTION HAS BEEN COORDINATED WITH ODACID AND ODENVY.
2. MEXICAN AUTHORITIES SHOULD INTERROGATE SILVIA DURAN TO EXTENT NECESSARY CLARIFY OUTSTANDING POINTS WHICH BEEN RAISED YOUR CABLED LAST 48 HOURS. YOU MAY PROVIDE QUESTIONS TO MEXICAN INTERROGATORS BUT WE DO NOT REPEAT NOT WANT ANY AMERICANS TO CONFRONT SILVIA DURAN OR BE IN CONTACT WITH HER.

A CIA translation of a report dated November 29, 1963, from the Mexican secret police reads:

SHE [Duran] REMEMBERED HIS NAME BECAUSE OF HIS UNUSUAL CHARACTERISTICS AND THE CIRCUMSTANCES OF HIS VISIT, I.E., HE WAS MARRIED TO A RUSSIAN AND SAID HE BELONGED TO THE 'FAIR PLAY FOR CUBA'; THAT SHE CHECKED HIS DATE IN THE CONSULATE'S ARCHIVES AND SHE WAS THEN SURE THAT IT WAS THE SAME PERSON. THAT HE IS BLOND, SHORT, POORLY DRESSED, THAT HIS FACE GETS RED WHEN HE TALKS, THAT HE WAS DENIED A VISA

BECAUSE THE CONSULATE TOLD HIM THAT IN ORDER TO OBTAIN ONE HE WOULD FIRST NEED A VISA FROM THE RUSSIAN CONSULATE AND THIS PROCEDURE WOULD TAKE ABOUT FOUR MONTHS AND URGED OSWALD TO LEAVE MEXICO. OSWALD BECAME ANGRY AND FOR THIS REASON SHE HAD TO CALL THE CONSUL WITH WHOM HE HAD AN ARGUMENT.

Blond?

A CIA document dated May 26, 1967, states that Silvia Duran had been recommended to the Cuban embassy by Teresa Proenza, by then in a Cuban jail for committing espionage on behalf of the CIA.

When arrested Oswald said that he had only been to Mexico once, to Tijuana when he was in the U.S. Marine Corps.

Suspicions that the man claiming to be Oswald in Mexico City was not really Oswald are also supported by the statements of pro-Castro student activist Oscar Contreras given to House Select Committee investigators. Contreras was a student at the time of the assassination at Mexico's National Autonomous University, and had friends who worked at the Cuban consulate in Mexico City. Contreras said that, one evening during September 1963, he and three friends were approached by a fellow claiming to be Lee Harvey Oswald. Oswald told them about his problems trying to get a visa to Cuba and maybe he and his friends could use their contacts inside the consulate to help him. He did not help the man and after the assassination, when he saw the photographs of Lee Harvey Oswald following his arrest in Dallas, Contreras came to the conclusion that the man who had approached him and his friends was not the real Oswald. Contreras described the man he had spoken to as older than 30, short, with *blond* hair. Contreras later became the editor-in-chief of the Mexican newspaper *El Mundo*.

In addition to visiting the Russian and Cuban consulates and the campus of the National Autonomous University of Mexico he was reportedly also seen, with two companions, attending a "twist party" at the home of Ruben Duran, the brother-in-law of consul secretary Silvia Duran.

According to the January 1964 issue of *Minority of One* magazine, William M. Kline, the chief of the United States Customs Bureau investigative services in Laredo, Texas, said on November 25, 1963, that Oswald's movements in and out of the United States were being watched at the request of a "Federal agency in Washington." Eugene Pugh, the U.S. agent in charge of the customs office on the U.S. side of the bridge into Mexico at Laredo said that Oswald had been checked by U.S. immigration officials on entering and leaving Mexico—which he admitted was not the usual procedure—because "U.S. immigration had a folder on Oswald."

(See also CENTRAL INTELLIGENCE AGENCY; HUNT, E. HOWARD; KOMITET GOSUDARSTVENNOY BEZOPASNOSTI; PHILLIPS, DAVID ATLEE; OSWALD, LEE HARVEY; SAUL; SCOTT, WINSTON MACKINLAY.)

Oswald in the Marines

Here is the official chronology of Lee Harvey Oswald's military service: Oswald dropped out of the tenth grade at Arlington Heights High School on September 28, 1956. He turned 17 on October 18 and enlisted in the U.S. Marines on October 24. Two days later he reported for duty in San Diego, California. There, he took aptitude tests, scoring above average in verbal, below average in math. He struggled on the firing range with his M-1 rifle.

Oswald reported to Camp Pendleton, California, on January 18, 1957. On March 18, 1957, Oswald reported to the Naval Air Technical Training Center in Jacksonville, Florida, where he was taught "radar theory" and "map reading."

On May 1 he was promoted to Private First Class. Two days later he reported to Keesler Air Force Base in Biloxi, Mississippi, where he took the aircraft control and warning operator course. It was here that he first picked up the nickname "Ozzie Rabbit."

On June 25, 1957, Oswald was given the military occupational specialty of aviation electronics operator. On July 9 he reported to the Marine Air Station in El Toro, California, as a replacement trainee.

On August 22, 1957, Oswald departed from San Diego, California, to Yokosuka, Japan, aboard the USS *Bexar.* He arrived in Yokosuka on September 12 and was assigned to Marine Air Control Squadron 1 (MACS-1)—a squadron of less than 100 men—in Atsugi, Japan.

On October 27, 1957, according to the official story, Oswald accidentally shot himself in the "left elbow" when he dropped a .22 caliber pistol while opening his locker. He was in a hospital, it is said, in Yokosuka until November 15.

On November 20, MACS-1 embarked for the Philippines for maneuvers. They left the Philippines to return to Atsugi on March 7, 1958. They arrived in Japan on March 18.

On April 11, 1958 Oswald was court-martialed for the gunshot incident—possession of an unauthorized weapon—and on April 29 he was sentenced to 20 days confinement with hard labor. That sentence was suspended, but he was stripped of rank and fined.

On June 20, Oswald again got in trouble, this time when he poured a drink over the head of a sergeant while drunk in the Bluebird Café in Yamato. A week later he was court-martialed for a second time, sentenced to 28 days confinement with hard labor, and forced to serve out his first sentence. He was confined until August 13.

From September 14 to October 5, 1958, MACS-1 sailed to Taiwan and then back to Atsugi. On October 6 he was transferred out of MACS-1. He departed Japan from Yokosuka on November 2 and arrived in San Francisco, California, on November 15. Upon his arrival he took one month's leave.

On December 22, 1958, he was assigned to MACS-9 in El Toro, California. On February 25 he was tested on his ability to speak Russian. Officially, he did very poorly on the test.

On March 9 he was promoted back to Private First Class. Ten days later he applied to Albert Schweitzer College in Churwalden, Switzerland, for the spring 1960 term. On August 17, 1959, he applied for a hardship discharge because his mother had, so the story goes, injured herself at work.

On September 4 he applied for a passport. Three days later he was released from active duty. On September 18, 1959, he left the United States bound for the Soviet Union.

A number of Lee Harvey Oswald's U.S. Marine Corps acquaintances have made statements, mostly to representatives of the Warren Commission, regarding their knowledge and opinion of Oswald at that time in his life.

Marine acquaintance Allen R. Felde said that Oswald was unpopular while stationed at Camp Pendleton. According to Felde, Oswald would go on bus trips with his fellow Marines to Tijuana, Mexico, and Los Angeles, California, but that he would go off by himself once he got there.

John E. Donovan was the first lieutenant in charge of Oswald's radar crew at El Toro Marine Base in California from November 1958 to September 1959. Prior to joining the marines, Donovan earned a B.S. degree in foreign service at Georgetown University, graduating in 1956. Donovan told the Warren Commission that Oswald read a Russian-language newspaper while in the marines, that he believed it to be a communist paper and that Oswald had a subscription to it. He testified: "I don't recall him being particularly excitable . . . He did not share a common interest with [his peers]. For better or for worse, the average young American male in that age is interested in saving enough money to go buy another beer and get another date. This I don't believe would characterize him at all. He read a great deal . . . the men always told me that he subscribed to a Russian newspaper . . . I never saw the newspaper . . . he did not apparently take this stuff as gospel . . . he thought [the Communist newspapers] presented a very different and perhaps equally just side of the international affairs in comparison with the United States newspaper . . . I think he enjoyed international affairs in all respects. He enjoyed studying them . . . he constantly brought up the idea that our Government must be run by many incompetent people . . . His bond with me was that I was a recent graduate of the Foreign Service School . . . He took great pride in talking to a passing officer . . . and in a most interested manner, ask him what he thought of a given [international] situation, listen to the officer's explanation and say, 'Thank you, very much.' As soon as we were alone again, he would say, 'Do you agree with that? . . . Now if men like that are leading us, there is something wrong— when I obviously have more knowledge than that man.' . . . His grave misunderstanding . . . is that these men were . . . supposed to be schooled in the field of warfare . . . not as international political analysts. And in some respect he was probably better informed than most people in the Marine Corps, namely, on international affairs. But I never heard him in any way, shape or form confess that he was a Communist, or that he thought of being a Communist. [Sure, he had sympathy for Castro] but on the other hand so did *Time* magazine . . . Harvard accepted him [Castro] *de facto,* at face value—which is one of our better schools. At any rate what he said about Castro was not an unpopular belief at that time . . . it was a godsend that somebody had overthrown Batista . . . [Oswald] was a wiseguy in the sense that he could be disrespectful in a way that you could accept. He would in a very respectful manner argue with someone . . . I don't think he ever asked information of anyone on foreign affairs, including me, whose opinion he particularly respected. He had his mind made up and was willing to discuss that point of view with anyone . . . I recall that he had a hardship discharge. We offered to get him a flight—that is hop from El Toro to someplace in Texas, his home. He refused. We considered that normal in that if you take a hop you sacrifice your transportation pay. We offered to take him to the bus or train station, he refused. But that is not particularly unusual either." Later in his testimony, Donovan was asked if he recalled a man named Thornley. Thornley was another marine who testified about Oswald to the Warren Commission, and is particularly noteworthy because he wrote a book based on Lee Harvey Oswald *before* the assassination. Donovan replied, "I don't recall the name at all." (See also THORNLEY, KERRY WENDELL.) Donovan told assassination researcher Edward Jay Epstein that he clearly remembered discussing the U-2's radar blips with Oswald—although the conversation took place at the Cubi Point base in the Philippines instead of in Japan. Although, officially, Oswald had a "confidential" clearance, Donovan says that it must have been higher than that. "He must have had 'Secret' clearance to work in the radar center, because that was the minimum requirement for all of us," Donovan said.

A marine friend of Lee Harvey Oswald, Nelson Delgado bunked "next door" to Oswald for almost a year (November 1958 to September 1959) at the El Toro Marine Base in California. Delgado told the Warren Commission that Oswald's proficiency with a rifle was minimal.

"It was a pretty big joke," Delgado said, "because he got a lot of 'Maggie's drawers,' you know, a lot of misses, but he didn't give a darn . . . [Oswald] wasn't as enthusiastic as the rest of us. We all loved—liked, you know—going to the range . . . He was mostly a thinker, a reader."

According to Delgado, Oswald once told him that the best way to escape U.S. law enforcement, should that become necessary, was to flee to Russia, via Mexico and Cuba.

Delgado testified: "We got to know each other quite well . . before Christmas, before I took my leave [1958] . . . He liked Spanish and he talked to me . . . in Spanish . . . I was kind of a loner myself . . . at the time he was commenting on the fight Castro was having at Sierra Madres . . . When I went on leave . . . coincided with the first of January [1959], when Castro took over. So when I got back, he was the first to see me . . . [He said,] 'Well, you took a leave and went there and helped them, and they all took over.' It was a big joke . . . He had trouble in one of the huts and he got transferred to mine . . . [The] way I understand it . . . came time for a cleanup . . . he didn't want to participate . . . griping all the time . . . the sergeant in charge of that hut asked to have him put out . . . they put him into my hut. He was a complete believer that our way of government was not quite right . . . he was for, not the Communist way of life, the Castro way . . . the way he was going to lead his people . . . he never said any subversive things or tried to take any classified information . . . he kept his [rifle] mediocre. He always got gigged (sic) for his rifle . . . very seldom did he pass an inspection without getting gigged for one thing or another . . . for him there was always another way of doing things, an easier way for him to get something done . . . I would say, 'Oz, how about taking care of the bathroom today?' Fine, he would do it. But . . . somebody from the outside saying, 'All right, Oswald, I want you to take and police up that area'—'Why? Why do I have to do it? Why are you always telling me to do it?' Well, it was an order, he had to do it, but he didn't understand it like that . . . He could speak a common Spanish like "How are you? I am doing fine . . which way is this?" . . . as far as getting involved in political argument . . . he couldn't hold his own . . . he bought himself a dictionary . . . After a while he got to talk to me . . . in Spanish. Then he kept asking me [how] he could go about helping the Castro Government. I didn't know what to tell him . . . get in touch with the Cuban Embassy . . . After a while he told me he was in contact with them . . . he didn't believe in God. He was a devout atheist. That's the only thing he and I didn't discuss because he knew I was religious."

Delgado testified that there had been an evening when Oswald was allowed to stand down from guard duty so he could meet for two hours with a stranger in an overcoat who appeared "Cuban."

Of his unit, including Oswald, Delgado said, "We all had access to classified information. I believe it was classified 'secret.'"

After the Warren Commission hearings, Delgado took his family to England, because he was fearful that "the conspirators might think I know more than I do."

Marine acquaintance Gator Daniels met Oswald aboard the USS *Bexar* on the way to Japan. Daniels told Edward Jay Epstein, "He was simple folk, just like I was . . . we were a bunch of kids—never been away from home before—but Oswald came right out and admitted that he had never known a woman . . . It was real unusual that a fellow would admit that . . . but he never was ashamed to admit it . . . He was just a good egg."

Marine acquaintance Richard Dennis Call lived in the ensign hut next to, and was on the same radar crew as, Oswald with MACS-9 from December 1958 to December 1959. Call told the Warren Commission: "I talked with Oswald each day . . . we were stationed together . . . [By] usual standards I was just an acquaintance. I was probably one of his best friends . . . I played chess with him about once a week . . . [He] was studying Russian . . . [We] kidded him about being a Russian spy; Oswald seemed to enjoy this sort of remark . . . I had a phonograph record of Russian classical pieces entitled 'Russian Fireworks.' When I would play this record Oswald would come over to me and say, 'You called?' I had a chess set which contained red and white chessmen; Oswald always chose the red chessmen . . . he preferred the 'Red Army.' . . . It was my opinion that the Staff Non-Commissioned Officers did not think Oswald was capable . . . a result of the fact that Oswald did not try to hide his lack of enthusiasm . . . it is difficult to tell how intelligent Oswald was, because of his refusal to communicate. It was clear, however, that Oswald wanted to be thought of as intelligent . . . Oswald's reactions to everything were subdued and stoic . . . I do not recall Oswald's making serious remarks with regard to the Soviet Union or Cuba."

Officially, Oswald purchased his rifle by mail order under the pseudonym Alec Hidell. The Warren Commission affirmed that Oswald made the name up, that it was just a variation of "Fidel." This may not be the case. John Heindel and Oswald were stationed together in Atsugi, Japan. Heindel's nickname was "Hidell." Heindel was living in New Orleans in 1963, as did Oswald. Heindel testified to the Warren Commission that Oswald was "often in trouble for failure to adhere to the rules and regulations and gave the impression of disliking any kind of authority . . . I was often referred to as 'Hidell'—pronounced so as to rhyme with Rydell rather than Fidel . . . indeed he may himself have called me Hidell . . . Although I generally regarded Oswald as an intelligent person, I did not observe him to be particularly interested in politics or international affairs . . . I do not recall Oswald's being called by any nick-names. Although our Air Marine Group was sent to Formosa . . . I am unable to remember Oswald's being there" Neither the Warren Commission nor the House Select Committee on Assassinations investigated the possibility that there might have been a relationship between Oswald and Heindel after they left the marines.

Paul Edward Murphy was present on the day that Oswald supposedly shot himself with an unauthorized weapon. He told the Warren Commission: "I was stationed at Atsugi, Japan, and thereafter at Santa Ana, California with . . . Oswald . . . Oswald was self-contained and withdrawn . . . I am of the opinion that he was generally in sympathy with Castro . . . One night in the barracks in Japan, I heard a shot in the adjoining cubicle. I rushed to the cubicle to find Oswald sitting on a foot locker looking at a wound in his arm. When I asked what happened, Oswald very unemotionally replied, 'I believe I shot myself.' Oswald was at that time in possession of a small caliber pistol which he was not authorized to possess . . . While at Santa Ana, Oswald had a subscription to a newspaper printed in English which I believe was titled either 'The Worker' or 'The Socialist Worker.' . . . I do not recall Oswald receiving other literature of a Socialist nature. I remember that Oswald could speak a little Russian, even when he was overseas . . . [He was] proficient at his assigned job, but was below average in . . . discipline and military courtesy. He was, however, personally quite neat . . . His temperament was such that he would push companions to the verge of fighting him, but seldom, if ever, actually took the step of engaging in a fight . . . While overseas, however, Oswald had an active social life . . . Oswald seldom left his post in Santa Ana."

Peter Francis Connor was stationed in Atsugi with Oswald. He told the Warren Commission: "When the fellows were heading out for a night on the town, Oswald would either remain behind or leave before they did. Nobody knew what he did . . . He often responded to the orders of his superiors with insolent remarks . . . I was of the opinion that Oswald was intelligent . . . I never heard Oswald make any anti-American or pro-Communist statements. He claimed to be named after Robert E. Lee, whom he characterized as the greatest man in history." Regarding the Atsugi shooting incident, Connor said that, in his opinion, the bullet missed Oswald altogether and struck the ceiling. The incident is believed by some to have been staged to covertly separate Oswald from the marines who knew him.

Marine Thomas Bagshaw was also present and, like Connor, believes Oswald faked shooting himself and that the bullet actually struck the ceiling.

Marine acquaintance David Bucknell told Mark Lane that Oswald had told him, while stationed in Atsugi, that

he had been alone in a bar when he was approached by a woman who was curious about the details of his "top secret" work. Oswald reported the incident to his superior officer, who arranged for Oswald to meet a civilian. The civilian told Oswald that the woman was a known KGB agent. The man gave Oswald money and told him he could do his country a great service by feeding the woman false information regarding the U-2 spy plane flown out of Atsugi. During Oswald's time in Japan he received medical attention for a venereal disease, contracted "in the line of duty." This would explain why.

Years later, CIA finance officer James A. Wilcott told the House Select Committee on Assassinations that Oswald had been recruited from the Marine Corps while stationed in Atsugi, Japan by the CIA "with the express purpose of a double-agent assignment in the USSR." Wilcott testified that he had personally handled the funding for Oswald's assignment. According to Jim Garrison, "Predictably, a chorus line of other agency witnesses, whose names Wilcott had mentioned, denied all knowledge of such a project. The committee did not pursue the lead."

Mack Osborne told the Warren Commission that Oswald "spent a great deal of his free time reading papers printed in Russian . . . with the aid of a Russian-English dictionary . . . [He] did not go out in the evening . . . he was saving his money, making some statement to the effect that one day he would do something that would make him famous, it was my belief—although he said nothing to this effect—that he had his trip to Russia in mind . . . [F]ellow Marines sometimes accused him of being a Russian spy. In my opinion, he took such accusations in fun."

David Christie Murray, Jr., was stationed with Oswald at Santa Ana, California. Murray told the Warren Commission: "Oswald did not associate with his fellow Marines . . . I personally stayed away from Oswald because I heard a rumor to the effect that he was a homosexual . . . [H]e was never satisfied with any event or situation. He was quietly sarcastic . . . was not a show-off; he did not want to be the center of attention. I regarded Oswald as quite intelligent . . . [and] was of the opinion that he had received a college education . . . [He] was studying Russian. He often made remarks in Russian; the less intelligent members of the unit admired him for this . . . He played chess a good deal."

Allen D. Graf was Oswald's platoon sergeant while stationed in Santa Ana. Graf told the Warren Commission, "Oswald seemed to me to resent all military authority. He also seemed narrow-minded, refused to listen to the views of others . . . with regard to his job . . . Oswald learned quickly . . . and kept his temper—if, indeed he had a temper—in check . . . Oswald never gave to me any indication of favoring Communism or opposing capitalism."

Daniel Patrick Powers told the Warren Commission that Oswald was "an individual you could brainwash, and quite easy . . . [but] I think once he believed in something . . . he stood in his beliefs . . . [he was] somewhat the frail, little puppy in the litter . . . [Oswald] would take the easy way out to avoid a conflict . . . a lot of his mannerisms were closely related to other homosexuals I had seen."

Marine acquaintance James Anthony Botelho told the Warren Commission that he "shared a room with Oswald [in Santa Ana] for about two months before his discharge. He was unusual in that he generally would not speak unless spoken to, and his answers were always brief. He seldom associated with others . . . It was common knowledge that Oswald had taught himself to read Russian . . . [Some] kidded him by calling him 'Oswaldkovich' . . . My impression is that, although he believed in pure Marxist theory, he did not believe in the way Communism was practiced by the Russians . . . My impression was that Oswald was quite intelligent . . . [His] clearance was taken away from him . . . I believe he was made company clerk . . . Before Oswald requested his hardship discharge, the Sergeant Major was planning to take steps to 'straighten Oswald out.' . . . I remember Oswald's having a date with a girl who spoke Russian. I believe Oswald liked the girl a great deal, but he was for some reason unable to get in touch with her thereafter."

Henry J. Roussel Jr. was stationed for "three or four months" with Oswald in MACS-9. Roussel told the Warren Commission, "I recall no serious political remarks on the part of Oswald. On occasion, however, Oswald when addressing other Marines, would refer to them as 'Comrade.' It seemed to me . . . that Oswald used this term in fun . . . [He] complained about the orders he was given, but no more than did the average Marine . . . [I thought he was] quite intelligent . . . I do not recall Oswald's having any dates other than the one I arranged for him with my aunt [Rosaleen Quinn]."

(See also QUINN, ROSALEEN.)

Oswald Look-Alikes

There were many reports of Oswald's whereabouts during the weeks leading up to the assassination alleging that the accused assassin had been in more than one place at the same time. Here is information regarding men involved in the assassination who may have had a physical resemblance to Lee Harvey Oswald.

John Thomas Masen in this case's most compelling Oswald look-alike. Masen was a Dallas gun shop owner. Wally Weston, Ruby's former Carousel Club emcee, told a 1976 national TV audience that, in September or October 1963, Oswald, or a man who looked like Oswald, came into the Carousel. Weston and Oswald got into a verbal altercation, during which "Oswald" called Weston a communist and Weston hit "Oswald." At that point Ruby inter-

jected and bounced "Oswald" from the premises, saying, "I told you never to come in here again." According to George Evica, Masen is the Oswald look-alike who was ejected from the Carousel that night. Masen furnished weapons to D.R.E., Alpha 66, and the SNFE (Segundo Frente del Escambray) through Manuel Rodríguez Orcarberro, according to a January 17, 1964, Secret Service document. According to Captain George Nonte (see PERRIN, ROBERT AND NANCY), Masen stood five feet five and weighed 130 pounds with a large nose, sandy-colored hair, and a receding hairline. His fingerprint chart from his November 20, 1963, arrest shows his height as five feet nine and a half inches and his weight as 156 pounds. Regarding Masen's alleged resemblance to Lee Harvey Oswald, Treasury agent Frank Ellsworth said, "Exactly the same facial features, hair—they could've passed for each other." According to an FBI document dated April 1, 1964, Masen told the FBI that he had spent much of the summer of 1963 in Mexico on vacation. In a 1976 interview with researcher Dick Russell, Masen said, "I've got some friends who are top marksmen who say it [the assassination] couldn't have happened as they said. I really don't believe this was the brainstorm of a deranged man. I think it was the sophisticated work of someone with a great deal of money who could buy a life." It is perhaps significant that no photographs of Masen have been found anywhere. Masen still lives in Dallas where he runs a gun part manufacturing company.

Ellsworth—who was present, with another Treasury agent, on the sixth floor of the Texas School Book Depository building at the time the rifle was found and was allegedly involved in Oswald's interrogation—told Village Voice writer Dick Russell in 1976 that he had knowledge of an "Oswald double" who had associated with right-wing Dallas Minutemen in 1963. Ellsworth told Russell the Oswald double was still alive and resided in Dallas. Ellsworth said this man (whom he did not name) was the man mistaken for Oswald repeatedly in and around Dallas during the weeks and months before the assassination. Ellsworth said this "twin" was a frequent traveler to Mexico, had associations with the family of oil billionaire H. L. Hunt, and had been convicted of a Federal arms violation. (According to a Warren Commission memo, the member of the Minutemen whom Ellsworth had been investigating was a "local gun shop owner.") Ellsworth said that the "twin" associated with anti-Castro Cuban exiles was associated with the anti-Castro group known as Alpha 66, who had admitted to supplying arms to a terrorist Cuban organization. Among the "twin's" other associates was General Edwin Walker. Ellsworth told Russell that he had gone undercover, posing as a criminal involved in Mexican smuggling, to track the Oswald twin—and had eventually gotten the twin convicted on a gun violation.

Masen told Ellsworth that he had once sold guns to Alpha 66 bigwig Manuel Rodríguez Orcarberro, and that Alpha 66 had developed a large cache of arms in Dallas. According to former CIA agent Robert D. Morrow, this group had their Dallas headquarters in the home of Jorge Salazar at 3126 Harlendale Avenue. (See also 3126 HARLENDALE.)

Curtis LaVerne Crafard worked for Jack Ruby at the Carousel Club. He was a theoretic Oswald look-alike (according to the Warren Commission), who lived at the Carousel while under Ruby's employ from mid-October until November 23, 1963. Crafard fled Dallas following the assassination. Before coming to Dallas, Crafard worked as a carnival barker with small-time freak-show acts like "the two-headed baby" and "the snake girl." According to *Time* magazine (January 13, 1992), Crafard "bummed around looking for roustabout jobs, [and] met his first wife at a Salvation Army mission. When she left him in the summer of 1963, he hitchhiked all the way from the West Coast to Dallas looking for her. He picked up some work at the Texas State Fair in a carnival sideshow called 'How Hollywood Makes Movies,' which featured some of Jack Ruby's strippers. Made some connections and soon found himself living in the back room at the Carousel Club." At 5:00 A.M., November 23, Crafard met with Ruby and his roommate George Senator in a Dallas garage. The three remained there for about an hour. Later that morning Crafard left Dallas and hitchhiked to Michigan with only seven dollars on him. Ruby returned to the garage later that morning where he was overheard on the phone discussing security for Oswald's transfer.

The Warren Commission said Crafard's sudden departure from Dallas following the assassination was not indicative of Ruby's involvement in a conspiracy. The *Warren Report* states: "[Crafard] made no attempt to communicate with law enforcement officials after Oswald's death; and a relative in Michigan recalled that Crafard spoke very little of his association with Ruby. When finally located by the FBI six days later, he stated that he left Ruby's employ because he did not wish to be subjected to further verbal abuse by Ruby and that he went north to see his sister, from whom he had not heard in some time . . . Although Crafard's preemptory decision to leave Dallas might be unusual for most persons, such behavior does not appear to have been uncommon for him."

While many researchers were searching for men who might have impersonated Oswald during the weeks preceding the assassination, the Warren Commission used Crafard's supposed resemblance to Oswald to diffuse rumors of conspiracy: "The testimony of a few witnesses who claim to have seen Ruby with a person who they feel may have been Oswald warrants further comment . . . Ruth Paine testified that Crafard's photograph bears a strong resemblance to Oswald." Photos of Crafard in the 26 volumes of published commission hearings and exhibits, however, *show no resemblance*. After the assassination, again according to *Time*, "the FBI followed Crafard to Michigan and questioned him repeatedly; he had to go back to Dallas for Ruby's trial; he never found the wife he'd lost. And then in the early 1980s, just when his life seemed to have settled down, renewed interest in the JFK case made his name the object of speculation again: it appeared in a book on the organized crime connections to Ruby and the assassination. His new wife read the book and began to get a little paranoid. She wondered about the serious car accident they had had: Was it really an accident? Eventually, things began to go awry: his marriage broke up, he lost his job. When last contacted, Crafard—his name now spelled Craford—was working 'as a night security guard in a mill, boarding with some people,' without a traceable phone number of his own."

According to David Scheim, "There is no possibility that Crafard could have been mistaken for Oswald since Crafard had 'no front teeth,' was 'creepy,' looked 'like a bum,' and had 'sandy hair,' as witnesses described him, whereas Oswald was good looking, had all of his front teeth, and had brown hair."

Billy Lovelady was an assassination witness and colleague of Oswald's who bore a strong physical resemblance to the alleged assassin. An Associated Press photo taken by James W. Altgens at the moment JFK was first shot shows a man standing in the doorway of the Texas School Book Depository building who looks remarkably like Oswald. (See also ALTGENS.) The Warren Commission said this couldn't have been Oswald because Oswald was on the sixth floor, and that this was actually Billy Lovelady. The photo seems to show the man wearing Oswald's clothes as well. The man in the picture is wearing a light T-shirt with a dark heavy-textured shirt over it, unbuttoned half way to the waist. This is what Oswald was wearing at the time of his arrest. Lovelady said that he was wearing "a red and white vertical striped shirt" that day. Also, witnesses near the doorway said that Lovelady was sitting at the time of the shooting. He could have stood up at the last second, of course. And no one stepped forward to say they saw Oswald in the doorway. Photos of Lovelady proved hard to obtain and, when one was finally made available, researchers learned that Lovelady did strongly resemble the accused assassin. Lovelady died in January 1979 from complications following a heart attack during the House Select Committee on Assassinations hearings.

Lovelady told the Warren Commission: "The shots came from right there around that concrete little deal on that knoll." He said the last time he saw Oswald was at 11:45 A.M. on the day of the assassination. As Lovelady rode down from the sixth floor on the elevator with coworker and assassination witness Bonnie Ray Williams, they heard Oswald call down for them to send the elevator back up when they were done with it. (See also WILLIAMS, BONNIE RAY.)

William Seymour—from Phoenix, Arizona—was thought by the Warren Commission to be one of the three men who visited Cuban exile Silvia Odio (one of whom was identified as Leon Oswald) on either September 25 or 26, 1963 when, officially, Oswald was on his way by bus to Mexico City. (See also ODIO INCIDENT, THE.) The *Warren Report* says: "On September 16, 1964, the FBI located Loran Eugene Hall in Johnsandale, Calif. Hall had been identified as a participant in numerous anti-Castro activities. He told the FBI that in September of 1963 he was in Dallas, soliciting aid in connection with anti-Castro activities. He said he had visited Mrs. Odio. He was accompanied by Lawrence Howard, a Mexican-American from East Los Angeles and one William Seymour from Arizona. He stated that Seymour is similar in appearance to . . . Oswald; he speaks only a few words of Spanish, as Mrs. Odio had testified one of the men did . . . [T]he Commission has concluded that . . . Oswald was not at Mrs. Odio's apartment in September of 1963."

House Select Committee on Assassinations chief counsel G. Robert Blakey writes that he interviewed Loran Hall, Lawrence Howard, and William Seymour and has "determined they could not have been the three visitors [to Sylvia Odio]." All three of these anti-Castro activists were members of INTERPEN (International Penetration Force), a soldier-of-fortune group used to obtain information by the Miami office of the FBI. Blakey writes: "In September 1963 Hall and Howard drove from Los Angeles headed to Miami with a trailer-load of arms, but they were forced to leave the trailer in Dallas for lack of a hiding place in Florida. In October Hall and Seymour, back in Dallas to retrieve the trailer, were arrested for possession of drugs; but with the help of an influential financial supporter, they were released. They took the arms back to Miami, but the mission for which they were intended, Hall told us, was aborted in late October when he, Howard, Seymour, and some Cubans were arrested by customs officials as they were driving to their embarkation point south of Miami. No charges were filed, but their arms and equipment were confiscated so they returned to Miami, frustrated, and in early November, headed west. All three swore they were at their respective homes—Hall and Howard in California, Seymour in Arizona—on November 22, 1963."

According to assassination researcher Paris Flammonde, however, Seymour "claimed—with some proof—to have been in Miami at the time [of JFK's death]."

According to the assassination researcher who wrote under the name William Torbitt, who claimed to have been an insider in the Garrison investigation, Seymour was also known as "Leon Oswald" and was the man who fired a rifle from the sixth floor of the Texas School Book Depository on November 22, 1963—and was, minutes later, the man whom Roger Craig and others saw leaving the School Book Depository and entering a Nash Rambler station wagon on Elm Street. According to Torbitt it was also Seymour who killed Officer J. D. Tippit and was later seen fleeing into the nearby Abundant Life Temple.

It has also been noted that Michael Paine, the Bell Helicopter employee whose estranged wife was living with Marina Oswald at the time of the assassination, bore a resemblance to Oswald—not only in appearance but also in voice and manner.

(See also DOWNTOWN LINCOLN-MERCURY; PAINE, RUTH AND MICHAEL R.)

Oswald's Historic Diary

Found among Lee Harvey Oswald's possessions following his arrest in Dallas was his "Historic Diary," which purports to be a day-by-day journal of his experiences in the Soviet Union.

David J. Purtell, House Select Committee on Assassinations handwriting expert, was called upon, along with Joseph McNally and Charles Scott, to assess the authenticity of the diary. They determined that, though the diary was written by Oswald, it was written in one or two sittings rather than in a daily manner.

Oswald's Jacket

During the pursuit of Officer J. D. Tippit's killer through the Oak Cliff section of Dallas about 45 minutes after the assassination, a jacket was found in a gas station parking lot near the rear entrance to the Abundant Life Temple. Since Oswald had been seen earlier by his cleaning lady Earlene Roberts putting on a jacket and he was arrested later without one, it has long been assumed that this was his jacket.

Dallas police captain W. R. Westbrook told the Warren Commission: "I had come down by the Texaco service station and at this time I had a shotgun. I had borrowed a shotgun from a patrolman—there is an old house there and some officers were looking it over. They had seen somebody go in it, and there were quite a few officers there so I didn't pay any further attention to it. I just hesitated a moment and then I walked on towards the parking lot behind the Texaco service station, and some officer, I feel sure it was an officer, I still can't be positive, and he said, 'Look! There's a jacket under the car. . . . So I walked over and reached under and picked up the jacket. I told the officer to take the make and the license number [of the car]."

With Westbrook was Sergeant H. H. Stringer, who radioed in, "The jacket the suspect was wearing over here on Jefferson bears a laundry tag with the letter B 9738. See if there is any way you can check this laundry tag."

The Warren Commission was unable to locate the laundry that issued this tag and Marina Oswald said she didn't remember her husband ever using professional laundry services.

In order to trace the laundry mark, the FBI checked 424 laundries in the Dallas/Fort Worth area and 293 more in New Orleans, with no success. In all of Lee Harvey Oswald's known clothing there was not another laundry mark. Whereas all of Oswald's known clothes were in size small, the jacket found in the parking lot was a medium.

Officer Thomas Alexander Hutson, in his Warren Commission testimony, recalls the finding of the jacket in this way: "We were searching the rear of the house in the 400 block of East Jefferson Boulevard at the rear of the Texaco station. Behind cars parked on a lot at this location, a white jacket was picked up by another officer. It looked like a white cloth jacket to me."

Westbrook—who retired from the Dallas police in 1966 and went on to serve in South Vietnam as a "police adviser"—told researcher Larry A. Sneed that the jacket "was kind of a tan, beige, or rye color, whatever you want to call it." Like many of the eyewitnesses to the assailant's flight, Officer Hutson thought the jacket was white. The jacket that became Warren Commission Exhibit No. 162 is gray.

According to the late Tippit researcher Larry Ray Harris, the officer who actually first picked up Oswald's jacket was John R. Mackey, who rode a three-wheeled motorcycle in the same squad with officers Hutson and J. T. Griffin.

Apparently the assailant wore a tan jacket, a white jacket was found, and a gray jacket was turned over to the Warren Commission.

Oswald's Wallet

According to the official scenario, Dallas police detective Paul Bentley pulled Lee Harvey Oswald's wallet out of Oswald's back pocket while sitting in the back seat of a Dallas police car outside the Texas Theatre where Oswald had just been arrested. The identification for Alec Hidell was allegedly found in that wallet, the ID that linked Oswald with the supposed assassination weapon as well as the gun that killed Officer J. D. Tippit. (Of course, there was no public mention of the Hidell ID until after Oswald was dead.)

This scenario of how Oswald's wallet was discovered is directly challenged in a number of ways. James P. Hosty, the FBI agent in charge of Oswald's case in Dallas, wrote in his book *Assignment: Oswald* that Dallas police captain W. R. Westbrook found the wallet containing the identification for both Oswald and Hidell at the scene of the Tippit murder.

In a 1996 interview with researcher Dale K. Myers, FBI agent Robert M. Barrett said: "I went on over there and Captain Westbrook was there with several of his officers. They were interviewing Helen Markham and some other witnesses in the area. Westbrook and I were well-acquainted, and he knew I worked criminal intelligence work. Now, you have to remember that at that time there were two distinct bodies within the FBI. There were those who worked security work, like Jim Hosty, and there are those who worked criminal work, which is where I was assigned. My job was criminal intelligence, keeping up with the organized crime and gambling element in the Dallas area. Westbrook knew this. Knew that I was well acquainted with the hoodlum element. . . . It hadn't been very long when Westbrook looked up and saw me and called me over. He had this wallet in his hand. Now, I don't know where he found it, but he had the wallet in his hand. I presumed that they had found it on or near Tippit. Westbrook asked me, 'Do you know who Lee Harvey Oswald is?' And, 'Do you know who Alek Hidell is?' And I said, 'No, I have never heard of them.'" Barrett said that he then went to the Texas Theatre, where he witnessed the arrest without ever knowing the man being arrested matched the ID found in the wallet at the Tippit murder scene. Barrett returned to the corner of Tenth and Patton in March of 1964 to conduct follow-up interviews and take photographs. Barrett says that he doesn't remember which witness it was, but one told him that he had seen Oswald pass something to Tippit through the passenger side window of the car. (That window is revealed to be closed in photographs of the car taken soon after the shooting.)

The wallet does appear in WFAA-TV film footage taken at the scene of the Tippit murder. Looking at the wallet in the footage are Sergeant Calvin B. "Bud" Owens (who died in 1984), and Westbrook and George Doughty, both of whom died in 1996. So it is impossible to corroborate Barrett's statements. The WFAA-TV film was recently examined by author Dale Myers, who noticed one frame which clearly showed Captain Westbrook and Special Agent Barrett examining a wallet. Myers has had that frame blown up and has compared it to a photograph of the wallet that was reportedly taken from Oswald outside the Texas Theatre and has concluded that they are two different wallets.

One of the key pieces of identification reportedly found in the Oswald wallet taken from Oswald outside the Texas Theatre was a Defense Department identification card bearing the number DD1173-N4,271,617. It was a type of identification card given only to personnel who were injured in the line of duty to make sure that they received their medical benefits following their discharge or for civilian employees who were to be working overseas. A similar identification card was found on Francis Gary Powers when his U-2 spy plane was shot down over the Soviet Union.

Officially, the contents of Oswald's wallet included: 1. a draft card in the name Lee Harvey Oswald; 2. a fake draft card in the name of Alek James Hidell; 3. a U.S. Marine Corps Certificate of Service in the name of Lee Harvey Oswald; 4. a fake Marine Certificate of Service in the name of Alek James Hidell; 5. a draft registration certificate in the name of Lee Harvey Oswald; 6. a Department of Defense identification card in the name of Lee Harvey Oswald bearing two postal cancellation stamps and a photo reported to have been taken in Minsk, Russia; 7. a "United States Forces Japan" identification card in the name of Lee H. Oswald, issued May 8, 1958; 8. a Social Security card in the name of Lee Harvey Oswald; 9. a card that reads: "Compliments GA—JO Enkanko Hotel, a special services hotel." On the reverse side of the card is handwritten "ED5-0755" and "92463"—the latter perhaps a date; 10. a white card with words handwritten: "Embassy USSR, 1609 Decatur NW, Washington, D.C., Consular Reznichenko; 11. a piece of paper with the words handwritten: "The Worker, 23 W. 26th St., New York 10, NY. The Worker Box 28 Madison Sq. Station, New York 10, NY"; 12. a "Fair Play for Cuba, New Orleans Chapter" card, issued to L. H. Oswald by chapter president A. J. Hidell; 13. a Dallas Public Library card stamped with the expiration date December 7, 1965, issued to Lee Harvey Oswald of 602 Elsbeth, Dallas. Oswald's place of business was listed as Jaggars-Chiles-Stovall and the witness had signed "Jack L. Bowen, 1916 Stevens Forest Drive, WH8-8997"; 14. a second Fair Play for Cuba card issued to Lee H. Oswald by V. T. Lee, the actual executive secretary of the organization; 15. a check stub from American Bakeries in Dallas dated 1960. Oswald was in the Soviet Union in 1960. It was reported that the tenant who preceded the Oswalds in their Neely Street apartment had worked for American Bakeries. Why the check stub was left behind and why Oswald kept it are unknown; 16. a photo of Oswald as a Marine; 17. a Marine Marksman's medal; 18. a photo of Marina Oswald; 19. a photo of June Oswald; 20. cash, one five-dollar bill and eight ones, for a total of $13.

Other Bullets

During the summer of 1966 an intact bullet was found by a man named William Barbee imbedded in the roof of a building at 1615 Stemmons Freeway, about a quarter of a mile from the Texas School Book Depository. The FBI lab determined that the bullet was a .30 caliber full-metal jacketed military bullet. According to researcher Ira David Wood III, this is the type of bullet that would have been used had the assassination been committed with a silenced M-1 .30 caliber carbine. There is no innocent explanation for its presence since any weapon that could have fired it would have been illegal for hunting.

In 1967 another bullet was found on the roof of the Massey Building, eight blocks east of the Texas School Book Depository on Elm Street. The roofer who found it was named Rick Haythorne, who gave it to his attorney who held it until turning it over to the House Select Committee on Assassinations. The Washington, D.C., Police Department ran tests on the bullet and determined it to be a .30 caliber jacketed soft-point bullet. This is a popular hunting bullet and the rifling marks on the bullet proved that it was not fired from the Mannlicher-Carcano found on the Depository's sixth floor.

In 1974 a bullet fragment was found by a man named Richard Lester in Dealey Plaza. The location of the discovery was reported as 61 yards east of the triple underpass and 500 yards from the Texas School Book Depository, although almost anything 500 yards from the Depository has to be outside Dealey Plaza. Although the fragment could have come from a 6.5 mm bullet, the rifling marks indicated that it was not fired by the sixth-floor Mannlicher-Carcano.

In 1977, a rusted shell casing was found on the roof of the Dal-Tex Building by a man repairing the building's air-conditioning system.

Oxford, J. L.

Dallas sheriff's deputy who watched the motorcade from the corner of Houston and Main Streets. After he heard the shots, Oxford ran across Dealey Plaza toward the grassy knoll.

Oxford has said, "When we got there, everyone was looking over into the railroad yards."

Later in the day, Oxford was among those who searched the home of Ruth Paine in Irving, Texas, where Marina Oswald had been living. It was during this search that the blanket that Marina said held Lee's rifle was found empty in the garage.

P

Paine, Ruth and Michael R.

Estranged couple who befriended the Oswalds just in time for the Oswalds' previous friends, the DeMohrenschildts, to move to Haiti. Ruth was responsible for getting Oswald his job at the Texas School Book Depository, calling building supervisor Roy Truly for him when she learned they were hiring.

The Paines had some very interesting relatives. Michael Paine's stepfather, Arthur Young, invented the Bell Helicopter—so it is not shocking that Michael Paine worked for Bell Helicopter, where he had a security clearance, at the time of the assassination. Young was born in Philadelphia and studied physics at Princeton. He disagreed with Einstein's Theory of Relativity and instead believed in something he called the "Theory of Process." He made a model of his helicopter and flew it right into Larry Bell's office. Bell was so impressed that he made Young the head of research and development at the brand-new Bell Helicopter Corporation. Young did a lot of research in UFOs and astrology and married Ruth Forbes Paine in 1948. She, Michael Paine's mother, was a school friend of Mary Bancroft (they even went to Europe together once on holiday). Mary was to become Allen Dulles's mistress. In the 1950s, Ruth Forbes Paine became involved in CIA agent Cord Meyer's New Federalists. Ruth Paine, Michael's wife, was visiting her in-laws, Arthur and Ruth, in New England during the summer of 1963 and it was from there that she wrote the letter to Marina inviting her to come live with her. Ruth Paine's dad, William Avery Hyde, was very political and was considered by the CIA in 1957 as a candidate to set up an "Educational Center" in South Vietnam. He worked for the Agency for International Development, a part of the State Department. Sylvia Hope, Ruth Paine's sister, was a CIA contract agent. Sylvia was in the U.S. Air Force and was under investigation to get a top-secret clearance in 1957. According to documents she was refused that clearance at that time because her mother-in-law had an acquaintance who was a communist. The whole investigation may have been a hoax since we know she ended up working for the CIA anyway. William Hyde became a contract agent for the CIA in the early 1960s, working in Peru (1964–67) for the Cooperative League as an insurance adviser, where he urged Peruvian leaders to set up a Latin American Common Market. Hyde's reports on Latin American business practices ended up in CIA files.

It has been noted that Lee Oswald and Michael Paine resembled one another, not so much facially as in body language, mannerisms, and the sound of their voices. The big difference between Oswald and Paine was height: Oswald was five-feet-nine; Paine six-feet-two.

There are more than 1,000 documents dealing with sightings of Oswald before the assassination. They fall into three groups: 1. Midwest; 2. New England and Mid-Atlantic; and 3. Louisiana and Texas. Interestingly, none of the sightings are west of Texas. Although the sightings do not have much relationship with Oswald's known movements, they do seem to follow the movements of Ruth Paine. One sighting, in August or September of 1963 in Yellow Springs, Ohio, near the College of Antioch (where Ruth and her brother Carl Hyde went to college) coincides with a visit there by Ruth and Carl. Oswald was spotted picketing a barber shop that wouldn't serve blacks. Carl Hyde says it wasn't Oswald, it was he—a remarkable coincidence.

FBI special agent Bardwell Odum knew Michael Paine before November 22, 1963, and Michael casually referred to Odum as "Bob."

Michael had worked at Bell Helicopter in Fort Worth since 1958, and he was under the supervision of former Nazi general Walter Dörnberger. Yet Michael was a member of the American Civil Liberties Union, and attended a meeting of that organization with Lee Oswald.

As if he were making room, Michael moved out of his Irving, Texas, home just before his wife took in Marina Oswald and her two children. Jim Bishop wrote that the separation of the Paines was a "friendly estrangement, difficult to define."

Paine says that he was having lunch with coworker Dave Noel at the time of the assassination, and they were discussing "the character of assassins" *before* they heard the news.

Michael arrived at his Irving home around 3:00 P.M. on the day of the assassination and the house was already being searched by police. He said, "As soon as I found out about it, I hurried over to see if I could help." The Dallas police tore up the house in search of evidence.

Dr. Charles Crenshaw writes that, on November 23, 1963, Paine was overheard talking on the phone to his wife. Michael reportedly said that he was sure Oswald had killed President Kennedy but didn't think Oswald was responsible.

"We both know who is responsible," he reportedly added. Since both sides of the conversation were overheard, a wiretap would best explain this knowledge.

Michael Paine and Lee Oswald had some things in common. Both have been suspected of being agent provocateurs, trying to identify leftists by pretending to be one themselves. Oswald, of course, tried to identify pro-Castro persons by passing out leaflets for the Fair Play for Cuba Committee, while Michael Paine tried to recruit members of the American Civil Liberties Union at Southern Methodist University.

Evidence that the Paines were not what they appeared to be comes from the fact that they lived in a simple, smallish suburban home despite the fact that both Michael and Ruth came from well-to-do families and Michael had a $300,000 trust fund.

Robert Oswald, Lee's brother, said in his testimony before the Warren Commission: "I still do not know how or why, but Mr. and Mrs. Paine are somehow involved in this affair."

Ruth Paine, Michael's wife, was a social member of Dallas' Russian-speaking community, perhaps the only member of that group who was not Russian. Ruth was reportedly fascinated with all things Russian. She learned Russian at the Berlitz School, and before meeting Marina she'd had a Russian pen pal named Ella in the Soviet Union. Lee, coincidentally, had dated a Russian woman named Ella before meeting Marina.

Ruth was enamored with Marina. Both had young children, husbands who were not around, and each could help the other with her second language. Ruth has said that she had with Marina an excellent relationship because she could help Marina with her English and Marina could help her with her Russian. This misrepresents the situation. Ruth had been studying Russian since 1957 and had even taught Russian at a prep school. They, according to Ruth, "comforted" one another.

Ruth and Michael Paine have been deemed suspicious by multiple researchers. The reasons: 1. Michael's connection with the military-industrial complex; 2. Ruth's convenient situation with her husband that allowed Marina to live with her indefinitely; 3. Ruth's responsibility for Oswald's employment in a building that overlooked the presidential motorcade route; and 4. the Paines' possession of evidence against Oswald—including the backyard photos of Oswald holding his weapons, as well as the blanket that supposedly held Oswald's rifle.

Ruth told the Warren Commission that it was decided in New Orleans around September 20, 1963, that Marina, pregnant with the Oswalds' second child, would stay at Ruth's house where better care for her and the expected baby was available.

Ruth spent the weekend with the Oswalds in New Orleans and on September 23, Marina, Ruth, and their children left for Irving, leaving Lee alone. Before they left, Lee told them that he was going to go to Houston, or possibly Philadelphia, to look for work. He mentioned having a friend in Houston.

Ruth and Marina had no contact with Lee between September 23 and October 4. Officially, during this time, Oswald is said to have traveled to Mexico City, but there are reports that he was elsewhere. (See ODIO INCIDENT, THE.)

On October 4, Lee hitchhiked from Dallas to Irving to visit, and from then until the assassination, he regularly visited on weekends. The only exception to this pattern would be the Thursday night Lee would spend at the Paines on the eve of the assassination.

In her Warren Commission testimony, Ruth said that one weekend in October, Lee asked to use her husband's drill press to drill a hole in a coin. Later, a peso turned into a necklace was found, and this, along with other souvenirs, was used as evidence that Lee had actually been in Mexico. Lee never verbally alluded to his trip to Mexico to Ruth.

Ruth claims that, two weeks before the assassination, Lee left a typed letter on her desk that she read. It mentioned his trip to Mexico, that while there he had had an interview with a "Comrade Kostine," and that "the FBI is not now interested in my activities." (See COMRADE KOSTIN LETTER.)

She said that she wanted to show the letter to the FBI immediately, but she never got around to it. Nobody saw the letter except Ruth until after President Kennedy's assassination. Ruth said that she made a handwritten copy of Oswald's letter, which had been typed on her typewriter. Her handwritten copy has never been seen.

Ruth told the commission that she recalled seeing the blanket that allegedly held the Mannlicher-Carcano rifle on the floor of her garage, but she said it appeared flatter than it would have if it had contained a rifle.

When asked about arranging the School Book Depository job for Oswald, Ruth said she'd called Roy Truly on October 14 or 15, since her neighbor Buell Wesley Frazier worked there. Lee applied for the job on the 15th and started work the next day.

On the evening of November 21, 1963, the only non-weekend night that Lee ever spent at the Paines, Ruth says she did not see Lee in the garage, where the rifle was allegedly kept—although she says she did notice that the garage light had been left on and had assumed that it was Lee who had forgotten to turn it off.

Ruth and Michael were not called as witnesses by the House Select Committee on Assassinations. Ruth currently lives in Florida and is said to make frequent trips to Nicaragua.

Paraffin Test

On November 22, 1963, the Dallas Police Department administered a paraffin test on Lee Harvey Oswald's hands and right cheek to determine whether or not he had fired a gun. The test showed that Oswald had nitrates on his hands but not on his cheek.

While a positive test is not conclusive evidence that a gun was fired, a negative response is good evidence that a gun was not fired. Therefore, this test would seem to indicate that Oswald might have fired a handgun but definitely did not fire a rifle on the day of the assassination. (Or, to consider other possibilities, the test does not rule out the possibility that Oswald fired a rifle left-handed.)

Parkland Hospital

Hospital where John F. Kennedy, John Connally, and Lee Harvey Oswald were taken following their shootings. It was also the location of J. D. Tippit's autopsy.

The T-shaped structure was built in 1954. In 1963 the emergency room at Parkland treated 1,271 gunshot wounds per year.

DOCTORS WHO TREATED JFK

Dr. Charles James Carrico was the first physician to attend to President Kennedy. He signed a hospital report on November 22 stating that Kennedy's throat wound was one of entrance. Like the other Parkland doctors, Carrico saw a gaping wound in the back of the president's head that does not appear on the official autopsy photographs. Although Carrico says he did a "brief manual examination" of President Kennedy's back, he found no wound there. No doctor at Parkland saw Kennedy's back wound.

Dr. Charles Crenshaw, a Parkland witness, authored, with Jens Hansen and J. Gary Shaw, *JFK Conspiracy of Silence* (Signet, 1992). Dr. Crenshaw told Geraldo Rivera on the *Now It Can Be Told* TV program on April 2, 1992, "The bullet [that killed Kennedy] entered from the right side [pointing to the right temple], coming down and coming across. It was a huge, blown-out hole [toward the back of Kennedy's head]. . . . If the bullet had come from the back, the cerebellum would have been destroyed." Crenshaw believed the fatal shot came from the grassy knoll. When the American Medical Association published a story saying that Crenshaw was a liar and had not even been in Trauma Room One when JFK was treated, Crenshaw sued. The suit was settled for almost $250,000. Crenshaw died of natural causes at his home in Fort Worth, Texas, on November 15, 2001.

Dr. Robert N. McClelland attended to Kennedy and later told a reporter that he and the other Dallas doctors were puzzled by the reconstruction of the crime by the authorities (that Kennedy had been shot exclusively from behind). Dr. McClelland said that he and his colleagues saw bullet wounds every day and that Kennedy's throat wound was an entrance wound. He wrote that the president died as a result of a gunshot to the "left temple." McClelland has repeatedly told researchers and members of the press that he recalls a gaping hole in the back of JFK's head, which does not appear in the autopsy photos. He said in a British television documentary, "[There was] a jagged wound that involved the right side of the back of the head. My initial impression was that it was probably an exit wound. So it was a very large wound. Twenty to twenty-five percent of the entire brain was missing . . . his head had almost been destroyed. His face was intact but very swollen . . A fifth to a quarter of the right back part of the head had been blasted out along with most of the brain tissue in that area."

Dr. Malcolm O. "Mac" Perry was the surgeon who performed a tracheotomy over the small wound in Kennedy's throat, thus inadvertently destroying evidence that this resembled an entry wound. Still, every medical professional who saw the president in Parkland described the throat wound as one of entry. Perry told a television reporter on the day of the assassination that there was "a large wound in his head in the right rear area." To the Warren Commission, he said that there was "a large avulsive wound on the right posterior cranium." Years later, when being interviewed by lone-nut theorist Gerald Posner, Perry reportedly said that he was no longer certain that the large skull wound was in the back of the head since the autopsy photos show it to be at the right side, adding, "I made only a cursory examination of the head."

Dr. David Stewart, an attending doctor who was not asked to testify for the Warren Commission, told researcher Harold Weisberg that "there was a small wound in the left front of the President's head and there was a quite massive wound of exit at the right back side of the head—and it was felt by all of the physicians at the time to be a wound of entry which went in the front."

Dr. Charles R. Baxter told the Warren Commission that it was "unlikely" that Kennedy's throat wound was one of exit, and that the president had a "large, gaping wound at the back of the skull."

Dr. Adolphe H. Giesecke Jr., a Parkland anesthesiologist, told researcher Harrison Livingstone that, when Kennedy was brought in, the back of his head "was missing."

Dr. Fouad Bashour, associate professor of medicine in cardiology, when shown the purported Kennedy autopsy photos in 1979, shook his head no. He had seen a big hole in the back of the president's head, a hole which does not appear in the photos. "Why do they cover it up?" he asked.

Dr. Marion T. Jenkins, Parkland witness, chief anesthesiologist, attended to Kennedy and told the Warren Commission that he did not see an entrance wound in the back of Kennedy's head, thus supporting allegations that the written and photographic autopsy evidence has been doctored to support Oswald's lone guilt. He said, "There was a great laceration on the right side of the head . . . even to the extent that the cerebellum had protruded from the wound . . . I would interpret it [as] being a wound of exit."

When Harrison Edward Livingstone showed the purported Kennedy autopsy photos to Dr. Jenkins, he disagreed with what they showed. Dr. Jenkins said, beating at the back of his head with his fingertips, "Well, that picture doesn't look like it from the back. . . . You could tell at this point with your fingers that it was scored out, that the edges were blasted out."

In Jenkins's written report, he noted that Kennedy had chest damage, a fact the Warren Commission had to disregard to sell the "single-bullet theory." That theory involved raising the wound in the president's back to the back of his neck so that it would correspond to Kennedy's throat wound, which in turn was changed from an entrance wound into an exit wound.

After years of having his own opinions differ so strongly with the "facts," Jenkins began to believe he was mistaken.

Jenkins later said, "The first day I had thought that the one bullet must have . . . gotten into the lung cavity, I mean, from what you say now, I know it did not go that way. I thought it did." Jenkins's waffling opinion does not alter the fact that, while JFK was in Parkland, a drainage tube was inserted into his chest.

Dr. Gene Coleman Akin, another Parkland anesthesiologist, told the Warren Commission: "the back of the right occipital-parietal portion of [JFK's] head was shattered, with brain substance extruding . . . I assume that the right occipital parietal region [right rear] was the exit." Dr. Akin initially believed the president was shot from the front.

Dr. Ronald Coy Jones, born in Harrison, Arkansas, a 1957 graduate of the University of Tennessee Medical School, and, at the time of the assassination, the chief resident in surgery at Parkland, treated Kennedy and gave a detailed written description of Kennedy's throat wound as a wound of entrance. Dr. Jones told the Warren Commission: "The hole was very small and relatively clean cut, as you would see in a bullet that is entering rather than exiting a patient. . . . [There] appeared to be an exit wound in the posterior portion of the skull. . . . There was a large defect in the back side of the head as the President lay in the cart with what appeared to be brain tissue hanging out of this wound with multiple pieces of skull noted next with the brain and with a tremendous amount of clot and blood." Dr. Jones told a conference in Dallas in 2000 that Trauma Room One was so crowded that he could not get from one side of the room to the other while the president was receiving treatment.

Years later, when Dr. Jones was shown the Kennedy autopsy photos by the *Boston Sun,* he said, "the wound was not the same as what he saw in 1963." He was interviewed in 1988 on KRON-TV in San Francisco, at which time he said that the official Kennedy autopsy X rays, reportedly shot at Bethesda Hospital, do not accurately represent the president's wounds. The autopsy X rays show a head with severe facial damage—an eye socket appears to be completely missing—yet Kennedy's face was intact in death.

Dr. Jackie H. Hunt told Harrison Edward Livingstone that the massive wound in Kennedy's head had to be in the rear portion of the head because she couldn't see it, and, because of the way they were positioned in the Parkland Emergency Room, the back of Kennedy's head was the only part she couldn't see.

Dr. William Kemp "High Pockets" Clark, Parkland chief of neurosurgery, officially pronounced the president dead. Dr. Clark later told the press that one bullet struck Kennedy at about the necktie knot. "It ranged downward in his chest and did not exit," he said. Kemp is reported to have said in the emergency room, "My God, the whole back of his head is shot off." Clark told the Warren Commission that JFK's skull wound was in the "right/occipital" portion of the president's head.

Dr. Robert G. Grossman told Ben Bradlee Jr. of the *Boston Globe* that Kennedy had a large wound, separate from his temple wound, in the back of his head—much too large to be an entrance wound. Dr. Grossman did not testify for the Warren Commission or the House Select Committee on Assassinations.

Dr. Joe D. Goldstrich, a fourth-year medical student at the University of Texas Southwestern Medical School who was standing by in the Parkland emergency room when the president was brought in, told Dallas reporter Bill Sloan that, upon entering Trauma Room One, "The first thing I saw was the President lying on his back on an operating table. I was standing very close to him on the left side of the table, and his face and the upper part of his body were clearly visible. I didn't have a clear view of the back of his head, but I have a vague recollection of seeing a portion of his brain exposed. He wasn't breathing and someone was doing CPR. . . . [The throat wound] was a small, almost perfectly round hole—somewhere between the size of a nickel and a quarter—and it was right in the middle of the front of the neck, just below the Adam's apple . . . I thought how curious it was that the wound was exactly the right size and in exactly the right spot to accommodate a tracheostomy tube. I saw the surgeons getting ready to do a tracheostomy, and I said to myself, 'Why not just slide the tube right into the hole? It's a perfect fit.' There was no need to make any sort of incision at all, and I couldn't believe it when I saw them start cutting on it." Goldstrich left Trauma Room One at this point, when one of the senior staff members in the room ordered him to fetch a defibrillator, a devise designed to regulate a failing heartbeat, from the hall. When he returned, "They had made a sizable diagonal incision, and I kept wondering, 'Why? Why?' . . . Dr. [William Kemp] Clark arrived about three or four minutes after I did. He walked into the midst of all this frantic activity and came directly to the head of the operating table where Dr. [Charles R.] Baxter was trying to resuscitate the President. I still remember Dr. Clark's exact words. He said, 'My God, Charlie, what are you doing? His brains are all over the table.' In other words, why are you trying to revive a dead man? Then, almost immediately, Dr. Clark looked up and saw Mrs. Kennedy standing there in one corner of the room, and I could tell that he was terribly embarrassed about what he had just said. I was standing approximately halfway between the two of them, and I could see the expressions on both their faces. I'm not sure she fully comprehended what Dr. Clark had said, because she was obviously in a state of shock, but I think that might have been the first time she realized her husband was beyond hope. . . . The more I thought about it, the more it haunted me. At first, I was like the majority of

other people. I didn't really believe in the idea of a conspiracy, but the more I realized how impossible it would have been for the neck wound I saw to have been an exit wound, the more I changed my mind . . . Except for telling a few personal friends, I've kept this thing to myself all these years, and until recently, I never intended to make it public. My reason for agreeing to tell the story now [1992] is that I feel there is room for more discussion, no matter what anyone else might say. . . . Nobody ever told me not to talk about it. On the other hand, nobody ever asked me about it either." Dr. Goldstrich is today a board-certified cardiologist and a practicing physician in Dallas.

Dr. Bill Midgett, a second-year ob-gyn resident, was one of the first doctors to see JFK outside the emergency room and helped roll JFK into Trauma Room One. Once again proving that Dallas was a very small world in 1963, Dr. Midgett also delivered Marina Oswald's baby on October 20, 1963.

Dr. Paul C. Peters was another of the Parkland doctors who testified to a large exit wound in the back of Kennedy's head. When asked if there was a smaller entrance wound in the back of Kennedy's head (as appears on the autopsy photographs supposedly taken later that day in Bethesda), he replied no.

When the Secret Service announced that they intended to return the president's body to Washington immediately—thus breaking a Dallas law requiring an immediate, locally performed autopsy in all cases of homicide—it was Dr. Earl Rose who physically attempted to stop the body from being removed. This started a vulgar shouting and shoving match (which took place in front of Jackie Kennedy) that Rose lost. (Dr. Rose also served on the House Select Committee on Assassinations' panel of medical experts, whose conclusions about JFK's wounds, and the shots that caused them, basically agreed with the Warren Commission.)

Twenty-seven-year-old Dr. Kenneth Everett Salyer set up the IV for Kennedy. Dr. Everett saw a "sucking wound" in Kennedy's neck; described the head wound as being in the "right temporal region."

Doctors Perry, McClelland, and Jones had about as stressful a weekend as can be imagined by a peacetime surgeon as all three were on duty and treated both JFK and Oswald.

PARKLAND WITNESSES, GOVERNOR CONNALLY
Dr. William Osborne, with Dr. John Parker, assisted the chief of orthopedic surgery, Dr. Charles Gregory, in operating on the wounds in Governor Connally's right wrist between 4:00 P.M. and 4:50 P.M. on November 22, 1963. According to the *Warren Report*, "The wound on the back of the wrist was left partially open for draining, and the wound on the palm side was enlarged, cleansed and

closed. The fracture was set, and a cast was applied with some traction utilized."

Dr. Charles Gregory, who died in April 1976 of a heart attack, told the Warren Commission, in a 1964 statement unknowingly critical of the "single-bullet theory," that the bullet that struck Connally "behaved as if it had never struck anything except him."

Dr. Ralph Don Patman, with doctors Robert McClelland and Charles Baxter, assisted Dr. George Shires in operating on the bullet wound in Governor John Connally's thigh between 4:00 P.M. and 6:00 P.M., November 22, 1963. The *Warren Report* says, "This puncture missile wound, about two-fifths of an inch in diameter (one centimeter) and located approximately five inches above the left knee, was cleansed and closed with sutures; but a small metallic fragment remained in the Governor's leg." This fragment is significant because of the pristine nature of Warren Commission Exhibit 399, the bullet that—according to the Warren Commission—caused Connally's thigh wound, along with all other nonfatal wounds suffered in JFK's limo.

Charles Harbison was a Texas state patrolman who told the House Select Committee on Assassinations that three bullet fragments fell from the wound in Governor Connally's leg, three or four days after the shooting, while he helped move the governor to another hospital room. Harbison said fragments were turned over to the FBI—thus casting further doubt on the plausibility of the "magic bullet." Officially, these fragments don't exist.

Henrietta M. Ross was a Parkland operating room technician who guarded the hallway while President Kennedy and Governor Connally were being treated. She told the Warren Commission that the last she saw of Connally's stretcher, it was being pushed up toward Trauma Room Three, which would leave it in the appropriate position to have the "magic bullet" found on it.

Dr. Robert Roeder Shaw treated Governor Connally's wounds and told the Warren Commission that the "magic bullet" couldn't have caused Connally's wounds because there would've been "more in the way of loss of substance to the bullet or deformation of the bullet."

Dr. George Shires treated Governor Connally's wounds and told the Warren Commission that he didn't think Kennedy and Connally were struck by the same bullet.

While Connally was recuperating from his wounds lead shields were placed over his hospital windows to prevent further assassination attempts.

PARKLAND HOSPITAL, OTHER WITNESSES

Audrey Bell was the supervising operating room nurse at Parkland Hospital when Governor Connally was treated. She said she removed "four or five" bullet fragments from Connally's wrist, and placed them in an envelope and gave

them to government agents. She said that "the smallest was the size of the striking end of a match and the largest at least twice that big. I have seen the picture of the magic bullet, and I can't see how it could be the bullet from which the fragments I saw came." Her statements corroborate the multitude of evidence that there was a large gaping wound in the back of Kennedy's skull at Parkland.

Aubrey (Al) Rike drove the ambulance that took Jerry Belknap—who apparently had a seizure in front of the Texas School Book Depository building moments before the assassination (a seizure suspected of being a diversion)—to Parkland Hospital. (See also EPILEPTIC FIT.) Coincidentally, Rike also drove the ambulance that took Kennedy's body from Parkland to Love Field. On the 1988 British television documentary *The Men Who Killed Kennedy* Rike described "pushing and shoving" between the Secret Service and Parkland officials as the federal agents attempted, and eventually succeeded, in illegally removing the body from the hospital so they could fly it back to Washington. Rike said that he had to hold onto the cross on the casket to keep it from falling off because of the way the casket was being pushed and pulled back and forth. He insists that when JFK's body left Parkland it was wrapped in a clear plastic sheet, such as one used to cover mattresses. This is odd, since when the body arrived at Bethesda for its autopsy it was wrapped in a military-type dark body bag.

Doris Mae Nelson, the supervising nurse, was delegated the task of removing Mrs. Kennedy from the overcrowded Trauma Room One during Kennedy's emergency treatment. Mrs. Kennedy left only temporarily, however, and reentered the room moments later, despite Nelson's protests. After the president was pronounced dead Nelson asked Mrs. Kennedy if she wanted to wash up and she declined, as she would to others who made the same suggestion during the course of the day. Moments later, Nelson asked the Secret Service agents what arrangements would be made for the body and was informed that the undertaker and casket were en route. When hospital staffers were having trouble with Kennedy's body—his massive head wound was still oozing, had already soaked through four sheets and they didn't want to stain the white satin interior of the casket—it was Nelson who suggested they "Go up to Central Supply and get one of those plastic mattress covers."

Nurse Diana Hamilton Bowron was 22 years old and from Great Britain. She saw President Kennedy arrive at Parkland and helped wheel him into the emergency room. She told the Warren Commission: "I saw the condition of his head . . . the back of his head . . . it was very bad . . . I just saw one large hole." Bowron was among the nurses who, after Kennedy died, washed the body and prepared it for the coffin. It was at that time that Nurse Bowron got her best view of JFK's corpse. In 1993, she told assassination researcher Harrison Edward Livingstone: "There was very little brain left. I had my hands inside his head, trying to clean it up so there wouldn't be more of a mess in the coffin. I put cloth inside [the head] and removed it. The brain was almost gone. . . . I first saw the large wound in the back of the head in the car. When we were preparing the body for the coffin I had the opportunity to examine it more closely. It was about five inches in diameter and there was no flap of skin covering it, just a fraction of skin along part of the edges of bone. There was, however, some hair hanging down from the top of the head which was caked with blood, and most of the brain was missing. The wound was so large I could almost put my whole left fist inside." Bowron said that there was no damage to President Kennedy's face. The only wounds she saw were the entrance wound in the throat, the exit wound in the back of the head, and an entrance wound in the back.

Parkland nurse Donna Willie told the *Jenkintown Times-Chronicle,* regarding the president's throat wound, "I know he was shot from the front."

Patricia (Hutton) Gustafson, the nurse who helped wheel Kennedy from the limousine into the emergency room, told the Warren Commission that there was a "massive opening in the back of the head." She later told Ben Bradlee Jr. of the *Boston Globe* that she was given instructions to apply a pressure bandage to Kennedy's head. "I tried to do so but there was really nothing to put a pressure bandage on. [The wound] was too massive. So he told me to just leave it be . . . [The wound was] in the back of the head." She was also one of the nurses who washed Kennedy's body in preparation for the coffin.

Margaret M. Hinchliffe (later, Margaret Hood; shown in the *Warren Report* as Henchcliffe), was the nurse who helped wheel Kennedy from the limousine into the emergency room, and later helped prepare the body for the coffin. She told reporters in 1981 that the President had a gaping wound in the back of his head and an entrance wound in his throat. With nurse Diana Bowron, she used surgical shears to cut off the president's clothes upon his arrival, removing everything except his underwear and his back brace. (Someone else later removed the brace, but the underwear remained on throughout the procedure, out of deference to the president's position.) After President Kennedy's death, she was ordered to clean the body. According to Jim Bishop, "The body was sponged carefully, the legs and arms still pliant. The cart drapes on the right hand side were heavy with brain matter. This was cleaned up and the edges of the massive wound in the head were wiped. The brown hair was slicked back. The body was lifted off the carriage and white sheets were placed underneath. Enough loose material was allowed to hang off the left side so that, when the President was placed in the box,

his head and neck wounds would not soil the white satin interior."

Father Oscar Huber of Holy Trinity Church in Dallas administered the Last Rites of the Catholic Church to the president. As reported by the *Philadelphia Sunday Bulletin* (November 24, 1963), Father Huber said that Kennedy had a terrible wound over his left eye.

Special agent Vincent Drain of the FBI briefly saw the president in Parkland and later said, "The head was badly damaged from the lower right base across the top, extending across the top of the ear. It appeared to me that the bullet had traveled upward and had taken off the right portion of the skull."

(See also AUTOPSY OF JOHN F. KENNEDY.)

Partin, Edward Grady

Baton Rouge, Louisiana, Teamster lieutenant under Jimmy Hoffa. Partin smuggled guns to Cuba and was an associate of Jack Ruby. According to the House Select Committee on Assassinations, "Hoffa and . . . Partin . . . did, in fact, discuss the planning of an assassination conspiracy against President Kennedy's brother, Attorney General Robert F. Kennedy, in July or August 1962. . . . In an interview with the Committee, Partin . . . stated that Hoffa had believed that having the Attorney General murdered would be the most effective way of ending the Federal Government's intense investigation of the Teamsters and organized crime . . . Hoffa . . . approached him about the assassination proposal because Hoffa believed him to be close to various figures in Carlos Marcello's syndicate organization." Partin passed a polygraph examination authorized by FBI director J. Edgar Hoover in 1962, soon after Partin first told the FBI about his discussion with Hoffa.

According to Partin's House Select Committee testimony, Hoffa discussed "the possible use of a lone gunman equipped with a rifle with a telescopic sight, the advisability of having the assassination committed somewhere in the South, as well as the potential desirability of having Robert Kennedy shot while riding in a convertible." Partin said that Hoffa believed "that by having Kennedy shot as he rode in a convertible, the origin of the fatal shot or shots would be obscured." Hoffa said this could be done only "upon the recruitment of an assassin without any identifiable connection to the Teamsters organization or Hoffa himself."

Paternostro, Sam

Dallas County assistant district attorney who watched the presidential motorcade from the second floor of the Dallas County Criminal Courts Building on the east side of Houston Street.

Paternostro was with court clerk Ruth Thornton and heard three shots, with a long pause between shots one and two. He told the FBI that he heard "a shot [come] from the depository or the Criminal Courts Building or the triple overpass [sic]."

Paul, Ralph

Business associate of Jack Ruby—he owned a portion of the Carousel Club—and owner of a drive-in restaurant called the Bull-Pen in Arlington, Texas—who spoke with Ruby by phone the night before Ruby shot Oswald. Paul did not testify as to what was said, but he was overheard by a waitress saying to Ruby "Are you crazy? A gun?"

Paul's girlfriend at the time of the assassination was Carousel Club stripper Nancy Powell, whose professional name was Tammy True.

According to a member of New Orleans district attorney Jim Garrison's investigation team, who wrote under the name William Torbitt, Paul was born in Kiev, Russia.

Paul was referred to by Carousel Club stripper Karen Carlin as Ruby's "friend from Chicago." Paul kept the Carousel Club open for a time after Ruby shot Oswald in hopes of capitalizing on Ruby's notoriety. Paul died in 1976 of a heart attack.

Pawley, William Douglas

Along with Claire Chenault, Pawley created the American Volunteer Group in China during World War II, a group of pilots who became better known as the Flying Tigers. Pawley was a world financier and ambassador, and a special envoy for several presidents. Pawley was involved in CIA-sponsored Cuban-exile raids on Cuba during the months before President Kennedy's death.

On January 7, 1977, at the dawn of the House Select Committee on Assassinations investigation, Pawley, who was bedridden at the time in his Miami mansion with a nervous condition, committed suicide with a gunshot to the chest. Carlos Prío Socarrás and George DeMohrenschildt, likewise sought by the House Select Committee, also allegedly committed suicide during this same time period.

Payne, Darwin

Payne was the first journalist to learn of the existence of the Zapruder film. At the time of the assassination he was a 26-year-old *Dallas Times Herald* general assignments writer and fill-in police reporter who, with rotund feature writer Paul Rosenfield, was assigned by City Editor Ken Smart to cover Dealey Plaza in the moments following the assassination.

"I ran all the way to Dealey Plaza," Payne told Dallas reporter Bill Sloan. "Although I had to slow down a time or two to let Paul catch up, we probably got [to Dealey Plaza] within five or six minutes after the shots were fired. . . . There were people wandering around everywhere, and I noticed two women standing over by the [School Book Depository] so I rushed over to them, all out of breath, told them who I was and asked them if they had seen anything. . . . One of them said, 'No, but our boss got the whole thing on film with his eight-millimeter movie camera.' . . . I said, 'Where is he now?' . . . And she said 'He went back up to his office. He was awfully upset. Come on. I'll show you.' . . . I still remember the scene [in Zapruder's office] in great detail. I'd never seen Zapruder before, but it was obvious that he was very distraught. He was slumped in a chair, staring at a television set turned to KRLD-TV. Channel 4, the CBS affiliate in Dallas. I knew it was CBS because Walter Cronkite was on the screen, saying that Kennedy had been wounded in an assassination attempt, but the extent of his wounds weren't known. . . . [A crying Zapruder said,] 'I know he's dead. I was looking right at him through the viewfinder and I saw his head explode like a firecracker. It was the worst thing I've ever seen. There's no way he could still be alive.'" Payne offered to buy Zapruder's film for his newspaper but Zapruder said, "No, I can't do that. I've got nothing against you or your paper, but I want to do the right thing where this film's concerned, and I feel like I ought to turn it over to the FBI or the Secret Service." Apparently someone in Zapruder's office had already called "the authorities," because, soon after it was announced that President Kennedy was dead, "six or seven" men in business suits, identified by Zapruder as the "Secret Service people" arrived and took Zapruder and his film into another room.

Perez, Eddie   See BAYO, EDDIE.

Permindex (Permanent Industrial Expositions)

A shady Swiss corporation suspected of involvement in assassination attempts upon Charles de Gaulle. Louis Mortimer Bloomfield—a Montreal, Quebec, Canada, resident—was, along with assassination suspect Clay Shaw, a board member for Permindex. French intelligence discovered that about $200,000 of the money to finance an assassination attempt on de Gaulle was sent to Permindex's accounts in the Banque du Crédit International. According to the Canadian newspaper *Le Devoir* (1967), Bloomfield was not only a major stockholder in Permindex but also in its sister corporation, Centro Mondiale Commerciale (CMC) as well. The paper reported that Bloomfield had been involved in "espionage" missions for the U.S. government. As for CMC and Permindex, *Le Devoir* wrote: "[CMC] was the creature of the CIA . . . set up as a cover for the transfer of CIA . . funds in Italy for illegal political-espionage activities. It still remains to clear up the presence on the administrative Board of the [CMC] of Clay Shaw and ex-Major [of the Office of Strategic Services] Bloomfield . . . [CMC is] the point of contact for a number of persons who, in certain respects, have somewhat equivocal ties whose common denominator is anti-communism so strong that it would swallow up all those in the world who have fought for decent relations between East and West including Kennedy."

According to Jay Pound, in his article "Who Told the TRUTH About KENNEDY?" in *Critique* (Spring/Summer 1986):

Both Permindex and CMC were directed by the same men, and their stated corporate purpose was to encourage trade between nations. They actually handled large sums of money, did little or no real legitimate business, and were constantly switching around the same group of men amongst their board of directors (as stated by an ex-member who resigned in disgust). Their real purposes were fourfold:

1) To fund the direct assassinations of European, Mid-East and world leaders considered to be threats to the Western World and to petroleum interests of the backers.

2) To furnish couriers, agents and management in transporting, depositing and rechanelling funds through Swiss banks for Las Vegas, Miami, Havana and the international gambling syndicate.

3) To co-ordinate the espionage activities of the Solidarists and Division 5 of the FBI with groups in sympathy with their objectives.

4) To receive and channel funds and arms from the financiers to the action groups (assassination teams)." All parenthetical interjections are Pound's, who continues: "The Swiss Corporation Permindex was used to head five front organizations that were responsible for furnishing personnel and supervisors to carry out the assigned duties. These five groups and their supervisors were:

1) The Czarist, Russian, Eastern European and Middle East exile organization known as Solidarists; headed by Ferenc Nagy, ex-Hungarian premiere and John [Jean] DeMenil, Russian exile from Houston, Texas—a close friend and supporter of Lyndon Johnson for thirty years. Nagy was living in Dallas at the time of the assassination. DeMenil ran Schlumberger Corp., whose ammunition dump was raided by David Ferrie and Gordon Novel in preparation for the Bay of Pigs invasion.

2) A section of the American Council of Christian Churches, headed by H. L. Hunt of Dallas, Texas, working with [Rev.] Carl McIntire.

3) A Cuban exile group called the Free Cuba Committee, headed by Carlos Prio Socarrus, ex-Cuban President; he worked closely with Jack Ruby and Frank (Fiorino) Sturgis of Watergate fame.

4) An organization of the United States, Caribbean and Havana, Cuba gamblers called The Syndicate, headed by Clifford Jons, ex-lieutenant Governor of Nevada and National Committeeman, and Bobby Baker of Washington, D.C., also a close friend of Lyndon Johnson. This group worked closely with the Mafia family headed by Joseph (Joe Bananas) Bonanno.

5) The Security Division of the National Aeronautics and Space Administration (NASA) headed by: Wernher von Braun, head of the German Nazi rocketry program from 1932 through 1945, when he was recruited by the USA in Operation Paperclip. Headquarters for this group were: the Defense Industrial Security Command located at Muscle Shoals Redstone Arsenal in Alabama, and also housed on East Broad Street in Columbus, Ohio.

According to former CIA-asset Robert Morrow, David Ferrie ordered the weapons he used to train Cuban exiles through Permindex.

Both Permindex and CMC lost their charters (in Switzerland and Italy, respectively) after Charles de Gaulle learned they had been involved in plots to assassinate him in 1961 and 1962. They were forced to set up new headquarters in Johannesburg, South Africa.

George Mandel—a.k.a. Mantello, Giorgio—was the founder of Permindex. Mandel was suspected by the assassination investigator who wrote under the name William Torbitt of being the "master cylinder" behind the JFK assassination. In 1959, Mandel (whose name was Italianized to Giorgio Mantello when he worked in Italy) created a Societa Italo-Americana, the purpose of which was announced as industry and commerce. The Italian newspaper *Paesa Sera* reported (March 4, 1967) that on November 14, 1959, Mandel inaugurated his "most important creation," the Italo-American Hotel Corporation. The object of the corporation was the building of the Exposition Universale Roma's Hotel du Lac. Three foreign credit groups were the corporation's largest shareholders. They were "represented in Italy by the *Banca Nazionale del Lavoro*, the *DeFamaco Astalde Vaduz* (Swiss), the *Miami Astalde Vaduz* (American), and the Seligman Bank of Basel. The DeFamaco and Seligman institutions were among the most powerful stockholders of the [CMC]."

Researcher Paris Flammonde wrote that Mandel was "a Hungarian refugee, Austrian citizen, functioning in Italy, Switzerland, and elsewhere with financial transactions reaching throughout Europe, Africa and America, who has, according to *Paesa Sera*, been condemned for his 'criminal activities' in Switzerland." Allegations of Mandel's "criminal activities" were first reported in the August 19, 1961, issue of *A-Z,* a Basel newspaper. Mandel filed a defamation suit against *A-Z* but then withdrew it. *A-Z* commented, "Too bad; we would have heard some great things at the trial."

Mario Ceravolo, a Christian Democrat and member of CMC's Board of Directors, wrote *Paesa Sera* a letter that appeared in the paper's March 11–12, 1967, issue. He said, in part, "To avoid misunderstandings and false interpretations, I ask that you please publish the fact that I left the administrative board of the CMC on 25 July 1962 because it was no longer possible to understand the sources of great sums of money obtained abroad by Mr. Giovanni [Giorgio] Mantelo, and the real destination of the money."

On March 6, 1967 *Paesa Sera* said: "It is certain that Clay Shaw . . . had a position on the board of the CMC in Rome. . . . It is certain that the CMC (taking advantage of the good faith of . . . Italians who were involved in that disasterous enterprise) has not fulfilled any of the activities for which it was originally projected. It is certain that an important shareholder in the CMC was an ex-official of the American service. . . Concerning the CMC and the organizations formed by Mandel, it is not clear on whose account many Hungarian refugees who were implicated in espionage activities were working, nor through what agencies large financial dealings in European political movements have been taking place."

Perrin, Robert and Nancy

Robert once ran guns by boat into Spain for Francisco Franco during the Spanish Civil War. In Dallas, in 1962, he was offered $10,000 at a meeting to use a boat to pick up Cuban refugees in Cuba and deliver them to Miami. The man carrying the cash at that meeting was Ruby. Perrin eventually declined the offer because there were too many "police types" involved. Robert married Nancy Zeigman, a Carousel Club bartender.

Perrin died on August 28, 1962, of arsenic poisoning. His death was ruled by the New Orleans's coroner's office, a suicide. It has been theorized—by Penn Jones Jr. and others—that Perrin faked his own death, and that the real corpse was a man named Starr, with whom Perrin switched places.

Nancy Perrin, formerly Nancy Zeigman and later Nancy Rich, was a former Carousel Club bartender. She told the Warren Commission that her husband Robert Perrin had been offered $10,000 by a group of men that included Ruby to smuggle Cuban refugees out of Cuba and into Miami by boat. The group had also included a "short, colonel with a big moustache." (Best guess is that this man was Captain George Charles Nonte Jr. who was, at the time, 37 years old. He stood five-feet seven-inches tall and had a walrus moustache. Captain Nonte was the commanding officer of D Company, 123rd Maintenance Battalion, Fort Hood, and later became editor-in-chief of *Soldier of Fortune* magazine.)

Nancy's background shows that she had created a small business for herself by "informing" for the police. She once volunteered her services to and obtained evidence for the Dallas police that led to the conviction of an abortionist. In Oakland, California, she had unsuccessfully attempted to help police by obtaining a nightclub job and informing on the owner. A polygraph examination given to Mrs. Rich regarding Ruby on December 5, 1963, was inconclusive due to her heavy drug use, although this may have been an overly harsh opinion of her condition based on the fact that the Warren Commission wanted none of her Ruby-running-guns-to-Cuba story. She was already Mrs. Rich by the time she testified and her testimony comes off as truthful and confessional at times as she admits that Robert was "turning her out" as a prostitute.

Pettit, Tom

Working for the National Broadcasting Company, Pettit was the only television reporter to be on the air live from the basement of the Dallas police station when Oswald was shot. He stood approximately six feet away.

Petit was the winner of three Emmy awards. A former executive vice president of NBC News, he died in 1996 at 64 in New York City of complications following surgery to repair a ruptured aorta.

Phase-One Cover-Up

According to Peter Dale Scott in *Deep Politics and the Death of JFK,* this term refers to any distortion of the truth designed to put forth "a false but plausible story of an international Communist conspiracy (supported by superficially credible evidence from intelligence sources too sensitive to be publicly disclosed)." Americans in power were scared by these pieces of disinformation because it was thought that public disclosure of the communist plot would begin a chain of events that could lead to World War III.

Gilberto Ugarte Alvarado was a Nicaraguan Secret Service agent in Mexico City, who told CIA officer David Atlee Phillips at the American embassy in Mexico City on November 24, 1963, that he had seen Oswald paid $6,500 by Cubans on September 18, 1963, and overheard Oswald and the Cubans, one of whom was a "Negro with red hair," discussing the assassination in the Cuban consulate. The story was proved false. The *Warren Report* included Alvarado's story, and his later admission that it was false, but never referred to Alvarado by name, instead calling him "D." The activities of anyone quick to proclaim Oswald part of a Communist conspiracy should be closely scrutinized. According to Anthony Summers, Alvarado's story was: "one of the first pieces of 'evidence' to sow the idea of Cuban conspiracy in the mind of President Johnson. . . . Under questioning by the Mexican authorities, [Alvarado] at first admitted that he had made up the entire story. . . . When American officials showed . . . interest, Alvarado reverted to his old story, claiming that the Mexicans had pressured him into a retraction. He agreed to a lie detector test. The polygraph . . . indicated that Alvarado might be lying . . . [and] the Nicaraguan began to crumble. He now said he 'must be mistaken,' was no longer certain about the date of the incident, and now talked only of having seen 'someone who looked like Oswald.'" According to Summers, Alvarado was "handled and debriefed by David [Atlee] Phillips, CIA Chief of Cuban Operations in Mexico." It was Alvarado's initial statements that were used by President Lyndon Johnson to impress upon the men he had chosen to serve on the Warren Commission that the assassination could be made to look like a communist conspiracy and be taken as an act of war. The next thing you knew, LBJ said, you had a nuclear war and 40 million Americans were dead. Better to squelch all those rumors. The possibility that one of the rumors might turn out to be true was not considered. President Johnson convinced seven men to serve on his blue-ribbon panel comprised of unimpeachable personnel and announced the commission on November 29, 1963. The following day, Director of Central Intelligence John McCone called LBJ and told him that this Alvarado fellow had retracted his claims. It turned out he had made up the whole thing. The tape of the telephone conservation picks up the new president's chuckle.

Oddly the "Negro with red hair" shows up also in the House Select Committee on Assassinations testimony of Elena Garro de Paz, a well-known and eccentric Mexican writer. She told the committee: "Garro de Paz . . . claimed that Oswald and two companions had attended a "twist" party at the home of Ruben Duran, brother-in-law of Silvia Duran, the secretary of the Cuban consul [Eusebio] Azcue who dealt with Oswald [or an Oswald impersonator] when he applied at the consulate for a Cuban visa. . . . The significance of the Elena Garro allegation, aside from its pointing to Oswald associations in Mexico City that the Warren Commission did not investigate, lay in her description of one of [Oswald's] companions [at the party] as gaunt and blond-haired. These are the characteristics that both Azcue and Duran attributed to the visitor to the Cuban consulate who identified himself as Lee Harvey Oswald. . . . The committee was unable to obtain corroboration for the Elena Garro allegation, although Silvia

Duran did confirm that there was a "twist" party at her brother-in-law's home in the fall of 1963 and that Elena Garro was there. She denied, however, that Oswald was there." Garro de Paz said the twist party was also attended by "a Latin American man with red hair."

On December 2, 1963, Mexico City credit investigator Pedro Gutierrez wrote to President Lyndon Johnson, telling him that he had also seen Oswald in the Mexico City Cuban embassy in September, and that Oswald had been passed a large wad of money. Research into Gutierrez's background revealed that he was a politically active anticommunist.

(See also OSWALD IN MEXICO; PHASE-TWO COVER-UP.)

Phase-Two Cover-Up

Peter Dale Scott's theory continues that a Phase-Two Cover-Up refers to any distortion of fact designed to put forth that Oswald was a lone gunman. Scott believes that Phase One and Phase Two were generated by many of the same individuals, a scheme designed to make frightened politicians leap at Phase Two after Phase One was raised as a terrifying possibility.

Phillips, David Atlee

A CIA propaganda specialist, Phillips was the former CIA Mexico City station chief who alleged before the House Select Committee on Assassinations that the CIA had reports of a meeting between Oswald and Cuban agents.

Phillips once worked with assassination suspect E. Howard Hunt in Havana. It has been alleged that Phillips's code name was "Maurice Bishop" and that he was "deeply involved" with Alpha 66, the Cuban exile/CIA assassination team plotting to kill Fidel Castro. CIA asset Frank Terpil said he was introduced to the man known as David Atlee Phillips by journalist (and fellow CIA asset) Hal Hendrix in the early 1960s, but that Phillips was introduced as a man named "Bishop."

During the November 3, 1978, House Select Committee on Assassinations deposition of E. Howard Hunt, Hunt said that the D.R.E., another anti-Castro group which included Oswald-acquaintance Carlos Bringuier, was being run by David Atlee Phillips. (See also D.R.E.)

Phillips told the House Select Committee that Oswald had offered information to the Russians while in Mexico City in September 1963 and had requested free passage to the Soviet Union.

Born on October 31, 1922, in Fort Worth, Texas, Phillips briefly attended William and Mary College in Virginia before returning to his home state to complete his education at Texas Christian University. He hoped one day to become an actor.

He served in the European theater during World War II, was captured by the Germans but escaped from a prisoner-of-war camp. Phillips says he was recruited by the CIA because he was fluent in Spanish. He was approached, he said, while living in Chile with his wife where he was performing in plays and running a small newspaper called the *South Pacific Mail*.

Phillips went on to play a key role in the overthrow of a leftist regime in Guatemala in 1954. It was during this mission that Phillips first worked with assassination suspect E. Howard Hunt. In 1960, Phillips was stationed in Havana, where he operated undercover as a public-relations consultant.

While headquartered in Washington, Phillips was head of the propaganda campaign leading up to the Bay of Pigs. From 1961 to the fall of 1963, Phillips was the chief of covert action in Mexico City.

Following Phillips's retirement from the CIA, he formed an organization called the Association of Former Intelligence Officers. On the board of directors for the organization was Clare Boothe Luce, the wife of the Time, Inc. board chairman.

Before testifying to the House Select Committee on Assassinations, Phillips told *Washington Post* reporter Ronald Kessler that he had heard the surveillance tapes made of Lee Harvey Oswald's alleged visit to the Soviet embassy in Mexico City during the fall of 1963, and that on the tape Oswald said, "I have information you would be interested in, and I know you can pay my way." Phillips says the tape was "routinely destroyed" before the assassination. However, FBI agents reported to J. Edgar Hoover after the assassination that they had heard the tapes and that the voice on the tape was not that of Oswald. How did the FBI hear tapes that had been routinely destroyed weeks before?

Phillips died in 1988 of cancer in Bethesda, Maryland.

(See also ALPHA 66; D.R.E.; HUNT, E. HOWARD.)

Piper, Eddie

Piper was the oldest employee of the Texas School Book Depository, where he worked as a janitor. Piper said that he last saw Oswald at noon on the first floor. Unkindly, the *Warren Report* referred to Piper as a "confused witness" without "exact memory of the events of that afternoon."

Pizzo, Frank   See DOWNTOWN LINCOLN-MERCURY.

Pool of Blood

Jerry Coley was a 30-year-old member of the *Dallas Morning News* advertising department who, along with his friend Charles Mulkey, went to see the Dallas motorcade before 11:30 A.M. Coley later said that he saw Jack Ruby in the *Dallas Morning News* cafeteria at 10:30 A.M. (According to Ruby's alibi he was still in the same cafeteria two hours later.) Coley and Mulkey stood on Houston Street in front of the Old Courthouse. Coley stood atop a portable stop sign. Both men heard the shots but neither realized that that was what they were. To find out what had happened the pair circled around behind the Texas School Book Depository and ended up on steps that led to a walk that in turn led to one end of the north pergola. At that location they found a large pool of dark red fluid, more than a pint. At first they thought it was a spilled soft drink until Mulkey poked a finger into the pool, tasted it, and determined that it was blood. When Coley returned to his office Ruby was still there crying into a telephone, standing near a window through which he could see the School Book Depository. Coley located *Dallas Morning News* photographer Jim Hood and the pair returned to the pool of blood and photographed it. Coley says he received threatening phone calls after that and, early in December 1963, he was interviewed by the FBI. Coley says one agent told him, "It never happened. You didn't see it. Someone got hurt and it's ridiculous to carry this thing any further. Someone just fell and got hurt and if you continue, you're just going to cause yourself a lot of problems." The FBI then took all of Hood's copies and negatives of the pool of blood, which have not been seen since.

Twenty-five-year-old Malcolm O. Couch told Warren Commission assistant counsel David W. Belin on April 1, 1964, that he, too, had seen the pool of blood. Couch, a part-time news cameraman with WFAA-TV, the American Broadcasting Company affiliate in Dallas, said the blood was "on the little sidewalk between the Book Depository property and the beginning of the parkway [pergola]. . . . This was the little walkway—steps and walkway that leads up to the corner, the west corner, the southwest corner of the Book Depository building." After clearly establishing that he saw the pool of blood on the sidewalk and steps on the east side of the pergola (as opposed to the steps and walk on the west side of the pergola that lead down the grassy knoll all the way to Elm Street) Couch told Belin that the blood appeared fresh and the pool was eight to 10 inches in diameter. He said that the blood was 50 to 60 feet from Elm Street and only about 10 to 15 feet from the southwest corner of the School Book Depository building. He said that he looked for objects near the ground that might offer an explanation or a clue and found nothing.

Attempts have been made to explain the pool of blood, all of which have placed the pool on the steps to the west of the pergola. This is where a couple smashed soda pop bottles during the assassination, according to witness Marilyn Sitzman. It is unlikely that Mulkey would have mistaken the taste of soda pop (sweet) for blood (salty), and it is even more unlikely that journalist Malcolm Couch would have failed to notice broken glass as a clue to explain a pool of blood. It must then be concluded that the pool of blood is an as-of-yet unexplained phenomenon.

Potter, Nolan H.

Potter was standing atop the triple underpass at the time of the assassination and is among those who saw smoke coming from the bushes atop the grassy knoll after the shooting sequence.

Potts, Walter Eugene

Potts was a member of the homicide division of the Dallas police department who participated in one police lineup with Oswald. Potts told the Warren Commission that Oswald complained bitterly during the lineup that he was in a T-shirt while the other "suspects" were all dressed nicely.

Potts was also involved in the search of Oswald's Beckley Street room. Others involved in that search were E. L. Cunningham, Bill Senkel, and F. M. Turner. Nothing incriminating was found.

Powell, John

Powell was on the sixth floor of the Dallas County Jail on Houston Street, where he was incarcerated, at the time of the assassination. Powell says that he, as well as other inmates, saw two men in the "sniper's nest" window before the shooting. One of the men appeared to be Latin, and that the men together appeared to be adjusting the scope on a rifle.

Powell, Nancy   See JACK'S GIRLS.

Powers, David

The presidential assistant who rode with the Secret Service in the presidential follow-up car, directly behind President Kennedy's limousine. Powers told the Warren Commission: "the first shot went off and it sounded to me as if it were a firecracker. I noticed then that the President moved quite far to his left after the shot, from the extreme right hand side where he had been sitting. There was a second shot and Governor Connally disappeared from sight and then there was a third shot which took off the top of the President's head and had the sickening sound of a grapefruit splattering against the side of a wall. The total time between the first and third shots was about five or six seconds. My first impression was that the shots came from the right and overhead but I also had a fleeting impression that the noise appeared to come from the front in the area of the Triple Underpass. This may have resulted from my feeling, when I looked forward toward the overpass, that we might have ridden into an ambush."

The others in that car were: George Hickey, Paul Landis, Glenn Bennett, John Ready, William McIntyre, Clinton Hill, Emory Roberts, Samuel Kinney, and Kenneth O'Donnell.

Powers accompanied JFK's casket on Air Force One from Dallas to Andrews Air Force Base and refutes the theory of David Lifton that the body was moved during the trip so that it could be secretly taken off the jet and altered before it arrived at Bethesda for the autopsy. Powers says that the casket was never left unattended so there was no opportunity for the body to have been moved or altered.

Presidential Limousine

More than 21 feet long, this was a stretched version of the standard 1961 Lincoln Continental convertible. The car had a hydraulically controlled rear seat and a special motorcade throttle that would maintain a speed of 10-to-12 miles per hour. The limo was called the X-100 by the Secret Service. The car had been flown into Texas on November 20 aboard an Army C-130 cargo plane.

Officially the car was driven by Secret Service agent George W. Hickey Jr. from Parkland Hospital to Love Field. The car was flown from Dallas to Washington, D.C., on the evening of November 22, 1963, and then driven from Washington to Dearborn, Michigan, just before Christmas of that year. From Michigan it was driven to Cincinnati, Ohio, where, on Christmas Eve, it was fitted with a new bulletproof bubbletop.

Carl Renas, who was the head of security for the Dearborn Division of the Ford Motor Company, says that he drove the car from Washington directly to Cincinnati and that during that time he noticed a full through and through bullet hole in the windshield. Officially the hole in the windshield was just a crack caused by a bullet fragment striking the glass on the inside. Renas says the Secret Service told him to keep his mouth shut.

Even while the limousine was still parked outside the emergency entrance to Parkland Hospital the full bullet hole in the windshield was being noticed. *St. Louis Post-Dispatch* reporter Richard Dudman said, "I could not approach close enough to see which side was the cup-shaped spot that indicates a bullet had pierced the glass from the opposite side." Dudman's colleague Frank Cormier of the Associated Press also saw the hole. Officer

Horribly stained with blood and gore, the backseat of the presidential limousine following the shooting. *(Collector's Archive)*

H. D. Freeman of the Dallas police said in an interview eight years after the assassination, "I was right beside it. I could have touched it. It was a bullet hole. You could tell what it was." Officer Starvis Ellis concurred: "You could put a pencil through it," he said.

Price, Jesse C.

At the time of the assassination, Price was standing on the roof of the Terminal Annex Building, which is on the south side of Dealey Plaza, at the southwest corner of Houston and Commerce.

Price told the Dallas Sheriff's Department 30 minutes after the shooting that he had heard a "volley of shots." After the shooting, he saw a man running from behind the wooden fence atop the grassy knoll toward the railroad cars.

He said the running man was about five-feet-six or five-feet-seven, 145 pounds, with long, dark hair and that he had something in his hand. He said he was about 25 years old and wore a white dress shirt and khaki-colored trousers. (This last statement is consistent with the testimony of witnesses Lee Bowers and Julia Mercer.)

On March 27, 1966, Price told Mark Lane, "He was bare-headed, and he was running very fast, which gave me the suspicion that he was doing the shooting, but I could have been mistaken. . . . [He ran] over behind that wooden fence past the cars and over behind the Texas School Book Depository." Price added that he was carrying something "in his right hand."

Prío Socarrás, Carlos   See SUSPICIOUS DEATHS.

Prouty, Fletcher

Prouty was chief of special operations for the Joint Chiefs of Staff. He was in New Zealand at the time of the assassination and bought a newspaper later in the day. The paper, the *Christchurch Star,* named Oswald as the assassin and included a photo of Oswald dressed in a suit and tie. Later, Prouty was reportedly horrified to discover that Oswald's biography (defection to Russia, pro-Castro, Russian wife, etc.) and photo (looking sharp) went out over the international news wire before Oswald was arrested by the Dallas police. Harrison Edward Livingstone checked out this claim and found that the info had actually gone over the wire two hours *after* Oswald's arrest. Still quick but hardly impossible.

Prouty was a consultant to Oliver Stone's film *JFK.* The character "X," played by Donald Sutherland, was based on Prouty. Prouty died June 6, 2001.

Prusakov, Ilya   See OSWALD, MARINA.

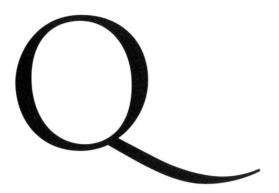

Quigley, John Lester   See FEDERAL BUREAU OF INVESTIGATION.

Quinn, Rosaleen
Quinn once dated Oswald while he was in the U.S. Marines. She was the aunt of Oswald's fellow marine in MACS-9, Henry Roussel Jr. Researcher Edward Jay Epstein wrote: "one Marine asked [Oswald] to have dinner with his aunt . . . an extremely attractive airline stewardess from New Orleans, because she was studying Russian for the State Department's foreign-language examination. She met Oswald in a cafeteria in Santa Ana [California] and they spoke Russian for about two hours. Although she had been studying Russian with a Berlitz tutor for more than a year, she found that Oswald had a more confidant command of the language than she did and could string entire sentences together without much hesitation. She asked how he had learned Russian, and he shrugged and said that he had "taught himself" by listening to Radio Moscow. . . . Just before she left Santa Ana, Oswald took her to see the film *South Pacific,* and afterward they had a drink at a neighborhood bar. Again they practiced their Russian and spoke of traveling. This time Oswald told her that he had plans to go to Europe, but he did not mention what they were."

After the assassination, the FBI interviewed Quinn and reported, "[She] recalled that Oswald was a quiet individual and that it was difficult to converse with him. . . . The evening date . . . did not prove to be a very interesting one . . . she concluded by stating that she has never seen nor heard from Oswald since."

Quiroga, Carlos   See D.R.E.

Raikin, Spas T.

It was Raikin who met the Oswalds in June 1962 at the New York City pier upon their arrival from the Soviet Union. The Warren Commission says Raikin was working for the Traveler's Aid Society and had been asked by the State Department to meet the Oswalds.

According to Jim Garrison, Raikin was then also the secretary-general of the "American Friends of the Anti-Bolshevik Bloc of Nations, Inc." That organization was a private [neo-Nazi] anti-Communist operation with extensive intelligence connections."

According to Peter Dale Scott, one of Raikin's associates was Maurice B. Gatlin, a frequent visitor to 544 Camp Street in New Orleans, an address that had once been stamped upon Fair Play for Cuba Committee leaflets distributed by Oswald.

(See also 544 CAMP ST.)

Rather, Dan

Rather, the current *CBS Evening News* anchorman, was then a 32-year-old bureau chief for the Columbia Broadcasting System affiliate in Dallas. Rather was in charge of setting up CBS's coverage of President Kennedy's visit to Dallas. Rather was on the west side of the triple underpass at the time of the assassination, waiting to pick up a reel of film shot during the motorcade.

Rather claims to be the first man to approach Abraham Zapruder following the assassination to acquire his film of the shooting. According to Warren Commission Counsel David W. Belin, "[Rather] took the film and was able to have the processing of the film expedited." All other sce-narios of Zapruder's film from camera to processing do not include Rather's participation.

Rather was, however, one of the first reporters to be allowed to see the film. After viewing it, he said that it showed President Kennedy's head snapping forward with the fatal shot. For years it was assumed that Rather had been purposefully misrepresenting the Zapruder film to the world, but with new evidence that the Zapruder film is a drastically altered document of the event, perhaps Rather was telling the truth about what the film showed at that time.

Rather was the first to report the name and background of the accused assassin—although he referred to the suspect as "Lee Henry Oswald," the same variation in name seen in several CIA documents. Rather's rise to the top was rapid from that point on.

In a February 6, 1992, Associated Press interview, Rather said he was "at the end of the motorcade route outside the plaza, waiting for the final 'film drop' for the motorcade's camera crew. . . . The motorcade never passed me. Here comes the limousine, but it seems to be going awful fast and it sort of streaks by in a blur. And I sensed that something was wrong. I had no idea. I had heard no shots." Rather ran into Dealey Plaza—he didn't say if he went under or over the triple underpass—and, "Now I had in front of me the grassy knoll, the School Book Depository. God, the chaos and confusion! People were on the ground, screaming. Police were running around. It was clear then . . . something was wrong."

The Associated Press reported that Rather "sprinted the few blocks back to the CBS affiliate, and heard the first radio bulletins that shots had been fired in Dealey Plaza.

. . . Rather called [Parkland] and confirmed the death with emergency room witnesses, breaking the story seventeen minutes before the official report that the president was dead."

Rayburn, Sam Taliaferro

According to FBI special agent Vincent Drain, Speaker of the House Rayburn was the person who arranged for Lee Harvey Oswald to receive a hardship discharge from the U.S. Marine Corps, ostensibly because Marguerite Oswald, Lee's mother, had been injured at work when she dropped a box on her foot. The injury was not real, and Oswald used his early discharge to get an early start on his plans to leave for the Soviet Union.

For 17 years, Rayburn was the U.S. Speaker of the House of Representatives. He was born January 6, 1882, in Roane County, Tennessee, the eighth of 11 children born to William Marion and Martha Waller Rayburn. His father, an illiterate Confederate veteran, learned to read from his wife at the kitchen table in their log cabin. The family moved to a 40-acre farm in Flag Springs, Texas, in 1887. From 1900 to 1903, Rayburn attended East Texas Normal in Commerce, the school now known as Texas A & M University. In 1906, Rayburn ran for and was elected to the Texas state House of Representatives. He was reelected for two additional terms, and while in Austin he attended law school at the University of Texas at Austin. He passed the bar in 1908 and served as speaker of the Texas House in 1911. Rayburn was first elected to the Congress of the United States in 1912, representing the Fourth District of Texas. He was reelected 24 consecutive times. He served as chairman of the Interstate and Foreign Commerce Committee, 1931–37, and was a major architect of Franklin D. Roosevelt's New Deal. He coauthored six important laws: the Railroad Holding Company Act, the Federal Communications Act, the Truth-in-Securities Act of 1933 (to prevent fraud in the sale of stocks and bonds), the Securities Exchange Act of 1934, the Rural Electrification Act, and the Public Utility Holding Company Act of 1935. On September 16, 1940, he was elected Speaker of the House of Representatives and held the position until 1961, except for the 80th and 83rd congresses when he was minority leader. Sam Rayburn served as Speaker for longer than anyone else. (The previous record was set by Henry Clay in the first quarter of the 19th century.) He was also chairman of the Democratic National Committee in 1948, 1952, and 1956. Rayburn died November 16, 1961, in Bonham, Texas, at the age of 79. His funeral was attended by President John Kennedy; two former presidents, Harry Truman and Dwight Eisenhower; and one future president, Lyndon Johnson.

Redbird Airport

An airport in the south Oak Cliff section of Dallas. According to Ricky White—who says his father, Roscoe, was one of the men who shot the president—Officer J. D. Tippit was to drive the assassins to the airport, where their getaway plane would be waiting. Researcher Matt Smith claims the pilot of that plane was to be John Crawford, the only known man to have been friends with both Jack Ruby (according to researcher Penn Jones Jr.) and Buell Wesley Frazier, the man who gave Oswald a ride to work on the morning of the assassination. Crawford and Frazier were longtime schoolmates in Huntsville, Texas. Since Crawford lived near Redbird Airport, Smith theorizes that it was Crawford who was assigned to fly the assassins out of town. Crawford's name joins a pilot list of suspects that includes Jules Ricco Kimble, Joe Cody, David Ferrie, Pat Kirkwood, Charles Frederick Rogers, et al. Crawford died in a plane crash near Huntsville on April 15, 1969. The circumstances surrounding the crash were most strange. Crawford was living at the time in a trailer home at the Huntsville airport. Investigators found the stereo still playing in his trailer. Six other people died in the crash, three men, a woman, and two children. All three men had left their keys in their cars and the woman had left her purse on the car seat.

The story is supported by Wayne January, who ran a plane-rental business at Redbird Airport. January told the FBI after the assassination that, on November 20, 1963, he was approached by two men (one of whom resembled Oswald) who wanted to rent a plane for a flight to Mexico on the afternoon of the assassination. January said he "didn't like the look of them" and refused to rent the plane.

Rich, Nancy Perrin   See PERRIN, ROBERT AND NANCY.

Rickerby, Arthur

Life magazine photographer who rode in the Dallas motorcade in Camera Car 2. Born in March 1921 in New York, New York, Rickerby served in the U.S. Navy during World War II. He carried a 35mm Nikon in the Dallas motorcade. Rickerby later said that he thought the first shot was a "giant firecracker." He said he saw "people diving to the ground, covering up their children or scurrying up the banks. We saw Secret Service men running with guns drawn, and thought they were chasing someone." Rickerby died in August 1972.

Roberts, Earlene

Oswald's housekeeper at 1026 North Beckley Street, where he lived on weekdays at the time of the assassination, registered under the name O. H. Lee. Mrs. Roberts told the Warren Commission that at about 1:00 P.M. on November 22, 1963, Oswald entered her rooming house in an unusual hurry. He came into the house in his shirtsleeves and left zipping up a jacket. He stayed only a few minutes. During the time Oswald was in the house, she said, a Dallas police squad car containing two uniformed policemen parked in front of the house. The car's horn was honked twice ("tit-tit," she described it), then drove off. After Oswald left the house, Roberts saw him standing at the bus stop on the east side of the street. The next time she looked out the window, he was gone.

Officer Tippit was shot to death sometime from eight to 12 minutes later. His murder took place about a mile away. The bus Oswald was supposedly waiting for did not go in the direction of Tippit's murder.

Roberts first said she thought the police car's number was 207. According to an FBI memo dated November 29, 1963, written by special agents Will Hayden Griffin and James C. Kennedy, "Mrs. Roberts advised after Oswald had entered his room at about 1 P.M. on November 22, 1963, she looked out the front window and saw Police Car No. 207 with two uniformed policemen in the car which slowed up and stopped in front of the residence at 1026 Beckley, and one of the officers blew the horn on the car and then drove slowly on Beckley toward Zangs Boulevard. Mrs. Roberts said the reason she recalled the number of the car was because she had worked for two policemen who drove Squad Car 170, and she looked to see if these were the two officers she knew parked in front of the residence."

Car 207 was supposedly at the Texas School Book Depository at that time. After receiving an argument from interrogators, she later listed other squad-car numbers as possibilities as well. The Dallas police said no police car was in that vicinity at the time.

The Warren Commission said Oswald went from his room to the scene of the Tippit killing on foot, which is moving at quite a clip. Some have speculated that Oswald got a ride from Tippit, who was driving Car 10. If so, who was the other man in the car?

Reporter Hugh Aynesworth says that he spoke with Mrs. Roberts on the afternoon of the assassination and that she made no mention of the police car stopping in front of the house and beeping its horn. The first mention of the incident comes in an interview Roberts gave to FBI agent Will Hayden Griffin on November 29, 1963.

According to a memo written by J. Edgar Hoover on May 25, 1964, "The reason for any police car honking the horn in front of this address is unknown, however, it is entirely possible this was a car in plant to determine if Oswald returned to his home."

Roberts was connected to the assassination in another way. Her sister, Mrs. Bertha Cheek, once considered buying a portion of Ruby's Carousel Club and had, on one occasion a few days before the assassination, visited the Carousel.

(See also HILL, GERALD LYNN; 1026 NORTH BECKLEY.)

Robinson, Marvin C.   See CRAIG, ROGER.

Robinson, Mike

Robinson was 14 years old in November 1963 and watched the Dallas motorcade from the corner of Main and Harwood Streets in front of the Dallas police headquarters. Robinson was with a friend whose father was a higher-up in the department. After the parade passed, the boys went to a movie—*not* at the Texas Theatre—and while there heard that the president had been shot. They headed back to the Dallas police station where Robinson had an opportunity to briefly see Lee Harvey Oswald as he was being led out of an elevator. During that same time Robinson saw motorcycle officer Bobby Hargis, still covered with blood and brain matter, slamming his helmet against a wall and going berserk so that he had to be restrained by other policemen. During the late afternoon, Robinson happened to use the men's room in the basement of the building and, while in a stall, claims he overheard a very disturbing conversation. Three other men were in the room. He heard one say, "You knew you were supposed to kill Lee—then, you stupid son of a bitch, you go kill a cop." There was a pause as another man came into the men's room and the conversation continued only after that newcomer had left. The concluding comment was, "Lee will have to be killed before they take him to Washington." Robinson lingered in the toilet long after the men had gone and upon leaving passed a policeman in the locker room who glared at him. Robinson later identified the glaring man as assassination suspect Roscoe White.

(See also HARGIS, BOBBY; WHITE, ROSCOE.)

Robinson, Tom

One of the morticians who prepared President Kennedy's body for burial, Robinson said that he used wax to plug up the bullet wound on the right side of Kennedy's forehead, a hole which officially did not exist. Robinson also stated that he had to plug three small holes in Kennedy's cheek, cause unknown, which he discovered only when embalming fluid began to leak through.

(See also AUTOPSY OF JOHN F. KENNEDY; PARKLAND HOSPITAL.)

Rockefeller Commission

Commission formed in January 1975 at the orders of then-president Gerald Ford to investigate improprieties by the CIA. The executive director of the commission was David Belin, an assistant counsel for the Warren Commission. It was during this commission's hearings that the world first learned of CIA plots to assassinate Fidel Castro as well as plots to assassinate Rafael Trujillo of the Dominican Republic and Patrice Lumumba of the Congo. The latter two were actually assassinated.

Rodriguez, Angelo   See CASTILLO, LUIS ANGEL.

Rodriguez, Mario   See CASTILLO, LUIS ANGEL.

Rodríguez Orcarberro, Manuel   See D.R.E.

Rogers, Charles Frederick   See THREE TRAMPS.

Roselli, Johnny

Roselli was a powerful asset to both organized crime and the CIA's efforts to rid Cuba of Castro. Assassination analysts who believe the CIA was responsible for JFK's death and those who believe organized crime was behind the crime share common ground here. (And, because the two groups had been working together since World War II, the theories cannot be mutually exclusive.)

Like Jack Ruby, Roselli started as a street hood in Chicago working for Al Capone. After John Martino was released from a Havana prison, having been arrested in the Bay of Pigs, he and Roselli started a new effort to combat Castro with its headquarters in Key Biscayne, Florida.

According to investigator Scott Malone, Roselli met with Jack Ruby twice during October 1963. Roselli had said that Ruby was "one of our boys" and that Ruby had killed Oswald to silence him. According to Charles Rappleye and Ed Becker in their book *All American Mafioso: The Johnny Roselli Story,* Roselli and Jack Ruby met at two small hotels in Miami during October 1963.

Roselli may have known Ruby as early as 1933, when both had dealings with Santa Anita Race Track in Los Angeles. After agreeing to testify to the Senate and speaking to columnist Jack Anderson, Roselli was garroted, stabbed, and dismembered, and left to float in an oil drum off the coast of Florida in August 1976. His date of death is officially listed as August 7, 1976.

(See also *GEMSTONE FILE, THE*; RUBY, JACK.)

Rowland, Mr. and Mrs. Arnold Louis

Assassination witnesses who were standing at the west entrance of the Dallas County Records Building on Houston Street, about 150 feet from the sixth floor of the Texas School Book Depository at the time of the shooting. In an FBI interview, Arnold said that, at 12:15, 15 minutes before the assassination, he saw a man with a "high-powered rifle" standing about five feet from the southwest corner window, on the other side of the building from the "sniper's nest." Rowland said the man was 140–150 lbs., light-complected, with short-cropped dark hair. He was wearing an unbuttoned light-colored shirt over a T-shirt and dark slacks. In the "sniper's nest" window, Rowland saw a second man, black, 55 years old, practically bald, and very thin.

The black man was there until five minutes before the assassination. Rowland assumed the men were Secret Service agents. When the shots were fired, he ran in the direction of the grassy knoll with everyone else.

Rowland's wife, Barbara, could not corroborate what her husband had seen. She is near-sighted and claims she was not wearing her glasses.

Ruby, Jack Leon (a.k.a. Rubenstein, Jack "Sparky")

Ruby murdered Lee Harvey Oswald in the basement of the Dallas police station on the morning of November 24, 1963, as Oswald was being transferred from the city to the county jail facilities.

The murder was committed on live television, the first homicide ever to be committed under those circumstances. Photographer Bob Jackson won a Pulitzer Prize for his photo of Ruby shooting Oswald. Photographer Jack Beers was nominated for a Pulitzer for his photo of the scene, taken a fraction of a second earlier and from a position to the right of and above Jackson's.

Ruby was born on March 25, 1911, in Chicago where he grew up around mobsters. Ruby made money as a youth by scalping tickets and running numbers for mobster Al Capone through his fellow organized-crime member Frank Nitti. Ruby grew into a man with a cleft chin and five o'clock shadow who wore diamond pinkie rings.

From as early as 1946, Ruby was a U.S. government informant and police-protected trafficker in narcotics. Ruby's vice activities put him in contact with top Texas oilmen and politicians.

Ruby talked to the Kefauver Committee in 1950 and, in exchange, the FBI eased up on their investigation of organized crime in Dallas. In 1959, he reportedly visited Florida mob boss Santos Trafficante in a Cuban prison.

The Warren Commission learned that Ruby's acquaintances included Benny Barish, a Democratic bagman in

San Francisco; Maurice "Frenchy" Medlevine, who was, along with Ruby, a member of the Dave Miller gang in Chicago, and who in 1970 was arrested as part of a national stolen-securities ring; and Irwin Weiner, who was reportedly a major organized crime financial figure in the Midwest. Ruby telephoned Weiner on October 26, 1963.

At the time of the assassination, Ruby lived with George Senator at 323 South Ewing Street in the Oak Cliff section of Dallas.

Ruby's connection with drugs has been largely ignored by assassination researchers. As far back as 1956 there were FBI memos from Los Angeles to Dallas with information that Ruby was working as a liaison between the Dallas police and Dallas' narcotics dealers. The informant's name was Eileen Curry. She said her husband wanted to move drugs into Dallas but first had to "get the okay" from Ruby. Ruby's friend Dallas crime boss Joe Civello served six years of a 15-year sentence on a narcotics conviction during the 1930s and got a pardon after Sheriff Bill Decker, an "old bootlegger" as one mobster called him, testified for Civello as a character witness.

Ruby worked at the Santa Anita racetrack during the 1930s. That track was run at the time by assassination suspect Johnny Roselli.

Leon Cooke, secretary-treasurer of the Waste Handler's Union in Chicago, was murdered in December 1939 in the presence of Ruby, who was arrested and held for a time as a suspect in the killing. That murder, Robert Kennedy later wrote, was instrumental in the mob's gaining control of the Teamsters' Central States Pension Fund. Cooke was replaced by a pro-Teamsters man named Paul Dorfman.

Paul Rowland Jones, a Chicago mobster, attempted to bribe the Dallas County Sheriff's Department and the Dallas district attorney into allowing organized crime to operate a nightclub/gambling casino in Dallas unhindered in 1946. Jones offered the Dallas officials a bribe, $1,000 a week. He was promptly arrested and charged with attempted bribery. Perhaps the problem was that the bribe was not large enough. Steve Guthrie of the Dallas Sheriff Department said in a 1963 statement that the man the mob planned to put in charge of their Dallas operation was Ruby. Ruby arrived in Dallas in 1947 and set up a nightclub. Jones later became known as the mob's "paymaster" in Dallas. Jones met with Ruby only days before the assassination.

In exchange for leaving organized crime in Dallas alone, Ruby reportedly appeared before the staff of the Kefauver Senate Rackets Committee in 1950, offering information about the Chicago mob.

According to an organized crime figure named Harry Hall (a.k.a. Haler, Haller and Helfgott), he and Jack Ruby once won a lot of money from Texas oil millionaire H. L. Hunt by betting with him on the outcome of the Cotton Bowl and Rose Bowl college football games.

Jack Ruby died in prison while awaiting a death sentence for the murder of alleged Kennedy assassin Lee Harvey Oswald. *(AP/Wide World Photos)*

Ruby's number of long-distance phone calls skyrocketed during November 1963. Ruby's phone list included men involved both in organized crime and influential with the Teamsters. Here is a rundown of some of the men Ruby called in the weeks leading up to the assassination:

On October 26, 1963, Ruby talked by phone to Irwin Weiner, a Chicago bail bondsman with alleged mob ties. The conversation lasted 12 minutes.

On October 30, 1963, Ruby called Nofia Pecora, a lieutenant to New Orleans organized crime boss Carlos Marcello.

On November 7, 1963, Ruby received a collect call from Robert B. "Barney" Baker, a strong-arm man for Jimmy Hoffa in Chicago, and talked for 17 minutes. Three of Baker's phone numbers were found in Ruby's notebook.

Ruby repeatedly called Breck Wall (a.k.a. Billy Ray Wilson), president of the Dallas council of AGVA, the union which Ruby's strippers were supposed to join. Wall was responsible for reviewing complaints by performers against nightclub operators. Ruby called Wall four times during November 1963. Wall later couldn't remember what the calls concerned. Wall told the FBI in 1963 that, back in 1960, he had almost worked a deal for a "nightclub review" he produced to appear at Ruby's Carousel Club, which was then called the Sovereign Club. Also in on the deal was James Henry Dolan, an AGVA/Mafia man from Denver. When Ruby refused to put the deal on paper, Wall backed out. This upset Ruby so much that he punched Wall's assistant Joseph Peterson—a man who Dolan described as "a little fairy." Wall appears in drag in the exploitation film *Naughty Dallas*, some of which was filmed in Ruby's Carousel Club.

Also on Ruby's phone list was Lewis J. McWillie, with whom Ruby had a history. McWillie was a prominent gambler in Havana, Dallas, and Las Vegas. Ruby traveled to Havana at McWillie's invitation in 1959. McWillie said that Ruby had once "mailed me a pistol." Ruby had told friends that McWillie was his idol. McWillie was also a close friend of Fort Worth nightclub-owner Pat Kirkwood, who entertained the Secret Service the night before the assassination in his beatnik nightclub called The Cellar. He was a business associate of Santos Trafficante and Meyer Lansky, both organized crime bigwigs, and ran the Tropicana Casino in Havana before Castro's takeover and was arrested by Castro after the revolution.

And perhaps most disturbingly, Ruby also called David Yaras, a Teamster hitman.

Ruby called his sister, Eileen Kaminsky, in Chicago about 90 minutes after the assassination. She later said that Ruby was "completely unnerved and crying about President Kennedy's death."

At 2:37 on the afternoon of the assassination, Ruby called his boyhood friend from Chicago Alex Gruber, who was at the time living in Los Angeles and an associate of one of Jimmy Hoffa's top officials. The conversation lasted for approximately three minutes and reportedly consisted of discussions regarding a dog Ruby had promised to give Gruber, Gruber's attempt to open a car wash, and how horrible the assassination was. Gruber had met with Ruby 10 days earlier in Dallas. (See also MATHEWS, RUSSELL D.)

Ruby's claim that he shot Oswald spontaneously is hindered by evidence that Ruby was stalking Oswald throughout the weekend. Ruby was at the midnight press conference in the Dallas police station where Oswald was presented to the world. FBI agent Vincent Drain, who knew and liked Ruby, recognized and spoke to Ruby at the midnight press conference.

Two witnesses say they saw Ruby outside the Dallas police station on the morning of Oswald's murder. Warren E. Richey and John Allison Smith, both Fort Worth television technicians sitting in a truck outside the police station, said that Ruby appeared twice, at 8:00 A.M. and 10:00 A.M.

Chief Justice Earl Warren and Congressman Gerald Ford personally traveled to Dallas to question Ruby in the county jail in June 1964. The questioners behaved like men afraid they would hear too much. Ruby acted as if he were desperate to talk but afraid for his life.

Ruby told them: "Is there any way to get me to Washington? [Warren says no.] I don't think I will get a fair representation with my counsel, Joe Tonahill, I don't think so. I would like to request that I go to Washington and you take all the [polygraph?] tests that I have to take. It is very important . . . Gentlemen, unless you get me to Washington, you can't get a fair shake out of me. If you understand my way of talking, you have to bring me to Washington to get the tests . . . I want to tell the truth, and I can't tell it here. I can't tell it here. Does that make sense to you? . . . Gentlemen, my life is in danger here. Not with my guilty plea of execution . . . Do I sound sober enough to you as I say this? . . . I will tell you gentlemen, my whole family is in jeopardy. My sisters, as to their lives. . . . There is a certain organization here, Chief Justice Warren, if it takes my life at this moment to say it, and [Dallas County Sheriff] Bill Decker said be a man and say it, there is a John Birch Society right now in activity, and [Major General] Edwin Walker is one of the top men of this organization—take it for what it is worth, Chief Justice Warren. . . . Unfortunately for me, for me giving the people the opportunity to get in power, because of the act I committed, has put a lot of people in jeopardy with their lives. Don't register with you, does it? [Warren says, "No, I don't understand that."] Would you rather I just delete what I said and just pretend that nothing is going on? . . . Well, I said my life, I won't be living long now. I know that my family's lives will be gone. . . You can get more out of me. Let's not break up too soon. . . . Mr. Bill Decker said be a man and speak up. I am making a statement now that I may not live the next hour when I walk out of this room."

According to the late Dallas reporter Seth Kantor, who saw Ruby at Parkland Hospital minutes following the assassination, there are 10 facts about Ruby which need further investigation. "1. Leading up to the assassination, Ruby was in debt and seeking money. 2. On the afternoon of Kennedy's assassination, Dallas bank officer Bill Cox saw Ruby with several thousand dollars in hand at the bank, but Ruby moved none of it into or out of his account. 3. Ruby's best sources of money were in organized crime and he met privately with syndicate paymaster Paul Rowland Jones . . . only hours before President Kennedy reached Texas. 4. Organized crime had a known history of control inside the [Dallas Police Department]. 5. When Ruby sprang at . . . Oswald, he came from behind a policeman . . . [W. J.] Blackie Harrison. 6. Harrison had been in position at two different times that Sunday morning to let Ruby know by telephone precisely what the plans were for moving the prisoner Oswald. 7. Ruby left his apartment on the route which led to the silencing of Oswald, after Harrison was in position to make the second and final telephone call to the apartment. 8. Harrison and his partner, detective L. D. Miller, became strangely reluctant witnesses. Miller acted more like a suspect than a witness, refusing at first to become a sworn witness—when all he had done was to have a coffee with Harrison on the morning of Oswald's murder. 9. The evidence shows Ruby lied about his entry to the [Dallas Police] basement. 10. Ruby then tried to conceal his private meeting with police officer Harry N. Olsen soon after Oswald was arraigned as a cop killer."

According to Penn Jones: "Ruby had $2000 on his person [when arrested] and the authorities found $10,000 in their search of his apartment. The statement by the authorities concerning money in Ruby's car was: 'The trunk was full of money.' . . . In a storeroom reserved for Jack Ruby at his apartment house, the police found a case of hand grenades, several M16 rifles, a Browning automatic rifle and several thousand rounds of ammunition."

On Tuesday, April 15, 1969, John Crawford, who was among Ruby's friends, died in a plane crash near Huntsville, Texas. One of Crawford's lifelong friends was Buell Wesley Frazier, Oswald's coworker at the Texas School Book Depository who gave Oswald a ride to work on the morning of the assassination.

Jones said, "Several high ranking telephone people in Dallas hurried to the police shortly after Jack Ruby killed Lee Harvey Oswald, with phone company records proving that Ruby and Oswald knew each other. . . . At Dallas police headquarters, the men were told to go home and forget it. All the phone company men were hastily transferred out of Dallas."

FBI director J. Edgar Hoover wrote a memo to Warren Commission general counsel J. Lee Rankin on February 27, 1964, saying, "Ruby had been contacted nine times by the FBI in 1959, from March 11 to October 2, 'to furnish information.'" Hoover asked that the Warren Commission keep this secret, and they agreed to do so.

In letters smuggled out of jail, Ruby said President Lyndon Johnson was the mastermind behind the assassination. Ruby wrote: "First you must realize that the people here want everyone to think I am crazy . . . isn't it strange that Oswald . . . should be fortunate enough to get a job at the Texas School Book Depository two weeks before. . . . Only one person could have had that information, and that man was Johnson . . because he is the one who was going to arrange the trip. . . . The only one who gained by the shooting. . . . They also planned the killing, by they I mean [President Lyndon] Johnson and the others . . . you may learn quite a bit about Johnson and how he has fooled everyone."

Tom Johnson was a former aide to Lyndon Johnson who was among the few allowed to interview Ruby. At that time Ruby said, "It is the most bizarre conspiracy in the history of the world. It'll come out at a future date. . . . I walked into a trap when I walked down there. I wasn't clean enough. It was my destiny. I'd taken thirty antibiotic and Dexedrine pills. They stimulate you."

Vincent Drain of the FBI claims he overheard Ruby say, "I didn't know they'd condemn me for this. I thought I'd be a hero and I'd be able to have a big restaurant like Jack Dempsey."

A very poor character reference comes from Dallas reporter Hugh Aynesworth, who told assassination researcher Larry A. Sneed, "I didn't like Jack Ruby at all and had known him for years. He was a whiner, a show-off, a showboat, a despicable person and not a very nice man. He was also a guy who would beat up on drunks. I once saw him beat a drunk over the head with a whiskey bottle in 1962. I was actually going to testify against him but had to be in court and the charges were dropped, and I've never seen those charges since. But all this guy tried to do was bum a quarter from Ruby and he hit him with a whiskey bottle and cut his head open."

KLIF reporter Gary DeLaune says, "Jack Ruby was kind of a nuisance guy, a little harmless creature. He hung around KLIF. He had a great friend there in Russ Knight, the 'Weird Beard.' He would hang around KLIF and they'd bowl every night at the Cotton Bowling Palace at Inwood and Lemmon Avenue." (See also WEIRD BEARD.)

Another charming character reference came from sheriff's deputy Jack Faulkner, who said, "Ruby more or less indicated to me that he was a homosexual, and I think he was. He was talking to me one day and said that one of his strippers was telling him that she was pregnant. He apparently told her, "You can't blame it on me! I don't think you can get that way from spit."

A kinder appraisal comes from Dallas police lieutenant Elmo L. Cunningham, who had been in the Texas Theatre at the time Oswald was arrested, who told assassination researcher Larry A. Sneed: "I knew Jack Ruby probably as well as any officer in Dallas. Jack came to Dallas, I guess, in 1946 and ran a little beer joint, dance hall type place on South Ervay Street which I understand was financed by his sister, Eva. I worked down there for him at least once or maybe two or three times." Cunningham said that he was paid by the city but "usually the guy running the joint would also give the officer a few dollars extra." Cunningham continued, "I became acquainted with Jack after working at his place a few times and then put him in jail later for pistol whipping one of his employees out in Oak Lawn. I recall putting him in jail one other time for some type of pistol offense."

Earl Ruby, Jack's brother, decided that Jack needed a "classy" defense lawyer and so hired famous San Francisco torts attorney Melvin Belli, who happened to be a friend of California mobster Mickey Cohen and had previously defended, on narcotics charges, Cohen's stripper girlfriend, Candy Barr, who at one time had worked for Jack Ruby. Earl Ruby paid Belli $25,000, much less than Belli was accustomed to working for—but he took the job anyway because he figured he would make up the difference with a book deal. Before 1964 was through, the David McKay Company had published *Dallas Justice: The Real Story of Jack Ruby and His Trial* by Melvin Belli.

Other members of Ruby's defense team were Sol Dann, who later claimed he quit because of death threats; the 300-pound Dallasite Joe Tonahill, who had also teamed up with Belli during his defense of Candy Barr; Elmer Gertz, who wrote the book *Moment of Madness: The People vs. Jack Ruby;* and Alan Adelson, who later wrote the book *The Ruby Oswald Affair.*

Presiding over the trial was Judge Joseph B. Brown. After the death verdict, however, Judge Brown had to disqualify himself from the case and a retrial was ordered, when it was learned that he too had been working on a book during the trial, the sales of which would have been enhanced by a quick conclusion of the proceedings. (Ruby did not live to see his second trial and Brown's book was never finished.) This is the same Judge Brown who granted columnist Dorothy Kilgallen permission to interview Ruby alone for 30 minutes during Ruby's murder trial. According to Penn Jones Jr., even Ruby's guards left the room during the interview. Kilgallen died before she could publish what she had learned.

"Dallas Justice," as Belli called it, definitely threw the Californian off his game. Judge Brown, at one point during the proceedings, admonished Belli during a sidebar meeting for "citing nigger cases." Belli (pronounced Bell-EYE) was further flustered by Dallas assistant district attorney Bill Alexander, who insisted on calling him "Mr. Belly."

As part of Ruby's defense, Belli put character witnesses on the stand to testify that Jack was a nice guy. Among these witnesses was Barney Ross (originally Barney Rasofsky), Ruby's childhood friend from Chicago who had gone on to become the welterweight boxing champion of the world. Ross testified that, when young, Ruby frequently had tantrums and was very easily aroused. Ross said Ruby's childhood was spent in a grim environment but, despite the squalor, Ruby was considered honest and reputable.

After Ruby's conviction, Ross helped raise funds for his substantial legal bills.

Another character witness was Roby A. Pryor, a printer for the *Dallas Times Herald* who once worked for Ruby at one of his nightclubs. Pryor established Ruby's emotional nature with an anecdote: Jack taking presents to a Catholic orphanage. Pryor also established Ruby's deteriorating mental state following the assassination by describing how he had run into Ruby at 4:00 A.M. on November 23, 15 and one-half hours after the assassination. Ruby, he said, had discussed the great loss to the nation and the Kennedy family. Ruby bragged that he had "scooped" other Dallas nightclub proprietors by changing his newspaper ad into a "memorial" to JFK. Ruby expressed his pleasure at having overheard Dallas district attorney Henry Wade talking on the phone and the way he had corrected one of Wade's factual errors. This incident actually occurred while Wade was speaking to reporters in the Dallas police station. Wade had erroneously stated that Oswald was a member of the "Free Cuba Committee." Ruby corrected him, saying that Oswald actually belonged to the "Fair Play for Cuba Committee." This incident is made more interesting by the fact that there really is a Free Cuba Committee, but it is not a pro-Castro organization such as the one to which Oswald supposedly belonged. It was, rather, right wing and anti-Castro, and reportedly not above suspicion in the assassination. (See also ALPHA 66.) Pryor testified, "Jack was happy about being able to feel like he could assist the District Attorney in making that correction, and he told me, he said that he knew Mr. Wade and that he knew influential people." On cross-examination, Pryor told the prosecution that Ruby thought it was a rare privilege to see Oswald in person at the midnight press conference and that Ruby described Oswald as "a little weasel."

Instead of concentrating on showing that Ruby had murdered Oswald without malice (premeditation), Belli attempted to prove that Ruby was temporarily insane because he suffered from "psychomotor epilepsy" due to head injuries he had received throughout his life. The jury didn't buy it. Belli was fired by the Ruby family after Jack was sentenced to death. Ruby became despondent and tried to commit suicide by sticking a wet finger into an electric socket and by banging his head against the walls of his cell.

Just before his appeal began (January 3, 1967), Ruby died of cancer. He told family members that he had been "injected with cancer cells."

In 1990, the .38 Colt Cobra that killed Oswald was for sale. The asking price: $130,000.

Ruby's Strippers   See JACK'S GIRLS.

Russo, Perry Raymond

Russo claimed to be a longtime acquaintance and "play-mate" of assassination suspect David Ferrie. We can corroborate that Russo knew Ferrie because, in a 10-page screed Ferrie wrote in February 1962 regarding his legal difficulties—Ferrie had been arrested on morals charges—Ferrie mentioned that he knew Perry Russo and that Russo was a "hard character."

According to historian Will Robinson, "Russo was born on May 14, 1941, to Francis Raymond Russo and Morie Kimbrell Russo. Perry spent most of his early years in the Gentilly section of New Orleans. He attended Our Lady of the Sea elementary school, maintaining about a C+ average, and then went on to Colton Junior High School. In 1959 he was graduated from McDonogh High School. Noting that he was very active in school affairs, his brother recalled that Perry once outpolled a fellow student 400 to seventy votes for the class vice-presidency. First enrolling at Tulane University, Russo remained for two years and then, because his Catholic father wished it, he transferred to Loyola University and took his political science degree there in 1964. Perry's mother died in 1963. Francis Russo, his father, lived at 4607 Elysian Fields and was employed as a machinist at the Champion Rings Service. His brother Edwin, twenty-eight years old, took a master's degree at Tulane, and became an engineering instructor at Louisiana State University while studying for his doctorate. Married, he had three children. Perry Russo worked for a financial division of the General Electric Company, but when he left his father's residence in 1966 to move to Baton Rouge he took a position as a salesman with the Equitable Life Assurance Society. Taylor Bernard, his superior, regarded Russo as one of the better newer sales persons, saying he was reliable and had done his job well. The Barry Goldwater campaign in 1964 drew Russo into his initial affiliation with the Republican party and he supported the Senator's Presidential efforts, although he has indicated that he might have been a little more at home with a more liberal candidate."

Russo was twenty-one years old in 1963. He became a key witness in Jim Garrison's prosecution of Clay Shaw for conspiracy to assassinate JFK in 1967 when he positively identified a photo of Clay Shaw as "Clem Bertrand," a man he had overheard discussing plans to assassinate JFK.

"Russo overheard Shaw and Ferrie engaging in a discussion of the prospective murder of John Kennedy," Garrison said. Under close medical supervision, Garrison had Russo hypnotized and given Sodium Pentothal (a truth serum), both of which revealed that Russo was telling the truth.

Russo said the meeting took place "somewhere around the middle of September 1963" in Ferrie's New Orleans apartment. Also at the meeting initially were several anti-Castro Cubans and a man who was introduced to him as "Leon Oswald."

According to Garrison, "The talk turned to the possibility of assassinating Fidel Castro. This conversation was speculative and strongly anti-Kennedy . . . [After the Cubans left, leaving Bertrand, Ferrie, Russo and "Oswald" alone] Ferrie, Russo said, was pacing back and forth, saying that they could get rid of Kennedy and blame it on Castro. Then there could be an excuse to invade Cuba. . . . All they had to do was get Kennedy out in the open . . . Ferrie emphasized that 'triangulation of crossfire' was the way to do it." At the Shaw trial, Russo's testimony was—apparently successfully—discredited by the defense attorneys with claims that Garrison had hypnotized and drugged Russo to influence his testimony. During cross-examination at the Shaw trial, Russo said: "Ferrie talked about so many things . . . there was some talk of the assassination last summer, but we talked about many things. He talked about a cure for cancer. You name it, he talked about it. I learned not to argue with him. I knew that he knew everything. . . . To me, he was a walking encyclopedia . . . he knew it all . . . all the answers . . . why should I question him?"

During earlier direct examination, Russo described the meeting as being in September 1963 in Ferrie's apartment. Present were Russo, Ferrie, Shaw (using the name Clem Bertrand) and "Leon Oswald."

Russo testified: "Ferrie took the initiative in the conversation, pacing back and forth as he talked . . . [He said] an assassination attempt would have to involve diversionary tactics . . . there would have to be a minimum of three people involved. Two of the persons would shoot diversionary shots and the third . . . would shoot the 'good shot.' . . . [You would have to create] a triangulation of crossfire. . . . If there were three people, one of them would have to be sacrificed."

On June 19, 1967, New Orleans Parish assistant district attorney Andrew Sciambra delivered to Garrison a "memorandum of information" supplied by Russo on June 19, 1967. The memo stated that Walter Sheridan and Richard Townley of the National Broadcasting Company and magazine writer James Phelan had made attempts to get Russo to desert Garrison and help them "destroy" Garrison and his case.

In January 1993, Russo told researcher Edward T. Haslam that he had been a coach of a neighborhood basketball team and met David Ferrie because Ferrie was in love with one of the boys on his team. Ferrie, Russo said, enticed the boy to live with him and, because Russo was friends with the boy's parents, he agreed to infiltrate Ferrie's homosexual circle and try to bring the boy back.

On page 132 of J. Gary Shaw's book *Cover-Up* there is a picture of a young man standing on the grassy knoll several minutes after the shooting who bears an uncanny resemblance to Russo.

Russo made a cameo appearance in Oliver Stone's movie *JFK*. He plays a man in a New Orleans bar who cheers when he learns of President Kennedy's death. Russo himself died soon after the making of the film, on August 16, 1995, in New Orleans of a heart ailment. He was 52.

Ryder, Dial D.   See IRVING SPORTS SHOP.

S

Santana, Emilio

Santana is an assassination suspect who was interviewed by New Orleans Parish district attorney Jim Garrison. According to the assassination researcher who wrote under the name William Torbitt, Santana told Garrison that he was an acquaintance of Jack Ruby, Clay Shaw, Gordon Novel, and William Seymour. (See OSWALD LOOK-ALIKES.) He said that he had been employed by Shaw and knew of one trip to Cuba that Shaw and Ruby had taken together in 1959. Santana also, reportedly, told Garrison that he had been staying at the home of Ruby-stripper Tammy True during the days preceding the assassination (see also JACK'S GIRLS). Santana also claimed to be a CIA agent and an employee of the alleged CIA-front organization known as the Double-Chek (sic) Corporation.

Saul

Hugh C. McDonald—a veteran of military intelligence, the FBI, and Hughes Aircraft—wrote that President Kennedy was shot and killed from the second floor of the Dallas County Records Building (see map) by a man whose code name was Saul.

McDonald says that assassination experts will recognize Saul as the unidentified man who was photographed exiting the Russian embassy in Mexico City in September 1963, whose photos were sent to the FBI in Dallas on the morning of November 22, 1963, before the assassination, mislabeled Lee Harvey Oswald. The code name "Saul" also appears in the Roscoe White theory.

McDonald claims that, after being told the "truth" about JFK's death by CIA agent Herman Kimsey in 1964,

he spent years trying to locate Saul. With the help of a European network of intelligence agents known to him as the "Blue Fox," McDonald finally tracked Saul down in London in 1972. McDonald claims Saul told him the whole story of how he had killed JFK. Saul, who admitted being a professional killer, said he was assigned the Kennedy hit by a man known to him as Trois (the number three in French), whom he had met in Guatemala and Haiti.

Saul reportedly said that he was paid $50,000, half of which he received in advance, the other half of which was kept for him in a Swiss bank account. Saul knew from experience that the assassination was the work of a very powerful group but had no real idea who he was working for when he shot the president.

To explain why Oswald, not a killer, did what he did on November 22, Saul reportedly said that Oswald had been told that he was to stage a fake assassination attempt to alert the government of the necessity for beefed-up Secret Service security. (This scenario is interesting because it explains both the slow Secret Service response to the shooting and the combination of gunfire that was deadly accurate with the bizarrely wide misses reported in Dealey Plaza.)

After Oswald fired and missed on purpose, Saul was to 1. shoot JFK, and 2. shoot Oswald. The Secret Service would get credit for killing "the assassin." When the Secret Service failed to return Oswald's fire, Saul didn't fire upon the sixth floor of the Texas School Book Depository either.

Saul reportedly told McDonald that he had been in Mexico City to observe Oswald, so that he would know whom to shoot when the time came. (This doesn't make sense. How many men would be shooting from that window?)

Saul reportedly told McDonald that he sneaked his weapon into the Records building assembled, loaded, and strapped to his body underneath his clothes. Saul said he used disintegrating ammunition that left little or no ballistic evidence. Therefore any ballistic evidence that was found would link the crime to Oswald's rifle.

Saul reportedly said he did his best to coincide his shots to Oswald's so that it would sound to earwitnesses as if only one man were shooting. According to this scenario, all three of Oswald's shots missed while Saul fired twice, the first shot causing all of the president's and Governor Connally's nonfatal wounds. The second blew out the right side of JFK's head. So McDonald's scenario, like that of the Warren Commission, asks us to believe in the magic bullet.

There is even a bigger problem with "Saul's" scenario. It would have been impossible to shoot President Kennedy from the second floor of the Dallas County Records Building. The windows in that building *do not open.*

(See also ARMY INTELLIGENCE; SECRET SERVICE.)

Schmidt, Larrie H.   See "WELCOME, MR. KENNEDY" AD.

Schmidt, Volkmar   See SOCONY MOBIL COMPANY.

Schrand, Martin
Schrand served in the U.S. Marine Corps with Lee Harvey Oswald in Biloxi, Mississippi, Santa Ana, California, and Cubi Point in the Philippines. While stationed at Cubi Point, Schrand was assigned to guard the U.S. spy plane used to fly over the Soviet Union, the U-2.

Officially, on January 5, 1958, Schrand fatally shot himself in the armpit while on duty. The Office of Naval Intelligence investigated Oswald in connection with Schrand's death and there was a rumor, according to marine Donald Camarata, that Oswald had been, in some way, responsible for Schrand's death.

Scott, Winston MacKinlay (a.k.a. Curtis, Willard)
Ex-FBI agent Scott was the CIA station chief in Mexico City at the time of the assassination. On October 9, 1963, Scott sent the following secret cable—now declassified but redacted—to Director of Central Intelligence McCone: "1. Acc [deleted] 1 Oct. 63, American male who spoke broken Russian said his name [was] Lee Oswald, stated he [was] at Sov[iet] Emb[assy] on 28 Sept when [he] spoke with

Consul whom he believed [to] be Valeriy Vladimirovich Kostikov. Subj[ect] asked Sov[iet] Guard Ivan Obyedkov [deleted] if there [was] anything new re telegram to Washington. Obyedkov upon checking said nothing received yet, but request had been sent. . . . 2. Have photos male appears [to] be American [deletion] 1 Oct. Apparent age 35, athletic build, circa 6 feet, receding hairline, balding top, wore khakis and sport shirt, source [deleted] . . . 3. No local dissem[ination]." (House Select Committee on Assassinations Hearings, Volume IV, p. 212.)

That the Oswald who visited the Soviet embassy in Mexico City was an imposter is supported by an FBI memo that was sent to the Secret Service on the day after the assassination, while Oswald was still alive. It read: "The Central Intelligence Agency advised that on October 1, 1963, an extremely sensitive source had reported that an individual identified himself as Lee Oswald, who contacted the Soviet Embassy in Mexico City inquiring as to any messages. Special Agents of this Bureau, who have conversed with Oswald in Dallas, Texas, have observed photographs of the individual referred to above and have listened to a recording of his voice. These Special Agents are of the opinion that the above-referred-to individual was not Lee Harvey Oswald."

(See also ANGLETON, JAMES JESUS; BOWEN, JACK LESLIE; CENTRAL INTELLIGENCE AGENCY; COLBY, WILLIAM; DULLES, ALLEN; HELMS, RICHARD; HUNT, E. HOWARD; MK/ULTRA; SAUL.)

Secret Service, U.S.
The performance of the U.S. Secret Service during President Kennedy's assassination was dismal. Looking at a series of President Kennedy's motorcades leading up to the one in Dallas, we find that JFK was uniquely insecure in Dallas. In addition, many of the men assigned to protect the president had been out all night drinking on the night before the assassination and were in no condition to perform their duties when the crisis arose.

The Secret Service were later criticized for not making any attempt to secure the buildings or overpasses along the motorcade route. Although Secret Service regulations prohibit turns sharper than 90 degrees in a presidential motorcade, JFK's limousine made a 120-degree turn onto Elm Street seconds before the shooting started. The turn forced the car to slow down, thus creating an easier target.

Forrest V. Sorrels, with Winston Lawson, were the agents who selected the motorcade route. Sorrels was in charge of protecting the motorcade. He sat in the backseat of the motorcade's lead car, an enclosed sedan. William Robert Greer was the driver of President Kennedy's limo, a Lincoln Continental convertible sedan, designation SS Car No. 100-X. Film of the assassination shows that, after the first shot struck the president, the limo's brake lights went

Eyewitness Jim Towner took this photo of Secret Service agent William Greer as he drove the presidential limousine slowly around the difficult turn from Houston Street onto Elm Street. The Dal-Tex Building can be seen in the background. *(Collector's Archive)*

on. Eyewitnesses say the car had almost stopped when the fatal shot was fired.

Greer has been severely criticized for being slow to react to the crisis. Greer was also not sympathetic to the Warren Commission's desire to prove that the assassination was the work of a lone nut. Greer told the Warren Commission, "If President Kennedy had, from all reports, four wounds, Governor Connally three, there have got to be more than three shots, gentlemen."

Sitting beside Greer was agent Roy Kellerman. Sitting behind the Secret Service men were the Connallys, Nellie on the left and the governor on the right, and in the back were President Kennedy on the right and the First Lady on the left.

According to author William Manchester, at Parkland Hospital immediately following the shooting, Greer burst into tears when he saw Mrs. Kennedy. He squeezed her head with both hands and said, "Oh, Mrs. Kennedy, oh my God! Oh my God! I didn't mean to do it, I didn't hear, I should have swerved the car, I couldn't help it! Oh, Mrs. Kennedy, as soon as I saw it I swerved the car. If only I'd seen it in time!" He then wept on the former first lady's shoulder.

There were almost 60 eyewitnesses to the assassination who commented that the presidential limousine slowed down or stopped after the shooting sequence began. However, on November 19, 1964, Greer said to author William Manchester, "After the second shot I glanced back. I saw blood on the Governor's white shirt. The blood was coming out of his right breast. When I heard the first shot I thought it was a backfire. I was tramping on the accelera-

tor at the same time Roy Kellerman was saying, 'Let's get out of here, fast.'" Greer retired in July 1966 because of a stomach ailment.

Agent Kellerman quoted President Kennedy as saying "My God, I am hit." No one else heard the president say anything at all after he was wounded. Kellerman attended President Kennedy's autopsy. Concerning that procedure, Kellerman later told the Warren Commission: "A Colonel [Pierre A.] Finck—during the examination of the President, from the hole that was in his shoulder, and with a probe, and we are standing right alongside of him, he is probing inside the shoulder with this instrument and I said, 'Colonel, where did it go?' He said, 'There are no lanes for an outlet of this entry in this man's shoulder.'" This does not sound like the same autopsy that determined that the bullet had not entered JFK's shoulder, but rather his neck, and that the bullet was not without outlet but rather exited through the throat. Kellerman died in March 1984 of undisclosed causes.

Clinton J. Hill, the agent in charge of protecting the First Lady, rode on the running board of the Secret Service presidential follow-up car, directly behind Kennedy's limo. It was Hill who climbed onto the back of the limousine and pushed Mrs. Kennedy back into her seat after she had crawled onto the trunk. In his Warren Commission testimony, Hill recalled the assassination as he was running toward the rear of the presidential limo, just reaching it: "there was another sound, which was different from the first sound as though someone was shooting a revolver

Amateur photographer Justin Newman took this photo outside the Trade Mart. Clinton J. Hill, the Secret Service agent in charge of protecting the first lady, rides on the back of the presidential limousine as it speeds toward Parkland Hospital. Hill later said, "I noticed a portion of the president's head on the right side was missing and he was bleeding profusely. Part of the brain was gone . . ." *(Collector's Archive)*

into a hard object—seemed to have some type of an echo . . . the second noise that I had heard had removed a portion of the President's head, and he had slumped noticeably to his left . . . I noticed a portion of the President's head on the right rear side was missing and he was bleeding profusely. Part of the brain was gone. . . . His brain was exposed . . . one large gaping wound in the right rear portion of the head."

John D. Ready rode on the right front running board of the Secret Service's presidential follow-up car. According to the *Warren Report,* "Ready . . . heard noises that sounded like firecrackers and ran toward the presidential limousine. But he was immediately called back by Special Agent Emory P. Roberts, in charge of the follow-up car, who did not believe he could reach the President's car at the speed it was traveling." At that point, the president's car was traveling approximately 11 miles per hour and was slowing up. Roberts, a former Baltimore policeman, exhibited unusual behavior after the assassination as well. While the agents assigned to Kennedy stayed with the body while the vice presidential agents stayed with LBJ, Roberts switched his allegiance to Johnson immediately.

Glenn Bennett rode in the car directly behind the presidential limo. Bennett said, "I looked at the back of the President. I heard another firecracker noise and saw the shot hit the President about four inches down from the right shoulder." This location for JFK's back wound agrees with the observations of the Parkland Hospital doctors, and places the entry wound too low for it to have been caused by the "magic bullet."

Samuel Kinney drove the backup car immediately behind JFK's limo.

George W. Hickey Jr. sat in the backseat of the presidential follow-up car. At the sound of gunfire, Hickey rose to his feet with his AR-15 machine gun, but saw nothing to shoot at. In a statement written several days after JFK's death, Hickey said that the first shot sounded to him like a firecracker. He wrote: "I stood up and looked to my right and rear in an attempt to identify it. Nothing caught my attention except people shouting and cheering . . . [When Kennedy] was almost sitting erect I heard two reports which I thought were shots and appeared to me completely different in sound than the first report and were in such rapid succession that there seemed to be practically no time element between them . . . the last shot seemed to hit his head and cause a noise at the point of impact which made him fall forward and to his left again."

Paul E. Landis Jr. was standing on the right running board of the presidential follow-up car and later said: "I heard what sounded like a report of a high-powered rifle from behind me . . . [I drew my gun and] I heard a second report and saw the President's head split open and pieces of flesh and blood flying through the air. My reaction at

that time was that the shot came from somewhere toward the front . . . and [I] looked along the right side of the road."

Thomas L. "Lem" Johns rode in the right rear of the vice presidential follow-up car, three cars behind President Kennedy's limo. In his written report, Johns said "On the right-hand side . . . a grassy area sloped upward . . I was looking to the right and saw a man standing and then being thrown or hit to the ground."

Jerry D. Kivett rode in the same car, on the far right of the front seat, immediately next to LBJ-aide Clifton C. Carter. Kivett wrote in a November 29, 1963, affidavit: "I heard a loud noise. . . . It sounded more like an extremely large firecracker, in that it did not seem to have the sharp report of a rifle. As I was looking in the direction of the noise, which was to my right rear, I heard another report— then there was no doubt in my mind what was happening."

Warren W. Taylor rode in that car also, on the left-hand side. In the famous Associated Press photo of the assassination taken by James Altgens, it is shown that a fraction of a second after the first shot was fired, Taylor had his door open. (Photos of the vice presidential follow-up car taken earlier in the motorcade show that door to be open at that point also, leaving open the possibility that the door was always left open, so the agents inside could be quicker to react to an emergency.) None of the agents in charge of guarding the president had yet made a move. Several had not reacted at all to the first report. Taylor wrote in a November 29, 1963, affidavit: "I heard a bang which sounded to me like a possible firecracker—the sound coming from my right rear. Out of the corner of my eye and off slightly to the right rear of our car, I noticed what now seems to me might have been a short piece of streamer flying in the air close to the ground, but due to the confusion of the moment, I thought that it was a firecracker going off."

Abraham Bolden, the first black member of the Secret Service, reported in early November 1963, that there was a plot by "four Cuban gunmen" to kill JFK in Chicago. He received this information from the FBI, who detailed the plot to kill the president with "high-powered rifles." No records exist of this report or the ensuing investigation (if there was one). After the assassination, Bolden charged the Secret Service with laxity in protecting JFK. Soon thereafter, Bolden was indicted by the federal government and charged with trying to sell government files. Bolden claimed the charges were "retaliation."

During the investigation of the assassination, it was agent John Joe Howlett's job to see if Oswald could have done in the first few seconds following the assassination what the Warren Commission claimed he did. The Secret Service conducted a test using Howlett: "[Howlett] carried a rifle from the southeast corner of the sixth floor along the east aisle to the northeast corner. He placed the rifle on the floor near the site where Oswald's rifle was actually found after the shooting. Then Howlett walked down the stairway to the second-floor landing and entered the lunchroom. The first test, run at normal walking pace, required one minute, eighteen seconds; the second test, at a 'fast walk' took one minute, fourteen seconds . . . Howlett was not short winded at the end of either test run."

Leon I. Gopadze was the Russian-speaking Secret Service agent who interrogated Marina Oswald extensively following the assassination. Gopadze reported that Marina didn't know if Oswald had ever used the alias "Alek Hidell." Six months later, when Marina testified for the Warren Commission, she not only remembered Oswald using the name but said that she had personally signed that name, at Lee's request, on Fair Play for Cuba Committee membership cards.

Gerald A. "Jerry" Behn spoke with Forrest Sorrels, head of the Dallas Secret Service, 10 hours after the assassination. "It's a plot," Behn said. "Of course," was Sorrels's reply.

According to Vince Palamara's book *The Third Alternative,* Forrest Sorrels reported that he had stayed with JFK's body at Parkland Hospital until it was transported to Love Field, but there is plenty of photographic and documentary evidence to indicate that this is not true. Sorrels, it is clear, actually left Parkland and returned to Dealey Plaza where he found two witnesses willing to say that the shots came from the Texas School Book Depository, "discovered" the erroneous fact that Lee Harvey Oswald was the only Texas School Book Depository employee who was missing from the building, and he accompanied Abraham Zapruder to the offices of Eastman Kodak so that his film could be developed. (Sorrels died on November 6, 1993.)

Secret Service agents investigated Jack Ruby following the assassination as well. Agent Lane Bertram filed a report on December 2, 1963, stating that Ruby had been seen by five witnesses on the 400 block of Milam Street in Houston for "several hours," while JFK was in town. Ruby was seen one block from JFK's "entrance route and from the Rice Hotel where [JFK] stayed."

On November 24, 1963, the day Ruby killed Oswald, agent Roger C. Warner interviewed Ruby-stripper Karen Carlin. In his report on the interview, Warner wrote, "Mrs. Carlin was highly agitated and was reluctant to make any statement to me. She stated to me that she was under the impression that . . . Oswald, . . . Ruby and other individuals unknown to her were involved in a plot to assassinate [JFK] and that she would be killed if she gave any information to the authorities." Carlin disappeared soon thereafter.

In Dallas, according to Dr. James H. Fetzer, many Secret Service regulations were violated. These included: 1. no coverage of open windows along the motorcade route; 2. a turn in the motorcade route of greater than 90 degrees (from Houston onto Elm); 3. no agents riding on the presidential limousine; 4. improper sequence of cars in the motorcade; 5. no military security present; 6. slowing and perhaps stopping the limousine after the shooting sequence began; 7. nonresponsiveness of the agents in the motorcade during the shooting sequence.

Secret Service agents were guilty of tampering with evidence several times at Parkland Hospital. The blood and brains on the backseat of the presidential limousine were immediately cleaned up, destroying what evidential value that material might have had. The cleanup job was done to keep people from seeing and possibly photographing the gore, but the same thing could have been accomplished by a tarp thrown over the car, which would have protected the president's privacy while preserving the evidence. The Secret Service also illegally took President Kennedy's body—also evidence—out of Parkland, and out of Texas.

There was a strange incident at Love Field just before the motorcade began involving Secret Service agents. American Broadcasting Company television film footage shows agent Henry J. Rybka ordered out of the motorcade by agent Emory P. Roberts. There is room for Rybka on the running board next to agent Paul E. Landis but every car goes by, leaving Rybka behind, throwing his arms up in frustration. Roberts was again involved during the shooting sequence. When agent John D. Ready jumped off the presidential follow-up car to run up to the presidential limousine, Roberts ordered him back onto the Secret Service vehicle. Secret Service agent Marty Underwood told researcher Vincent Palamara in 1991 that the CIA, the FBI, and the Mafia all had foreknowledge of the assassination and that he got his information from Mexico City CIA station chief Winston Scott.

There were 15 agents in the motorcade protecting President Kennedy, Mrs. Kennedy, Vice President Johnson, and Mrs. Johnson. Only three of them moved to offer protection during the assassination's shooting sequence. Those three were: Clint Hill, Lem Johns, and Rufus Youngblood, who threw himself over Lyndon Johnson.

Sharp, William

Sharp was apprehended by Dallas police after the assassination because, according to J. R. Leavelle of the Dallas Police Department, "he had been in the building across the street from the [Texas School Book Depository] without a good excuse." This is very similar to what happened to assassination suspect Eugene Hale Brading.

Shaw, Clay (a.k.a. Clay Bertrand, Clem Bertrand)

The only man ever tried (and acquitted) in connection with the assassination. New Orleans Parish district attorney Jim Garrison arrested Shaw and he was indicted following a grand jury hearing. Shaw's trial began on February 6, 1969, and lasted for 39 days. The jury acquitted him without deliberation, stating that Garrison had proved a conspiracy but failed to show that Shaw was part of it. Shaw had been, until 1965, the general manager of the International Trade Mart in New Orleans—the position he held at the time of the assassination.

A CIA memo dated September 28, 1967, and made public in 1977, stated that the CIA's Domestic Contact Services in New Orleans had "received reports" from Shaw regarding international trade and political activities. Shaw had visited and then "reported on" places that included Nicaragua, Argentina, East Germany, and Peru. There were 30 reports in all from Shaw to the CIA, dated from 1949 to 1956. Shaw introduced Deputy Director of Central Intelligence Charles Cabell, brother of the Dallas mayor, when Cabell spoke to a private right-wing organization called the New Orleans Foreign Policy Association in May 1961. There is no evidence that Shaw was still doing work for the CIA at the time of the assassination, but it has been suspected that his past relationship with the organization—especially since he had done work for the Office of Strategic Services, the father of the CIA, during World War II—would have been enough to the agency to help with his defense during his trial.

Shaw told *Who's Who in the South and Southwest* on December 1, 1962, that he was a director of a Swiss corporation called Permindex, a company suspected of being a CIA-front involved in the assassination attempts on French president Charles de Gaulle in 1961 and 1962.

The Warren Commission gathered evidence that Permindex was suspected of funding political assassinations and laundering money for organized crime. Shaw was also on the Board of Directors of Permindex's first cousin, Centro Mondiale Commerciale (CMC). Paris Flammonde wrote that CMC was "composed of channels through which money flowed back and forth, with no one knowing the sources or the destination of these liquid assets." Jim Garrison wrote that CMC was "representative of the paramilitary right in Europe, including Italian fascists, American CIA, and other interests."

Shaw's personal address book was seized at the time of his arrest, along with many of his other possessions, on March 1, 1967. In it was this entry:

Lee Odom
PO Box 19106
Dallas, Tex

The number 19106 (preceded by a pair of Cyrillic figures) appeared in Lee Harvey Oswald's address book.

Shaw died in August 1974, possibly of cancer. No autopsy was performed.

(See also CLINTON, LOUISIANA, INCIDENT; FERRIE, DAVID; GARRISON INVESTIGATION; PERMINDEX; RUSSO, PERRY.)

Shelley, William H.

Texas School Book Depository manager and Oswald's immediate supervisor who was standing just outside the main entrance to the building at the time of the assassination. Shelley told the FBI that School Book Depository employee and Oswald-look-alike Billy Lovelady was seated on the steps in front of him at the time of the shooting. Shelley said he thought the shots came from "west of the Depository."

While Oswald was being questioned by the Dallas police following his arrest, he reportedly said he encountered Shelley just outside the Depository after the shooting. According to the official version of Oswald's statements, Oswald said he then went home because Shelley told him there would be no more work that day. Shelley denies this, but admits to being in the right place for the encounter to have occurred.

Sherman, Dr. Mary

Born in 1913 in Evanston, Illinois, as Mary Stults. At 16, she traveled to France to attend L'Ecole de M. Collnot. She studied there for two years and later taught French while studying for her master's degree at the University of Illinois. She then attended medical school at the University of Chicago. She did groundbreaking research into botanical viruses and her articles on the subject continue to be heavily quoted in botanical literature. During the 1940s she became an associate professor of Orthopedic Surgery and practiced medicine at the University of Chicago's Billings Hospital, one of the few hospitals that participated in ultra-secret plutonium experiments during the 1940s and 1950s in which unsuspecting patients were injected with the radioactive material. In 1952, Sherman was approached by Dr. Alton Ochsner of New Orleans, who asked her to be a partner in his private clinic, where she would be the head of her own cancer laboratory and be named associate professor of Tulane Medical School. She accepted and moved to New Orleans. By the 1960s, Dr. Sherman was recognized as one of the United States's leading cancer experts.

Dr. Sherman, a widow living alone, was murdered on July 21, 1964. At first it was reported in the local press that an intruder had forced his way into her apartment—which was near the corner of St. Charles Avenue and

Louisiana Avenue—had stabbed her to death and then set fire to her body. A neighbor named Juan Valdez had smelled smoke and called the police. The police found an apartment filled with smoke and called the fire department. The fire department broke into the apartment and found the fire limited to a mattress upon which was Dr. Sherman's body. She had been stabbed repeatedly. No murder weapon was found but a large butcher knife was missing from the kitchen. The initial newspaper reports quoted detectives as saying that the apartment door had been forced open, that Dr. Sherman's wallet was empty, and that her car was missing. The next day, these stories were corrected. There was no sign of a forced entry and Dr. Sherman's burglary alarm had been turned off. None of the neighbors had heard a thing.

The newspapers found irony in the paintings that adorned Dr. Sherman's apartment, one of which depicted a frightened woman with her hands to her throat and another which showed a Roman warrior stabbing a woman with a sword.

On July 22 the newspapers began to refer to the murder as a "mutilation slaying," with a quote from a New Orleans police captain saying, "Obviously, some perverted mind was involved." Dr. Sherman's car had been found eight blocks from her home with a palm print on it that has never been identified. Following the autopsy the public learned that, though the body was mutilated, there was no evidence of rape. On August 11, a press blackout on the case was announced and no new information was forthcoming. However, in 1992, researcher Edward T. Haslam acquired the police reports and learned more about Dr. Sherman's strange murder. From these documents we learn that Dr. Sherman's feet were pointing toward the head of the bed when she was discovered. She had received stab wounds to the left arm, in the torso, and on the right thigh just above the knee. The most fascinating news was that, despite the limited nature of the fire in Dr. Sherman's apartment, her right side, from the hip to the shoulder and including the entire right arm, had been burned completely away, exposing internal organs. The cause of death was determined to be a stab wound to the chest that penetrated the heart. There was also a one centimeter laceration of the labia minora, apparently the "mutilation" that had been earlier mentioned. The homicide report was written in two sections, with one dated October 29, 1964, and the other dated November 3, 1964. The body was found nude. Her clothes had been bundled up and placed on her torso, and they were partially burned. There was no sign of a struggle in the apartment. It has never been satisfactorily explained how a fire, which merely charred a portion of Mary's mattress, could at any time have become so hot as to destroy the complete upper right extremity. It has been theorized that whatever took off her right arm—an experimental laser perhaps—was not in her apartment and that her body must have been placed in her apartment with the arm already gone and then perhaps cut and set on fire to cover-up what had happened. The burning is so selective as to be peculiar, with a portion of her scalp charred, yet the hair immediately adjacent to that area not even singed. The heat source must not only have been intense but focused as well. During the press blackout police spent most of their time, it would appear, trying to prove that Dr. Sherman was a lesbian and that her killing had a sexual motive. One of the witnesses with whom police spoke was David Gentry of 4919 Magazine Street. He had seen Dr. Sherman on the day before she was murdered, and sold her an ash tray. Gentry also was once Lee Harvey Oswald's next door neighbor, when Oswald lived on Magazine Street and in 1967 became a witness at the Clay Shaw grand jury hearings, testifying that he had been to parties at Clay Shaw's house.

According to New Orleans Parish district attorney Jim Garrison, Dr. Sherman was involved in her cancer research with assassination suspect David Ferrie. Garrison also said that Dr. Sherman was a financial backer of anti-Castro Cuban causes.

(See also FERRIE, DAVID; OCHSNER, DR. ALTON, SR.)

Simmons, James L.

Simmons stood atop the triple underpass at the time of the assassination and, like other witnesses in that area, saw a puff of smoke drifting over the grassy knoll. Simmons said to researcher Mark Lane in 1966, "[The shot] sounded like it came from . . . toward the wooden fence. And there was a puff of smoke that came from underneath the trees on the embankment directly in front of the wooden fence."

After the shooting, Simmons ran behind the wooden fence atop the grassy knoll. There, he saw footprints behind the fence. There were also footprints on the two-by-four railing of the fence and "on a car bumper there, as if someone had stood up there looking over the fence."

Simmons was a prosecution witness at the Clay Shaw trial at which he said the presidential limo was forced to slow down during the shooting sequence because the motorcycle patrolman at the left front of the car got in the way.

Sitzman, Marilyn

The receptionist for Abraham Zapruder who stood on the pergola's pedestal and steadied Zapruder as he took the most famous home movie of all time. Sitzman told assassination researcher Josiah Thompson in 1966: "There was nothing unusual until the first sound, which I thought was a firecracker, mainly because of the reaction of President

Kennedy. He put his hands up to guard his face and leaned to the left—and the motorcade proceeded down the hill. The next thing I remember is the shot that hit him directly in front of us . . . and we could see his brains come out . . . it exploded his head more or less."

Before the shooting she noticed a young black couple sitting on a park bench next to the concrete steps on her right, drinking cokes, and eating bag lunches. (The park bench is no longer there but there is photographic proof that the bench was there on November 22, 1963.) Sitzman told Thompson: "The main reason I remember 'em is after the last shot . . . I heard a crush of glass and I looked over there and the kids had thrown down their Coke bottles, just threw them down, and just started running towards the back." The couple has never been identified, but they may be responsible for the image on photographs that has come to be known as "Black Dog Man" as well as the "running assailant" seen from across the street by Jean Hill.

Sitzman is not the only one to see the running couple. George Carter in the November 22, 1963, edition of the *Dallas Times Herald* wrote that: "Reporters following the President said a man and woman were seen scrambling on a walk over the underpass." Radio reports on the afternoon of the assassination said that the couple had been chased up "an embankment" by a policeman on a motorcycle.

(See also BLACK DOG MAN; HILL, JEAN; ZAPRUDER, ABRAHAM.)

Skelton, Royce G.

A railroad worker who stood atop the triple underpass during the Dallas motorcade. Skelton wrote in a November 22, 1963, affidavit, "I saw something hit the pavement to the left rear of the [presidential limo] . . . and I heard two more shots . . . then heard another shot and saw a bullet hit the pavement. The concrete was knocked to the south away from the car. It hit the pavement in the left or center lane."

Skelton said he thought the shots came from "around the President's car."

Smith, Edgar Leon, Jr.

Smith was an accident investigator for the Dallas police who joined the department in 1956. At the time of the assassination he was standing on the southeast corner of Houston and Elm Streets, in front of the Criminal Records Building and across from the Texas School Book Depository.

Smith had been assigned to crowd control. He said he heard three shots and thought they came from the pergola on the north side of Elm Street. After the shooting, he ran to that pergola, searched the area, and found nothing.

Later, after the official scenario came out—three shots, all from the Depository—he became unsure of the shots' source.

Years after the assassination, Smith spoke to researcher Larry A. Sneed, saying, "It seemed like a lot of time elapsed between the three shots. . . . Certainly it didn't seem to me that they came from the sixth floor, but things just seem to echo around there. At the time of the shooting I was looking more toward the grassy knoll. However, it was sort of obstructed because there were other cars going by. . . . I reacted by running across the street from the south side of Elm toward the underpass, then cut across the street . . . I followed the crowd with my pistol drawn but holstered it before I crossed Elm headed toward the grassy knoll. I don't recall the amount of time that elapsed, but we did check out the area behind the grassy knoll. . . . We had police officers from different divisions there. There were also, what I assumed, Secret Service and FBI agents there simply because they had loaded carbines and were in civilian clothes. They ran with me toward the grassy knoll, so I'm assuming that some of them came off the cars that followed the presidential limousine. When I got into the parking lot, there were a number of other officers there also. I didn't spend a lot of time back there, but there was a search, which was very unorganized, that took place. I recall looking in some of the cars, but I don't recall going into the cars or looking in the trunks. . . . I was in the railroad yards for just a short time." Smith then reported back to the front of the Texas School Book Depository.

Smith retired from the Dallas Police Department in 1983.

Smith, Joe

A Fort Worth photographer who says he arrived at Dealey Plaza on November 22, 1963 at 2:15 P.M. to photograph the aftermath of the assassination. Minutes after his arrival he photographed the now notorious three tramps as they were escorted from the railroad yards near Dealey Plaza to the Dallas County Sheriff's Office. If Smith is correct about the time of his arrival, this eliminates the often assumed scenario that the tramps were arrested moments following the shooting before they had had an opportunity to escape. The tramps, whoever they were, were obviously not in a hurry to get away if they were still in Dealey Plaza one hour and forty-five minutes after the assassination. Other photographers who took "tramp" photos were Jack Beers and William Allen.

Smith is a separate individual from Joe Marshall Smith.

Smith, Joe Marshall

The Dallas police patrolman who stood at the corner of Elm and Houston Streets, in front of the Texas School

Book Depository at the time of the assassination. Smith thought the shots came from "the bushes of the overpass."

After the shooting, Smith ran toward the triple underpass. He says he smelled gunpowder when he got behind the wooden fence on top of the grassy knoll.

On December 9, 1963, Smith told the FBI that he ran into a man in the parking lot behind the stockade fence. Smith said, "I pulled my pistol from my holster, and I thought, this is silly, I don't know who I am looking for, and I put it back. Just as I did he showed me he was a Secret Service agent."

All real Secret Service agents had followed the motorcade to Parkland Hospital.

Smith, L. C.

The Dallas deputy sheriff who was standing in front of the sheriff's office at the corner of Main and Houston Streets at the time of the shooting. He later wrote in his official report, "I heard a woman unknown to me say . . . the shots came from the fence on the north side of Elm."

Smith, Merriman

The United Press International White House reporter who rode in the Dallas motorcade. The day after the assassination, Smith filed this report: "I was riding in the . . . White House press 'pool' car, a telephone company vehicle equipped with a mobile radio-telephone. I was in the front seat between a driver from the telephone company and Malcolm Kilduff, acting White House press secretary for the President's Texas tour. Three other pool reporters were wedged in the back seat. . . . Suddenly we heard three loud, almost painfully loud cracks. The first sounded as if it might be a large firecracker. But the second and third blasts were unmistakable. Gunfire . . . The President's car, possibly as much as 150 or 200 yards ahead, seemed to falter briefly. We saw a flurry of activity in the [Secret Service] follow-up car. . . . Our car stood still for probably only a few seconds, but it seemed like a lifetime . . . [then] we saw the big bubble-top [JFK's limo] and a motorcycle escort roar away at high speed."

While their car was still on the way to Parkland Hospital, Smith called the United Press International operator and dictated a news flash regarding the shooting. The story was on the wire at 12:34, four minutes following the shooting. Smith's initial report said that there had been automatic gunfire in Dealey Plaza, and that he had heard three "bursts" of gunfire. Also in the car was Associated Press reporter Jack Bell, who was unable to get his story in because Smith would not give up the phone until the car reached Parkland, at which time the line was dead.

Sniper's Nest

Area found in the southeast corner of the Texas School Book Depository's sixth floor, where boxes had been stacked, theoretically to keep others on the floor from seeing that corner. Those boxes consisted of an 18-inch by 12-inch by 14-inch box with the word "BOOKS" written on it that was placed near the window. On top of this was a 13-inch by nine-inch by eight-inch box with "10 ROLLING READERS" written on it. Resting on the brick casing next to the window sill was another "ROLLING READERS" box, forming the "gun rest."

According to the official scenario it is from this sniper's nest that Lee Harvey Oswald committed the assassination. The theory was that Oswald himself had stacked the boxes in that fashion. However, evidence exists that the boxes had been stacked that way by a crew of men who were laying a new plywood floor on the sixth floor during the morning of the assassination. As the new flooring was laid down, boxes on that floor were moved steadily eastward. The exact configuration of the boxes surrounding the sniper's nest is also in question as photographs published by the Warren Commission show three different configurations of boxes near that window, indicating that the boxes were moved after the sniper's nest was discovered by police.

One of the best-known pieces of evidence found by the Dallas police were the three empty shells found at the "sniper's nest." However, a close look at early documents and photographs of the scene seems to indicate that in fact, two empty shells and one live round were found. If this is true the live round turned into an empty shell when police quickly figured out that they had to account for at least three shots. According to the chain of evidence, Detective Richard M. Sims originally picked up the shells and turned them over to Dallas police lieutenant J. C. Day.

It is interesting to note that the first two men to reach the sixth floor following the assassination—Dallas police officer Marrion Baker and Texas School Book Depository superintendent Roy Truly did not report smelling gunpowder.

Though the sniper's nest window is shown as fully open in FBI and Secret Service re-creations of the assassination, photographs taken from both inside and outside at the time of the shooting prove that the window was only half open when it was supposedly used as a rifleman's perch.

Experienced riflemen who have been in that corner of the sixth floor complain that it is not a comfortable place from which to shoot, because of the lowness of the window sill, and because of the closeness of the window to the side wall, forcing the gunman to press his back against a steam pipe to get into position.

(See also FLOOR-LAYING CREW, THE.)

Snyder, Richard Edward

Snyder was the Foreign Service officer stationed in the United States embassy in the Soviet Union, 1959–61, and the first consul to whom Oswald spoke after his arrival in the USSR. That meeting took place on October 31, 1959.

Oswald told Snyder he wanted to renounce his U.S. citizenship. Snyder refused to accept his renunciation and told Oswald that he would have to return "to complete the necessary papers."

Before Oswald left the embassy, he gave Snyder his passport and a handwritten statement requesting that his U.S. citizenship be revoked. During that first 40-minute conversation, Oswald told Snyder that he had been a U.S. Marine Corps radar operator and intimated that he might know things that were of value to the Soviets. Oswald, however, never did file a formal renunciation.

On Monday, July 10, 1961, almost two years later, Oswald met with Snyder again this time in connection with leaving the USSR and returning to the United States. Since Oswald had not officially expatriated himself, his passport was returned.

Snyder testified to the Warren Commission that he could "recall nothing that indicated Oswald was being guided or assisted by a third party when he appeared in the Embassy in July 1961. On the contrary, the arrogant and presumptuous attitude which Oswald displayed in his correspondence with the Embassy from early 1961 until June 1962, when he finally departed from Russia, undoubtedly hindered his attempts to return to the United States. Snyder . . . testified that although he made a sincere effort to treat Oswald's application objectively, Oswald's attitude made this very difficult."

Socony Mobil Company

Offshoot of Standard Oil that, after urging JFK to increase U.S. involvement in Vietnam, eventually took over that company's Asian operations. The controlling stock for this company was owned by the Rockefellers. It was at a party sponsored by Socony Mobil where Lee and Marina Oswald met Ruth Paine. Socony also employed Volkmar Schmidt, who hosted the party. Schmidt once told assassination researcher Edward Jay Epstein that he was fascinated with the "techniques of hypnosis." Schmidt admitted to "studying and living with Dr. Wilhelm Kuetemeyer, a professor of psychosomatic medicine" who was involved in a 1944 "plot to assassinate Hitler." Schmidt was introduced to the Oswalds by George DeMohrenschildt.

Solidarists   See WHITE RUSSIANS.

Solon, John

Solon watched the assassination from the Main Street entrance to the Old Courthouse. Solon says he heard three shots, couldn't tell where the shots came from, and heard a pause between the first and second shots. Solon said the second and third shots came close together.

Souetre, Jean   See CORSICAN MOB.

Specter, Arlen   See MAGIC BULLET.

Sports Drome Rifle Range

Many witnesses saw a man who resembled Oswald practicing at the Sports Drome Rifle Range in Dallas during the weeks leading up to the assassination. Garland Glenwill Slack saw Oswald at the range on November 10, 1963, accompanied by a tall, dark-haired, complected man with a full beard. The rifle range was run by Floyd Guy Davis and his wife Virginia Louise, and they too saw the man resembling Oswald. Slack took special note of the man, becoming irritated with him because "Oswald" was shooting at Slack's target rather than his own. Slack said the man received a ride to the range from a man named "Frazier" from Irving, Texas. (Buell Wesley Frazier denies having done this.) Amazingly, Slack was also an assassination witness. He was standing on Houston Street during the shooting and later said that he knew instantly that it was a high-powered rifle shot and that the shot had hit something. A great majority of the other earwitnesses thought they had heard a firecracker. Slack died September 1978 during the House Select Committee on Assassinations hearings.

Malcolm H. Price Jr. saw Oswald on several occasions at the Sports Drome between late September and early November 1963. Price got a good look at the individual, as he helped "Oswald" adjust the scope on his rifle, and was confident that the man he had seen was Oswald. Dr. and Mrs. Homer Wood also saw the man and swore that he looked like Oswald. The Warren Commission concluded this wasn't Oswald because one of the sightings took place while the "real" Oswald was in Mexico City.

Stark, J. W. "Dub"   See TOP 10 RECORD STORE.

Stemmons Freeway Sign

One of the most enduring mysteries about November 22, 1963, is what happened to the Stemmons Freeway sign that had been on the north side of Elm Street in front of the pergola at the time of the assassination. It disappeared hours after the assassination and was not replaced.

The sign is most famous because it appears to obscure Abraham Zapruder's view of the presidential limousine during a key portion of the shooting sequence. Photographic experts have said that the sign appears larger in the Zapruder film than it should have, perhaps because the film was altered and those who altered it used the sign to cover up the limousine during a moment they did not want seen.

Others have theorized that there was a bullet hole in the sign that would have been impossible to explain while sticking dogmatically to a lone-nut theory.

(See also ZAPRUDER, ABRAHAM.)

Stoughton, Cecil William

Stoughton was an assassination witness, born on January 18, 1920, in Oskaloosa, Iowa. In 1963, Stoughton was a White House military photographer. He rode in the motorcade in the eighth car behind the presidential limousine. It was a 1964 Chevrolet Impala convertible. Stoughton sat directly behind the driver. Stoughton said he heard three shots as the car he was in turned from Main Street onto Houston. He photographed the grassy knoll moments after the shooting. He then went to Parkland Hospital where he photographed activity outside the emergency entrance. His most famous photograph of the day was taken in Air Force One as Lyndon Baines Johnson was sworn in as president of the United States. Another photo, also taken on Air Force One, just before or after President Johnson was sworn in, appears to show Lady Bird Johnson attempting to stifle a smile while Congressman Albert Thomas, who was in charge of the National Aeronautics and Space Administration budget, winks at LBJ.

Stuckey, William Kirk

New Orleans radio-program director who arranged for a radio debate on August 21, 1963, between anti-Castro activist Carlos Bringuier and pro-Castro activist Lee Harvey Oswald.

"I was a columnist with the *New Orleans States-Item* with an interest in Latin America," Stuckey told the Warren Commission. "I had been looking for representatives of the Fair Play for Cuba Committee [in New Orleans] . . . There haven't been any. Most of the organizations that I had contact with were refugee organizations, very violently anti-Castro groups . . . I was in the bank and I ran across a refugee friend . . . Carlos Bringuier . . . he said that a representative of the Fair Play for Cuba Committee had appeared in New Orleans and that he had had an encounter with him . . . [Oswald] said somehow he knew

Bringuier was connected with the Revolutionary Student Directorate [D.R.E.], how I don't know. But at any rate . . . he offered his services . . . Bringuier told me . . . he ran into this young man again . . . distributing literature, handbills . . . 'Join the Fair Play for Cuba Committee in New Orleans, Charter Member Branch' . . . Bringuier, who was rather an excitable fellow, . . . got into a shouting match . . . on the street corner, and I think some blows were exchanged, I'm not sure . . . [Bringuier told me] the police arrived on the scene and took everybody down to the jail . . . I was interested in locating the fellow and . . . Bringuier gave me his name . . . and he lived on Magazine Street, somewhere in the 4000 block . . . It was [Saturday] August 17 when I went by [Oswald's] house . . . So we had a few cursory remarks about the organization. [He showed me his card which] identified him as the secretary of the New Orleans chapter . . . and it was signed A. J. Hidell, president . . . I never thought of the name again until after the assassination when Mr. Henry Wade [Dallas District Attorney], on Dallas television on Sunday [November 24, 1963] I believe, mentioned that Oswald purchased a rifle from a Chicago mail order house and had used the name A. Hidell in purchasing the rifle. . . . As I recall, [Oswald] insisted he was . . . the Fair Play for Cuba Committee secretary and this other gentleman, Hidell, was the president. . . . He appeared to be a very logical, intelligent fellow, and the only strange thing about him was his organization . . . he did not seem the type at all . . . I was arrested by his cleancutness. I expected a folk-singer type . . . a beard and sandals . . . instead I found this fellow who was neat and clean . . . I asked him to meet me at the radio station . . . and he agreed . . . [There] was to be a recorded interview prior to a broadcast . . . instead of just interviewing him for five minutes, I would just let him talk . . . this was a thirty-seven-minute rambling interview between Oswald and myself . . . we played it back . . . He was satisfied . . . and I think he had scored quite a coup. Then I went back over it in his presence . . . we had a couple of his comments . . . and the rest was largely my summarizing . . . and [four-and-a-half minutes of it] was broadcast on schedule that night . . . next Monday I called the News Director . . . and he said . . . there would be more public interest if we did not run this tape at all, but instead arrange a . . . debate panel show with some local anti-Communists on 'Conversation Carte Blanche' . . . a twenty-five-minute public affairs program that runs daily . . . I picked Mr. Edward S. Butler . . . Executive Director . . . of an anti-Communist propaganda organization . . . (See also INFORMATION COUNCIL OF THE AMERICAS) a friend of mine. I knew him as a columnist . . . [F]or the other panelist I asked Mr. Bringuier . . . During that day, Wednesday, August 21, one of my news sources called me up and said, 'I hear you are going to have Oswald on Carte Blanche. . . . We have some information on Mr. Oswald, the fact that he lived in Russia for three years.' [Oswald] had omitted reference to this in the thirty-seven-minute previous interview and in all of our conversations . . . [In the thirty-seven-minute interview Oswald lied:] 'I entered the Marine Corps in 1956. I spent three years in the Marines working my way up through the ranks to the position of buck sergeant, and I served honorably having been discharged. Then I went back to work in Texas and have recently arrived in New Orleans with my family.' . . . [When he arrived at the station he] was unaware [we knew he had lived in Russia.] During that day Mr. Butler called and said he too had found out the same thing . . . his source was the House Un-American Activities Committee or something like that. At any rate, we thought this was very interesting and we agreed together to produce this information on the program that night . . . so it was a somewhat touchy exchange there between Bringuier and Oswald. Bringuier started . . . 'You know I thought you were a very nice boy. You really made a good impression on me when I first met you . . . I cannot understand how you have allowed yourself to become entangled with this group . . . I don't think you know what you are doing.' Oswald said something to the effect that, 'I don't think *you* know what *you* are doing.' And back and forth . . . Bringuier said, 'Anytime you want to get out of your organization and join mine there is a place for you.' And again Oswald says, 'I hope you see the light.' . . . I left . . . to get Bill Slatter . . . the official moderator of the program, and we came back and picked up our participants and went into the broadcast room."

Warren Commission interrogator Assistant Counsel Albert Jenner at this point offered Stuckey a copy of the transcript of the WDSU radio debate to refer to before he continued.

Stuckey testified, "I would like to say this about the transcript. I think it is very unfair. These people have put in all of Oswald's hesitations, his 'er's' and that sort of thing. . . . They were apparently trying to make him look stupid. Everyone else was using 'er's', but they didn't put those in . . . I think it's an unfair thing."

Stuckey then returned his comments to the debate itself: "the principle thing that came out . . . aside from the Russian residence . . . was his admission that he was a Marxist. We asked him if he was a Communist—we were always doing this—he was very clever about avoiding the question. He would usually say, 'As I said before, I belong to no organization other than the Fair Play for Cuba Committee.' . . . and I asked, 'Are you a Marxist?' and he said, 'Yes.' . . . The program largely consisted of speeches by Bringuier, and Butler, and Oswald did not have a chance to ramble much or talk much as he had, and most of the answers are rather short . . . It was my impression that he had done a lot of reading . . . [He seemed] confident, self-assured, logical . . . very well qualified to handle questions, articulate . . . if he could use a six-syllable word instead of a two-syllable word he would do so . . . his manner was sort of quasi-legal . . . as if he were a young attorney."

Jenner asked Stuckey if the debate became heated. Stuckey replied: "Yes, it did. Mr. Butler in particular . . . took the offensive and tried to trip him up . . . and Mr. Oswald handled himself very well, as usual. I think we finished him on that program. I think that after that program the Fair Play for Cuba Committee, if there ever was one in New Orleans, had no future there, because we had publicly linked the Fair Play for Cuba Committee with a fellow who had lived in Russia for three years and who was an admitted Marxist . . . Oswald seemed like such a nice, bright boy and was extremely believable before this. We thought the fellow could probably get quite a few members if he was really indeed serious about getting members. We figured after this broadcast of August 21, why, that was no longer possible. After all, you have to recognize that Oswald—they were ganging up on him. . . . There were three people who disagreed with him, and he was only one man, and the fact that he kept his composure with this type of environment indicates discipline."

(See also BUTLER, EDWARD S.; D.R.E.)

Sturgis, Frank (a.k.a. Fiorini, Frank)

According to the sworn statements of former Castro-mistress and CIA asset Marita Lorenz, Sturgis, a soldier of fortune who had done jobs for the CIA, was one of the men who conspired to kill President Kennedy.

Sturgis and Lorenz have also been linked romantically—and were lovers at the time Sturgis sent her into Cuba with a poison capsule to attempt to assassinate Fidel Castro. Later, Sturgis became well known after his arrest in connection with the Watergate break-in.

Depending on the interview, Sturgis has said that he was in Miami or Washington, D.C., at the time of the assassination. In both of his alibi's versions, he was watching TV at the time. According to Mark Lane, Sturgis admitted having been offered a contract by the CIA to kill someone in the United States.

According to Sturgis, the FBI interrogated him soon after the assassination because they said, "Frank, if there's anybody capable of killing the President of the United States, you're the guy who can do it."

Sturgis was born Frank Angelo Fiorini in Norfolk, Virginia, but grew up with his mother's family in Philadelphia's Germantown. He took the name Frank Anthony Sturgis from his stepfather.

Sturgis was good friends with exiled Cuban President Carlos Prío. He died December 4, 1995, in Miami, Florida, of lung cancer.

(See also THREE TRAMPS.)

Styles, Sandra

Texas School Book Depository employee who watched the presidential motorcade from a fourth-floor window in that building. She said she couldn't tell from which direction the shots came.

After the shooting, she ran down the School Book Depository stairs and did not hear anyone else using them. In the official scenario, which says that Lee Harvey Oswald got from the sixth floor of the Depository to the second floor within 90 seconds of the assassination, the alleged assassin ran down those same stairs after the shooting. If Styles and Oswald were on the stairs at the same time, Oswald must have been moving silently.

If Oswald was on the sixth floor to begin with, certainly a matter of doubt, we know he must have taken the stairs down because both of the building's elevators were at the top of the building when police entered.

(See also BAKER, MARRION L.)

Sullivan, William

According to the House Select Committee on Assassinations Report, Sullivan "had been one of several FBI officials and agents who were disciplined by Director J. Edgar Hoover for what the Inspection Division determined to have been defective performance in the investigation of Oswald prior to the assassination. The disciplinary action was kept a Bureau secret. Not even the Warren Commission was informed of it. Within Sullivan's Domestic Intelligence Division, the investigation of Oswald and a possible conspiracy was assigned to a team of agents from the Bureau's Soviet section because Oswald had been an avowed Marxist who had defected to the Soviet Union. While numerous experts on Cuban affairs and exile activities were assigned to the Domestic Intelligence Division, the committee found that they were seldom consulted on the assassination or asked to participate in the investigation, despite the reported connections between both Oswald and Ruby and individuals active in Cuban revolutionary activities."

Sullivan was head of the FBI's Division Five (counterespionage and domestic intelligence). He was the former number-three man in the FBI and was in Washington, D.C., at the time of the assassination. By 6:00 P.M. on the day of the assassination, Sullivan was, according to Jim Bishop, "in charge of the internal security aspects—and background—of . . . Oswald." Sullivan died just prior to the House Select Committee on Assassinations investigation in November 1977 in a "hunting accident." The man who shot him said, "I thought he was a deer."

(See also FEDERAL BUREAU OF INVESTIGATION.)

Summers, Malcolm

An assassination witness who was standing on the south side of Elm Street across from the grassy knoll at the time of the shooting. Summers, born and raised in Dallas, happened to be the brother-in-law of former deputy sheriff Al Maddox.

He owned a direct mail business in 1963 and had just been to the Terminal Annex Building at Houston and Commerce Streets when he went to see President Kennedy's motorcade.

In a 1991 statement, Summers said: "I was right next to the car when Jackie crawled on the back and helped pull the FBI guy [actually Secret Service]. I heard three shots. The first shot came right after the car turned the corner [from Houston onto Elm]—and I thought it was more like the sound of a firecracker . . . I thought, 'Well, that's a cheap trick.' And I saw the FBI guys [again, he means Secret Service] looking around on the ground like that was what they thought too. . . . Then came the second and third shot and they came so close together that I thought they were coming from different directions. I didn't know where they were coming from initially—but I certainly did think there was more than one [person] shooting. A motorcycle cop came by me and he was looking in my direction so I hit the ground because I thought there might be someone shooting from behind me and I didn't want to get caught in the crossfire there. After the motorcade got by, I ran across the grassy knoll because there was some people beginning to run toward the railroad tracks. I was stopped by a guy, a well-dressed person—he had a top coat on his shoulder—he said, 'Y'all better not come up here or else you could get shot.' He had a gun under that raincoat. All I could see was the barrel of it and I couldn't tell you what kind of gun it was. I didn't argue with the man because there wasn't any reason to argue with him. He seemed in authority and he was stopping people there—so I went back to the postal annex so I could call my wife and tell her what happened. After a couple of days, I reported this to the Sheriff's office. One of the main reasons that I came forward was because when I went back to the postal annex, there were three men, what I call Mexicans, getting in a car and driving off toward Oak Cliff at a high rate of speed. I never did know where the shots came from but I do know that the second and third shots came so close together that there's no way one man could do it."

During his interview with researcher Larry A. Sneed, Summers said that he had run into the man with the gun under his coat at the east end of the pergola, or the end closest to the Texas School Book Depository. (See also POOL OF BLOOD.) Summers also told Sneed, "There was another event connected with my getting home. I happened to live in the 400 block of East Twelfth Street. By the time I arrived home and pulled in my driveway, there was just dozens of squad cars in that area. Then I didn't know what the reason for all that was. Later they said something about this policeman being shot over on the 400 block of East Tenth."

Suspicious Deaths

It didn't take long for the suspicious deaths of those connected in some way with the assassination to start. Maurice "Monk" Baker was a Dallas police officer and a friend of Jack Ruby. He lived on North Beckley, the same street that Oswald lived on at the time. Baker reportedly killed himself with a bullet to the brain on December 3, 1963, less than two weeks after the assassination. On that same day, Captain Michael D. Groves, a member of the honor guard at JFK's funeral, dropped dead while eating dinner.

Jack Zangretti was the manager of a casino/hotel located at Lake Lugert, Oklahoma, called the Red Lobster. On November 23, 1963, Zangretti reportedly told friends that a fellow named Ruby would shoot Oswald and that Frank Sinatra's son would be kidnapped to draw attention away from the assassination. Ruby did shoot Oswald and Frank Sinatra's son was kidnapped. Approximately a week later Zangretti was shot in the chest and dumped in Lake Lugert.

An internal Dallas police report dated December 11, 1963, contained the following: (A confidential) "source states that she was told by another person that a mechanic from a garage in the downtown area who regularly services Jack Ruby's automobile, had stated that subject (Lee Harvey Oswald) had driven Ruby's car several times prior to the assassination of President Kennedy." An unattributed footnote rejected the content of the report and stated that "subject did not know how to drive an automobile." Perhaps because of that footnote, no action was taken for almost three months. Another Dallas police internal report (dated April 3, 1964) repeated the content of the first, adding that the mechanic had mentioned that Oswald "had been driving Jack Ruby's automobile for approximately two months and that he (the mechanic) knew this because Oswald had brought Ruby's car to his garage for repairs." The report named the mechanic as William J. Chesher and stated that the previous day, April 2, 1964, Detectives Biggio and Stringfellow had attempted to contact him (presumably for the first time) but "the officers were informed that subject (Chesher) had died on March 31, 1964 of a heart attack."

Jim Koethe (pronounced "Koty") was a 30-year-old reporter for the *Dallas Times Herald*. William Hunter was a reporter from the *Long Beach Independent Press Telegram*. After 48 hours of covering the assassination the men decided they needed a drink. They went to Bill Martin's TV Bar in Dallas on the afternoon of November 24, 1963. In the bar were three men who in the past had done legal work for Jack Ruby. They were C. A. Droby, Jim Martin, and Tom Howard. Howard will be discussed further later. The three men were waiting for Ruby's roommate George Senator to arrive. When Senator arrived, the reporters asked him if he had a picture of Ruby so Senator invited everyone to the apartment he and Ruby shared. "It was just a dumpy apartment," Koethe later said. The meeting in Senator and Ruby's apartment, at which all parties agree nothing significant happened, is important because Hunter, Koethe, and Howard all died soon thereafter, two of them violently. Droby received death threats that only ceased when he agreed not to represent Jack Ruby. Hunter was the first to go, "accidentally shot" by a policeman while sitting in the press room of the Long Beach police station at two A.M. on the morning of April 23, 1964. At first the police detective whose .38 had been fired said that he accidentally dropped it and it went off, the bullet going through Hunter's heart and fatally wounding him. Later the detective changed his story to say that the gun had gone off during "horseplay." Two detectives were fired from the police department and charged with manslaughter in the case and both received three-year probated sentences. According to A. L. Goodhart in the *Law Quarterly Review* (January 1967), "Hunter was shot accidentally by a detective he had known closely for years while the latter 'was clowning foolishly' with a revolver in the station pressroom. It may be remembered that at that time the dangerous game 'Quick on the draw' was popular in the West."

Koethe died seven months later, on September 21, 1964, murdered in his Dallas apartment, reportedly just as he had stepped out of the shower. According to Goodhart, "Koethe was a beer-drinking bully who liked to hang out with thugs; he had been strangled, not 'karate-chopped,' (as some reports have said) and police suggested that homosexuality might have been the motive."

Thomas Hale Howard, Ruby's attorney who met with Senator was the third to go. He died at age 48 of a heart attack in Dallas on March 27, 1965. How suspicious is this death? According to Goodhart, not at all: "The connection between Howard's heart attack and the conspiracy seems to be . . . remote because he was not at Ruby's apartment that night." Howard was the first lawyer to represent Ruby after he shot Oswald. Howard was a man who had once been fined $50 by Judge Joe Brown of Dallas for having a fistfight with Assistant District Attorney Fred Bruner in the courtroom in 1951, and who once was prosecuted in federal court for violations of the Mann Act. He had been asked to handle the case by Ruby's friend and business associate Ralph Paul. Elmer Gertz, who later represented Ruby and wrote a book about it, writes, "Like Ruby himself, [Howard] was a 'little' man of great aspirations. The striking difference between the two was that Howard was highly successful in his small way, whereas Ruby was a spectacular flop in all that he did. Howard's clients were pimps and prostitutes and murderers and unimportant people. He lost no clients to the electric chair, however, and he was reasonably certain that he would not lose Ruby either." Howard was no longer involved in the case by the time Ruby was convicted of murder with malice and sentenced to death. Ruby believed he had "no class." Howard, who had been in the Dallas police basement moments before Ruby shot Oswald, died soon after Ruby's trial began.

John Garrett "Gary" Underhill worked as an Office of Strategic Services agent during World War II. He attended Harvard and was the former military affairs editor for *Life* magazine. On November 28, 1963, Underhill told friends in New Jersey that he knew who had ordered the assassination, claiming it was "a Far Eastern group in the CIA." Underhill died soon thereafter, on May 8, 1964, in his Washington, D.C., apartment with a bullet in his brain. The death was ruled a suicide in spite of the fact that the bullet entered the right-handed Underhill's head behind the left ear.

Hugh F. Ward, investigator for Guy Banister, died on May 23, 1965, when the plane he was flying crashed near Ciudad Victoria, Mexico. According to assassination investigators Sybil Leek and Bert R. Sugar, Ward was taught to fly by assassination suspect David Ferrie. It was the same plane crash that killed New Orleans mayor DeLesseps Morrison.

Dorothy Kilgallen was a *New York Journal-American* columnist and game-show (*What's My Line?*) panelist. She was given permission by Judge Joe Brown in Dallas to have a private interview with Jack Ruby. After meeting with Ruby in prison, she said she was going to "break open the Kennedy case." Soon thereafter (November 8, 1965), before an exposé could be written, Kilgallen died at age 52 in her New York home of a drug overdose. It took eight days to officially determine the cause of death as "ingestion of alcohol and barbiturates."

Kilgallen's good friend and confidante, Mrs. Earl Smith, died only three days later, on November 11, 1965, at the age of 45, of a cerebral hemorrhage. Mrs. Smith wrote a column for the *New York Journal-American* under the pen name "Miss Florence Pritchett."

Lieutenant Commander William Bruce Pitzer reportedly attended JFK's autopsy (although his name does not appear on the official list of those present) and, according to several accounts, filmed the Bethesda autopsy. On October 29, 1966, Pitzer was found dead of a .45 caliber pistol wound in his Bethesda office. According to assassination researchers Harrison Edward Livingstone and Robert Groden, Pitzer was murdered as a

warning to all autopsy witnesses not to talk about what they had seen. Pitzer was found dead just before he was scheduled for retirement after 28 years in the service. Just before his death, Pitzer had been offered a job working for a "network television station" for $45,000 a year. Livingstone and Groden say, "His family was told that his death was a suicide, and no one in his family believes it. The government refuses to give up a copy of the autopsy report. . . . His widow stated . . . that Pitzer left . . . notes for the smallest thing and would have left a suicide note. . . . His widow said that his left hand was so mangled that they could not remove his wedding ring to give it to her, but he was right-handed. The question is, if he shot himself in his office with his right hand, how could his left hand be mangled?" According to the Waukegan (Illinois) *News-Sun* on May 1, 1975, Pitzer had taken the JFK autopsy photos and had been repeatedly threatened because of what he had seen. According to Dennis David, a medical corpsman who officially attended the autopsy, "Pitzer filmed in detail the Kennedy autopsy." Pitzer's death came on the *same day* that the "autopsy materials" were transferred from the Kennedy family to the National Archives, the day the footlocker was opened and it was discovered that President Kennedy's brain was missing.

On November 9, 1966, assassination witness James Richard Worrell died in a motorcycle accident at the age of 22. A female passenger was also killed. Worrell had seen a man running out of the back of the Texas School Book Depository.

Suspicious characters David Ferrie and Eladio Cerefine Del Valle, a Cuban exile and friend of Ferrie's, both died on February 22, 1967. Del Valle's occupation was unknown, but he was possibly a freelance pilot. He died just hours after Ferrie, found with a split open head and a gunshot to the heart. Del Valle's head wound appeared to have been caused by a machete. At the time of Del Valle's death, Jim Garrison was searching for him to testify against Clay Shaw. According to ex-CIA agent Harry Dean, the shooters of JFK were Loran Hall and Eladio del Valle, who were hired to do the job by the John Birch Society. According to assassination researcher Anthony Summers, Del Valle was the leader of Florida's Free Cuba Committee who had "links" with Floridian mobster and assassination suspect Santos Trafficante, who was also later murdered. According to CIA agent Robert Morrow, Del Valle told him on November 10, 1963, that "Kennedy's going to get it in Dallas."

A witness to the flight of J. D. Tippit's murderer, Harold Russell, was killed during February 1967 by a police officer during a "barroom brawl."

Nicholas Chetta was the New Orleans medical examiner during the Garrison investigation. Chetta performed autopsies on assassination suspect David Ferrie, associate of Ferrie Dr. Mary Sherman, and Ruby-connection Robert Perrin, all who died before they had a chance to testify for Garrison. Dr. Chetta died of a heart attack, at 10:20 P.M., Saturday, May 25, 1968, before Garrison had finished his investigation. He was 50.

On January 26, 1969, Professor Henry Delaune, Chetta's brother-in-law who worked in the coroner's office, was murdered. Another potential Garrison prosecution witness was Philip Geraci, a friend of Perry Raymond Russo who was also said to have knowledge of a Lee Harvey Oswald/Clay Shaw connection and who had been a witness to a meeting between Oswald and D.R.E. member Carlos Bringuier. Geraci died before he could testify when he was accidentally electrocuted during August 1968.

The Reverend Clyde Johnson was a Kentwood, Louisiana, preacher who once ran for Louisiana governor on an anti-JFK platform. Johnson was also said to know of a David Ferrie/Oswald/Shaw connection. On February 17, 1969, the day before Johnson was scheduled to testify in New Orleans against Clay Shaw, he was severely beaten up. He never testified. In earlier conversations, Garrison says Johnson claimed that he had, on September 2, 1963, from 2:00 P.M. to 9:00 P.M., spoken with Jack Ruby, Clay Shaw, and Lee Harvey Oswald at the Jack Tar Capital House in Baton Rouge, Louisiana. On July 23, 1969, Johnson was killed at age 37 in a shotgun attack by his wife's second cousin near Greensburg, Louisiana.

Steve Pieringer was a KRLD-TV reporter and photographer who filmed police surrounding the Jefferson Branch Library, thinking they had captured J. D. Tippit's killer, and later filmed the scene outside the Texas Theatre just before Oswald was apprehended. Pieringer was killed in 1966 while covering a Dallas-area gas tanker explosion.

Edward Voebel was a friend of Lee Harvey Oswald when he was a teenager, and was in the Civil Air Patrol with him. He told the Warren Commission that "Captain Ferrie"—that is, David Ferrie—had been the leader of their group at the time he and Oswald were in it. Voebel died at the age of 31 of a blood clot in 1971.

Assassination suspect Roscoe White died on September 24, 1971, in a fire.

Warren Commissioner Hale Boggs's plane disappeared and was never heard from again over Alaska on October 16, 1972.

On December 8, 1972, Dorothy Wetzel Hunt, wife of assassination suspect E. Howard Hunt, died together with 60 others in Chicago, Illinois, when the United Airlines 737-222 jetliner she was in crashed on landing.

Thomas Eli Davis III ran guns and jeeps to Cuba with Ruby. In December 1963, Davis was jailed in Tangiers for running guns. He was released through the efforts of a CIA agent code-named QJ/WIN (see CENTRAL INTELLIGENCE

AGENCY). After Ruby's arrest, his lawyer asked Ruby if there was anyone who could hurt his defense that he killed Oswald spontaneously. Davis's was the only name Ruby mentioned. Davis died on September 9, 1973, electrocuted while stealing wire from a warehouse in Wise County, Texas.

Roger Craig, the sheriff's deputy who saw Oswald run out of the School Book Depository and enter a Nash Rambler station wagon, endured several attempts on his life and committed suicide on May 15, 1975. (See also CRAIG, ROGER.)

According to author Robert D. Morrow, an anti-Castro Cuban exile named Rolando Masferrer was the man putting together the assassination teams to kill Castro for Florida mobster Santos Trafficante. Morrow claims that Masferrer, along with JFK assassination suspect Eladio del Valle and Mario Kohly "assist[ed] in the implementation of the JFK assassination scheme." Masferrer died on October 31, 1975, when a dynamite bomb blew up his car.

On June 9, 1976, William King Harvey, the head of the CIA's assassination program, died at age 60 of a heart attack. A former FBI man, some say he never stopped reporting to J. Edgar Hoover. (See also CENTRAL INTELLI-GENCE AGENCY.)

On August 7, 1976, assassination suspect Johnny Roselli was found murdered. (See also ROSELLI, JOHNNY.)

Cold warrior William Douglas Pawley committed suicide on January 7, 1977. He was a right-wing lobbyist who, along with General Charles Willoughby, was a member of the American Security Council.

Oswald's friend George DeMohrenschildt was found by a reporter and by an investigator from the House Select Committee on Assassinations. He committed suicide with a shotgun on March 30, 1977. (See also DEMOHRENSCHILDT, SERGEI "GEORGE" S.)

That same month, the leader of White Russians in Dallas, Paul M. Raigorodsky, died of natural causes.

Carlos Prío Socarrás, the former president of Cuba and head of the anti-Castro organization called the Free Cuba Committee, was also being sought by the House Select Committee on April 5, 1977 because of his supposed knowledge of alleged ties between anti-Castro Cubans and Ruby, when he died of a pistol shot on April 5. Official cause of death: suicide.

In June of 1977 Louis Nichols, who some say was the number-three man in the FBI at the time, died of a heart attack. He had just been scheduled to be interviewed by the House Select Committee. Francis Gary Powers, the U-2 pilot who was shot down over the Soviet Union, died on August 1, 1977. Chief Steward of Air Force One at the time of the assassination, Joseph C. Ayres, also died in August 1977, in a "shooting accident." That same month also claimed James C. Cadigan, who had told the Warren

Commission (Exhibit 364) that the paper bag they were showing witnesses was not found on the sixth floor of the Texas School Book Depository building, but had rather been constructed by Dallas FBI agents to show to witnesses. He died in a fatal fall in his home.

On July 16, 1978, William Sullivan, the head of the FBI's Division Five (counterespionage and domestic intelligence), was killed, also in a hunting accident. The man who shot him said, "I thought he was a deer."

(See also CHERAMIE, ROSE; RUBY'S GIRLS.)

T

Tague, James T.

The third man wounded in the assassination, Tague—an employee of Chuck Hinton Dodge on Lemmon Avenue in Dallas—was standing near the entrance to the triple underpass at the time of the shooting. One bullet apparently struck a curb and kicked up a piece of concrete that cut Tague on the chin. It has been estimated that the shot resulting in Tague's wound missed the presidential limousine by 33 feet. That is bad aiming.

This is how Tague told the story to researcher Larry A. Sneed, "So I was standing to the front of the car on the cement where it narrows to go under the triple underpass between Main and Commerce streets. I could see [JFK's] car turn left onto Elm Street, then I heard three shots. When I heard the first shot, I thought somebody had thrown a firecracker and was standing there wondering what had happened. Then I heard another sound which was a little different. The third shot sounded the same as the second. At that point, I realized that they were possibly gunshots, so I ducked behind the concrete support and peeked out just as the presidential limousine was passing into the triple underpass."

The bullet must have missed the presidential limo. This is important because Tague's wound forced the Warren Commission to admit that at least one shot missed, thus creating the necessity for the "magic-bullet theory" that one bullet had caused all of the nonfatal wounds in the limousine.

The FBI, which had released its theory as to the explanation before the Warren Commission first convened, did not recognize Tague's wound as a real thing and didn't factor it into their shooting scenario. The FBI concluded that

President Kennedy was hit in the back with the first shot, Governor Connally was wounded with the second shot, and the third shot was the fatal one to President Kennedy's head.

Tague told the commission that the shots came from "behind the concrete monument" between the Texas School Book Depository and the grassy knoll.

Years after the assassination, Tague told his story to Dallas reporter Bill Sloan. Tague remembered that, in November 1963 he was 27 years old and had been divorced from his first wife for three years. On the day of the assassination he had a date with a "pretty little redhead" who later became his second wife. "That was the only thing I was thinking about when I swung off Stemmons Freeway onto Commerce Street and promptly got stalled in a huge traffic jam. At first I didn't have the slightest idea what was going on, but it seemed obvious that nobody was going to be going anywhere for a while, so I got out of my car. I was right at the edge of the triple underpass and I stepped onto the narrow section of curb between Commerce and Main streets to see if I could tell what was going on. Just then I saw the President's car turn onto Houston Street off Main, and it dawned on me what the traffic jam was all about. It was maybe ten seconds later, just as the car had turned onto Elm Street, that I heard the first shot. For some reason I remember glancing up at that instant at the Hertz sign [on the School Book Depository roof]. Later everybody said that the assassination took place at 12:30, but I distinctly remember that sign. It said 12:29. Then I heard two more shots." Tague told Sloan that the first shot sounded differently from the others and he thought it was a firecracker. He didn't realize what had happened until he encountered a man in Dealey Plaza, perhaps Charles Brehm, who was crying and repeating, "His head exploded! His head exploded!" Soon thereafter Tague ran into sheriff's deputy Buddy Walthers who noticed that Tague's face was bleeding.

Tague was acquainted with Jack Ruby, having been in the Carousel Club a couple of times. It is a strange coincidence, however, that Tague's roommate, a professional guitar player named Jody Daniel, was dating the Carousel Club stripper who worked under the name Tammy True, the same stripper who was said to be the steady girlfriend of Ruby's friend and business partner Ralph Paul.

In the years since the assassination Tague has heavily researched the assassination and has become an expert in the events of that weekend.

(See also JACK'S GIRLS; PAUL, RALPH.)

1026 North Beckley

The address of the rooming house where Oswald lived at the time of the assassination. He moved in on October 14, 1963, registering as O. H. Lee, and agreeing to pay $8 a week as rent. The housekeeper was Earlene Roberts, a key eyewitness. The building was owned by Arthur and Gladys Johnson, an estranged couple. Mrs. Johnson took care of the business. Although Mrs. Johnson testified to the Warren Commission before her ex-employee Earlene Roberts did, her statements were used to discredit Roberts' later claims. Roberts testified that about a half hour after the assassination, while Oswald was inside the rooming house putting on a jacket, a Dallas police squad car stopped directly outside, twice honked its horn, then drove on. Mrs. Johnson said she fired Roberts because she "had a lot of handicaps" like "talking, just sitting down and making up tales . . . have you ever seen people like that? Just have a creative mind, there's nothing to it, and just make up and keep talking until she makes a lie out of it."

(See also ROBERTS, EARLENE.)

Terry, L. R.

Assassination witness of unknown gender, found and protected by assassination researcher Jim Marrs. Terry stood on the south side of Elm Street across from the Texas School Book Depository to view the motorcade. He or she saw a rifle sticking out of an upper floor window, but

Oswald's rooming house at 1026 North Beckley. *(MacIntyre Symms)*

could only see the shooter's hand. Terry added, "There was a man with him."

Texas School Book Depository

Today known as the Dallas County Administration Building, the Texas School Book Depository building sits on land that was a part of the original Dallas townsite formed in 1844. The land was part of that owned by John Neely Bryan, Dallas's first settler. In 1849 Bryan sold the land to a homesteader for $50. The property was sold to the Southern Rock Island Plow Company in 1894. A five-story warehouse was built in 1898 at the current site, but that building was struck by lightning and burned. The current seven-story building was built in the old warehouse's place in 1901. It was constructed in an architectural style called "Commercial Romanesque Revival." Made of salmon-colored brick, the top floor, the seventh, is separated from the other six by masonry and brick dentil work. The top floor's windows are taller and are flanked by sets of thin double brick pilasters. A wide cornice with eight-sided louvered vents delineates the roof. The building was purchased in 1937 by the Carraway-Byrd Corporation.

That corporation defaulted on its loan and the property was purchased in 1939 by Colonel D. Harold Byrd at a public auction for $35,000. Byrd owned the building until 1970. Byrd was a right-wing Texas oil tycoon, and the nephew of Admiral Byrd. Interestingly, Byrd is also credited with founding the Civil Air Patrol, the organization through which conspiracy suspect David Ferrie met accused assassin Lee Harvey Oswald. Byrd purchased 130,000 shares of Ling-Temco-Vought, a defense contractor, weeks before the assassination for $13–$19 a share. With the coming of the Vietnam War following the assassination, those same shares became, by 1967, worth $203 per share. Byrd was a board member for the Dorchester Gas Producing Company, owned by Jack Crichton, an army intelligence reservist who met with H. L. Hunt soon after the assassination and was among the first persons to interview Marina Oswald.

The building had been under lease to the Texas School Book Depository Company for only a few months at the time of the assassination. It had been under lease to the Binyon O'Keefe Storage Company and then to John Sexton & Company, before it was leased to the Texas School Book Depository Company. The building is occasionally referred to as the "Sexton Building" in FBI documents, always without an effort to point out that the structure by that time was much better known under another name. The Sexton Company dealt in groceries and during that company's stay the floors in the building became oily, so much so that the oil was doing damage to books that were being

The Texas School Book Depository. The sniper's nest window is the one on the far right, second from the top. *(MacIntyre Symms)*

stored there by the new tenant. That is why plywood was being put down on the floors of the building, and why the sixth floor's floor was being repaired by a work crew on November 22, 1963.

At the time of the assassination, the Depository had books stored on the first, fourth, fifth, and sixth floors. The third floor was office space that had been rented out to other publishing companies. Sometime during 1963 the Hertz Rent-a-Car time/temperature clock was placed on the roof.

On November 22, 1963, 69 people worked in the building, 33 of them for the Depository, the others for the

TEXAS SCHOOL BOOK DEPOSITORY'S 6TH FLOOR LAYOUT

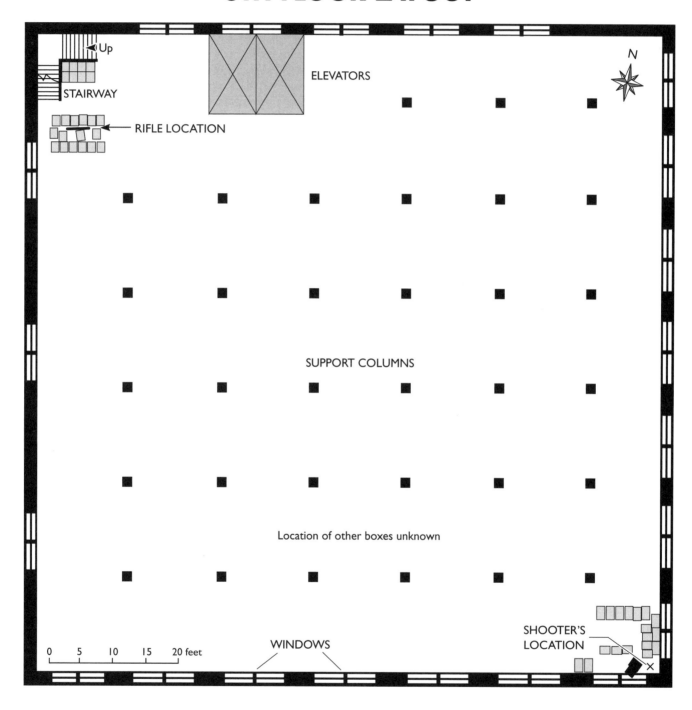

building's tenants. The main lunchroom was located on the first floor. This room was also known as the "domino room." The small room with the soda pop and vending machines in which Oswald was seen only seconds after the assassination was for the use of employees of the publish-

ing companies and was rarely used by Depository employees like Oswald.

It has been said that one of the reasons the police were looking for Oswald was because he was the only Texas School Book Depository employee to be absent at a roll call taken after the assassination. But, according to Warren Commission exhibit 2003, 11 Depository employees left the building following the shooting and did not return.

Byrd sold the building in 1970 to Aubrey Mayhew, a Nashville promoter. The book company vacated the premises in 1971 and Mayhew began an unsuccessful campaign to have the building converted into a museum. An arsonist's fire on July 20, 1972, caused $5,000 worth of damage to the building. Mayhew didn't make his loan payments and the property reverted back to Byrd on August 1, 1972. There were calls to have the building torn down but the city of Dallas refused to issue a demolition permit. Byrd tried and failed to sell the building. Dallas County picked up an option to buy the building in 1977, a move made because the county's main offices are also on Dealey Plaza. In 1977, Dallas County voters, by a two-to-one margin, approved a $1.8 million bond package that included $400,000 to purchase the building. Following the purchase, the building, with the exception of the sixth floor, was turned into county office space. The sixth floor was closed to the public.

In 1979, a study panel funded by the National Endowment for the Humanities recommended that the sixth floor be transformed into a major cultural exhibit on the assassination and legacy of JFK, and the county commissioners approved it. The first two floors were restored and renovated in 1981 by Burson, Hendricks and Walls, a Dallas architectural firm. At that time the building was renamed the Dallas County Administration Building.

A second arson attempt, during the Republican National Convention held in Dallas during the summer of 1984, caused minimal damage.

In 1988, Dallas County commissioners approved $2.2 million to build the exterior elevators behind the building and the Visitors Center entrance, so the new museum could be accessed without disrupting business in the rest of the building.

The building is a Texas Historical Landmark. On the 30th anniversary of the assassination, November 22, 1993, the building became part of the Dealey Plaza Historic Landmark District as designated by the National Park Service.

Texas Theatre

The site of Lee Harvey Oswald's arrest, located at 231 West Jefferson Boulevard, in the Oak Cliff section of Dallas, the Texas Theatre was built in 1931. It was at one time part of a chain of theaters owned by Howard Hughes. The building has a "Spanish eclectic" design.

Almost a half hour had passed since the assailant fleeing the scene of the Tippit killing was last seen, when a man we presume to be Lee Harvey Oswald was spotted outside

Hardy's Shoe Store on Jefferson Boulevard by store manager Johnny Calvin Brewer. After hearing a news flash that a policeman had been shot nearby, Brewer saw a man acting suspiciously (turning his face toward the window when a police car drove by), then sneaking into the Texas Theatre. Brewer asked the ticket taker to call the police and then identified Oswald when the lights went up in the theatre.

When Brewer saw the man enter the theatre, he informed Julia Postal, who was working in the ticket booth. She was out of the booth at the time though, having stepped out to see what the commotion was. Postal called the police between 1:40 and 1:45 P.M. In minutes, the theater was surrounded by police and Oswald was arrested inside. Postal claimed that she had seen the man as he "ducked into" the theater, but she did not react until Brewer told her that the man appeared to be trying to evade the police. There has never been an official explanation for why it took Oswald between 24 and 29 minutes to make the short walk from the scene of Tippit's murder.

The original report that the man who had sneaked into the theater was in the balcony came from Warren "Butch" Burroughs, a mentally handicapped adult who worked behind the candy counter. Oswald apparently bought popcorn from Burroughs, who originally said that the man who was arrested came in before 1:00. Burroughs later recalled seeing Oswald's hands being brought up high and tight against his spine as he was led from the theater.

Theater patron Jack Davis said that, in a large theater with only a handful of customers, Oswald, upon entering, sat in the seat right next to him. After a while he got up and moved to a seat immediately next to another customer. Oswald was obviously trying to make contact with someone.

Bernard J. Haire, who owned Bernie's Hobby House a few doors east of the Texas Theatre, was standing in the alley behind the theater while Oswald was being apprehended. Haire saw the police bring a man out into the alley and put him in a squad car. The man appeared flushed but Haire could not tell if he was handcuffed. Until Haire learned that Oswald had been brought out the front of the building and put into a squad car parked on Jefferson Boulevard, he believed that he had seen Oswald's arrest. There is no record of anyone else being taken into custody at the Texas Theatre and it remains unknown exactly what Haire saw.

One of the persons whom Oswald reportedly sat next to as he moved from seat to seat was a pregnant woman. However, no pregnant woman was listed among the patrons who were questioned by police and reporters. According to one list, there were seven patrons in the theater at the time Oswald was arrested, six not counting the accused assassin. Another list says 14. There were two boys who were sitting half way down the center section; Jack Davis, who sat in the right rear of the theater; another unknown person who sat across the aisle from Davis; George Applin, who sat six rows from the back in the center section; and John Gibson who sat one row from the back on the far right side of the theater. This list does not include those in the balcony.

Sergeant Gerald Hill, among those in on Oswald's arrest, said, "One of the main reasons that some of the witnesses at the theater were never interviewed were that they were hookey shooters [children illegally skipping school] and when we came in the front, they ran out the back."

"The back"—which was actually on the left hand side of the sitting arena since the theater aisles ran parallel to Jefferson Boulevard—comprised of an alley, the same alley that ran between the Abundant Life Temple and the parking lot where "Oswald's jacket" was found, was filled with the policemen. That kids could just "run out" seems impossible.

The Texas Theatre as it appeared in the early 1990s.
(MacIntyre Symms)

George Jefferson Applin Jr., 21 years old at the time, says he was sitting a few rows in front of Oswald when the alleged assassin was arrested. Applin claims that he saw Jack Ruby in the Texas Theatre at the time of Oswald's arrest. (Applin did not mention Jack Ruby's name until 1979. He referred to the individual only as "the man" in his Warren Commission testimony.) He also told the Warren Commission that Oswald fought with four or five policemen before he was handcuffed. One of the policemen, Applin said, struck Oswald in the back with the butt end of a shotgun. According to the *Warren Report*, Applin is the only witness who saw Oswald struck by a gun, although journalist Jim Ewell did say he saw a long arm being raised above the scuffle in an unusual way.

Witness John Gibson, a patron inside the theater, saw an officer grab Oswald. According to the *Warren Report*: "[Gibson] claims he heard the click of a gun misfiring. He saw no shotgun in the possession of any policemen near Oswald."

Among the witnesses was Hugh Aynesworth, who saw as much as any single reporter that weekend. Aynesworth, who later went on to become a reporter for *Newsweek,* was a witness to the assassination, Oswald's arrest, and Oswald's murder.

At the time of the arrest there were 16 policemen in the theater. Patrolmen M. N. "Nick" McDonald, Thomas Alexander Hutson, Charles T. Walker, and Ray Hawkins entered the theater through the rear entrance. (Among Ruby's possessions found after his arrest was Ray Hawkins's signed permanent pass to the Carousel Club.) Walker, in a twist of fate, had been watching news of the assassination at the fire station at Tenth Street and Jefferson Boulevard, past which the assailant in J. D. Tippit's murder reportedly fled, one block from the murder scene. But he had decided to leave the fire station and go to Dealey Plaza to see what he could do, and then returned to Oak Cliff when he heard of the Tippit shooting.

McDonald is the officer who eventually arrested Oswald. When the two emerged from the theater Oswald had a battered face and McDonald had a deep scratch running down the right side of his face.

Here's how Officer Paul Bentley recalls the arrest: "McDonald walked up in the row in front of this particular suspect . . . and as he walked in front of him, Oswald jumped up and pulled a pistol from his waist. At that instant, I dove over about three or four rows of seats and came down on the side of Oswald grabbing for the pistol. Either my finger or hand or McDonald's prevented the pistol from firing because there was a slight indentation in the shell where the firing pin had come down, but it didn't explode the shell . . . Oswald suffered a slight abrasion above his right eye on his forehead which I think came from the ring I still wear when I grabbed for him."

The alley behind the Texas Theatre. It is the same alley that runs between the Abundant Life Temple and the parking lot where "Oswald's jacket" was found. *(MacIntyre Symms)*

Outside the theater when Oswald was brought out was Jim MacCannon, whose photos of the incident are in the Warren Commission exhibits labeled as Hill Exhibits A and B."

After the police brought Oswald out of the theater and put him into the backseat of a police car, it was Officer Paul Bentley who, according to the official story, while going through Oswald's wallet, discovered the "Hidell" identification that linked Oswald with the purported murder weapons of JFK and Tippit. However, Bentley did not report the Hidell ID in his written report of the arrest, nor did Sergeant Gerald Hill, who was also in the squad car at the time the wallet was searched. Hill and Bentley claim that they radioed in the Hidell information at the time the ID was discovered, but the transcript of the Dallas police tapes shows no record of such a call.

The driver of that police car was Officer Bob K. Carroll. According to Hill's Warren Commission testimony, Carroll got into the car with the handgun reportedly taken from Oswald. Carroll handed the gun to Hill, who held the gun until they got to the police station.

Bentley remembers that he sat behind the driver with Oswald on his right. Officer K. K. Lyons sat on the other side of Oswald, with Hill and Charles T. Walker sitting on the front seat. Bentley's adrenaline was such that he made it all the way to the police station before he realized that, while diving over the seats in the Texas Theatre, he had severely damaged the ligaments in one ankle and that that ankle had swollen to twice its normal size. Bentley ended up wearing a cast on that ankle, leading many of his fellow officers to assume in the years since that he had broken the ankle in the theater.

As of 2001, the movie theater is closed for business, however an organization called the Oak Cliff Foundation has raised $2.4 million to purchase and renovate the building with plans to make it an active movie theater again, with the seat that marks Oswald's position when he was arrested still in place.

(See also HILL, GERALD LYNN; OSWALD'S WALLET.)

30th of November Group

Anti-Castro Cuban exile group whose most powerful members included Homer S. Echevarria, Carlos Rodriguez Quesada, and Rolando Masferrer. The group dissolved soon after President Kennedy's assassination. A Secret Service memo out of their Chicago office dated several days after the assassination states that, according to an informant, Echevarria had put a certain arms deal on hold and would get back to it, as he reportedly said, "as soon as we take care of Kennedy."

This group, like D.R.E and Alpha 66, received financial backing from a Chicago-based group called JGCE, run by Paulino Sierra Martinez. According to the Cuban government, this group was responsible for two assassination attempts on Castro.

(See also ALPHA 66; D.R.E.)

3128 Harlendale   See also ALPHA 66.

Thomas, Albert   See STOUGHTON, CECIL.

Thornley, Kerry Wendell

Thornley, a suspected Oswald look-alike (even though he was several inches taller than Oswald) was the only man to write a book (albeit a novel) about Lee Harvey Oswald before President Kennedy's assassination.

Thornley's number of connections with the assassination are well above the national average. He was in the U.S. Marines at the El Toro Annex in California in 1959 when he met Oswald.

He wrote the novel *The Idle Warriors* in 1962. The novel was about a disgruntled marine who defects to the Soviet Union. Thornley called his Oswald-based hero Private Johnny Shellburn. The book was not published until 1991. After the assassination, Thornley did publish a book about the assassination, but it was a nonfiction account.

After meeting Oswald, Thornley became obsessed with him, and from that point on their lives formed an interesting parallel. Thornley was stationed in Atsugi, Japan. So was Oswald (although not at the same time). A military LSD/mind-control program known as MK/ULTRA is reported to have been headquartered in Atsugi.

Thornley was interviewed by agents of the FBI two days after President Kennedy's assassination. The FBI was drawn to him because of the manuscript he had been vigorously shopping to publishers.

Thornley testified for the Warren Commission and a copy of his manuscript was placed in the National Archives. He told the commission that he was a "close acquaintance" but not a "good friend" of Oswald in the marines.

Thornley quoted Oswald as saying that "the Marxist morality was the most rational morality," and that communism was "the best system in the world." He said that Oswald's assignments were primarily janitorial during the spring of 1959 as he had lost his clearance.

According to Thornley, Oswald's interests included "philosophy, politics, [and] religion." Since both Oswald and Thornley were atheists, they once got into a conversation about atheism. During the conversation, Oswald asked, "What do you think about Communism?"

"I replied I didn't think too much of Communism," Thornley testified. "And he said, 'Well, I think the best religion is Communism.' And I got the impression at the time . . . he was playing the galleries . . . he said it very gently. He didn't seem to be a glassy-eyed fanatic by any means . . . I did know at the time he was learning the Russian language. I knew he was subscribing to *Pravda*. . . . All of this I took to be a sign of his interest in the subject, and not as a sign of any active commitment to the Communist ends . . . I didn't feel there was any rabid devotion . . . His shoes were always unshined. . . . He walked around with the bill of his cap down over his eyes . . . so he wouldn't have to look at anything around him . . . to blot out the military. . . . It was well-known in the outfit that . . . Oswald had Communist sympathies. . . . Master Sergeant Spar, our section chief, jumped up on a fender one day and said, 'All right, everybody gather around,' and Oswald said in a very thick Russian accent, 'Ah ha, collective farm lecture,' in a very delighted tone. This brought him laughs at the time."

Oswald understood the distinctions between Marxism, communism, and democracy "as well as most reasonably educated people do," Thornley testified, adding that Oswald was "extremely unpredictable" when it came to personal relationships.

"He and I stopped speaking before I finally left the outfit," Thornley testified. He described the incident that led to the tension between them: "It was a Saturday morning. . . . Every now and then we had to give up our Saturday morning liberty to go march in one of those parades . . . [and] to look forward to a morning of standing out in the hot sun and marching around, was irritable. So, we were involved at the moment in a 'hurry up and wait' routine . . . waiting at the moment . . . sitting. Oswald and I happened to be sitting next to each other on a log . . . he turned to me and said something about the stupidity of the parade, . . . and I said, I believe my words were, 'Well, come the revolution you will change all that.' At which time he looked at me like a betrayed Caesar and screamed, screamed definitely. 'Not you too, Thornley.' And I remember his voice cracked as he put his hands in his pockets, pulled his hat down over his eyes and walked away . . . and sat down someplace else alone . . . and I never said anything to him again and he never said anything to me again. This happened with many people, this reaction of Oswald's and therefore he had few friends. . . . He seemed to guard against developing real close friendships."

Thornley's Warren Commission testimony includes this intriguing statement: "there was someone else in the outfit who spoke Russian, don't ask me who, they used to exchange a few comments in the morning at muster and say hello to each other."

New Orleans States-Item reporter Don Hudson quoted Thornley on November 27, 1963, as saying that Oswald "was very resentful of the military; he was very much the type of man who would 'play' the role of assassin. But I'm still not sure he committed the assassination. He never showed any tendency toward violence, he was more of a talker."

In Thornley's own nonfiction book, *Oswald,* Kerry wrote: "When news of Oswald first began to appear, I wondered how any man could have changed so thoroughly in a few short years. A national news magazine called him a psychopath, a schizoid, a paranoid, and a probable homosexual—all in the same single column of print. Suddenly I was reading that he was constantly fighting with his fellow Marines and that in the service he displayed a conspicuous yen for physical violence. I observed no such traits. That an appendix of the Warren Report had to be devoted to speculation and rumors is in my mind argument enough that a good deal of fabrication and exaggeration was involved somewhere along the line. While Oswald had his psychological problems, I doubt that he would have been found legally insane had he lived to face a jury."

Thornley moved to New Orleans after being discharged from the marines, as had Oswald. Oswald and Thornley simultaneously lived in New Orleans. Thornley, however, claims he never ran into Oswald there. Regarding his and Oswald's proximity in New Orleans during the summer of 1963, Thornley wrote that Oswald "was even reputedly stopping in now and then at a bar where I hung out. We may have passed each other on the street but, if so, we didn't recognize each other. Only after the assassination did I realize that Oswald had been right under my nose for over two weeks."

New Orleans Parish district attorney Jim Garrison didn't believe this to be true. Garrison said there was at least one eyewitness (Barbara Reid) who placed Thornley and Oswald together in a New Orleans restaurant just weeks before the assassination.

Garrison called Thornley as a witness at the Clay Shaw trial and later charged Thornley with perjury. Garrison's claims against Thornley were: 1. Thornley and Oswald were involved together in covert CIA operations. 2. Thornley impersonated Oswald as early as 1961. 3.

Thornley's writings about Oswald were actually CIA disinformation. Garrison eventually dropped the perjury charge, although his second claim is worth considering, in light of the fact that Thornley made a short visit to Mexico City in September 1963, just as Oswald is supposed to have done.

Thornley, while living in New Orleans, became an admitted acquaintance of Guy Banister and David Ferrie. After living in New Orleans, Thornley moved to Los Angeles where he got a job as a doorman at the building where Johnny Roselli lived. (See also BANISTER, WILLIAM GUY; FERRIE, DAVID; ROSELLI, JOHNNY.)

It was while living in Atlanta that Thornley told authorities that, back in New Orleans before the assassination, he had been told by a man named Gary Kirstein that President Kennedy and Martin Luther King Jr. would be murdered.

Thornley came to suspect that Kirstein was actually E. Howard Hunt. After telling this story, Thornley claimed he was pistol-whipped by ski-masked intruders at a friend's birthday party. The only thing the intruders stole was Thornley's identification.

According to the *New York Press,* Thornley's odd life eventually caused a mental breakdown. Thornley came to believe, at least publicly, that "he and Lee Harvey Oswald were products of genetic tests carried out by a secret proto-Nazi sect of eugenicists, the Vril Society . . . that a bugging device was implanted in his body at birth, and that both he and Oswald were secretly watched and manipulated from childhood by shadowy, powerful Vril overlords."

On September 28, 1967, Thornley gave a sworn affidavit in Los Angeles that read: "The famous 'U-2 incident' occurred when I was stationed with MACS-11, which was then on maneuvers in the Philippines from the 'home' base at Atsugi, Japan. While at Atsugi, before going on maneuvers, my fellow Marines and I frequently observed what later turned out to be the U-2 taking off and landing at Atsugi. At the same time I was there, this was referred to, among the noncoms as the 'blackbird' or the 'mystery plane,' because it had no markings on it and was black in color. . . . It was kept in a hangar which, rumor had it, was guarded by civilians. At one time, when I was in the vicinity of this hangar, I was asked politely to leave the area by such a civilian. Most of us assumed, myself included, that this black airplane was some kind of experimental aircraft. We did not realize its true function until the story broke in the newspapers and hence that information was declassified."

On the February 25, 1992, edition of the television program *A Current Affair* Thornley said that he was part of a conspiracy to assassinate President Kennedy and that his co-conspirators were men he called "Brother-in-law and Slim."

Thornley stated that he was offended by Jim Garrison's claims that he had set up his former friend Oswald. "I would gladly have killed Kennedy, but I would never have betrayed Oswald," Thornley said. "I wanted him dead. I would have shot him myself. Two weeks before the assassination, Brother-in-law had it all planned out. The only question, as far as Brother-in-law was concerned, was who to frame it on. Brother-in-law said, 'We'll pin it on some jailbird.' I said, 'Why don't you frame some Communist?' and smirked."

(See also APPENDIX C.)

Three Tramps

For years it was believed these hobos were released without any permanent record of their identities—very interesting since the three men were photographed being escorted by men in Dallas police uniforms across Dealey Plaza.

The hobos all had recent haircuts and shoes with good leather. Dallas police records released in 1992, however, say the hobos were really hobos, and were held four days for vagrancy.

According to Dallas police sergeant David V. Harkness, he arrested six to eight hobos in the rail cars behind the grassy knoll but none of them were the three famous tramps whose "pictures were in the magazine."

JFK assassination files released by the Dallas police in February 1992, and discovered by assassination researchers Ray and Mary LaFontaine indicate that the three tramps were Gus Abrams, 53 years old, John F. Gedney, 38, and Harold Doyle, 32. The FBI, checking into this matter, discovered that Abrams was dead. Doyle and Gedney, however, were still alive and were located. The FBI has now concluded, according to the *New York Daily News* (March 4, 1992) that these three men were indeed the tramps and that they were actually tramps.

Over the years, the tramps have been positively identified as several people often thought to be suspects. Soldier-of-fortune Frank Sturgis and CIA agent E. Howard Hunt, later arrested in the Watergate break-in, were identified in *Coup d'Etat in America* by Michael Canfield and Alan Weberman as two of the three suspicious "tramps" apprehended near Dealey Plaza soon after the assassination.

On November 17, 1991, during a JFK assassination conference in Dallas, Lois Gibson, a forensic artist used by the FBI and the Houston Police Department—with private investigator John Craig and researcher Phillip Rogers—positively identified the "three tramps" as professional killer Charles Harrelson, confessed "tramp" and former CIA asset Chauncy Marvin Holt, and wanted murderer Charles Frederick Rogers.

Chauncy Marvin Holt is unique in that he does not deny being a tramp. He insists he was a tramp. Agreeing with forensic artist Lois Gibson, he says the other two tramps were assassination suspect Charles Harrelson and a man he knew as Richard Montoya, whom the Houston police believe to be a wanted murderer named Charles Rogers. According to Craig, Holt is a career criminal, a genius, a pilot who has worked for large segments of organized crime, a master forger, and a man who has been tried and acquitted of murder. Holt was born in Kentucky in 1921, enlisted in the U.S. Army before World War II, and was incarcerated after a court martial. After the war, he did time as a civilian as well, and through prison friends met mobster Peter Lacavoli, who in turn, introduced him to Meyer Lansky. According to Craig: "Holt went to Florida where he was an accountant for Lansky. After some years there in Miami, the Kefauver Hearings began. He was transferred away from there because he knew what was coming. Lansky arranged for him to work as a controller for an outfit called the International Rescue Corporation Committee, which was a proprietary of the CIA. After a time he realized what he was involved in. He forged documents for the CIA. He was transferred to California and in 1963 he provided Oswald with his Hidell I.D. and his Fair Play for Cuba Committee leaflets. He claims he was in Dealey Plaza that day delivering the Secret Service pins and other I.D. to individuals who were in the Plaza. Holt says he encountered assassination suspect Eugene Hale Brading soon after Brading was released by the Sheriff's Department and together they went to Lacavoli's Grace Ranch."

According to Phillip Rogers: "Holt was under the impression that some sort of incident was to be staged in Dallas that would be blamed on pro-Castro forces. When the shots rang out he says he was behind the pergola and he did not see Kennedy or Connally get hit. He immediately ran to the box car as instructed, the ninth box car from the engine. There he met the other two tramps who identified themselves as agents. Together, they were escorted from the scene. It has occurred to Holt that they might have been alternative patsies in case Oswald had escaped."

Craig adds: "Holt runs an art studio in San Diego. He also operates a shooting school. Even at the age of seventy he is still a master marksman. For many years, he taught at a shooting school for a proprietary of the CIA. . . . Holt arrived at a parking lot [behind the grassy knoll] in an Oldsmobile station wagon. This fits with the observations of Lee Bowers. The parking lot was supposed to have been secured. Holt says that he had a key. The Secret Service identification bars have a color of the day, which is why Holt had to forge the I.D. at the last minute, because he did not know until then what color would be valid for that day."

Craig and Rogers then presented evidence that the third tramp, the one who was photographed with his collar up and is sometimes referred to as "Frenchy," was actually Charles Frederick Rogers, the sole suspect in the double homicide of his own mother and father on Father's Day, June 23, 1965, in Houston, Texas.

According to Craig, Rogers has worked for the CIA since 1956. He was a physicist with graduate training in nuclear physics, a linguist, and a close personal friend of assassination suspect David Ferrie. He was born in 1921. He was a member of the Civil Air Patrol in the mid-1950s. He was a seismologist for Shell Oil for nine years after World War II. He graduated from the University of Houston with a degree in physics and was a member there of the Sigma Phi Sigma fraternity. Craig said, "He has been active with the CIA since he murdered his parents. The last place we have [placed] him is in 1986 in Guatemala where he was still working in the Iran-Contra program. He is a pilot and flew for Air America." Police were alerted to the death house of Rogers parents in June 1965 after a cousin became concerned about Fred and Edwina Rogers' whereabouts. According to Craig: "The police initially could not find the couple. A nephew had called and said that no one had heard from them in a couple of days. When Officer Bullock first opened the refrigerator, he thought that what he had seen was a butchered hog. When Officer Bullock, who was a young patrolman at the time, bent down to look in the crisper, he discovered the severed head of Edwina Rogers. Their viscera had been removed, diced up and flushed down the commode. The father's head and hands had been placed in a sack and he was in the process of attempting to dispose them. . . . The mother had confronted the son because of her deep concern over phone calls. Charles Rogers had disappeared for several months after the incident in Dallas, he had left the country in a CIA plane to South America. We know what airport he was at. He stayed down there and he did not contact his parents. It was quite unusual for him to do this. The refrigerator was filled with body parts except for peanut butter and baby food. The pistol that was used was a government issue high standard. This is the gun primarily used by the CIA as an assassination weapon. This had been issued to him and he had left it in a room upstairs. He had beaten his mother to near death in a locked room upstairs after a confrontation. He then went downstairs and beat his father to death with a hammer. He went back upstairs and hauled his mother down to the downstairs bathroom to begin the butchering process. Believe it or not, she was still alive. He took his .223 and put one round behind her ear. All of this was deduced by the Houston Medical Examiners. He used a saw to cut them up. In the house they found a very sophisticated short-wave radio set up and a wire that led up into the attic where there was a half-wave antenna for

broadcasting. The radio found upstairs was not a usual short wave but an unusual piece of equipment developed for government use. . . During World War II, Rogers served with the Office of Naval Intelligence. When the Navy tested him at the start of the war he scored at genius level on an I.Q. test. He spent thirty months in the South Pacific on two ships upon which he was the chief cryptographer. He had been trained in cryptography by Naval Intelligence. He even did work for Shell Oil in that field."

In 1975, Rogers was declared legally dead so that his estate could be probated. Craig continued, "Fred Rogers was also brilliant. He was one of the first men in the country to receive a degree in electrical engineering, which he did at Texas A&M. There were no jobs in that field, however, so he became a salesman and later worked from 1954–63 as a bookie in Galveston under the auspices of [New Orleans mobster] Carlos Marcello."

The tramp who resembled Frank Sturgis is the same tramp who resembles assassination suspect Charles V. Harrelson, so either Sturgis or Harrelson (or, of course, both) are not one of the three tramps. (See also STURGIS, FRANK.)

According to assassination investigators Sybil Leek and Bert R. Sugar, Gerry Patrick Hemming has identified the tall tramp as a member of the Minutemen named John Bloomer. Hemming has also said that "Frenchy," the short, young tramp with the upturned collar, is Ted Slack, an Office of Naval Intelligence instructor in the Miami area.

Public attention was first brought to the photos of the tramps by business-computer expert Richard E. Sprague. In February 1967, Sprague sent copies of the tramp photos to New Orleans district attorney Jim Garrison, who was then conducting an assassination investigation.

The House Select Committee on Assassinations assigned forensic anthropologists to analyze the tramp photos along with photographs of the men suspected of being the tramps, to see if any of them were identical. The study ruled out all of the suspects, with the exception of Fred Lee Crisman, whom, the report said, strongly resembled the oldest tramp.

The tramp photos were not taken moments after the assassination as is usually assumed. We know this because one of the photographers who took photos of the tramps being escorted across Dealey Plaza was George Smith of Fort Worth, Texas, and he says that he did not even arrive in Dealey Plaza until 2:15 P.M., one hour and 45 minutes after the shooting.

(See also CRISMAN, FRED LEE; HARRELSON, CHARLES VOYD; HUNT, E. HOWARD.)

Tilson, Tom G., Jr.

A Dallas police officer who had the day off on November 22, 1963. Just after the assassination, Tilson said he was involved in a strange car chase. At 12:30, Tilson said he and his daughter were driving downtown and had just turned east on Commerce Street from Industrial Boulevard (just west of the triple underpass) when he heard reports of the shooting on his police radio.

Tilson told the *Dallas Morning News* on August 20, 1978: "I saw all these people running to the scene of the shooting. By that time I had come across under Stemmons. Everybody was jumping out of their cars and pulling up on the median strip. My daughter Judy noticed [President Kennedy's] limousine come under the underpass. They took a right turn onto Stemmons toward Parkland Hospital. Well, the limousine just sped past [this] car parked on the grass on the north side of Elm Street near the west side of the underpass. Here's one guy coming from the railroad tracks. He came down that grassy slope on the west side of the triple underpass, on the Elm Street side. He had (this) car parked there, a black car. And, he threw something in the back seat and went around the front hurriedly and got in the car and took off. I was on Commerce Street right there across from [the car], fixing to go under the triple underpass going into town. I saw all this and I said, 'That doesn't make sense, everybody running to the scene and one person running from it. That's suspicious as hell.' So, I speeded up and went through the triple underpass up to Houston . . . made a left . . . [came] back on Main . . and caught up with him because he got caught on a light. He made a left turn, going south on Industrial. I told my daughter to get a pencil and some paper and write down what I tell you. By this time, we had gotten to the toll road [then the Dallas-Fort Worth Turnpike, now Interstate 30] going toward Fort Worth. I got the license number and description of the car and I saw what the man looked like. He was stocky, about five-foot-nine, weighing 185 to 195 pounds and wearing a dark suit. . . . If that wasn't Jack Ruby, it was someone who was his twin brother."

Tilson later called in the information. According to Jim Marrs, "Tilson's story is corroborated by his daughter, now Mrs. Judy Ladner, although photos taken west of the triple underpass at the time do not show a black car. . . . Also, Dallas police logs for the day do not indicate any alert for such a car as described by Tilson."

Dallas police homicide detective James R. Leavelle does not think that Tilson is telling the truth. According to Leavelle, Tilson "is a nut from the word go. . . . I have no idea where Tommy was that day, but I can tell you one thing: not a bit of it happened as he said, not a bit! In fact, he's changed his story at least three times."

The same Tommy Tilson said that J. D. Tippit had a girlfriend who lived on Tenth Street.

Tippit, J. D.

Born September 18, 1924, Tippit volunteered for the U.S. Army on June 21, 1944, and served in the European The-

ater of World War II as an ammo bearer for the 17th Airborne Division. He was honorably discharged on June 30, 1946. He joined the Dallas Police Department in June 1952. After the birth of his second son he took a job working security at college football games at the Cotton Bowl on Saturday afternoons and in 1961 took another moonlighting job working as a security guard at Austin's Barbecue at 2321 West Illinois Street in the Oak Cliff section of Dallas.

Tippit was shot four times and killed immediately in front of his police car on Tenth Street between Denver Street and Patton Avenue in Oak Cliff between 40 and 46 minutes following the assassination. He was one of very few policemen in Dallas that day who had not been called to Dealey Plaza to help investigate the assassination. He was the so-called officer-at-large, in charge of covering whatever came up.

In 1967, Dallas police dispatcher Murray Jackson tried to explain to CBS-TV why Tippit was where he was at the time he was murdered: "I realized that we were draining the Oak Cliff area of available police officers. If there was an emergency, such as an armed robbery or a major accident to come up, we wouldn't have had anybody there." According to the Warren Commission, Tippit called Oswald over to his car at 1:15 P.M., 45 minutes after the assassination, for questioning (theoretically because Oswald resembled the description of the assassin that had been broadcast on police radio).

Tippit got out of the car and walked around the front toward Oswald, who was standing on the passenger side. When Tippit got in front of his car, Oswald (according to the eyewitness Helen Markham) shot him dead.

Tippit's death may be the least investigated homicide of a police officer in history. It was assumed that Oswald did it, and no one questioned the matter until critics of the *Warren Report* began to see the Tippit killing as a possibly penetrable crack in the suspected assassination conspiracy.

There are witnesses who saw Tippit and Ruby together in the weeks and months before the assassination who claim that they were close friends. Tippit was killed only a few blocks from Ruby's apartment. Some witnesses claims that two men fled the scene after Tippit was shot and that one of them was a short, heavy middle-aged man.

Jack Hardee Jr., a runner for a Dallas numbers operations, told the FBI that J. D. Tippit was "a frequent visitor to Ruby's nightclub." The FBI deposed Hardee on December 26, 1963, at the Mobile (Alabama) County Jail, where he was incarcerated. The FBI reported: "Hardee stated that he has spent some time in Dallas, Texas, and he had met Jack Ruby during the course of his contacts in Dallas. He stated that approximately one year ago, while in Dallas, Texas, he attempted to set up a numbers game, and he was advised by an individual, whom he did not identify, that in

J. D. Tippit. *(Author's Collection)*

has so far given the Tippit widow and children more than $50,000."

(See also HARRIS, LARRY RAY; TIPPIT, MURDER OF; TOP 10 RECORD STORE.)

Tippit, Murder of

The star witness to the Tippit killing, as far as the Warren Commission was concerned, was Helen Louise Markham, a waitress in downtown Dallas. She told the commission that, at the time of Tippit's murder, she was standing on the northwest corner of Tenth Street and Patton Avenue in the Oak Cliff section of Dallas waiting for traffic to pass. It was approximately 1:15 P.M., about 45 minutes after the assassination. She was waiting to cross Tenth, heading toward her bus stop on her way to work, when she spotted a man at the opposite (southeast) corner of the intersection just about to step up onto the curb. She was approximately 50 feet away from the man, whom she says walked away from her—that is, eastward—slowly along Tenth.

The *Warren Report* says, "Mrs. Markham saw a police car slowly approach the man from the rear and stop alongside of him. She saw the man come to the right window of the police car. As he talked he leaned on the ledge of the right window with his arms. The man appeared to step back as the policeman 'calmly opened the car door' and very slowly got out and walked toward the front of the car. The man pulled a gun. Mrs. Markham heard three shots and saw the policeman fall to the ground near the left front wheel."

Mrs. Markham says she saw the man "fooling with" the gun (probably ejecting the shells) and then heading "in kind of a little trot" down Patton toward Jefferson Boulevard, which was a block away.

According to her story, she immediately ran to the policeman's side. He was lying in a pool of blood and tried to talk to her as the attempted to comfort him. All other evidence points to the fact that Tippit was killed instantly by the gunfire.

An edited version of Markham's Warren Commission testimony was used to "convict" Oswald of the Tippit murder. However, a transcript of her testimony casts serious doubts on what Markham saw and didn't see that afternoon.

She was hysterical—one officer felt it necessary to slap her—after the Tippit shooting. "She was just out of her gourd," Jez told researcher Dale K. Myers in 1996. "I shook her and she just kept screaming and carrying on and finally I smacked her across the cheeks and it brought her back in the world. And she started rattling it off. Exactly what he looked like, what he was wearing, what happened."

order to operate in Dallas it was necessary to have the clearance of Jack Ruby. He stated that this individual . . . told him Ruby had the 'fix' with the county authorities, and that any other fix being placed would have to be done through Ruby. . . . Hardee also stated that the police officer whom Harvey Lee Oswald [sic] allegedly killed after he allegedly assassinated the president was a frequent visitor to Ruby's night club, along with another officer who was a motorcycle patrol in the Oaklawn [sic] section of Dallas. Hardee stated from his observation there appeared to be a very close relationship between these three individuals . . . Hardee stated that he knows of his own personal knowledge that Ruby hustled the strippers and other girls who worked in his club. Ruby made dates for them, accepting the money for the dates in advance, and kept half, giving the other half to the girls. The dates were filled in the new hotel in downtown Dallas and the Holiday Inn in Irvington, where Ruby had an associate, whom Hardee could only identify as a Negro who drove a big Cadillac."

United Press International reported in 1964, "(Tippit's widow) stands to collect $225 a month in pension money, half to her and half to the three children. A grateful world

DALLAS POLICE OFFICER J.D. TIPPIT MURDER SCENE

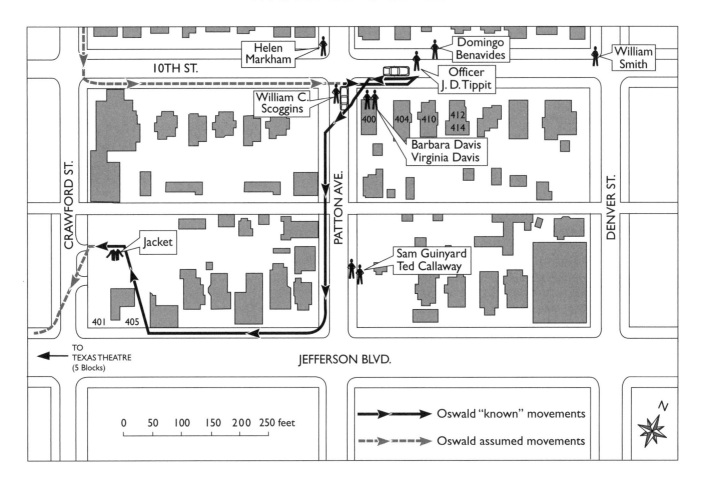

Photos of the crime scene show that, at some point, Mrs. Markham removed her shoes and placed them on top of Dallas Police car number 10, Tippit's patrol car.

She remained in a state of extreme agitation all the way through the time she was taken to the police station to view Oswald in a lineup. Here is one exchange that took place during her Warren Commission testimony:

Q: Did you recognize anyone in the lineup?
Markham: No, sir.
Q: You did not? Did you see anybody—I asked you that question before—did you recognize anybody from their face?
Markham: From their face, no.
Q: Did you identify anybody in these four people?
Markham: I didn't know nobody.
Q: I know you didn't know anybody, but did anyone in that lineup look like anybody you had seen before?

Markham: No. I had never seen none of them, none of these men . . .
Q: Was there a number two man in there?
Markham: Number two is the one I picked.
Q: I thought you just told me that you hadn't—
Markham: I thought you wanted me to describe their clothing.
Q: You recognized him from his appearance?
Markham: I asked—I looked at him. When I saw this man I wasn't sure, but I had cold chills run all over me.

This is what the commission called a "positive identification." Markham said she was "the only" witness to the shooting and that she remained for 20 minutes with the dying officer. Every other witness to the shooting said that the officer was killed immediately and that a crowd of people gathered "quickly" around the crime scene.

Also present at the scene of the crime was automobile repairman Domingo Benavides. The *Warren Report* says, "[Benavides] heard the shots and stopped his pickup truck on the opposite side of the street about twenty-five feet in front of Tippit's car. He observed the gunman start back toward Patton Avenue, removing the empty cartridge cases as he went. Benavides rushed to Tippit's side. The patrolman, apparently dead, was lying on his revolver, which was out of its holster. Benavides promptly reported the shooting to police headquarters over the radio in Tippit's car. The message was received shortly after 1:16 P.M."

Benavides said, describing the gunman, "the back of his head seemed like his hairline sort of went square instead of tapering off. His hair didn't taper of. It kind of went down and squared off." Photographs confirm that Oswald's hair tapered off. In fact, Oswald's hair was growing down the back of his neck so far that his colleagues at the Texas School Book Depository teased him about it.

Although Benavides had a clear view of the fleeing assailant, he wasn't asked by the Dallas police to view a lineup because, according to Warren Commission counsel David Belin, "he didn't think he was very good at identifying people."

Benavides said that, at the time of the shooting, there was a man between 25 and 30 years old sitting in a red 1961 Ford Falcon, parked about six cars from Tippit's car. This man has never been located. Benavides was threatened after the Tippit killing.

Benavides's brother, Edward, was shot to death in a Dallas bar in February 1964 at the age of 29. It is unlikely that this shooting had anything to do with Domingo's eyewitness status as Edward was shot by a drinking buddy who served 20 months for manslaughter.

The other witness closest to the crime was Dallas cab driver William W. Scoggins, who was parked on the east side of Patton Avenue facing north, a few feet from the corner of Tenth Street. Scoggins says he didn't see the shooting itself because of shrubbery in the way. He told the Warren Commission: "I saw him coming kind of toward me . . . I could see his face, his features, and everything plain . . . kind of loping, trotting . . . He had a pistol in his left hand . . . I heard him mutter something like 'poor damn cop,' or 'poor dumb cop.' He said that over twice."

After the shooting, Scoggins got out of his cab, then hid behind it when he saw the assailant approaching. The man cut across a lawn, ran into some bushes, and then passed within 12 feet of his cab. The man proceeded south on Patton Avenue. Scoggins later identified the man as Oswald. He said the assailant had been walking west when he first encountered Tippit's car, which was heading east on Tenth Street and had just passed directly in front of Scoggins's cab. (Scoggins died March 25, 1990.)

The Warren Commission insists that Oswald had to have been walking east on Tenth at the time he encountered Tippit since he didn't have time to make it there if he were coming from the other direction, that is, if he had made the entire journey from his rooming house on foot. The bulk of the eyewitness evidence, however, suggests that the assailant was walking west when the police car approached, and perhaps turned and started walking east at that point, this abrupt about-face perhaps being the behavior that aroused Tippit's suspicion.

Two other witnesses to the immediate aftermath of the murder were Barbara Jeannette Davis and her sister-in-law Virginia R. Davis, who lived in a house at the southeast corner of Tenth Street and Patton. They heard shots and ran to the door, where they saw a man cutting across their lawn twenty feet away, and then turning south on Patton Avenue. Two shells found near their house were handed over to Dallas policemen. Both women positively identified the man they had seen as Oswald. Why would a killer empty shells from his revolver and "hide" them close to the crime scene?

Warren Allen Reynolds of Reynolds Motor Company—a used-car dealership on East Jefferson Boulevard, one block away from the crime scene—saw the assailant fleeing the murder scene. At first Reynolds refused to identify the man as Oswald but, after he was shot in the head and recovered, he decided that, yes, it was Oswald he had seen fleeing. Reynolds was shot on the night of January 23, 1964. He was locking up his basement office when he was shot in the temple by a .22 caliber bullet. A man carrying a rifle pushed past him and ran up the stairs. A man by the name of Sonny Carty, who had an apartment on Jefferson Boulevard, heard the shot and ran out onto his balcony to see what was going on. He saw a man carrying a rifle run out of the back of the car lot and head south on Patton Street. He described the man as white, five-feet five-inches tall, and wearing khaki-colored pants and a blue flowered shirt. There had been no robbery.

An FBI memo dated March 5, 1964, stated that Reynolds "wanted to advise the FBI that on the afternoon of March 2, 1964, General Edwin A. Walker had telephonically contacted him at his place of business, at which time General Walker read an article from some Boston newspaper to him. According to Reynolds, this newspaper article was written by Bob Considine and indicated that it was unusual that Reynolds had been shot because he had 'fingered' Oswald. Reynolds stated that he had not 'fingered' Oswald. Reynolds stated that General Walker asked Reynolds if he would come to see General Walker because General Walker did not want to talk on the telephone." Reynolds did visit Walker and later told the FBI that, during that meeting, Walker emphasized that his shooting must have had something to do with the Tippit murder, even though Reynolds had no other reason to believe that was true.

Reynolds, on the other hand, may have known that the shooting did not have to do with the JFK assassination. The man accused of shooting Reynolds reportedly had tried to sell Reynolds a car earlier on the day of Reynolds's shooting and the Warren Commission heard rumors that the used-car dealer sometimes dealt in stolen and stripped cars. Still, making the public believe that the shooting was Tippit-related might serve to keep eyewitnesses from speaking out about what they had seen, which might have been what General Walker had in mind.

Reynolds's employee L. J. Lewis told the FBI that he had seen the man running from the scene *several minutes* after he heard the shots and that the man was trying to conceal "an automatic pistol or a revolver" in his belt. Lewis could not identify the man. Lewis's time reference does not agree with any of the other witnesses, who agree that Tippit's murderer fled immediately.

Harold Russell, another employee of Reynolds Motor Company, saw a man fleeing south on Patton Avenue toward Jefferson with a handgun in his hand moments after hearing shots, but he could not identify the man. Russell died in police custody in February 1967 after going berserk at a party screaming that he was going to be killed.

Ted Callaway, a veteran of the battle of Iwo Jima as well as the Marshall Islands, who worked at a used-car lot on Jefferson Boulevard and Patton Avenue, and his assistant B. D. Searcy also saw the assailant fleeing the scene. Searcy and Callaway watched the gunman approach them on Patton, then turn right on Jefferson Boulevard. Searcy said he couldn't identify the man. Callaway reported the murder to Dallas police over Tippit's car radio. The police called the Dudley Hughes Funeral Home, not because they presumed the officer to be dead but because the funeral home also functioned as the primary ambulance dispatch for the southern regions of Dallas. The call was taken by Hughes himself, who sent J. C. "Clayton" Butler and William "Eddie" Kinsley to the scene of the Tippit killing. Callaway helped put Officer Tippit's body in the ambulance, saw the assailant fleeing the scene with a gun in his hand, and later that day identified Oswald as the man. He said that he did not see Helen Markham—the Warren Commission's star witness—at the scene immediately following the murder. Callaway got into Scoggins's cab on the passenger seat and tried to talk Scoggins into chasing the murderer in his cab. But, according to Callaway, Scoggins was too nervous to be much good and had trouble just getting the car started because his hands were shaking so badly. Finally, Scoggins got the car into gear and running. The men turned west on Tenth Street, south on Crawford, to Jefferson and then west on Jefferson toward Beckley.

Jimmy Earl Burt, a soldier on leave, was standing in front of his house at the corner of Denver and Tenth—about a block east of the murder scene—talking to a friend, when he noticed a man walking west on Tenth. Burt, who died at 39 in a 1983 car crash in Florida, saw the man coming from the direction of the Town and Country Cafe, which is at 604 East Tenth Street. Moments later, he saw the same man talking with Tippit, then heard gunfire and saw the man run away. This statement is important because, officially, the assailant was walking east on Tenth (or, generally, from the direction of Oswald's rooming house) when he encountered Tippit. Burt's friend was William Arthur Smith, and his statements corroborate Burt's. Burt's observations are also corroborated by Scoggins, who also says the gunman was walking west.

There was a construction site directly across the street from Burt. Working on the site was William Lawrence Smith, who was walking east toward the Town and Country Cafe on Tenth Street when he passed a man he identified as Lee Harvey Oswald walking west.

He said this happened at 1:04 P.M. According to the official scenario, Oswald was walking east on Tenth Street and was still at the corner of Zang and Beckley, the location of his rooming house, at 1:04 P.M.

Mary Brock was the wife of a mechanic who worked at a Jefferson Boulevard gas station. She saw a man fleeing the scene of the Tippit shooting and described the man as white, five-feet ten-inches tall, and wearing light clothing and a light-colored jacket who was walking fast with his hands in his pockets. She last saw the man in the parking lot directly behind the gas station—the parking lot where a light-colored jacket was later found. During an FBI interview conducted on January 21, 1964, she positively identified the man as Oswald.

Jack Ray Tatum, who had driven to the scene in a red 1964 Ford Galaxie 500, told researchers that the Warren Commission's star witness to the Tippit killing, Helen Markham, was anxious to leave the scene of the crime because she did not want to miss the 1:12 bus that would take her to work.

In a 1983 interview with assassination researcher Dale K. Myers, witness Tatum said that, after the first three shots, "the man acted as if he was going to leave, and hesitated, and went back around behind the squad car, back up toward the front where the officer was laying. He didn't walk back, he hurried back, and cautiously approached him, and then shot him again—in the head." Tatum estimated that it was between six and 10 seconds between the first three shots and the fourth. "After shooting the officer in the head, the man hesitated—he stopped and looked around briefly, looked toward the lady up there on the corner, Mrs. Markham, and looked up in my direction.

And I was right there, right past the intersection, and it was only about a half a block, and he started a slow trot, or kind of a hurried run, in my direction. I thought he was coming after me, so I put my car in gear and moved forward away from the gunman." It has been theorized that witnesses to this murder who thought they saw a man in a getaway car actually remember Tatum getting away from the gunman.

Dallas resident Temple Ford "Thomas" Bowley was driving and had just turned west on Tenth Street when he encountered the Tippit murder scene. "I looked at my watch and it said 1:10 P.M.," Bowley said. That would mean the officer was already down only six minutes after Oswald, officially, left his rooming house on foot one mile away.

Acquila Clemons, who lived at 327 East Tenth Street, watched the shooting from her house on the north side of Tenth Street, four houses west of Patton Avenue. She saw two men talking with Tippit just before he was shot. One of the men shot Tippit, then both fled the scene in opposite directions. The gunman, she said, was "kind of a short guy and kind of heavy." The other man, she claimed, was tall and thin in khaki trousers and a white shirt. Clemons was warned by Dallas police members not to say what she saw because if she did, "she might get hurt." She was not called as a Warren Commission witness.

Thayer Waldo, a staff reporter for the *Fort Worth Star-Telegram,* told attorney Mark Lane that on the evening of November 14, 1963, he knew of a two-hour meeting at the Carousel Club between Ruby, Tippit, and Bernard Weissman, a Dallas right-winger who signed a full-page anti-JFK ad that ran in the *Dallas Morning News* on November 22. Lane refused to give the Warren Commission his source concerning the information on the November 14 meeting. The commission failed to ask Waldo where he had gotten the information.

Two other eyewitnesses who saw things not in sync with the official scenario are Frank and Mary Wright who lived at 501 Tenth Street. Mrs. Wright said she put in the call for an ambulance just after Tippit was shot. Neither were interviewed by the FBI or asked by the Warren Commission to testify. According to New Orleans Parish district attorney Jim Garrison, "Mr. Wright, who had been inside the house, came out in time to see . . . Tippit roll over on the ground, probably the last move of his life. Wright observed another man looking down on the fallen officer. Then the man circled around the police car and got into an old, gray car on the other side of it. He drove off rapidly."

Here is a rundown of some of the Dallas police officers who were involved, in one way or another, with the Tippit killing, and what their observations were:

Officer Murray James Jackson had been a friend of Tippit's for 20 years. He was the dispatcher at the time and the one who, according to Dallas police transcripts of police radio recordings ordered Tippit to patrol Oak Cliff when virtually all other mobile personnel had been ordered to Dealey Plaza. The official scenario of why Tippit was where he was doesn't make sense. All mobile personnel had been called to the Dealey Plaza area except Tippit, who was in charge of the rest of Dallas. That this one patrol car happened past the fleeing assassin stretches credibility.

One of the dispatchers at the time the Tippit murder was called in by Ted Callaway was Clifford E. Hulse. The other was Gerald Henslee. Hulse, who died on May 6, 1982, answered the call.

Officer J. M. Poe was one of the first policemen at the scene and was handed two shells by witness Domingo Benavides. Poe was ordered by Sergeant Gerald Hill to "mark them for evidence."—initial them so they could be identified later. Poe, when shown the shells on June 12, 1964, which did not bear his initials, said that he wasn't sure if he had initialed them. Thus, he made himself look incompetent rather than offering evidence that the shells might have been switched. The shells that did not bear Poe's initials were those which ballistically matched the gun reportedly found on Oswald at the time of his arrest in the Texas Theatre. Either Poe forgot to initial the shells or the shells were switched. (Although the Dallas district attorney probably had a better case against Oswald in the murder of Tippit than in the assassination, the problems with the evidence found at the scene might have caused a jury to pause. Not only were the cartridges manufactured by a different company than the four bullets found inside Tippit's body, but the bullets could not be ballistically matched to Oswald's gun.)

Dallas police sergeant Willie E. Barnes was called to the site of the Tippit shooting and took photographs of Tippit's car that showed the driver's window rolled up. This is significant since witness Helen Markham's Oswald-damaging testimony says Oswald spoke to Tippit before the shooting through that open window. Barnes initialed two of the shell cartridges that he received from Officer J. M. Poe at the scene of the Tippit killing. Like Poe, Barnes was later unable to identify the shells he had been given because his initials were missing.

Patrolman H. W. Summers was riding in patrol car number 221 and was involved in the immediate search for Tippit's murderer. Soon after the killing was reported Summers radioed in from Oak Cliff that he had "an eyeball witness to the getaway man." The assailant was described as having black, wavy hair and wearing dark trousers, a white shirt, and a light-colored Eisenhower jacket. He reported in that the suspect was "apparently armed with a .32, dark finish automatic pistol." Moments later, Sergeant Gerald Hill of the Dallas police went on the air stating "the shell at the scene indicates that the suspect is armed with an automatic .38 rather than a pistol."

The third and fourth shells at the scene were reportedly found later than the first two. The third shell was discovered some time after the shooting by Captain George M. Doughty. Doughty died on July 31, 1996, age 79. This shell was found under one of the bedroom windows on the Patton Avenue side of the house. The fourth shell was discovered by Virginia Davis herself near the sidewalk leading to her front door. This shell was turned over to George M. Doughty and Charles W. Brown of the Dallas police at 7:00 P.M. on November 22.

FBI firearms identification expert Charles L. Killion examined the four cartridges reportedly found at the scene of the Tippit killing and determined that they came from the revolver reportedly found on Oswald at the time of his Dallas arrest. FBI ballistics expert Cortlandt Cunningham told the Warren Commission it was impossible to ballistically match the bullets recovered at the scene of the Tippit shooting with the gun allegedly belonging to Oswald, but that he could match the four shell casings (the ones with the missing initials) found near the scene with "Oswald's" handgun, "to the exclusion of all other weapons."

According to Craig Roberts—an assassination researcher who has worked as a Marine sniper in Vietnam with 18 confirmed kills, and later as a sniper for the Tulsa police—the .38 super cartridge cases found at the scene of Tippit's murder couldn't have come from ammunition that was usable in Oswald's gun.

One of the physicians who attended to Tippit at Methodist Central Hospital was Dr. Paul C. Moellenhoff. In a 1983 interview with researcher Dale K. Myers, Dr. Moellenhoff said: "I opened up his clothes. There was a bullet, I believe it was in his, I can't remember, right or left chest, under a rib. The bullet was right there. You could feel it as well as you could feel a rib at least, and it wasn't any trick to get it out. I just reached in there with the hemostats and dug it out. It had carried his uniform button in with it, and I pulled this bullet out, with the uniform button still around it and handed it to the police officer." The bullet was handed to Second Platoon Commander Captain C. E. Talbert, who handed the slug to Officer Robert A. Davenport, who took the bullet to the police identification bureau.

The body was moved to Parkland Hospital for autopsy. Tippit's autopsy was performed by Dr. Earl F. Rose. He said there was a wound to the right temple and one near the right nipple that passed through the heart and would have been fatal if the head wound hadn't been there. A third wound was in the extreme right side of Tippit's

chest. The fourth wound was superficial and in the center of Tippit's abdomen. This is the wound caused by the bullet pushing a button from Tippit's uniform inside his body.

(See also ABUNDANT LIFE TEMPLE; OSWALD'S JACKET; TEXAS THEATRE; TOP 10 RECORD STORE.)

Top 10 Record Store

Located at 338 West Jefferson Boulevard, in the Oak Cliff section of Dallas, across the street and a block and a half west of the Texas Theatre where Oswald was arrested. Special Agent Carl E. Walters of the FBI wrote a memo on December 3, 1963, addressed to the special agent in charge, Dallas. It said, "On 12/3/63, Mr. John D. Whitten telephonically advised that he heard Lee Harvey Oswald was in the Top 10 Record Shop on Jefferson at 7:30 A.M. on the morning of 11/22/63. Oswald bought a ticket of some kind and left. Then, some time later, Oswald returned to the record shop and wanted to buy another ticket. Whitten requested that his name not be mentioned in any way, as it could hurt his business." The story was confirmed by Dallas reporter Earl Golz in an interview with Louis Cortinas, who was an 18-year-old employee of the record store at the time of the assassination.

In 1997, the store's owner, J. W. "Dub" Stark (born 1910) told researcher Dale K. Myers that he recalled the incident. Stark said that "Oswald" was waiting at the store when he arrived that morning at 7:30. Oswald, he said, had bought a ticket to a Dick Clark show and had left by bus. Stark said that Tippit was not in the store at the same time as Oswald, but had come in later to make a telephone call. Interestingly, Stark said that he had never heard of a man named Whitten. (Best bet here is that Stark and Whitten are one and the same, and the FBI agent who wrote the memo got the name wrong.)

Cortinas and Stark agreed that J. D. Tippit entered the store at about 1:10 P.M. on November 22, 1963—or only minutes before his death—and had hurriedly pushed his way past customers to get to a phone booth. Tippit made a call and his party apparently wasn't home. He hung up and left the store. Tippit got in his squad car and was last seen on Sunset, heading toward Beckley Avenue.

According to the official story, Oswald was never in Oak Cliff on the morning of November 22, as he had spent the night in Irving and had been given a ride directly to downtown Dallas and the Texas School Book Depository by Buell Wesley Frazier. The report of Tippit being in the store does fit in with his known movements, although the estimate of the time of the incident may be off by a few minutes.

(See also HARRIS, LARRY RAY; TIPPIT, J. D; TIPPIT, MURDER OF.)

Torbitt Document, The

A lawyer from the American Southwest who claims to have worked on the Garrison investigation wrote a book in 1969 called *Nomenclature of an Assassination Cabal* under the nom de plume William Torbitt. The book was published in 1996 by Adventures Unlimited as *NASA, Nazis & JFK*. The book states that the assassination was accomplished by Division Five of the FBI, along with elements of the Defense Intelligence Agency acting on behalf of the Joint Chiefs of Staff. The DIA division involved was called the Defense Industrial Security Command (DISC), which did intelligence work for NASA, the Atomic Energy Commission, and defense contractors doing work for the Pentagon. Also involved was the international finance organization known as Permindex. Agents of DISC, according to the document, included Lee Harvey Oswald, Jack Ruby, Clay Shaw, Guy Banister, and Permindex's L. M. Bloomfield.

Another organization participating was the American Council of Christian Churches (ACCC). Comprised predominantly of innocent churches, the organization was run by Carl McIntire, a friend of J. Edgar Hoover, as a cover for spying and propaganda activities. The document contains the claim that the Abundant Life Temple, near the site of the Tippit killing, was a member of the ACCC—and it was into this building that Tippit's killer was seen to flee. Another agent for the ACCC, the document states, was Albert Osborne, the man who reportedly accompanied Oswald or an Oswald look-alike to Mexico City on a bus during September 1963.

The document states that Oswald, while a U.S. Marine, was taken to an Office of Naval Intelligence base in Memphis, Tennessee, where he was given the highest level of covert espionage training.

Other guilty parties mentioned in the document include Lyndon Johnson, Ruby's friend L. J. McWillie, anticommunist New York lawyer Roy M. Cohn, rocket engineer Wernher Von Braun, John Connally, and oilmen Clint Murchison Sr. and H. L. Hunt.

(See also ABUNDANT LIFE TEMPLE; ARMY INTELLIGENCE; FEDERAL BUREAU OF INVESTIGATION; GARRISON INVESTIGATION, THE; MURCHISON, CLINT; OSBORNE, ALBERT; PERMINDEX; SHAW, CLAY; WHITE RUSSIANS.)

Towner, James M. and Tina

Assassination witnesses James M. Towner and his daughter Tina lived in the Oak Cliff section of Dallas, just northwest of Red Bird Airport. James brought a 35mm camera with him to the motorcade while Tina carried an 8mm movie camera. They stood at the southwest corner of Elm and Houston Streets directly across from the Texas School Book Depository. In one of the Towners' photographs taken after the assassination, it appears that a dark-

Jim Towner's photograph of the grassy knoll taken seconds after the shooting. Note that the man standing on the sidewalk has something resembling a walkie-talkie sticking out his pocket. This man, who'd earlier been standing next to the "Umbrella Man," had raised his fist as the President passed. *(Author's Collection)*

skinned man is wearing a walkie-talkie device stuck inside the back of his pants. The man is the same one who had been standing in front of the Umbrella Man with his right fist raised when the president passed.

(See also UMBRELLA MAN.)

Trafficante, Santos

Florida Mafia boss based in Tampa who controlled mob operations in Cuba before Castro's revolution and maintained close ties to the paramilitary Cuban exiles after Castro took over.

Jack Newfield, in the January 14, 1992, edition of the *New York Post,* quoted Trafficante's lawyer of 27 years, Frank Ragano, as saying that Jimmy Hoffa had sent him to New Orleans to instruct Trafficante and New Orleans mob boss Carlos Marcello to kill the president.

The House Select Committee on Assassinations reported that: "Trafficante, like [assassination suspect Carlos] Marcello, had the motive, means and opportunity to assassinate President Kennedy . . . Trafficante was a key subject of the Justice Department crackdown on organized crime during the Kennedy administration, with his name being added to a list of the top ten syndicate leaders targeted for investigation. [RFK's] strong interest in having Trafficante prosecuted occurred during the same period in which CIA officials, unbeknown to the Attorney General, were using Trafficante's services in assassination plots against . . . Fidel Castro. The committee found that . . . Trafficante's stature in the national syndicate of organized crime, notably the violent narcotics trade, and his role as the mob's chief liaison to criminal figures within the Cuban exile community, provided him with the capability of formulating an assassination conspiracy against President Kennedy. Trafficante had recruited Cuban nationals to help plan and execute the CIA's assignment to assassinate Castro. (The CIA gave the assignment to former FBI agent Robert Maheu, who passed the contract along to Mafia figures Sam Giancana and John Roselli. They, in turn, enlisted Trafficante to have the intended assassination carried out.)"

Trafficante admitted to his role in the plot to kill Castro during his House Select Committee on Assassinations testimony, but "categorically denied ever having discussed any plans to assassinate President Kennedy."

Regarding Trafficante's association with Ruby, the House Select Committee reported, "Ruby may have met with Trafficante at Trescornia prison in Cuba during one of his visits to Havana in 1959, as the CIA had learned but had discounted in 1964. While the committee was not able to determine the purpose of the meeting, there was considerable evidence that it did take place."

The CIA sent a copy of a memo to Lyndon Johnson aide McGeorge Bundy on November 28, 1963, stating that, in 1959, Trafficante had been visited by Ruby in jail in Cuba.

A July 21, 1961, Treasury Department memo made public in 1976 stated that there were "unconfirmed rumors in the Cuban refugee population in Miami that when Fidel Castro ran the American racketeers out of Cuba and seized the casinos, he kept . . . Trafficante . . . in jail to make it appear he had a personal dislike for Trafficante, when in fact Trafficante is an agent of Castro. Trafficante is allegedly Castro's outlet for illegal contraband in this country."

Anthony Summers wrote that Ruby arrived in Havana on August 8, 1959, having told his doctor that he was going to make some money gambling at the (Havana) Tropicana, where he was subsequently seen by many witnesses in the company of Lewis McWillie, who was managing the Tropicana for Trafficante.

Soldier-of-fortune Gerry Patrick Hemming has said that Ruby met with an American close to Castro to help secure Trafficante's release. One of Trafficante's fellow inmates, English journalist John Wilson Hudson, remembers seeing Ruby bring food to Santos.

Trafficante died following triple-bypass surgery in 1987 in Houston, Texas. On his death bed, he told his lawyer,

Frank Ragano, "Carlos [Marcello] fucked up. We should not have killed Giovanni [John]. We should have killed Bobby."

According to an FBI wire tap, following Johnny Roselli's death in August 1976, Trafficante said, "Now only two people are alive who know who killed Kennedy and they're not talking."

(See also GIANCANA, SAM; MARCELLO, CARLOS.)

Triple Underpass   See DEALEY PLAZA.

Truly, Roy Sansom

Texas School Book Depository superintendent who hired Oswald. Truly watched the assassination from the north curb of Elm Street, in front of the School Book Depository and told the Warren Commission that he thought the shots came from the direction of the concrete monument (pergola) adjacent to the wooden fence atop the grassy knoll. Truly saw Oswald about 90 seconds after the shooting on the Depository's second floor, calmly drinking a Coke.

Truly says that it was he who first noticed that Oswald was absent and drew that to the attention of the police. He told the Warren Commission that after assisting with the search of the floors, he returned to the first floor. "At first I didn't see anything except officers running around, reporters in the place," he testified. "There was a regular madhouse . . . I noticed some of my boys in the west corner of the shipping department, and there were several officers over there taking their names and addresses and so forth. . . . I noticed that Lee Oswald was not among these boys. So I picked up the telephone and called Mr. Aiken down at the warehouse who keeps our application blanks. . . . So [Depository Vice President] Mr. Campbell is standing there, and I said, 'I have a boy over here missing. I don't know whether to report it or not.' Because I had another one or two out then. I didn't know whether they were all there or not. . . . So I picked the phone up then and called Mr. Aiken, at the warehouse, and got the boy's name and general description and telephone number and address at Irving. . . . I knew nothing of this Dallas address. I didn't know he was living away from his family."

A few days before the assassination, according to Oswald, Truly was seen showing off a rifle inside the Texas School Book Depository.

U

Umbrella Man

As JFK's motorcade made the slow turn off of Houston Street onto Elm Street under the bright Dallas sunshine, one spectator, standing just on the west side of the "Stemmons Freeway" sign on the north side of Elm between the Texas School Book Depository and the grassy knoll, behaved very peculiarly.

Instead of waving at the president, or folding his arms and frowning (as men in Dallas were prone to do), this fellow opened an umbrella and held it over his head. Once the shooting began, the man began to pump the umbrella up and down.

After the shooting was over, and part of JFK's skull lay on Elm Street only a few feet away from him, the man calmly closed the umbrella and sat down on the curb to watch the chaos.

Standing beside the "Umbrella Man" was a dark-skinned man in a cap. When the president passed, this man raised a defiant-looking fist in the air. After the shooting, this man sat down on the curb beside the Umbrella Man and, according to a photo taken by assassination witness Jim Towner, began to talk into a walkie-talkie, which he later shoved partially down the back of his pants. After a few moments, the two strange men stood up and walked away from the scene in opposite directions.

What were these two up to?

Since the men were standing in a position that was visible both from the buildings behind the president and from the grassy knoll, it has been theorized that they were giving visual signals to the assassins. After the first shot, perhaps the Umbrella Man pumped his umbrella up and down to signal that the shot had not been fatal and that more shots were necessary.

Some think that the Umbrella Man's odd movements were symbolic. Since the sight of a man pumping up and down his umbrella may very well have been the last thing President Kennedy ever saw, some think the umbrella represented the umbrella of air coverage that JFK failed to supply at the disastrous Bay of Pigs operation.

According to veteran assassination researcher R. B. Cutler, among others, JFK was wounded in the throat by a paralyzing dart fired *from* the umbrella. It sounds wild—but there is evidence to support this theory: 1. the hole in the front of JFK's throat was "almost too small to be a bullet wound," according to one doctor who treated JFK at Parkland Hospital. 2. CIA weapons specialist Charles Senseney told researcher Jim Marrs that the CIA had developed by 1963 a dart-firing umbrella. The weapon operated silently and fired its darts through the webbing while the umbrella was open. According to Senseney, 50 such weapons were operational at the time of the assassination.

Who was the Umbrella Man? During the House Select Committee on Assassinations investigation, a warehouse manager named Louis Steven Witt stepped forward and said that he was the Umbrella Man. Witt did resemble the man in the photographs. He told the House Select Committee that he had opened the umbrella while JFK passed to "annoy" the president. Witt even brought *the* umbrella along with him so that he could show the committee, and a national TV audience, that the thing could not fire darts. That provided everyone with a good guffaw. Witt told the committee that he pumped his umbrella up and down as the president passed because JFK's father had been a friend of Neville Chamberlain, who sought to appease the Nazis during World War II. British people had been known to protest Chamberlain's actions by pumping their umbrellas up and down when he made public appearances, so that was what Witt was doing, protesting JFK's policies.

The trouble is, Witt also told the committee that he did not actually see the shooting because the umbrella was covering his face, a claim that contrasts sharply with the photographic evidence.

Photographic expert Jack White said during a lecture in Dallas on October 25, 1992, that he thought Gordon Novel, a man suspected by Jim Garrison of having involvement with the case, might be the Umbrella Man. He then used a portion of his slide show to demonstrate that Novel and the Umbrella Man have similarly shaped heads and hairlines. White said that he used to claim that Novel *was* the Umbrella Man, but stopped doing so after Novel threatened his life. Now he will only strongly emphasize the strong resemblance between the two.

Underwood, James R.

The assistant news director at KRLD-TV in Dallas who rode in Camera Car 3 during the Dallas motorcade. That car was still on Houston Street at the time of the shooting. Underwood was born in 1922 in Oklahoma City, Oklahoma. He served in the U.S. Marine Corps from 1940–43. He hopped out of his car in Dealey Plaza and spoke to fif-teen-year-old assassination witness Amos L. Euins. Euins told him that he had seen a man with a rifle in the Texas School Book Depository and that the man was black. (By the time Euins testified to the Warren Commission, the shooter's color was ignored.) A little more than a half hour after the assassination, Underwood was put on the air on CBS-TV to give his eyewitness report over a telephone in the Old Courthouse Building at the corner of Main and Houston. Underwood traveled from Dealey Plaza to the Dallas police headquarters where he arrived in time to ride up in the elevator with the just-arrested Lee Harvey Oswald. Underwood heard Oswald say, "I didn't kill anybody." Underwood died on September 3, 1983, of heart failure from the effects of diabetes.

United Fruit Company

The Boston-based company that controlled much of the Central American fruit business and was said to have played a strong anticommunist role in Central America for 100 years, including during the cold war. Large quantities of stock in United Fruit were owned by both Allen and John Foster Dulles. United Fruit had a close relationship with Tulane University.

(See also DULLES, ALLEN; OCHSNER, ALTON; SHERMAN, MARY.)

V

Vaganov, Igor "Turk" (a.k.a. Nicholson, John; Kullaway, Kurt; Carson, Vince; Bagavov, Igor)

Vaganov was a Latvian émigré who lived in Philadelphia but who suspiciously moved to Dallas two weeks before the assassination—then left Dallas immediately following the assassination.

A witness to the murder of J. D. Tippit, Domingo Benavides, testified that he had seen a red 1961 Ford with a man sitting in it, parked about six cars away from Tippit's car at the scene of the murder.

Vaganov drove a red Thunderbird that day. He lived near the site of the crime and was dressed the same that day as a man placed at the scene by another witness to the Tippit killing, Acquila Clemons. Vaganov cannot adequately account for his whereabouts at the time of Tippit's death.

According to John Berendt, writing in the August 1967 edition of *Esquire*, "He was tall and thin, and his green eyes were set beneath a high forehead in a perpetual squint. The corners of his mouth were habitually turned down. . . . A hitch in the Navy had left him with just enough polish, just enough superficial cool, to get by on. . . . Born in Latvia, he had lived in Germany during [World War II] and had come to America when he was about nine. He spoke four languages."

In late September 1963, Vaganov worked as a credit manager in a branch of General Electric Credit Corporation in suburban Philadelphia. Suddenly, he requested a transfer to Dallas. He was turned down. In October he asked again. Again he was denied. In the first week of October, Turk met 18-year-old Anne Dulin, a soda jerk at Doc Ornsteen's drug store in Village Green, where Turk hung out because he shared an interest in citizen band (CB) radios with Doc. Anne and Turk began to date. In Turk's red Thunderbird convertible, he had a CB radio worth $225 with enough power to exceed FCC regulations. The radio was strong enough to broadcast five-to-eight miles in a city with tall buildings.

Acquaintances say Turk was a crack shot with a rifle and owned a "250-3000"—only 6/1000 of an inch smaller in caliber than the Mannlicher-Carcano rifle reportedly owned by Oswald.

Turk's first wife, from whom he was already divorced by 1963, said his other hobbies included torturing dogs and cats. On November 5, Vaganov made his third request to be transferred to Dallas. He was again turned down, so he quit his job and made plans to go to Dallas anyway.

According to Berendt, Vaganov went to his apartment at 1116 Seventh Avenue in Swarthmore and "spent the next day and a half selling his furniture and packing his clothes. . . . Anne could go with him if she liked, and she did, so the two of them left town on November 7 in his Thunderbird. . . . With him also went his two-way radio, the rifle in the trunk and $800 in his pocket. . . . In addition Vaganov carried a .38 caliber pistol. Loading one bullet into it, he placed it between himself and Anne on the front seat, 'Just in case we see any deer.' Anne was frightened, she admitted later, but she didn't let on. . . . They were married in South Carolina and, stopping briefly in Georgia and Alabama to visit two of Vaganov's friends, they arrived in Dallas on the tenth or eleventh of November. On the twelfth they took an apartment at Sunset Manor in the Oak Cliff section of town."

Each day in Dallas, Turk dressed in a suit and tie and left the apartment at 7:30 A.M. He didn't return until 5:00 P.M. He never told anyone precisely what he did. He told his wife he was looking for a job, and his landlady that he had been transferred from Philadelphia. Still, he paid the bills and even opened up a bank account.

Anne's sister met Turk for the first time during this period. She was disturbed by his attitudes. He told her he hated "niggers and Jews" and "was proud to be a member of the master race."

On Tuesday, November 19, a short, stocky man came to the Vaganov home while Turk was out. Turk later would not discuss who the man was. (According to Anne, Turk told her in 1965 that the man was "Mike from the CIA.")

On the eve of the assassination, Anne called her sister, who lived in Conroe, Texas. She screamed into the phone: "Turk is going to do something horrible tomorrow!" She didn't elaborate.

On the morning of the assassination Turk slept in, not getting up until noon, breaking his pattern of getting up at seven and "looking for work." According to his landlady, he wore khaki pants and "possibly a white shirt or jacket."

By all accounts, Turk didn't leave the apartment until 12:45, 15 minutes after the assassination. While he was coming down the stairs, his landlord told him that President Kennedy had been shot.

Turk was reportedly "elated" at the news and ran back upstairs. He watched television for several minutes with his wife, then, at 12:50 P.M., he suddenly left, telling her that he had to go to the bank.

Bank records show that he never arrived. Less than a half hour later, Tippit was murdered with a .38 pistol. Domingo Benavides said he saw a red car at the scene. Acquila Clemons said she saw two men flee the murder: one a "heavy . . . short guy," the other a tall, thin man in a white shirt and khaki pants.

Berendt notes, "The first description fitted Vaganov's mysterious caller; the second fitted Vaganov."

About an hour and a half after he had left, Turk returned home. Anne says that when she told Turk a cop had been shot nearby, "he seemed to know it." Later in the afternoon, the couple got in the car and toured the sites of both murders—a popular pastime in Dallas on that day and ever since.

At 4:30 P.M., two FBI agents visited the Vaganovs. Anne's sister had called the FBI because of Anne's hysterical phone call the night before. The FBI interviewed the Vaganovs, checked Turk's rifle and pistol, determined that they had not been fired, seemed satisfied and left.

That evening, Turk told his wife that he had to return immediately to Philadelphia to "take care of a few things with General Electric." Anne, nearly hysterical again, called her sister, who picked her up and took her home with her.

Turk was out of Dallas by the next morning, on the road heading toward Philadelphia. He stayed in Philadelphia for only a few days, then moved back in with his first wife in Atlanta.

According to the FBI investigation of Vaganov, his wife went through his pockets soon after the assassination and found receipts for long-distance phone calls made from the Holiday Inn in Hapeville, Georgia; a three-inch-square piece of paper with the following notes written in pencil: "EL6-6111, E. STRAZDS, 353-1539, ARVIDS, JZAKS; and a King of Spades playing card with staple holes at the top that had been torn in half."

Now the story gets stranger. Six months after the assassination, the FBI discovered "a bundle of Vaganov's clothes" in a phone booth in Dallas.

In 1967, Vaganov attempted to explain his suspicious movements to *Esquire* magazine: "Vaganov says he wanted to go to Dallas because he believed his first wife was living in Garland, Texas, with her grandmother. He says that once he got there with a new wife, he felt obligated to her and did not go to visit the first. . . . During the week he was in Dallas, Vaganov said he worked at two places. He worked half a day at Art Grindle Motors. Grindle has since sold his business and moved, so it was impossible to check. Vaganov says that at Art Grindle's there were too many salesmen on the line, and that's why he left. Then he worked a day and a half at the Texas Consumer Finance Corporation. Vaganov says he left that job on the second day (the day before the assassination), when a report from General Electric in Philadelphia reached his new employer, telling them about the items he had stolen back East. General Electric insisted that they could not give him a favorable recommendation unless he returned and straightened out matters with them. Discouraged, Vaganov slept late the next day (the day of the assassination) and went back to Philadelphia that night."

Esquire checked the story and discovered that the Texas Consumer Finance Corporation could find no record of having hired Vaganov. They said, however that, because Vaganov's job had lasted for less than two shifts, the records may have been routinely destroyed. Vaganov applied for that job in an office at 1310 Commerce Street, Dallas—which was only a few doors away from Ruby's Carousel Club.

Vaganov denied torturing animals and being a crack shot. He said he didn't know the short and heavy man who came to see him in Dallas, and that "Mike" was actually an ex-cop he'd met in Los Angeles well after President Kennedy's assassination.

Turk said the phone call his wife had made to her sister concerned a domestic fight. Anne had been afraid that he was going to hurt her or himself. The call, he said, didn't have anything to do with the assassination.

Vaganov told *Esquire* where he had been at the time of the Tippit murder: "According to him, he left the apartment just before one o'clock, [about] twenty minutes before Tippit was killed. He did intend to go to the bank, but first he went downstairs and took his car around the corner to have two front tires replaced for the return to Philadelphia. He got back to his apartment an hour or an hour and a half later, at which time the FBI arrived."

Turk's landlady says he returned to the apartment a full two hours later than he said he did. *Esquire* talked to the gas station attendant who could have provided Turk with an alibi—his name was Jack Griffis.

Griffis said that, though he remembered that he changed the tires on a car at about the time of the assassination, he could remember neither the make of the car nor the appearance of the driver.

For a time it was suspected that the discarded jacket found near the Tippit murder, which officially belonged to Oswald, might actually have been Vaganov's. This theory, however, was discarded when it was learned that Vaganov wore 36-inch sleeves, while the jacket in the National Archives had 32$\frac{1}{2}$-inch sleeves.

Vaganov had no explanation for why a bundle of his clothes might have been found in a phone booth six months after he left Dallas.

Esquire concluded: "True, Vaganov tells a tall tale once in a while, he has acute fuzz paranoia [fear of police] and there are coincidences which lend sinister implications to his visit to Dallas. But his lies are usually the self-aggrandizing type, his fear of cops stems from his bad-check days and his coincidental movements are no fault of his own. Vaganov's willingness to be questioned, to have his picture published in a national magazine [such a photo accompanies the *Esquire* article], to go to Dallas and face the Tippit eyewitnesses [for a fee] would by themselves tend to rule him out. Furthermore, there is not one shred of evidence linking him with either killing that day or with any of the principals involved. If indeed he was involved in something shady in Dallas, it was something other than the assassination."

Vallee, Thomas Arthur

A lithographer who was arrested on November 2, 1963, in Chicago, the day President Kennedy was to ride through Chicago in a motorcade. The charge was carrying a concealed weapon (an M-1 rifle) and ammunition.

Vallee drove a car with New York State license plate number 311-ORF. The FBI has restricted all information regarding that number—although Chicago legal researcher Sherman Skolnick claims the number was registered to a man calling himself "Lee Harvey Oswald."

Vallee's arrest, at the corner of Wilson and Damen Streets, was witnessed by Secret Service agent Abraham Bolden.

(See also SECRET SERVICE.)

Veciana Blanch, Antonio

Former Cuban bank accountant and founder of the militant anti-Castro Cuban group, Alpha 66, a group that received heavy CIA support.

In a March 2, 1976, interview with Church Committee investigator Gaeton Fonzi, Veciana said that, sometime during September 1963, he saw Oswald in the company of a CIA-man he knew as Maurice Bishop. Veciana spotted the two together in the crowded lobby of a Dallas skyscraper (most likely the 42-story Southland Center). Although the composite drawing of Bishop based on Veciana's description greatly resembled CIA propaganda and disinformation expert David Atlee Phillips, Veciana has always denied that they are one and the same.

After the assassination, when newspaper stories reported that Oswald had been seen in Mexico City with a young couple and that the wife spoke excellent English, Bishop told Veciana to offer his cousin and his wife a large sum of money to claim that they were the couple Oswald had been seen with.

Soon after testifying, Veciana was shot in the head but survived the attack—and now refuses to comment further on the subject.

Veciana graduated from the University of Havana with a degree in accounting—and became assistant to Cuba's primary banker, Julio Lobo.

Veciana's organization, Alpha 66, was considered to be the most dangerous of the anti-Castro groups.

(See also ALPHA 66; PHILLIPS, DAVID ATLEE.)

Vidal Santiago, Felipe

Anti-Castro Cuban, accused by Colonel William C. Bishop of military intelligence of being a conspirator in President Kennedy's assassination. According to CIA documents, Vidal worked with that company until 1961, when the relationship was terminated because the CIA did not like some of the people Vidal was associating with. Vidal was reportedly in Dallas from November 8–13, 1963, and during that time had a meeting with General Edwin Walker regarding the "Cuban situation."

(See also BISHOP, WILLIAM C.; WALKER, EDWIN.)

Voebel, Edward

Voebel went to Beauregard Junior High School in New Orleans, Louisiana, with Lee Harvey Oswald. Voebel testified before Warren Commission staffer Albert E. Jenner on April 7, 1964. When he told of being together with Oswald at two or three Civil Air Patrol meetings, Jenner asked, "Who was the majordomo of the Civil Air Patrol unit that you attended?" To which Voebel replied, "I think it was Captain [David] Ferrie. I think he was there when Lee attended one of those meetings, but I'm not sure of that. Now that I think of it, I don't think Captain Ferrie was there at that time, but he might have been. That isn't too clear to me."

It was Voebel who called the New Orleans Police Department and the FBI after the assassination to report that Ferrie was a suspicious character who had known Oswald in the Civil Air Patrol.

Once, in the ninth grade, Oswald was punched by an older high school student and received a bloody lip and a loosened tooth. After this incident, Voebel took Oswald back to school to attend to his wounds. The pair developed a "mild friendship" because of this incident. He told the Warren Commission that Oswald had once had a plan to cut the glass out of a store window and steal a pistol, although this was probably normal adolescent fantasy. Voebel said Oswald "wouldn't start any fights, but if you wanted to start one with him, he was going to make sure that he ended it, or you were really going to have one, because he wasn't going to take anything from anybody."

(See also O'SULLIVAN, FREDERICK; SUSPICIOUS DEATHS.)

Wade, Henry Menasco

Wade was the Dallas district attorney in 1963 and had formerly been Governor John Connally's college roommate. Critics of the *Warren Report* have long wondered why the Dallas police made a beeline for Oswald after the assassination. This misstatement made by D. A. Henry Wade on November 24, 1963, has added to the confusion: "A police officer, immediately after the assassination, ran in the building and saw this man [Oswald] in a corner and started to arrest him, but the manager of the building [Roy Truly] said that he was an employee and was all right. Every other employee was located but this defendant, of the company. A description and name of him went out by police to look for him." A careful study of the facts finds several things wrong with this statement. Oswald was not in a "corner" when first approached by police, was not a suspect "by name" until after he was arrested, and was not the only employee of the Texas School Book Depository missing from the building after the assassination.

Wade was also the district attorney in charge of prosecuting Ruby in the years preceding the assassination for various vice and assault charges, a task Wade performed without tenacity, never achieving a conviction. Wade is perhaps most famous as the prosecuting attorney in the landmark abortion case *Roe v. Wade*.

Wade died in Dallas of complications from Parkinson's Disease on March 1, 2001, at the age of 86.

Walker, General Edwin

Walker—born November 10, 1909, in Kerr County, Texas—was a right-wing activist whose beliefs were so extreme that he was forced to retire from the U.S. Army in 1961 not long after it was discovered he had been showing right-wing films to the troops under his command.

Marina Oswald told the Warren Commission that her husband took a shot at General Walker on April 10, 1963, from outside Walker's home at 4011 Turtle Creek Street near Avondale in Dallas. (The shooting really happened, the bullet missing Walker completely.)

Among the effects reportedly found in Oswald's possession after his arrest was a photograph of Walker's home. By the time that photograph was released by the FBI, a hole had been cut into it, obliterating the license plate on a car parked in the driveway.

Other than Marina's testimony, there is nothing to connect Oswald with the attempted shooting of Walker. The balance of the evidence indicates that Oswald probably had nothing to do with the Walker incident, and that perhaps the incident had been staged to make Walker appear a "target of the enemy" to his supporters.

When the shooting first happened, police said that the bullet was a steel-jacketed 30.06. When that bullet was subjected to neutron activation analysis, it was found not to match the bullets reportedly used in the assassination.

At the time of the assassination, General Walker was aboard a Braniff flight out of New Orleans. When the assassination was announced, Walker reportedly walked up and down the aisle on the plane reminding his fellow passengers that he was there and that they were his alibi witnesses.

Walker died on October 30, 1993, age 84, in Dallas of a lung ailment.

Wall, Breck (a.k.a. Wilson, Billy Ray)

Friend of Jack Ruby and president of the Dallas council of AGVA who was responsible for reviewing complaints by performers against nightclub operators. Ruby called Wall four times during November 1963. Wall later couldn't remember what the calls concerned. One of the calls from Ruby to Wall came at 11:44 P.M. on November 23, 1963, the night before Ruby shot Oswald. Wall says that the call was about Ruby's concern that Abe Weinstein had kept his Colony Club, the strip club next to Ruby's Carousel Club, open despite the assassination. Wall told the FBI in 1963 that, back in 1960, he had almost worked a deal for a "night club review" he produced to appear at Ruby's Carousel Club, which was then called the Sovereign Club.

Also in on that deal was James Henry Dolan, an AGVA/Mafia man from Denver. When Ruby refused to put the deal on paper, Wall backed out. This upset Ruby so much that he punched Wall's assistant Joseph Peterson—a man who Dolan described as "a little fairy."

Wall and Peterson were in Dallas at the time of the assassination but left soon thereafter and went to Wall's mother's house in Galveston, Texas. At 11:00 P.M. on November 23, assassination suspect David Ferrie had checked into a hotel in Galveston.

During November 1963 Wall and Peterson had a show playing at the Adolphus Hotel, which was adjacent to Ruby's Carousel Club. The show was called "Bottoms Up."

Wall appears in drag in the exploitation film *Naughty Dallas*, some of which was filmed in Ruby's Carousel Club.

Wallace, Malcolm E. "Mac"

LBJ-confederate Billy Sol Estes, in a 1984 letter to the U.S. Justice Department, implicated Wallace as the assassin of JFK. Estes's charges are corroborated by the statements of one Loy Factor, who said that he, Lee Harvey Oswald, Malcolm Wallace, and a beautiful Latina with a walkie-talkie were all on the sixth floor of the Texas School Book Depository at the time of the assassination. Estes also said that he, LBJ, Wallace, and Cliff Carter had foreknowledge of or were involved in the murders of Department of Agriculture official Henry B. Marshall (whose death was officially called a suicide despite the fact that he was shot five times with a rifle), and others.

Wallace was convicted in 1952 of killing Kinser, who had been having an affair with Wallace's wife. He was defended at his trial by John Cofer, a friend of Lyndon Johnson, and received a five-year suspended sentence.

Wallace wore black horned-rim glasses in 1963.

Wallace graduated from the University of Texas in Austin in 1947, where he had been president of the student body during his senior year. (George DeMohren-schildt also attended the University of Texas at Austin in 1944, but it is unknown if he knew Wallace.) A native of Mount Pleasant, he had lived in Dallas for 30 years. He had also lived for almost 10 years in California. Wallace served in the U.S. Marine Corps from 1939–40 and was discharged because of an unknown injury. Wallace had been a manager of the purchasing department of Ling-Temco-Vought, Inc., an electronics company in Anaheim, California. According to one of Wallace's coworkers there, Wallace was sent to Stanford University on business, where they were building a particle-beam accelerator. Wallace was, for a time, an economist for the U.S. Department of Agriculture.

Wallace died January 7, 1971, in a car accident in Pittsburg, Camp County, Texas. According to the Texas Department of Public Safety, Wallace's car ran off the road three and a half miles south of Pittsburg on U.S. 271. At the time of his death, Wallace lived at 610 Tennison Memorial Drive in Dallas.

(See also CARR, RICHARD RANDOLPH; SHERMAN, MARY.)

Walter, William S.

FBI night clerk in the New Orleans office who, during the early morning hours of November 17, 1963, received a memo via telex warning of a plot to kill JFK. He told five agents about the memo and considered his job done. Walter's story was authenticated in 1976 when researcher Mark Lane successfully invoked the Freedom of Information Act to get a copy of the telex. It read:

> URGENT: 1:45 AM EST 11–17–63 HLF 1 PAGE/TO: ALL SACS/FROM: DIRECTOR/THREAT TO ASSASSINATE PRESIDENT KENNEDY IN DALLAS TEXAS NOVEMBER 22 DASH THREE NINETEEN SIXTY THREE. MISC INFORMATION CONCERNING. INFORMATION HAS BEEN RECEIVED BY THE BUREAS [sic] BUREAU HAS DETERMINED THAT A MILITANT REVOLUTIONARY GROUP MAY ATTEMPT TO ASSASSINATE PRESIDENT KENNEDY ON HIS PROPOSED TRIP TO DALLAS TEXAS NOVEMBER TWENTY TWO DASH TWENTY THREE NINETEEN SIXTY THREE. ALL RECEIVING OFFICES SHOULD IMMEDIATELY CONTACT ALL CIS, PCIS LOGICAL RACE AND HATE GROUP INFORMANTS AND DETERMINE IF ANY BASIS FOR THREAT. BUREAU SHOULD BE KEPT ADVISED OF ALL DEVELOPMENTS BY TELETYPE. OTHER OFFICES HAVE BEEN ADVISED. END AND ACK PLS.

Walter told the House Select Committee on Assassinations, "I immediately contacted the special agent-in-charge who had the category of threats against the President and read him the teletype. He instructed me to call the agents that had responsibility and informants, and as I called them I noted the time and the names of the agents that I called." In 1995 Walter told assassination researchers Ray and Mary LaFontaine that he had personally seen an FBI memo that specified Oswald as their information source for their investigation into the D.R.E.'s supply of arms.

(See also D.R.E.)

Walther, Carolyn

She told author Josiah Thompson that she saw two men in an upper-floor window in the Texas School Book Depository moments before the assassination and that one of them had a rifle. She did not think the men were as high as the sixth floor. Walther was not asked to testify before or submit an affidavit to the Warren Commission. She said the man with the gun "was wearing a white shirt and had blond or light brown hair" and that the other was "a man in a brown suit coat." Witnesses James Worrell

and Richard Randolph Carr also saw the man in the brown coat.

Walthers, Eddy Raymond "Buddy"

Walthers, a playboy with an abrasive personality, was a Dallas County deputy sheriff and the first law enforcement official to speak to James Tague, the spectator who was wounded during the assassination. Walthers searched the area near the mouth of the triple underpass, where Tague had been standing, and found a bullet mark "on the top edge of the curb on Main Street near the underpass."

Walthers appears in photographs taken on the south side of Elm Street, across the street from the pergola, exactly 10 minutes after the shooting. In the photos are Walthers and two men in business suits, assumed to be federal agents of some sort. In the sequence of photos, one of the suited men appears to reach down and pick something up out of the grass, clutch it firmly in his palm, and then slip it into his pocket. Walthers originally reported

In the first photo, taken on the south side of Elm Street 10 minutes following the shooting, sheriff's deputy Buddy Walthers (lighting cigarette) and Dallas policeman J. W. Foster stand over a spot where an apparent shot had kicked up a clump of grass. *(Collector's Archive)*

(This page and next) Walthers examines the spot and then is joined by a man wearing an earpiece, who picks an object up out of the grass and puts it in his pocket. These photos were taken by newsmen William Allen and James Murray. *(Collector's Archive)*

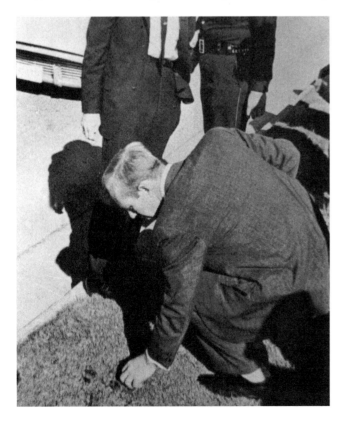

(Collector's Archive)

that a bullet had been found and then, for reasons unknown, withdrew this statement, saying it actually was a piece of JFK's head that had been found. Officially, the object doesn't exist.

After Ruby was arrested for shooting Oswald, his possessions were searched and among them was Walthers signed permanent pass to the Carousel Club.

Walthers died January 10, 1969, in a gunfight at a motel on Samuel Boulevard in Dallas. Officially, he was shot through the heart by escaped prisoner James Walter Cherry.

According to Deputy Sheriff Al Maddox, "Buddy had been known to pull your leg, but at one time he did show me a bullet that he claimed he found in Dealey Plaza which he may have eventually given to his son. When he first told me about it, I was very apprehensive and didn't pay much attention to it. But he'd never lied to me before."

Warren Commission, The

The Warren Commission was formed by Executive Order No. 11130 on November 29, 1963, and, from February 3, 1964, until September 15, 1964, commission members and their staff asked 109,930 questions of 488 witnesses. White House phone recordings indicate that the concept of a "blue-ribbon panel" of unimpeachable personnel to rubber stamp the FBI report of a lone nut killed by a lone nut came from Eugene Rostow, dean of Yale Law School, who called the White House on November 24, 1963, citing the poor behavior of the Dallas police as a reason to squelch the "nasty rumors" that threatened to tear the country apart. Only hours later Dean Acheson, who had been President Harry Truman's secretary of state and was considered one of the architects of the cold war, was also

on the phone with the president pushing the blue-ribbon panel concept. Clearly, from the start, the commission was a tool established to declare a political truth rather than to determine the facts, a package designed to placate, to make it all better, as much as was possible, because that was what was best for the country. Lyndon Johnson announced the establishment of the commission on November 29, and telephone recordings reveal that the president did not tell FBI director J. Edgar Hoover that the commission was going to exist until minutes before the announcement. Hoover, whose FBI had provided what was supposed to be the definitive investigation, didn't feel that anything was necessary to rubber stamp the FBI's determination, and the FBI had determined that Oswald acted alone within hours of the assassination, at least publicly.

The seven members of the Warren Commission were:

1. Earl Warren, the Chief Justice of the Supreme Court. Warren's chief contribution to the Warren Commission's investigation was his light-handed and noninquisitive interrogation of Ruby in the Dallas County Jail. During the Warren Commission hearings, Warren apparently took a liking to Marina Oswald. He would accompany her to press conferences holding her by the arm and referring to her as "my child." Warren did not want this job and declined when President Johnson first asked him. LBJ had to convince Warren that the commission was in the best interests of the nation before he would agree to do it, and he was reportedly in tears soon after taking the job.

2. Allen W. Dulles, who had been for eight years the director of Central Intelligence, until he was fired by JFK. (See also DULLES, ALLEN W.)

3. Gerald R. Ford, chairman of the House Republican Conference; later U.S. president. In his book *Portrait of the Assassin* he defends the Warren Commission's methods and conclusions. Still, Ford's writings indicate the commission was more concerned with preserving national unity and tranquility than it was with finding the truth.

Ford worked as liaison between the commission and the FBI during the investigation. In 1997 it was revealed that Ford had been responsible for a key edit in the *Warren Report* that helped to bolster the magic-bullet theory. In describing JFK's back wound, the commission's staff had originally written: "A bullet had entered the back at a point slightly above the shoulder and to the right of the spine." Ford changed this to: "A bullet had entered the base of the neck slightly to the right of the spine." This edit raised JFK's wound, thus making it more likely that a shot from above and behind could have entered at that spot and exited the

Warren commissioner and later president of the United States Gerald R. Ford. *(Author's Collection)*

front of his throat. "My changes had nothing to do with a conspiracy," Ford said in 1997. "My changes were only an attempt to be more precise."

4. Representative Hale Boggs, Louisiana Democrat and majority party whip. He was among those on the commission who never accepted the single-bullet theory. Boggs's plane disappeared over Alaska on October 16, 1972.

5. John Jay McCloy, former president of the World Bank, former assistant secretary of defense, former U.S. high commissioner for Germany, he represented "business" on the commission. According to Kai Bird's book *The Chairman: John Jay McCloy*, McCloy described his agenda on the Commission as showing that America was not "a banana republic, where a government can be changed by conspiracy." Also on McCloy's resume are the facts that he watched the 1936 Olympics from Adolf Hitler's private box and that, during World War II, he supervised the Japanese-American internment program. McCloy's box at the Berlin Olympics was not the only Commission connection with Hitler. The official commission historian, Otto Winnaker, had been one of Hitler's official historians.

6. Senator Richard B. Russell, Georgia Democrat; chairman of the Armed Services Committee of the Senate.

7. Senator John Sherman Cooper, Kentucky Republican, and former U.S. ambassador to India. He objected strongly to the "magic-bullet" theory, saying, "there is

no evidence that both men [Connally and JFK] were hit by the same bullet."

In addition to the commissioners, J. Lee Rankin was general counsel with a staff of 14 assistant counsel and 12 others, including a historian, lawyers, and Internal Revenue Service officials. Rankin was the former solicitor general of the United States. Thirty-seven other lawyers, clerks, and secretaries were also employed.

The staff included Leon Jaworski, from Texas, and a future Watergate special prosecutor; Albert Jenner, from Indiana; David Belin, who would later become the executive director of the Rockefeller Commission on the CIA; Arlen Specter, father of the "single-bullet theory" and later a candidate for president; and William Coleman, the only black man on the staff, later named to President Gerald Ford's cabinet.

That the conclusions of the *Warren Report* did not match the evidence gathered by the commission is supported by this: Of the 266 known witnesses to the assassination, the commission questioned 126. Of these, 51 thought the shots came from the direction of the grassy knoll, 32 said that they came from the Texas School Book Depository. Thirty-eight did not offer an opinion, but most of these witnesses were not asked. The remaining five thought the shots came from more than one location.

The commission concluded its work on September 24, 1964, submitting an 888-page report to the president. In addition to the report were 15 volumes containing the testimony of 488 people whom the commission had questioned, and 11 books of exhibits, mostly FBI documents. In total, there were 17,000 pages of information. The material that was not published was placed in the National Archives, under orders that it would remain sealed for 75 years.

Warren Report, The

The *Warren Report*, the 888-page summary of the Warren Commission's findings, concluded that only three shots had been fired, all by Lee Harvey Oswald with a 6.5 mm Mannlicher-Carcano rifle from the sixth floor of the Texas School Book Depository; that one bullet missed, one bullet struck JFK in the head and killed him, and one bullet caused all of the nonfatal wounds to both JFK and Governor Connally; that Jack Ruby shot Oswald; and that both Oswald and Ruby committed their act without the aid or foreknowledge of any other individuals.

The evidence the Warren Commission used to "convict" Oswald consisted of: 1. recovered mail-order forms that indicated Oswald bought the assassination rifle under a pseudonym; 2. Oswald's palm print on the rifle indicating that Oswald had handled the rifle when it was disassembled; 3. fibers found on the rifle that were found to be similar to those in a shirt Oswald was supposed to be wearing at the time of the assassination; 4. photographs taken in Oswald's backyard showing him holding communist literature, a rifle, and a handgun; 5. eyewitness testimony that Oswald brought with him to work on the morning of the assassination a "long and bulky package"; 6. a near pristine bullet found in Parkland that could be ballistically matched to the rifle found on the sixth floor of the School Book Depository; 7. the fact that Oswald resisted arrest when apprehended in the Texas Theatre; and 8. Marina Oswald's testimony that he had also shot at and missed General Edwin Walker in Dallas during April 1963, thus showing his proclivity toward violence. Technically, the *Warren Report* is not a legal document. Defense attorneys for Claw Shaw tried to use the *Warren Report* as evidence that Oswald assassinated JFK alone and therefore Shaw could not be guilty of conspiracy. But Louisiana courts determined in January 1969 that the report was "hearsay piled upon hearsay" and could not be entered as evidence in a court of law.

Weatherford, Harry

Dallas County deputy sheriff who was in Dealey Plaza at the time of the assassination. At 3:00 P.M., November 22, Weatherford was involved in the search and seizure of evidence at the Paine home in Irving, Texas, where Marina Oswald lived. It was here that police found the backyard photographs of Oswald holding a rifle—photographs that Marina later claimed she took. Also found was a rolled blanket in the garage that Marina claimed had held Oswald's rifle. Oswald claimed he owned no rifle.

According to Penn Jones, Weatherford was a "crackshot" and was on top of the Dallas County jail building at the time of the assassination. A researcher once asked him if he shot President Kennedy. As evidence of nothing but attitude, Weatherford replied, "You little son of a bitch, I shoot lots of people." Jones also wrote that a custom-made rifle silencer had been delivered to Weatherford "a few weeks" before the assassination.

In a 1990 interview, Dallas County sheriff James C. Bowles verified Weatherford's position at the time of the shooting. Bowles said, "Yes, Harry Weatherford was on the roof with a second deputy, and he had a rifle. They were assigned there for security. My first recollection of the suggestion that Weatherford might have been implicated was from the imagination of Penn Jones who, so far as I know, never worried about the other deputy. It would seem strange that a hit man would be stationed with a living witness. It does not fit reason."

Weatherford, however, reported that he was on ground level at the time of the shooting, saying, "I thought to myself that this was a rifle and I started towards the corner when I heard the third report. . . . By this time I was running toward the railroad yards where the sound seemed to come from."

Webster, Robert E.

An American citizen who told officials he planned to defect to the Soviet Union, less than two weeks before Oswald did the same. A former navy man, Webster was an ex-employee of the CIA-connected Rand Corporation. He was a young plastics expert who went to Moscow to work at an American trade exhibition and did not return with his colleagues.

While in the Soviet Union, Webster—already married in the United States—lived with a Russian woman. The couple had a child. Like Oswald, Webster became "disenchanted" with Soviet life and returned to the United States "about the same time" as Oswald.

According to researcher Jim Marrs, "Years later in America, Marina [Oswald] told an acquaintance that her husband had defected after working at an American exhibition in Moscow. This, of course, reflects Webster's story, not Oswald's. After the assassination, when American intelligence was looking into Marina's background, they discovered an address in her address book matching that of Webster's Leningrad apartment."

Was Webster an Oswald doppelgänger?

(See also OSWALD, MARINA.)

Wecht, Dr. Cyril

Dr. Wecht was the president of the American Academy of Forensic Scientists and chief coroner of Allegheny County in Pennsylvania whose dissenting view to the House Select Committee on Assassinations shattered the "single-bullet theory."

A pathology expert, he was a member of the House Select Committee on Assassination's nine-man forensic pathology panel, which frequently voted eight to one on matters regarding the numbers and direction of the bullets fired in Dealey Plaza, with Wecht being the lone dissenter. Dr. Wecht wrote: "Despite the semantical sophistry and intellectual gymnastics of the forensic pathology panel report, it is clear that the single-bullet theory can no longer be maintained as an explanation for the bullet wounds in JFK's back and neck, and all of the bullet wounds in Governor John B. Connally. The angles at which these two men were hit do not permit a straight-line trajectory (or near straight-line trajectory) of Commission exhibit 399 (the so-called magic bullet) to be established. Indeed, quite the opposite is true. In order to accept the single-bullet theory, it is necessary to have the bullet move at different vertical and horizontal angles, a path of flight that has never been experienced or suggested for any bullet known to mankind."

Today, Dr. Wecht remains a passionate speaker at JFK assassination symposia.

Weigman, Dave

Born in 1926 in Baltimore, Maryland, Weigman was a National Broadcasting Company television cameraman who rode in the seventh car of the motorcade, Camera Car 1. Weigman had with him his 16mm FILMO Bell & Howell 70 DL movie camera. When he saw chaos erupt in Dealey Plaza he hopped out of the car he was in but kept his camera rolling. He ran up onto the grassy knoll. Before the public got to see the Zapruder film, Weigman's herky-jerky motion picture of the assassination scene, which lasted 36 1/2 seconds, was the most famous view, since it was repeatedly shown on NBC during the days following the assassination.

It is claimed that, when Weigman's film is examined frame by frame, there is one shot—just as the presidential limousine disappears into the tunnel—that shows puffs of smoke coming from the bushes atop the grassy knoll.

Weigman retired from NBC during the 1980s.

Weird Beard

Dallas disc jockey on station KLIF who was a "bowling buddy" of Jack Ruby. His real name was Russell Lee Moore, but he was also known as Russell Lee Knight. Ruby visited KLIF at 1:45 A.M. on November 23, 1963. Ruby stayed for 45 minutes. Ruby and the Weird Beard left together.

The Weird Beard says that, while standing outside the station, Ruby handed him a radio script entitled "Heroism" from a conservative radio program called *Life Line*. The *Warren Report* says that the script "extolled the virtues of those who embark on risky ventures and stand firmly for causes they believe to be correct."

Ruby asked the Weird Beard's opinion on the script and then warned the disc jockey that a group of "radicals" in Dallas may have been responsible for President Kennedy's assassination.

Because of the script's nature and Ruby's possible misuse of the word "radical," the disc jockey was unclear if Ruby was referring to left- or right-wingers. The Weird Beard said that his conversation with Ruby ended and Ruby got in his car and left alone.

The Weird Beard next heard from Ruby in the early evening of November 23. Ruby called him at the radio station and asked him who Earl Warren was.

(See also RUBY, JACK.)

Weissman, Bernard   See "WELCOME, MR. KENNEDY" AD.

Weitzman, Seymour

Dallas County deputy constable who ran toward the wooden fence atop the grassy knoll following the shooting. He encountered, as did others in that area, a man carrying Secret Service identification. (Weitzman later identified this man as CIA asset and Watergate burglar Bernard Barker.)

While there, a railroad worker told him that he had seen a man behind the fence throw something into a bush. The railroad worker was never identified and, as far as we know, nothing of note was ever found in the bushes. Behind the wooden fence, Weitzman saw "numerous kinds of footprints that did not make sense because they were going different directions."

Weitzman was witness to the discovery of a portion of JFK's skull on the south side of Elm Street. After that discovery, he moved to the Texas School Book Depository where he was involved in the discovery of the sixth-floor rifle.

Weitzman signed an affidavit to the effect that the rifle found in the Texas School Book Depository was a 7.65 Mauser (rather than a Mannlicher-Carcano as is officially claimed). Once a gun-shop owner, Weitzman should have known the difference.

"Welcome, Mr. Kennedy" Ad

On the morning of the assassination, an aide showed President Kennedy a black-bordered full-page ad with a sardonic headline in the *Dallas Morning News*. "Welcome, Mr. Kennedy to Dallas," it read. In 13 rhetorical questions, something called the "American Fact-Finding Committee" accused the administration of selling out the world to communism. The chairman of the committee was listed as Bernard Weissman.

The ad was written by Weissman, along with his partners William Burley, Joseph Grinnan, and Larrie H. Schmidt.

"Oh, you know, we're heading into nut country today," the president said. The black border was the publishing industry's symbol for death.

Months later, explaining that ad, Weissman said to the Warren Commission: "It is rather simple. A group of individuals in Dallas, friends of mine, got together and decided to express our feeling about the domestic and foreign policy of the Kennedy administration, and we felt that picketing, anything of the nature of picketing, and so forth, wouldn't go, since the Stevenson incident. We decided that the best way to get our point across would be to run an ad."

About his organization, Conservatism, USA (CUSA), Weissman said, "CUSA intends to do everything it can to destroy communism. CUSA is against any philosophy, any organization, any group, any individual which threatens the freedom, way of life, or congressional government of the United States. CUSA is against any tyranny, whatever its skin or title; against anything indecent, unlawful, or harmful to man. Can anyone join CUSA? Any citizen of the United States who believes in what CUSA is trying to do and who is not a demagogue or dishonest, may join CUSA regardless of race, religion, creed, or ethnic origin. CUSA does not believe that patriotism is contingent upon skin, color, or religion or family background. Let me say again that this was prepared in 1961 and in its essence has been followed through . . . up until the 22d of November 1963, and this, I think, would give some reasons or give you several answers as to why the ad was placed, why it read as it did."

Weissman, Burley, and Schmidt had served together in the U.S. Army in Munich in 1962. (Grinnan was an independent Dallas oil operator and local John Birch Society coordinator.) According to the *Warren Report,* "Schmidt was the first [of the three] to leave the service; settling in Dallas in October 1962, he became a life insurance salesman and quickly engaged in numerous [right-wing] political activities." Larrie's brother Bob worked as General Edwin Walker's driver and Walker told author Dick Russell that he had received information that the Schmidt brothers may have been, along with Oswald, involved in the shooting at Walker's house on April 10, 1963.

According to assassination researcher and theorist Peter Dale Scott, Schmidt's mentor was General Charles Willoughby, the right-winger who went from being on General Douglas MacArthur's intelligence staff to being the chief of intelligence for Texas oil millionaire H. L. Hunt.

(See also DEAN, HARRY; HUNT, H. L.; RUBY, JACK; WALKER, EDWIN; WILLOUGHBY, CHARLES.)

WerBell, Mitchell Livingston, III

Born in Philadelphia, son of a Czarist officer, WerBell worked in the China-Burma theater with the Office of Strategic Services during World War II. WerBell wore a handlebar moustache and sometimes a monocle. During the time of the assassination he was the designer of the CIA's most sophisticated weapons and was an innovator in the field of silenced weapons. He was reportedly close friends with Lieutenant Colonel Lucien Conein.

He participated in Cuban exile missions against Castro, and he was a representative of the Nugan Hand Bank, which, according to Jonathan Kwitney in his book *The*

Crimes of Patriots (Norton, 1987), has been connected to both intelligence and drug operations.

Werbell died in 1983.

(See also CONEIN, LUCIEN; WEATHERFORD, HARRY.)

West, Dr. Louis Jolyan   See MK/ULTRA.

West, Robert H.

A Dallas County surveyor who was standing on Houston Street near Main Street. West said the first shot sounded like a "motorcycle backfire." That sound, he said, was followed by three reports sounding like rifle shots. According to Jim Marrs, West said the shots sounded as if they were coming from the "northwest quadrant of Dealey Plaza."

Westbrook, W. R.   See TIPPIT, MURDER OF.

Whaley, William Wayne

Dallas cabdriver who, according to the Warren Commission, was instrumental in Oswald's flight from the assassination scene. According to Whaley's logbook he took a passenger from the Greyhound Bus Station near Dealey Plaza to 500 North Beckley from 12:30 P.M. to 12:45 P.M., on November 22.

If this passenger was Oswald, as Whaley later said it was, this meant that Oswald was dropped off four-tenths of a mile from his rooming house, and that he would have boarded the cab at just about the time the president was being shot. Whaley later said that the man was relaxed and not in a hurry, even at one point offering to give up the cab to an older woman.

Whaley is included by many researchers on the list of suspicious deaths involving witnesses to the events of the assassination weekend. He was killed at age 57 in an accident in his cab on December 18, 1965, the first Dallas cabdriver to die on duty since 1937. Although taxicab fatalities were rare in Dallas, the circumstances of Whaley's accident aren't peculiar: Whaley was crossing a bridge across the Trinity River during a rain storm, when an 83-year-old driver coming the other way, swerved into his lane, and hit him head-on. The old man and Whaley were killed and Whaley's passenger was critically injured.

White, Roscoe

Did Roscoe Anthony "Rock" White kill JFK? His son thinks he did. And, before she died, his wife Geneva said she thought he did, too—but more about her later. Were they telling the truth or was it just a money-making scheme?

The Roscoe White story first became public on August 6, 1990, when 29-year-old unemployed oil-equipment salesman Ricky Don White claimed that his father was, in fact, JFK's assassin. White based his claims on a reportedly detailed description of the assassination plot that was allegedly in Roscoe's diary. The diary, Ricky says, disappeared after it was inspected by the FBI—but not before Ricky and three others read it.

Before we get further into Ricky and Geneva White's claims, let's examine the known documented facts, regarding Roscoe:

1. White served in the U.S. Marine Corps with the accused assassin, Lee Harvey Oswald. They traveled from California to Japan at the same time on the same ship. The pair was stationed at the time in Marine Air Wing 1 at Japan's Atsugi Air Base. Atsugi was the home of the U.S. top-secret U-2 spy plane operation, and was also allegedly the base of operations for the CIA's mind-control program, code-named MK/ULTRA.

2. White attained a position with the Dallas Police Department just two months before the assassination, and left their employ less than two years later. (Just before joining the Dallas police, White worked at Clay Page's drug store on Jefferson Boulevard in the Oak Cliff section of Dallas.) No one seems precisely sure what White did for the Dallas police.

3. White was acquainted with Officer J. D. Tippit, who was murdered in Dallas approximately 45 minutes after the assassination.

4. White, who was born on November 18, 1935, died suspiciously on September 24, 1971, of injuries suffered in a fire. On his death bed, White told a local minister (Reverend Jack Shaw, who himself has been linked with U.S. intelligence) that several months earlier he had made known his desire to sever his affiliation with U.S. intelligence. He also confessed that he was a professional killer.

5. White owned a 7.65 German Mauser, which he gave to his son before his death. (The rifle found on the sixth floor of the Texas School Book Depository—Oswald's alleged firing position—soon after the assassination was originally identified as a 7.65 German Mauser by several police officers, all of whom had to recant their identification later when it was discovered that the weapon was "actually" an Italian Mannlicher-Carcano.)

6. Among Geneva White's possessions after her husband's death was a previously unknown photo of Lee Harvey Oswald. The photo was one of a series of shots which purport to show the accused assassin in varying poses holding weapons and communist literature.

According to Geneva, Roscoe told her to hang onto the photo as it was apt to be valuable one day. According to the Warren Commission, these photos were taken by Lee's wife, Marina Oswald, in their Neeley Street backyard. Oswald, after his arrest, said that the series of photos were fake, and that his face had been pasted onto someone else's body. Many photographic experts agree that the photos are phony, citing differences in the shadow patterns, the ratio of the size Oswald's head to his body, and other inconsistencies. Two of the photos were made public, one appearing on the cover of *Life* magazine, where it did much to convince the public of Oswald's guilt. The third, apparently, belonged exclusively to Roscoe White. (Photographic experts, including Robert Groden, who have studied the famous backyard photos of Oswald holding a rifle, have noticed that there appears to be a lump on Oswald's right wrist. Photographic evidence indicates that, while Oswald did not have such a lump on his wrist, Roscoe White did. Was Oswald's head pasted onto Roscoe White's body?) According to researcher and author Anthony Summers (*Conspiracy*) the Dallas police must have, at one time, known about the White photograph, as they used Oswald's pose in that photo in their reenactments.

7. Geneva White had, at one time, worked for Jack Ruby as a stripper.

8. Roscoe knew Ruby.

9. Roscoe was a superb marksman.

10. Geneva later claimed that she was given electroshock treatment in an attempt to make her forget what she knew about the assassination. It can be documented that Geneva was given electroshock treatments and it is a chilling coincidence that those treatments started on November 22, 1966.

11. According to an FBI report, Roscoe was on duty for the Dallas police on the morning of the assassination, investigating a burglary in North Dallas.

12. Roscoe quit the Dallas Police Department on October 19, 1965, to manage a drug store in suburban Dallas. White eventually became a foreman at the M&M Equipment Company on the east side of Dallas and it was here that he died in an explosion on September 24, 1971.

Ricky Don White says he first learned of his father's involvement in the assassination in 1978 when a family friend, who was admittedly involved with U.S. intelligence, told Ricky to be prepared for a shock. He told the boy that Roscoe had killed Kennedy and that this fact was bound to become public sooner or later. Ricky refused to believe the man.

Then, in 1982, Ricky says he discovered his father's military footlocker. In it was a handwritten diary and a key to a safety deposit box. In 1988, Ricky contacted the Dallas district attorney seeking help in finding the safety deposit box. The district attorney notified the FBI and Ricky was interrogated. After one of these interrogations, the diary was discovered to be missing. He said he had no intention of telling what he knew regarding Roscoe's diary until the FBI began to persistently question him.

In 1990, Ricky says he searched his grandfather's empty house in Paris, Texas, and there discovered a steel container. In it were three cablegram-type messages alluding to the JFK assassination. These were apparently Roscoe's orders to eliminate a "National Security threat." The messages bore Roscoe's code name "Mandarin" and his military serial number.

This is what the cables said.:

1) Navy Int.
Code A MRC
Remarks data
1666106
NRC VDC NAC
(Illegible) 63
Remarks Mandarin: Code A
Foreign affairs assignments have been cancelled. The next assignment is to eliminate a National Security threat to world wide peace. Destination will be Houston, Austin or Dallas. Contacts are being arranged now. Orders are subject to change at any time. Reply back if not understood.
C. BOWERS
OSHA

2) NAVY INT.
CODE A MRC
REMARK data
1666106
Sept. 63
Remarks Mandarin: Code A
Dallas destination chosen. Your place hidden within the department. Contacts are within this letter. Continue on as planned.
C. Bowers
OSHA
RE-rifle code AAA destroy/on/

3) NAVY INT.
CODE A mrc
Remark data
1666106
NRC VDC NAC
Dec. 63

Remarks Mandarin: Code G
Stay within department, witnesses have eyes, ears and mouths. You (illegible) do of the mix up. The men will be in to cover up all misleading evidence soon. Stay as planned
wait for further orders.
C. Bowers
RE-rifle Code AAA destroy/on/

Here are the remainder of Ricky's claims, all based on entries in Roscoe's missing diary:

1. Roscoe shot twice at the president with his Mauser from behind the wooden fence atop the infamous grassy knoll, in front of, and to the right of, JFK at the time of the assassination. One of those two shots struck JFK in the right temple and killed him instantly. (See also MOORMAN PHOTO.)
2. Roscoe was one of three shooters in Dealey Plaza that day, according to the diary. Roscoe's code name was Mandarin, and the other two shooters, who are referred to only by code name, were called Saul and Lebanon. These two men allegedly shot at the president from two locations to the president's rear—one from the Texas School Book Depository, and the other from the Dallas County Record Building, on the east side of Houston Street, catty-corner from the Depository.
3. Roscoe killed Dallas police officer J. D. Tippit in the Oak Cliff section of Dallas approximately 45 minutes later. Ricky said Oswald was involved in the plot but did not fire any shots. Roscoe and Oswald were attempting to convince Tippit to give them a ride to Redbird Airport, where a getaway plane was waiting for them. Tippit, hearing about the assassination on the radio, put two and two together and refused to take the men to the airport. Roscoe killed Tippit and Oswald fled the scene on foot. According to Harrison Edward Livingstone, in his book *High Treason 2*, "There is a report that an extra police shirt was found in the backseat of Tippit's car, and we surmise that this belonged to Roscoe, who changed his clothes there. It is also thought that Tippit's car was the one that stopped at Oswald's house and beeped, and then picked him up down the street."
4. The White family was sent to Paris, Texas, after the assassination while Roscoe hid out with his fellow assassins in Dripping Springs, Texas.

Now we get to Roscoe's wife—and Ricky's mother—Geneva White. Her story alone would be enough to raise eyebrows. For starters, Geneva worked for Jack Ruby at the Carousel Club for a short period in September 1963, two months before the assassination.

In August 1990, while Geneva lay on her deathbed (she would succumb soon thereafter to lung cancer), she was interviewed by journalist Ron Laytner in the presence of Harrison Edward Livingstone. During that interview, she claimed that, while working at the Carousel, she had overheard Roscoe and Ruby plotting to kill JFK. When they caught her eavesdropping, Ruby wanted to kill her but Roscoe talked him out of it, saying they should just give her electroshock treatments until she forgot what she had heard. This was apparently done, and although the effects of the treatments were successful for awhile, she did later recall the incident. She was, however, plagued with mental health problems for the remainder of her life.

Geneva's other claims included:

1. She once went to a rifle range with Roscoe and Oswald and that Oswald was a "real bad shot."
2. After the assassination, she went to New Orleans without Roscoe and, while there, was threatened by mobster Charles Nicoletti, who said that her children would be tortured and killed if she ever talked.
3. She and Roscoe knew the Tippits well and that the conspirators "took care" of Tippit's wife and kids after Tippit's death.

During the interview, Geneva offered her opinion as to who was behind JFK's death: "We at first thought the assassination was more Mob [but later realized] it was more CIA."

Marie Tippit, widow of J. D., usually doesn't grant interviews but did come forward during the 1990s to point out that, as far as she knew, her husband did not know Roscoe White.

After weighing the evidence, the question is: If Rock White didn't kill JFK, what *did* he do?

White, T. F.

On December 14, 1963, FBI special agent Charles T. Brown Jr. filed the following report: "Mr. T. F. White, Mechanic, Mack Pate's Garage, 114 West 7th Street, Dallas, Texas, was interviewed regarding a red 1957 Plymouth reportedly seen by him on the parking lot of the El Chico Restaurant on the afternoon of November 22, 1963. Mr. White was advised Mr. Wes Wise, Sports Department, KRLD-TV, Dallas, had furnished information which Mr. Wise obtained from Mr. White reflecting the individual driving the red 1957 Plymouth was believed to be Lee Harvey Oswald. Mr. White stated he saw the red car at approximately 2:00 P.M. on the parking lot of the El Chico Restaurant. He stated he now believes the car to have been a red 1961 Falcon and he believed the automobile had 1963 Texas License PP 4537. White said he observed the man driving the car from the side of his face, and when he saw television pictures of Lee Harvey Oswald on the night of November 22, 1963, he believed the man he saw at the El Chico Restaurant parking lot was identical with Oswald. He said the man sat in the car for a short period of time and then left at a high rate of speed, going west on Davis Street. Mr. White was advised that

the license number furnished by him had been checked and ascertained to be assigned to the 1957 Plymouth automobile which had been observed by an FBI Agent and determined to be light blue over medium blue in color. Mr. White was also advised that Lee Harvey Oswald had been captured at the Texas Theatre in Dallas at approximately 2:00 P.M., after having shot Dallas Police Officer J. D. Tippit at approximately 1:18 P.M. Mr. White was further advised witnesses have stated they observed Oswald fleeing from the scene of the Tippit shooting on foot and he was observed by other witnesses to enter the Texas Theatre shortly after the shooting. Mr. White said he thought he had obtained the correct license number on the car, and, upon seeing Oswald on television on the night of November 22, 1963, he thought Oswald was possibly identical with the man he had seen driving the red automobile on the afternoon of November 22, 1963." This report could be chalked up as another case of mistaken identity except for a bizarre coincidence. The light blue over medium blue 1957 Plymouth with license number PP4537 belonged to Carl Mather, a close and longtime friend of J. D. Tippit. When the FBI arrived at the Mather's house the 1957 Plymouth was in the driveway and Mrs. Mather explained that they also owned a light blue 1954 station wagon. Mrs. Mather could not explain White's report, adding that from 3:30 until 5:00 P.M. on the day of the assassination the Mathers were at the Tippit's house offering their condolences.

Another strange connection between Mather and this case stems from the fact that he was a longtime employee of Collins Radio, a company that in April 1963 announced that it was going to build a modern communications system linking Laos, Thailand, and South Vietnam. Lee Harvey Oswald and George DeMohrenschildt once visited the home of retired admiral Henry Bruton who was a Collins Radio executive. On November 1, 1963, a ship called the *Rex*, which was leased by Collins Radio, was captured in the waters off Cuba by Castro's troops. It turned out that the Collins Radio connection was all a front and that the *Rex* was actually smuggling weapons to anti-Castro soldiers inside Cuba.

White Russians

A group of White Russian immigrants lived in Dallas, and seemed to almost universally thrive. White Russians represent about seven percent of the population of the Russian Empire, what was the former name of the Soviet Union. The term, in Russia, is considered synonymous with Belorussia. As a group, the White Russians in Dallas were said to have felt sorry for Marina—although often unimpressed with her personality—and very hostile to Lee, whom they saw as a communist and a wife-beater. The church that the Dallas Russian-speaking community belonged to was reportedly subsidized by the CIA because of the constituency's strong anticommunist feelings.

Peter Paul Gregory was a consulting petroleum engineer, a part-time Russian instructor at the Fort Worth Public Library who was born in Chita, Siberia, and came to the United States in 1923. He attended the University of California at Berkeley. One of Gregory's most interesting observations was that Oswald spoke with a Polish accent. Gregory was contacted by Oswald in June 1962 soon after Lee and Marina returned from the Soviet Union. Gregory noted that Oswald was wearing a wool suit, inappropriate summer garb in Dallas. Oswald got Gregory's name from the Texas Employment Commission in Fort Worth. Oswald was seeking a "letter certifying to his proficiency in the Russian language." Marina became a Russian tutor for Gregory's son, Paul. Gregory introduced the Oswalds to George Bouhe and Anna Meller. Soon, the Oswalds were acquainted with 30 Russian-speaking Texans, including Ruth Paine and George and Jeanne DeMohrenschildt. Sometime before the assassination, Marguerite Oswald, Lee's mother, signed up for and attended Gregory's Russian classes, presumably so that she could better communicate with Marina. Gregory was Marina's initial translator during her interrogation by the Secret Service following the assassination. On November 24, with her world torn apart by events, Marguerite called Gregory and asked Gregory for a place to stay. Gregory died in January 1982 of natural causes.

George Alexandrovitch Bouhe, according to the *Warren Report,* "attempted to dissuade Marina from returning [to Oswald] in November 1962, and when she rejoined him, [as he did not like Oswald] . . . became displeased with her as well." In the latter part of 1962 "relations between Oswald and his wife became such that Bouhe wanted to 'liberate' her from Oswald." Among other things, Bouhe is involved in the mystery of how Oswald met his Dallas-mentor George DeMohrenschildt. DeMohrenschildt says that Bouhe introduced him to Oswald. Bouhe denies it.

Teofil and Anna N. Meller were two of the first members of the Dallas Russian-speaking community to meet Lee and Marina. The Mellers, staunch anticommunists like their friends, became concerned about the Oswalds when Anna visited them in their apartment and spotted a copy of Karl Marx's *Das Kapital* on a table. Teofil called the FBI, who informed the Mellers that Lee was "all right."

Paul M. Raigorodsky was a leading member of Dallas' Russian-speaking community, who was referred to by that community as "The Czar." An oil millionaire, he became another unlikely acquaintance of Lee and Marina Oswald and a leading Dallas socialite, who often appeared in the papers in tails and hat attending select gatherings. In 1968, Raigorodsky co-hosted a party given in Dallas by Mrs.

Clint Murchison Jr. He was director of the Tolstoy Foundation, which reportedly sent Russian emigrants back to Russia to gather intelligence against the USSR—and which received $400,000 annually from the U.S. government. Raigorodsky died during March 1977, at the height of the House Select Committee on Assassinations investigation. He died during the same month as George DeMohrenschildt.

Mr. and Mrs. Igor Vladimir Voshinin were friends of DeMohrenschildt. Igor was an influential White Russian working in petrochemicals. According to the *Haagse Post* (September 30, 1967), "The only one of the Russian community who seems to have been *au courant* with the whole affair was a certain Igor Voshinin."

Mrs. Voshinin was 45 years old at the time of JFK's death. She was born in Labinsk, Russia, and became a naturalized American in 1955. She held a degree in geology. It was Mrs. Voshinin who described for the Warren Commission a feud within the Dallas Russian community over church liturgy (whether services should be in Old Church Slavic or in English) and said they were no longer on speaking terms with George Bouhe because of this. She was first employed in the United States by geologist George DeMohrenschildt as a secretary. She later told the Warren Commission that DeMohrenschildt was very politically provocative and could switch from the left to the right depending on the situation. She said she never met the Oswalds because she believed Lee was a Soviet agent. She got this notion from Marguerite Oswald. Mrs. Voshinin told the commission that she felt DeMohrenschildt was visiting some "politically unsavory" character during his frequent trips to Houston.

Igor was 58 years old and employed by Mullen & Powell as a structural engineer. He told the Warren Commission that George DeMohrenschildt was friends with a rich oil man in Mexico named Tito Harper, and that DeMohrenschildt also befriended Mikoyan (a top communist and "Butcher of the Stalin times") in Mexico. Like his wife, Igor said that he had never met the Oswalds.

Declan P. and Katherine N. Ford were also acquaintances of the Oswalds in Texas. He was a self-employed consulting geologist for various oil companies. Marina Oswald stayed at their home for several days after a fight with Lee. Both told the Warren Commission that, because of Oswald's boorish behavior, as of January 1963, "Marina and her husband" were 'dropped' from their social scene. Declan told the commission that Oswald was "really a screwy nut." On the morning of November 24, 1963, the Fords visited the FBI office in Dallas on their own and, while there, told FBI agent James Hosty that there was a Russian-speaking community in Dallas built around the Russian Orthodox Church and that they had befriended Marina when they heard she was in Dallas because she had grown up in Leningrad. The Fords told Hosty that Lee had been an abusive husband, and that he "took a pro-Communist stance on everything."

Dorothy Gravitis was a 74-year-old Russian-speaking acquaintance of Marina Oswald's housemate Ruth Paine. Dorothy was born in Latvia and came to United States in 1949. She taught Russian at the Berlitz School, where Ruth was both a friend and student. She had never met Lee or Marina, but discussed Marina with Ruth on the phone.

Lev Aronson was the Dallas Symphony Orchestra cellist. He attended a 1962 Dallas party at Katherine Ford's house, along with many members of the Russian-speaking community and Lee and Marina Oswald. Aronson's date for the evening was a Japanese woman named Yaeko Okui, with whom Lee "spoke at length." Lee had been stationed in Japan in the marines. Okui told federal investigators that, after that party, she never saw the Oswalds again.

Lydia Dymitruk, a 37-year-old resident of Fort Worth, Texas, at the time of the assassination, was born in Russia and raised in Belgium. She divorced a White Russian who brought her to the United States from Belgium. Lydia was a friend of Anna Meller, whom she met through George Bouhe. Lydia met Marina Oswald through Meller and Bouhe, and it was Lydia who took Marina and her newborn daughter Rachel to the hospital when Rachel had a fever.

Ilya A. Mamantov was Marina's interpreter during her interrogation by Dallas police on the evening of November 22, 1963. Ruth Paine, who had accompanied Marina to the police station, was not allowed to interpret for Marina because she too was a witness in the case.

Thomas M. and Natalie Ray were also acquaintances of the Oswalds in Dallas. Natalie was born in Stalingrad, and sent to Germany by the Nazis in 1943. She had become a writer. She said she met the Oswalds at a party. She commented that Lee spoke excellent Russian and later wondered if he were a Soviet agent. Thomas was a commission salesman for Gulf Oil of Paris, Texas, at the time of JFK's death. He also testified for the Warren Commission but didn't have much of interest to say. "Well frankly, I just didn't pay much attention to the guy," he said of Oswald.

Also named Ray was Valentina A. Ray, who was originally from the Ukraine. She met the Oswalds in November 1962 and told the Warren Commission that Marina told her Lee was mean to her and hit her. Valentina testified that Oswald was "rather arrogant."

Another Texas acquaintance of the Oswalds was Max E. Clark, a retired U.S. Air Force Colonel, attorney and former security officer for General Dynamics. Clark's wife Katya, was born Princess Sherbatov, a member of the Russian royal family. The Clarks were once dinner guests at the Oswalds' apartment in Dallas at which Marina prepared the meal.

For reasons unknown, translators Peter Gregory and Ilya Mamantov *both* mistranslated Marina Oswald's words to lead everyone to believe that Oswald's rifle in Dallas was the same as the one he had had in the Soviet Union.

(See also DEMOHRENSCHILDT, SERGEI "GEORGE" S.; PAINE, RUTH AND MICHAEL R.)

Whitworth, Mrs. Edith

Mrs. Whitworth was an operator of the Furniture Mart in Irving, Texas. She told the Warren Commission that, in early November 1963, a man she later came to believe was Oswald came into her store with his wife and two small children to inquire about having his rifle fixed. Marina Oswald denied that she ever went to this place with her husband and children. Whitworth later positively identified Marina as the woman she had seen with Oswald. The Warren Commission chose to believe Marina.

(See also OSWALD, MARINA.)

Wilcott, James A.

CIA finance officer who told the House Select Committee on Assassinations that Oswald had been recruited from the U.S. Marine Corps while stationed in Atsugi, Japan, by the CIA "with the express purpose of a double-agent assignment in the USSR." Wilcott testified that he had personally handled the funding for Oswald's assignment. According to Jim Garrison, "Predictably, a chorus line of other agency witnesses, whose names Wilcott had mentioned, denied all knowledge of such a project. The committee did not pursue the lead."

William B. Reily Company, The

William B. Reily was the owner of the company. A subsidiary of the company was the Standard Coffee Company, which was big enough to have two locations—at 725 and 640 Magazine Street. Lee Harvey Oswald reportedly worked at the 640 site from May 9 until July 19, 1963. There is evidence, however, that Oswald's job was actually a cover for other activities. According to Jim Garrison Reily had "actively supported the anti-Castro movement for years."

According to Peter Dale Scott, "at least some of Oswald's alleged paychecks from the Reily company are apparently not genuine." In the Warren Commission Hearings (Volume 22, page 208) there is an FBI document stating that Oswald's Reily paycheck #1684, dated June 14, 1963, was cashed by Roland Martin of Martin's Restaurant in New Orleans, yet the check itself was endorsed by

Oswald to Foltz Tea & Coffee, Inc., in New Orleans (Volume 22, page 288).

While Oswald worked for Reily he supposedly spent a lot of time at the Crescent Garage talking to employee Adrian Alba about guns, specifically how to order guns by mail. Alba told the Warren Commission so. But no one else at Reily remembers Oswald ever talking about guns.

Four of Oswald's coworkers at the coffee company were working at NASA a year later. According to assassination researcher Paris Flammonde, one of those coworkers, Dante Marachini, was a friend of assassination suspect Clay Shaw.

Williams, Bonnie Ray
Born in Carthage, Texas, Williams was a 20-year-old Texas School Book Depository employee who watched the presidential motorcade from the building's fifth floor with coworkers James Jarman and Harold Norman, directly below the "sniper's nest." Williams admits to eating his lunch on the sixth floor that day, leaving at 12:20 P.M., only 10 minutes before the shots were fired. The remains of this lunch (a brown paper bag once containing chicken, bread, and a bag of corn chips) were reportedly found near the sniper's nest—although WFAA cameraman Tom Alyea insists they were actually found on the fifth floor, which makes more sense because we know from photographs taken seconds after the assassination that this is the floor from which Williams watched the motorcade. The bag-lunch evidence, wherever it was found, was initially treated as if it had been left in the spot by the assassin.

As of 12:20, according to Williams, there was no sign of Oswald on the sixth floor. Williams told the FBI on the day of the assassination that he heard two shots, but later changed his story to three.

Williams told the Warren Commission, "Well, the first shot—I really did not pay any attention to it, because I did not know what was happening. The second shot, it sounded like it was right in the building, the second and third shot . . . it even shook the building, the side we were on. . . . We saw the policeman and people running—there are some tracks on the west side of the building, railroad tracks. They were running towards that way . . . since everybody was running, you know, to the west side of the building, towards the railroad tracks, we assumed maybe somebody was down there."

Williams had been working for the Texas School Book Depository since September 9, 1963. He started working at the other Depository building at the end of Houston Street, a block and a half north of Elm Street, but had been moved to the building on Elm "three or four weeks" before the assassination to help lay new floors on the fifth and sixth floors of the building.

(See also FLOOR-LAYING CREW; JARMAN, JAMES; NORMAN, HAROLD.)

Williams, Harold Richard
Chef at the after-hours Mikado Club in Dallas, a competitor of Ruby's clubs. Williams was arrested and roughed up during a vice raid at the Mikado during the early part of November 1963. He later claimed that when he was placed in a police car, Officer J. D. Tippit was driving and Ruby was riding shotgun. The driver referred to the passenger as "Rube," Williams claims. This would imply that Ruby was working with Tippit in a scheme to harass his competition. After the assassination, Dallas Police Department members threatened Williams, telling him that he would be charged with a serious crime that "they would make stick" if he didn't stop talking about seeing Tippit and Ruby together. Williams never made his statements under oath.

Williams, Otis N.
Assassination witness who had been working in the Texas School Book Depository since 1953. At the time of the assassination he was the Book Depository's credit manager. Williams stood on the Depository's front steps during the shooting sequence. He always maintained that he heard three shots and that they sounded as if they had come from the direction of the triple underpass. Williams is now deceased.

Willises, The
A family of assassination witnesses who stood on either side of Elm Street during the shooting. Phillip L. Willis—born August 2, 1918—is the only known person to have been an eyewitness to both the Japanese attack on Pearl Harbor to initiate American involvement in World War II and the assassination of President Kennedy. He had been assigned to the 86th Observation Squad at Bellow's Field in Oahu, Hawaii, and managed to get his plane airborne during the first Japanese attack there on December 7, 1941. Later, he was involved in the capture of the first Japanese prisoner of war when the prisoner's submarine ran into a reef off Bellow's Field. Later in the war, Willis served at the battles of Midway and Guadalcanal, flew 52 combat missions, and earned a silver star. He retired as an air force major. During the late 1940s, Willis was twice elected to the Texas state House of Representatives representing Kaufman County. During that time he met Lyndon B. Johnson and Sam Rayburn. Philip and his family moved to Dallas in 1960. That year he and his wife met presidential candidate John F. Kennedy at a fund-raising luncheon. On November 22, 1963, Philip Willis was employed at Down-

town Lincoln-Mercury, an establishment not far from Dealey Plaza that shows up with disproportionate frequency in the assassination literature for a variety of reasons.

For the motorcade, Willis was standing on the south side of Elm Street across the street from the Texas School Book Depository. With him was his Argus 35mm Autronic I, Model 35156-M camera, with an F 2.8 Cintar lens, loaded with Kodachrome slide film, ASA 25. Willis took 12 pictures around Dealey Plaza before, during, and after the assassination, all of which were published (although some were cropped) in the Warren Commission's 26 volumes of testimony and exhibits. Immediately following the shots, Willis yelled, "Ring the building!" Meaning the Texas School Book Depository, but that does not mean that Willis believes the Depository to be the sole source of the shots. Willis told researcher Richard B. Trask in 1985: "I don't care what any experts say. They're full of baloney. I've shot too many deer. I've hit a deer in the head and his horns fly twenty feet in the direction of the bullet. No one will ever convince us that the last shot did not come from the right front, from the knoll area."

Willis himself designated slide number eight as one of significance since it shows a man who greatly resembles Ruby at the assassination scene minutes after the shots were fired. In the Warren Commission's 26 volumes, that photo is cropped right through the face of that man. Willis

commented on the photo to an investigator for the Citizens' Committee of Inquiry, "It looks so much like him [Ruby], it's pitiful." Other photos of the scene, taken by other photographers, reveal the man not to be Ruby.

Phil's wife Marilyn watched the assassination from the north side of Elm Street in front of the pergola. With Mrs. Willis were her parents, Mr. and Mrs. William Stubblefield. Phillip's daughter Linda Kay Willis was with her father on the south side of Elm Street; she told Jim Marrs in 1978, "[the] shots came from somewhere other than the Depository. And where we were standing, we had a good view." His daughter Rosemary is easily identifiable on the Zapruder film in her white sweatshirt, running alongside the president's limo, then stopping and looking back, apparently in reaction to a shot.

Phillip and Marilyn Willis were both prosecution witnesses at the trial of Clay Shaw in New Orleans, Louisiana, and both were interviewed by the House Select Committee on Assassinations in Washington, D.C.

(See also DOWNTOWN LINCOLN-MERCURY.)

Willmon, Jim

A *Dallas Morning News* ad salesman who was standing on Houston Street during the shooting. According to Jim Marrs, Willmon thought the first shot was a backfire. "People ran toward the grassy knoll," Willmon added.

Phil Willis, the only man to be a witness to both the Japanese attack on Pearl Harbor and the assassination of John F. Kennedy, speaks to an assassination symposium in Dallas during the early 1990s. *(MacIntyre Symms)*

Willoughby, Charles (a.k.a. Tscheppe-Weidenbach, Adolf)

General Willoughby was born in 1892 in Heidelberg, Germany, as Adolf Tscheppe-Weidenbach and came to the United States in 1910. In the United States, Willoughby became a Counter Intelligence Corps agent, a major general in the U.S. Army, and General Douglas MacArthur's chief of intelligence during the Korean War. After the war, Willoughby worked out of a Washington, D.C., headquarters. Author Dick Russell writes, "his domestic associations extended from the Cuban exile community to the H. L. Hunt family." Willoughby reportedly ran H. L. Hunt's private intelligence network. MacArthur reportedly referred to Willoughby as "my little Fascist." Willoughby formed the ultra-secret intelligence agency known as FOI, which theoretically specialized in rooting out communist spies. Willoughby worked with "Japanese Warlords," "German Nazis," and CIA director—and later Warren commissioner—Allen Dulles in an attempt to establish a "global anti-Communist alliance."

Russell writes: "The case of Willoughby's involvement in the Kennedy conspiracy can be no more than circumstantial. But Willoughby was a master of intrigue who . . .

was assuredly in a position to make the right connections from his Washington domain."

According to Korean War historian Bruce Cumings: "Willoughby was a thoroughly loathsome person whose entire world view consisted of piles of ethnic stereotypes; he was apparently capable of anything." Cumings writes that, after World War II, Willoughby retained his ties with Japanese militarists, including germ-warfare specialist General Ishii.

Cumings also says: "After MacArthur's sacking by U.S. President Harry Truman, Willoughby frequently visited Spain and claimed to have been involved in the American military base negotiations with Francisco Franco. He set up a kind of right-wing *internationale* called the 'international *comité*,' using money from the Hunt brothers in Texas, linking Spain and Portugal together with German right-wingers, the Hargis Crusade, and others. He was an agent for Hunt Oil in seeking offshore rights in the Portuguese colony of Mozambique."

Willoughby was a member of a right-wing fraternal organization known as the Sovereign Order of Saint John of Jerusalem, more popularly known as the "Shickshinny Knights," because they were headquartered in Shickshinny, Pennsylvania. The group claims to be the original Knights of Malta, a fraternal order that dates back to the Crusades. Willoughby knew and worked with Nazi intelligence mastermind Reinhard Gehlen during the cold war.

According to researcher Peter Dale Scott, "In late 1963 the most conspicuous transnational feature of the Hunt-Willoughby network was their close identification with Madame Nhu, the widow of the recently assassinated Ngo Dinh Nhu in Vietnam."

(See also BISHOP, WILLIAM C.; CORSO, PHILIP; HUNT, H. L.; PERMINDEX; WALKER, EDWIN.)

Wilson, Billy Ray See WALL, BRECK.

Wilson, Eugene M. See DOWNTOWN LINCOLN-MERCURY.

Wilson, Steven F.
Wilson watched the Dallas motorcade from a third-floor window (second window from the east) in the Texas School Book Depository. On March 25, 1964, Wilson told an FBI agent that "the shots came from the west end of the building or from the colonnade (pergola) located on Elm Street across from the west end of our building. The shots really did not sound like they came from above me." He said he heard three shots and that the entire shooting sequence took less than five seconds.

After making this statement, Wilson was visited repeatedly by the FBI. "I couldn't get any work done. They were always there," he said. He refused to change his statement and was not called as a Warren Commission witness. None of the Texas School Book Depository employees who thought the shots came from elsewhere other than their building were called as Warren Commission witnesses.

Winborn, Walter L.
Winborn was standing atop the triple underpass at the time of the assassination. He told researcher Stewart Galanor in May 1966 about the "smoke that [had] come out from under the trees on the right-hand side of the motorcade. . . . It looked like a little haze, like somebody had shot firecrackers or something like that. . . . It looked like it was ten feet long and about two or three feet wide."

Winnipeg Airport Incident See GIESBRECHT, RICHARD.

Wise, Wesley
KRLD reporter in Dallas who later became mayor of Dallas. Wise reported seeing Ruby near the Texas School Book Depository moments after the assassination. He testified at Ruby's murder trial for the prosecution that at 3:00 P.M. on November 23, 1963, Ruby had tapped on the glass of Wise's mobile TV unit near the School Book Depository and had suggested that he take shots of the two Dallas police officers who had been assigned to the assassination investigation.

(See also COUCH, MALCOLM; MATHER, CARL; WHITE, T. F.)

Wiseman, John
Dallas County deputy sheriff who claims to have confiscated assassination-witness Mary Moorman's Land camera photograph taken moments before the assassination that shows the "Oswald" window. Wiseman turned the photo over to his superior (Chief Criminal Deputy Sheriff Allan Sweatt), who then turned it over to the Secret Service.

(See also FEATHERSTON, JIM; HESTER, CHARLES; HILL, JEAN; MOORMAN, MARY.)

Witt, Louis Steven See UMBRELLA MAN.

Wood, William C. See GARRISON INVESTIGATION.

Woodward, Mary Elizabeth (later Pillsworth, Mary)

A *Dallas Morning News* employee who was standing in front of and just to the left of the wooden fence atop the grassy knoll at the time of the assassination. She was the journalist closest to the president at the moment of the fatal shot. She wrote her first version of her story—which has remained unchanged—minutes after the shooting. Woodward wrote that "suddenly there was a horrible, ear-shattering noise from behind us and a little to the right," indicating that the shots came from the north side of Elm Street somewhere between the pergola and the triple underpass. She believes the first shot missed. Woodward completed writing her story before President Kennedy's death was announced.

She told a conference at Southern Methodist University on November 20, 1993, that "the car, after that first shot, had come practically to a stop. Later on, looking back at it, I said I could not believe how well-trained Secret Service people reacted so slowly. I would have expected that from ordinary human beings, but I expected that they would have reacted much quicker."

Worrell, James Richard "Dickie," Jr.

Worrell was walking along Houston Street just after the assassination when he saw a man running from the back of the Texas School Book Depository wearing a brown sport or suit coat. The man headed south on Houston.

Worrell's observances of the man in the brown coat are corroborated by witnesses Carolyn Walther and Richard Randolph Carr. Worrell died on November 9, 1966, at the age of 23 in a car and motorcycle accident in which his female passenger was also killed.

Wulf, William E.

In 1954, when Lee Harvey Oswald was 15 years old, he became interested in the New Orleans Amateur Astronomy Association, a local organization for high school students. Wulf was the association's president at the time and later recalled that Oswald "started expounding the Communist doctrine and saying that he was highly interested in communism, that communism was the only way of life for the worker, etc."

This occurred at Wulf's home. Oswald and Wulf got into an argument. Wulf testified, "my father came into the room, heard what we were arguing on communism, and that this boy was loud-mouthed, boisterous, and my father asked him to leave the house, and that is the last I have seen or spoken with Oswald."

Y

Yaras, Dave   See RUBY, JACK.

Yarborough, Senator Ralph W.
Senator Yarborough rode in the vice presidential limousine, two cars behind President Kennedy's limousine, in the Dallas motorcade. Yarborough smelled gunpowder as his limousine approached the triple underpass, indicating that at least one shot came from ground level rather than from a sixth-floor window. (Interestingly, not one of the police officers who searched the sixth floor of the Texas School Book Depository ever mentioned smelling smoke or gunpowder or anything else that might indicate that this was the source of the shots.)

On November 21, 1963, there was a fight between President Kennedy and Vice President Johnson regarding the seating in the next day's motorcade. According to Craig Zirbel, LBJ "wanted Connally out of JFK's car and his enemy . . . Yarborough to sit in Connally's seat."

YMCA
One of the ways that assassination theorists have linked Lee Harvey Oswald and Jack Ruby was through the YMCA in Dallas. The associate director of the YMCA Health Club in Dallas, Richard Leroy Hulen, told the Warren Commission that Jack Ruby was a short-term member of the club. Hulen used YMCA records to confirm that Oswald stayed there for a short time, on October 3 and then again from October 15–19, but said Oswald never used the club facilities. Jack Lawrence, who worked at Downtown Lincoln-Mercury and behaved suspiciously after the assassination, was also reported to have stayed at the same YMCA.

(See also DOWNTOWN LINCOLN-MERCURY.)

Z

Zangretti, Jack   See SUSPICIOUS DEATHS.

Zapruder Film, The

Abraham Zapruder was an assassination witness who stood on a pedestal at the westernmost section of the pergola and took the most famous film of the assassination. A freemason, Zapruder was born in Russia on May 15, 1905. Of the Jewish faith, Zapruder came to the United States in 1920. His company, Jennifer Juniors, Inc., occupied the fourth and fifth floors of the Dal-Tex Building on the northeast corner of Elm and Houston, 501 Elm Street. In 1963, Zapruder lived in the University Park section of Dallas.

With Zapruder when he shot his film was the receptionist at his office, Marilyn Sitzman. She climbed up onto the pedestal with him, standing behind him and steadying him, so that he could concentrate on filming the president and not have to worry about falling off of the four-foot pedestal.

The camera Zapruder used that day was a Model 414 PD Bell & Howell Zoomatic Director Series Camera, serial number AS 13486, purchased in 1962 at the Peacock Jewelry Company on Elm Street. The camera was loaded with Kodachrome II Safety film.

On the morning of the assassination Zapruder saw that it was raining and decided not to bring his movie camera. However, after he arrived at work that morning, the weather greatly improved. He consented to drive the 14-mile roundtrip to his home and back to get his movie camera to stop the friendly but persistent badgering that was coming from his secretary Lillian Rogers.

Zapruder later said that he went out to the north side of Elm Street by himself and ran into Sitzman by accident near the pergola. The concrete perch upon which Zapruder and Sitzman stood while the film was being shot is 65 feet from the center of Elm Street and 185 feet from the southwest corner of the Texas School Book Depository. The motorcade sequence of the film lasts for $26^1/2$ seconds, or 486 frames.

The Warren Commission would have had a much easier time selling the American public its version of the facts if the Zapruder film had not existed. Zapruder told the FBI he thought the shots had come from directly behind him.

Secret Service agent Forrest Sorrels contacted Zapruder at 2:00 P.M. on the day of the assassination, requesting copies of the film. Zapruder told Sorrels to come up to his office. Moments later members of the Dallas Police arrived at Zapruder's office in the Dal-Tex Building carrying shotguns and demanding the film. Zapruder refused to give it to them, saying he had already promised it to the Secret Service. Soon thereafter Sorrels arrived and took the undeveloped film. Four film positives were developed that afternoon, and three reversal duplicates were developed at the Jamison Film Company using Kodachrome II camera stock provided Jamison by the Eastman Kodak Company. Zapruder and his partner, Erwin Swartz delivered one copy of the film to the Secret Service office in Dallas with the understanding that it was to be sent immediately to FBI headquarters in Washington, D.C. That same night, the night of the assassination, oil billionaire H. L. Hunt bought an original copy of the film through his security guard Paul Rothermel Jr. At midnight on the day of the assassination, Richard B. Stolley of *Life* magazine contacted

Zapruder and asked if he could view the film. Zapruder told him to come by 9:00 A.M. on November 23. The original copy of the film taken by Sorrels was given to Secret Service inspector Thomas Kelley on November 23. Kelley loaned it to the FBI on December 4 and it was returned to the Secret Service office in Dallas on December 4.

After viewing the film on Saturday morning, Stolley purchased the rights to publish the film from Zapruder. The price was originally announced as $50,000, but Zapruder eventually received $150,000 for the film. Stolley's copy of the film was flown to *Life* magazine's Chicago offices and that afternoon 10 black and white prints from the frames were made to publish in the magazine. While this was going on, a copy of the film went to New York where it was viewed by *Life* publisher C. D. Jackson, who was reportedly so upset by the images that he decided the public should never see them. He ordered that all rights to the film be purchased from Zapruder and the film never to be shown publicly.

Contrary to the official history of the film, Homer McMahon and Bennett Hunter, CIA employees of the National Photographic Interpretation Center say that Zapruder's film was developed at Kodak headquarters in Rochester, New York, rather than in Dallas, Texas, and that the original was taken to the NPIC for study. This version doesn't explain how Zapruder and others could repeatedly watch the developed film in Dallas on the weekend of the assassination.

The key piece of information here is that H. L. Hunt purchased a copy of the film before there would have been an opportunity to make changes. Therefore, the Hunt copy of the film, if it still exists, is a duplicate of the film in its pristine state.

There is now conclusive evidence that the Zapruder film, as it is currently seen, is an altered document, thus throwing into question every conclusion that previously could have been made based on its viewing. For example, the driver of the presidential limousine William Greer is looking straight ahead at frame 302, but has turned back to look over his shoulder at frame 303. It has been proven that it is physically impossible for a human being to turn his head so far in 1/16th of a second, which is the time that would have elapsed between those two frames if the Zapruder film were not altered. More likely is the theory that frames that originally existed between frames 302 and 303 have been removed.

Harrison Livingstone rebuts the notion that Bill Greer turns his head 180 degrees in only one frame. Livingstone, somewhat nonsensically, says that this is true only in one version of the film. The film that was purchased by *Life* and is kept in the National Archives shows that the head turn takes three or four frames, which is within the realm of physical possibility. If Greer's head turn is different but

all other motion in the film remains the same, this argument tends to support alteration. There can be only one version of an unaltered document.

Other evidence that the Zapruder film does not record reality comes from eyewitnesses who reported the presidential limousine slowing down or coming to a complete stop following the start of the shooting sequence. Yet, in the Zapruder film, the car maintains a steady speed of approximately 11 miles per hour throughout the shooting sequence. (Indeed, those who may argue that the film is authentic but that Zapruder's camera was malfunctioning, causing the skipped frames, would be stymied by the constant speed of the limousine. The frames are not skipped randomly but rather schematically, to affect a scenario that did not occur.) Another indication that the limousine did stop but the Zapruder film was altered to not show this is the fact that there are incidences on the film of adjacent frames in which the limousine is in focus, but in one the background is blurred while in the other the background is sharp and in focus. The only way this is possible is if in one image the car was moving and in the other it was stopped.

Though a huge piece of the back of JFK's head was found on Elm Street and eyewitnesses report blood and brain tissue blowing out the back of JFK's head, the Zapruder film shows the back of JFK's head remaining intact, while the blood and brain tissue exploded forward.

According to photographic expert Jack White, there is "in the Zapruder film as it exists today, people who were present at the time are no longer present, people who were not present at the time are present; the sun changes its position in the sky and casts false shadows; people remain mysteriously motionless when they should be moving; small people grow tall and tall people shrink; people make impossibly rapid movements; signboards and lampposts reposition themselves; on and on—impressive evidence of alteration that emerges from the extant photographic record."

Taking into consideration the way the Moorman photograph was framed in the camera, the photographer's height, the height of the street, and the grass mall on and next to Elm Street, it has been determined by White that Mary Moorman must have stepped off the curb and into the street before she took her famous photograph. Moorman's own recollections of taking the photograph are that she was standing in the street when she took it. But the Zapruder film shows Moorman standing on the grass. This is evidence, according to White, that the movements in the foreground and background of the Zapruder film are no longer synchronized.

As an eyewitness, Zapruder described what he had seen through the viewfinder of his camera to Warren Commission counsel Wesley J. Liebeler during July 1964: "I heard the first shot and I saw the President lean over and grab himself like this [clutches chest]. . . . for a moment I thought it was 'Oh, he got me!' when you hear a shot . . . and then I saw—I don't believe the President is going to make jokes like this, but before I had a chance to organize my mind, I heard a second shot and then I saw his head open up and the blood and everything came out and I started—I can hardly talk about it." Zapruder became choked up at this point in his testimony but soon continued: "Then I was yelling, 'They killed him! They killed him!' and I just felt that somebody had ganged up on him and I was still shooting the pictures until he got under the underpass—I don't even know how I did it." Regarding the direction of the shots, Zapruder told Liebeler, "I assumed that they came from back there [behind the wooden fence] because as the police starting running back of me it looked like it came from the back of me."

Frames 208–211 of the original film were destroyed while the film was in the possession of *Life* magazine. The only copies we have of those frames come from the original copies made of the original film before the frames were destroyed by *Life*. Two adjacent frames were also damaged in the incident. Frames 155 and 156 are also missing in the original and there is a splice at 157.

The FBI used Zapruder's camera to help analyze the film and re-creations of the assassination until June 23, 1964, when it was returned. Zapruder gave the camera back to federal authorities on December 7, 1966, and it has resided ever since in the National Archives in Washington, D.C.

The film was shown 10 times during the Clay Shaw trial. Zapruder appeared as a prosecution witness at that trial on February 13, 1969. The film was first shown on television on March 6, 1975, on NBC's *Good Night America* show, hosted by Geraldo Rivera, and with guests, photographic expert Robert Groden and comedian/political activist Dick Gregory.

There are some aspects of Zapruder's story that make him seem that he might have had a different role in the assassination from that which is perceived, which is not to say that he was a knowing member of any conspiracy. But it has been noted that there was a certain urgency in the office that "Mr. Zapruder bring his camera to work." Conspiracy theorists delight in noting that in 1953 Zapruder had worked at Nardis of Dallas, alongside Jeanne DeMohrenschildt, wife of George DeMohrenschildt, the man who claims to have been asked by the CIA to keep an eye on Lee Harvey Oswald after his return from the Soviet Union. Also, Madeleine Brown, a top-notch prostitute at the time of the assassination, who mingled with the top power in Texas, says that oil billionaire H. L. Hunt was a friend of Abraham Zapruder. And then there's the opinion of snipers who have surveyed Dealey Plaza and have deter-

mined that the best place to shoot JFK from behind was from the fourth floor of the Dal-Tex Building, which just happened to be where Zapruder had his offices. Zapruder's partner was Erwin Swartz who was close friends with the Campisi brothers, Dallas crime bosses who owned the Egyptian Lounge.

Abraham Zapruder died on August 30, 1970, at Presbyterian Hospital in Dallas at age 66 of stomach cancer.

Zed

The code name of an alleged assassin who, according to an August 1971 article in a French newspaper, killed President Kennedy under the orders of Nazi war criminal Martin Bormann, who was still alive and living in South America. Zed, according to this story, shot JFK in the head with a .45 caliber weapon.

Zoppi, Tony

Dallas Morning News columnist (1950–65) and friend of Jack Ruby. Zoppi met Ruby in 1951 and was introduced by Ruby to Chicago television personality Irv Kupcinet. Zoppi was visited by Ruby a little more than one hour before the assassination. Here, Ruby said, he "obtained a brochure on his new master of ceremonies that he wanted to use in preparing copy for his advertisements." Ruby spent two or three hours in the *Dallas Morning News* building, reportedly before, during, and after the assassination, spending much of that time in Zoppi's office. Strangely, Ruby later denied that Zoppi was there, telling the Warren Commission that he'd been told Zoppi was in New Orleans for a couple of days. Zoppi, on the other hand, says that he was there and that Ruby seemed too calm to be part of the assassination. Both Ruby and Zoppi were later spotted at Parkland Hospital.

Zoppi watched the motorcade from under the marquee of the Hotel Adolphus, holding a transistor radio. Zoppi was at a bar on the mezzanine level of the hotel when he heard the president had been shot. Zoppi later wrote: "As a newspaperman, my first reaction was to cover the story. I dashed down to the *News*, volunteered my services to John King, the city editor, and he asked me to go to Parkland Hospital and act as liaison between city desk personnel and photographers. Phone service was nil, and I was asked to relay stories and photos by car, if necessary. When I arrived at Parkland, I was stopped at the door of the emergency entrance and asked for credentials. I had none, and the Secret Service turned me away. Moments later, an O'Neal Ambulance drove up. Two men tried to unload a heavy bronze casket. The scene was a significant one—the President was dead. Up until that moment, there was speculation about the extent of his injuries. I had to get that news back to the paper. Instinctively, I grabbed a corner of the casket and helped balance it on some wheels. The very Secret Service men who had turned me away moments before, now urged us to hurry into the hospital with our ghastly cargo. We raced down the hall, waved on by the FBI, City Police and Secret Service. A thought hit me at once. I was going to be the first newspaperman to see the president! But a foot from the door to the room where he lay, a young Secret Serviceman stopped our party and said: 'That's all gentlemen, we'll take it from here.' Once more, I was turned away, but I was inside Parkland Hospital. I got on a phone but was told there would be no outside calls. I searched for the switchboard, identified myself to the operator and told her it was absolutely imperative I call the *Dallas News*. She said she was a reader of my night club column, and put me through. 'This is Tony Zoppi at Parkland,' I told the City Desk. 'I know the President is dead, because I just helped carry in his coffin.' There was a click and the phone went dead. The FBI was obviously monitoring all calls. But the message got through."

As a friend of Jack Ruby's, Zoppi recalled events following the death of Lee Harvey Oswald: "I was at my desk that Sunday morning the news of Oswald's murder was announced. I rushed into the City Room in time to hear Ruby's name mentioned and a shiver went up my spine. Ruby and I were friends and he visited my office the day the President was shot. . . . The last time we met he told me of his plans to move from his old apartment to the swanky high-rise building at 21 Turtle Creek. 'It'll cost me $175 a month, he said, 'but what the hell, I've worked hard all my life and now I want to live a little.". . . I dashed down to City Hall and was immediately deluged by newsmen radio, TV and detectives. I was the first person to enter the building who knew Ruby intimately. Following hours of interviews, I returned to my office where several long distance calls awaited me. One was from my friend Ed Sullivan who wanted to know about Ruby. He was also interested in Bill DeMar, an entertainer who had played Ruby's night club and claimed he saw Oswald in the audience ten days prior to the murder. Ever on the alert for new talent, Sullivan paused for a moment, then said: 'What kind of an act does he do?' It was the first time I laughed that day. I assured Sullivan this performer was merely seeking publicity and he let it drop."

Zoppi says he received a phone call from Ruby during the days before Ruby's murder trial: "I received a mysterious phone call from Ruby while lunching at King's Club one day. We chatted for nearly an hour and he rambled on about his youth, the good things he had done for charity around Dallas, the events leading up to the assassination, and—why he shot Oswald. I asked him the last thing he remembered, prior to pulling the trigger and he said: 'I'd better not say.'"

Zoppi left the *Dallas Morning News* in 1965 to become the director of publicity and advertising for the Riviera Hotel in Las Vegas, Nevada. He returned to Dallas in 1982 to operate his own talent booking agency.

ZR/Rifle   See CENTRAL INTELLIGENCE AGENCY.

APPENDIXES

APPENDIX A
JFK ASSASSINATION ORGANIZATIONS

APPENDIX B
JACK RUBY'S WRITTEN STATEMENT

APPENDIX C
JFK ASSASSINATION IN FILM AND VIDEO

APPENDIX D
CONCLUSION OF THE HOUSE SELECT
COMMITTEE ON ASSASSINATIONS

APPENDIX A

JFK ASSASSINATION ORGANIZATIONS

Assassination Archives and Research Center (AARC)
918 F Street, N.W.
Room 510
Washington, D.C. 20004
(202) 393-1917

The Assassination Records Review Board
600 E Street, N.W.
Second Floor
Washington, D.C. 20530
(202) 724-0088
Fax: (202) 724-0457

The Conspiracy Museum
110 South Market Street
Dallas, Tex. 75202
(214) 741-3040
Fax: (214) 741-9339
tcm95@altinet.net

Coalition on Political Assassinations (COPA)
P.O. Box 772
Ben Franklin Station
Washington, D.C. 20044-0772
(202) 785-5299

CTKA
P.O. Box 5489
Sherman Oaks, CA 91413
(310) 838-9494

Committee for an Open Archive (COA)
P.O. Box 6008
Washington, D.C. 20005

(202) 310-1858

Dallas '63
2 Wingrave Way
Liverpool, L11-2UB
United Kingdom
johnr@mail.cybase.co.uk (Secretary John Rudd)

Dealey Plaza UK
Contact: Ian Griggs, Secretary
igriggs@easynet.co.uk
011-44-1992-719805

The Fourth Decade
State University of New York
Fredonia, N.Y. 14063
Editor: Dr. Jerry Rose

JFK/Deep Politics Quarterly
P.O. Box 174
Hillsdale, N.J. 07642
Editors: Jan Stevens and Walt Brown
Associate Editor: Vince Palamara

JFK Lancer Productions and Publications
332 NE 5th St
Grand Prairie, Tex. 75050
(214) 264-2007
jfklancr@flash.net
jfklancr@exo.com

Justice for JFK Committee
214 West 92nd Street, #3E
New York, N.Y. 10025
(212) 496-1472
Contact: Professor R. D. Morningstar

APPENDIX B

JACK RUBY'S WRITTEN STATEMENT

When Ruby's lawyers were preparing his initial defense on murder with malice charges, they asked Jack to write down his experiences during the period November 22–24, 1963. Here, verbatim (with some explanatory notes in brackets), is what Jack wrote:

I. 11/22/63

11:00 A.M. FRI. Went to Tony Zoppi office to pick up Weimar brochure.

11:10 Talked to salesman about the owner of the Castaway Club.

12:00 Saw John Newman [Newnam] at the [Dallas Morning] news talked to him for few minutes, and then saw different people running back and forth, and went to watch the television set, and then heard the tragic news.

Called Eva [his sister] at home and she was hysterical John was standing nearby and knew Eva was crying so put the receiver to John's ear. Phone was ringing constantly and people were complaining about [the anti-JFK] ad in paper—Then John Newman comment to someone that they shouldn't have taken the ad, and he said that were his superiors and their was nothing he could do about it, and he said to someone standing nearby "that you saw the fellow when he paid for part of the ad.—called Chicago spoke to [his other sister] Eileen [Kaminsky].

II. Then I called Andy [Armstrong] at the club and told him I would be there in a little while. Left the news and drove back to the club, told Andy to call everyone that we wouldn't be open tonite. Larry [Crafard] was their also.

Called Alice [Nichols] at her office, and left RI2-6189 for her to call back.

Phoned Ralph Paul.

Called Al Druber in Calif. and apologized for not sending dog, and started to cry and had to hang up.

Delivery boy from Gibson's came by and I paid for some records and gave him some cards to take back with him.

2:30 P.M. Went to Rita delicattessen and bought quite a few [groceries] to take to Eve [Eva],

Arrived at Eves house and received a call from Andy to call Don Saf[f]ran, I called Don and he asked me if we were going to close, that the Cabena & Century Rooms were closing, and that he asked the other two clubs and didn't know yet, and I answered that I've made up my mind to close, and I didn't have to ask if anyone else was closing. That I already had decided to close by around 1:30 P.M. and then he asked me about Sat. and I said I didn't know yet, he said he would be there for another 45 min. that I could phone him back, and I hung up, and I said to her that were going to close, and I called Don back immediately and told him we were going to close Fri. & Sat. & Sun. and that it didn't take me long to make up my mind to decide. Then I called back again and spoke to Mr. Porter and to told him to tell Don that I wish we wouldn't tell the other clubs what I was going to do, that let them decide for themselves whether or not they should close.

I called the Morning news and the composing room, and [told] them to change my ad.

I called Dr. Jacobson about going to Synogaugue and asked what time service would be, also I called the synogaugue to inquire the time of the services.

7:30 Then had gone home to dress and go to the services. Stayed for services and said greetings to Rabbi and talked about Eve.

9:30 P.M. Then went into reception room and had some refreshments and said hello Joe Col[e]man, and Elaine.

11:15 From their went to Phils Delecatteson told counter man to make up sandwiches—called Sims of homicide, if he wanted sandwiches, and he said they were winding everything up and was going to tell the boys about my thoughts for them.

11:30 Then wanted to find phone number for K.L.I.F., because I wanted to bring sandwiches there.

Looked through my clothing and every place I could think of but couldn't find Russ' number.

Tried to look for Russ Knight's number [(See WEIRD BEARD.)] but couldn't find it, then called information, but somehow couldn't remember Russ's real name. However, I dialed information and tried anyway, and mentioned that his name was Roberts and that he lived on Northwest Highway, but she couldn't help me.

Then I decided to call the Gordon McLendon home, and asked a young lady if anyone else was at home, and told her my name, but she said there wasn't anyone else at home, and I asked her name, and I think she said Christine, and told her I wanted to bring sandwiches to the station and could she get me the number, and she said her mother already had brought some food, then she left and gave me a Riverside number which was discontinued. I had made so many calls that the woman behind the counter asked if I would like to use the business phone, but I told her I was through.

The counter man helped me with the sandwiches, and thanked him for making such wonderful sandwiches for a good cause, and told him if he ever wanted to come down to the club he was welcome.

Drove down to the station to look for Joe Long [actually Gary DeLaune] to try to find the number so I could get into the radio station, parked car with dog on corner of Harvard & Commerce, and thought I would run up for a minute just to get number.

12:00 MID. Taken the elevator to 2nd or 3rd fl. and asked policemen if he knew Joe Long from K.L.I.F., and he let me go by.

Ran into some officers I knew, and even had asked a police-officer if he could help me, and he called out loudly through the hall, but no answer to the page.

At different intervals I would spot check and ask someone if they were Joe Long.

Then as I was standing in the hallway they brought the prisoner [Oswald] out, that was the first time I had ever seen him, I don't recall if he was with Capt. Fritz or Chief Curry or both.

Then the reporters shouted if there was a better place they could gather so as to have room for all the reporters.

The authorities said they would go down to the assembly room in the basement, and that is where I had gone too.

They brought the prisoner out and he mumbled something unintelligable and it wasn't [long] before they had taken him back again.

Then Henry Wade started to answer many questions whether or not he was the man.

Then everyone left the room, and two fellows walked by as I was walking out of the room, one I had recognized who had worked at a service station across from the Vegas Club but I asked the other fellow if he was Joe Long, and he asked why, and I said I had some sandwiches to bring to K.L.I.F. and I couldn't get in, unless I had the right phone number and he said we are from K.B.O.X. what about them, and I said next time, and he did give me the number, and I spoke to the other fellow for a minute and was surprised he was working for radio, I believe his name was Sam.

I went around the desk and dialed the number, and spoke to some disk jockey by name of Ken, and I told him I had sandwiches for the boys, and he was very [pleased] about it, but then I suddenly said you would like to talk to Henry Wade and to have his tape ready, and he became very excited and said definitely yes. Wade was on the phone talking to New York I believe, to another radio station I surely though[t] he wouldn't object to talking to this other disk-jockey, and I shouted to Mr. Wade just as he was about to hang up the receiver, or perhaps they were waiting for someone to come to the phone, and I did get him to leave and he did talk to this fellow, when they had finished I got on the phone again and he was thrilled and didn't know how to thank me enough, and said if I would leave immediately they would leave the door open for me.

As I was leaving and walked up one flight of stairs, I saw Russ Knight talking to someone and he seemed to be asking for information. What he was asking was where the assembly room was, and then he saw me, and I immediately told him that I got an interview with Henry Wade for his station and replied that is what he come for, and I said follow me, and taken him to Henry Wade and shouted here is Russ Knight Henry and he answered Oh! The Weird Beard!!!

Then I left and drove over to K.L.I.F. but the door was closed, because I had taken too much time getting there. Waited for Rus[s] for about 15 minutes and we both had gone up, he was so happy for what I had done that he definitely was going to tell Gordon McLendon what I had accomplished.

They started to work in splicing the tape in bringing both interviews together somehow. They called the New York and told them they had a story for them.

We all started in on the sandwiches and soft drinks, and they certainly enjoyed them.

We talked about a number of things, and I mentioned how much respect I had for Gordon, that he was the only one who came out with an editorial after the incident with Adlai Stevenson. Russ Knight had agreed with me. Mentioned that the prisoner resembled a very popular movie actor [Paul Newman]. Also that he had a scratch on his forehead and a little discoloring around his eye.

2:00 Russ had made the 2:00 A.M. news bulletin and put the Henry Wade interview on the air.

Russ and I had left and we spoke on the way to my car, and I mentioned that I had some literature I picked up at the H. L. Hunt's exhibit at the Texas States Invention at Market Hall. Told him he could have some, that I was certain I had copy for myself. Also mentioned the way Hunt was told he could pull out of the New York's World Fair.

Said good nite to Russ and drove on . . .

Went to the Times Herald to bring a twist board I had promised to Pat Godosh for some time. Went to composing room and demonstrated board, a few of printers gathered around and they enjoyed my agile way of doing it.

2:30 Then the subject came with a woman who works in a little anteroom about the big ad the news had taken, and I remarked don't worry, the phones were ringing off the desks, and people were cancelling subscriptions, and ads from all over the United States.

Told Pat to put my ad in that I was closing.

I had taken the elevator down and spoke to the nite watchman at the door for a few minutes, and got in my car and drove home, and then awakened George [Senator], and he said he had seen my ads in the newspaper that I was closing for three days, and we talked about the tragedy, and he was heartbroken too!

3:30 A.M. I made him [Senator] get out of bed and told him I wanted him to go with me, and called Larry [Crafard] at the club got him out of bed and asked him if he knew how to work a polaroid camera, and he said yes, I told him to be down in the garage in ten minutes with the camera and bring plenty of film and bulbs. George and I got to the garage and he wasn't there, and I became impatient thinking that he may have gone back to bed again, and had nite man call him, and he said he would be right down.

4:00 A.M. We drove to E. Ross and Expressway and took photos of a billboard that read

IMPEACH EARL WARREN
WRITE TO BELTHAM
BOX 1757 MASS.

The above sign was above another sign that read POTTER'S WROUGHT IRON, Located somewhere on Expressway.

We had taken three snapshots of same, then stopped at post-office asked man how does it happen that they have given a box to person placing an ad of that sort in the newspaper. He said he didn't have a thing to do with it. He went and checked again and said their was a person and that is all he could answer me. I went to look at the amount of mail that Box 1792, and tried to make certain I would remember if the contents would be removed the next time I'd stop by. George was with me, and Larry was sitting in the car.

From there we had gone to Habb's Coffee Shop in the Southland Hotel, they had some coffee and I had some juice. I spoke to the owner for about a minute. I don't recall what I had said to him, perhaps about hunting?

However, when I got back to the apartment I decided I would go to bed.

It wasn't long before I got a phone call, and it was Larry, and I asked him what did he want very angrily, and he wanted to know what kind of dog food he should buy, then I asked what time it was, and when [he] said 8:30 A.M. I bawled the heck out of him for getting me up at this early hour forgetting that I had mentioned that I wasn't going to bed, and then hung up on him. 8:30 A.M. SAT.

11:00 A.M. That same morning I phoned Andy or he may have called me and he said that Larry had left, that he had given the key to Mac at the garage and to tell me thanks for everything, and later Andy said that he took seven dollars from the cash register, and I felt quite sad and guilty because [he] was a wonderful person.

That same morning I think George also had stayed in the apartment and watched television, and we watched all of the dignitaries pull up in their limousines to go and pay their last respects, and my heart was just broke, because of all these wonderful people. And how they grieved for their friend and beloved president.

Then I watched on television a memorial given by some synogaugue and a Rabbi Saligman of New York for Sabbath services in honor of the late President Kennedy, and it just tore me apart when he said to think that our president had untold courage to combat anything and everywhere and then to be struck down by some enemy from behind.

I really don't know what time I left the apartment, and Andy said that he phoned me or I phoned him.

I drove towards town and either had gone to the club first or had gone to look at the wreaths?

I pulled my car north on Houston St. past Elm St. to park my car, their was a policeman on that corner guiding the heavy traffic, and I walked down Elm St. toward the underpass and saw officer Chaney their, I've known him for many years, and had asked him which one of the windows was used and he pointed or described it to me. We talked for a few minutes and then I couldn't talk anymore and had to walk off because I was choking and holding my tears back.

Walked up on the north bank of Elm to look at the wreaths and started to cry when I read the car[d] on one that read "We Grieve For You."

Then I said to myself that I was going to send flowers.

Walked a little further down Elm closer to the underpass and started to make it across the other side where the Plaza is located so as to see the rest of the wreaths, but the traffic was bearing down to[o] fast and had to wait a minute. However, I was determined to get across regardless of what would happen to me, and I finally dashed across recklessly, and people driving must have thought I was crazy, because the cars were speeding very fast at that point.

Saw the wreaths on the Plaza and started to cry again. Crossed over to the other side of Houston St., and walked north to cross over Elm.

As a reached the other side of Elm and about 50 ft. from the corner, I ran into Wes Wise parked in a K.R.L.D. News car, and stopped to talk and he mentioned that I get a scoop for K.L.I.F. and I said it was just a little something that happened, and didn't talk more about it.

3:00 P.M.? Got into my car and must have circled back either to the club first or had gone to Sol's Turf Lounge, I had gone their to look up my accountant Abe Kleinman went in and heard a lot of comment about the big ad in the news, and they were complaining why a newspaper would take such an ad. Mr. Kleinman was their and jewelry designer by name of Be[l]loc[c]hio. It became quite a discussion, and heard Belochio say that he is leaving Dallas and was very emphatic about it, that his mind was made. I jumped all over him telling him that Dallas was good enough for him when he was making his living here, and now he wants to quit and run. I kept repeating don't say that because you will start something we won't be able to stop.

Then I had taken out my three photos of impeach Earl Warren, and he could not believe that it could happen here, and he became very beligerent that he wanted one and I practically had to fight him off from taking one from me. I said I've got a special purpose for these. I'm going to give them to Gordon McLendon so he can run an editorial on soon. He insisted that I show the picture to a fellow sitting at the bar, because he knew the Potter's and surely they wouldn't allow something like that. Abe Kleinman was witness to all this. SAT. 3:30 P.M.

From there we went to sister Val's [Eva?] apartment, and told her I wanted to send some flowers to the Plaza, but she said not to have the same place when I ordered for her when she was at Caston Hosp. The nurse told her one of plants or flowers were stale.

Then I told Eve I was tired after watching television for awhile and took the phone with me to her bedroom and called Russ Knight and told him I had more pictures and he said that was swell to hold them for awhile, that this wasn't the time for it. That he would tell Gordon about it. Their was also something about Leonard Woods and Eve and I spoke about my visiting Chicago 3 days.

Then I must have called Stanley Kaufman and also told him about the photos, and he thought that was wonderful as to what I was going to do with them. I believe he told me that some persons checked about the person that placed the ad. Didn't have any residence in Dallas that their wasn't any such person in this area. I told him how I checked the box number etc.

SAT. Then I think I had taken a nap, and awakened and then had gone down to the club, and Andy was cleaning, and he thought he was going to get off early, and I insisted that he will have to stay until 9:00 P.M. and gave him an ultimatum that it would have to be that way. I may have called Ralph Paul and told him we were closing.

I called the Adolphus Hotel and asked for Joe Petersen, they said he left town for three days, they gave me the phone number in Galveston and I called and talked to Joe or Breck [Wall]? and told them that I had closed for three days and they said they also wanted to get away.

SAT. 8:00 P.M. Had gone back to my apartment and showered and shaved. Phoned Andy and told him about the new girl and to go over and catch the show over at the Colony Club, and to see about the audition show and I would give them their money back.

10:20 SAT. Phoned Eve and asked her if she was watching television.

10:30 P.M. Drove to town and drove out to Bob Horton at the Pogo Club, and a girl came over and asked me what I would like and I ordered a coke but didn't feel like drinking it, I sat for about 15 or 20 minutes, and didn't want anyone to recognize me, because I didn't want to explain to anyone why, if I didn't want to dance or to have a drink. I sort of sat in a shell and didn't want to be recognized. Bob Horton came over and apologized saying he didn't know I was there or he would have been there sooner. 11:00 P.M.

We talked and he started to explain why he remained open etc. I stopped him and didn't want to hear any of it. That was his business.

Told him that my type of entertainment was different than his, my was burlesque, and I wouldn't want the performers to put on our type of show at a time like this. Anyway, I liked Bob too much as a friend to make him feel uneasy in my presence. SAT.

He gave me $25.00 and I asked him for what, and he explained and I refused to take it but he insisted. Said good-nite and drove downtown and pulled into the garage asked the attendant something and then drove to my apartment. SAT.

12:40 A.M. Phoned Eve and told her something asked why she didn't go to bed. SUN.

SUN. 10:00 A.M. Received call from Lynn [Karen "Little Lynn" Bennet Carlin], said she had to have some money, told her that I don't have to let her draw money, that all I'm obligated to do was to pay her salary, but she said she had to pay her rent, and then it dawned on me that we are going to be closed tonite, and thought she may desperately need some money and then I said how can I get the money to you, and I think she said she will come to my apartment but I certainly didn't want that because of her supposed to be husband, and that is all I would need for them to know where I live. I took time to ask her how to send it, because all I know her by was Little Lynn, I think I wrote her name out and spelled it Karren Bennet, and asked her if she knew where the Western Union was in Ft. Worth. By the way she said she was broke, and didn't have a penny, and I asked her if she get it somewhere else, and she could return it the next day, and then I think I asked her where

husband was and I thought he would let her have the money but I think she said he was out of town.—Anyway I told her it would be in care of Will Call Western ($25.00) George Senator was there during all this. SUN. A.M.

Then left the apartment and spoke to a neighbor for a minute—Curtiss?—about some fences I promised him then left to go to Western Union to send money to Lynn. 10:45 A.M.

Was always in the habit of taking the freeway straight down Commerce St., but since the tragedy have been going by to see the wreaths, and remember their would be more traffic on Main St., because it is where their is more activity going on than Commerce St., and if I was in a hurry to get anywhere I certainly would have stayed on Commerce, especially Sunday, the street is dead. 10:45 A.M.

Anyway I passed the intersection where I was to turn left and then right on Industrial, so I could pass where the wreaths were and at the same time drive towards the Western Union. I backed up in reverse, so as to make correct turn.

10:50 Did pass where all the wreaths were and then passed the County Jail on the left and saw the largest crowd I had ever seen there, and thought to myself that they already have transferred the prisoner, and continued to drive on the Western Union, and pulled in to a parking lot on the left. Waited my turn, because the clerk was waiting on someone else, and I filled out a form to send money. When I passed by the station, I looked down the ramp to my right and saw a lot of people down in the basement so when I finished with the Western, I had walked west and down the ramp just out of curiosity. When I walked by to go down the ramp I saw this officer guide a car out of the upper portions of the ramp, and thought the officer was there only to guide the cars coming out. I continued walking down the ramp and just hit the bottom part of the ramp. That is all I remember.

APPENDIX C

JFK ASSASSINATION IN FILM AND VIDEO

The American Assassins (1975)   Columbia Broadcasting System. Dan Rather, host. Originally shown on CBS on November 25, 1975.

Best Evidence, The Research Video (1990)   Rhino Video. Shows many of the interviews used in David Lifton's book of the same name.

Beyond JFK: Question of Conspiracy (1992)   Directors: Danny Schechter and Barbara Kopple. Attempts to present Jim Garrison's case in the larger context of political ferment in the 1960s, the other political assassinations of the era, and the Oliver Stone movie *JFK*.

CBS New Inquiry: The Warren Report (1967)   Columbia Broadcasting System. Walter Cronkite, host. Originally broadcast on CBS in four parts on June 25–28, 1967.

Confession of an Assassin: The Murder of JFK (1996) This documentary features an interview with one James E. Files. Files claims to be one of JFK's assassins. (See also FILES, JAMES E.)

Deep Politics in the United States: The Banana Connection (1993)   Cinema Guild. Interviews with Peter Dale Scott.

Executive Action (1973)   Director: David Miller; featuring Burt Lancaster, Robert Ryan, Will Geer, John Anderson, Ed Lauter, and Dick Miller. This film theorizes multiple shooters hired by a wealthy conservative idealogue (seemingly in the energy industry) for whom the president's policies are distasteful. Based on the book by Mark Lane and Donald Freed.

Fake (1990)   JFK Video Group. Video by Jack White about the backyard photos of Oswald.

Fatal Deception: Mrs. Lee Harvey Oswald (1993)   Director: Robert Dornhelm; featuring Helena Bonham Carter as Marina Oswald and Frank Whaley as Lee Harvey Oswald. Made for television (NBC).

Four Days in Dallas (See *Ruby and Oswald*.)

Four Days in November (1964)   Wolper Productions/United Artists. Compilation of news and amateur film footage depicting events in Dallas and Washington, D.C., during the assassination weekend.

Image of an Assassination: The Zapruder Film (1994) The first commercially available video version of the legendary 26-second "Zapruder Film." Digitally re-mastered, this film includes a frame-by-frame analysis of the original 8mm film and some additional footage from Dallas that day.

In the Line of Fire (1993)   Director: Wolfgang Petersen; featuring Clint Eastwood, John Malkovich, Rene Russo, Dylan McDermott, and Gary Cole. This fictional account of an aging Secret Service agent desperate to protect a president under threat refers to the JFK assassination in the past tense. The agent was with the motorcade in Dealey Plaza on the fateful day, and failed to save the president's life.

JFK (1991)   Director: Oliver Stone; featuring Kevin Costner as Jim Garrison, Joe Pesci as David Ferrie, Kevin Bacon as a composite character based on Perry Raymond Russo and Vernon Bundy, Tommy Lee Jones as Clay Shaw, Ed Asner as Guy Banister, Jack Lemmon as Jack Martin, John Candy as Dean Andrews. In this well-made docudrama, Stone postulates a military-industrial plot to kill JFK in order to goad LBJ into escalating the war in Vietnam. Based on Jim Garrison's book, *On the Trail of the Assassins*, Stone focuses on the New Orleans suspects surrounding Clay Shaw. Garrison himself appears in the film portraying Chief Justice Earl Warren. This film was heavily criticized in the mainstream media many months before its release. The film was credited with inciting public opinion leading to creation by Congress of the JFK Records Review Act.

Cast of the 1991 Oliver Stone film *JFK*.   *(Author's Collection)*

The JFK Assassination: The Jim Garrison Tapes (1992)
This film by John Barbour accurately portrays the New
Orleans district attorney's case for a combined FBI, CIA,
and Cuban exile collaboration conspiracy theory. Includes
a candid interview with Garrison himself. A Blue
Ridge/Film Trust Film, released on video by Vestron Video.

The JFK Conspiracy (1992)   James Earl Jones hosts this
documentary, which contains photographs, documents,
most of the Zapruder film, and interviews with eyewitnesses. The selling point, however, is a brief interview with
Oliver Stone. All American Communications.

The Manchurian Candidate (1962)   Director: John Fran-
henheimer; featuring Frank Sinatra and Laurence Harvey.
This fictional account of a veteran army captain of the
Korean War who discovers that he and his men were
brainwashed by communists has the quiet distinction of
being the first movie about the assassination of JFK that
was actually made before the assassination. It also happened to be one of Kennedy's favorite movies. In this
movie, a sargeant is transformed into an assassin. For
those theorists who are concerned with mind control and
MK/ULTRA, this is a perfect example of how that program
might have worked.

The Many Faces of Lee Harvey Oswald (1991)   JFK
Videos. Video by Jack White.

The Mark Lane Tapes (1992)   Grey Wizard Videos.

The Men Who Killed Kennedy (1995)   A&E Home Video.
Director: Nigel Turner. This five-part documentary was
originally made for and aired on the A&E network. It
explores many different conspiracy theories, but finally
settles on the Corsican assassin Jean Soutre. Turner shows
many of the most interesting photographs of the event,
and the interviews are of a higher caliber than most. See
also *The Truth Will Set You Free.*

Naughty Dallas (1994 re-release)   Director: Larry
Buchanan; featuring Jada, Breck Wall, and Toni Shannon.
This fictional film is the story of Toni Shannon, a small-
town Texas girl who goes to the big city to become an
exotic dancer. An early 1960s nudie movie, many of the
people in the film were to be associated with the assassination through Jack Ruby, whose Carousel Club was used as
one of the locations in the film. Jada was one of Ruby's
dancers, and Breck Wall was a friend of Ruby's. One audience shot shows a man who bears an uncanny resemblance
to Oswald-look-alike Kerry Wendell Thornley. Remarkable.

The Parallax View (1974)   Director: Alan J. Pakula; featuring Warren Beatty, Hume Cronyn, Paula Prentiss, and
William Daniels. A fictional account of a journalist's

exploration of an assassination atop Seattle's Space Needle. In pursuit of the truth, the journalist stumbles upon a corporate assassination cabal, called Parallax. (See PERMINDEX.)

The Plot to Kill JFK (1966)   MPI Home Video. Formerly known as *Rush to Judgment*, and made to accompany Mark Lane's book of that name.

Reasonable Doubt (1988)   White Star Videos. Can be seen frequently on the A&E cable television network.

Ruby (1992)   Director: John Mackenzie; featuring Danny Aiello as Jack Ruby and Sherilyn Fenn as a fictional stripper who works in his club. The assassination told from the point of view of Jack Ruby. The film entertains a broad conspiracy theory, including Cuban exiles, the CIA, and, most important (for Ruby), the mob. No overarching solution to the riddle of who was behind the conspiracy is addressed. The film does portray Ruby as a professional killer who once killed a man in Cuba with a gun that looked like a movie camera.

Ruby and Oswald (1978)   Director: Mel Stuart; featuring Michael Lerner as Jack Ruby, Doris Roberts as sister Eva, and Frederic Forrest as Lee Harvey Oswald. Made for TV docudrama, this speculative reenactment of the days leading up to the JFK assassination sticks to the known "facts," eschewing any particular conspiracy theories. Also known as *Four Days in Dallas*.

The Trial of Lee Harvey Oswald (1964)   Director: Larry Buchanan; featuring Arthur Nations and George Russell. Imaginary docudrama presenting a possible version of Oswald's trial (had he only lived long enough!). Actual newsreel footage is mixed with courtroom scenes in this clueless recapitulation of the Warren Commission's conclusions. By the director of *Naughty Dallas!*

The Trial of Lee Harvey Oswald (1978)   Director: Richard Freed; featuring John Pleshette as Lee Harvey Oswald, Ben Gazzara, Lorne Green, Frances Lee McCain. Made for TV

imaginary docudrama based on Amram Ducovny and Leon Friedman's play of the same name. This speculative courtroom drama imagines a trial wherein the flimsy evidence against Oswald is exposed as such. No particular theories as to what really happened are entertained, only Oswald's acquittal is obvious.

"The Truth Will Set You Free" (1995)   A&E Home Video. Produced by Nigel Turner, this is actually episode 6 of *The Men Who Killed Kennedy*.

"The Warren Omission", episode 12 of *Dark Skies* (1997) Director: Perry Lang; featuring Eric Close, Megan Ward, and J. T. Walsh. Fictional TV series episode postulates the UFO Majestic-12 conspiracy as the true purpose behind both Kennedy assassinations.

Who Killed JFK? Facts Not Fiction (1992)   Another attempt to prove the lone-gunman theory. A "Special CBS News Home Video Presentation of a '48 Hours' Production." Host: Dan Rather. Released by Fox Video.

"Who Really Killed President Kennedy?" *Geraldo* TV episode (1991)   Relatively inconsequential documentary put together by TV journalist Geraldo Rivera. Interviews some eyewitnesses, but fails to offer any new revelations.

"Who Was Lee Harvey Oswald?" (1993)   Producers: William Cran, Mike Sullivan, and Ben Loeterman. Reporters: W. Scott Malone, Gus Russo. Originally shown on the Public Broadcasting System show *Frontline*, this three-hour documentary attempts to shed light on Oswald's confusing life, with a special focus on his stay in the Soviet Union, using recently released Soviet files on Oswald.

Winter Kills (1979)   Director: William Richert; featuring Jeff Bridges, John Huston, and Anthony Perkins. Based on the novel by Richard Condon this fictional drama—or is it a black comedy?—tells the tale of a younger brother of an assassinated U.S. president who investigates his brother's murder, only to find his own life threatened by the very same political forces that took his brother's life.

APPENDIX D

CONCLUSION OF THE HOUSE SELECT COMMITTEE ON ASSASSINATIONS

The Committee believes, on the basis of the evidence available to it, that president John F. Kennedy was probably assassinated as a result of a conspiracy. The committee is unable to identify the other gunman or the extent of the conspiracy.

Supreme Court Justice Oliver Wendell Holmes once simply defined conspiracy as "a partnership in criminal purposes." That definition is adequate. Nevertheless, it may be helpful to set out a more precise definition. If two or more individuals agreed to take action to kill President Kennedy, and at least one of them took action in further-ance of the plan, and it resulted in President Kennedy's death, the President would have been assassinated as a result of a conspiracy.

The committee recognizes, of course, that while the word "conspiracy" technically denotes only a "partnership in criminal purposes," it also, in fact, connotes widely varying meanings to many people, and its use has vastly differing societal implications depending upon the sophis-tication, extent and ultimate purpose of the partnership. For example, a conspiracy to assassinate a President might be a complex plot orchestrated by foreign political powers; it might be the scheme of a group of American citizens dis-satisfied with particular governmental policies; it also might be the plan of two largely isolated individuals with no readily discernible motive.

Conspiracies may easily range, therefore, from those with important implications for social or governmental institutions to those with no major societal significance. As the evidence concerning the probability that President Kennedy was assassinated as a result of a "conspiracy" is analyzed, these various connotations of the word "con-spiracy" and distinctions between them ought to be con-stantly borne in mind. Here, as elsewhere, words must be used carefully, lest people be misled.

A conspiracy cannot be said to have existed in Dealey Plaza unless evidence exists from which, in Justice Holmes' words, a "partnership in criminal purposes" may be inferred. The Warren Commission's conclusion that Lee Harvey Oswald was not involved in a conspiracy to assas-sinate the President was, for example, largely based on its findings of the absence of evidence of significant associa-tion between Oswald and other possible conspirators and no physical evidence of conspiracy. The Commission rea-soned, quite rightly, that in the absence of association or physical evidence, there was no conspiracy.

Even without physical evidence of conspiracy at the scene of the assassination, there would, of course, be a conspiracy if others assisted Oswald in his efforts. Accord-ingly, an examination of Oswald's associates is necessary. The Warren Commission recognized that a first premise in a finding of conspiracy may be a finding of association. Because the Commission did not find any significant Oswald associates, it was not compelled to face the diffi-cult questions posed by such a finding. More than associa-tion is required to establish conspiracy. There must be at least knowing assistance or a manifestation of agreement to the criminal purpose by the associate.

It is important to realize, too, that the term "associate" may connote widely varying meanings to different people. A person's associate may be his next door neighbor and vacation companion, or it may be an individual he has met only once for the purpose of discussing a contract for a murder. The Warren Commission examined Oswald's past and concluded he was essentially a loner. It reasoned, therefore, that since Oswald had no significant associa-tions with persons who could have been involved with him in the assassination, there could not have been a con-spiracy.

With respect to Jack Ruby, the Warren Commission similarly found no significant associations, either between Ruby and Oswald or between Ruby and others who might have been conspirators with him. In particular, it found no connections between Ruby and organized crime, and it reasoned that absent such associations, there was no conspiracy to kill Oswald or the President. The committee conducted a three-pronged investigation of conspiracy in the Kennedy assassination. On the basis of extensive scientific analysis and an analysis of the testimony of Dealey Plaza witnesses, the committee found there was a high probability that two gunmen fired at President Kennedy.

Second, the committee explored Oswald's and Ruby's contacts for any evidence of significant associations. Unlike the Warren Commission, it found certain of these contacts to be of investigative significance. The Commission apparently had looked for evidence of conspiratorial association. Finding none on the face of the associations it investigated, it did not go further. The committee, however, conducted a wider ranging investigation. Notwithstanding the possibility of a benign reason for contact between Oswald or Ruby and one of their associates, the committee examined the very fact of the contact to see if it contained investigative significance. Unlike the Warren Commission, the committee took a close look at the associates to determine whether conspiratorial activity in the assassination could have been possible, given what the committee could learn about the associates, and whether the apparent nature of the contact should, therefore, be examined more closely.

Third, the committee examined groups, political organizations, national governments and so on that might have had the motive, opportunity and means to assassinate the President.

The committee, therefore, directly introduced the hypothesis of conspiracy and investigated it with reference to known facts to determine if it had any bearing on the assassination.

The committee examined a series of major groups or organizations that have been alleged to have been involved in a conspiracy to assassinate the President. If any of these groups or organizations, as a group, had been involved in the assassination, the conspiracy to assassinate President Kennedy would have been one of major significance.

As will be detailed in succeeding sections of this report, the committee did not find sufficient evidence that any of these groups or organizations were involved in a conspiracy in the Kennedy assassination. Accordingly, the committee concluded, on the basis of the evidence available to it, that the Soviet government, the Cuban government, anti-Castro Cuban groups, and the national syndicate of organized crime were not involved in the assassination. Further, the committee found that the Secret Service, the Federal Bureau of Investigation, and the Central Intelligence Agency were not involved in the assassination.

Based on the evidence available to it, the committee could not preclude the possibility that individual members of anti-Castro Cuban groups or the national syndicate of organized crime were involved in the assassination. There was insufficient evidence, however, to support a finding that any individual members were involved. The ramifications of a conspiracy involving such individuals would be significant, although of perhaps less import than would be the case if a group itself, the national syndicate, for example, had been involved.

The committee recognized that a finding that two gunmen fired simultaneously at the President did not, by itself, establish that there was a conspiracy to assassinate the President. It is theoretically possible that the gunmen were acting independently, each totally unaware of the other. It was the committee's opinion, however, that such a theoretical possibility is extremely remote. The more logical and probable inference to be drawn from two gunmen firing at the same person at the same time and in the same place is that they were acting in concert, that is, as a result of a conspiracy.

The committee found that, to be precise and loyal to the facts it established, it was compelled to find that President Kennedy was probably killed as a result of a conspiracy. The committee's finding that President Kennedy was probably assassinated as a result of a conspiracy was premised on four factors:

(1) Since the Warren Commission's and FBI's investigation into the possibility of a conspiracy was seriously flawed, their failure to develop evidence of a conspiracy could not be given independent weight.

(2) The Warren Commission was, in fact, incorrect in concluding that Oswald and Ruby had no significant associations, and therefore its finding of no conspiracy was not reliable.

(3) While it cannot be inferred from the significant associations of Oswald and Ruby that any of the major groups examined by the committee were involved in the assassination, a more limited conspiracy could not be ruled out.

(4) There was a high probability that a second gunman, in fact, fired at the President.

At the same time, the committee candidly stated, in expressing its finding of conspiracy in the Kennedy assassination, that it was "unable to identify the other gunman or the extent of the conspiracy."

The photographic and other scientific evidence available to the committee was insufficient to permit the committee to answer these questions. In addition, the committee's other investigative efforts did not develop evidence from which Oswald's conspirator or conspirators could be firmly identified. It is possible, of course, that the extent of the conspiracy was so limited that it involved only Oswald and the second gunman. The committee was not able to reach such a conclusion, for it would have been based on speculation, not evidence. Aspects of the investigation did suggest that the conspiracy may have been relatively limited, but to state with precision exactly how small was not possible. Other aspects of the committee's investigation did suggest, however, that while the conspiracy may not have involved a major group, it may not have been limited to only two people. These aspects of the committee's investigation are discussed elsewhere. If the conspiracy to assassinate President Kennedy was limited to Oswald and a second gunman, its main societal significance may be in the realization that agencies of the U.S. Government inadequately investigated the possibility of such a conspiracy. In terms of its implications for government and society, an assassination as a consequence of a conspiracy composed solely of Oswald and a small number of persons, possibly only one, and possibly a person akin to Oswald in temperament and ideology, would not have been fundamentally different from an assassination by Oswald alone.

(1) It might be suggested that because of the widely varying meanings attached to the word "conspiracy," it ought to be avoided. Such a suggestion, however, raises another objection the search for euphemistic variations can lead to a lack of candor. There is virtue in seeing something for what it is, even if the plain truth causes discomfort.

(2) The Warren Commission devoted its Appendix XVI to a biography of Jack Ruby in which his family background, psychological makeup, education and business activities were considered. While the evidence was sometimes contradictory, the Commission found that Ruby grew up in Chicago, the son of Jewish immigrants; that he lived in a home disrupted by domestic strife, that he was troubled psychologically as a youth and not educated beyond high school; and that descriptions of his temperament ranged from "mild mannered" to "violent." In 1963 Ruby was 52 and unmarried. He ran a Dallas nightclub but was not particularly successful in business. His acquaintances included a number of Dallas police officers who frequented his nightclub, as well as other types of people who comprised his clientele.

(3) The committee found associations of both Ruby and Oswald that were unknown to the Warren Commission.

(4) If the conspiracy were, in fact, limited to Oswald, the second gunman, and perhaps one or two others, the committee believes it was possible they shared Oswald's left-wing political disposition. A consistent pattern In Oswald's life was a propensity for actions with political overtones. It is quite likely that an assassination conspiracy limited to Oswald and a few associates was in keeping with that pattern.

Further, it is possible that associates of Oswald in the Kennedy assassination had been involved with him in earlier activities. Two possibilities: the attempt on the life of Gen. Edwin A. Walker in April 1963 and the distribution of Fair Play for Cuba Committee literature in August 1963. With respect to the Walker incident, there was substantial evidence that Oswald did the shooting, although at the time of the shooting it was not sufficient to implicate Oswald or anyone else. It was not until after the Kennedy assassination that Oswald became a suspect in the Walker attack, based on the testimony of his widow Marina. Marina's characterization of Oswald is more consistent with his having shot at Walker alone than his having assistance, although at the time of the shooting there was testimony that tended to indicate more than one person was involved. Further, it is not necessary to believe all of what Marina said about the incident or to believe that Oswald told her all there was to know, since either of them might have been concealing the involvement of others.

According to a general offense report of the Dallas police, Walker reported at approximately 9:10 P.M. on April 10, 1963, that a bullet had been fired through a first floor window of his home at 4011 Turtle Creek Boulevard, Dallas. Detectives subsequently found that a bullet had first shattered a window, then gone through a wall and had landed on a stack of papers in an adjoining room. In their report the detectives described the bullet as steel-jacketed of unknown caliber.

Police located a 14-year-old boy in Walker's neighborhood who said that after hearing the shot, he climbed a fence and looked into an alley to the rear of Walker's home. The boy said he then saw some men speeding down the alley in a light green or light blue Ford, either a 1959 or 1960 model. He said he also saw another car, a 1958 Chevrolet, black with white down the side, in a church parking lot adjacent to Walker's house. The car door was open, and a man was bending over the back seat, as though he was placing something on the floor of the car.

On the night of the incident, police interviewed Robert Surrey, an aide to Walker. Surrey said that on Saturday, April 6, at about 9 P.M., he had seen two men sitting in a dark purple or brown 1963 Ford at the rear of Walker's house. Surrey also said the two men got out of the car and walked around the house. Surrey said he was suspicious and followed the car, noting that it carried no license plate.

If it could be shown that Oswald had associates in the attempt on General Walker they would be likely candidates as the grassy knoll gunman. The committee recognized however, that this is speculation, since the existence, much less identity, of an Oswald associate in the Walker shooting was hardly established. Further, the committee failed in its effort to develop productive leads in the Walker shooting.

With respect to the Cuba literature incident, Oswald was photographed with two associates distributing pro-Castro pamphlets in August, 1963. As a result of a fight with anti-Castro Cubans, Oswald was arrested, but his associates were not. Of the two associates, only one was identified in the Warren Commission investigation. Although the second associate was clearly portrayed in photographs, the Commission was unable to identify him, as was the case with the committee.

Select Committee on Assassinations

Louis Stokes, Ohio, Chairman

Richardson Preyer, North Carolina
Walter E. Fauntroy, District of Columbia
Yvonne Brathwaite Burke, California
Christopher J. Dodd, Connecticut
Harold E. Ford, Tennessee

Floyd J. Fithian, Indiana
Robert W. Edgar, Pennsylvania
Samuel L. Devine, Ohio
Stewart B. Mckiney, Connecticut
Charles Thone, Nebraska
Harold S. Sawyer, Michigan

Subcommittee on the Assassination of John F. Kennedy

Richardson Preyer, Chairman

Yvonne Brathwaite Burke
Christopher J. Dodd
Charles Thone
Harold S. Sawyer
Louis Stokes, Ex Officio
Samuel L. Devine, Ex Officio

Staff

G. Robert Blakey, Chief Counsel and Director

Gene Johnson, Deputy Chief Counsel
Gary Cornwell, Deputy Chief Counsel

BIBLIOGRAPHY

Abrahamsen, David, M. D. "A Study of Lee Harvey Oswald." *New York Academy of Medicine Bulletin* 43, no. 10 (October 1967): 861–888.

Abrams, Malcolm. "I'm Being Framed As JFK's Killer," *Midnight/Globe,* November 29, 1977. Article concerns Frank Sturgis.

Adelson, Alan. *The Ruby Oswald Affair.* Seattle, Wash.: Romar Books, 1988. Written by one of Jack Ruby's lawyers.

Adler, Bill. *The Weight of the Evidence: The Warren Report and Its Critics.* New York: Meredith, 1968.

"Afterword: The Search for 'Maurice Bishop.'" *Lobster* 10, January 1986, p. 13.

Alleged Assassination Plots Involving Foreign Leaders: An Interim Report of the Select Committee to Study Governmental Operations with Respect to Intelligence Activities, U.S. Senate, Washington, D.C.: U.S. Government Printing Office, 1975.

"Alleged Oswald Letter Checked for Its Authenticity by FBI Agents." *Dallas Morning News,* February 6, 1977.

Altman, Lawrence K. "Doctors Affirm Kennedy Autopsy Report." *New York Times,* May 20, 1992, p. A1, B7.

Alvarez, Luis. "A Physicist Examines the Kennedy Assassination Film." *American Journal of Physics,* September 1976, pp. 813–827.

"A Matter of Reasonable Doubt." *Life,* November 24, 1966.

Ambrose, Steven E. "Writers on the Grassy Knoll: A Reader's Guide." *New York Times Book Review,* February 2, 1992, pp. 23–25.

"American Communist Chief Dies." *Daily News,* October 17, 2000, p. 70. Obituary of Gus Hall, head of the American Communist Party.

"A New Theory: 3 French Gangsters Killed JFK." *Dallas Morning News,* October 26, 1988.

Angers, Bob. "Louisiana Editor Reports on Bringuier's Challenge to Mark Lane and James Garrison." *Lafayette (Louisiana) Advertiser,* January 14, 1968. Jim Garrison's name, by the way, was legally Jim, not James.

Anson, Robert Sam. "JFK the Movie: Oliver Stone Reshoots History." *Esquire,* November 1991.

———. *"They've Killed the President!"* New York: Bantam, 1975. The quotes are part of the title.

"Any Oswald-Rubenstein Tie in Dallas Sought by Police." *Dallas Morning News,* November 26, 1963.

Artwohl, Robert R. "JFK's Assassination: Conspiracy, Forensic Science, and Common Sense." *Journal of the American Medical Association* (March 24–31, 1993): 1540–1543.

"Assassination Inquiry Stumbling—Is Fensterwald a CIA Plant?" *Washington Star,* October 4, 1976.

"Assassination: Now a Suicide Talks." *Time,* April 11, 1977. About the death of George DeMohrenschildt.

"Assassination Story—The Reaction in Japan." *March of the News,* June 15, 1964.

"Assassination: The Trail to a Verdict." *Life,* October 2, 1964.

"Author Not the First to Ask Exhumation." *Fort Worth Star-Telegram,* January 11, 1979. The author is Michael H. B. Eddowes; the exhumation Oswald's.

"Autopsy on the Warren Commission." *Time,* September 16, 1966.

"Autopsy Photos Put in Archives by the Kennedys." *New York Times,* November 3, 1966, p. 1.

"Autopsy Studied Again." *New York Times,* April 26, 1975, p. 12. Article concerns JFK's autopsy, or lack thereof.

Autry, James A. "The Garrison Investigation: The Established Facts." *New Orleans,* April 1967, p. 8.

Aynesworth, Hugh. "Assassination in Dallas." *D Magazine,* November 1983.

———. "The JFK Conspiracy." *Newsweek,* May 15, 1967.

"Back Channels Talks with Gerry Hemming." *Back Channels,* Winter 1992, p. 22.

Backes, Joseph. "Rediscovering the DCA Film: President Kennedy's Last Hour." *The Third Decade,* May 1993, pp. 7–8.

Banta, Thomas J. "The Kennedy Assassination: Early Thoughts and Emotions." *Public Opinion Quarterly,* Summer 1964.

Barkdoll, Robert. "Kennedy Case Figure Died As He'd Lived." *Los Angeles Times,* April 3, 1977. Article about the death of George DeMohrenschildt.

Barry, Bill. "Assassination Idea Taped." *Miami News,* February 2, 1967. Regarding the taped statements of Joseph Milteer.

Battaile, Janet. "C.I.A. Says It Ousted Officer after a Search of House Unit's Files." *New York Times,* June 18, 1979. Regarding CIA Liaison Officer Regis Blahut who allegedly rifled the files of the House Select Committee on Assassinations.

Belin, David W. "The Case against Conspiracy." *New York Times Magazine,* July 15, 1979, p. 40.

———. "Connally's Wounds Held No Secrets." *New York Times,* June 25, 1993, p. A31.

———. *Final Disclosure.* New York: Charles Scribner's Sons, 1988. Oswald-did-it-alone book.

———. *November 22, 1963: You Be the Jury.* New York: Quadrangle Books, 1973.

Belli, Melvin, with Maurice C. Carroll. *Dallas Justice: The Real Story of Jack Ruby and His Trial.* New York: David, 1964.

Benson, Michael. *Who's Who in the JFK Assassination.* New York: Citadel, 1993.

Berendt, John. "'If They've Found Another Assassin, Let Them Name Names and Produce Their Evidence.'—Allen Dulles, July 1966; Name: Igor 'Turk' Vaganov. Evidence: See Below," *Esquire,* August 1967.

Bethell, Tom. "Conspiracy to End Conspiracies." *National Review,* December 16, 1991.

Bianculli, David. "Hoffa, Mob Killed JFK: Frontline." *New York Post,* November 17, 1992, p. 68–69. Review of that date's PBS *Frontline* broadcast, which names Hoffa as the mastermind behind JFK's death, while accusing Jim Garrison of being a disinformation artist, erroneously and egregiously pointing the guilty finger at the CIA.

Bickel, Alexander M. "The Failure of the Warren Report." *Commentary,* October 1966.

Billings, Richard N. "Garrison and the JFK Plot." *Long Island Press,* May 15, 1968. Billings is the author of the House Select Committee on Assassinations report. Interestingly, Billings, then an editor at *Life* magazine, according to Peter Dale Scott, accompanied a CIA-sponsored "hit team" to Cuba in 1963.

———. "Garrison Convinced of Plot." *Miami Herald,* May 22, 1968.

Bishop, Jim. *The Day Kennedy Was Shot.* New York: Funk and Wagnalls, 1968.

Blakey, G. Robert, and Richard N. Billings. *Fatal Hour.* New York: Berkley, 1992.

———. *The Plot to Kill the President.* New York: New York Times Books, 1981. Subtitled: "Organized Crime Assassinated JFK—The Definitive Story."

Bloomgarden, Henry S. *The Gun.* New York: Bantam Books, 1976.

Blum, Andrew. "JFK Conundrum." *National Law Journal* 14, no. 16 (December 23, 1991).

Blumenthal, Sid, and Harvey Yazijian. eds. *Government by Gunplay.* New York: New American Library, Signet, 1976.

Blythe, Myrna, and Jane Farrell. "Marina Oswald—Twenty-five Years Later." *Ladies Home Journal,* November 1988.

"Body of JFK Assassin Is Under Guard in FW." *Fort Worth Press,* November 25, 1963.

Bonafede, Dom, and Stuart L. Loory. "Ruby Knew Tippit, Killer's Sister Says." *Boston Globe,* December 2, 1963, p. 17.

Bonner, Judy W. *Investigation of a Homicide: The Murder of John F. Kennedy.* Indianapolis, Indiana: Droke House, 1969.

Bowart, Walter. *Operation Mind Control.* New York: Dell Publishing Co., 1978. See MK/ULTRA.

Bower, Thomas. *The Paperclip Conspiracy.* Boston, Mass.: Little, Brown, 1987.

Boyles, Peter. "Fear and Loathing on the Assassination Trail." *Denver Magazine,* November 1980.

Brancato, Paul. *Coup d'État.* Forrestville, Calif.: Eclipse Enterprises, 1991.

Brashler, William. *The Don: The Life and Death of Sam Giancana.* New York: Harper and Row, 1977.

Brener, Milton E. *The Garrison Case: A Study in the Abuse of Power.* New York: Clarkson N. Potter, 1969.

Brennan, Howard, L., with J. Edward Cherryholmes. *Eyewitness to History.* Waco, Tex.: Texan Press, 1987. Book "written" by the only man to identify Oswald as the man in the sixth-floor window.

Breo, Dennis L. "JFK's Death—The Plain Truth from the Doctors Who Did the Autopsy." *Journal of the American Medical Association,* May 27, 1992.

Breslin, Jimmy. "A Death in Emergency Room No. One." *Saturday Evening Post,* December 14, 1963.

Bringuier, Carlos. *Red Friday: November 22nd, 1963.* Chicago: Chas. Hallburg and Co., 1969.

Brown, Ray "Tex," with Don Lasseter. *Broken Silence: The Truth about Lee Harvey Oswald, LBJ and the Assassination of JFK.* New York: Pinnacle Books, 1996. Mass market paperback. Tex says he taught Ruby and Oswald how to "use guns" during the weeks before the assassination and that, afterward, LBJ paid him to keep his mouth shut. A candidate for worst-written and least-trustworthy book ever written about the Kennedy assassination.

Brown, Walt. *The People v. Lee Harvey Oswald.* New York: Carroll and Graf, 1992.

———. *Treachery in Dallas.* New York: Carroll and Graf, 1995.

Buchanan, Thomas G. *Who Killed Kennedy?* London: Secker and Warburg, 1964.

Burney, Peggy. "I Saw Him Die, Woman Cries." *Dallas Times Herald,* November 22, 1963.

Burnham, David. "Assassination Panel Facing Budget Trim." *New York Times,* January 25, 1977, p. 17.

———. "Assassination Panel Is Warned on Its Techniques." *New York Times,* January 6, 1977, p. 15.

———. "Assassination Panel's Fate in Doubt As Sprague Faces New Allegations." *New York Times,* February 12, 1977, p. 11.

———. "Assassination Study Requests $13 Million." *New York Times,* December 10, 1976, p. 19.

———. "Gonzalez, Assailing His Committee, Quits As Assassination Inquiry Head." *New York Times,* March 3, 1977, p. 1.

———. "House Gives Assassination Panel Authority to Continue Temporarily." *New York Times,* February 3, 1977, p. 21.

———. "New Assassination Panel Is Blocked." *New York Times,* January 12, 1977.

———. "Sprague Ouster Is Upset by Panel on Assassination." *New York Times,* February 10, 1977, p. 1.

"Bush Inks Law Opening JFK Files." *New York Post,* October 28, 1992, p. 16.

"Bus Stub Traces Oswald in Mexico." *New York Post,* August 31, 1964, p. 4.

Callahan, Bob. *Who Shot JFK?* New York: Simon and Schuster, 1993. A guide to the major conspiracy theories. Trade paperback, illustrated by Mark Zingarelli.

Campbell, Alex. "What Did Happen in Dallas?" *New Republic,* June 25, 1966.

"Cancer Work Slain Doctor's Main Interest." *New Orleans States Item,* July 21, 1964, Section 1, p. 1. Regarding the death of Dr. Mary Sherman.

Canfield, Michael, with Alan J. Weberman. *Coup d'État in America: The CIA and the Assassination of John F. Kennedy.* New York: Third Press, 1975.

"Capture: It's All Over Now." *New York Herald Tribune,* November 23, 1963.

"Carlos Marcello, 83, Reputed Crime Boss in New Orleans Area." *New York Times,* March 3, 1993. Obituary regarding March 2, 1993, death. Says "Mr. Marcello's name had been mentioned in media accounts about the assassination of President John F. Kennedy in 1963, but no official link was ever made."

Carter, Bill. "ABC Finds K.G.B. Fickle on Oswald." *New York Times,* November 21, 1991.

"Castro Aide: JFK Killing a Conspiracy." *New York Daily News,* November 28, 1993. According to Reuters, General Fabian Escalante Font, a Cuban Interior Ministry officer, says that "the shots fired on November 22, 1963 numbered four to five from various locations." The assassins were two anti-Castro Cubans and three Chicago gangsters. He did not disclose the evidence upon which he based his conclusions.

"Chagra Says Harrelson Told Him He Also Killed JFK." *Fort Worth Star-Telegram,* November 2, 1982. Regarding assassination suspect Charles V. Harrelson.

Chambaz, Jacques. "This French Terrorist Accused of Murdering Kennedy." *Le Quotidien de Paris,* January 1, 1984. Regarding Jean Souetre.

Chapman, Gil, and Ann Chapman. *Was Oswald Alone?* San Diego, Calif.: Publisher's Export Co., 1967.

Chariton, Wallace O. *Unsolved Texas Mysteries.* Plano, Tex.: Worldware Publishing, 1991. Used for information about the mysterious pool of blood.

Christensen, Dan. "JFK, King: The Dade County Links." *Miami Magazine,* September 1976, pp. 20–25. Regarding the taped statements of J. A. Milteer.

"CIA Withheld Details on Oswald Call." *Washington Post,* November 26, 1975. Regards tapes allegedly made of Oswald in Mexico City in September 1963.

"The Clamour Rises for Kennedy X Rays." *London Observer,* August 7, 1966, p. 10.

Clifford, Timothy. "JFK Assassin Theories Kept CIA Bustling." *New York Newsday,* August 24, 1993, p. 4.

———. "Oswald acted alone: Clinton." *New York Daily News,* November 23, 1993, p. 2.

Cohen, Jeff. "The Oswald Tapes." *Crawdaddy,* August 1975, p. 40. Regarding Oswald's New Orleans radio debate.

Cohen, Jacob. "The Warren Commission Report and Its Critics." *Frontier,* November 1966.

———. "What the Warren Report Omits: Vital Documents." *The Nation,* July 11, 1966.

———. "Conspiracy Fever." *Commentary,* October 1975.

Cohen, Joel. "The Two Assassins: Booth and Oswald." *Back Channels,* Winter 1992, p. 16.

Columbia Journalism Review, Winter 1964. (Entire issue dedicated to media coverage of the JFK assassination.)

"Congress OKs Release of JFK Files." *New York Post,* October 1, 1992, p. 9.

Connally, John. "Why Kennedy Went to Texas." *Life,* November 24, 1967.

"Connally's Bullet Sought." *Newsday,* June 17, 1993, p. 129.

"Connick to Turn Over the Garrison Files?" *Probe: The Newsletter of Citizens for Truth about the Kennedy Assassination,* May/June 1996, p. 1.

Considine, Bob. "Violent Dallas: A New Chapter." *New York Journal American,* February 23, 1964.

"Conspiracy 'Profs' Teaching JFK 101." *New York Post,* August 21, 1997, p. 22. Washington conspiracy theorist Michael Collins Piper was approved by the South Orange County Community College District of Mission Viejo, California, to be one of four speakers at a three-day course on JFK's assassination. The approval was controversial because of Piper's contention that the Mossad, Israeli Intelligence, masterminded JFK's hit.

Cooper, Milton William. *Behold a Pale Horse.* Sedona, Ariz.: Light Technology Publishing, 1991. Useful for those who believe JFK was murdered to cover-up the fact that aliens from outer space control the world, as well as for those interested in other forms of mind control.

Corliss, Richard. "Who Killed J.F.K.?" *Time,* December 23, 1991.

Cowan, Edward. "New Study Urged in Kennedy Death." *York Times,* July 21, 1975, p. 27.

Craig, John R., and Philip A. Rogers. *The Man on the Grassy Knoll.* New York: Avon, 1992. Book about assassination suspect Charles Frederick Rogers.

Cranor, Milicent. "The Magician's Tools." *Probe: The Newsletter of Citizens for Truth about the Kennedy Assassination,* November/December 1995, p. 9. Article about the possible use of silencers in Dealey Plaza.

Crawford, Kenneth. "The Warren Impeachers." *Newsweek,* October 19, 1964.

Crenshaw, Charles A., M.D., with Jens Hansen J. Gary Shaw. *JFK Conspiracy of Silence.* New York: Signet, 1992.

Crewdson, John M. "Rockefeller Unit Said to Check Report of CIA Link to Kennedy Assassination." *New York Times,* March 8, 1975, p. 11.

Crile, George. "The Mafia, the CIA, and Castro." *Washington Post,* May 16, 1976, p. C4.

———. "The Riddle of AMLASH." *Washington Post Outlook,* May 2, 1976, p. C1.

Cruz, Humberto, and Hilda Inclan. "'El Tigre' Died As He Lived—by Violence." *Miami News,* November 1, 1975. Regarding the death of Rolando Masferrar.

"Cuban Criticizes Writer on Kennedy Assassination." *New Orleans Times-Picayune,* January 5, 1968. The "Cuban" is Carlos Bringuier. The writer is Mark Lane.

Cumings, Bruce. *The Origins of the Korean War.* Vol. 2. Princeton, N.J.: Princeton University Press, 1990. Used for information regarding General Charles Willoughby.

Cunniff, Albert B. *JFK Assassination: Nothing but the Truth.* Baltimore, Md.: Books Unlimited, 1994.

Curry, Jesse. *JFK Assassination File.* Dallas, Texas: American Poster and Publishing Company, 1969. Out of print book by the Dallas chief of police.

Cushman, Robert F. "Why the Warren Commission?" *New York University Law Review* 40, no. 3 (May 1965): 477–503.

"Dallas Cop Named As Assassin." *National Examiner,* October 13, 1992, p. 45. Regarding Roscoe White.

"Dallas Ex-police Chief Alleges an FBI Cover-up on Oswald." *New York Times,* September 2, 1975, p. 12.

"Dallas Man Claims FBI Had Oswald Film." *Fort Worth Star-Telegram,* September 20, 1978.

Dallas, Tita, and Jeanira Ratcliffe. *The Kennedy Case.* New York: Popular Library, 1973.

Dallos, Robert E. "New Witness Alleges That He Was Offered Money to Aid Garrison in Investigation of Assassination." *New York Times,* June 19, 1967, p. 27.

Daniel, Jean. "When Castro Heard the News." *The New Republic,* December 7, 1963.

Davies, Col. *Named! For the First Time, The Master Spy and Hit-men Who Shot J.F.K.* Melbourne, Australia: Bookman Press, 1993.

Davis, John H. *The Kennedy Contract: The Mafia Plot to Assassinate the President.* New York: HarperPaperbacks, 1993. Book suggests that New Orleans crime boss Carlos Marcello ordered the assassination. Davis, who is the first cousin of Jackie Kennedy, told journalist Jack Anderson in 1988, "An informant witnessed Oswald in Marcello's headquarters, the Charles Guthrie Hotel, in New Orleans receiving what appeared to be a payment from a Marcello lieutenant. This is a scandalous story because Oswald's relationship with organized crime was completely withheld from the American people and the Warren Commission."

Addressing a JFK assassination symposium in Dallas on November 16, 1991, Davis said: "Since Dallas was under the Mafia jurisdiction of Carlos Marcello—who operated out of New Orleans, but who also controlled Dallas and Houston—Jack Ruby would not have been allowed to operate in those areas without Marcello's permission. . . . As the House Select Committee on Assassinations discovered in 1978, Ruby was closely connected in Dallas with at least three associates of Carlos Marcello. One was Joseph Civello, who represented Marcello at the Apalachin Crime Conference in 1957. . . . Then there were the Campisi brothers, Joe and Sam. Joe ran the Egyptian Lounge in Dallas and Ruby ate at Joe's restaurant on the night before the assassination. Joe was one of the first people to visit Ruby in jail after he killed Oswald . . . Ruby, we have found out, also knew several members of the Marcello organization in New Orleans. One of them was Carlos Marcello's brother, Pete, who also ran a nightclub in the French Quarter. . . . He knew one of Ruby's chief lieutenants, Nofio Pecora. He phoned him about a month before the assassination. He also knew two French Quarter operators—one of whom, Frank Caracci, incidentally, is running the rackets now in the French Quarter.

"But Ruby's mob connections extended all over the nation. He knew Mickey Cohen in California. He knew Johnny Roselli, the front man in Las Vegas. He knew Santos Trafficante, the mob boss in Florida. And he knew several henchmen of Sam Giancana and Jimmy Hoffa, who, of course, was under the influence of Giancana. . . . Phone records indicate that he called *all* of these people in the months leading up to the assassination. Ruby actually met with Roselli in Miami about a month before the assassination.

"One of Ruby's activities was cultivating the Dallas police. He was what is called a 'police buff.' It has been estimated that Jack Ruby was on a first name basis with more than 50 officers on the Dallas police force. It's hard to believe. He bought the men on the night watch deli sandwiches. He arranged loans for certain officers in need of financial assistance. He introduced officers to the sexiest striptease dancers in his nightclub, acting in a sense as a pimp. Many members of the Dallas police force were beholden to Jack Ruby in one way or another. This, of course, made Ruby extremely useful to the conspirators once Oswald was arrested and jailed by the Dallas police.

"At the time of the assassination he owed upwards of $40,000 to the IRS in back taxes and penalties. In other words, he was desperate for money. This is why we believe he allowed himself to become an instrument in a conspiracy to assassinate President Kennedy."

Addressing another assassination symposium in Dallas, this one in 1992, Davis announced that he had new evidence, which at first sounded impressive: Davis had reason to believe that both Tammy True and Karen "Little Lynn" Carlin, Ruby strippers who show up on the "mysterious deaths" list—faked their own deaths and are, in reality, still alive. (See also JACK'S GIRLS.) Furthermore, both women had called him on the phone. Gary Shaw first heard from Karen Carlin. Tammy True called John Davis out of the blue and said, "Hi, it's Tammy!" Davis said that Tammy had spoken to him on the phone four times, but she still hadn't left an address or a phone number.

Davis, Marc, and Jim Mathews, eds. *Highlights of the Warren Report.* Covina, Calif.: Collectors Publishers, 1967.

Davis, William Hardy. *Aiming for the Jugular in New Orleans.* Port Washington, N.Y.: Ashley Books Co., 1976.

Davison, Jean. *Oswald's Game.* New York: W. W. Norton and Co., 1983.

Davy, Bill. "Case Distorted: Posner, Connick, and the *New York Times.*" *Probe: The Newsletter of Citizens for Truth about the Kennedy Assassination,* March–April 1996, p. 5. Response to Gerald Posner's article "Garrison Guilty" in the *New York Times* on August 6, 1995. Connick refers to Harry Connick, New Orleans Parish district attorney.

———. "Clay Shaw's DCS Career: An Analysis of a Recent File Release." *Probe: The Newsletter of Citizens for Truth about the Kennedy Assassination,* May–June 1996, p. 6.

"The Deadly Kennedy Probe: Execution for the Witnesses." *Rolling Stone,* June 2, 1977.

Delfiner, Rita. "FBI Memo: Castro Says It Took 3 to Kill JFK." *New York Post,* March 31, 1995, p. 10. According to an FBI document, a memo to J. Edgar Hoover from a New York agent dated June 12, 1964, Fidel Castro believed that "about three" people were shooting in Dealey Plaza during JFK's assassination. "The Cuban president, who prided himself in being a sharpshooter, ran his own ballistics tests to back up his theory."

Demaris, Ovid, and Gary Wills. *Jack Ruby.* New York: New American Library, 1968.

Denson, R. B., ed. *Destiny in Dallas*. Dallas Tex.: Denco Corporation, 1964.

Devlin, Lord. "Death of a President: The Established Facts." *Atlantic Monthly,* March 1965, pp. 112–118.

DiEugenio, James. *Destiny Betrayed: JFK, Cuba, and the Garrison Case*. New York: Sheridan Square Press, 1992.

———. "Mockingbird: The Next Generation?" *Probe: The Newsletter of Citizens for Truth about the Kennedy Assassination,* March–April 1996, p. 12.

———, "Nagell Update." *Probe: The Newsletter of Citizens for Truth about the Kennedy Assassination,* March–April 1996, p. 26.

———, and John Armstrong. "The Albert Schweitzer Documents." *Probe: The Newsletter of Citizens for Truth about the Kennedy Assassination,* March–April 1996, p. 7. Analysis of the Swiss "school" where Oswald applied for admission near the end of his stint in the U.S. Marines, and which, following his acceptance, he used as an excuse to travel overseas when he was actually planning to go to the Soviet Union.

DiMaio, Vincent J. M. "The Exhumation and Identification of Lee Harvey Oswald." *Journal of Forensic Sciences* 29, no. 1 (January 1984).

"Dispute on JFK Assassination Evidence Persists." *Boston Sunday Globe,* June 21, 1981.

"District Attorneys Pay for Dinner, Garrison Cancels It." *New York Times,* March 17, 1968, p. 78.

"Docs in Dispute on JFK Wounds." *New York Daily News,* April 3, 1992.

Donnelly, Judy. *Who Shot the President?* New York: Random House, 1988.

Donovan, Robert J. *The Assassins*. New York: Harper and Bros., 1964.

Dorman, Michael. "Soviet JFK Files a 'Breakthrough.'" *Newsday,* June 23, 1999, p. A22.

———. "Warren 'Draft' Draws Theories." *Newsday,* September 19, 1996. Family of J. Lee Rankin kept early draft of *Warren Report* and are now releasing it to the Assassination Records Review Board.

Dudman, Richard. "Commentary of an Eyewitness." *The New Republic,* December 21, 1963, p. 18.

Duffy, James R. *Who Killed JFK?* New York: Shapolski Publishers, 1988.

Dugger, Ronnie. "The Last Voyage of Mr. Kennedy." *The Texas Observer,* November 29, 1963.

Duncan, Tom. "Intrigue at 'No Name' Key." *Back Channels,* Spring 1992, p. 13.

Eddowes, Michael H. B. *Khrushchev Killed Kennedy*. Dallas: self-published, 1975. The thesis here is that Lee Harvey Oswald went to the Soviet Union and, while there, was replaced by a Soviet agent, who returned to the United States and assassinated President Kennedy. As evidence, Eddowes offers the fact Oswald's height was recorded repeatedly in the U.S. Marines as five feet eleven inches and the accused assassin was no taller than five feet nine inches. Years later Eddowes successfully called for Oswald's exhumation, which resulted in Oswald's corpse being officially declared as Oswald's. Eddowes claims the man called Oswald's assignments upon his return to the United States were to 1. deceive Oswald's

brother and mother that he was really Lee; 2. establish that he may have been an American agent when he went to Russia and that he and Marina were both thoroughly disgusted with life in the Soviet Union; 3. infiltrate the White Russian community in Dallas and gain employment at Jaggars-Chiles-Stovall in time for the Cuban Missile Crisis in October 1962; 4. appear on bad terms with Marina so it was more difficult for observers to conceive of them as an agent team. According to Harrison Livingstone publication of this book was financed by anticommunist benefactor and oil billionaire H. L. Hunt.

———. *November 22, How They Killed Kennedy*. London: Neville Spearman Ltd., 1976.

———. *The Oswald File*. New York: Clarkson N. Potter, 1977.

Edginton, John, and John Sergeant. "The Murder of Martin Luther King, Jr." *Covert Action Information Bulletin,* No. 34, Summer 1990.

Ellis, David. "Did JFK Really Commit Suicide." *Time,* April 13, 1992, p. 64.

Epstein, Edward Jay. *The Assassination Chronicles: Inquest, Counterplot and Legend*. New York: Carroll and Graf Publishers, Inc., 1992. Epstein's first three books about the assassination and its aftermath, now assembled into a single volume.

Epstein, Edward Jay. "Who's Afraid of the Warren Report?" *Esquire,* December 1966.

Evica, George Michael. *And We Are All Mortal*. West Hartford, Conn.: University of Hartford Press, 1978. One of the best.

"Evidence against Oswald Described As Conclusive." *York Times,* November 24, 1963, p. 2.

Faso, Frank, and Paul Meskil. "Operation Amlash." *New York Daily News,* January 27, 1977, p. 47.

"FBI: Gov's Body May Hold Clue to JFK Murder." *The Daily News,* June 18, 1993, p. 9. The FBI sought to remove metal fragments from the body of Governor John Connally to see if they disproved the single-bullet theory. Permission to do so was angrily denied by Connally's widow, Nellie.

"FBI Shaken by a Cover-up That Failed." *Time,* November 3, 1975, p. 9. Regarding Oswald's pre-assassination note to FBI special agent James Hosty.

Feinsilber, Mike. "JFK Conspiracy Theorists Seize upon Ford's Editing." *New Orleans Times-Picayune,* July 4, 1997, G-10.

Feldman, Harold. "Oswald and the FBI." *The Nation,* January 27, 1964, pp. 86–9.

Fensterwald, Bernard, Jr., and Michael Ewing. *Coincidence or Conspiracy?* New York: Kensington Publishing, 1977.

Fensterwald, Bernard, and George O'Toole. "The CIA and the Man Who Was Not Oswald." *New York Review of Books,* April 3, 1975, p. 24.

Ferrell, Mary. "'Concerding' the Oswald Letter." *The Continuing Inquiry,* March 1977, pp. 7–8, 13.

Fetzer, James H., ed. *Assassination Science: Experts Speak Out on the Death of JFK*. Peru, Ill.: Catfeet Press, 1998. A collaborative study of various assassination topics by 11 physicians, scientists, and other serious students of the crime.

———. *Murder in Dealey Plaza: What We Know Now That We Didn't Know Then about the Death of JFK*. Peru, Ill.: Catfeet Press, 2000.

"Fidel Fretted over Invasion after JFK Slay." *New York Post,* August 20, 1997. In a National Security Agency two-page report entitled "Top Secret Dinar," released by the Assassination Records Review Board, it was revealed that a European secret agent sent a dispatch home on November 27, 1963, a dispatch that was intercepted by the agency, which said that Fidel Castro was "terrified" about the assassination because he feared it would justify internationally an invasion by the United States of Cuba.

"Film Crew Reexamines JFK Shoot Theory." *New York Daily News*, September 4, 1998, p. 9.

Flammonde, Paris. *The Kennedy Conspiracy.* New York: Meredith Press, 1969.

Fonzi, Gaeton. *The Last Investigation.* New York: Thunder's Mouth Press, 1993. Inside look at the House Select Committee on Assassinations investigation. Fonzi concludes, "So in the end, the House Select Committee on Assassinations, like the Warren Commission before it, produced a report that *looked* comprehensive and complete, but which failed the American people."

———. "Who Killed JFK?" *The Washingtonian*, November 1980, p. 167.

Footlick, Jerrold D. "Jim, Do You Really Believe All This Stuff?" *National Observer,* January 22, 1968, p. 1. Attack on Garrison.

Ford, Gerald, with John R. Stiles. *Portrait of the Assassin.* New York: Simon and Schuster, 1965.

"Former Indianola Man Assassination Witness." *The Record Herald and Indianola Tribune*, November 28, 1963, p. 1.

Fox, Sylvan. *The Unanswered Questions about President Kennedy's Assassination.* New York: Award Books, 1965.

Francescani, Christopher. "JFK's 'Mob Mistress' Exner Is Dead at 65." *New York Post,* September 26, 1999, p. 4.

Freedman, Lawrence Zelic. "Profile of an Assassin." *Police,* March–April 1966.

Freese, Paul L. "The Warren Commission and the Fourth Shot: A Reflection on the Fundamentals of Forensic Fact-Finding." *New York University Law Review* 40 XL, no. 3 (May 1965): 424–465.

Freund, Charles Paul. "Who Killed JFK? And Why We Still Have to Ask." *McCall's*, January 1992, p. 70.

Gage, Nicholas. "Roselli Called a Victim of Mafia Because of His Testimony." *New York Times,* February 25, 1977, p. 1.

"Garrison Assails Tokyo Words of Chief Justice." *New Orleans Times-Picayune*, September 5, 1967.

"Garrison Arrests an Ex-Major in Conspiracy to Kill Kennedy." *New York Times,* March 2, 1967, p. 24. Re: The arrest of Clay Shaw.

Garrison, Jim. *A Heritage of Stone.* New York: G. P. Putnam's Sons, 1970.

———. *On the Trail of the Assassins.* New York: Sheridan Square Press, 1988.

———. "The Murder Talents of the CIA." *Freedom Magazine,* April–May 1987.

"Garrison Record Shows Disability." *New York Times,* December 30, 1967, p. 28.

"Garrison Says Assassin Killed Kennedy from Sewer Manhole." *New York Times,* December 11, 1967, p. 28.

"Garrison Says CIA Knows the Slayers." *New York Times,* May 23, 1967.

"Garrison Says Kennedy Was Killed in Crossfire." *New York Times,* May 24, 1967, p. 50.

"Garrison Says Oswald Gave FBI a Tip Before Assassination." *New York Times,* December 27, 1967.

"Garrison Says Some Policemen in Dallas Aided Kennedy Plot." *New York Times,* September 22, 1967, p. 28.

"Garrison Seeks High Court Help." *Fort Worth Star-Telegram,* February 20, 1969.

Gauzer, Bernard, and Sid Moody. *The Lingering Shadow.* Dallas, Tex.: Dallas Times-Herald, 1967.

Gertz, Elmer. *Moment of Madness.* Chicago: Follett Publishing Company, 1968. Three of Jack Ruby's lawyers wrote books: Melvin Belli, Alan Adelson, and Elmer Gertz.

Giancana, Charles, and Sam Giancana. *Double Cross: The Explosive History of the Mobster Who Controlled America.* New York: Warner Books, 1992. Written by Mafia don Sam Giancana's brother and nephew. Book alleges that Ruby worked for Giancana while running guns for the CIA; Ruby once gave David Ferrie a job at the Carousel Club; Oswald had ties to both organized crime and the CIA; Oswald was recruited into intelligence by Civil Air Patrol captain David Ferrie, Lyndon Johnson, Richard Nixon, a Bay of Pigs officer, and a right-wing Texan were involved; several cities were considered, including Los Angeles, Chicago, and Miami; the team in Dealey Plaza included Charles Harrelson, Jack Lawrence, Richard Cain, Charles Nicoletti, and Felix "Milwaukee Phil" Alderisio, with Cain and Nicoletti shooting from opposite ends of the Texas School Book Depository's sixth floor, Cain in the "sniper's nest" window; CIA shooters in Dealey Plaza included Roscoe White and J. D. Tippit, with Frank Sturgis and Lee Harvey Oswald also being involved in nonshooting roles. Wasn't anybody there just to see the parade?

Gibson, Donald. "The Creation of the 'Warren Commission.'" *Probe: The Newsletter of Citizens for Truth about the Kennedy Assassination*, May–June 1996, p. 8.

Goldberg, Alfred. *Conspiracy Interpretations of the Assassination of President Kennedy: International and Domestic.* Los Angeles: University of California Press, 1968.

Goldberg, Jeff. "Waiting for Justice." *The Continuing Inquiry,* March, 1980.

Goldberg, Jeff, and Harvey Yazijian. "The Death of 'Crazy Billy' Sullivan." *New Times,* July 24, 1978.

Golden, Charles. "Mystery Miami Murder Linked to JFK Plot." *National Enquirer,* April 30, 1967. Concerns the death of assassination suspect Eladio del Valle.

Golz, Earl. "After 17 Years of Silence, FBI Oswald Agent Speaks Up." *Dallas Morning News,* December 8, 1980, p. 1. Regarding James Hosty.

———. "Alleged Oswald Letter Checked for Its Authenticity by FBI Agents." *Dallas Morning News,* February 6, 1977. Regarding the "Dear Mr. Hunt" letter.

———. "Classmates Doubt 'Run-of-the-Mill' Cop Gunned Down JFK." *Austin American-Statesman,* August 5, 1990, p. A1. Regarding Roscoe White.

———. "Cubans' Friend Believes Oswald Contacted Exile Leader." *Dallas Morning News,* June 10, 1979, p. 1AA. Regarding a note allegedly written by Oswald to Pedro Gonzalez.

———. "Dallas Camera Disappeared during FBI Investigation." *Dallas Morning News,* June 15, 1978.

———. "November 22, 1963: Another Story Blurs the Facts." *Austin American-Statesman,* August 5, 1990, p. A1. Regarding Roscoe White.

———. "Oswald Pictures Released by FBI." *Dallas Morning News,* August 7, 1978.

Goodhart, Arthur L. "The Warren Commission From The Procedural Standpoint," *New York University Law Review* 40, no. 3 (May 1965): 405–423.

Groden, Robert J. "Argosy Discloses: 'The JFK Evidence That Nobody Wanted to Reveal!'" *Argosy Magazine,* August 1977, pp. 28–34. Regarding the taped statements of Joseph Milteer.

———. "A New Look at the Zapruder Film." *Rolling Stone,* April 24, 1975, pp. 35–36.

———. *The Search For Lee Harvey Oswald.* New York: Penguin Books, 1995. Misquotes author Michael Benson three times.

Groden, Robert J., and Harrison Edward Livingstone. *High Treason.* New York: Berkley Books, 1990.

Groden, Robert, and Peter Model. *J.F.K.: The Case for Conspiracy.* New York: Manor Books, 1967.

Guinn, Vincent. "JFK Assassination: Bullet Analyses." *Analytical Chemistry,* April 1979.

Gun, Nerin. *Red Roses from Texas.* London: Frederick Muller, 1964.

Hanson, William H. *The Shooting of John F. Kennedy.* San Antonio, Tex.: Naylor, 1969.

Haseltine, Nate. "Kennedy Autopsy Report." *Washington Post,* December 18, 1963, p. A3.

Haslam, Edward T. *Mary, Ferrie & the Monkey Virus: The Story of an Underground Medical Laboratory.* Albuquerque: Wordsworth Communications, 1995. The story of David Ferrie, his associate cancer researcher Dr. Mary Sherman, and their possible connection to the origin of AIDS. As a child Haslam learned from his father that research regarding deadly monkey viruses from Africa was taking place at Tulane University in New Orleans, Louisiana. In November 1964, with the opening of the Delta Regional Primate Center, the research moved from downtown New Orleans to 500 wooded acres near Covington, Louisiana. Following the death of David Ferrie, Haslam learned that Ferrie, in the course of his cancer research, had been injecting mice with monkey viruses.

Healy, Paul. "The President Is Assassinated As Dallas Multitude Hails Him." *New York Daily News,* November 23, 1963, p. 3.

Hemenway, Phillip. *Riding the Tiger's Back: A Footnote to the Assassination of JFK.* Chico, Calif.: Heidelberg Graphics, 1992.

Hepburn, James. *Farewell America.* Vaduz, Liechtenstein: Frontier Publishing Company, 1968. Hepburn is a pseudonym. Hepburn's book says, "Ten hours after the assassination, Secret Service Chief James Rowley knew that there had been three gunman, and perhaps four, firing in Dallas that day. . . . Robert Kennedy . . . learned that evening from Rowland that the Secret Service believed the President had been the victim of a powerful organization." According to researcher William Turner, this book was commissioned by Robert Kennedy and Senator Daniel Patrick Moynihan, who asked French president Charles de Gaulle to launch an investigation into President Kennedy's assassination using French intelligence. This book was the result. Some assassination researchers who have been quick to criticize this book have later been found to work for Hunt Oil, which would naturally want to deflect suspicion in the assassination away from the political right wing.

Herbert, Bob. "A Historian's View." *New York Times,* June 3, 1999, p. A27. After all these years, William Manchester still sees no evidence of a conspiracy. Item written in reaction to news that JFK's coffin was dropped by helicopter into the ocean.

Hewitt, Carol. "Captain George Nonte's Cartridge Conversions and Those 'Cute' Mannlichers." *Probe: The Newsletter of Citizens for Truth about the Kennedy Assassination,* March–April 1996, p. 14.

———. "The Paines Know: Lurking in the Shadows of the Walker Shooting." *Probe: The Newsletter of Citizens for Truth about the Kennedy Assassination,* November–December 1997, p. 13.

———. "Silencers, Sniper Rifles and the CIA." *Probe: The Newsletter of Citizens for Truth about the Kennedy Assassination,* November–December 1995, p. 7.

———, Steve Jones, and Barbara LaMonica. "The Paines: Suspicious Characters." *Probe: The Newsletter of Citizens for Truth about the Kennedy Assassination.* May/June 1996, p. 14.

Hinckle, Warren, and William Turner. *The Fish Is Red.* New York: Harper and Row, 1981. Reissued in 1992 by Thunder's Mouth Press as *Deadly Secrets: The CIA-Mafia War against Castro and the Assassination of JFK.*

Hlavich, Laura, and Darwin Payne, eds. *Reporting the Kennedy Assassination: Journalists Who Were There Recall Their Experiences.* Dallas, Tex.: Three Forks Press, 1996. Transcript of a conference at Southern Methodist University on November 20, 1993.

"Hoffa 'Plot' to Kill R.F. Kennedy Alleged." *New York Times,* April 12, 1964, p. 1.

"Hoover Is Said to Have Been Told Oswald Disclosed Plans to Cubans." *New York Times,* November 12, 1976.

Horrock, Nicholas M. "CIA Data Show 14-Year Project on Controlling Human Behavior." *New York Times,* July 21, 1977, p. 1. About the MK/ULTRA mind-control program.

Horrock, Nicholas M. "CIA Documents Tell of 1954 Project to Create Involuntary Assassins." *New York Times,* February 9, 1978. Real-life Manchurian Candidates.

Hosty, James P., Jr. *Assignment: Oswald.* New York: Arcade Publishing, 1995. Story of the assassination through the eyes of the FBI agent assigned to investigate Oswald prior to JFK's death.

Hougan, Jim. *Secret Agenda.* New York: Ballantyne Books, 1984. Looks at Watergate.

"House Allows for Opening of JFK Files." *Variety,* October 5, 1992, p. 16.

House Select Committee on Assassinations. *The Final Assassinations Report.* New York: Bantam Books, 1979.

Hurt, Henry. *Reasonable Doubt.* New York: Holt, Rinehart, 1986.

Irwin, T. H., and Hazel Hale. *A Bibliography of Books, Newspaper and Magazine Articles Published in English Outside the United States of America, Related to the Assassination of John F. Kennedy.* Belfast, Ireland/Leeds, England: The Editors, 1975.

"Is This the Man Who Killed JFK?" *National Enquirer,* November 22, 1983. Regarding Jean Souetre.

Jackman, Frank. "FBI Files: No Link between Ruby, Oswald." *New York Daily News,* December 15, 1993. On December 14,

1993, the National Archives released 21,224 pages of FBI files. Amazingly, none of those pages told us anything we didn't already know.

Jaffe, Louis L. "Trial by Newspaper." *New York University Law Review* 40, no. 3 (May 1965): 504–524.

James, Rosemary, and Jack Wardlaw. *Plot or Politics: The Garrison Case and Its Cast.* New Orleans, La.: Pelican Publishing House, 1967.

"JFK Assassination Secrets Bared." *New York Post,* August 24, 1993, p. 2.

"JFK Assassins Got $$ from Kennedy-Hating Billionaire." *National Enquirer,* June 14, 1977, p. 4. Regarding H. L. Hunt.

"JFK Probers: Remove Connally Bullet Parts." *New York Post,* June 17, 1993.

"JFK X-Rays Called Fake." *Newsday,* May 29, 1992, p. 8. By autopsy witness and X ray technician Jerrol Custer.

"Jimmy Hoffa Vanishes." *Newsweek,* August 11, 1975, pp. 19–21.

Joesten, Joachim. *The Garrison Enquiry.* London, Peter Dawnay Ltd., 1967.

———. "Highlights and Lessons of the Clay Shaw Trial." *Truth Letter,* June 15, 1969.

———. *Marina Oswald.* London: Peter Dawnay Ltd., 1967.

———. *Oswald: Assassin or Fall Guy?* New York: Marzani and Munsell, 1964.

———. *Oswald: The Truth,* London: Peter Dawnay Ltd., 1967.

Johnson, Bob. "Too Busy for Tears." *The A.P. World,* August 1972, pp. 16–17.

Johnson, Richard. "The Booziest JFK Murder Theory." *New York Post,* August 21, 1996, p. 8. Regarding Michel Roux.

Johnston, David. "F.B.I. Backs Plan to Remove Fragments from Connally." *New York Times,* June 18, 1993, p. A28.

Jones, Jr., Penn. "Disappearing Witnesses." *The Rebel,* November 22, 1983.

Jones, Jr., Penn. *Forgive My Grief.* Vols. 1–4. Midlothian, Tex.: Self-Published, 1966, 1967, 1969 (revised 1976), 1978.

Kantor, Seth. *Who Was Jack Ruby?* New York: Everest House, 1978.

Katz, Joseph et al. "Lee Harvey Oswald in Freudian, Adlerian, and Jungian Views." *Journal of Individual Psychology* 23 (May 1967): 19–52.

Keith, Jim, ed. *The Gemstone File.* Atlanta: IllumiNet Press, 1992.

Kellogg, Mary Alice. "The Marina Oswald Story." *TV Guide,* November 13, 1993, p. 26.

Kempster, Norman. "Warren Report Omitted Oswald Offer to FBI." *Washington Star,* October 8, 1975.

The Kennedy Assassinations: A commemorative booklet. A booklet published by the (Rochester, N.Y.) *Times-Union* and *Democrat & Chronicle.* No date of publication.

"Kennedy Family Had First JFK Coffin Dumped Off Atlantic Coast in 1966." *Washington Times,* June 2, 1999, p. A3.

"Kennedy Was Hit First, Says Governor's Wife." *New York Daily News,* November 23, 1963, p. 10.

Kirk, Don. "Book 'Shuts' JFK case." *New York Daily News,* August 23, 1993, p. 16. Discusses the book *Case Closed* by Gerald Posner (Random House).

Kirkwood, James. *American Grotesque.* New York: Simon and Schuster, 1970. A look at the Clay Shaw trial.

"KGB Bigs Had Jitters over Oswald: Mailer." *New York Daily News,* April 3, 1995, p. 22. Publicity-generated item preceding release of Norman Mailer's book, *Oswald's Tale: An American Mystery.* "In the Soviet Union, Lee Harvey Oswald was a klutz who couldn't shoot straight."

Kristi, Amanda, and G. J. Rowell. "The Mysterious Mannlicher-Carcano CIA Tapes II." *The Investigator,* February–March, 1993.

Kritzberg, Connie. *Secrets from the Sixth Floor Window.* Tulsa, Okla.: Under Cover Press, 1994.

Kross, Peter. "DeMohrenschildt and Oswald." *Back Channels,* Spring 1992, p. 2.

———. "JFK and the French Connection." *Back Channels,* October 1991, p. 3.

———. "John Wood Murder Case." *Back Channels,* Spring 1992, p. 8. The case that put assassination suspect Charles Harrelson behind bars.

———. "The Assassination Archives." *Back Channels,* October 1991, p. 23.

———. "Top Hat and Fedora—Two Peas in a Pod?" *Back Channels,* October 1991, p. 11.

———. "The Tragedy of Roger Craig." *Back Channels,* Winter 1992, p. 3.

Kurtz, Michael L. *Crime of the Century: The Assassination from a Historian's Perspective.* Knoxville: University of Tennessee Press, 1982.

———. "Lee Harvey Oswald in New Orleans: A Reappraisal." *Louisiana History,* Winter 1980.

La Fontaine, Ray, and Mary La Fontaine. *Oswald Talked: The New Evidence in the JFK Assassination.* Gretna, La.: Pelican Publishing Company, 1996. Breaking the John Elrod story.

Landsman, Susan. *A History Mystery: Who Shot JFK?* New York: Avon, 1992. Book for children.

Lane, Mark. "The Assassination of President John F. Kennedy: How the CIA Set Up Oswald." *Hustler,* October 1978.

———. "CIA Conspired to Kill Kennedy." *Los Angeles Free Press,* 1, 1978.

———. *A Citizen's Dissent.* New York: Dell, 1975.

———. "The Mysterious Death of a Key JFK Witness." *Gallery,* November 1977. Story about George DeMohrenschildt.

———. *Plausible Denial.* New York: Thunder's Mouth Press, 1991.

———. *Rush to Judgment.* New York: Holt, Rinehart and Winston, 1966, 478 pages. Subtitled: "A Critique of the Warren Commission's Inquiry into the Murders of President John F. Kennedy, Officer J. D. Tippit and Lee Harvey Oswald."

Lardner, George Jr. "Connallys Tell of 'Terrible Ride.'" *Washington Post,* September 7, 1978, p. A1.

———. "Experts Track Mystery JFK Bullet." *Washington Post,* December 22, 1978, p. A1.

———. "50-50 Chance of a 4th Shot in Dallas, JFK Panel Is Told." *Washington Post,* September 12, 1978, p. A2.

———. "JFK Panel Gets Evidence of Conspiracy." *Washington Post,* December 21, 1978, p. A1.

———. "The Mysterious Death of a Key Witness." *Gallery,* November 1977, p. 41. About the death of George DeMohrenschildt.

———. "New Tests to Match Fragments in Kennedy, Connally." *Washington Post,* September 9, 1978, p. A3.

———. "Second JFK Gunman, Experts Say." *Washington Post,* December 31, 1978, p. A1.

———. "Warren Commission Backed." *Washington Post,* September 8, 1978, p. A1.

———. "CIA Officer Rifled Assassination Files." *Los Angeles Times,* June 18, 1979. Regarding CIA liaison officer Regis Blahut.

Lattimer, John K. "Factors in the Death of President Kennedy." *Journal of the American Medical Association,* October 7, 1966, pp. 327–333.

———. *Kennedy and Lincoln—Medical and Ballistic Comparisons of Their Assassinations.* New York: Harcourt Brace Jovanovich, 1980.

———. "The Kennedy-Connally Single Bullet Theory." *International Surgery,* December 1968.

———. "Observations Based on a Review of the Autopsy, Photographs, X-rays, and Related Materials of the Late President John F. Kennedy." *Resident and Staff Physician,* May 1972.

Lawrence, Lincoln. *Were We Controlled?* New Hyde Park, N.Y.: University Books, 1967.

Leary, Timothy. "The Murder of Mary Pichot Meyer." *The Rebel,* November 22, 1983.

"Lee Harvey Oswald in Mexico: New Leads." *Lobster* 6, November 1984.

Lee, Martin A., and Bruce, Shlain. *Acid Dreams: The CIA, LSD and the Sixties Rebellion.* New York: Grove Press, 1985.

Leek, Sybil, and Bert R. Sugar. *The Assassination Chain.* New York: Corwin, 1976. First book to use evidence to link the assassinations of John Kennedy, Martin Luther King Jr., Robert Kennedy, and the shooting of George Wallace. Comes to the conclusion that Howard Hughes (or the power behind the Hughes empire) was responsible.

Lehmann-Haupt, Christopher. "Books of the Times: Catalogue of Accusations against J. Edgar Hoover." *New York Times,* February 15, 1993. Review of *Official and Confidential: The Secret Life of J. Edgar Hoover* by Anthony Summers (G. P. Putnam's Sons).

Lehmann-Haupt, Christopher. "Books of the Times: Kennedy Assassination Answers." *New York Times,* December 9, 1993, p. C18. Review of *Case Closed* by Gerald Posner (Random House).

Lemann, Nicholas. "The Case against Jim Garrison." *GQ,* January 1992.

Lewis, Ron. *Flashback: The Untold Story of Lee Harvey Oswald.* Roseburg, Ore.: Lewcom Productions, 1993.

"The Life and Death of Richard Case Nagell." *Probe: The Newsletter of Citizens for Truth about the Kennedy Assassination.* November–December 1995, p. 1.

Lifton, David S. *Best Evidence: Disguise and Deception in the Assassination of John F. Kennedy.* New York: Penguin Books, 1992. Troubled by the gross discrepancy between the descriptions of JFK's wounds at Parkland and Bethesda (in Dallas, Kennedy appeared to have been shot from the front, in Maryland the president appeared to have been shot from the rear), Lifton obtained frightening evidence that JFK's body was tampered with somewhere between Parkland and Bethesda. Lifton's best theory maintains that between 2:18 and 2:32 P.M., 14 minutes during which "it appeared, from the public record, that the coffin was. . . . unattended," JFK's body was removed from its coffin and hidden until Air Force One landed at Andrews Air Force Base in Washington. At that time, Lifton alleges—while the nation watched an empty coffin being removed, accompanied by Jacqueline and Robert Kennedy—JFK's body was deplaned through a right-front door and loaded onto a helicopter. The body was flown to Walter Reed Hospital and while there it was altered. According to Harrison Edward Livingstone and Robert G. Groden, "Mandatory to this hypothesis is the necessity for the coffin to have been left unattended . . . Dave Powers, a long-time friend and close aide of President Kennedy, told . . . Harrison Livingstone on June 23, 1987 that 'the coffin was never left unattended . . . I never had my hands or eyes off of it during that period [Lifton] says it was unattended.'"

———. ed. *Document Addendum to the Warren Report.* El Segundo, Calif.: Sightext Press, 1968.

Liss, Dan. "Oswald's Ghost." *Back Channels,* Spring 1992, p. 18. Article about Kerry Wendell Thornley.

Livingstone, Harrison Edward. *High Treason 2.* New York: Carroll and Graf, 1992.

———. *Killing Kennedy and the Hoax of the Century.* New York: Carroll and Graf, 1995.

———. *Killing the Truth.* New York: Carroll and Graf, 1994. Author concludes that the plotters were J. Edgar Hoover, Lyndon B. Johnson, Clint Murchison, General Charles Cabell, Mayor Earle Cabell, and David Atlee Phillips.

Lueck, Thomas J. "Seth Kantor Is Dead; Reporter, 67, Fought to Protect Sources." *New York Times,* August 19, 1993. Kantor died in a Washington hospital of cardiac arrest on August 17. He had entered the hospital for "tests."

Lundberg, George. "Closing the Case in JAMA on the John F. Kennedy Autopsy." *Journal of the American Medical Association,* October 7, 1992, pp. 1736–1738.

Lyons, Gene. "Conspiracy Killer." *Entertainment Weekly,* September 24, 1993, p. 82. Review of *Case Closed* by Gerald Posner (Random House).

McBirnie, William Stewart. *What Was Behind Lee Harvey Oswald?* Glendale, Calif.: Acare Publications, no date.

McDonald, Hugh. *Appointment in Dallas.* New York: Zebra, 1975. See SAUL.

McDonald, N. M. "Officer Recalls Oswald Capture." *Dallas Morning News,* November 24, 1963.

MacFarlane, Ian. *The Assassination of John F. Kennedy: A New Review.* Melbourne, Australia: Book Distributors, 1974.

MacFarlane, Ian. *Proof of Conspiracy in the Assassination of President Kennedy.* Melbourne, Australia: Book Distributors, 1975.

Machirella, Henry. "Leftist Accused of Murders of Kennedy and Dallas Cop." *New York Daily News,* November 23, 1963, p. 3.

McMillan, Priscilla J. *Marina and Lee.* New York: Harper and Row, 1977. Author's full name: Priscilla Mary Post Johnson McMillan. She is one of the few people to have met both President Kennedy and his accused assassin. Ms. Johnson interviewed Lee Harvey Oswald in the Soviet Union on November 16, 1959, for the North American Newspaper Alliance. She says she was impressed that, while Oswald was outspoken about his desire to renounce his American citizenship, he never bothered to follow through with the necessary paperwork. Before writing her book, she lived for a time with Marina Oswald.

McNamara, Sean, and Steve Marshall. "Inspiration for 'JFK' dies." *USA Today*, October 22, 1992. Garrison obit.

Mailer, Norman. *Oswald's Tale: An American Mystery*. New York: Random House, 1995.

Manchester, William. *The Death of a President*. New York: Harper and Row, 1967.

Mandel, Paul. "End to Nagging Rumors: The Six Critical Seconds." *Life*, December 6, 1963, p. 52F.

Marchetti, Victor, and John Marks. *The CIA and the Cult of Intelligence*. New York: Knopf, 1974.

Marcus, Raymond. "Blow Up! November 22, 1963." *Los Angeles Free Press*, November 24, 1967, p. 1. See "Number-Five Man."

———. *The Bastard Bullet*. Los Angeles, Calif.: Randall Publications, 1966.

Marks, Stanley J., and Ethel M. Marks. *Yes, Americans, A Conspiracy Murdered JFK!* San Marino, Calif.: Bureau of International Affairs, 1992.

Marrs, Jim. *Crossfire: The Plot That Killed Kennedy*. New York: Carroll and Graf, 1990. One of three books, Anthony Summers' *Conspiracy* and Jim Garrison's *On the Trail of the Assassins* are the others, upon which Oliver Stone's film *JFK* was based.

———. "Ex-agent 6th to Die in Six-Month Span." *Fort Worth Star-Telegram*, November 10, 1977. Article about the death of William Sullivan.

Meagher, Sylvia. *Accessories after the Fact*. Indianapolis: Bobbs-Merrill, 1967. Shows, point by point, how the evidence, often the very evidence presented by the Warren Commission itself, does not support the *Warren Report's* conclusions.

———. *Subject Index to the Warren Report and Hearings and Exhibits*. New York: Scarecrow Press, 1966. Outraged that the Warren Commission published its 26 volumes without an index, she published one herself.

Melanson, Philip H. "High Tech Mysterious Deaths." *Critique* 4, nos. 3, 4 (Fall–Winter 1984–85).

———. *Spy Saga: Lee Harvey Oswald and U.S. Intelligence*. New York: Praeger, 1990.

Menninger, Bonar. *Mortal Error*. New York: St. Martin's Press, 1992.

Merrill, Laurie C. "Fidel Shot at Solving JFK Case." *New York Daily News*, March 31, 1995, p. 8.

Meunier, Robert F. *Shadows of Doubt: The Warren Commission Cover-up*. Hicksville, N.Y.: Exposition Press, 1976.

Meyer, Lawrence, and Joel D. Weisman. "Giancana, Linked to CIA Plot, Slain." *Washington Post*, June 21, 1975, p. 1.

Miller, David. "Who Murdered DeMohrenschildt?" *Yipster Times*, October–November 1977.

Miller, Laura. "Oswald's Daughter." *Dallas Observer*, February 27, 1992, p. 5. Story about Rachel Oswald.

Morrow, Robert D. *Betrayal*. Chicago: Henry Regnery Co., 1977.

———. *First Hand Knowledge: How I Participated in the CIA-Mafia Murder of President Kennedy*. New York: S.P.I. Books, 1992.

———. *The Senator Must Die*. Santa Monica, Calif.: Roundtable, 1988. About the conspiracy to murder Robert F. Kennedy.

Myers, Dale K. *With Malice: Lee Harvey Oswald and the Murder of Officer J. D. Tippit*. Milford, Mich.: Oak Cliff Press, 1998.

Myers, Laura. "Mob Officer to Kill Castro for Free." *New Orleans Times-Picayune*, July 2, 1997, p. A-1.

Nash, H. C. *Citizen's Arrest: The Dissent of Penn Jones, Jr., in the Assassination of JFK*. Austin, Tex.: Latitudes Press, 1977.

Nash, George, and Patricia Nash. "The Other Witnesses." *The New Leader*, October 12, 1964. pp. 7–8.

NBC News, Seventy Hours and Thirty Minutes. New York: Random House, 1966.

Nechiporenko, Colonel Oleg Maximovich. *Passport to Assassination: The Never-Before-Told Story of Lee Harvey Oswald by the KGB Colonel Who Knew Him*. New York: Birch Lane Press, 1993.

"New Book Disputes Conspiracy Theories of Kennedy Killing." *New York Times*, August 23, 1993, p. A16. Discusses the book *Case Closed* by Gerald Posner (Random House).

Newfield, Jack. "'I Want Kennedy Killed!' Hoffa Shouted. . . ." *Penthouse*, May 1992, p. 31. Regarding the statements of Hoffa lawyer Frank Ragano.

Newfield, Jack; Jim Nolan; and Leo Standora. "Did Mob Use Gay Pix to KO Hoover's JFK-Slay Probe?" *New York Post*, February 8, 1993, p. 2. Information based on the February 9, 1993, episode of *Frontline* entitled "The Secret File on J. Edgar Hoover," broadcast over the Public Broadcasting System. Interestingly, the only person presented on the program who claimed to have actually seen the photographs of Hoover partaking in homosexual activity, was Gordon Novel—a man who was suspected of involvement in the JFK assassination by New Orleans Parish district attorney Jim Garrison.

Newman, Albert H. *The Assassination of John F. Kennedy: The Reasons Why*. New York: Potter, 1970.

Newman, John M. *JFK and Vietnam*. New York: Warner Books, 1992. Did JFK's reluctance to get drawn into a prolonged war in Vietnam contribute to his demise? For 20 years, Newman was a military intelligence officer with the National Security Agency.

———. *Oswald and the CIA*. New York: Carroll and Graf, 1995.

Nobile, Philip, and Ron Rosenbaum. "The Mysterious Murder of JFK's Mistress." *New Times*, July 9, 1976, pp. 22–33. Regarding Mary Pinchot Meyer.

Norden, Eric. "The Death of a President." *The Minority of One*, January 1964, pp. 16–23.

North, Mark. *Act of Treason*. New York: Carroll and Graf, 1991. Regarding J. Edgar Hoover.

"Novel Will Be Returned–Ohio." *New Orleans Times-Picayune*. May 10, 1967. Garrison attempts to extradite Gordon Novel.

Noyes, Peter. *Legacy of Doubt*. New York: Pinnacle, 1973.

The Official Warren Commission Report on the Assassination of President John F. Kennedy. Garden City, N.Y.: Doubleday, 1964.

Oglesby, Carl. "The Conspiracy That Won't Go Away." *Playboy*, February 1992, p. 75.

———. *The Yankee and Cowboy War: Conspiracies from Dallas to Watergate*, Mission, Ks.: Sheed Andrews and McNeel, 1976.

"The Oswald Affair." *Commentary*, March 1964, pp. 55–65.

"Oswald Called It My 'Historic Diary'—And It Is." *Life*, July 10, 1964.

"Oswald-Ferrie Link Made by Ex-cabbie." *Fort Worth Star-Telegram,* March 10, 1967. The ex-cabbie is Perry Raymond Russo.

"Oswald Friend Labeled CIA Informant in Memo." *Dallas Times Herald,* July 27, 1978. The friend is George DeMohrenschildt.

"Oswald Grave Now Battle Site." *Fort Worth Star-Telegram,* October 19, 1979.

"Oswald Pictures Released by FBI." *Dallas Morning News,* August 7, 1978.

Oswald, Robert L. with Myrick and Barbara Land. *Lee: A Portrait of Lee Harvey Oswald.* New York: Coward-McCann, 1967.

"Oswald Tags Self As Marxist, Denies He's a Commie." *New York Daily News,* November 23, 1963, p. 10.

"Oswald Widow in JFK Flip." *New York Daily News,* November 22, 1996, p. 30. Three-paragraph item which previews that day's appearance on the Oprah Winfrey Show by Marina Oswald Porter during which Marina says she now believes Lee to have been innocent. The article also announces the release to the public of a film taken by presidential aide David Powers during the motorcade from the presidential follow-up car. Powers, however, ran out of film before the motorcade reached Dealey Plaza.

"Oswald's Camera Disappeared during FBI Investigation." *Dallas Morning News,* June 15, 1978.

"Oswald's Mother Asks Exhumation." *Fort Worth Star-Telegram,* November 17, 1967.

"Oswald's Prints Revealed on Rifle Killing Kennedy." *Dallas Times Herald,* November 25, 1963.

O'Toole, George. *The Assassination Tapes.* New York: Penthouse Press, 1975. O'Toole is a former CIA agent. In his book, O'Toole uses an instrument called a Psychological Stress Evaluator (PSE) to determine, from the sound of their voice on tape recordings, if people are telling the truth. The author concludes that "at least some of the people who framed Lee Harvey Oswald were members of the Dallas police."

O'Toole, George, and Paul Hoch. "Dallas: The Cuban Connection." *The Saturday Evening Post,* March 1976.

Palamara, Vince. "59 Witnesses: Delay on Elm Street." *The Dealey Plaza Echo,* July 1999, pp. 1–7. Regarding whether or not the presidential limousine stopped during the shooting sequence. Palamara has a theory that the Secret Service agents in Dallas were told that a "security-stripping test" was to take place that day. We know from Secret Service chief James J. Rowley that there were studies underway regarding presidential protection. Palamara's theory is that certain Secret Service agents were told that a fake assassination was to take place, a covert operation to precipitate a Cuban invasion, and *not* to respond.

Parshall, Gerald. "The Man with a Deadly Smirk." *U.S. News & World Report,* August 30–September 6, 1993, p. 62. Introduction to the magazine's excerpt from Gerald Posner's book *Case Closed* (Random House).

Pease, Lisa. "The Formation of the Clark Panel: More of the Secret Team at Work?" *Probe: The Newsletter of Citizens for Truth about the Kennedy Assassination,* November–December 1995, p. 13. Article argues, by examining the backgrounds of the members and those who nominated them, that the fix was in when the attorney general convened in 1968 a medical panel to examine the JFK assassination medical evidence. After two days of work the panel concluded that there was no evidence of conspiracy.

———. "Manipulating Reality: Operation Mockingbird." *Probe: The Newsletter of Citizens for Truth about the Kennedy Assassination,* March–April 1996, p. 10. Discussion of the use, by American intelligence agencies, of journalists to alter the public's perception of history.

———. "David Atlee Phillips, Claw Shaw & Freeport Sulphur." *Probe: The Newsletter of Citizens for Truth about the Kennedy Assassination,* March–April 1996, p. 16.

Phelan, James R. "Rush to Judgment in New Orleans." *Saturday Evening Post,* May 6, 1967, pp. 21–25.

"Pierre Finck & the Secret Team." *Probe: The Newsletter of Citizens for Truth about the Kennedy Assassination,* November–December 1995, p. 10. Evidence that JFK's autopsy may not have been the only one fixed by the titular medical examiner.

Policoff, Jerry, ed. "The JFK Assassination." supplement to *Gallery,* July 1979.

Popkin, Richard H. "Garrison's Case." *New York Review of Books,* September 14, 1967, p. 28.

———. *The Second Oswald.* New York: Avon, 1966.

Posner, Gerald. *Case Closed: Lee Harvey Oswald and the Assassination of JFK.* New York: Random House, 1993. Tunnel vision, psycho-babble and selective use of the evidence again leads to the lone-nut scenario.

———. "Garrison Guilty: Another Case Closed." *Probe: The Newsletter of Citizens for Truth about the Kennedy Assassination,* August 6, 1995. Another brief for the prosecution from Posner. For rebuttal, see Bill Davy's "Case Distorted."

Powledge, Fred. "Is Garrison Faking?" *New Republic,* June 17, 1967, p. 16.

———. "Texas Investigation into Kennedy Death Put Off Indefinitely." *New York Times,* December 7, 1963.

"The Private Correspondence of Richard Case Nagell." *Probe: The Newsletter of Citizens for Truth about the Kennedy Assassination,* November–December 1995, p. 5. First publication of a letter, written by Nagell to his friend Arturo Verdestein on October 8, 1967.

Prouty, L. Fletcher. "The Betrayal of JFK Kept Fidel Castro in Power." *Gallery,* February 1978.

———. "An Introduction to the Assassination Business." *Gallery,* September 1975.

———. "The Guns of Dallas." *Gallery,* October 1975.

———. *JFK: The CIA, Vietnam and the Plot to Assassinate John F. Kennedy.* New York: Birch Lane Press, 1992.

———. *The Secret Team: The CIA and Its Allies in Control of the United States and the World.* New York: Prentice-Hall, 1973.

———. "Visions of a Kennedy Dynasty." *Freedom Magazine,* April–May 1987.

Raskin, Marcus. "JFK and the Culture of Violence." *American Historical Review,* April 1992, pp. 487–499.

Raum, Tom. "Deputies Arrest Thornley on Fugitive Warrant." *Tampa Times-Tribune,* February 22, 1968. (See THORNLEY, KERRY WENDELL.)

Rawls, Wendell, Jr. "Assassination Panel Is Given Right to Bypass House." *New York Times,* October 17, 1977, p. 15.

———. "Cornell Professor Is Named As Assassination Panel Counsel." *New York Times,* June 21, 1977, p. 21. Regarding G. Robert Blakey. (See HOUSE SELECT COMMITTEE ON ASSASSINATIONS.)

———. "Dutch Journalist in Kennedy Case Is 'Half Showman,' Colleague Says." *New York Times,* April 12, 1977. Regarding Willem Oltmans, who claimed to have 12 hours of taped interviews with Oswald-associate George DeMohrenschildt.

———. "Ex-Castro Soldier Balks at House Inquiry on Kennedy." *New York Times,* June 8, 1977. Story about Loran Hall.

———. "House Inquiry Reported Fruitless on Kennedy-King Assassinations," *New York Times,* June 6, 1977, p. 1.

"Reopen the Warren Commission." *Midlothian Mirror,* March 31, 1966, p. 2.

Report of the Select Committee on Assassinations. U.S. House of Representatives, 1979.

Richards, Guy. "Mystery New York 'Contact' of Oswald Revealed." *New York Journal-American,* December 18, 1963. About Fair Play For Cuba Committee executive director V. T. Lee.

Ringgold, Gene, and Roger LaManna. *Assassin: The Lee Harvey Oswald Biography.* Hollywood, Calif.: Associated Professional Services, 1964.

Risen, James. "K.G.B. Told Tall Tales about Dallas, Book Says." *New York Times,* September 12, 1999. Regarding *The Sword and the Shield,* a book written by Christopher Andrew and former KGB officer, Vasily Mitrokhin, and their claim that the "Dear Mr. Hunt" letter was a KGB plant intended to incriminate CIA agent E. Howard Hunt.

Roberts, Gene. "Arrests in Kennedy Case Delayed for Months, New Orleans Prosecutor Says." *New York Times,* February 21, 1967, p. 20.

———. "Figure in Oswald Inquiry Is Dead in New Orleans." *New York Times,* February 23, 1967, p. 19. Obituary of David Ferrie in which it states that Ferrie was hairless because of "burns."

———. "Businessmen Aid Inquiry on Plot." *New York Times,* February 25, 1967, p. 56. Reveals that Jim Garrison's assassination probe is being privately funded.

———. "The Case of Jim Garrison and Lee Harvey Oswald." *New York Times Magazine,* May 21, 1967.

———. "Figure in Oswald Inquiry Is Dead in New Orleans." *New York Times,* February 23, 1967, p. 22. Report on the death of David Ferrie.

———. "Investigator Quits Garrison's Staff and Assails Inquiry into Plot." *New York Times,* June 27, 1967, p. 25.

———. "Louisiana ACLU Scores Garrison." *New York Times,* March 7, 1967, p. 21.

———. "Suspect in 'Plot' Linked to Oswald." *New York Times,* March 3, 1967, p. 22.

Roffman, Howard. *Presumed Guilty.* Cranbury, N.J.: Fairleigh Dickinson University Press, 1975. Reissued in 1976 by A. S. Barnes (New York).

Rogin, Michael. "JFK: The Movie." *American Historical Review,* April 1992, pp. 500–505.

Rose, Jerry D. "Agent 179: The Making of a Dirty Rumor." *The Third Decade,* May 1985, pp. 14–19.

———. "Important to Hold That Man." *The Third Decade,* May 1986, pp. 17–20.

———. "Jack Ruby and J. D. Tippit: Coincidence or Conspiracy?" *The Third Decade,* March 1985.

———. "Martin Schrand." *The Third Decade,* January 1988, pp. 15–19. Was Marine Schrand Oswald's first murder victim?

———. "The Trip That Never Was." *The Third Decade,* July 1985.

———. "They Got Their Man on Both Accounts." *The Third Decade,* March 1988, pp. 1–8.

———. "We've Been Expecting You." *The Third Decade,* January 1990, pp. 14–17.

Rosenstone, Robert A. "JFK: Historical Fact/Historical Film." *American Historical Review,* April 1992, pp. 506–511.

Rothstein, David A., M.D. "Presidential Assassination Syndrome." *Archives of General Psychiatry* 11, no. 3 (September 1964): 245–254.

"Ruby Lawyers Claim Perjury; Ask Retrial." *Rochester Democrat & Chronicle,* June 25, 1966, p. 12. In theory, the perjurer was Patrick Dean.

"Ruby, Oswald Slayer, Dies of a Blood Clot in Lungs." *New York Times,* January 4, 1967, p. 20.

Rush, George. "Autopsy-Turvy over JFK Photos." *New York Daily News,* October 14, 1993, p. 22. Reported furor over plans by Robert Groden to publish color versions of the alleged JFK autopsy photos in his tabletop book, *The Killing of a President.*

Russell, Dick. "Is the 'Second Oswald' Alive in Dallas?" *Village Voice,* August 23, 1976, p. 23. Article concerns alleged Oswald look-alike John Thomas Masen.

———. "Loran Hall and the Politics of Assassination." *Village Voice,* October 3, 1977, p. 23.

———. *The Man Who Knew Too Much.* New York: Carroll and Graf, 1992. The story of CIA contract agent Richard Case Nagell.

———. "This Man Is a Missing Link." *Rolling Stone,* August 14, 1978, p. 1.

———. "What Was in the CIA's Declassified JFK File?" *Village Voice,* April 16, 1976, pp. 17–20.

"Russo Says: David W. Ferrie Was a Marxist." *The Councilor* (Shreveport, Louisiana), June 15, 1967.

Salandria, Vincent. "The Impossible Tasks of One Assassination Bullet." *Minority of One,* 1966. Salandria was a Philadelphia attorney who wrote magazine articles regarding the medical and ballistic evidence and the impossibility of the official version of the facts when comparing the evidence to the Zapruder film.

———. "A Philadelphia Lawyer Analyzes the President's Back and Neck Wounds." *Liberation,* March 1965.

———. "Warren Report (Parts 1&2)." *Liberation,* January and March, 1965.

"Salesman Insists FBI Discounted Facts on Oswald." *Dallas Morning News,* May 8, 1977.

Sample, Glen, and Mark Collom. *The Men on the Sixth Floor.* Garden Grove Calif.: Sample Graphics, 1995.

Sauvage, Leo. *The Oswald Affair.* Cleveland, Ohio: World Publishing Co., 1966.

Savage, Gary. *JFK: First Day Evidence.* Monroe, La.: Shoppe Press, 1993. Based on the collections and recollections of former Dallas police crime lab detective R. W. (Rusty) Livingston.

Scott, Peter Dale. *Crime and Cover-up.* Berkeley, Calif.: Westworks, 1977.

————. *Deep Politics and the Death of JFK.* Berkeley: University of California Press, 1993.

————. "From Dallas to Watergate—the Longest Cover-up," *Ramparts,* November 1973.

Seay, Theresa M. "What Better Alibi?" *Back Channels,* Winter 1992, p. 3. Discussion of spurious Secret Service agents at the scene of the JFK assassination.

"The Separate Connally Shot." *The Minority of One.* April 1966, p. 13.

Severo, Richard. "John Connally of Texas, a Power in 2 Political Parties, Dies at 76." *New York Times,* June 16, 1993, p. A1.

Shaw, J. Gary, and Larry R. Harris. *Cover-up: The Governmental Conspiracy to Conceal the Facts about the Public Execution of John Kennedy.* Cleburne, Tex.: self-published, 1976.

————. "The Dallas Mystery Man." *The Continuing Inquiry,* August 1979.

————. "Is the FBI Shielding a JFK Assassin?" *The Continuing Inquiry,* November 22, 1977.

Sheatsley, Paul B., and Jacob J. Feldman. "The Assassination of President Kennedy." *The Public Opinion Quarterly,* Summer 1964.

Sheehy, Maura. "The Searchers." *Details,* January 1992. Story about assassination researchers.

Shuster, Mike. "George de Mohrenschildt." *Seven Days,* May 9, 1977.

Sibley, Robert. "The Mysterious, Vanishing Rifle of the JFK Assassination." *The Third Decade,* September 1985, pp. 16–18.

Siemaszko, Corky. "Second Gun at JFK Slay, Authors Say." *New York Daily News,* November 7, 1994. According to new research by Anthony and Robbyn Summers, there exists an FBI memo reporting that a .38 snub-nosed Smith & Wesson was found in a brown paper sack in the Texas School Book Depository on the morning of November 23, 1994. The gun, according to the report, had the word England written on it next to the serial number.

Simon, Art. *Dangerous Knowledge: The JFK Assassination in Art and Film.* Philadelphia, Pa.: Temple University Press, 1996.

Sites, Paul. *Lee Harvey Oswald and the American Dream.* New York: Pageant Press, 1967.

Sloan, Bill. *JFK: Breaking the Silence.* Dallas, Tex.: Taylor Publishing, 1993.

Sloan, Bill, with Jean Hill. *JFK: The Last Dissenting Witness.* Gretna, La.: Pelican Publishing Co., 1992.

Sloyan, Patrick J. "Desperately Seeking Link to Castro." *New York Newsday,* August 24, 1993, p. 4.

Smith, Liz. "Who Killed Kennedy?" *Newsday,* May 12, 1997. Gossip item regarding JFK's personal secretary Evelyn Lincoln.

Sprague, Richard E. "The Assassination of President John F. Kennedy: The Application of the Photographic Evidence." *Computers and Automation,* May 1970.

————. "The Assignment of G. Robert Blakey." *The Continuing Inquiry,* March 1981.

————. *The Taking of America 1-2-3.* Self-published, 1976.

Squires, James D. "Cuban Guerrilla Team Killed JFK, Garrison Thinks." *Nashville Tennessean,* June 22, 1967.

Stafford, Jean. *A Mother in History—Three Incredible Days with Lee Harvey Oswald's Mother.* New York: Pharos Books, 1992. (Originally published in 1965.)

Stern, Laurence, and Alfred E. Lewis. "As a Schoolboy, Oswald Pinched and Bit . . . But Grown, He Was a Model Roomer." *Washington Post,* December 1, 1963.

"The Story of Abraham Zapruder." *The Kennedy Quarterly Newspaper* 1, no. 2 (Autumn 1992): 1.

"The Strange Deaths of JFK Assassination Figures." *The Kennedy Quarterly Newspaper* 1, no. 2 (Autumn 1992): 1.

Streitfeld, David. "Book Report: Conspiring to Publish." *Washington Post* (Book World Section), Sunday, June 13, 1993. Preview of JFK assassinations books due to be published in the fall of 1993, to commemorate the 30th anniversary of JFK's death.

Summers, Anthony. *Conspiracy.* New York: Paragon House, 1989. One of three books, Jim Marrs's *Crossfire* and Jim Garrison's *On the Trail of the Assassins* are the others, upon which film director Oliver Stone based his film *JFK.*

————. *Official and Confidential: The Secret Life of J. Edgar Hoover.* New York: G. P. Putnam's Sons, 1993.

————. "Who Killed JFK?" *The Independent,* February 15, 1992.

Sussman, Barry. "New Probe into 'Lost Warning' on JFK." *New York Post,* October 1, 1975, p. 22. Regarding the November 17, 1963, telex message from FBI headquarters warning that a political hate group planned to kill JFK in Dallas.

Swank, Patricia. "A Plot That Flopped." *Look,* January 26, 1965, pp. 28–29. Article concerns ultra-conservative Larrie Schmidt, who is a suspect in the attempted shooting of General Edwin Walker.

Szulc, Tad. "Friend of Oswalds Knew Mrs. Kennedy." *New York Times,* November 24, 1964. Story about George DeMohrenschildt.

"Tape Sez LBJ Saw Fidel Tied to Slay of JFK." *New York Daily News,* October 6, 1997, p. 13. According to the just-then-published book *The Johnson White House Tapes, 1963–64,* by historian Michael Beschloss, LBJ said that he suspected Castro of playing a role in JFK's death, but feared a retaliation would lead to nuclear war. The tapes also reportedly contain a tape of LBJ speaking to Warren commissioner Senator Richard Russell that he, like Russell, did not believe in the commission's conclusions.

Tatro, Edgar F. "Who's Afraid of the Grassy Knoll South?" *Continuing Inquiry,* July 22, 1981, pp. 10–11. Assassins visible on the grassy knoll again, but this time on the other side of Dealey Plaza.

Taubman, Bryna. "JFK Mystery Buried with John Connally." *New York Post,* June 19, 1993, p. 5.

Thomas, Evan, with Patrick Rogers and Adam Wolfberg. "Who Shot JFK?" *Newsweek,* September 6, 1993, pp. 14–17.

Thomas, Ralph D. *Photo Computer Image Processing and the Crime of the Century: A New Investigative and Photographic Technique.* Austin, Tex.: Thomas Investigative Publications, Inc., 1992.

Thomas, Ralph D. *Missing Links in the JFK Assassination Conspiracy.* Austin, Tex.: Thomas Investigative Publications, Inc., 1992.

Thompson, Josiah. *Six Seconds in Dallas: A Micro-Study of the Kennedy Assassination,* New York: Bernard Geis, 1967. Thompson was an assistant professor of philosophy at Haverford College in Pennsylvania. Thompson was the first to postulate that two shots might have hit President Kennedy in the head almost simultaneously, one from the back and one from the front, as evidenced by the Zapruder film, frames 310-315. Thompson was also the first to see two figures in the sixth-floor windows of the Texas School Book Depository in the Hughes film. *Life* magazine granted Thompson permission to use frames from the Zapruder film in this book but withdrew the rights shortly before publication. Thompson was forced to replace the slides with artist's facsimiles. Thompson's shooting scenario is that there were three shooters: one in front on the grassy knoll, one in the County Records Building, and one in the School Book Depository "sniper's nest." There were five shots: the first hit President Kennedy in the back, the second hit Governor Connally, the third was a wild miss, the fourth was a head shot from the rear, and the fifth was a head shot from the front, the last two being nearly simultaneous.

———. "Why the Zapruder Film Is Authentic." *JFK Deep Politics Quarterly,* April 1999.

Thompson, W. C. *A Bibliography of Literature Relating to the Assassination of John F. Kennedy.* San Antonio, Tex.: The Editor, 1968 (with 1971 supplement).

Thornley, Kerry. *Oswald.* Chicago: New Classics, 1965. (See THORNLEY, KERRY WENDELL.)

"Three Patients at Parkland." *Texas State Journal of Medicine,* 1964, pp. 60–74.

Trento, Joe, and Jacquie Powers. "Was Howard Hunt in Dallas the Day JFK Died?" *Wilmington Sunday News Journal,* August 20, 1978.

Troelstrup, Glenn. "New Light on the Assassination: A Secret Agent's Story." *U.S. News & World Report,* June 8, 1964, pp. 38–39. Japanese intelligence's input into the FBI's "investigation" of JFK's death.

Tuchman, Mitch. "Kennedy Death Films." *Take One,* May 1978, p. 21.

Turner, William W. "The Garrison Commission on the Assassination of President Kennedy." *Ramparts,* January 1968, p. 52.

———. *Power on the Right.* Berkeley, Calif.: Ramparts Press, 1971.

———. "The Press versus Garrison." *Ramparts,* August 1968, p. 12.

———. "Some Disturbing Parallels." *Ramparts,* June 1968. Common denominators between the JFK and MLK killings.

Twyman, Noel. *Bloody Treason.* Rancho Santa Fe, Calif.: Laurel Publishing, 1997.

Van Bemmelen, J. M. "Did Lee Harvey Oswald Act without Help?" *New York University Law Review* 40, no. 3 (May 1965): 466–476.

Van Der Karr, Richard K. "How Dallas TV Stations Covered Kennedy Shooting." *Journalism Quarterly* 42 (1965): 646–647.

Verhovek, Sam Howe. "Family Bars Exhuming of Connally." *New York Times,* June 19, 1993. Beside this story was a photograph of Warren Commission counsel Arlen Specter, now a senator, giving a thumbs up sign. He has a bandaged head and is wearing a baseball cap. Reading the caption, you learn that he is celebrating his release from the hospital after having a benign tumor removed from his skull.

Waldron, Martin. "Garrison Charges CIA and FBI Conceal Evidence on Oswald." *New York Times,* May 10, 1967.

"Walker Escapes Assassin's Bullet." *New York Times,* April 12, 1963, p. 12. (See WALKER, EDWIN.)

Ward, Geoffrey C. "The Most Durable Assassination Theory: Oswald Did It Alone." *New York Times Book Review,* November 21, 1993, p. 15.

"Warren Commission Will Ask Mrs. Oswald to Identify Rifle Used in the Kennedy Assassination." *New York Times,* February 5, 1964, p. 19.

"Warren Foresees Trial News Curbs." *New York Times,* September 5, 1967.

Wecht, Cyril. "JFK Assassination: A Prolonged and Willful Cover-up." *Modern Medicine,* October 28, 1974.

———. "A Pathologist's View of the JFK Autopsy: An Unsolved Case." *Modern Medicine,* November 27, 1972.

———. "Why Is the Rockefeller Commission So Single-Minded about a Lone Assassin in the Kennedy Case?" *Journal of Legal Medicine,* July–August 1975.

Weeks, Anthony Edward. "Late Breaking News on Clay Shaw's United Kingdom Contacts." *Lobster,* November 1990.

Weiner, Tim. "C.I.A. to Release 90,000 Pages on Kennedy's Assassination." *New York Times,* August 20, 1993.

———. "Papers on Kennedy Assassination Are Unsealed, and '63 Is Revisited." *New York Times,* August 24, 1993, p. 1.

Weinstein, A., and Olga G. Lyerly. "Symbolic Aspects of Presidential Assassination." *Psychiatry* 32, no. 1 (February 1969): 1–11.

Weisberg, Harold. *Oswald in New Orleans.* New York: Canyon Books, 1967. Weisberg was a political warfare specialist for the Office of Strategic Services during World War II. After the war, he worked in intelligence for the U.S. Department of State, but he was fired from that position because of reported leftist allegiances. According to assassination researcher Harrison Edward Livingstone, Weisberg, after JFK's death, provided information regarding the assassination to right-wing Texas oil billionaire H. L. Hunt. Livingstone says, "Weisberg . . . seems more to function as a 'watcher' of others in the case." Weisberg, Livingstone believes, was paid by Hunt Oil to distract the public away from any evidence that the right wing was involved in JFK's death.

———. *Photographic Whitewash—suppressed Kennedy Assassination Pictures.* Frederick Md.: self-published, 1967, 1976.

———. *Whitewash.* (Vols. 1–4.) Hyattstown Md.: self-published, 1965, 1966, 1967, 1974.

———. *Post-Mortem.* Frederick Md.: self-published, 1975.

Weisz, Alfred E., M.D., and Robert L. Taylor, M.D. "The Assassination Matrix." *Stanford Today,* February 1969, pp. 11–17.

"What the Warren Report Actually Says." *The Kennedy Quarterly Newspaper* 1, no. 2.

Wilber, Charles G. *Medicolegal Investigation of the President John F. Kennedy Murder.* Springfield, Ill.: Charles G. Thomas, 1978.

Wills, Garry. "JFK Papers Won't Change Attitudes." *Rochester Times-Union,* August 30, 1993, p. 6A. Columnist opines that theories regarding JFK's death reveal more about peoples' prejudices and ways of thinking than about the "facts" of the crime.

———. "JFK Slaying Probe: CIA, FBI Had Secrets to Keep." *New York Post,* November 23, 1993, p. 19.

Wills, Gary, and Ovid Demaris. *Jack Ruby*. New York: New American Library, 1967.

Wilonsky, Robert. "The Man Oswald Missed." *Dallas Observer,* November 18–24, 1993, p. 21. The last interview of Major General Edwin Walker before his death from lung disease at 83 in his modest north Dallas home, during which the general defends his place in history.

"Witness in Assassination Plot Hints at Cuban Link." *New York Times,* April 4, 1967.

Zelizer, Barbie. *Covering the Body: The Kennedy Assassination, the Media, and the Shaping of Collective Memory.* Chicago: University of Chicago Press, 1992.

Zirbel, Craig I. *The Texas Connection.* Scottsdale, Ariz.: The Texas Connection Company, 1991. Book argues that LBJ was behind the assassination.

Zoglin, Richard. "More Shots in Dealey Plaza." *Time,* June 10, 1991, pp. 64, 66. Re: *JFK* by Oliver Stone.

Zoppi, Tony. "I Know the President Is Dead." *Dallas Morning News,* November 17, 2000. First person account first published in 1964.

INDEX

Boldface page numbers indicate major treatment of a subject. Page numbers in *italics* denote an illustration.